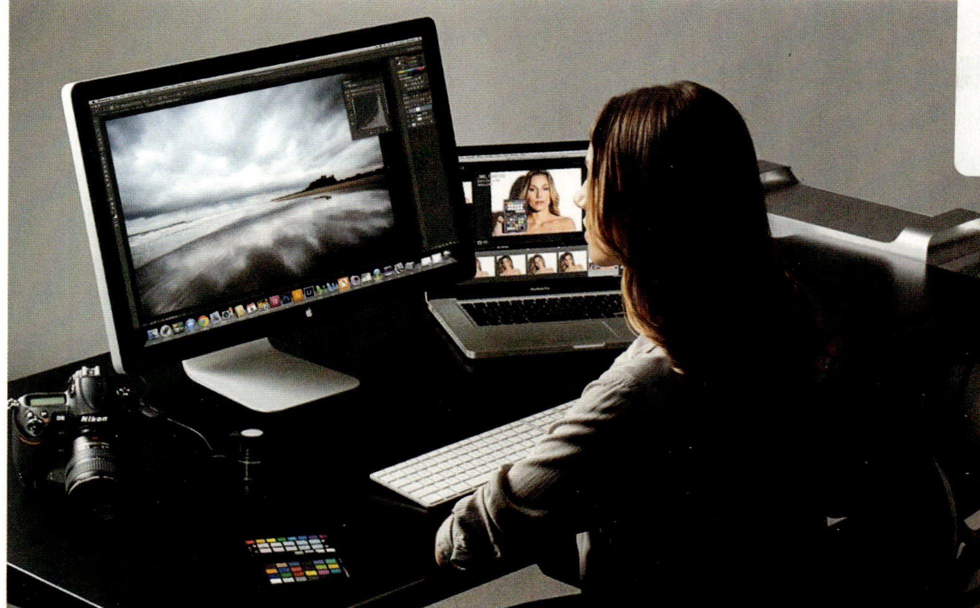

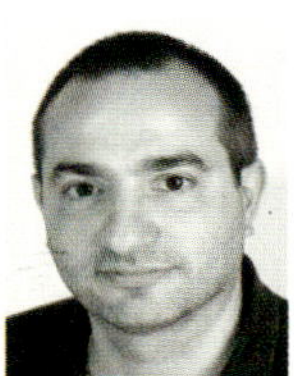

"The creation of a photograph rarely stops when you press the shutter. While a great photographer needs the skills to capture brilliant pictures with their camera, they often need to polish their in-camera creations during post-production. With film, it used to be that any necessary edits and enhancements were done in the darkroom. Now, with digital, it's done on a computer, usually accompanied by an Adobe editing software. Regardless of the type of digital camera you use, once you have your images on your PC or Mac, Lightroom and Photoshop allow you to organise, enhance and manipulate to your heart's content. Whether using Adobe's beginner-focused Elements or its powerhouse software, Photoshop, there are countless ways to improve or transform your photographs. Add to these the intuitive workflow system of Lightroom, and a variety of versatile plug-ins, and you've all you need for efficient editing. While these programs can be bought standalone, Photoshop and Lightroom can now be leased as an affordable bundle called Creative Cloud, meaning you always have the most up-to-date software at hand. Of course, such sophisticated tools require time and effort to master, which is where *The Photographers' Guide to Photoshop and Lightroom* will help. Produced by photographers for photographers, this guide is an ideal jargon-free introduction to Adobe's imaging software, packed with practical and creative techniques to help you get the most from your images. All the best!"

DANIEL LEZANO, EDITOR

Meet our team of Photoshop experts

All our experts are team members or regular contributors to *Digital SLR Photography* magazine. For more expert advice and inspiration, pick up the latest issue available on the second Tuesday of every month. For further information visit the magazine's website at www.digitalslrphoto.com

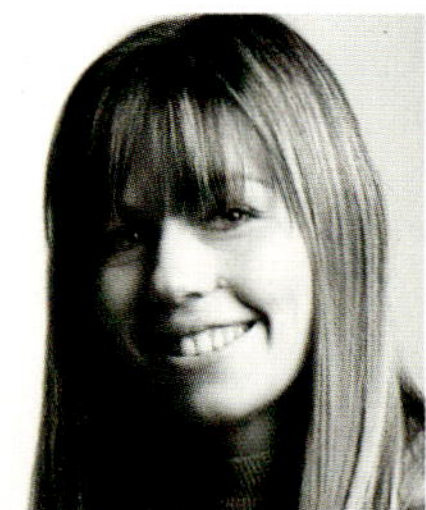

CAROLINE SCHMIDT
An avid portrait photographer, Caroline has developed in-depth knowledge of Adobe editing software and creative skills in post-production to add extra impact and polish to her pictures.

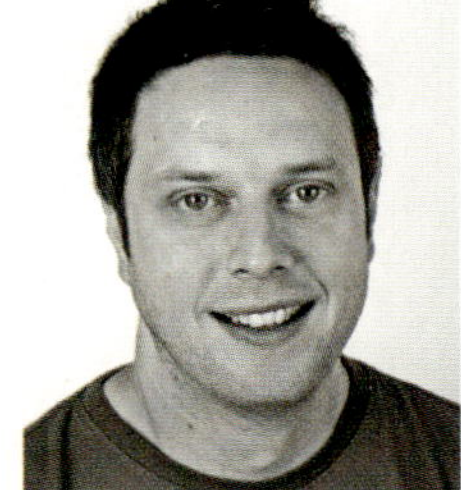

LUKE MARSH
As well as being a keen DSLR photographer, Luke is also the creative genius behind the look of *Digital SLR Photography* magazine and this MagBook, as well as a Photoshop expert.

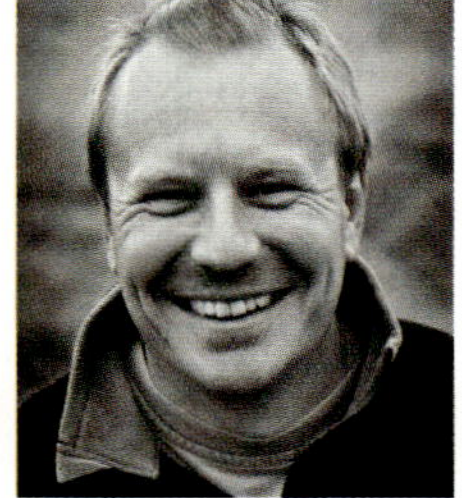

LEE FROST
A professional photographer and writer for two decades, Lee regularly combines his in-camera skills with Photoshop to get the very best from his images. *www.leefrost.co.uk*

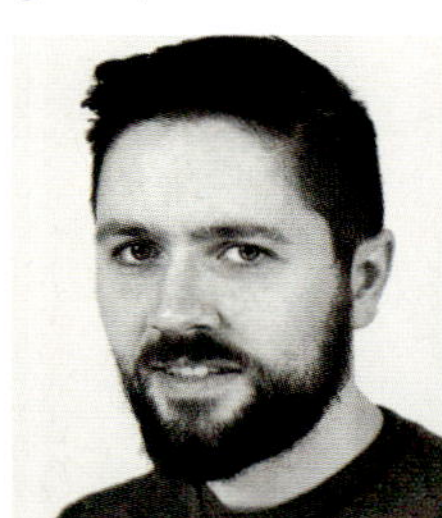

JORDAN BUTTERS
With his roots in shooting motorsport, Jordan's passion for photography has evolved to include Photoshop. He is highly skilled in creating stunning images in post-production.

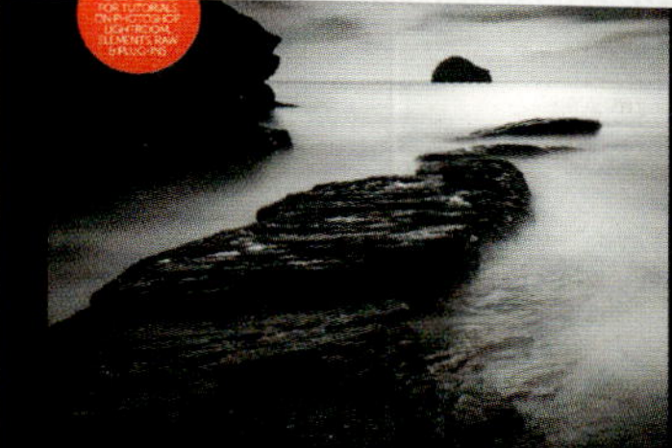

The Photographers' Guide to Adobe Photoshop & Lightroom (Vol. 2)
Produced by *Digital SLR Photography*
Editorial queries: enquiries@dslrphotomag.co.uk
Online: www.digitalslrphoto.com

Editorial
Editor Daniel Lezano
daniel.lezano@dslrphotomag.co.uk
Art Editor Luke Marsh
luke.marsh@dslrphotomag.co.uk
Senior Contributing Editor Caroline Schmidt
caroline.schmidt@dslrphotomag.co.uk
Contributing Editor Jordan Butters
jordan.butters@dslrphotomag.co.uk
Editorial Consultant Jo Lezano
jo.lezano@dslrphotomag.co.uk
Other editorial contributors:
Lee Frost, Ross Hoddinott and Paul Ward

Advertising & Production
Display & Classified Sales: 020 7907 6651
Commercial Brand Manager Alex Skinner
alex_skinner@dennis.co.uk
Account Manager Finan Tesfay
finan_tesfay@dennis.co.uk
Senior Production Controller Anisha Mogra
anisha_mogra@dennis.co.uk
Digital Production Manager Nicky Baker
nicky_baker@dennis.co.uk

Management
MAGBOOK PUBLISHER DHARMESH MISTRY
OPERATIONS DIRECTOR ROBIN RYAN
MD OF ADVERTISING JULIAN LLOYD-EVANS
NEWSTRADE DIRECTOR DAVID BARKER
MD TECHNOLOGY & IMAGING JOHN GAREWAL
CHIEF OPERATING OFFICER BRETT REYNOLDS
GROUP FINANCE DIRECTOR IAN LEGGETT
CHIEF EXECUTIVE JAMES TYE
FOUNDER FELIX DENNIS

The Photographers' Guide to Adobe Photoshop & Lightroom is produced for Dennis Publishing Ltd by Red Creative Media Ltd.

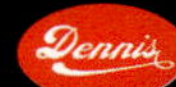

The Photographers' Guide to Adobe Photoshop & Lightroom (Vol.2)
ISBN 1-78106-489-X
Licensing & Syndication. To license this product please contact Carlotta Serantoni on +44 (0) 20 7907 6550 or email carlotta_serantoni@dennis.co.uk. To syndicate content from this product please contact Anj Dosaj Halai on +44(0) 20 7907 6132 or email anj_dosaj-halai@dennis.co.uk

The paper used within this MagBook is produced from sustainable fibre, manufactured by mills with a valid chain of custody
Printed by Southern Print

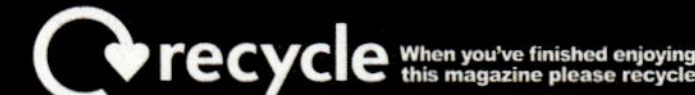

CONTENTS

THE PHOTOGRAPHERS' GUIDE TO PHOTOSHOP & LIGHTROOM **2ND EDITION**

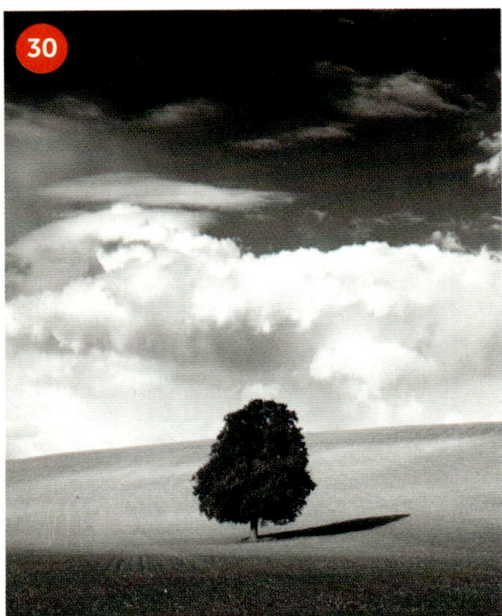

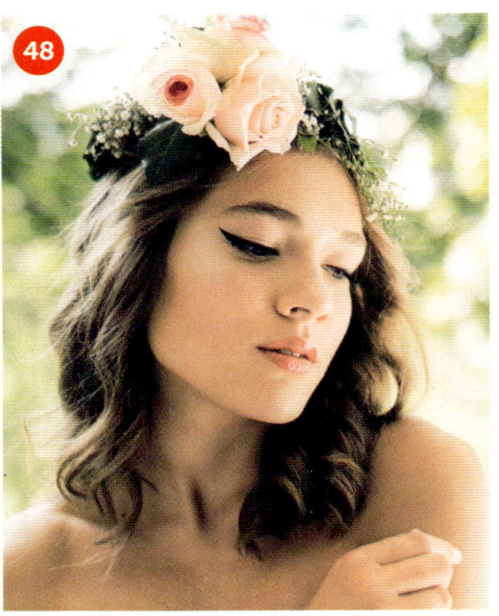

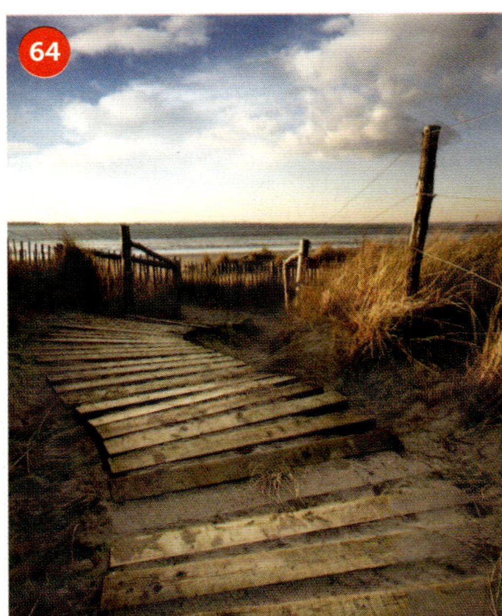

TURN TO PAGE 122 TO FIND OUT ABOUT OUR FANTASTIC SUBSCRIPTION OFFERS

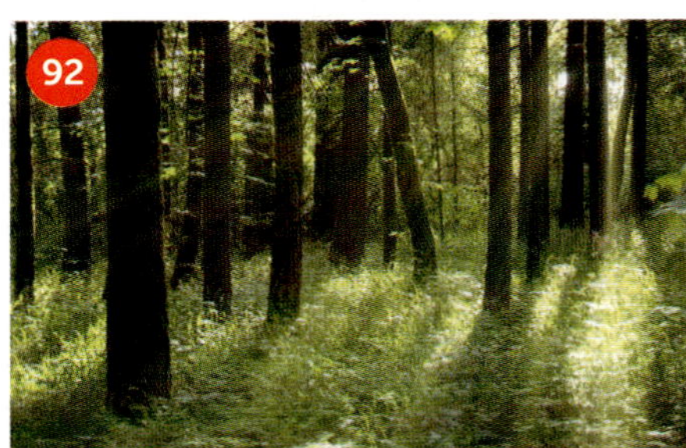

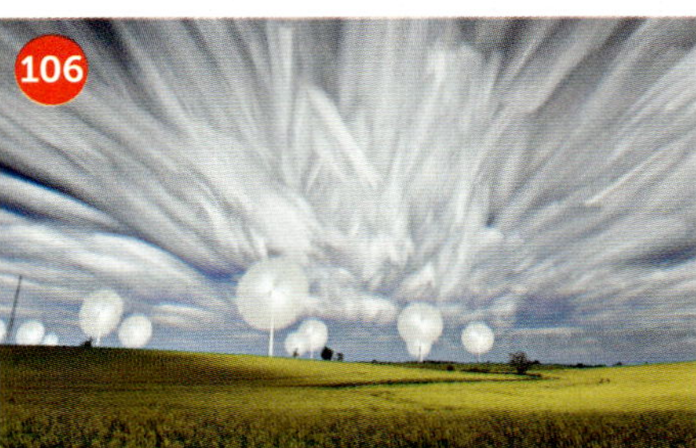

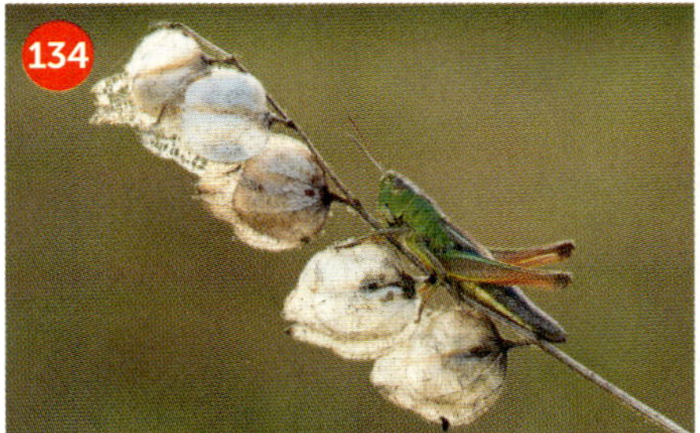

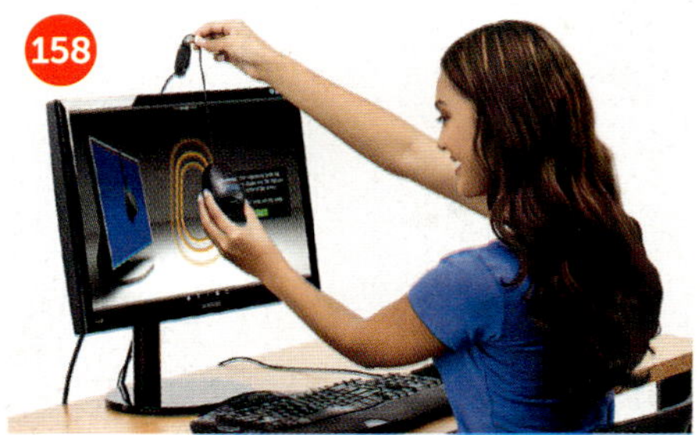

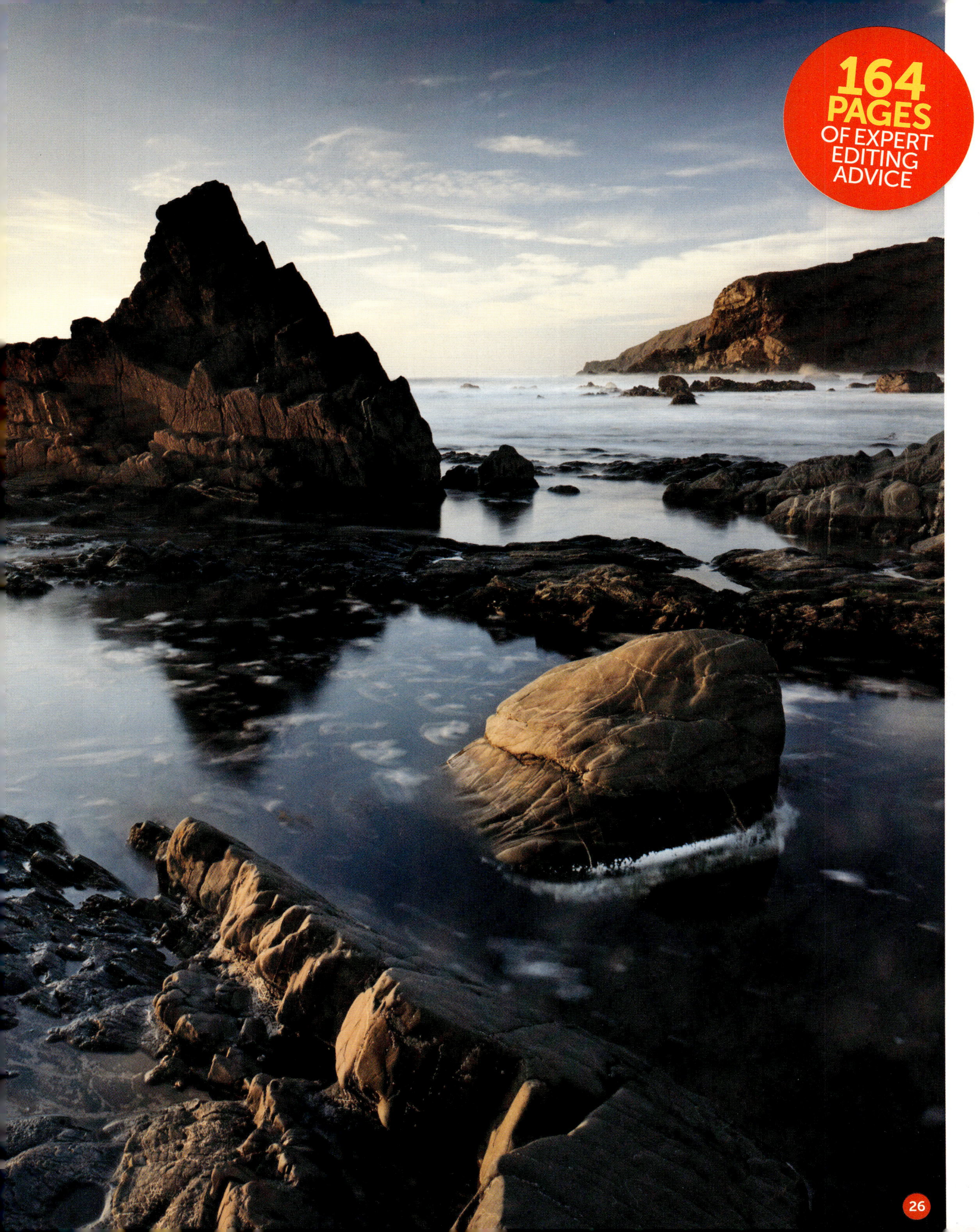
164
PAGES
OF EXPERT
EDITING
ADVICE

PHOTOSHOP. THE DIGITAL PHOTOGRAPHERS' CHOICE!

PHOTOGRAPHY IS ABOUT creativity, always has been. Since its inception, photographers haven't simply been content to document their surroundings but have sought to enhance, embellish, beautify and distort their imagery, be it via the darkroom or with in-camera techniques. Adobe Photoshop, Elements and Lightroom are just tools in the creative arsenal, though they happen to be damn good ones – the best possible. Everything that was done in the film darkroom can be recreated in these softwares, and far more besides. Images that are now appearing in this digital age are really pushing the boundaries of the imagination. So if you haven't already jumped on the Adobe bandwagon, it's really time to take that leap. You're missing out on the chance to explore your creative self. Even if your ambitions are modest, you'll find that there isn't an image in the world that can't be improved by editing in some manner, even if it's a matter of simple contrast tweaks or basic blemish removal. And the best way to learn is just to get stuck in. After, of course, you've familiarised yourself with the basics in our feature-packed guide to the best imaging software on the planet! Here are our favourite reasons for using Photoshop…

1) Raw conversion: All digital cameras come with their own brand software to help convert Raw files into an editable image state (ie JPEG or TIFF). However, these are often basic. Adobe Photoshop, Elements and Lightroom all come with their own Raw converter, Adobe Camera Raw (ACR), which happens to be rather good! Most people tend to plump for the Adobe engine rather than the camera manufacturer's own, not least because of its seamless integration with the rest of the software.

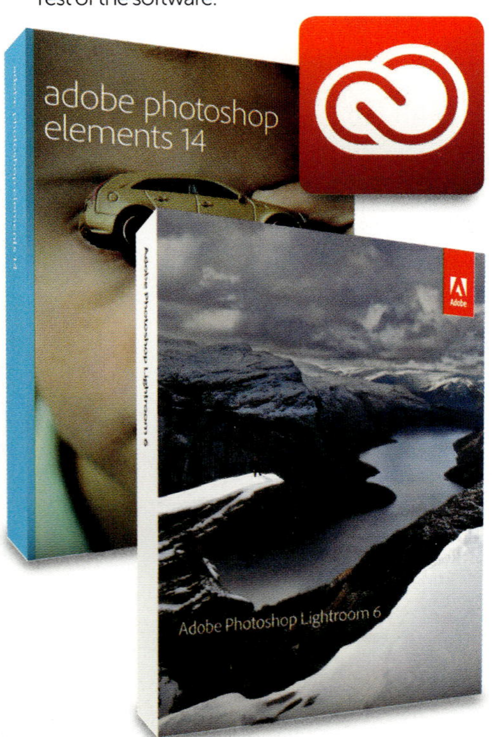

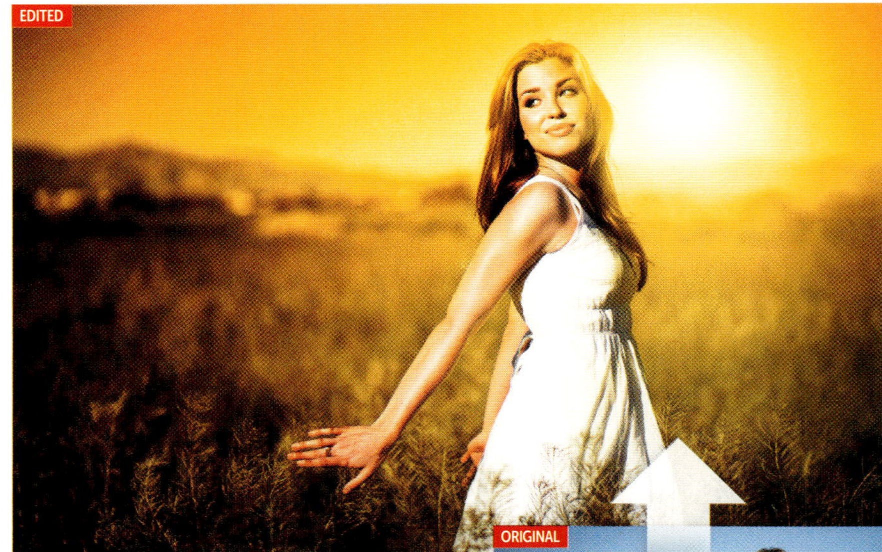

2) Exposure control: Adobe's editing software gives you the kind of exposure control that darkroom enthusiasts could have only dreamed of. Not only can you lighten or darken the image as a whole, but you can work on specific tones, lightening the highlights or darkening shadows, for example. You can also 'dodge' and 'burn' specific areas in the traditional darkroom manner – darkening a sky perhaps, or bringing out more detail in a landscape foreground.

3) Colour control: We're not just talking about warming things up or cooling them down. You can tweak colours in any way imaginable and locally as well as globally, changing the colour of someone's eyes, hair, or perhaps the colour of a particularly bad tie. And you can control colour saturation as well as hue, so you can make those sunsets really burn.

4) Better black and white: Yes, you can shoot black and white in camera but, no, it won't do. First, you'll be shooting JPEG and secondly, all you're doing is performing a basic desaturation, which means you'll be discarding vital information. Anyone who's printed in the traditional darkroom knows there's a bit more to mastering monochrome. Adobe's software lets you control specific colour channels in the way that black and white filters did for film cameras.

5) Blemish removal: On a basic level, this means polishing portraits a little by removing spots, moles and wrinkles, but this process can be extended to pretty much anything with the clever combination of Clone Stamp and Healing Brush Tools. You can remove a telegraph pole from an otherwise picture-perfect landscape, an unwanted reflection from a window, and so on.

6) Montage: Layers allow you to montage (otherwise known as composite) different images, in the same way that you might have once cut and pasted family photos together. But Photoshop allows you to go that extra mile. You can change a cloudy sky for a clear one, add trees where there were none, or even place a person in a completely different background scene. This type of montage is also known as compositing and has grown in popularity with amateur users and professionals alike.

7) Subject enhancement: As well as taking out aspects you don't really like and sticking in stuff that wasn't really there, you can also enhance what you've already got. Aside from the colour and exposure controls for whitening teeth or pulling out grey hairs, you could change the shape and size of parts of your image with various Transform commands. And yes, that can mean slimmer hips and bigger biceps, but it could also mean ironing out the converging verticals of a tall building or scaling down a hand that's too close to a wide-angle lens.

8) Web preparation: If you want to post your photos in a forum, an online gallery or your website, Adobe imaging software will come in handy. You can resize them, sharpen them, convert them to sRGB mode and save them with the appropriate JPEG quality setting.

9) Special Effects: Photoshop, Elements and Lightroom all have a massive array of filters and plug-ins to enable you to achieve special effects. Turn photos into watercolour paintings, add film effects, frames and borders, the list goes on.

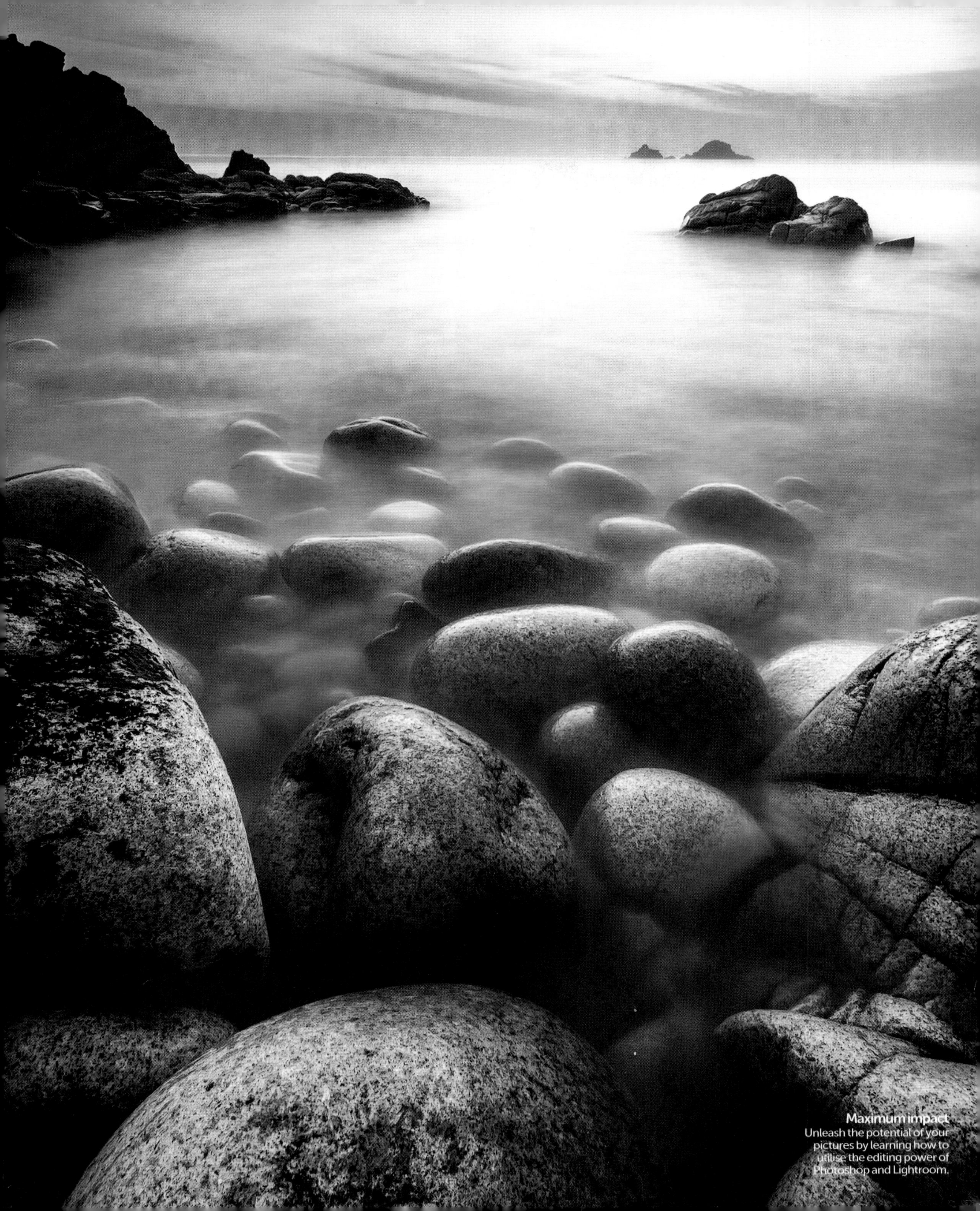

Maximum impact
Unleash the potential of your pictures by learning how to utilise the editing power of Photoshop and Lightroom.

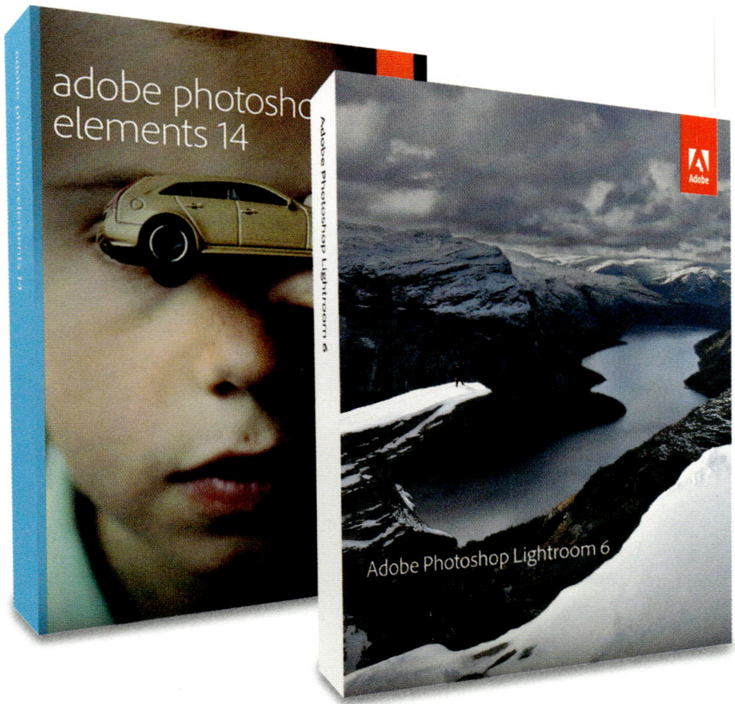

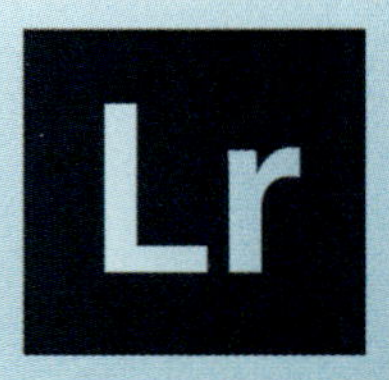

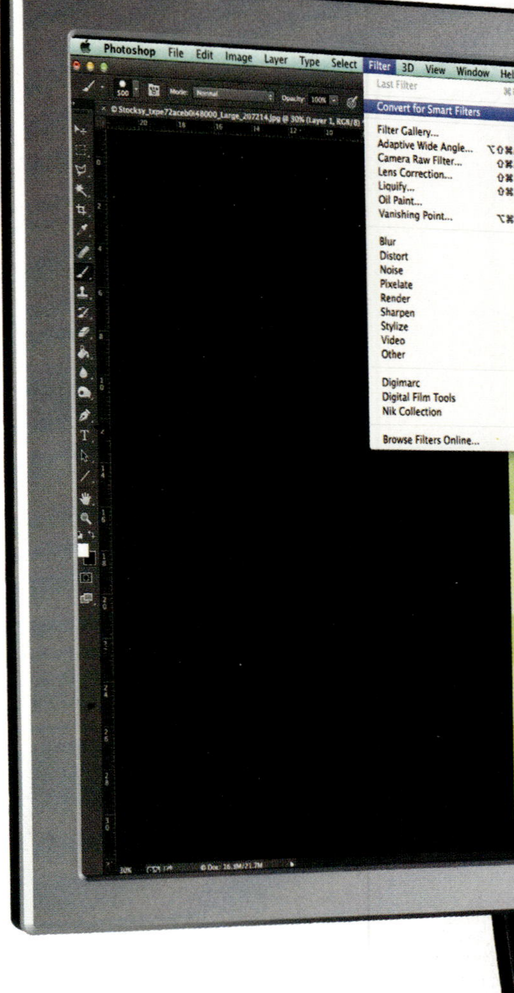

Which software is right for me?

THERE ARE TWO types of Photoshop, designed for different levels of user. You have Adobe's editing powerhouse, Photoshop, and the scaled-down Photoshop Elements, which is designed for those new to editing.

While you can still buy the standalone versions of Photoshop for several hundred pounds from some retailers, Adobe has now bundled it with the latest version of Lightroom – their popular editing and workflow system – into what's now known as Photoshop Creative Cloud, or CC. It's a monthly subscription-based service, costing less than £9 per month, and ensures you always have the latest version of the softwares. It's the choice of many professionals but really suits any photographer who wants to catalogue large volumes of images and have tools and scope to do more advanced image retouching.

The beginner-friendly Photoshop Elements – now in version 14 – is still offered as a standalone package costing around £75 and suits most photographer's needs for basic image enhancements. It's a teacherly program that guides you through the available tools and adjustments, including the use of Layers.

If Elements 14 is more your skill level, but you want the professional workflow and a few more advanced editing features, you might also want to consider buying the standalone Adobe Lightroom 6 for £110 as you can still link these two softwares seamlessly. Still wondering your best option? Turn over to learn more...

Photoshop interface
While the Elements interface is a little different from Photoshop CC, there are enough similarities so that photographers upgrading from one to the other won't find it alien.

Which Photoshop: New or old?

If you're a first-time buyer who wants a standalone package, there's little incentive to buy earlier versions than Photoshop CS6 or Elements 14 as there isn't much difference in price and you'll avoid camera compatibility problems that can come with earlier versions. If you're not planning to upgrade your camera and already own a copy of Elements or Photoshop, weigh up the price against the features you'll be gaining before you buy a newer version. There are some features that make the upgrade worth it, if they're of use to you, such as Layers in Elements 9, Photomerge for panoramics in CS3, CS4's Clone Stamp Tool, CS5's Content-Aware Fill function and CC's Camera Shake Reduction. Remember to check the compatibility of your operating system, too, as what supports CS3 may not be recent enough to use CS5 or CS6. Also many plug-ins are only compatible with the latest versions of Lightroom and Photoshop. Bear in mind, too, that Raw support for new cameras will only be added to Lightroom and Photoshop CC, so the subscription-based service is your best bet if you want to ensure future compatibility – Adobe will not add support for new cameras to older versions.

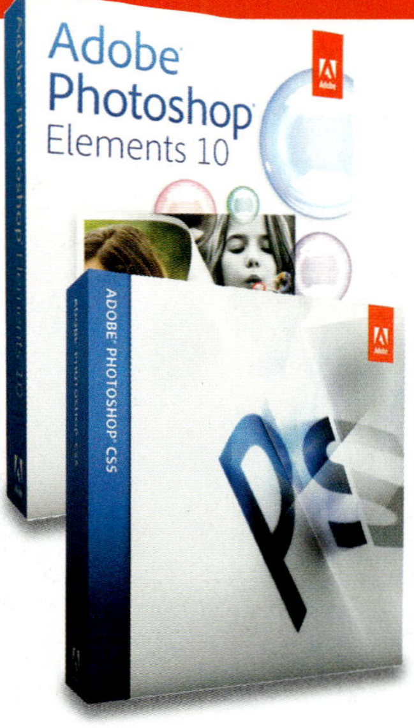

File formats

Check out the File Format drop-down list in the Photoshop Save As dialogue and get a shock at the multitude of options available. Panic not, though; there are only really four formats worth discussing.

✓ Photoshop
Photoshop EPS
JPEG
Large Document Format
Photoshop PDF
Photoshop 2.0
Photoshop Raw
Scitex CT
TIFF
Photoshop DCS 1.0
Photoshop DCS 2.0

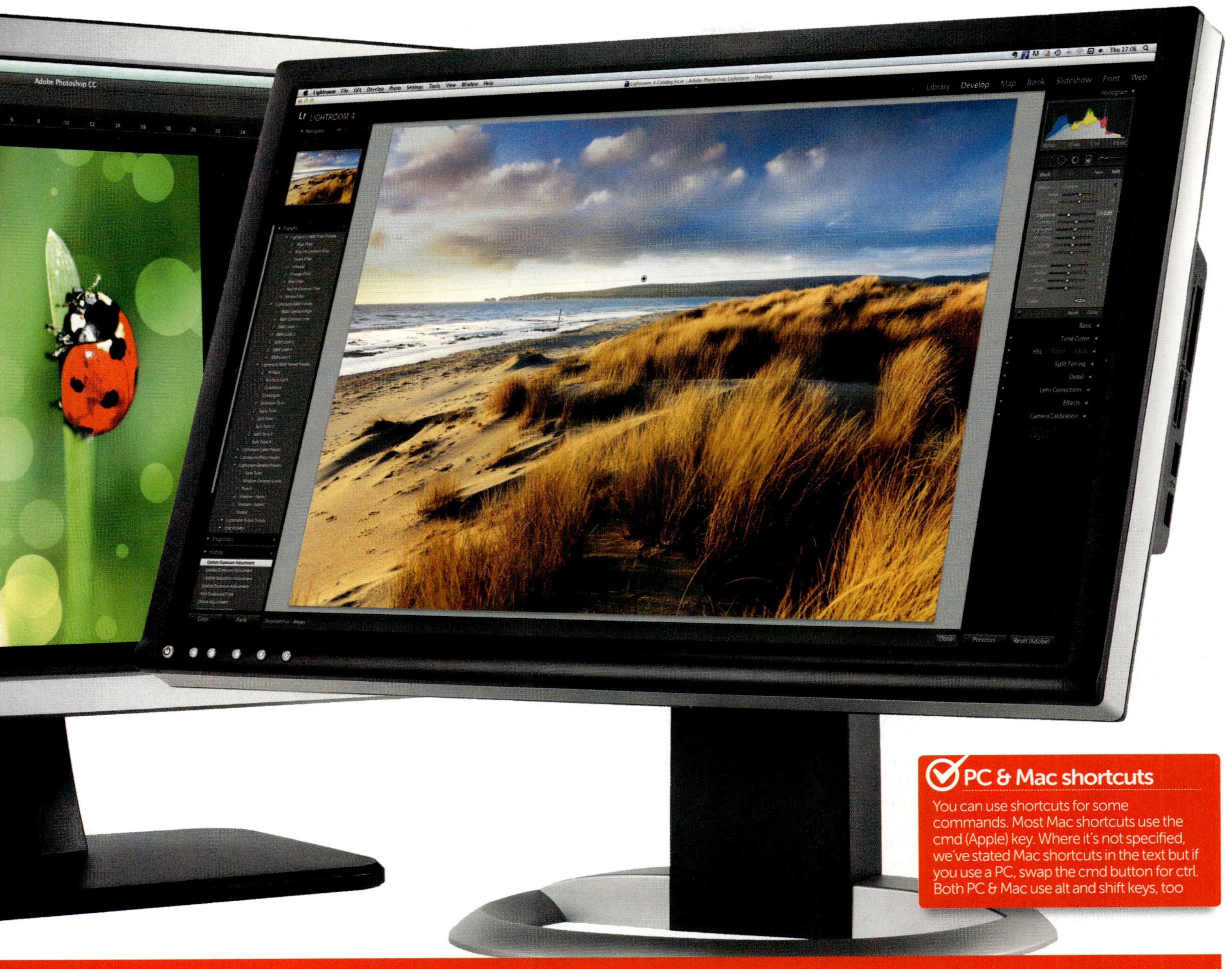

PC & Mac shortcuts

You can use shortcuts for some commands. Most Mac shortcuts use the cmd (Apple) key. Where it's not specified, we've stated Mac shortcuts in the text but if you use a PC, swap the cmd button for ctrl. Both PC & Mac use alt and shift keys, too

RAW

This is the catch-all term given to the different proprietary file formats direct out of a camera when shooting in Raw (a Canon EOS 5D Mk II Raw file, for example, has the extension .CR2). These files need converting into editable information via a Raw converter, such as Adobe Camera Raw (ACR), which comes with Photoshop, Elements and Lightroom. Shooting Raw allows access to the full range of information recorded by the camera sensor, giving more room to correct for exposure mistakes and to make edits to your image without chancing visible degradation. Raw files give you access to 16-bits of information, as opposed to a JPEG's 8-bits.

PSD

The PSD file is a Photoshop format that allows all Photoshop information, such as layers and saved selections, to be easily stored and re-accessed at a later date. It's an uncompressed format and maintains the full 16-bits of information. While TIFF files do give you the option of including Photoshop layers, the file size increases disproportionately, making PSD the file format of choice for editing your images. When the image is finally flattened, it can be saved as a TIFF or JPEG, although it's always a good idea to keep the PSD file with all the layers of work you've done in case you need to make any additional changes at a later date.

JPEG

The JPEG is a compressed file format, designed to keep file size as low as possible with as little quality loss as possible. It uses what's termed a 'lossy' version of compression, meaning image information is thrown away for good. The amount discarded depends on the compression setting. A JPEG file retains only 8-bits rather than 16-bits of information, making it less useful as a format for image editing; the decrease in available information can produce signs of degradation if adjustments are pushed particularly hard. The reduced file size makes JPEGs great for web reproduction, email and even magazine reproduction, with a quality setting of 9 or more.

TIFF

The TIFF is generally an uncompressed file format (though there is a 'lossless' compression option), and an alternative to the JPEG for distributing images once you've made all your edits in Photoshop and flattened the layers. File sizes are considerably bigger than JPEGs, so it's used as a maximum quality option if you're prepared to distribute images on a CD or upload them via FTP – forget email! Those without a copy of Photoshop are normally able to open a TIFF file without any problems. It can hold 16-bits of information, but as it's not generally used for editing, it's better to convert your images to 8-bits before saving as a TIFF to keep down the file size.

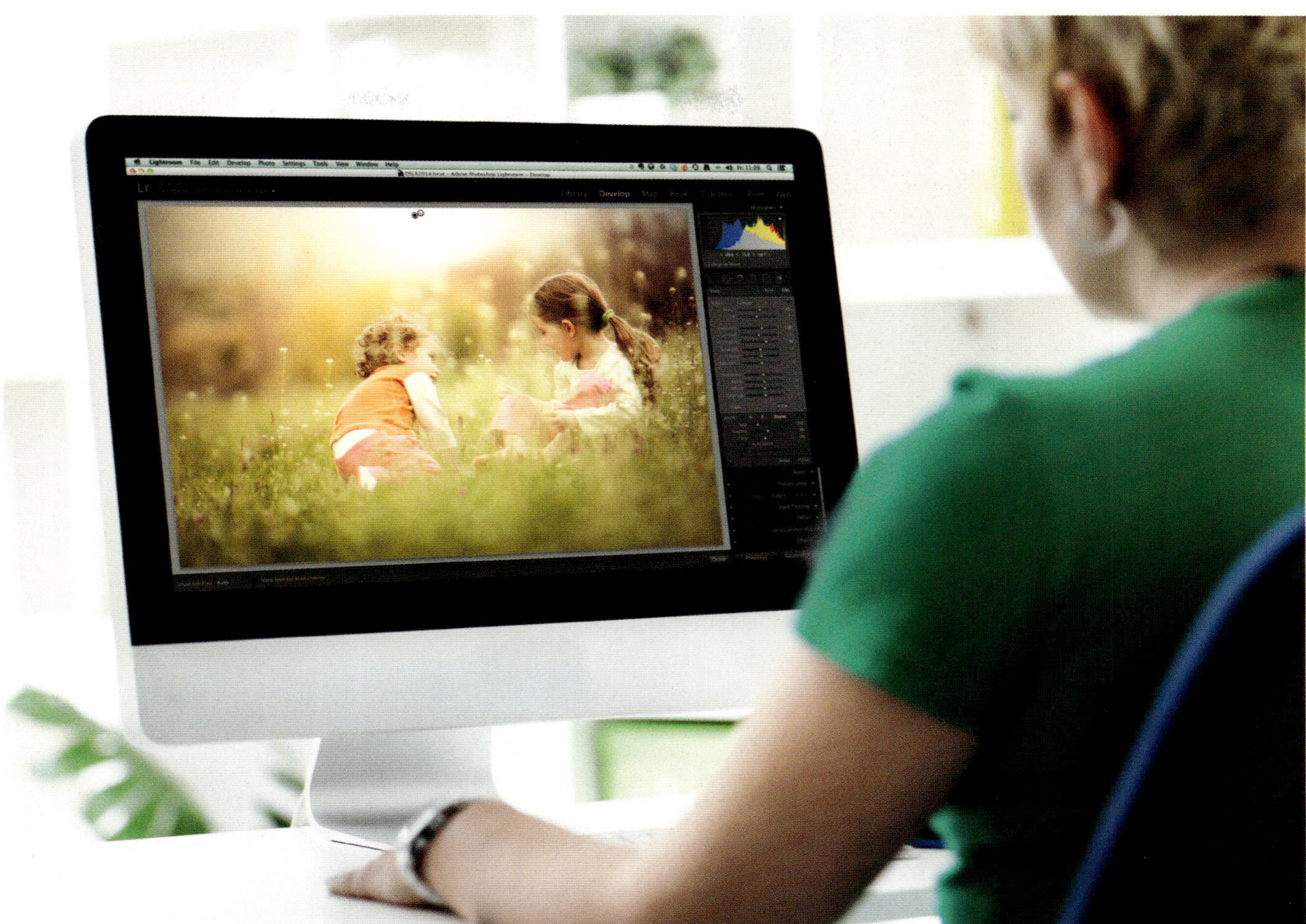

Which Adobe editing software is right for you?

You know you need software to improve image quality and express your creativity, but you're unsure which to choose. We explain the similarities and differences of each editing program so you can make a sound decision

LIGHTROOM, ELEMENTS OR Photoshop Creative Cloud (CC)? It's a question many photographers ask themselves, especially now the full version of Photoshop is more affordable than ever thanks to a monthly subscription. Many who once recoiled at the hefty price might be tempted to give it a go, but is it the right choice for you when compared to Lightroom or the even more affordable Elements 14? That's what we aim to help you decide here.

Photoshop and digital photography are the perfect pair to the point that the noun 'Photoshopped' has become synonymous with most types of photo editing. However, while professional image quality is expected with Photoshop CC, the extensive tools in Lightroom and even Photoshop Elements may be more than adequate depending on your budget and level of skill. Some enthusiast and many professional photographers find combining Lightroom, as a way to manage their workflow, with Photoshop CC gives them everything that they need. However, Elements 14 offers similar organising, editing and sharing features at a much lower cost, but as a less sophisticated and scaled-down version of the two top-dog programs. While there are other photographers that find Lightroom's editing suite sufficient as an all-in-one software and have no need for Elements or Photoshop. Which are you?

If you want access to the advanced editing features of Photoshop and like to have the latest tools, plus the benefit of Lightroom's workflow features, the monthly subscription to CC could be the way to go. However, if you prefer to own your program rather than get locked-in to a pay-monthly contract, Elements and Lightroom can still be bought as standalone packages. It's worth noting, though, that while updates for Elements are available, Adobe has kept the monopoly on Lightroom by stopping available upgrades, unless you subscribe to CC. Unless you plan to upgrade your camera, and need the latest software for compatibility, it's unlikely this will be a problem as Lightroom 6 is already highly capable with a sophisticated toolkit.

To help you further in your decision, we've an overview of all three choices...

Photoshop Elements 14

Photoshop Elements offers guidance for all levels of photographer, with a focus on beginners to make learning the ropes as easy as possible

Buy for: £79.10
Upgrade for: £64.81
Best for: New photographers and those with limited editing skills or basic ambitions for their editing

"CAPTURE THE MOMENT now. Perfect the photo later': it's Adobe's sell for the latest version of Elements and it's suitably fitting given it's designed for photographers who prefer auto over manual mode, or find their skills in their infancy.

In essence, Elements is a stripped-down version of Photoshop CC that's much easier to use but is still loaded with easy-to-use features, such as one-click Quick editing options as well as Guided and Expert platforms for when you progress in skill. The Guided interface is ideal for new amateur photographers, while the Expert mode looks and functions similar to Photoshop CC, making it perfect for budget-conscious Weekend Photo Warriors. It's the cheapest option by far – you can own Elements for the same cost of renting Photoshop CC for eight months and have access to many of its features, including Layers and Layer Masks (available since Elements 9).

For new photographers, or those new to digital editing, Elements is a powerful software designed to guide you through basic editing, enhancements and printing. Based on the same excellent image editing code as Photoshop CC, Elements gives you room to improve as well as easily corrects rookie mistakes. For instance, a new feature for Elements 14 allows you to remove camera shake caused by too slow a shutter speed for steady handholding. While earlier versions of the software feature tools for replacing backgrounds, recomposing images and removing colour casts. For the most part, the program's features are automated or provide clear step-by-step on-screen instructions on how to use properly. While this makes it easy for amateur photographers, it's somewhat restrictive and frustrating for more advanced editors who find creativity and refinement in specific manual controls. If you like to do compositing, for instance, while Elements 14 does offer an improved Quick Selection Brush to create more refined selections of tricky edges, it's still a less sophisticated tool than what you can find in Photoshop CC.

Even if you do advance quickly, however, and want more control, Elements offers extensive Raw editing options – not as many as Photoshop CC, but enough to continue to progress developing your image quality. And, if you find yourself outgrowing the system, you could buy Elements XXL (Windows only) – a plug-in that adds up to 430 features to Elements, previously only available in Photoshop CC, such as Curves, the Properties panel for editing Layer Masks, Warp filter and Channels panel.

New features

- A one-click solution for removing camera shake from unsteady hands.
- Remove the common haziness from your landscape images for saturated skies.
- Better selection tools for complex composites, however Photoshop still has the edge.
- Even more creative options to make simple toning and special effects easy to apply.
- It's capable of organising photos by events, places and even the people in the images.
- New editing styles: Elements analyses the subject, colour and lighting and gives you five effects that fit perfectly to the image.

TAKE A GUIDED TOUR

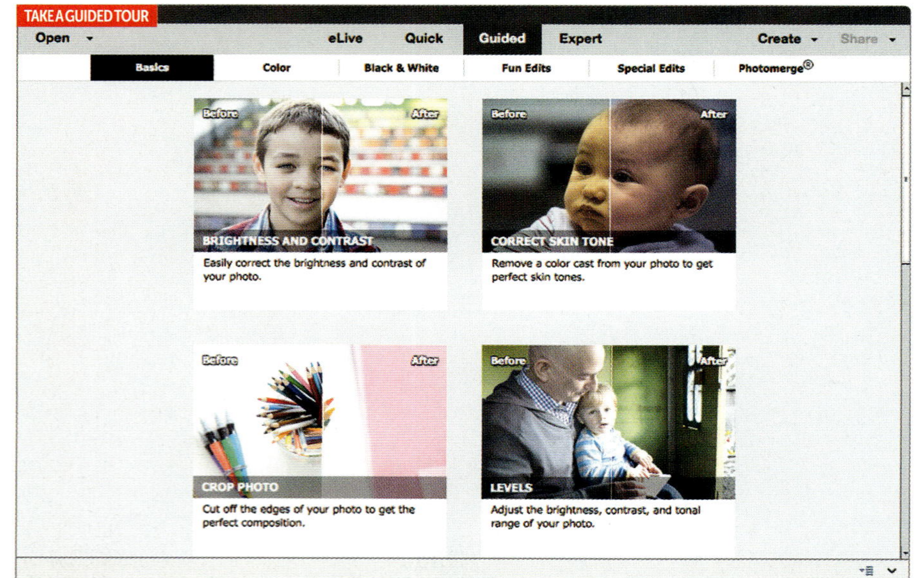

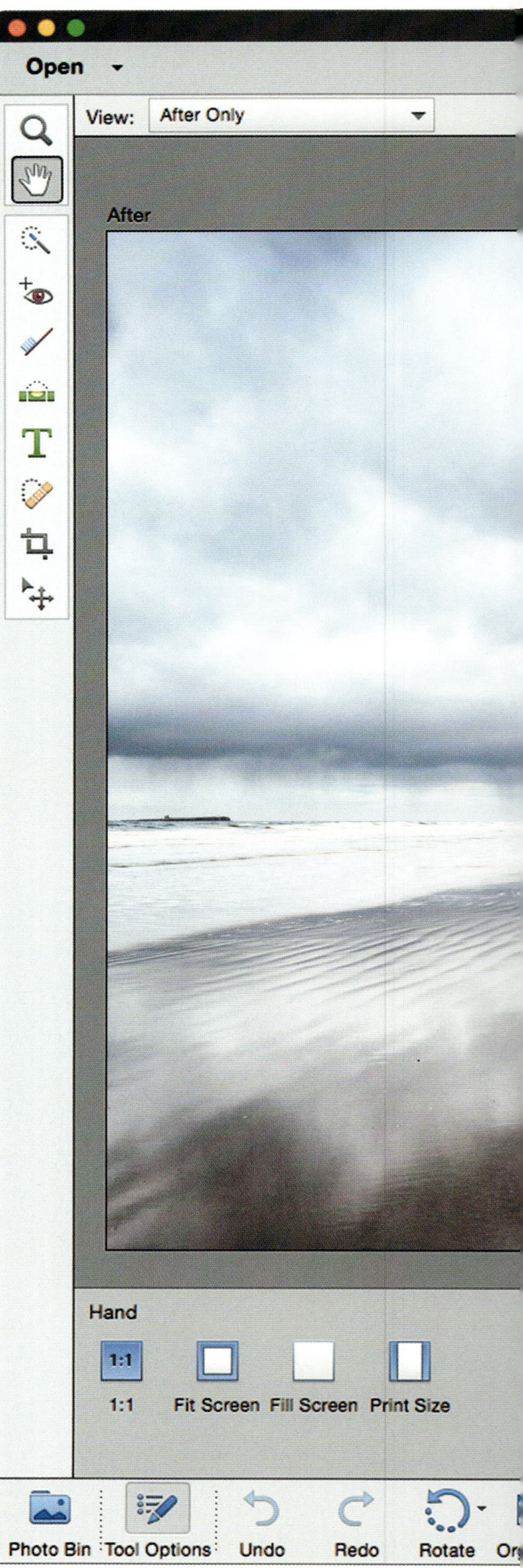

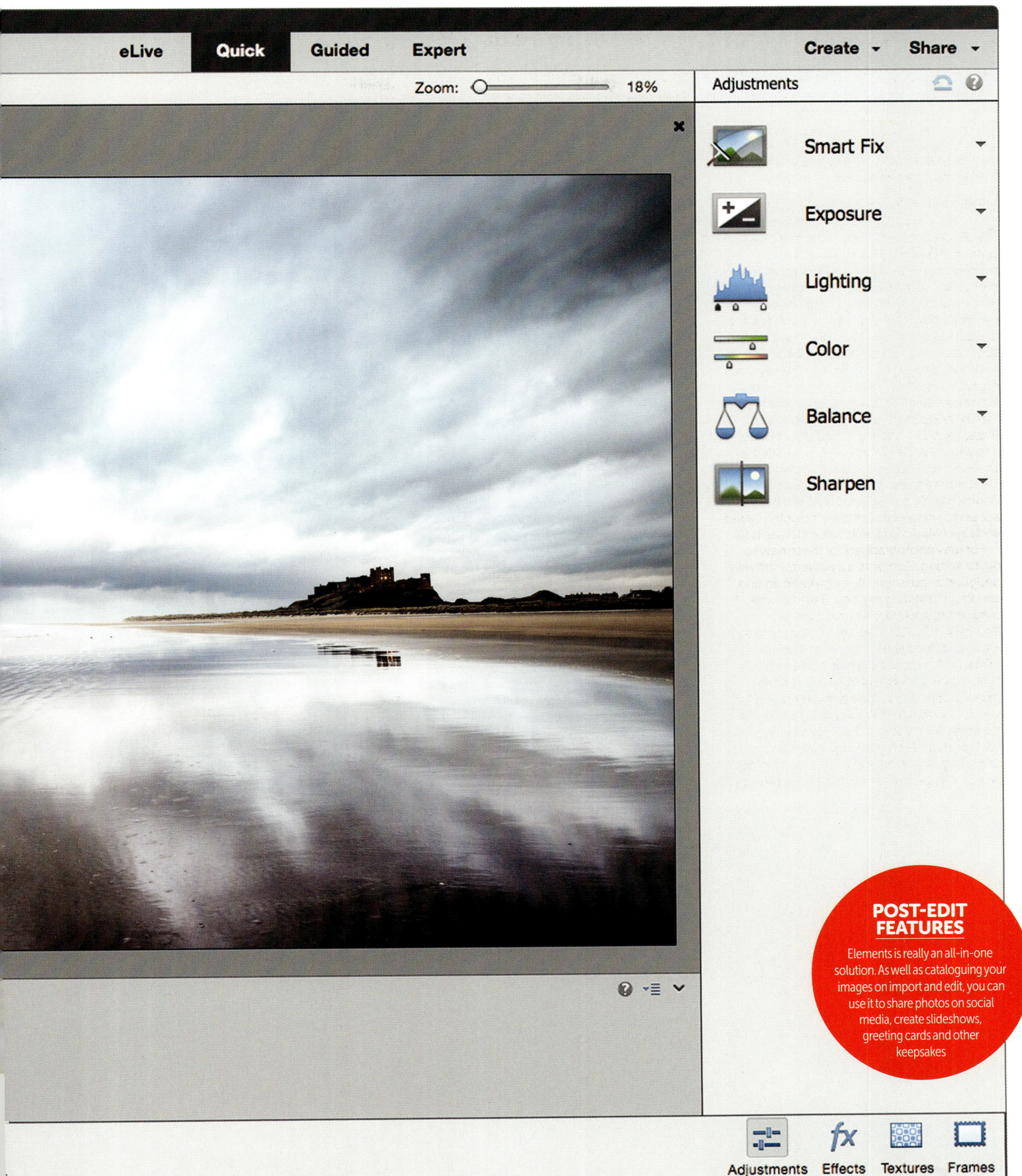

POST-EDIT FEATURES

Elements is really an all-in-one solution. As well as cataloguing your images on import and edit, you can use it to share photos on social media, create slideshows, greeting cards and other keepsakes

Lightroom CC

Photoshop Lightroom is a professional's tool for organising and processing digital images, but could not be more simple to master

Buy for: £110 (Lightroom 6 or earlier)
Rent for: £8.57 per month (as part of CC package)
Best for: Enthusiast and pro photographers who want advanced editing as well as cataloguing

THINK OF LIGHTROOM as the ultimate digital darkroom where you can organise and edit your negatives. It's a system for serious enthusiast and professional photographers alike; it's the first stop and often the only stop for photographers due to its arsenal of editing and cataloguing features.

Many pro photographers use Lightroom to download their memory cards, filter their image selection and then do all – or 90% – of their editing using the Develop module. You can quickly organise your entire library of photos, efficiently make common global edits and even make selective tweaks using the Adjustment Brush – frankly, there's very little you cannot do, so why do you even need Photoshop CC?

If your shots need no significant changes, well, you don't – Photoshop is for when you want to manipulate images, to remove elements or use high-end editing techniques like Frequency Separation for skin retouching. For photographers who prefer more options, advanced techniques and wider scope for creativity – Photoshop is their polishing cloth. For everyone else, you may just find Lightroom has all you could ever want.

Aside from a slew of useful features to correct lens distortion and to adjust exposure, colour and tone, there are also extensive output options for printing, contact sheets, photos books and web publishing, making it similar to Elements. But the pinnacle of Lightroom for many is its presets; it's fully loaded set of colour toning, image enhancing and mono-converting features that you can apply to your images individually or in batches. It's the ultimate system for efficient editing, which is why it is many a pro's preferred software. If you're concerned about all your images looking too uniform or common, Lightroom has a plethora of features to create your own presets, uploading actions and tools to help you customise your signature look. But that's not the best part...

We all know that the more edits we make, the more it diminishes image quality, but with Lightroom you don't have to worry about it. Every edit you make in Lightroom is nondestructive, that means you can see and alter the changes you make to your images without making those changes permanent. Brilliant! It uses the same genius interface as Adobe Camera Raw, so if you're familiar with editing in ACR, you'll circumnavigate Lightroom with ease as it has many of the same tools and is of a similar layout. The depths of Lightroom are so expansive, from cataloguing to editing, that we've dedicated an entire section of this MagBook (pages 39-61) to help you get to grips with it by taking you through all the main features and functions in this amazing program.

Best features

- Efficiently organises images on import by creating folders, collections and tagging.
- Offers a superb array of professional-grade one-click toning solutions for fast workflow.
- You may not have Layers, but you can still make small, precise edits using the Adjustment Brush
- All images are edited in their raw format and any editing is completely nondestructive
- Provides easy export solutions such as slideshows, book publishing and to the web.

MAKE PRECISE ADJUSTMENTS

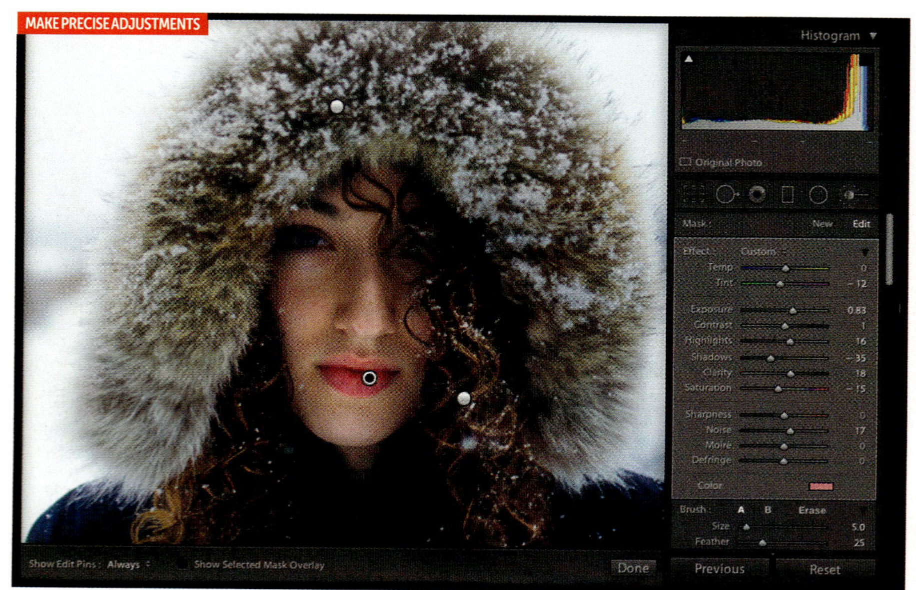

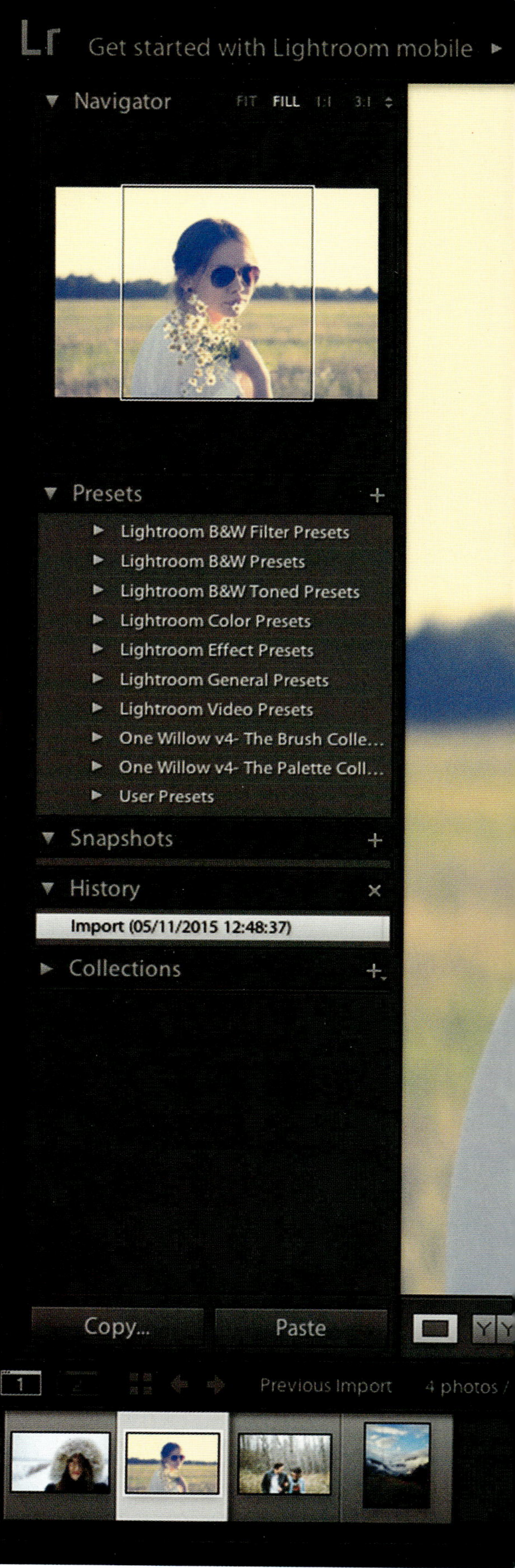

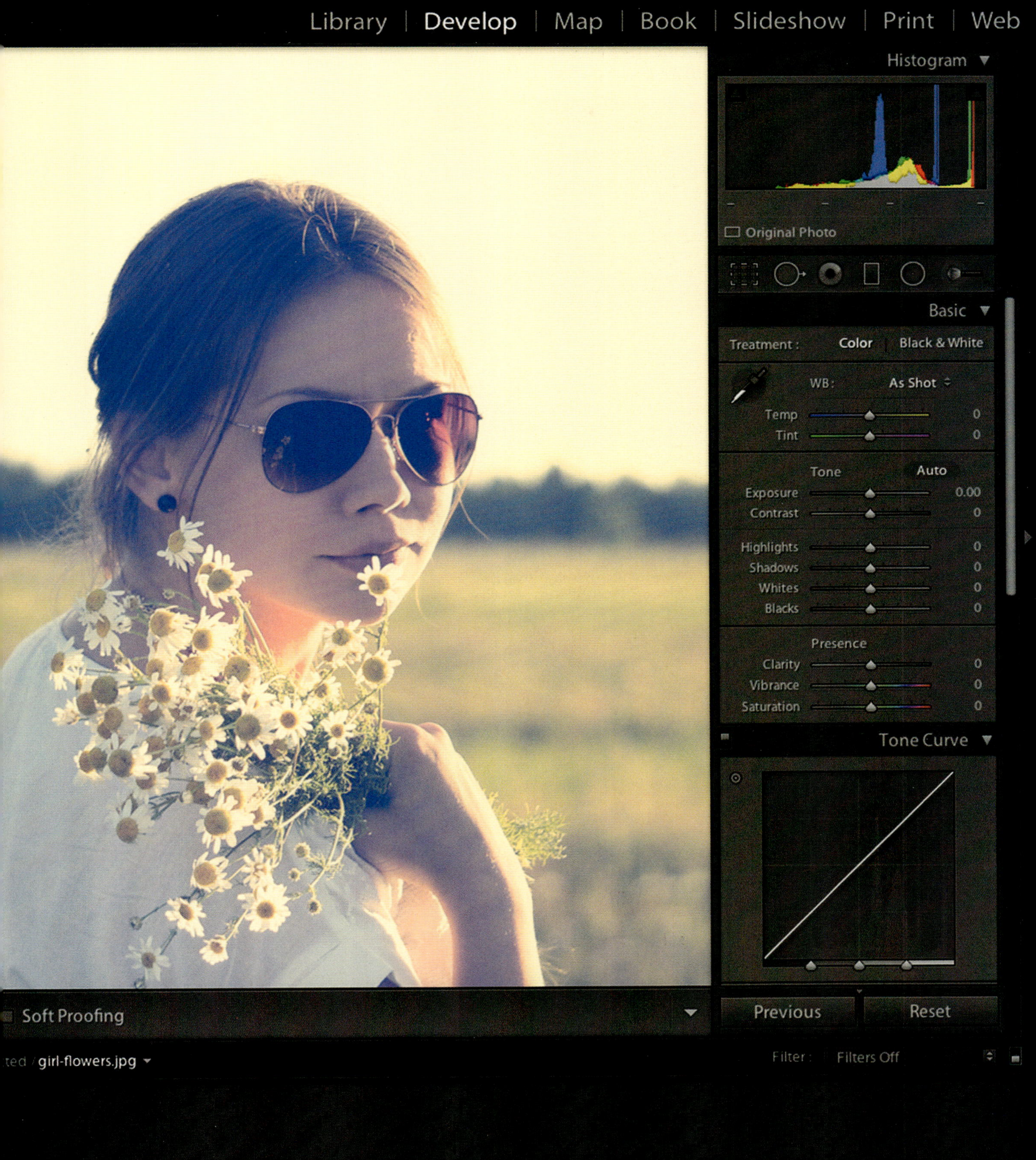
Library
Develop
Map
Book
Slideshow
Print
Web
Histogram
Original Photo
Basic
Treatment :
Color
Black & White
WB :
As Shot
Temp
0
Tint
0
Tone
Auto
Exposure
0.00
Contrast
0
Highlights
0
Shadows
0
Whites
0
Blacks
0
Presence
Clarity
0
Vibrance
0
Saturation
0
Tone Curve
Soft Proofing
Previous
Reset
girl-flowers.jpg
Filter :
Filters Off

Photoshop CC

The top-dog of editing software, Photoshop CC has the most extensive set of features to enable professional quality and creativity for photographers

Buy for: £799 (Photoshop CS6)
Rent for: £8.57 per month (as part of CCI package)
Best for: Advanced photographers and those who want precise and unlimited control over their editing

IF YOU'RE STILL UNSURE, or contemplating investing in a Creative Cloud subscription, you probably want to know what all the fuss is about for Photoshop CC. Frankly, it's probably a bit misdirected unless you're an advanced photographer, designer or animator. The answer whether you need it or not depends on how intricate you want your editing to be. If you plan to create complex composites or simply want access to a wider selection of tools and better features, then it's worth it. There are at least three or four ways to do any one thing in Photoshop, which is arguably two to three more ways than in Elements, so you can choose and control your preferred method of working. If you want that creative flexibility, then subscribing to Creative Cloud is perhaps your best option.

If you're a complete beginner, Photoshop CC will be a steep learning curve to conquer. It's a huge program that offers no on-screen user guidance, and has very few automated controls to ease you through. But when it comes to sophisticated tools and editing potential, it cannot be beat. You've got the tools to manipulate colour channels, access advanced features like Curves as well as create and use actions, to name just a few.

The decision between buying Elements 14 and licensing Photoshop CC is pretty simple, but choosing between Lightroom and Photoshop is a little trickier. You can own Lightroom, which is capable of doing at least 90% of a photographer's editing, for almost the same cost of a year's subscription to Creative Cloud – that's quite the saving over the long term. However, when it comes to making changes to a photo, there is nothing you can do in Lightroom that you can't do in Photoshop, but the same cannot be said the other way around. Here are five reasons you may prefer Photoshop:

- **COMPOSITING:** While Lightroom has Adjustment Brushes for selective, nondestructive editing, Photoshop has Layers and Layer Masks, making it easier to control your selective editing and to reassess your workflow. Without Layers, it's also impossible to composite or blend images.
- **SHARPENING:** Lightroom has a basic sharpening panel and sharpening output function, while Photoshop has several global methods of sharpening as well as tools for localised sharpening.
- **REPLACING:** Photoshop has Content Aware Fill, which lets you select an area of an image and Adobe's genius fills it based on the information surrounding the area.
- **RETOUCHING:** Anyone who has used Lightroom and Photoshop will tell you that the Clone Stamp and Healing Brush Tools are far superior in Photoshop. When it comes to evening out skin tones, removing blemishes and other intricate retouching, the combination of Photoshop's tools make it the superior option for flawless results.
- **EXTENSIVE SET OF TOOLS:** Compared to Lightroom, Photoshop has a far more expansive set of features to pick from giving you multiple ways to work.

Lightroom & Photoshop CC

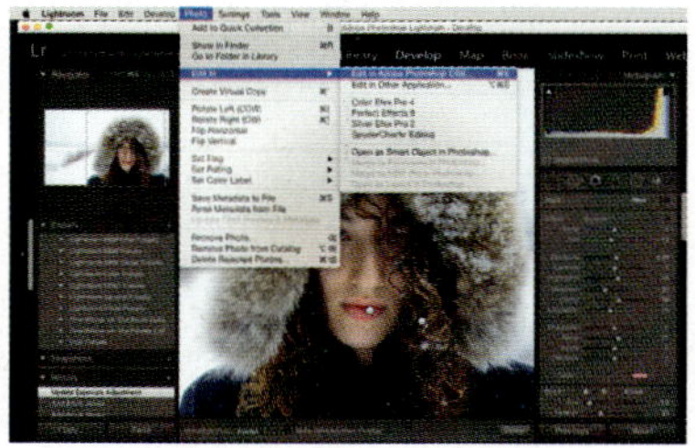

How easy is it to work in Lightroom and Photoshop CC? Very easy – the programs seamlessly work together. Most photographers import their images into Lightroom to organise and back up their library, make most of their global and selective edits in the Develop module, then if there's more to do that need specific Photoshop tools, all they need to do is go to ***Edit in>Photoshop*** to transfer the image.

PRO-QUALITY RETOUCHING

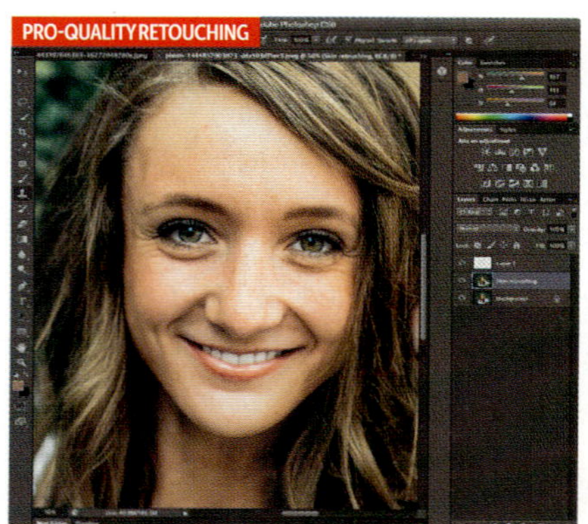

ADVANCED LAYER FEATURES

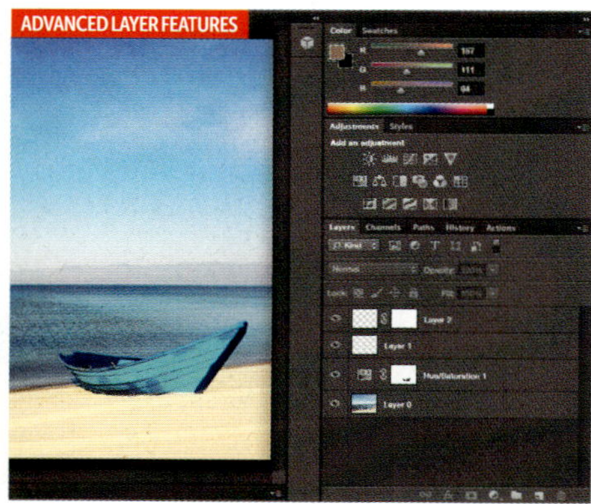

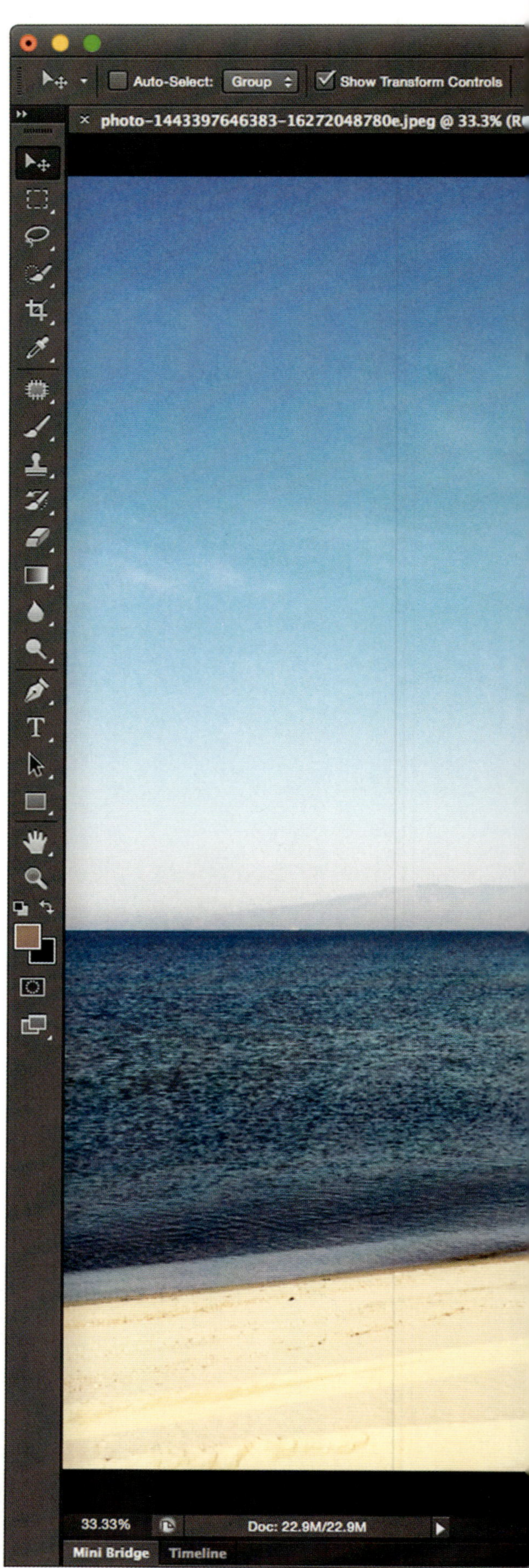

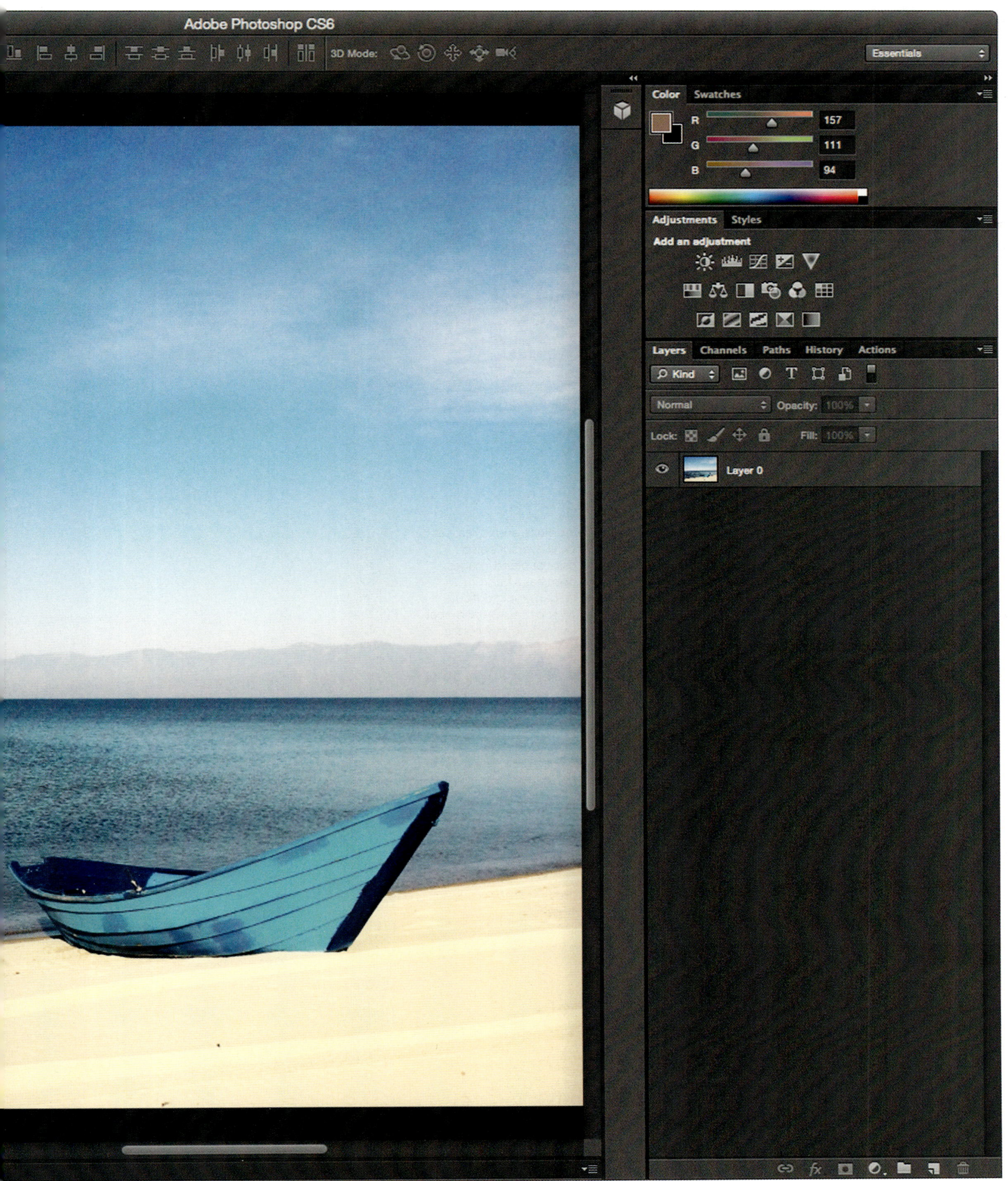
Adobe Photoshop CS6
3D Mode:
Essentials
Color
Swatches
R
157
G
111
B
94
Adjustments
Styles
Add an adjustment
Layers
Channels
Paths
History
Actions
Kind
Normal
Opacity:
Lock:
Fill:
Layer 0

MENUS, TOOLS & PALETTES

THE PHOTOSHOP workspace can be a daunting place at first, with its vast array of features. However, once you grasp a basic understanding of just a few key areas, you'll be up and running in no time. Here we'll be looking at the Expert workspace of Photoshop Elements 14 and although there are differences between Elements' interface and Photoshop's, Adobe does a great job with crossing over packages to encourage a progression as users become more experienced.

Some of the tools here also carry over into Adobe Lightroom. The four key areas to understand are the Toolbar (which runs vertically on the left side), the Tool Options at the bottom of the interface, the Menu bar (which runs along the top) and the Panel Bin, which sits to the right-hand side and holds palettes such as Layers and Effects. Also on the right are Create and Share for when you're ready to export your images. Most of these items can be hidden or made visible via the Window tab, which allows the user to customise the workspace to suit.

Top tip

Customise your space The Photoshop interface is fully customisable. If there are palettes you don't use, simply hide them in the Window menu. Also, you can drag and drop them into positions that suit you!

The Toolbar

Photoshop's tools are generally easy to understand as their descriptions usually outline their function well, you can also identify each by hovering over the icons.

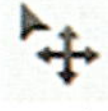

Move This tool can be used to move pixel information on a layer, text or an active selection. Just click and drag.

Zoom Click to zoom in, or press *alt* and click to zoom out. You may also choose to use *ctrl* (PC) or *cmd* (Mac) plus the + or – keys.

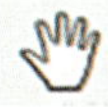

Hand Use for moving around your image when zoomed in. Access quickly by holding down the *spacebar*.

Color Picker Select a colour from your image by clicking on the areas. Use the Tool Options to choose whether the picker samples a single pixel or an average from a 3x3 or 5x5 area.

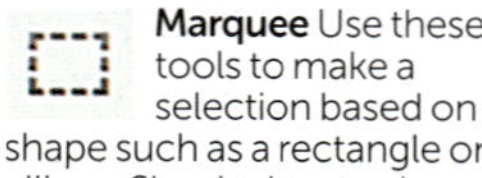

Marquee Use these tools to make a selection based on a shape such as a rectangle or ellipse. Simply drag to size.

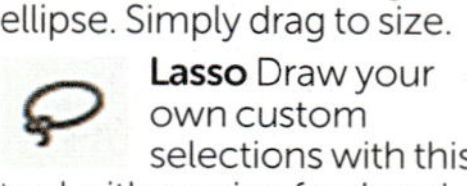

Lasso Draw your own custom selections with this tool, either using freehand, polygonal or magnetic points.

Quick Selection Houses the Quick Selection, Selection Brush and Magic Wand Tools for semi-automated selections. You can adjust the brush controls in the Tool Options bar.

Type Add text directly onto your image using any of the installed fonts. Type horizontally or vertically and create selections based on your type.

Crop Crop out unwanted aspects from your image. Set a width-to-height ratio if needed in Tool Options. Also houses the Cookie Cutter Tool, used for cutting shapes out of your images.

Spot Healing Brush Replace blemishes with nearby clean pixel information and have it blend in with surrounding pixels. Also houses the Healing Brush Tool for manual corrections.

Clone Stamp Allows you to copy and paste pixels from one area to another without the blending of the Healing Brush. Also houses the Pattern Stamp Tool.

Eraser Remove pixel information manually or in a semi-automated manner using the Background or Magic Eraser Tool.

Brush A useful tool, particularly when combined with Layer Masks. Control its Opacity and Size via Tool Options. Houses the Impressionist Brush and Color Replacement Brush too.

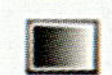

Gradient Draw gradients directly onto layers or their masks. You can edit the gradients in Tool Options.

Blur Soften selected areas of your image or Sharpen and Smudge them with the two other useful tools which are housed within Blur.

Custom Shape Draw shapes or lines using any one of the default shapes, or choose another with the Custom Shape Tool.

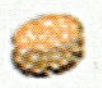

Sponge The Sponge Tool increases or decreases colour saturation. There's also the Dodge Tool for lightening and the Burn Tool for darkening.

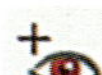

Red Eye Removal A quick fix for removing red eye (or pet eye) caused by an on-camera flash. Tool Options allows you to adjust pupil size and darken the eyes too.

Smart Brush Part selection tool, part adjustment brush, the Smart Brush allows you to quickly enhance select parts of your images. Also houses the Detail Smart Brush Tool.

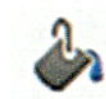

Paint Bucket Used for replacing an area of colour with another single colour. Adjust the Opacity and Tolerance in Tool Options, or choose the Pattern option to fill with a pattern.

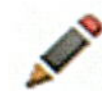

Pencil Draw pixels onto your image. Can also be used on Layer Masks but creates harder edged lines than the Brush Tool. Useful for annotating images or making notes on a blank layer.

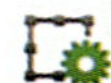

Recompose A combination of crop and transform tools. Allows you to mark areas to preserve and areas to transform before changing the composition or crop.

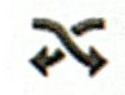

Content Aware Move Allows you to select an element of your image and move it. Elements will fill the space left by the element using surrounding pixel data.

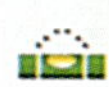

Straighten Draw a line to straighten wonky images. Select Autofill Edges in Tool Options to use Content Aware Fill to fill any spaces.

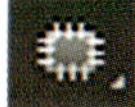

Patch (CS/CC only) A combination of the Lasso and Healing Brush Tool. Select Content Aware from the options bar for seamless blending with the surrounding area.

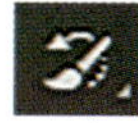

History Brush (CS/CC only) Go back in time by painting previous states into your image in conjunction with the History palette.

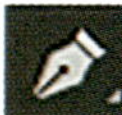

Pen (CS/CC only) Allows the user to create curved or straight selections to precisely outline solid-edge subjects.

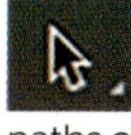

Path Selection (CS/CC only) Use to select and move paths created with the Pen and Shape Tool.

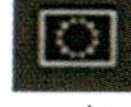

Quick Mask Mode (CS/CC only) View selections as a red mask rather than marching ants. When active, paint with a Black or White brush to add or subtract from the mask.

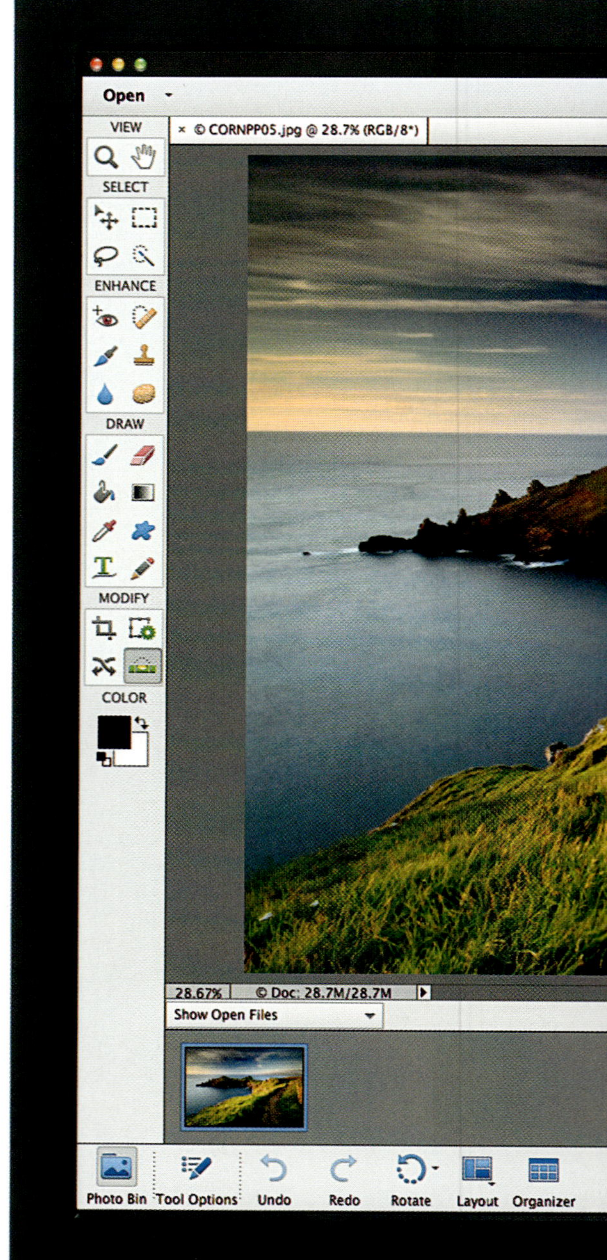

Elements workspace
Elements' interface is a simplified version of the one found in Photoshop. Many of the tools within are the same too.

The Menu bar

EDIT As well as hosting options for general preferences and keyboard shortcuts, the Edit menu is home to Undo, Redo, Cut, Copy, Paste and Delete, though all these are accessed easier via their respective keyboard shortcuts. You can also define new patterns and brushes here too.

IMAGE The Transform commands are located here, allowing you to perform things such as Free Transform, Skew, Distort and Perspective. You can also Rotate, Flip and Straighten from here, as well as Crop and Recompose. There's also controls to change the Image and Canvas Size and Mode and Color Profile.

LAYER The Layer menu is home to popular layer-based commands like Merge Layers and Flatten Image, and you can also add Fill or Adjustment Layers from here. In truth, virtually everything in this menu is quicker accessed by keyboard shortcuts or buttons on the Layers palette itself.

SELECT Everything to do with selections is here, such as Select All, Deselect and Select Inverse. You can also modify selections via this menu with commands like Expand, Contract and, most commonly, Refine Edge and Feather. This menu also gives access to the very useful Transform Selection command.

FILTER Along with being home to a variety of special-effects filters and adjustments, the Filters menu also includes two of the most often used tools in Photoshop – Correct Distortion and Gaussian Blur. There's also High Pass, which can be used with different Blend Modes for sharpening an image or dramatic effect.

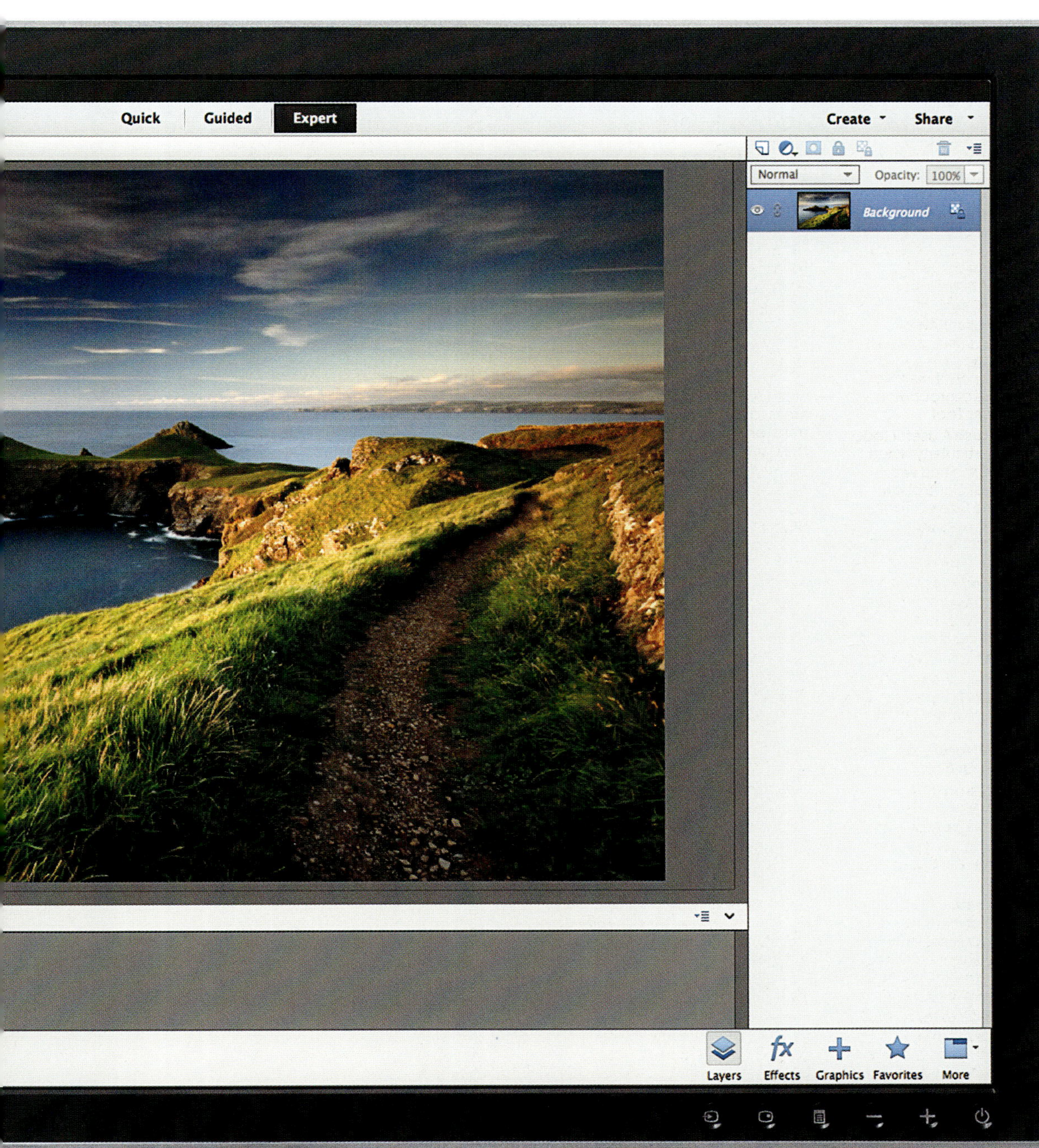

Palettes

The right-hand side of your Elements workspace contains an interchangable palette. Here are some of the main features...

Layers This palette contains all your pixel, vector and Adjustment Layers, as well as their masks. You can reorder and delete these layers at any time, organise layers into groups, turn them on and off with the visibility icon and, of course, add Layer Styles from the palette itself. There's also a context menu for more commands, such as Flatten Image.

Effects Changes the Layers palette into the Effects palette. Contains a host of one-click editing options and filters, complete with example thumbnails. Some of great, while others leave a lot to be desired!

More This button in the lower right corner brings up a menu of all of the other palettes that you might need while editing your images, including Actions, Adjustments, Color Swatches, Histogram, History, Info and Navigator. Click on any one to open a floating window and switch between the palettes using the tabs at the top.

Photo Bin/Tool Options (PSE)

The Photo Bin in Photoshop Elements is an organisational tool that shows thumbnails of all the files you have open in the workspace. Underneath the thumbnail you'll see the file name, and when you click on a thumbnail, that file becomes the active document. Right-click on a thumbnail and you can minimise, close or rotate the image, create a duplicate file or access the image's original camera data. Switching to Tool Options shows you all of the available parameters that you can adjust for your selected tool.

First adjustments

The first changes you may need to make to an image are correcting any distortions and to crop. Here are a selection of basic techniques and tools to help you with these initial edits

The basics...

REFORMAT

The Crop Tool is more versatile than you might think and should be your first step for reformatting images. Select the ***Crop Tool*** from the toolbar (or press the ***C*** key), then click and drag over the area that you wish to include in the composition. You don't have to get it right first time; the changes aren't applied until you commit to them. You can use the anchor points around the bounding box to expand or contract the crop as needed. If you would like to maintain your image's aspect ratio, hold down the ***shift*** key when making your initial selection or you can preset the size or ratio using the ***Width*** and ***Height*** input boxes in the top toolbar. You can also use the Crop Tool to rotate an image by hovering your cursor outside one of the corner points: the cursor will change to a curved arrow and you can then click and rotate the selection. Finally, commit to your crop by clicking on the green ***tick*** or by pressing ***Enter***.

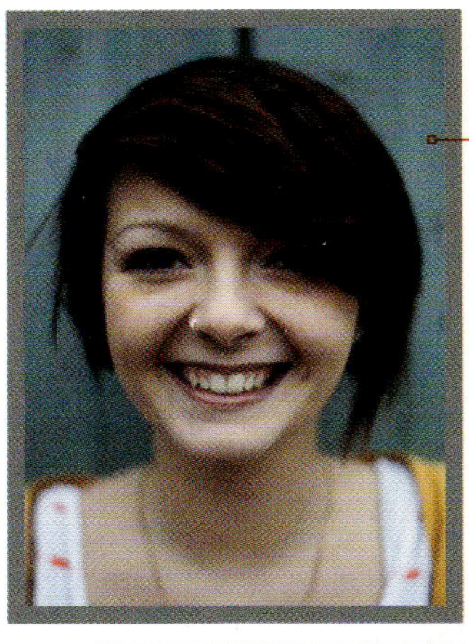

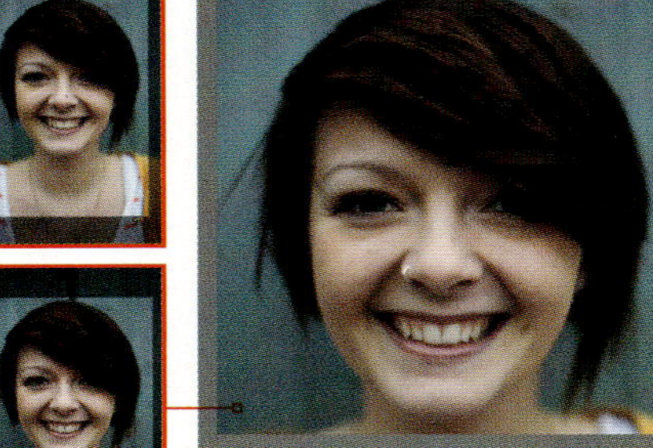

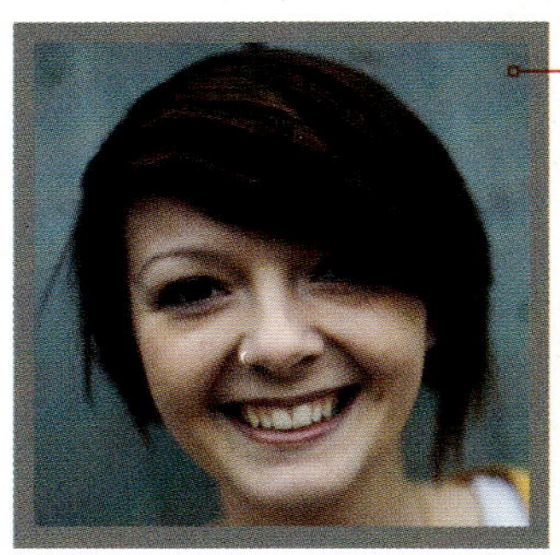

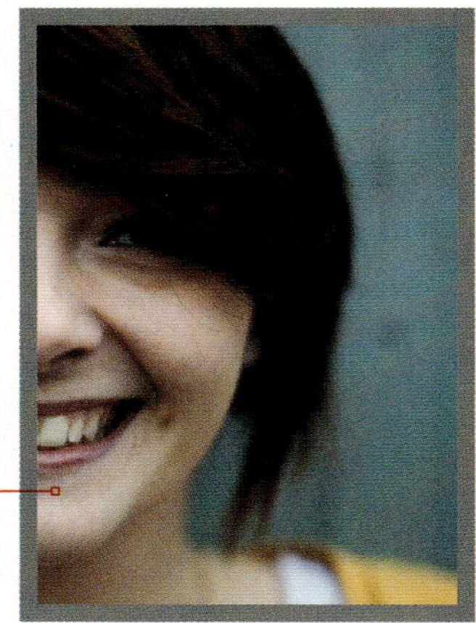

ORIGINAL

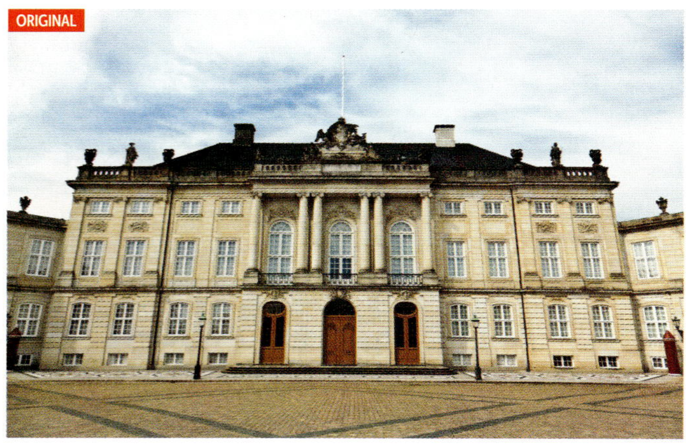

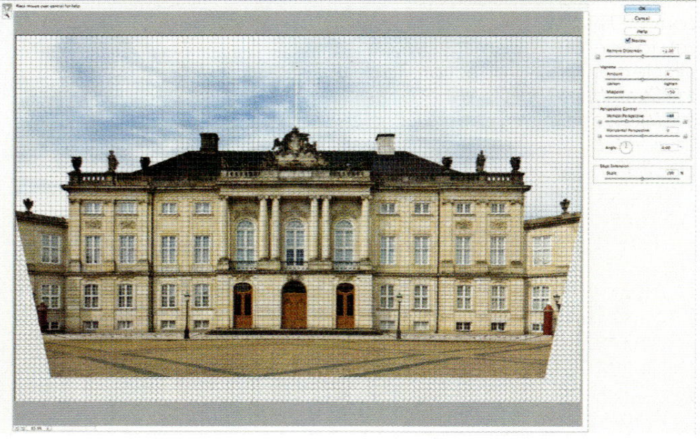

CORRECTED

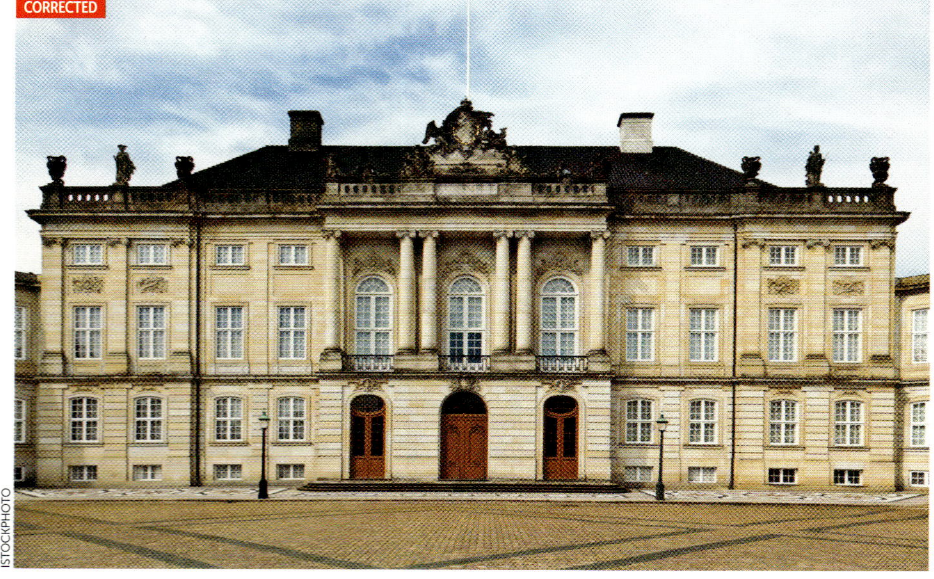

ISTOCKPHOTO

CORRECT DISTORTION

When you capture an image using a wide-angle lens, pictures can often be subject to perspective distortion. One telltale sign that your image is distorted is converging verticals, which is more obvious when the image contains straight lines. By going to ***Filters>Correct Camera Distortion*** you can fix distortion, remove vignetting, correct perspective and even rescale your image. Your preview image allows you to easily assess any changes made. Use the ***Remove Distortion*** slider to correct barrel or pincushion distortion. Move the ***Amount*** slider to adjust the edges' tonality and the ***Midpoint*** slider to select the size of the area to be affected. Use the ***Perspective Control*** sliders for correcting any vertical or horizontal tilting and the ***Vertical Perspective*** slider to correct images taken from a low angle. Finally, use the ***Scale*** slider under ***Edge Extension*** to resize your image to remove any empty areas created by the corrections.

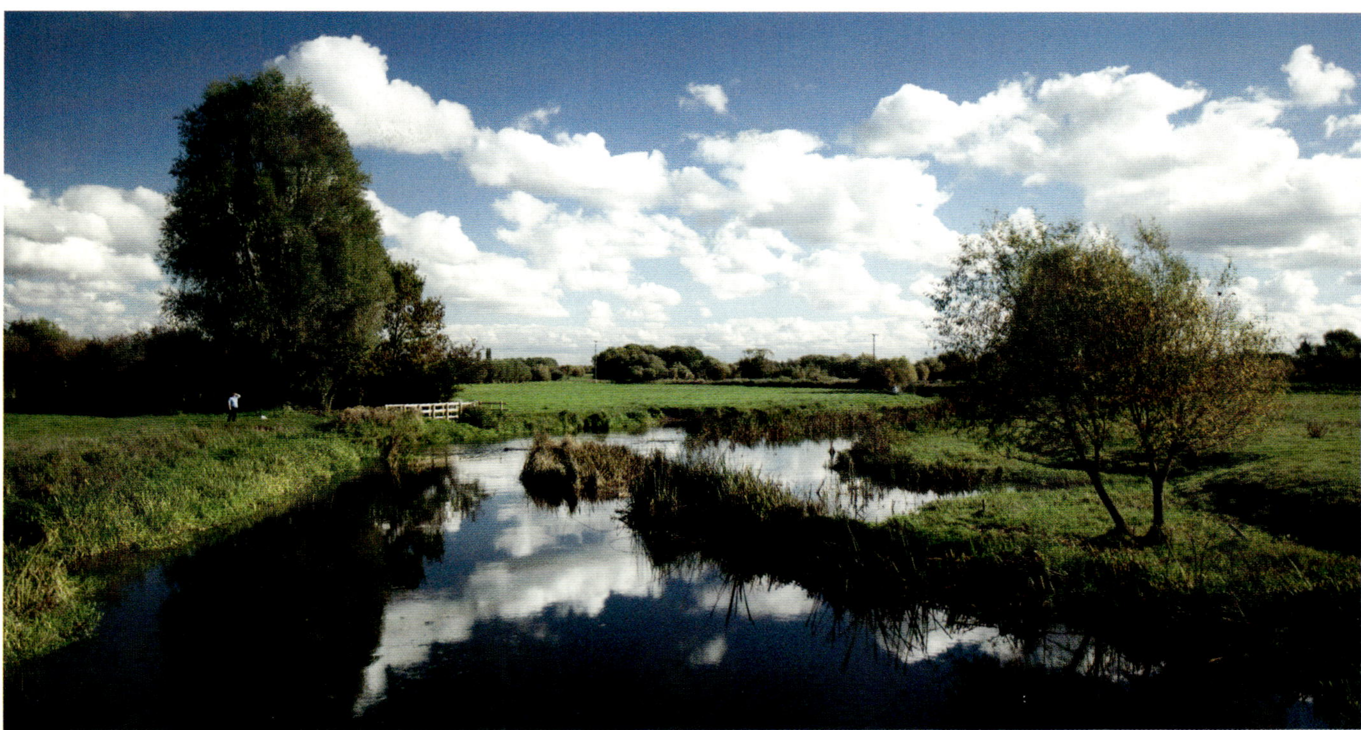

STRAIGHTEN

A wonky horizon is an error that's hard to ignore, but it's also easy to correct. The Straighten Tool allows you to level out your images with a simple drag-and-drop action. To do this, select the ***Straighten Tool*** from the toolbar (or press the *P* key) and then make your choice of three ***Canvas Options*** from the top toolbar. ***Grow or Shrink Canvas to Fit*** rotates the image and then increases or decreases the size of the canvas to fit the area. ***Crop to Remove Background*** rotates the image while cropping out excess background. ***Crop to Original Size*** rotates the image while keeping the original dimensions. Once you have chosen your method, click and drag along the image's horizon. Hold ***shift*** to restrict the adjustment to 45° increments as you rotate an image. If you're not sure if your image needs horizon correction, go to ***View>Grid*** to activate guidelines – you'll immediately see if it's straight.

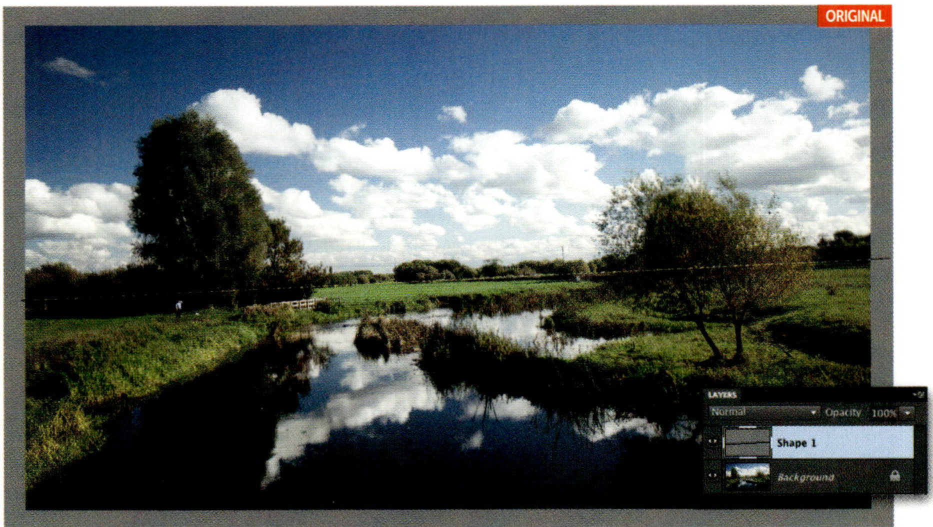

Other software

PHOTOSHOP CS5, CS6 & CC

A step up from the correction tools in Elements, CS5, CS6 & CC offers all the Transform tools plus Warp Tool, which allows you to manipulate different parts of your image independently. You can also correct converging verticals by selecting the ***Perspective*** option in the top toolbar when using the ***Crop Tool***.

LIGHTROOM 6

The same adjustments can be made in Lightroom as they can in Elements and CC. As well as manual settings to correct distortion, Lightroom also allows you to apply the exact correction needed via ***Lens Correction>Profile*** by selecting the camera and lens you used.

TRANSFORM

If you want to be able to access most of these corrective functions at once, you can use the Transform commands for precise manual adjustments. To access them, go to ***Image>Transform>Free Transform*** (or press ***cmd/alt*** and *T*). You can then use the anchor points around the bounding box, along with a shortcut key, to do a range of actions such as perspective alterations, skew and distortion. As Free Transform can be tricky to master, though convenient once you do, we suggest you select each command (***Skew***, ***Distort*** and ***Perspective***) individually via the ***Image>Transform*** menu. You can also rotate or flip your picture via the ***Image>Rotate*** menu. As the Transform commands affect image pixels, you degrade the quality every time you apply a transformation. To minimise this damage, make all your adjustments before committing to them.

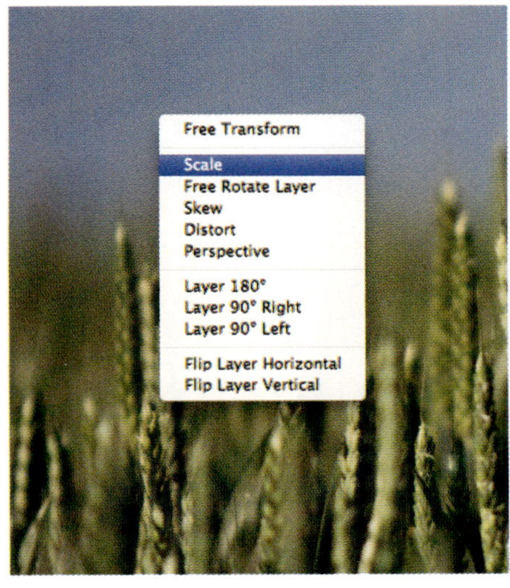

Using Levels and Curves

Learn how to use Levels, Curves and Blend Modes to take control of your picture's exposure and contrast

GETTING YOUR EXPOSURE right in-camera is always the preferred way to capture images, but while it's a discipline we'd all like to master, sometimes it doesn't work out.

It may be that you dialled in the wrong settings or it could be that tricky lighting conditions fooled your camera's metering system and you didn't have time to adjust – nevertheless, it's better to capture the moment and correct the exposure afterwards than to miss the picture altogether. Of course, overexposure isn't always a mistake – by exposing your images to the right and pulling them back during processing, you'll retain far more detail than a standard 'good' exposure out of the camera – providing you haven't clipped your highlights. If you're using Elements 12 onwards, all steps are best made in the Expert Photo Editor mode, as this allows for more adjustments, though all of these steps also apply to Elements 4 and above as well as the full-blown Photoshop software, but some menus may be structured differently.

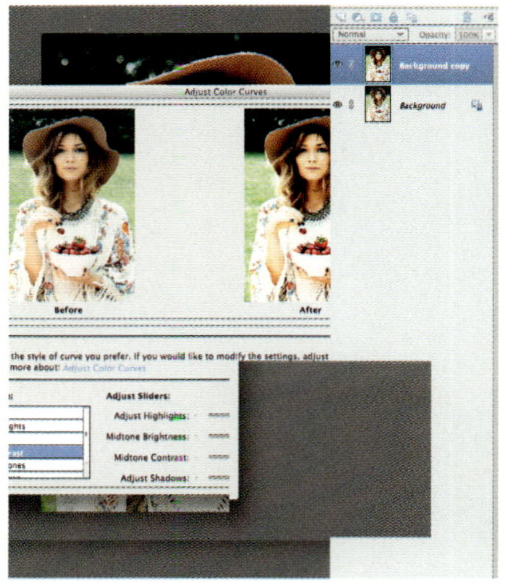

1 Create a Levels adjustment This image is overexposed, but the histogram (***Window>Histogram***) shows that the highlights aren't clipped, which means the exposure can be fixed. In the Layers palette (***Window>Layers***), click on the ***Create new fill or adjustment layer*** button and select ***Levels***.

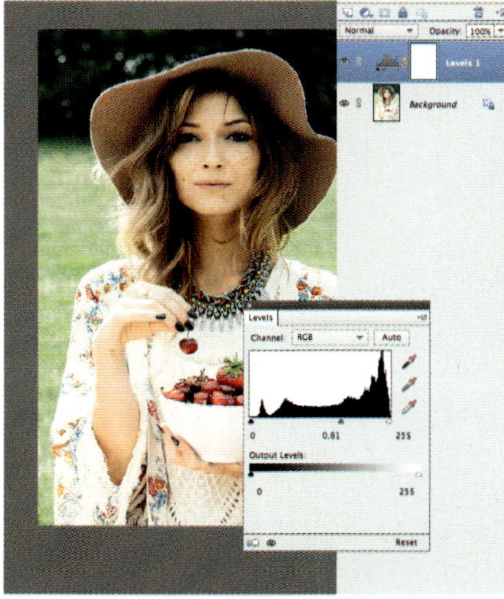

2 Adjust the Levels In the Levels palette, click on the middle (grey) slider and drag it to the right to darken the exposure (alternatively, drag it to the left to lighten the exposure). This middle slider concentrates on the midtones while retaining the highlights and shadows as best it can.

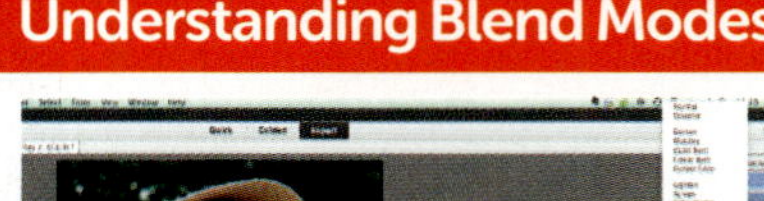

Understanding Blend Modes

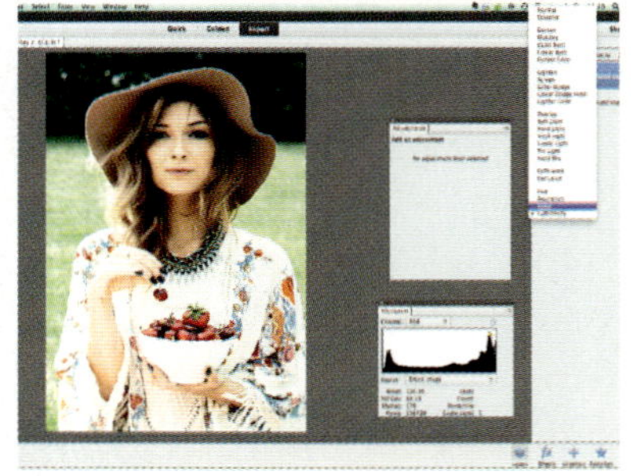

The Blend Mode you choose completely changes how that layer affects the image. Two useful Blend Modes when adjusting contrast (via Levels or Curves) are Luminosity and Color. Luminosity discards all colour information and only deals with highlight and shadow – perfect for adjusting contrast, without affecting the colours. Color does the opposite – it discards exposure information and just affects colours, allowing you to tweak colour contrast without affecting your image's overall exposure.

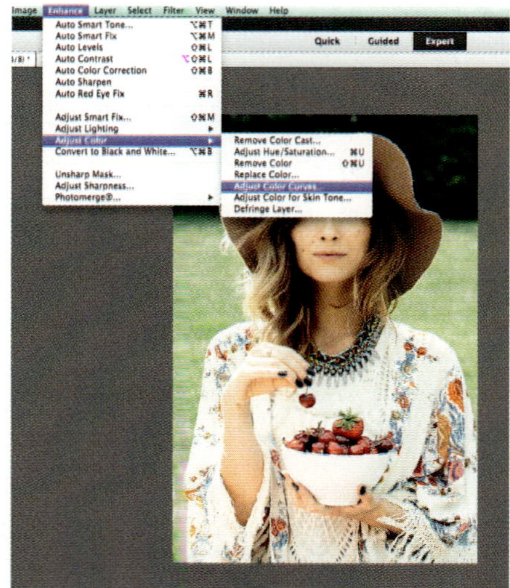

3 Merge and duplicate With the exposure corrected it's time to add some contrast. First, go to ***Layer>Merge Visible*** to flatten your image, then create a duplicate of this layer by going to ***Layer>Duplicate Layer*** and clicking ***OK***. Then go to ***Enhance>Adjust Color>Adjust Color Curves...***

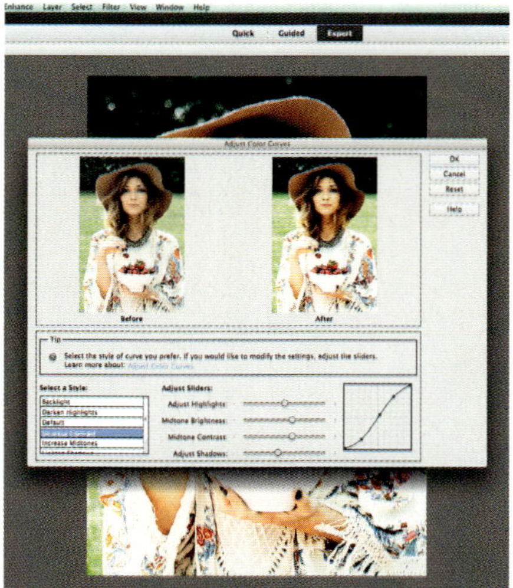

4 Adjust Curves In the Color Curves window, use the ***Increase Contrast*** preset on the left to boost contrast. You can then tweak the curve further using the sliders. Here, we've increased the Midtone Contrast and Brightness slightly and decreased the Adjust Shadows slider.

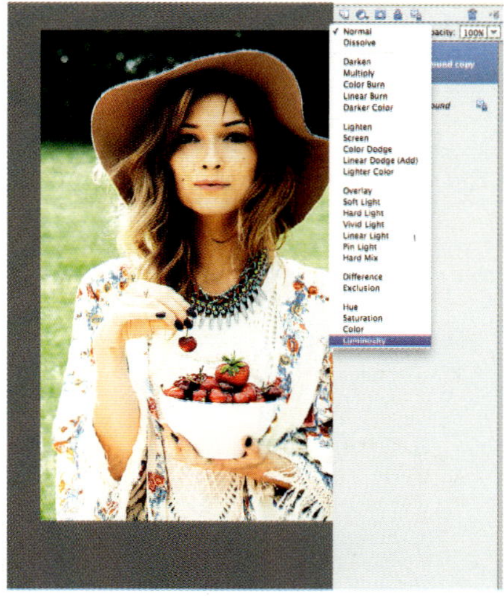

5 Change the Blend Mode You'll notice that increasing the contrast so much has also increased the saturation here, making the skin look orange. Back in the Layers palette, change the Blend Mode of this layer to ***Luminosity*** – the Curves adjustment will now only affect contrast, not colour.

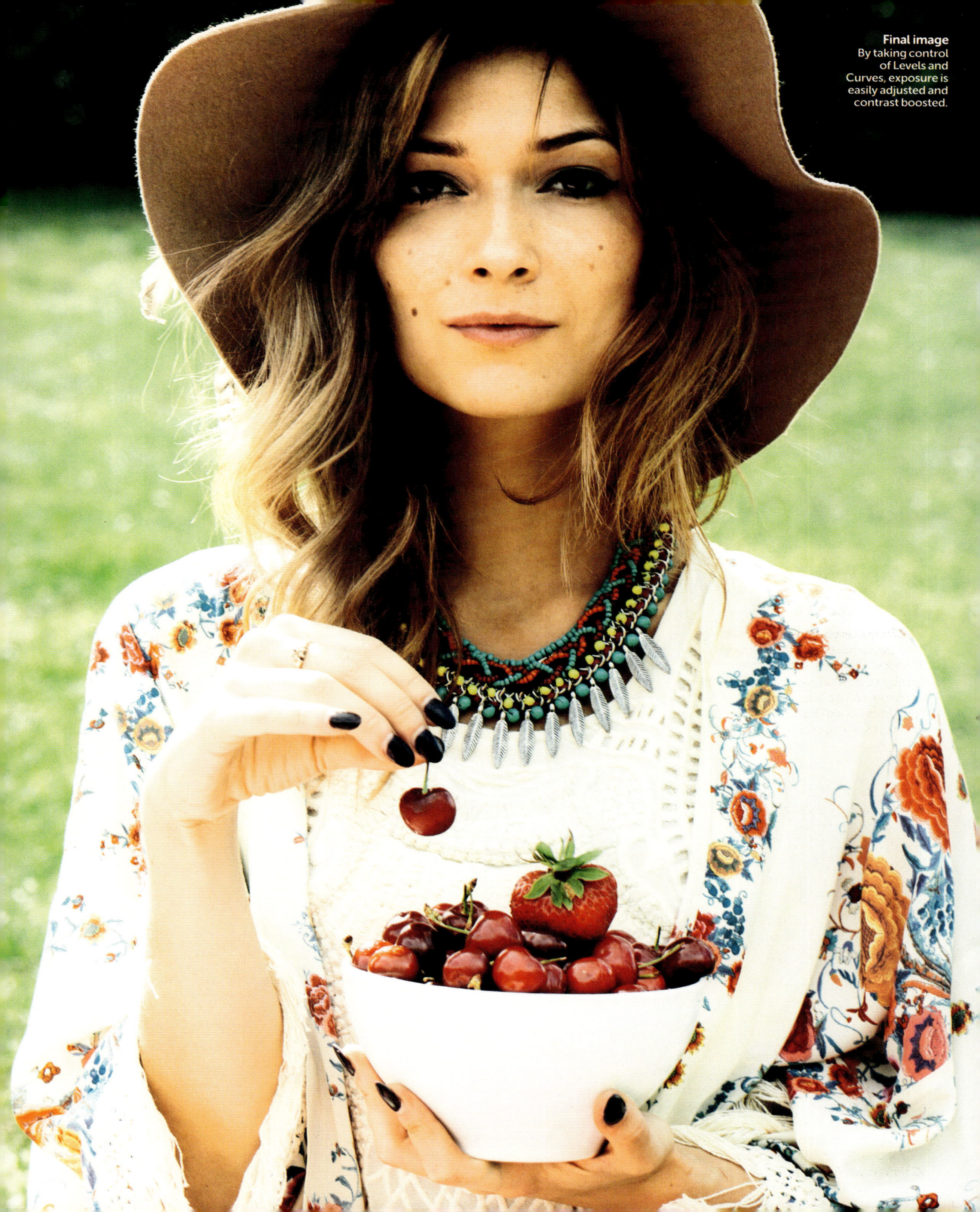

Final image
By taking control of Levels and Curves, exposure is easily adjusted and contrast boosted.

Extend dynamic range with precise control

Learn how to use layer masks to dodge and burn without destruction

PICK ANY ADJUSTMENT that you can make in Photoshop Elements and we guarantee that there will be at least three ways to carry out that alteration. We would always advocate using methods that are both nondestructive and easy to revisit and adjust as required. This is where the strengths of Layer Masks and Adjustment Layers really shine through.

When you apply an Adjustment Layer to your image you aren't affecting the image itself, so any changes that you make can be done without detrimental effect to image quality, or fear of making an irreversible mistake. When you then use a Layer Mask on that Adjustment Layer you can apply the changes selectively – what's more, even the Layer Mask itself is reversible, so you can paint over it to change the areas that the Adjustment Layer affects time and time again.

Here, we're going to use Levels to dodge and burn this studio portrait to bring it to life.

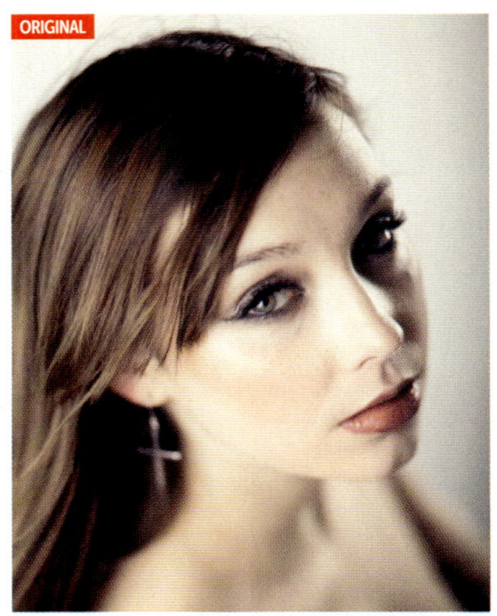

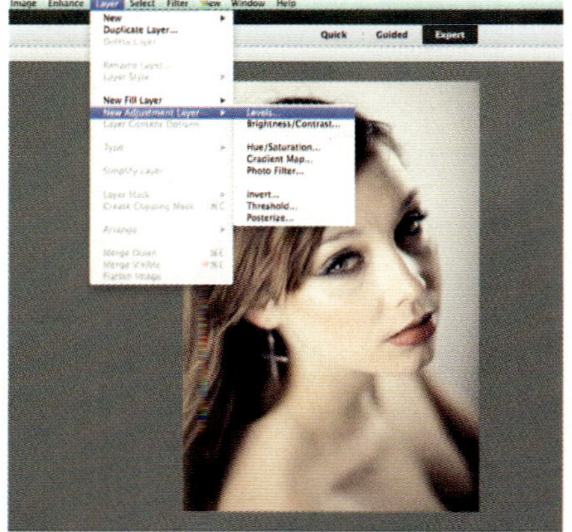

1 ADD AN ADJUSTMENT LAYER Start by adding your first Adjustment Layer – go to ***Layer>New Adjustment Layer*** and choose your adjustment from the list. Here, we're going to use a ***Levels*** adjustment layer to dodge and burn our image, starting with dodging (increasing exposure).

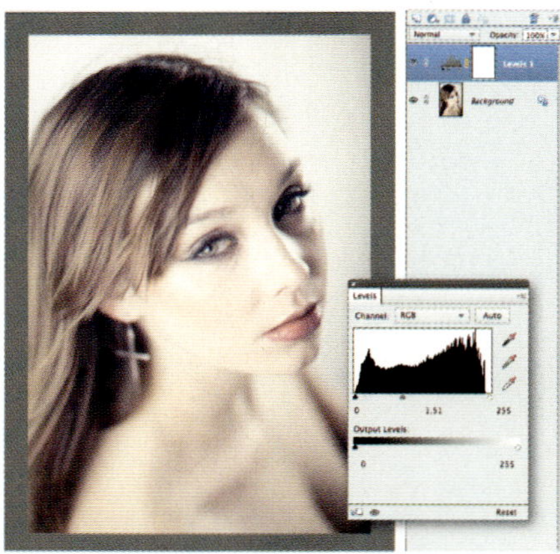

2 MAKE THE ADJUSTMENT In the Adjustments palette, drag the ***mid-tone slider*** left to lift the mid-tones. Then select the attached Layer Mask in the Layers palette, hold down the ***cmd*** key (Mac) or ***ctrl*** key (PC) and press the ***I*** key to invert the mask to hide the effect – next we'll brush it back in.

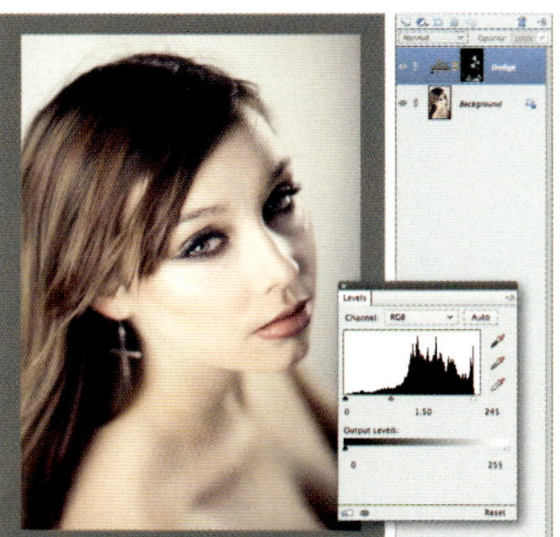

3 BRUSH TO REVEAL Select the ***Brush Tool*** and, within Brush Settings along the top toolbar, set the ***Hardness*** to ***0%***, ***Opacity*** to ***20%*** and choose a brush ***Size***. With ***White*** set as your ***Foreground Color***, brush on areas of the image that need to be brightened slightly, like eyes and skin.

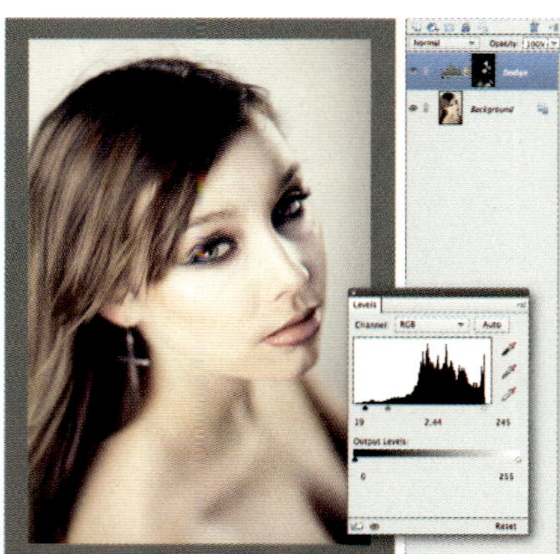

4 TWEAK SETTINGS Adjustment Layers allow you to go back and tweak the settings. Click on the Adjustment Layer in the Layers palette and make any changes. Once happy, add another Adjustment Layer, choosing ***Levels*** again. This time we'll take care of burning (decreasing exposure).

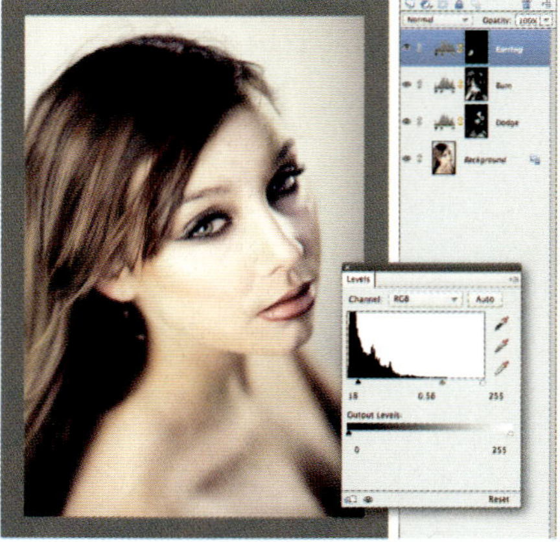

5 USE MORE LAYERS Repeat steps 2 and 3, this time moving the ***mid-tone slider*** to the right before editing the Layer Mask in the same manner. This multiple layer technique can also be used to target very specific image areas; we added a third Levels adjustment to darken the distracting earring.

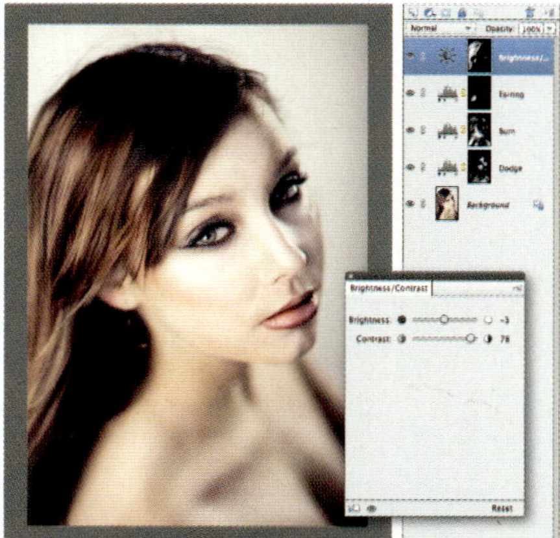

6 WORK SELECTIVELY You aren't just limited to dodging and burning. Any Adjustment Layer can be applied alongside a Layer Mask, allowing you to target parts of your image. Here, we've used a Brightness/Contrast adjustment layer to boost just the model's hair, eyes and mouth, masking off the skin.

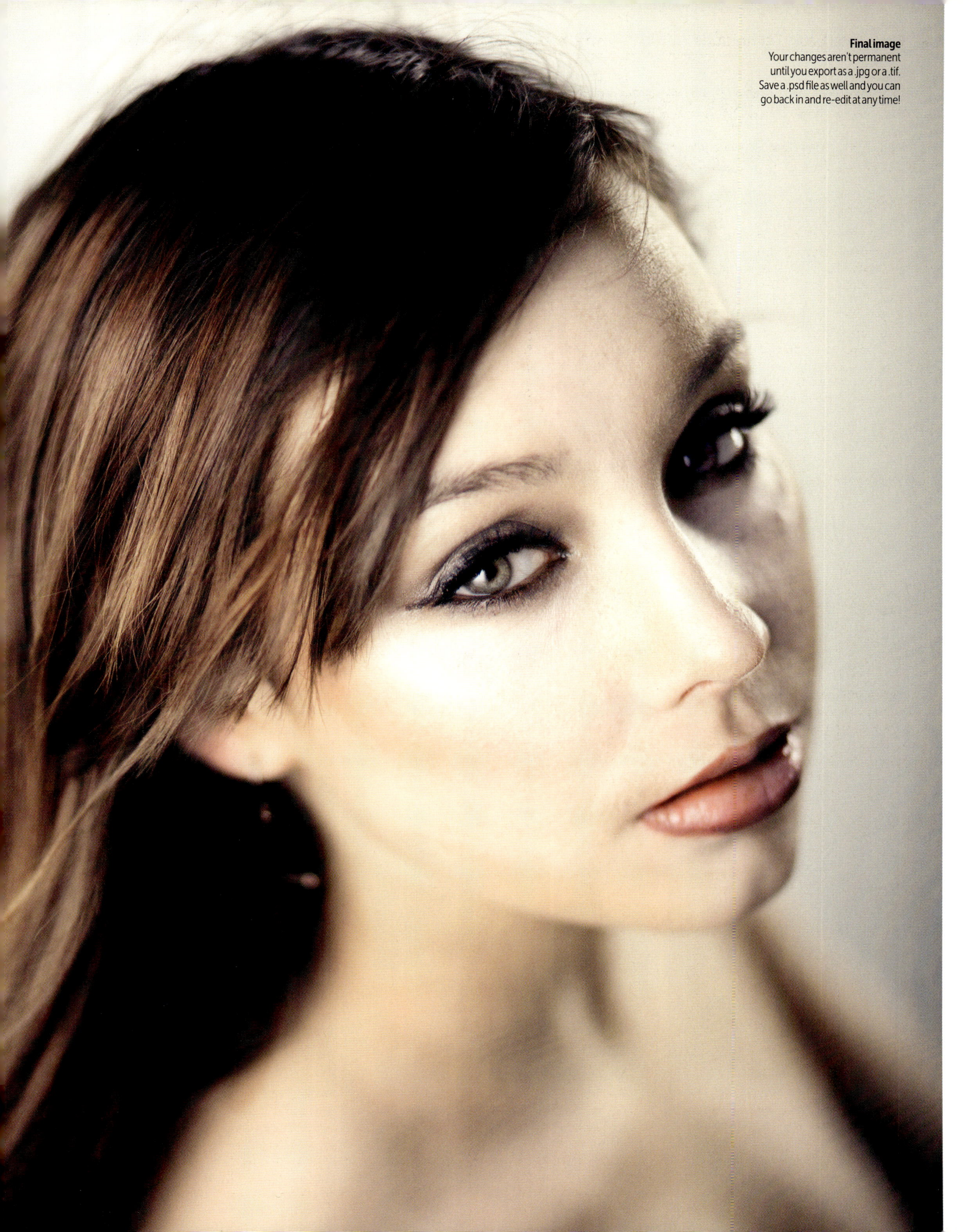

Final image
Your changes aren't permanent until you export as a .jpg or a .tif. Save a .psd file as well and you can go back in and re-edit at any time!

Mastering masking

The real power of Adobe's Elements is evident when using multiple layers and adjustments. Power is nothing without control and this is where Layer Masks help...

THE WORLD OF multiple layers and masking can be a daunting one if you've never used them before. However, in reality, the concept of using Layer Masks is incredibly simple – they do exactly as their name implies – they act as a mask in front of a layer, which you can edit and manipulate to reveal as much or as little of the layer as you want. On the surface, masking might sound very similar to using the Eraser Tool – it is, but with one crucial difference: Layer Masks are nondestructive, so any changes you make can be undone without altering the original image.

Layer Masks can be applied to Adjustment Layers to selectively edit your image or, depending on the version of Elements that you're using, they can be applied directly to image layers – useful when combining exposures or creating a composite image. Early versions of Elements didn't offer this functionality, but see above for a workaround.

Secrets unlocked

MASKING IN EARLIER VERSIONS

Elements 8 and earlier sadly do not offer Layer Masks. There is a way to get around this though, which works like this: place your image layer directly on top of a Levels adjustment layer and go to ***Layer>Create Clipping Mask***. Then edit the Levels' Layer Mask using the ***Brush Tool***. The mask will be applied to both layers, but as no Levels adjustments were made, only the image layer is masked.

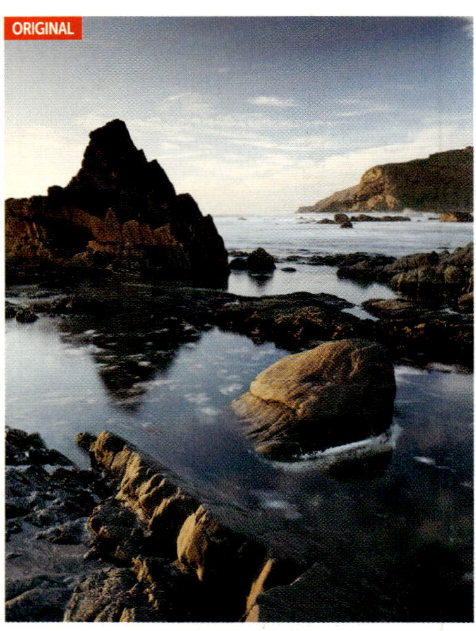

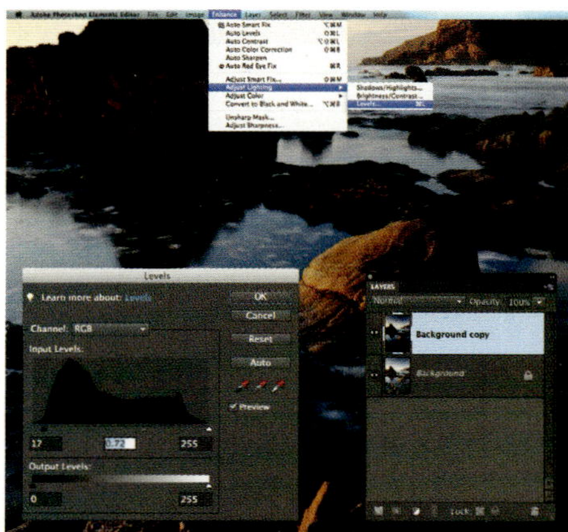

1 Duplicate the image We want to boost the contrast in the sky and water without affecting the rocks in the image. First go to ***Layer>Duplicate Layer***. Then select ***Enhance>Adjust Lighting>Levels*** and tweak the ***Black***, ***Grey*** and ***White*** points to boost the contrast in the image. Once you're happy with how it's looking, click ***OK***.

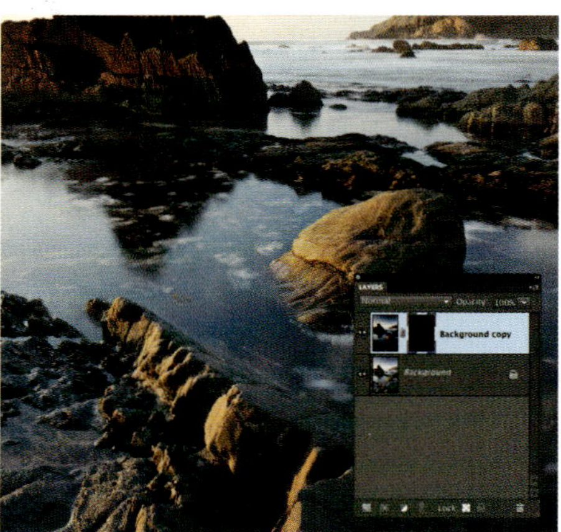

2 Add the Layer Mask Hold down the ***option*** key (Mac), or ***alt*** key (PC) and click on the ***Add layer mask*** button in the Layers palette to add a ***Hide All Layer Mask*** – the layer will then be completely hidden. Conversely, if you select the ***Add layer mask*** button without holding down the key, you add a ***Reveal All Layer Mask***.

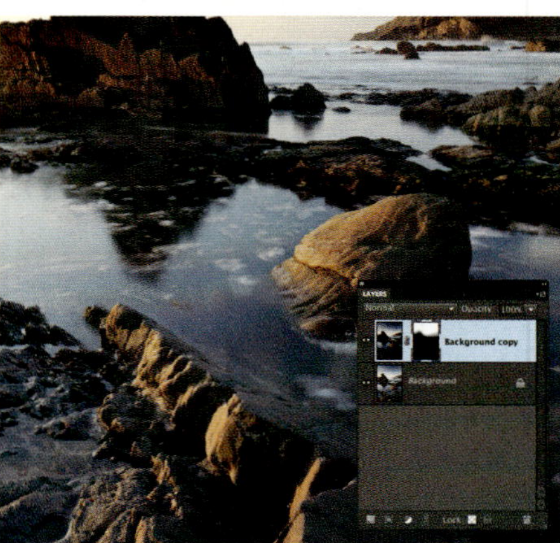

3 Brush onto the mask Select the ***Brush Tool*** and set ***White*** as your ***Foreground Color***. Use the top toolbar to set the appropriate brush ***Size*** and ***Hardness*** and start to brush the sky back in. Use the top menu again to lower the brush ***Opacity*** when you're approaching the horizon to blend in the higher contrast layer.

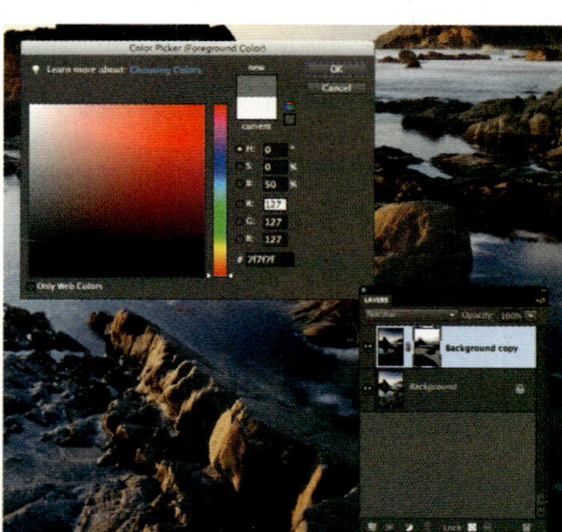

4 Reveal parts of the image Layer Masks can be used to partly reveal a layer at a lower opacity, too. Change your ***Foreground Color*** to a mid-grey and brush onto your Layer Mask again. Here, we have chosen to use 50% grey on the water in my image to add some of the contrast back in, but without going over the top.

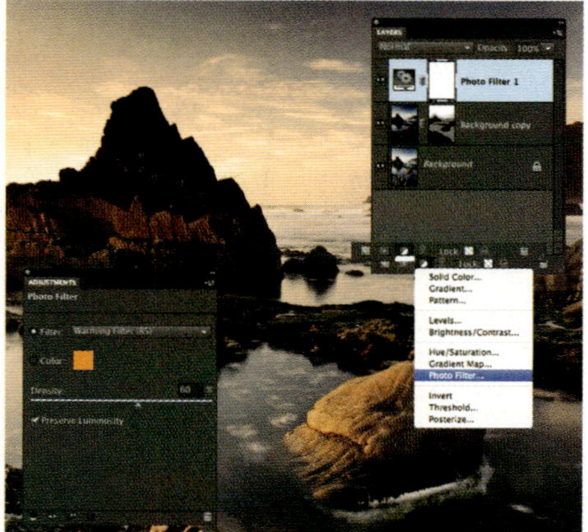

5 Add an Adjustment Layer Layer Masks can also be used with Adjustment Layers. Click on the ***Create new fill or adjustment layer*** button in the Layers palette and then select ***Photo Filter***. We're going to use a Warming filter, which will enhance the sunset's orange glow on the rocks. Adjust the ***Density*** of the filter to suit your image.

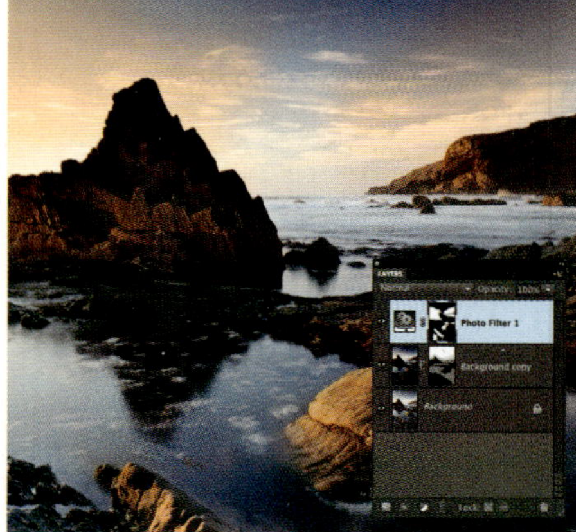

6 Mask the adjustment A Reveal All Layer Mask is automatically added to any Adjustment Layer. Select the ***Brush Tool*** and set ***Black*** as your ***Foreground Color***. Brush over any areas where you don't want the adjustment to be applied – for this image, we brushed over the sky, water and shadow areas of the rocks.

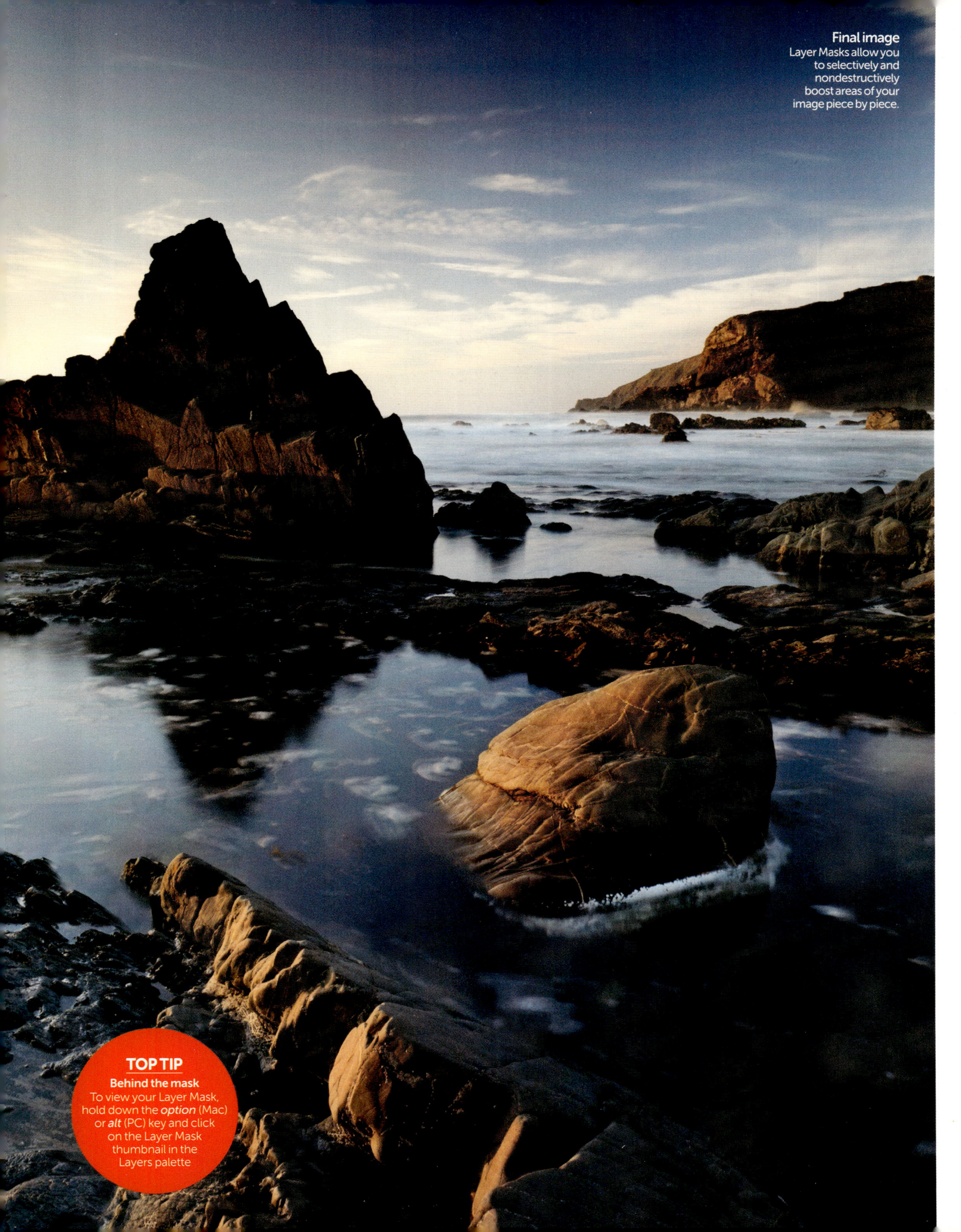

Final image
Layer Masks allow you to selectively and nondestructively boost areas of your image piece by piece.

TOP TIP

Behind the mask

To view your Layer Mask, hold down the ***option*** (Mac) or ***alt*** (PC) key and click on the Layer Mask thumbnail in the Layers palette

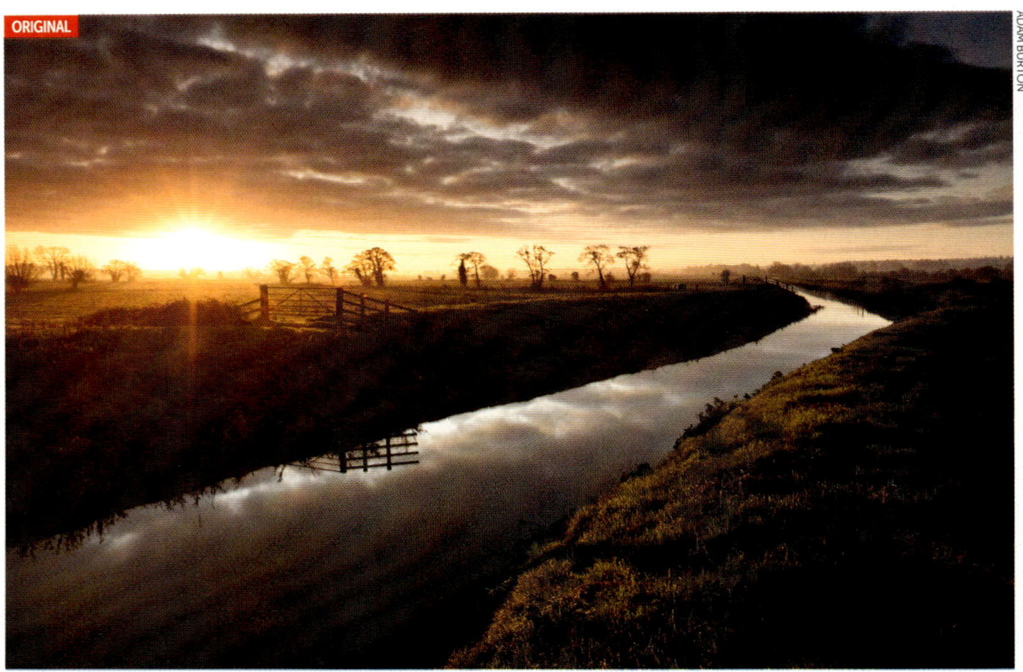

ADAM BURTON

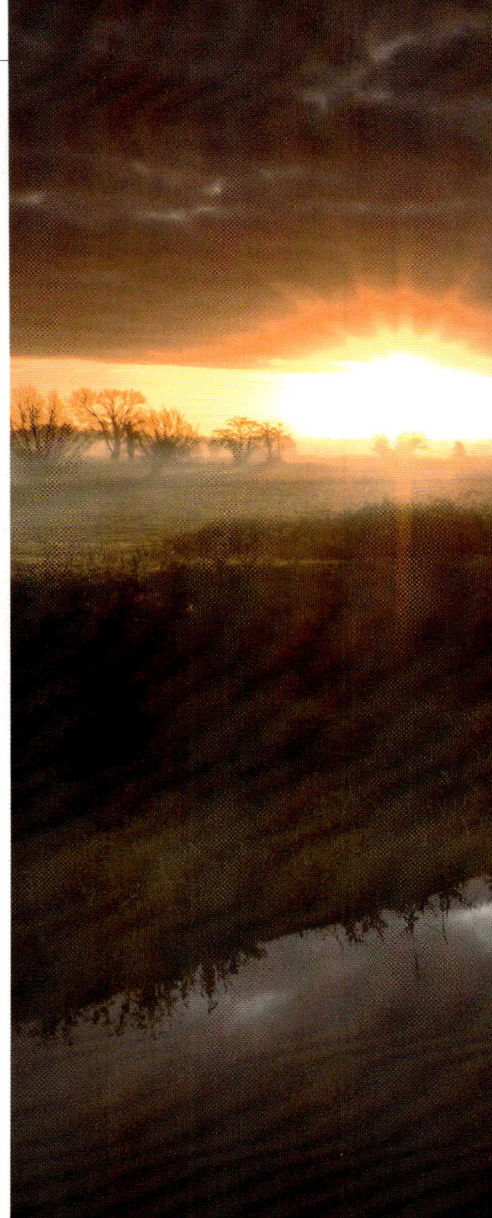

Add mist to your pictures

Have you mist an opportunity to capture fog? Don't worry, you can add a blanket of atmosphere to your early morning landscapes using Photoshop Elements

MIST IS MANY a landscape photographer's favourite phenomenon. Forming when heat rising from the ground meets cold air on a clear night, mist is best captured at sunrise as the first rays of light cut through the air. The trouble is, it doesn't always form when expected, and when it does it can dissipate before you've had time to compose your shot. Fear not – using this handy technique it's easy to add a touch of cloudy atmosphere to your landscape images.

As with any technique, when you're adding to or changing the climatic conditions in your image, it's important to choose the right type of scene to work with. It's no use adding blankets of mist to a shot taken at midday in the height of summer, you'll fool no one! This technique is best applied to images taken at sunrise in locations where mist is likely to form. We've used Photoshop Elements, but the technique applies to other variants of Photoshop too, although some tools sit in different places.

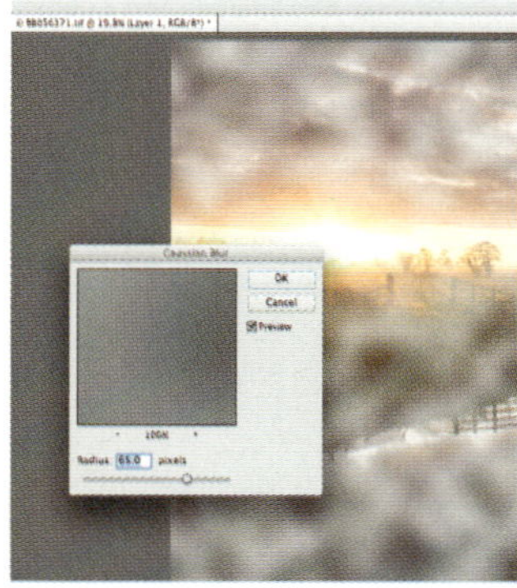

1 ADD A FILTER Duplicate your Background layer by pressing ***cmd + J*** (Mac) or ***ctrl + J*** (PC). Next, go to ***Filter>Render>Clouds***. In the Layers palette, set the ***Blend Mode*** of this layer to ***Screen***, before going to ***Filter>Blur>Gaussian Blur*** and adding a blur of around ***65 pixels***, depending on your image.

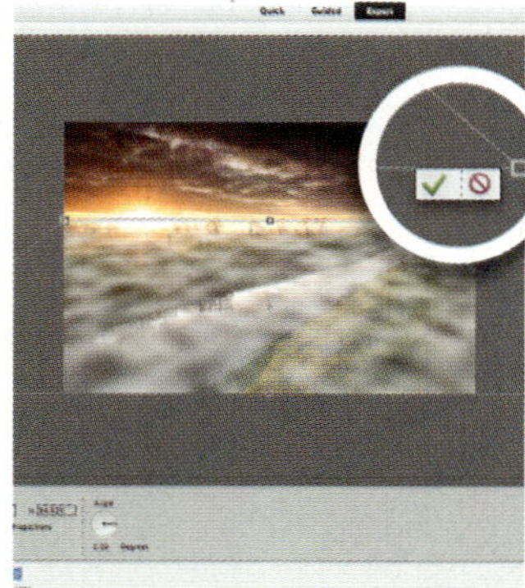

2 TRANSFORM THE MIST Go to ***Image>Transform>Free Transform***. Right-click on your image and select ***Perspective***. Drag the lower corners of your mist image outwards. Right-click again and select ***Distort,*** then drag the centre-top point down to match the perspective of your scene, as shown. Click the ***green tick*** to confirm the placement.

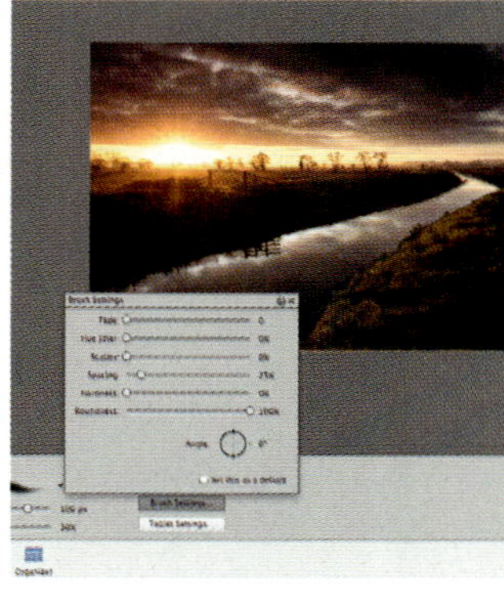

3 MASK THE MIST Go to ***Layer>Layer Mask>Hide All*** to mask this layer. Select the ***Brush Tool*** and, in ***Tool Options***, set ***Hardness*** to ***0%*** and ***Opacity*** to ***30%***. Press ***Shift + 3*** to set your flow to ***30%***. Choose ***White*** as your ***Foreground Color*** and start brushing in the mist, concentrating on the foreground and middle distance.

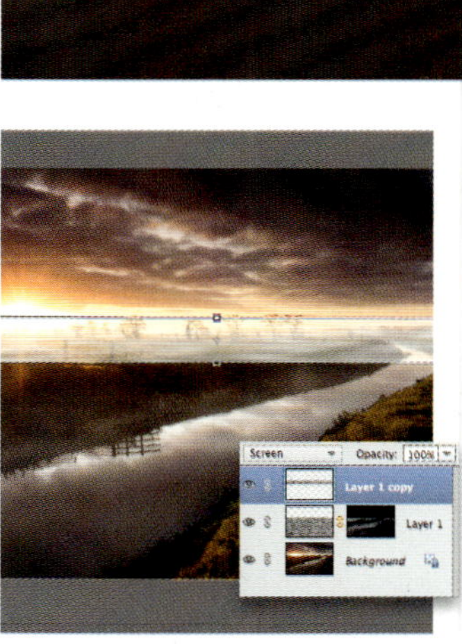

4 ADD A SECOND LAYER Press ***alt + J*** (Mac) or ***ctrl + J*** (PC) to duplicate this layer. In the Layers palette, drag the Layer Mask thumbnail up to the ***Delete layer*** button and click ***Delete*** when prompted. Enter ***Free Transform***, as before, but this time drag the centre-bottom anchor to compress the mist layer – this forms the distant mist.

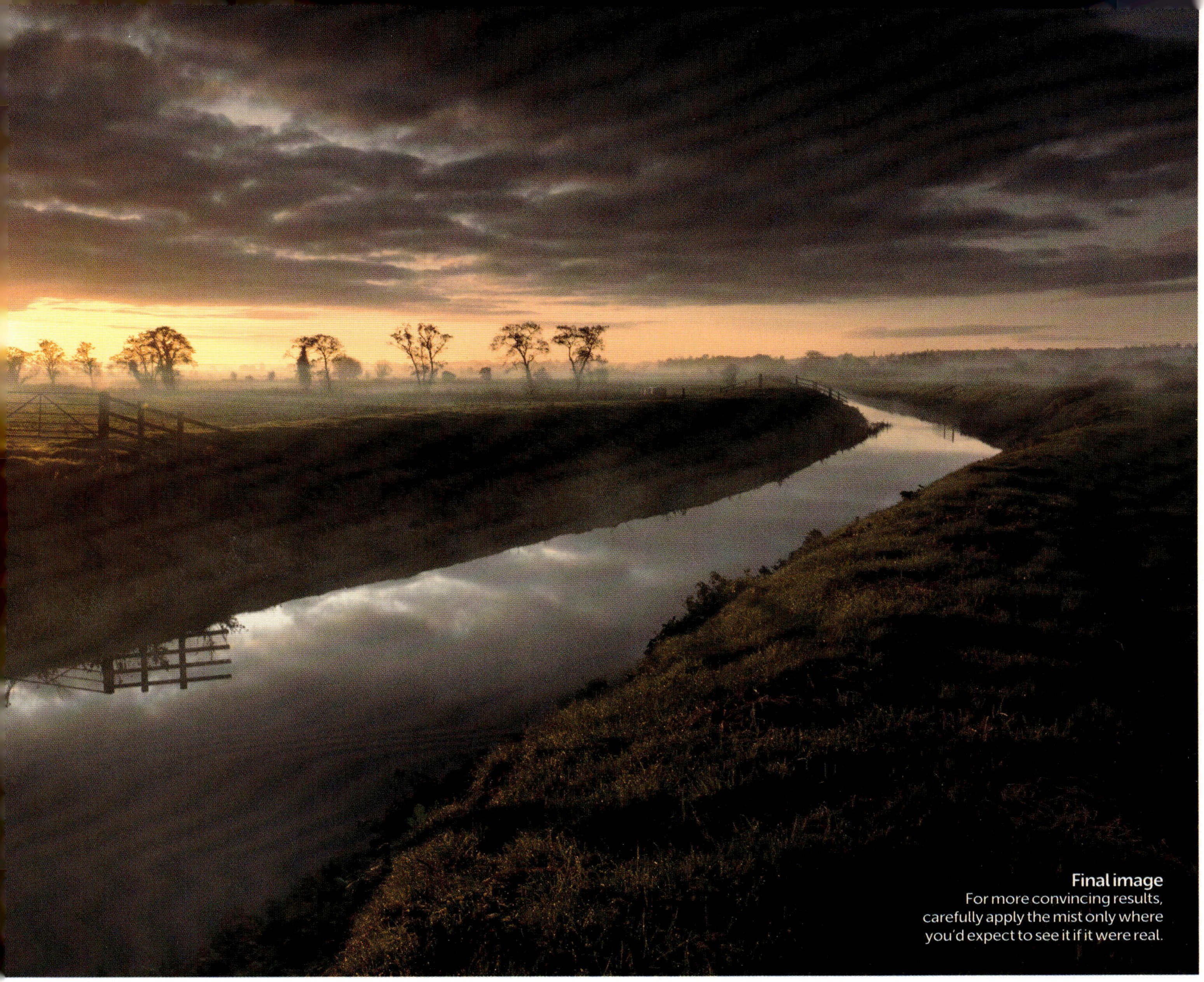

Final image

For more convincing results, carefully apply the mist only where you'd expect to see it if it were real.

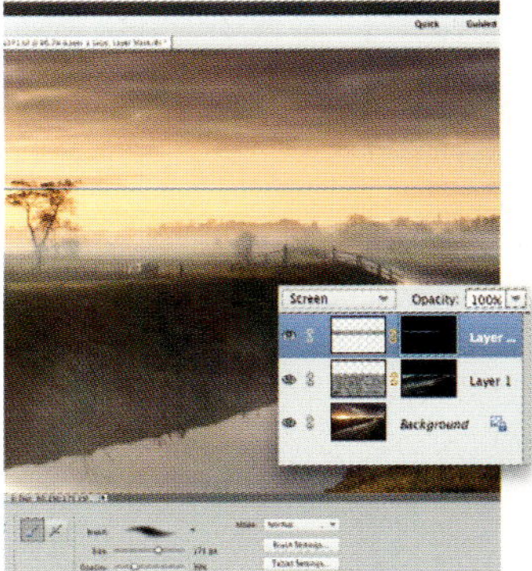

5 MASK THIS LAYER Add a Layer Mask to this layer, as before, and use the *Brush Tool* to gradually reveal the distant mist, focusing on the horizon. If you go too far or make a mistake, switch your *Foreground Color* to *Black* and paint back over the mistake on the Layer Mask. Once happy, go to *Layer>Merge Down* and click *Apply*.

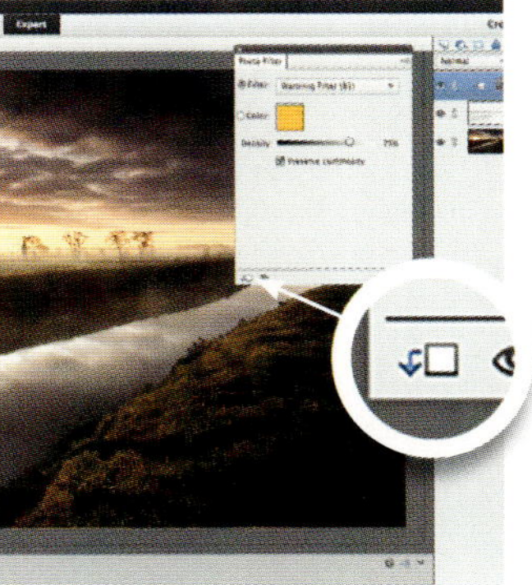

6 WARM THE MIST Click on the *Create new fill or adjustment layer* button in the Layers palette, selecting *Photo Filter*. In the Adjustment palette, select a *Warming Filter* and increase the *Density* to *75-100%*. Click on the *Clip to layer* button (shown above) so that the filter only affects the mist and warms it to match the sunrise.

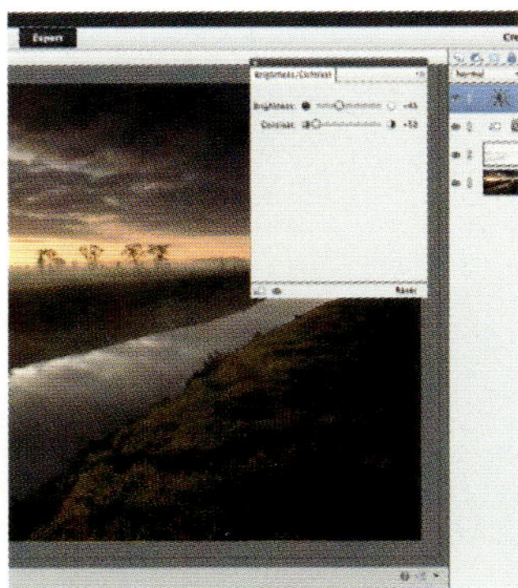

7 ADJUST THE CONTRAST Mist results in reduced contrast. Select your *Background* layer in the Layers palette and choose *Brightness/Contrast* from the *Create new fill or adjustment layer* menu. In the Adjustments palette, decrease the *Contrast* all the way down to *-50* and lower the *Brightness* to about *-45*, or whatever suits your image.

Use the Opacity

Take full control over every Adjustment Layer by using the Opacity slider in the Layers palette. From here you can adjust the strength of each layer of mist, as well as the potency of any Adjustment Layers.

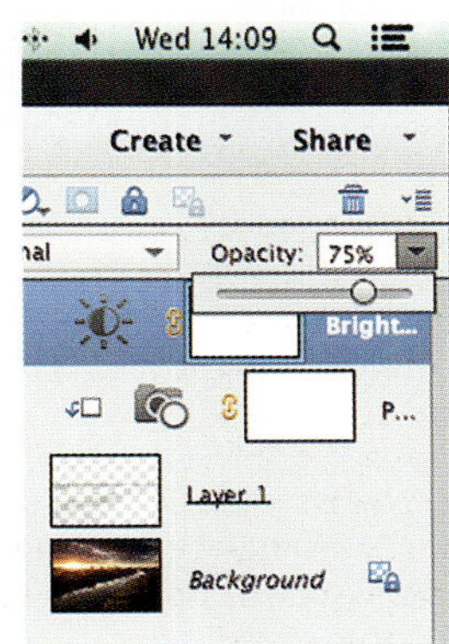

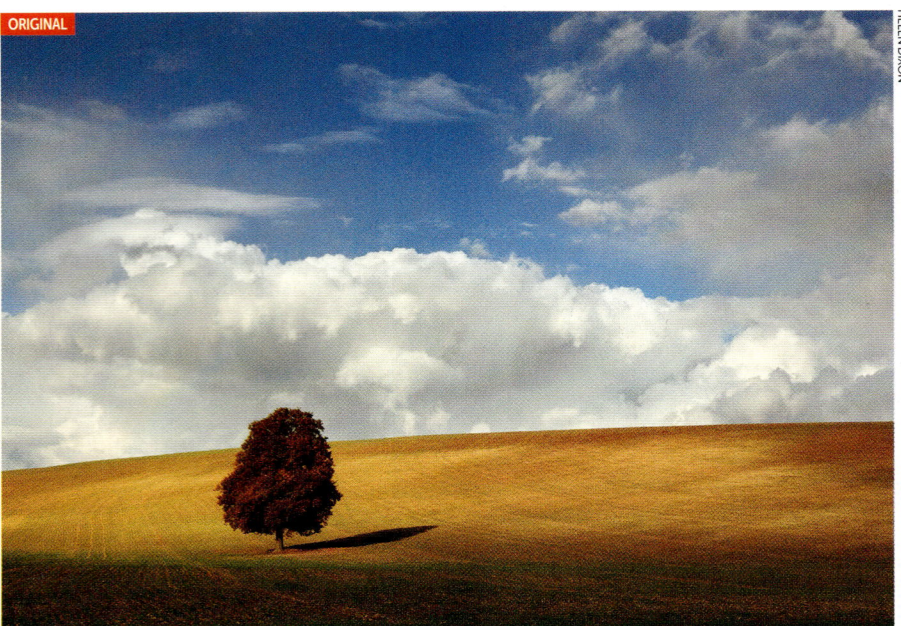

HELEN DIXON

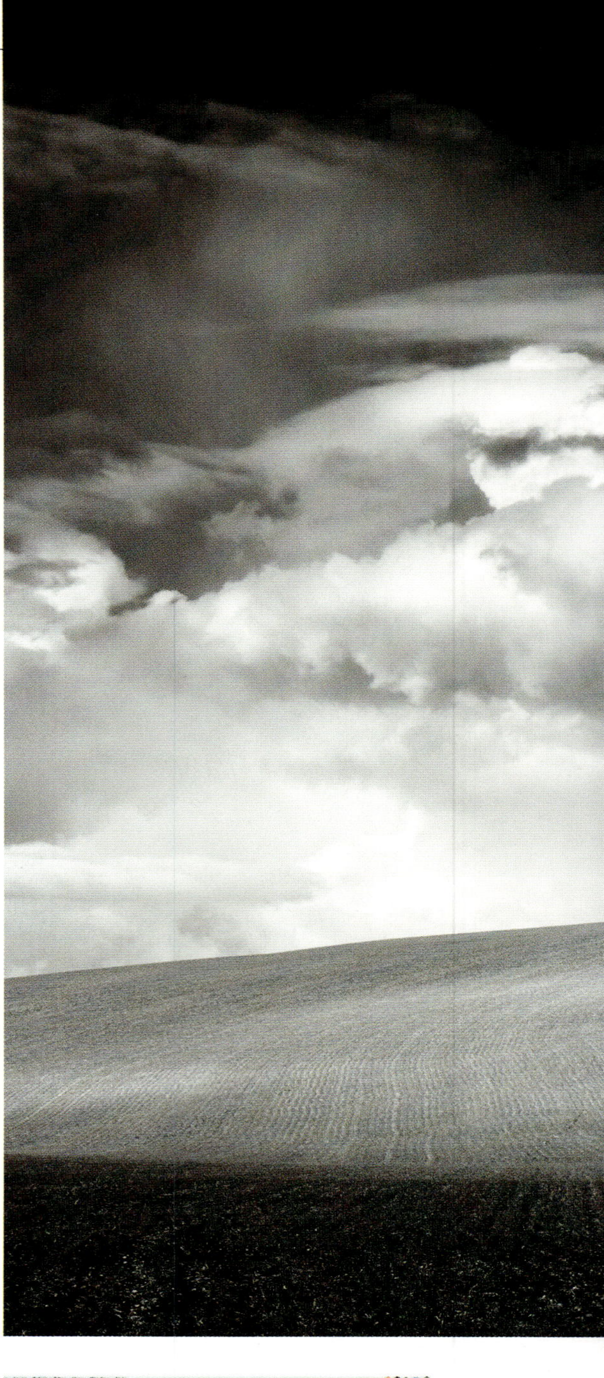

Using Gradient Maps

Learn how to create a tone-rich black & white image with ease in Photoshop Elements using the powerful Gradient Map tool

THEY SAY THERE'S more than one way to skin a cat. We've always found this idiom to be a bit on the gruesome side so from now on we're going to use – there's more than one way to convert an image to black & white in Photoshop. While not as catchy an utterance, it's just as true. There are numerous ways that you can go about transforming your images into black & white masterpieces – while some methods offer more control, others are fast and easy one-click solutions. Some methods allow you to control each colour channel individually, while others let you tweak the tonality of your shadows, mid-tones and highlights to a greater degree. There's no right or wrong way to do it, but knowing the different approaches allows you to be best informed and pick one that works for you.

Here we're going to cover creating a tone-rich monochrome image using Gradient Maps. It might sound complex, but a Gradient Map is simply a method of converting the tones in your image to match those along a simple gradient – in this case, black to white. When used in conjunction with the Histogram, the Gradient Map method of converting to monochrome helps ensure that your shadows are dark and rich, your highlights are bright and your mid-tones are exactly where you want them to be. Here's how you do it...

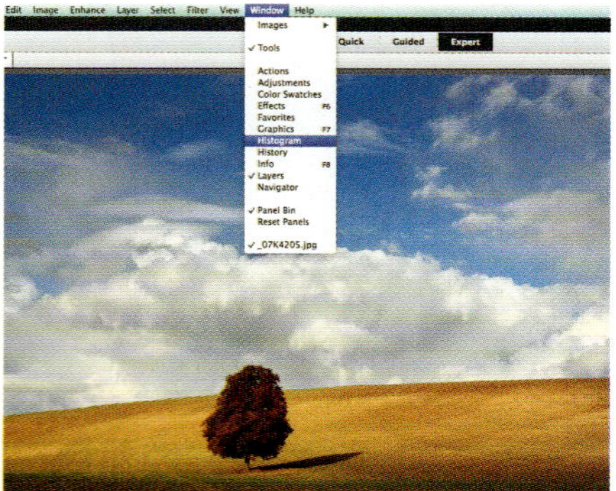

1 SET UP THE WORKSPACE With your image loaded, select *Expert* mode at the top to allow you access to all of Elements' features. First, go to *Window>Histogram* to enable the Histogram and then *Window>Layers* to enable the Layers palette. Then, press the *D* key to reset your colour palette to default.

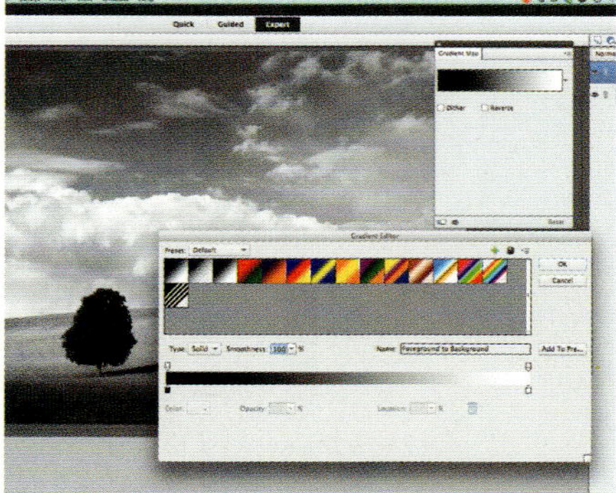

2 ADD A GRADIENT MAP In the Layers palette, click on the ***Create new fill or adjustment layer*** button and select *Gradient Map*. This converts your image to black & white and opens the Gradient Map Adjustment palette. Within the Adjustment palette, ***double-click*** on the thumbnail to open the Gradient Editor.

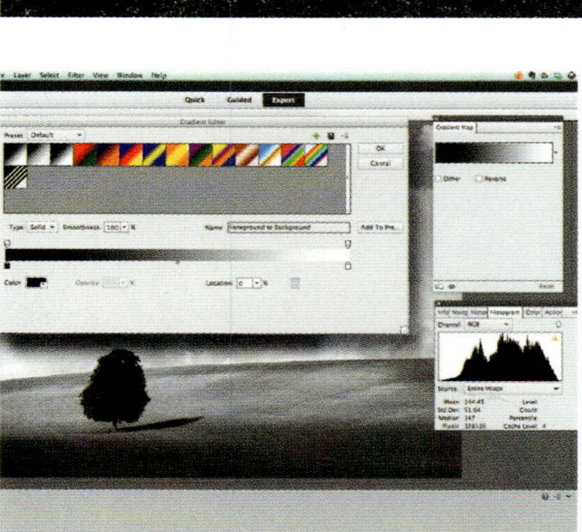

3 USE THE HISTOGRAM Move the Gradient Editor window to ensure that you can see the Histogram too. The horizontal bar at the bottom allows you to set the shadows, mid-tones and highlights. We're going to add a second adjustment for the sky later, so only concentrate on the foreground for now.

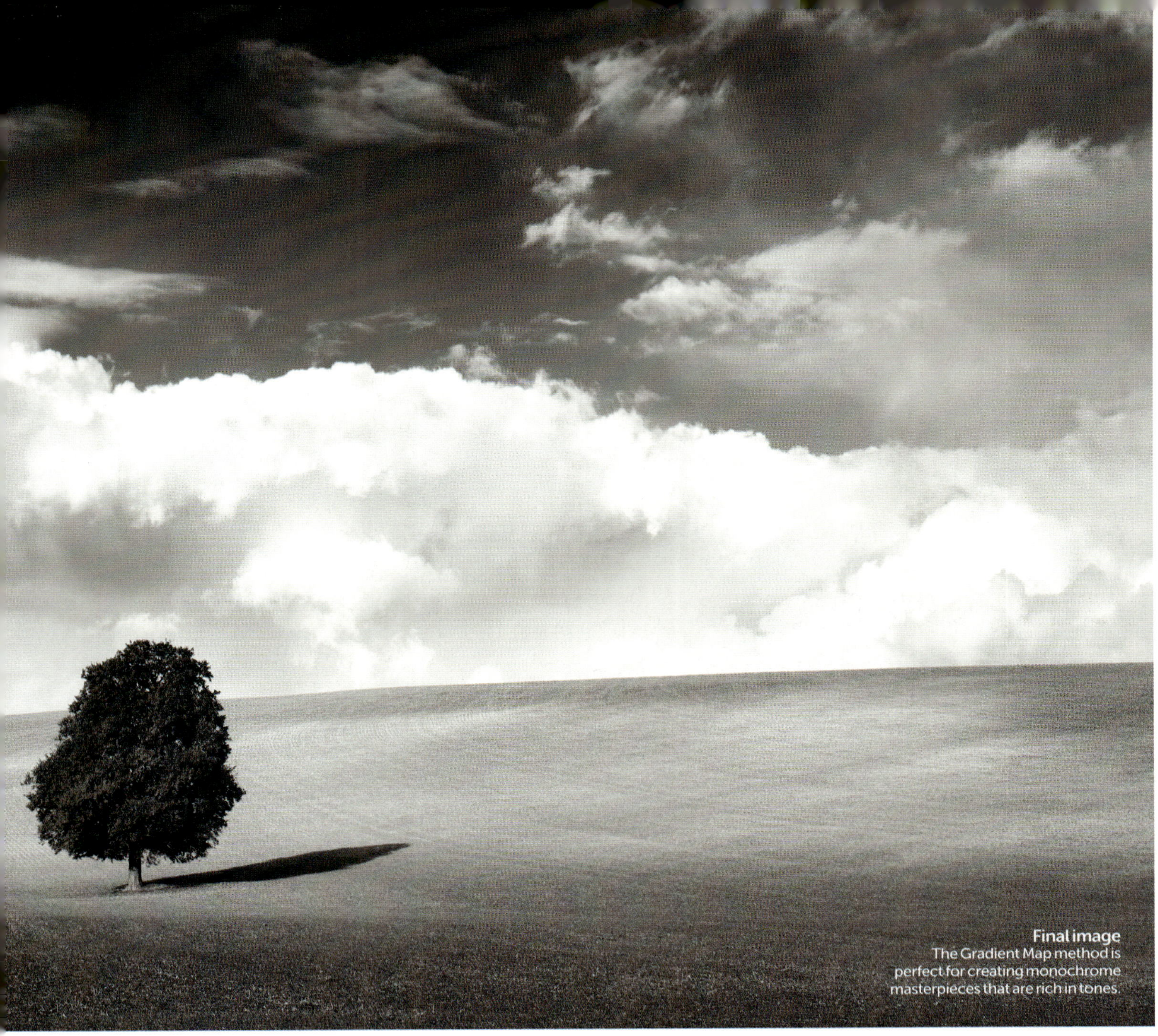

Final image
The Gradient Map method is perfect for creating monochrome masterpieces that are rich in tones.

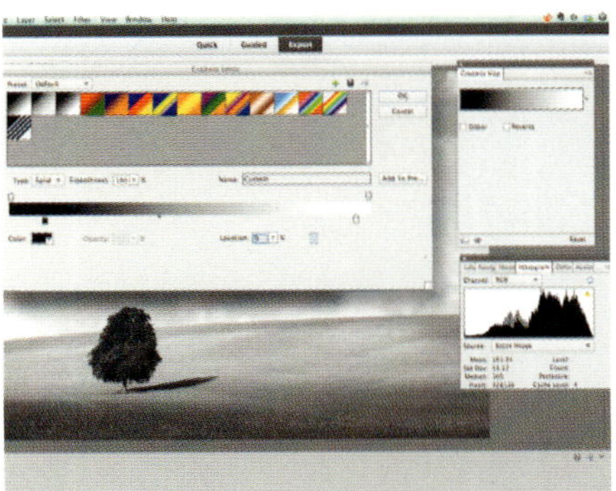

4 MAKE ADJUSTMENTS Drag the *Black Color Stop* to the right to darken the shadows. Watch the Histogram and stop before the graph touches the left edge. Next, adjust the mid-tones using the *Color Midpoint*. Finally use the *White Color Stop* to regulate the highlights, watching the Histogram again.

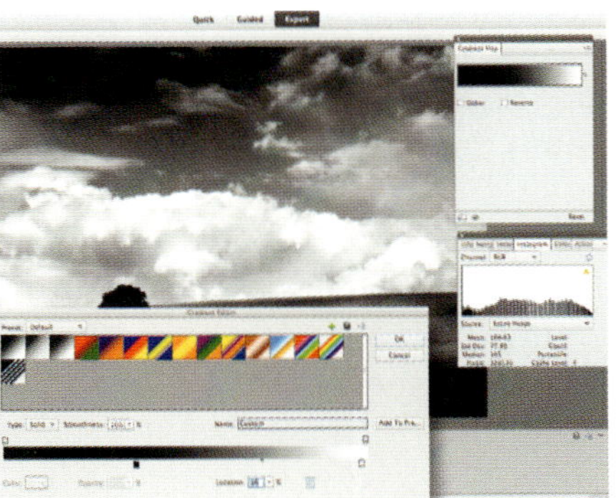

5 ADD A SECOND GRADIENT MAP Add another Gradient Map, as in step two. Back in the *Gradient Editor*, adjust the *Black Color Stop* and *Color Midpoint* to add drama, concentrating on the sky, ignoring the effect on the foreground. Once done, click *OK* and select the *Gradient Tool* from the toolbar.

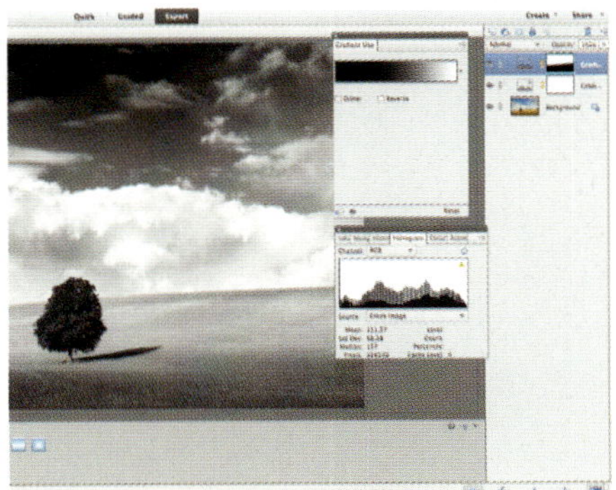

6 ADD A LAYER MASK Set your *Foreground Color* to *White* and your *Background Color* to *Black*. Make sure that *Linear Gradient* is selected in *Tool Options* and then drag from sky to foreground to blend the Gradient Maps. Click and drag as many times as required until you are happy with the effect.

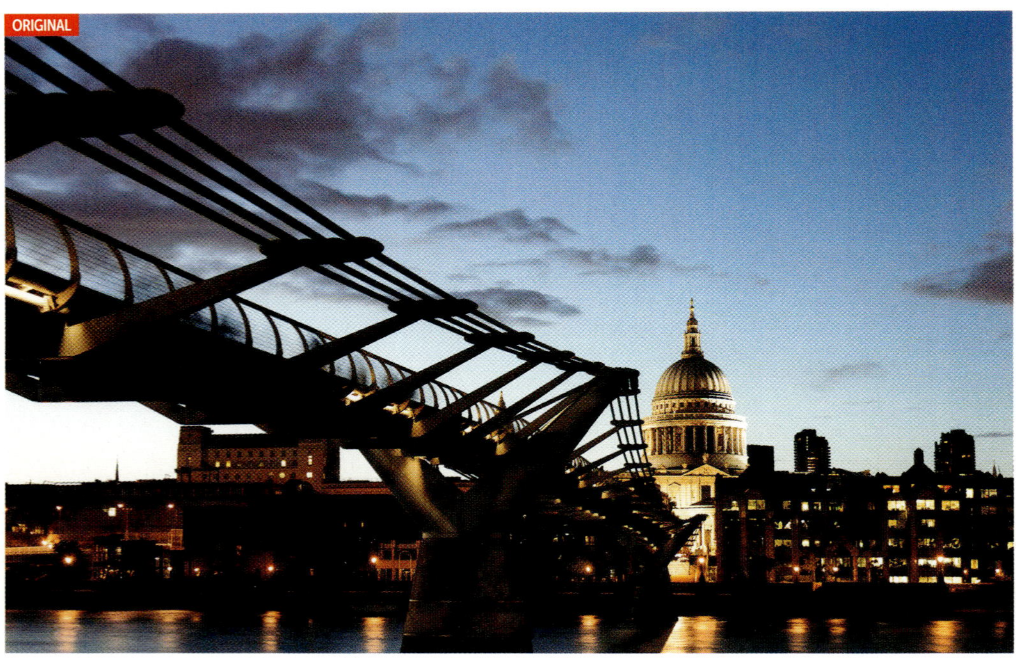

STOCKSY

Narrow down your focus

Add special interest to images without the outlay of specialist tilt-shift lenses – all you need is Photoshop Elements, creativity and little a bit of patience...

A SHALLOW DEPTH-OF-FIELD and a shifted plane of focus are telltale signs that an image has been shot on an expensive, specialist tilt-shift lens. In reality, these sort of optics are a pipe dream for most of us. However, there is a way that you can recreate the sort of effects created by tilt-shift lenses in Photoshop Elements. The finish isn't exactly the same as the in-camera results you'd get from using expensive glass but, when applied with care and precision, can turn an everyday image into something that grabs people's attention.

The type of image that you apply this effect to largely dictates the outcome. When applied to images shot from a raised vantage point, a tilt-shift effect can make photographs look like miniature-scale models. When used on images shot from ground-level, as we have done here, the result is a selective focus that draws the viewer into the image. If your picture was taken during the day, the first four steps are all you'll need, as the final two steps only apply to shots containing bokeh.

There are a number of different ways to achieve a similar effect in Elements, such as using Gaussian or Lens Blur alongside a Layer Mask, but here we're going to concentrate on the Blur Tool, which we've found gives a more realistic and controllable result.

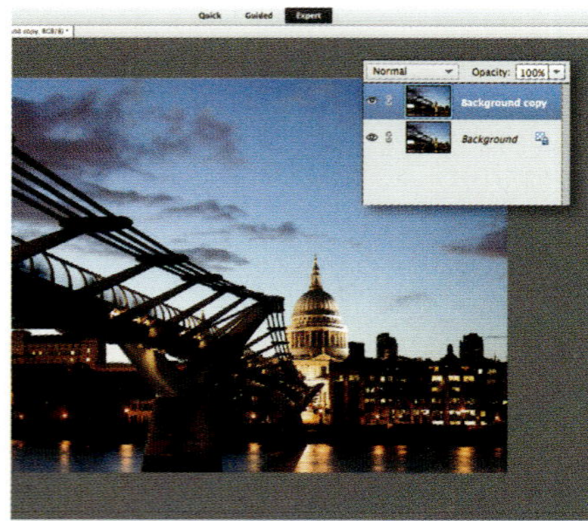

1 DUPLICATE YOUR LAYER Blurring is a destructive process – once an area is blurred, it cannot be unblurred! Before you start, create a copy of your image layer by going to ***Layer>Duplicate Layer***. This leaves the original image intact underneath. Once done, select the ***Blur Tool*** from the toolbar.

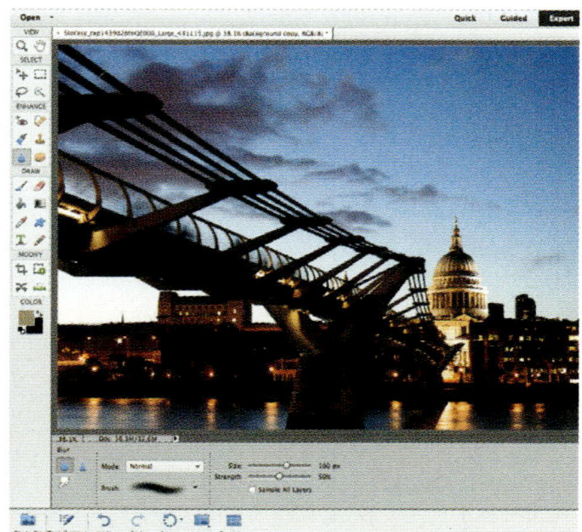

2 CUSTOMISE THE TOOL In *Tool Options*, set the ***Strength*** to ***50%***. You can select the brush size using the ***Size*** slider, but most people find it easier to use the ***[*** and ***]*** keys to adjust the size as they edit. The idea is to focus your viewer on one element; St Paul's Cathedral is our focal point.

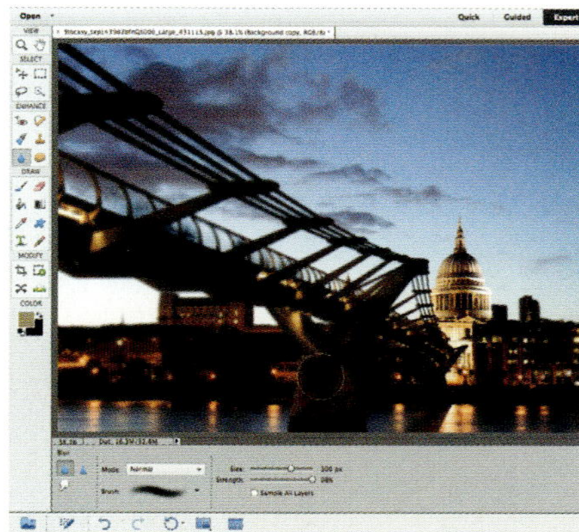

3 START BLURRING Brush over your image, increasing the ***Strength*** of the blur the further away from your focal point you get. Brushing over the same area multiple times will also increase the amount of blur. Objects closer to the camera should be blurred more than those closer the focal point.

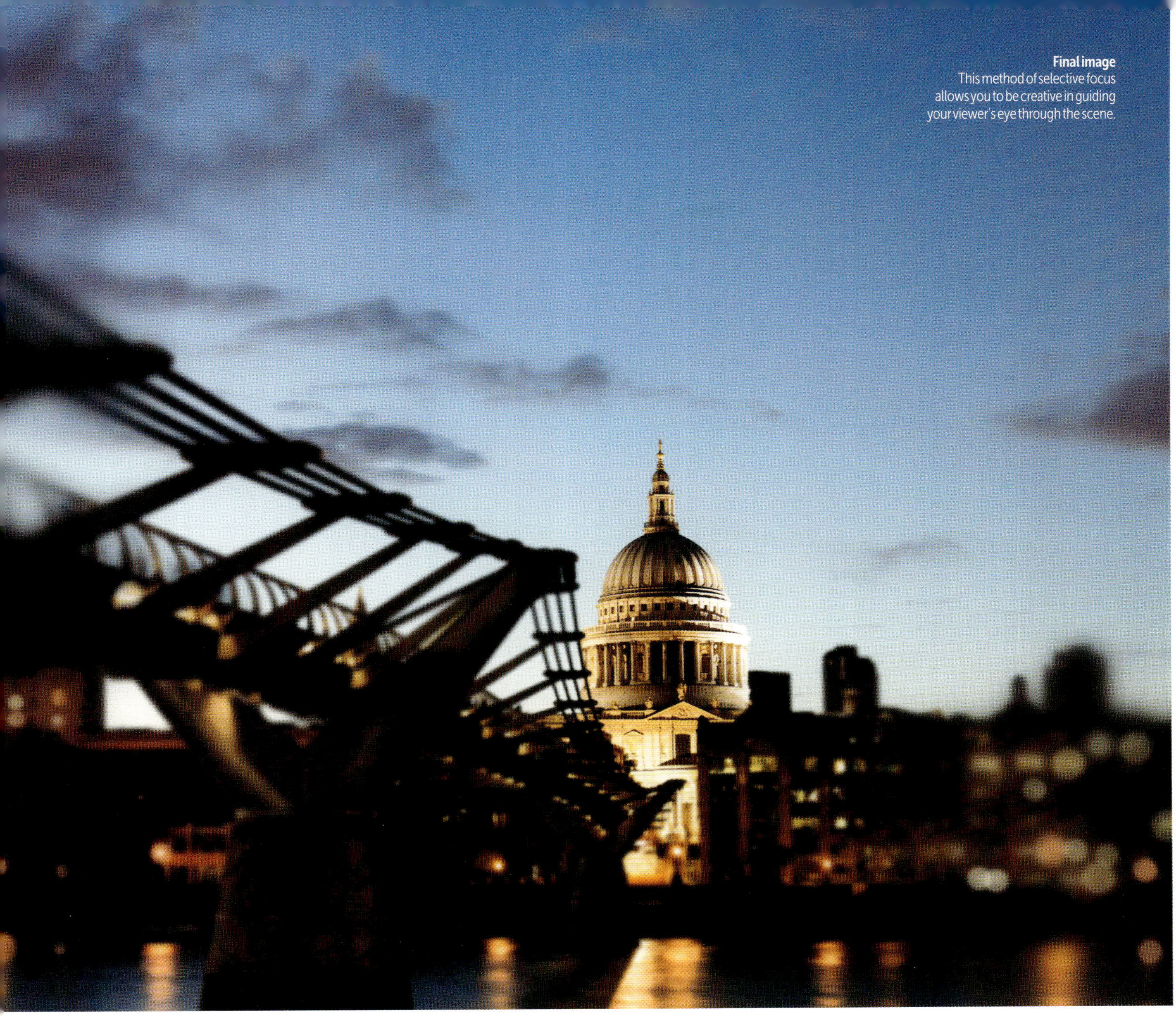

Final image
This method of selective focus allows you to be creative in guiding your viewer's eye through the scene.

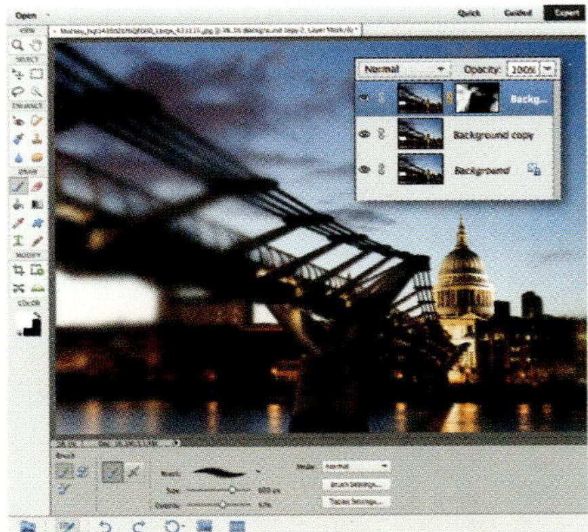

4 EXTRA BLUR If the Blur Tool lacks power in places, duplicate your blur layer again, then go to *Filter>Blur>Gaussian Blur*. Add a *Radius* of *20 pixels*. Go to *Layer>Layer Mask>Hide All*. Select the *Brush Tool* and, with *White* set as your *Foreground Color*, add extra blur at a low opacity.

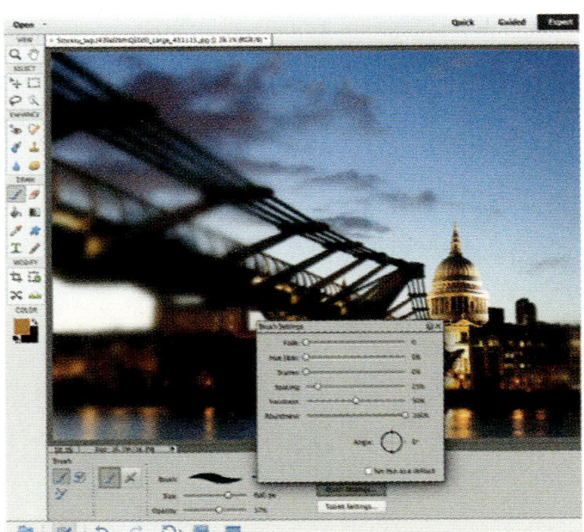

5 BOOST NIGHTTIME SHOTS Click on *Layer>Merge Visible* to flatten your image. Choose the *Color Picker Tool* and pick the colour of one of the bright highlights in your image. Select the *Brush Tool* and, in *Tool Options*, click the *Brush Settings* button. Set the *Hardness* slider to *50%*.

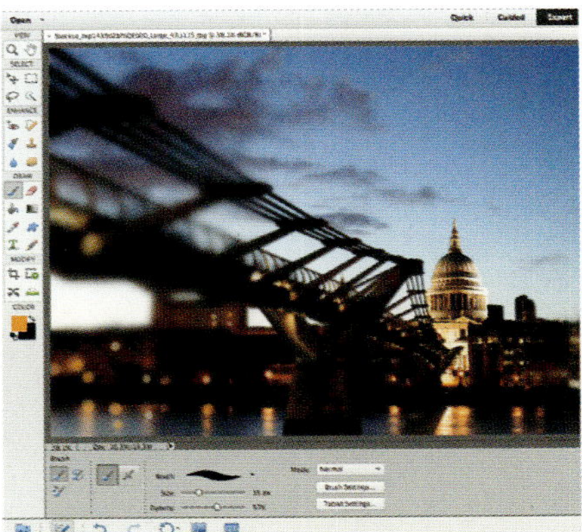

6 ADD BOKEH Set your brush's *Opacity* to *100%* and the *Size* to be slightly larger than the light source, before clicking once or twice to add a ball of bokeh. Repeat for each light source, remembering that areas with more blur should have more pronounced bokeh than areas with less blur.

Easy collages in Elements

Creating photo collages is a great way to show off multiple images at once, but they can be tricky to produce. Take the complexity out of a collage by using Elements 14's automated solution

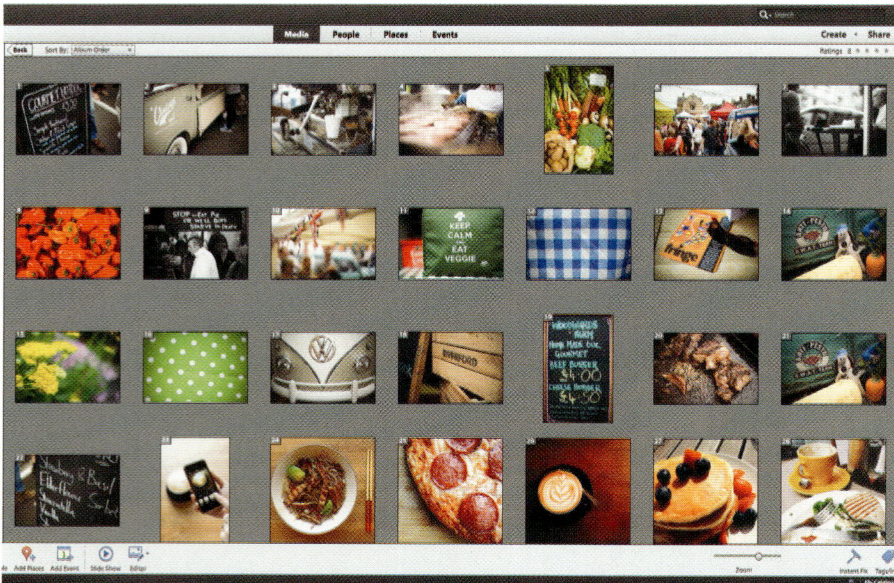

ONE OF THE MOST effective ways to display a collection of images as one is a collage. They can be used to tell the story of a day out, event or family holiday. They can also be used to tie together several images with an underlying theme or topic. However, they can be tricky to put together manually. Not only do you have to upload all of your images at once and decide on a layout, but you then have to resize and crop each image to the right size and shape to fit!

Elements offers a quick-and-easy solution. Sure, it's not as flexible as creating your own collage from scratch, and you are limited to a set number of sizes, layouts and borders, but it is much easier to do – less time spent in front of a computer and more time spent out shooting can only be a good thing!

For the purposes of this tutorial we've used Photoshop Elements 14, though earlier versions of Elements offer very similar functionality, albeit with less options for customising. As an Elements user this is your chance to be smug – the full version of Photoshop doesn't offer the Photo Collage option! Let's get stuck in...

Create your own designs

The choice of preset layouts that Elements offers depends on the number of images that you've selected in the Organizer and the output size that you choose in step two. However, each of these layouts are merely templates, so feel free to get in amongst it and move the frames and images around to suit your needs to come up with your own layouts and designs.

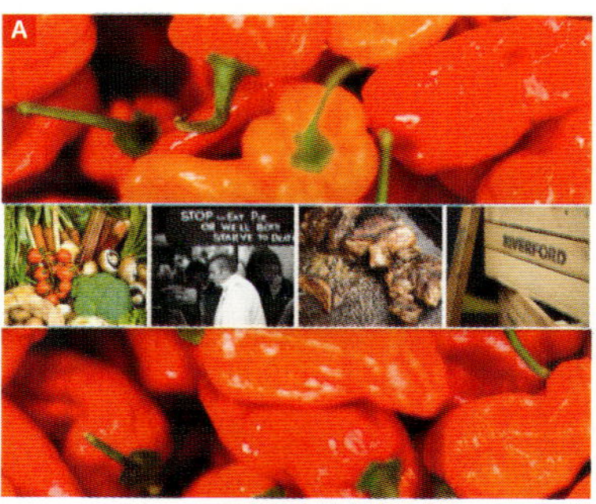

A

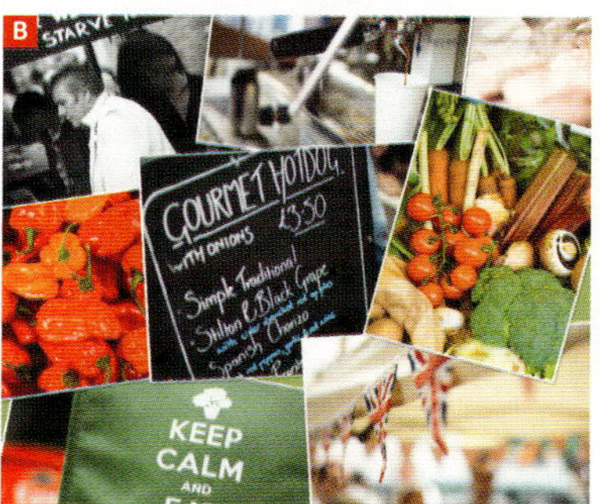

B

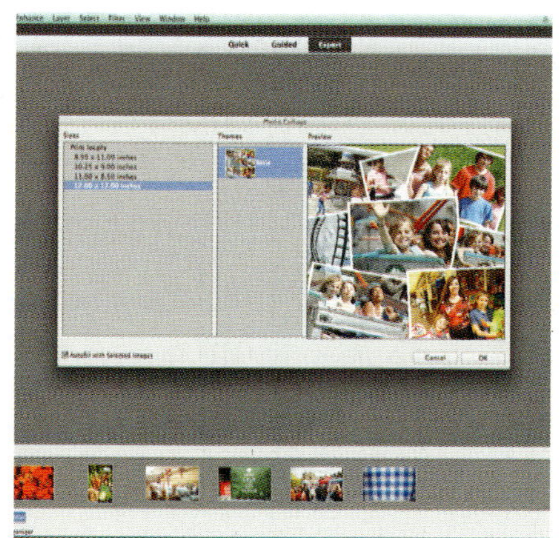

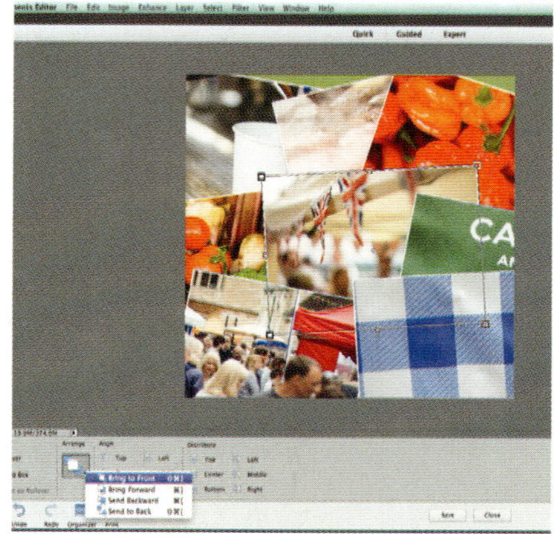

1 CHOOSE YOUR IMAGES Open the Elements Organizer and click on *File>Import* in the top left – from here you can either import files from your computer, or directly from your camera or card reader. Once imported, hold down the *ctrl* key (Windows) or *cmd* key (Mac) and select the files that you want to include in your collage.

2 SELECT THE SIZE Once done, click on the *Create* menu in the top right and select *Photo Collage*. In the Photo Collage window, choose your output size – different sizes will have different layout options available. We've selected *300 x 300mm* for now. Click *OK* and Elements will start putting together your collage image.

3 CUSTOMISE THE COLLAGE The images will be displayed in a jumbled format. You can add extra images into the boxes by clicking on them. Single-click on an image to adjust the frame, and double-click to adjust or change the image within the frame. To bring an image to the front, select it and use the *Layer>Arrange* menu to select *Bring to Front*.

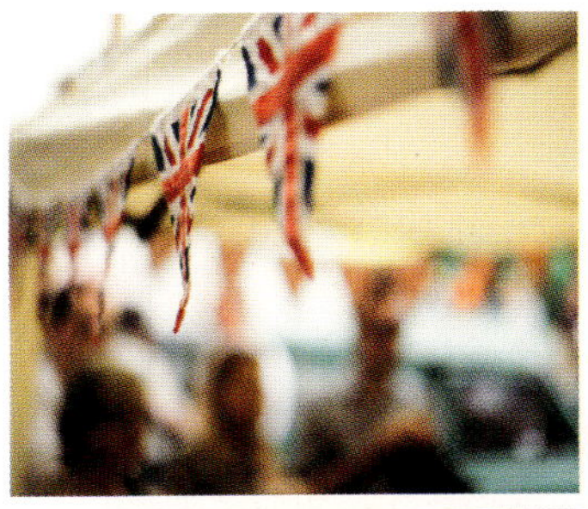
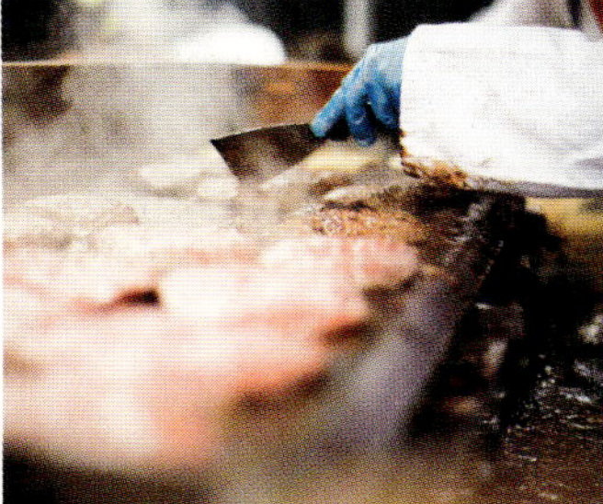
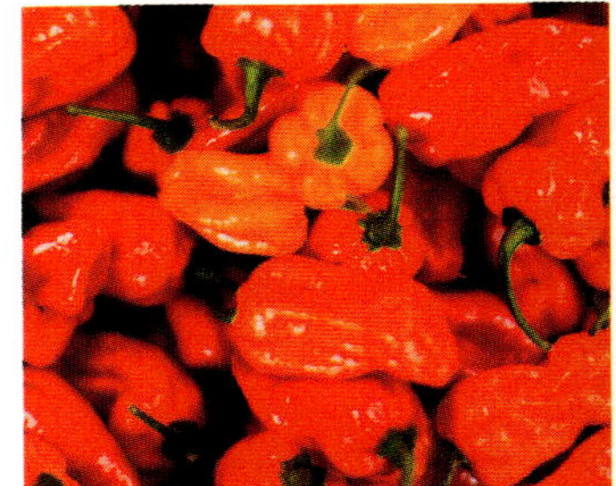
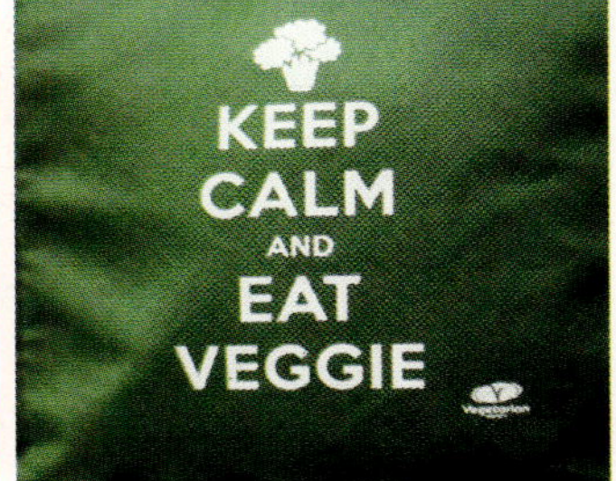

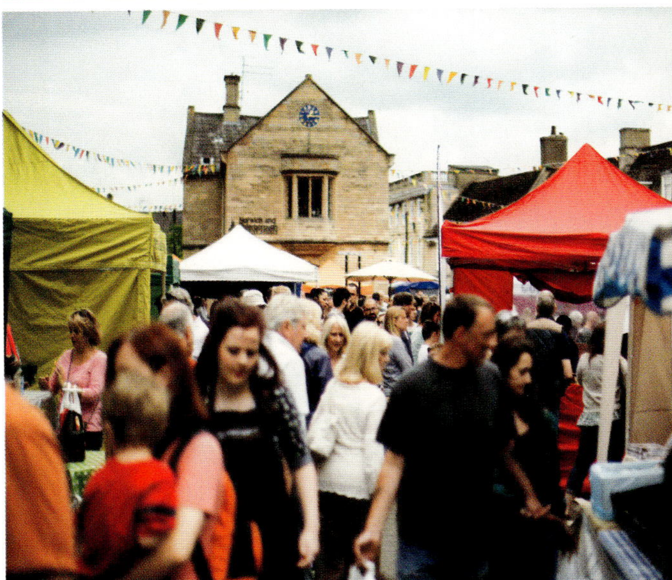
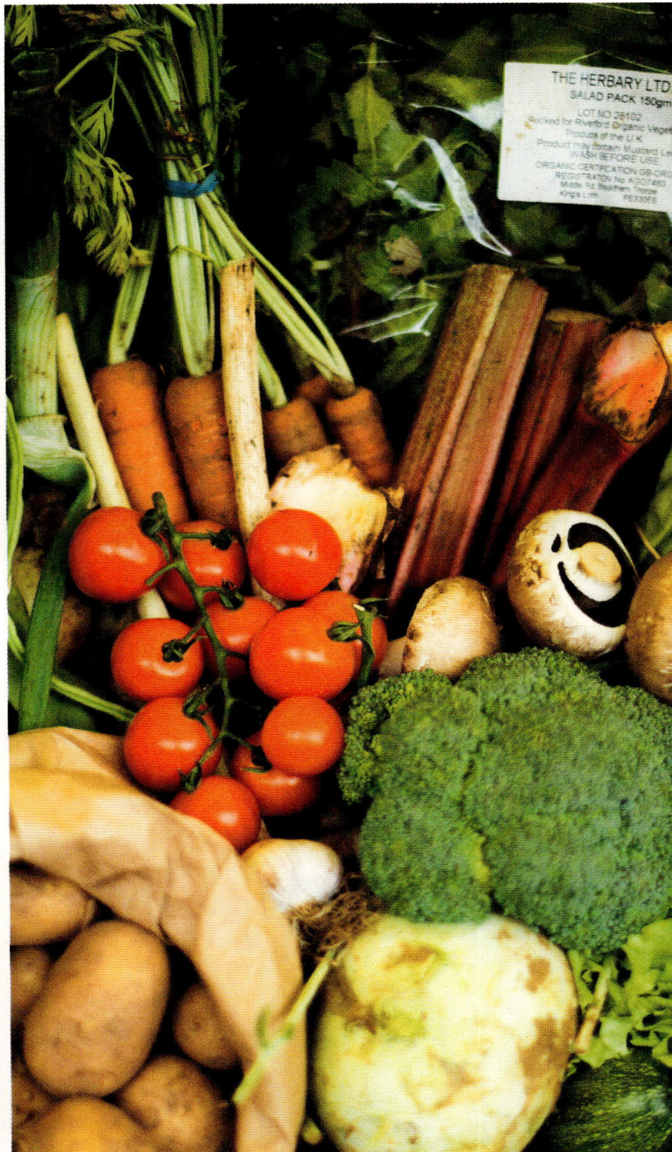

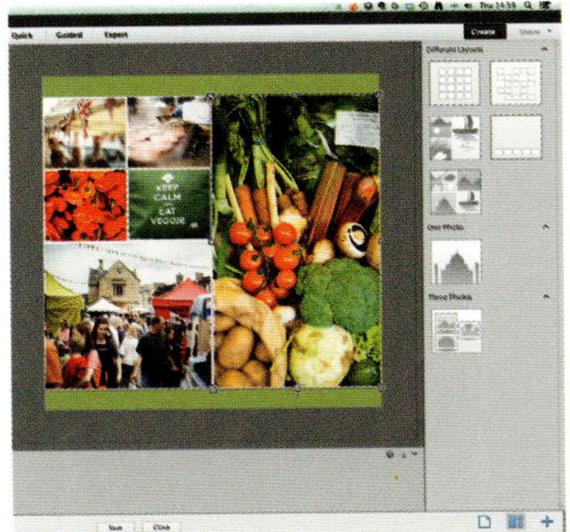

4 CHANGE THE LAYOUT To add order to your collage, click on ***Layouts*** in the bottom corner. Choose a layout that you like and double-click on it. You can rearrange the layout to suit your tastes, as in the previous step. Blank space is filled with a background – to change this, click on ***Graphics*** in the bottom corner and choose a different one.

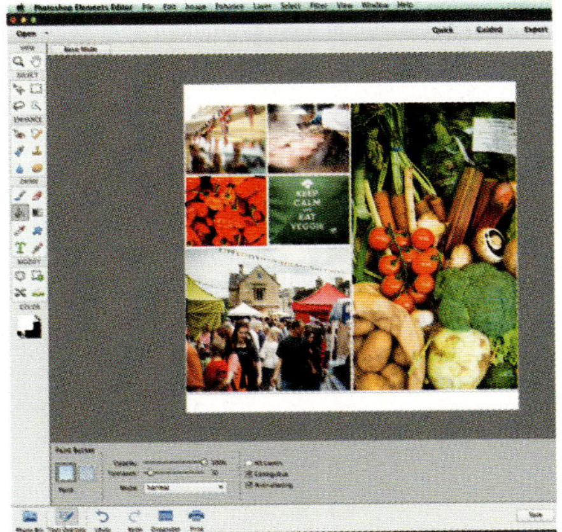

5 TAKE MORE CONTROL If you want more advanced control of your collage, click on ***Advanced Mode*** in the top left. You can then click on ***Layers*** in the bottom-right corner and edit the individual layers. Here, we've opted for a plain white rather than a textured background by using the Paint Bucket Tool on the Background layer.

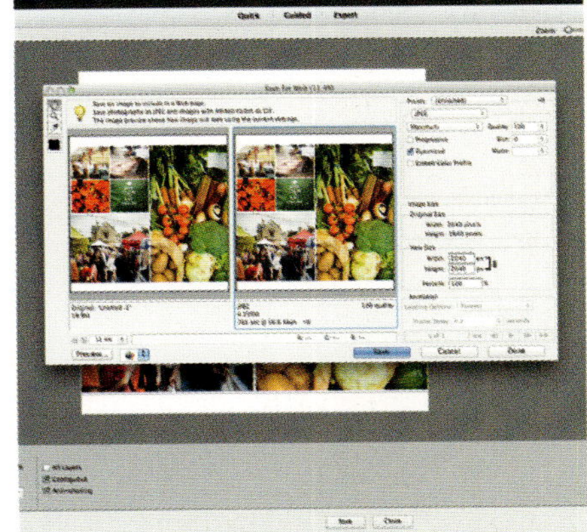

6 SAVE YOUR WORK By clicking on the ***Save*** button at the bottom of the window your collage will be saved as a Photo Project Format (.pse) file – this allows for further editing. To save for web use go to ***File>Save for Web***. In the window that opens set the ***File Format*** to ***JPEG*** and ***Quality*** to ***100***, before clicking ***Save***.

Basic compositing

Get to grips with the basics of image compositing by adding new elements to your photographs for more visual interest

PHOTOSHOP ELEMENTS IS a fantastic tool for tweaking and perfecting your digital images. However, it's also incredibly fun to use if you want to add extra elements into a scene that were not there when you captured the image – more commonly referred to as a composite image.

Composites are commonplace in professional advertising photography, as it's often the case that the campaign calls for either an impossible scenario to be shot, or when logistically it's expensive or difficult to place the item or person that you want photographed in the location that you want them in. These types of composites are very complex and often take teams of retouchers tens of man hours to compile. While this tutorial doesn't go to these lengths, it serves as a good introduction to the world of basic compositing, using one of the simplest types of image to composite – a silhouette. In order to give this technique a go, you'll need a main image, such as the landscape shot we've chosen here and an object to add to the image – we've opted for a flock of birds in flight. One of the most crucial aspects of compositing is that the direction of lighting in your two images are closely matched. Both of my scenes are backlit, so basic adjustments to the bird image are all that's required.

The only limit is your imagination when it comes to compositing, so give it a go – start with the basics as we've done here and see what creative scenes you come up with!

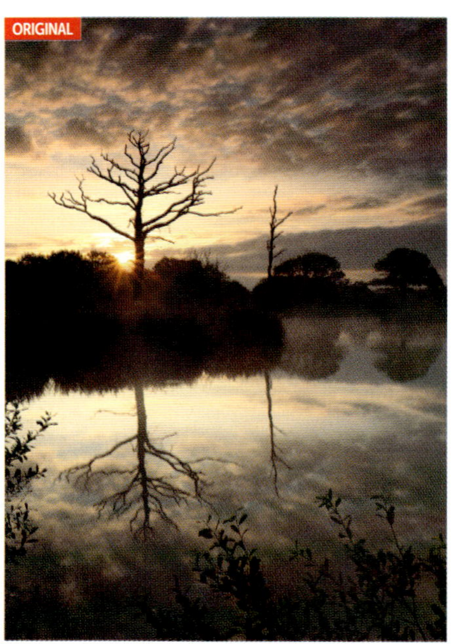

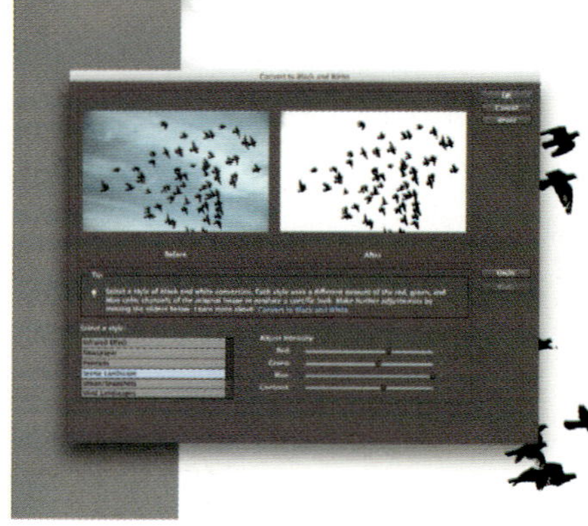

1 Create a silhouette First, your bird image needs to be as near to silhouette as possible. With the image open, go to *Enhance>Convert to Black and White*. In the Convert to Black and White box that opens, increase the *Contrast* to darken the shadow and lighten the highlights. I've also increased the *Blue* slider to render the blue sky almost completely white. Click *OK*.

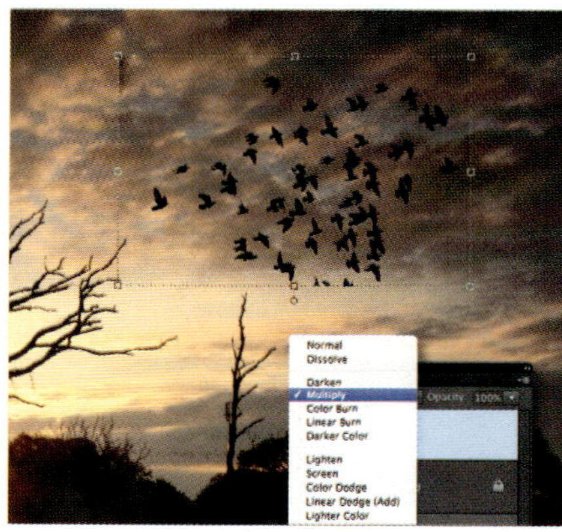

2 Scale the birds to fit Go *Select>All* and then *Edit>Copy*. Open your landscape image and go to *Edit>Paste*. Select the *Move Tool* and click and drag one of the corner anchors to scale the birds to fit your image – making sure that *Constrain Proportions* in the top menu bar is checked. Once done, change the *Blend Mode* of this layer to *Multiply*.

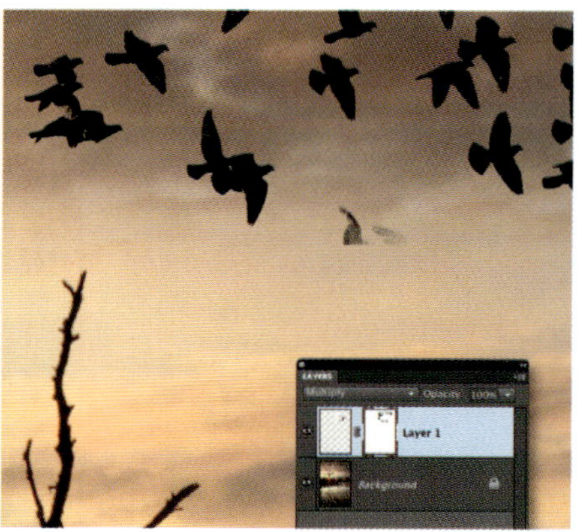

3 Mask the birds There may still be areas of the sky from your bird image visible, depending on how good a job you did of silhouetting it. If so, go to *Layer>Layer Mask>Reveal All*. Select the *Brush Tool*, set *Black* as your *Foreground Color* and brush over the areas of sky still remaining. There are some birds cropped on my image, so brush over these too to remove them.

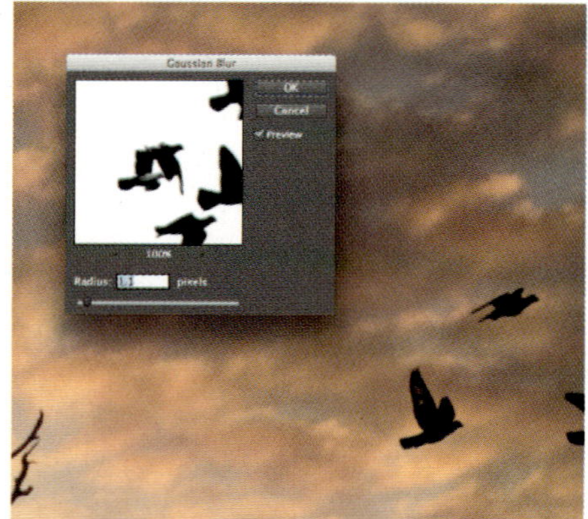

4 Add some blur Your birds may look a bit too crisp in relation to the image. If so, go to *Filter>Blur>Gaussian Blur*. Increase the blur until the sharpness of the birds match with other elements in the scene. This may be all that is required for your image however, as this image contains a reflection there are a couple more steps that are needed.

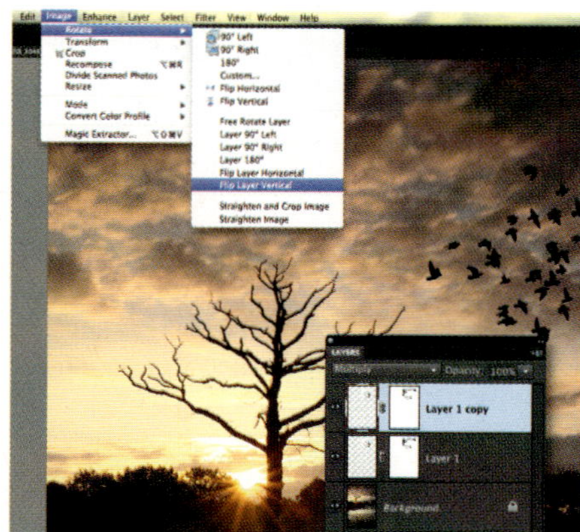

5 Add a reflection Right-click on your bird layer in the Layers palette and select *Duplicate Layer...* Go to *Image>Rotate>Flip Layer Vertical*. Using the *Move Tool*, hold down the *shift* key and drag the birds down into the reflection in a mirrored position. Reduce the *Opacity* of this layer in the Layers palette to between *30-70%*, depending on your image.

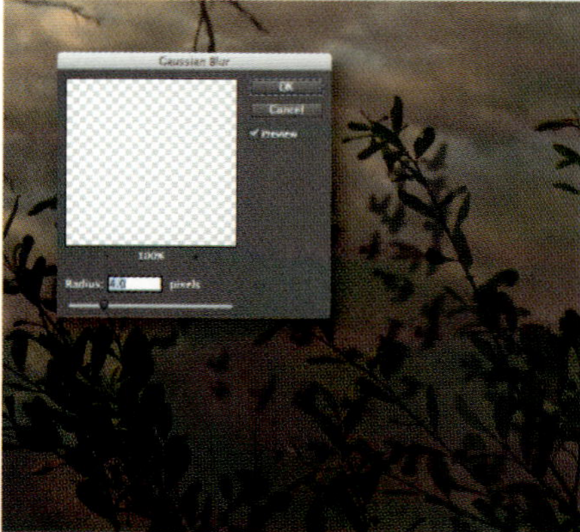

6 Mask the reflection The reflection may require a little more blur to look natural, so go to *Filter>Blur>Gaussian Blur* and increase the blur – I found 4.0 pixels worked. Finally, click on the Layer Mask thumbnail on your reflection layer in the Layers palette, select the *Brush Tool* with *Black* as your *Foreground Color*, and mask areas where the reflection wouldn't appear.

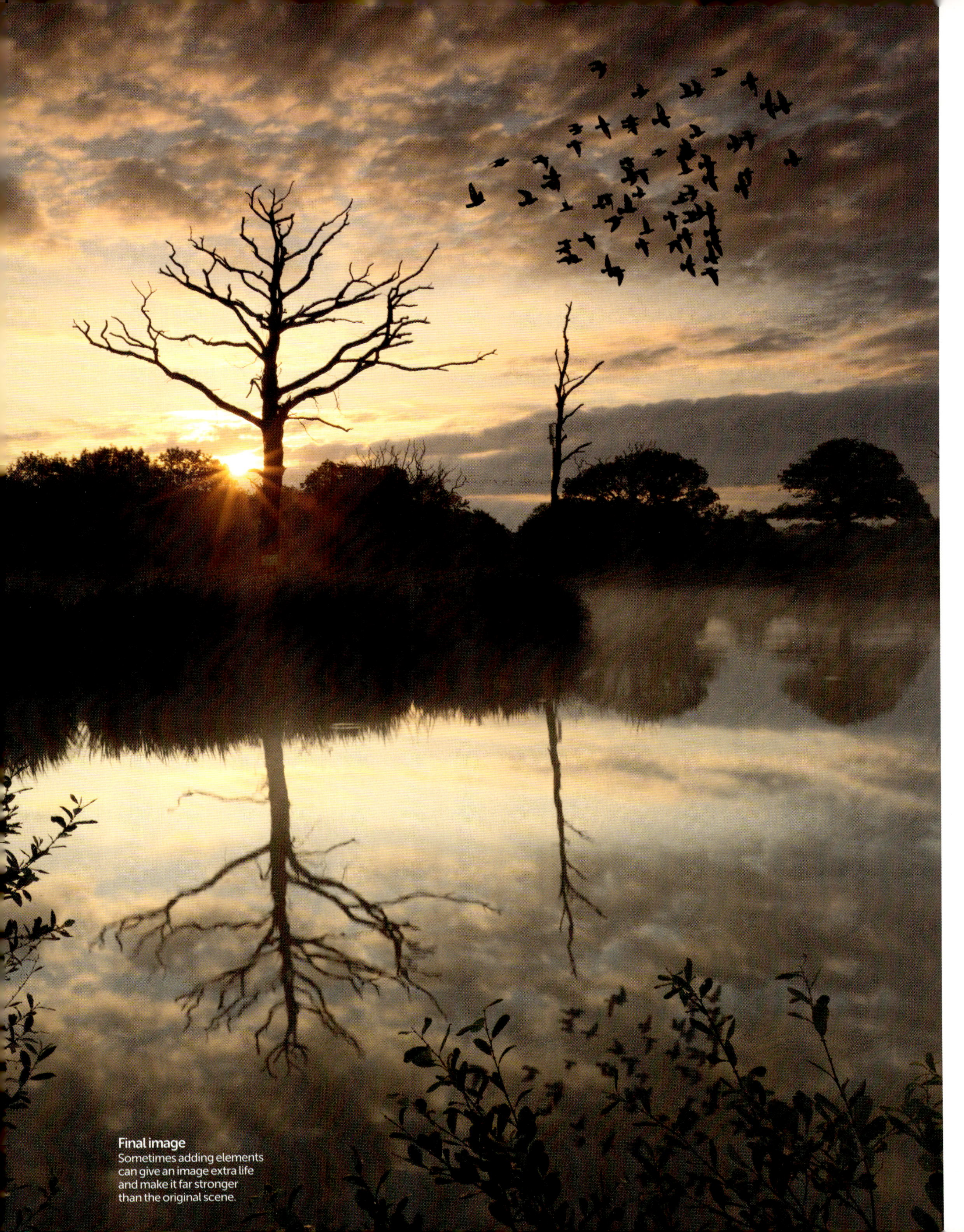

Final image
Sometimes adding elements can give an image extra life and make it far stronger than the original scene.

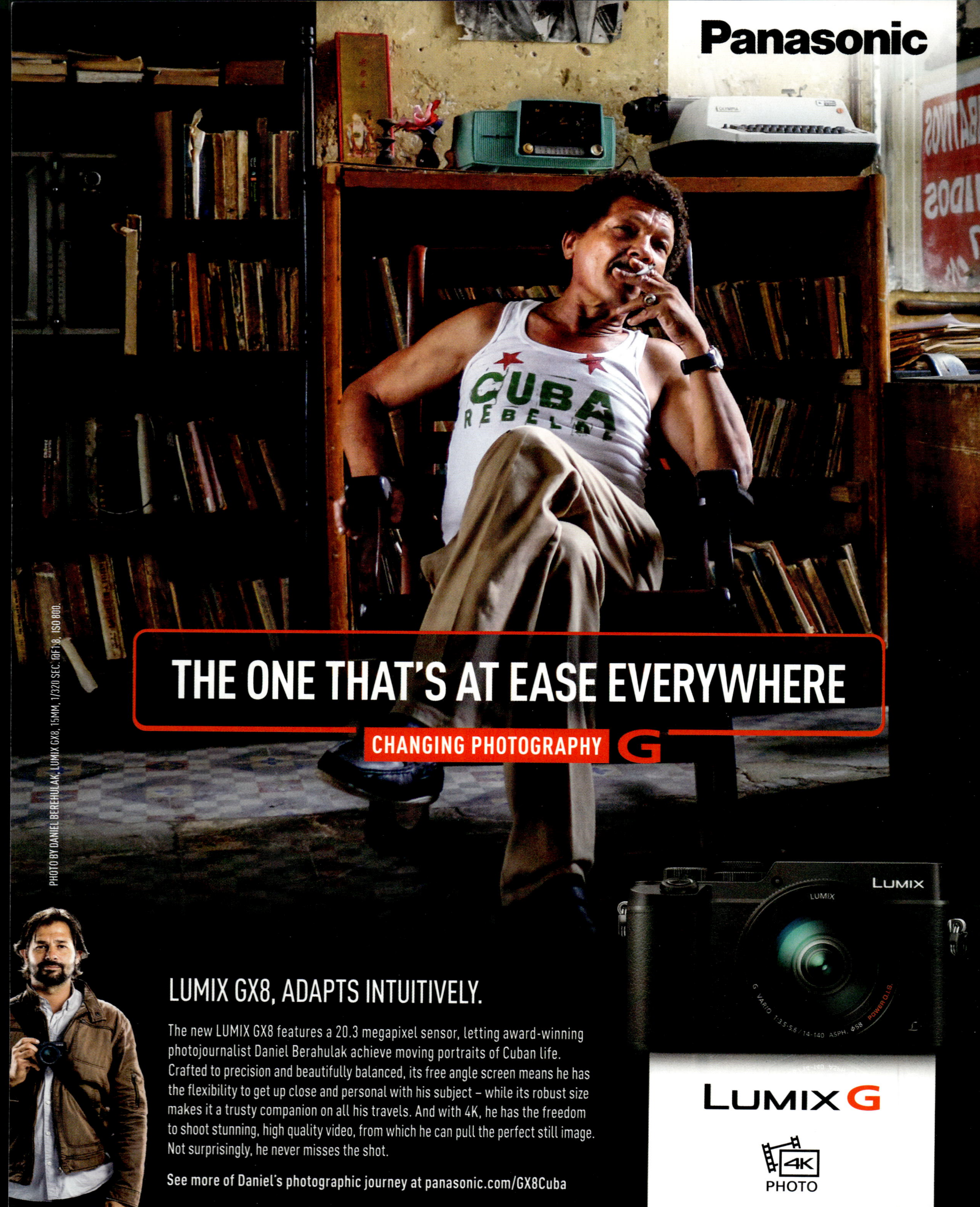

Panasonic
CUBA
REBELDE
THE ONE THAT'S AT EASE EVERYWHERE
CHANGING PHOTOGRAPHY G
LUMIX GX8, ADAPTS INTUITIVELY.
The new LUMIX GX8 features a 20.3 megapixel sensor, letting award-winning photojournalist Daniel Berahulak achieve moving portraits of Cuban life. Crafted to precision and beautifully balanced, its free angle screen means he has the flexibility to get up close and personal with his subject – while its robust size makes it a trusty companion on all his travels. And with 4K, he has the freedom to shoot stunning, high quality video, from which he can pull the perfect still image. Not surprisingly, he never misses the shot.
See more of Daniel's photographic journey at panasonic.com/GX8Cuba
LUMIX
LUMIX G
4K
PHOTO

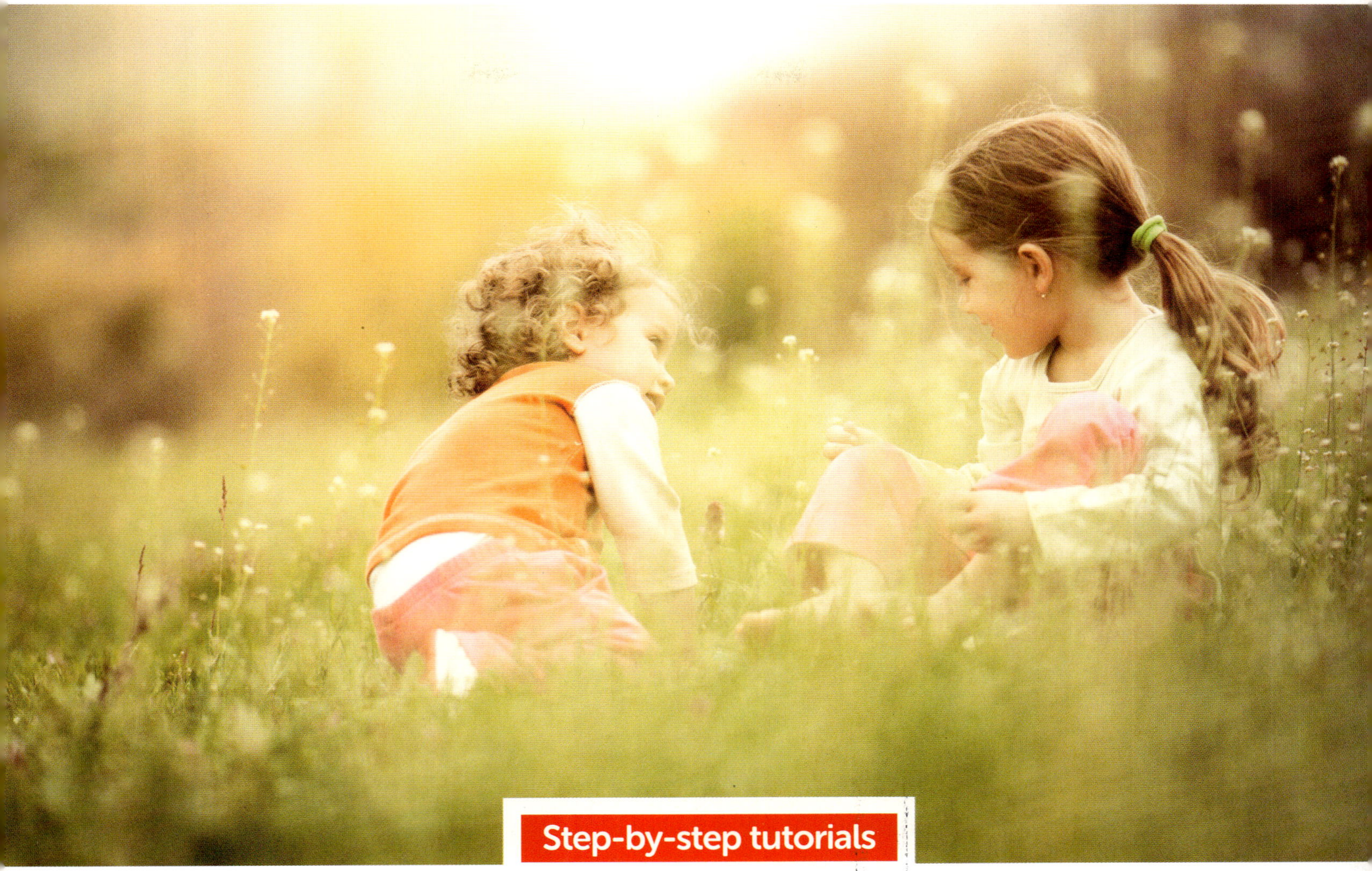

Step-by-step tutorials

LIGHTROOM

Master your workflow with expert advice and tutorials for using Adobe Lightroom

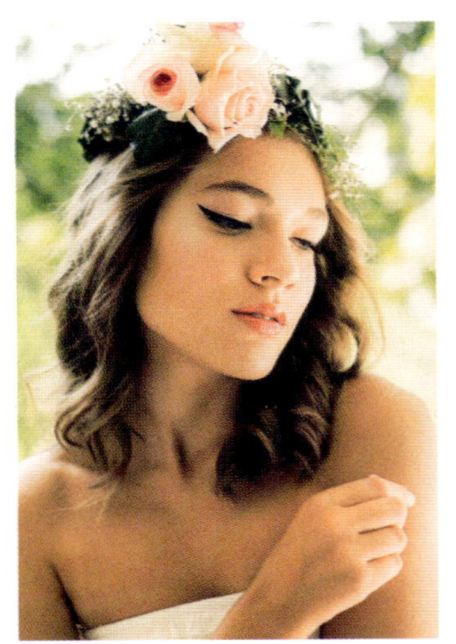
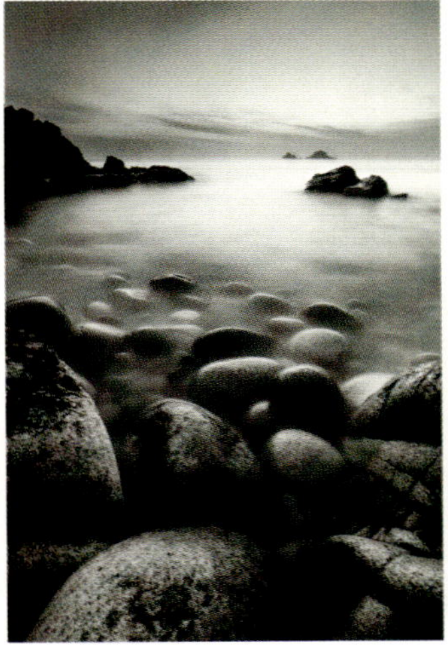
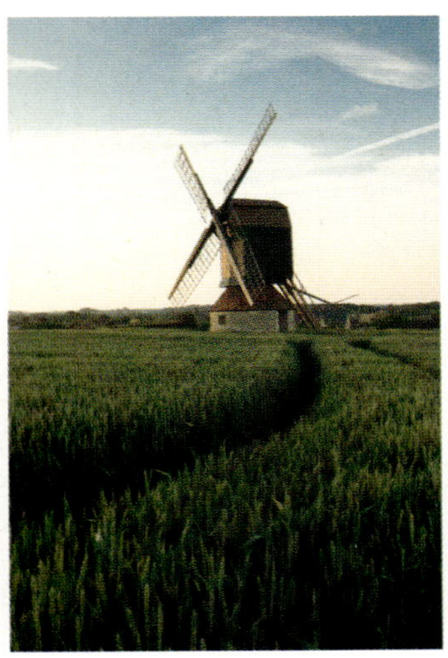
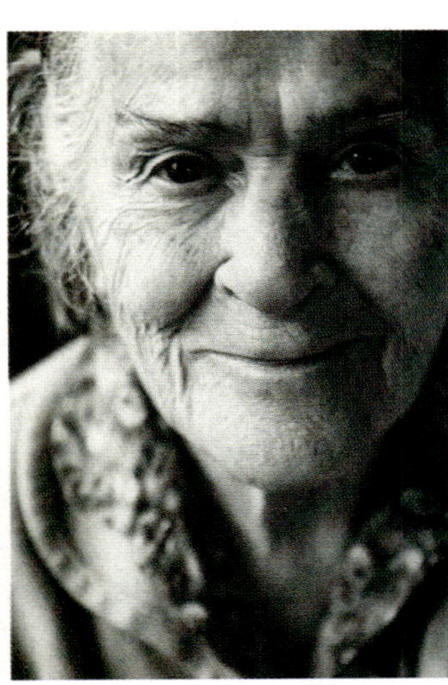

Workflow Part 1

It's time to get organised! Here we show you how to use Lightroom to catalogue all your pictures

DIGITAL PHOTOGRAPHY IS a curse and a blessing as, unless you're ruthless with your picture taking, it's easy to become shutter-happy and take hundreds of images, which then need sorting, organising and editing. Thankfully, Lightroom helps you do just that: offering an array of tools to make your workflow simple, logical and quick. In part one of our two-part feature on Lightroom workflow, find out how to efficiently import and organise your image collection. Over the page, we show you how to index, make quick edits and publish your pictures.

1 Import your image Upon connecting your camera or card reader to your computer, Lightroom will automatically open the Import interface. If you are importing from the hard drive, click on the *Import* button at the bottom of the Library module to open the import window. You can start sorting your images by deselecting pictures that you don't want to import. Once you've selected your collection, click on *Keywords* on the right-hand side and give your collection a name. You may also want to add your copyright details via the *Metadata* tab, too. Click *Import* to open the images in the Library.

2 Review your images Now in the Library, it's time to get ruthless with your images to separate the good from the bad. Lightroom 6 offers several ways to preview and compare images, accessible via the buttons at the bottom of the Library module. Grid View displays thumbnails of your image collection, which you can increase or decrease in size using the Thumbnail slider. The Loupe View loads a selected image on the page and allows you to zoom in and out by clicking on the image. The Compare View allows you to preview two images side by side and is useful if you have two similar images to choose between. And, finally, the Survey View displays a group of images you've selected from the Filmstrip, using the shift or cmd keys.

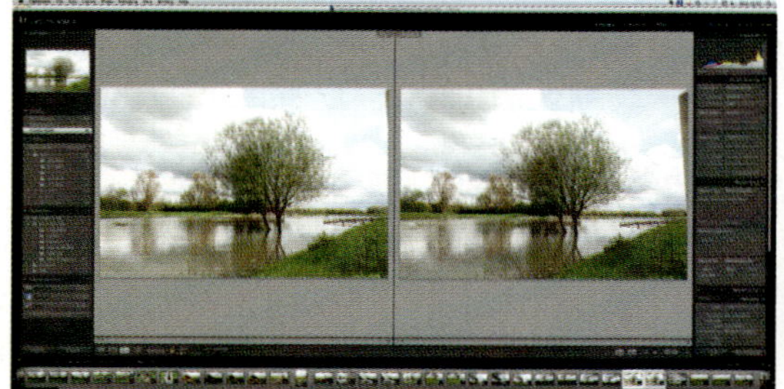

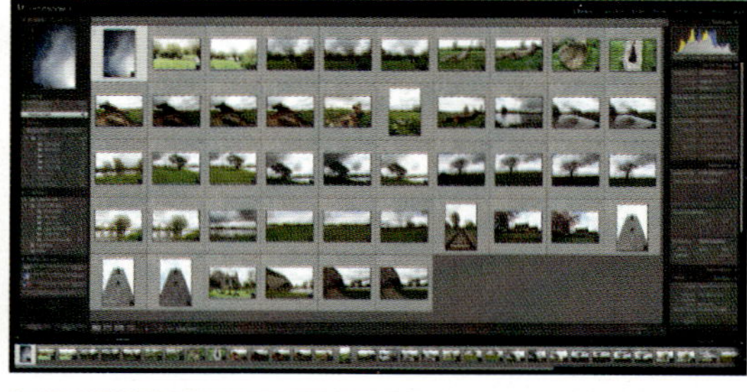

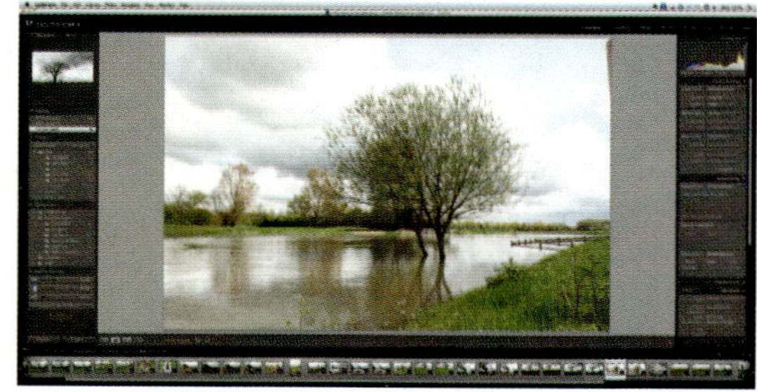

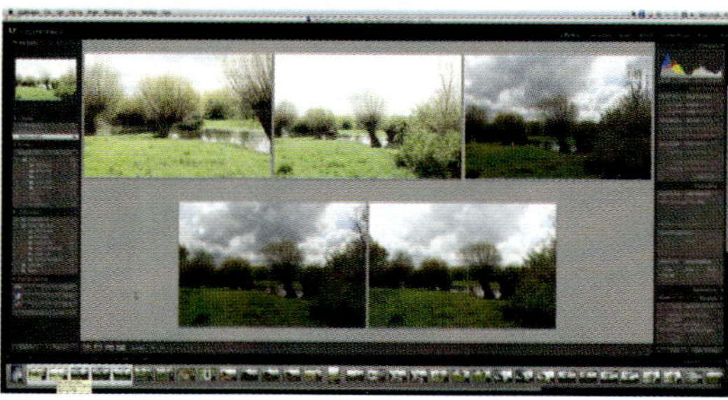

3 Flag images The term 'Flagging' refers to markers that you can assign to your images for quick and efficient organisation. You can Flag an image as Picked or as Rejected by pressing the *P* key or *X* key respectively – you'll see either a white flag (Picked) or a black flag with a cross (Rejected) appear in the corner of the image. Once your images have been Flagged, you can quickly sort them using the Filter selection to the right of the filmstrip: by clicking on the different Filter flags, you can view Flagged images, Flagged and unflagged photos, and Rejected images only.

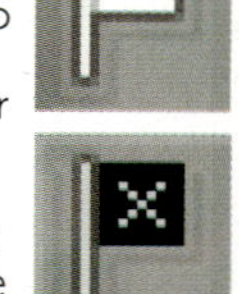

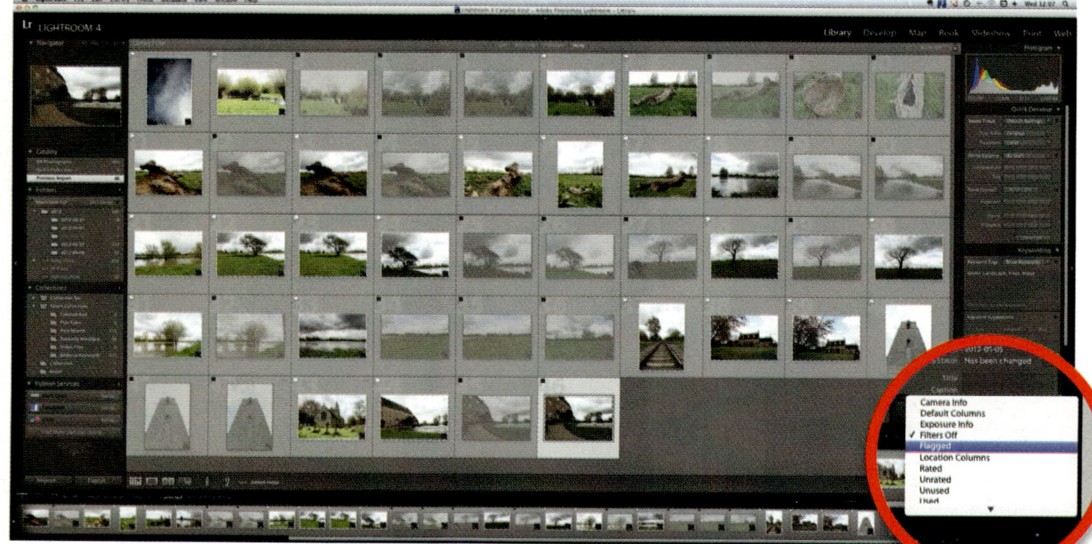

4 Remove the rejects Now you can view your Rejected images and review them once more before removing them from your library. Once your selection is final, go to ***Photo>Delete Rejected Photos***. The dialogue box that appears will give you the option to Remove the image from your library, which removes it from Lightroom but leaves the image on your hard drive, or Delete From Disk, which deletes the Raw file from both your hard drive *and* the library. Rather than assigning a choice to all the images, you can select them individually instead.

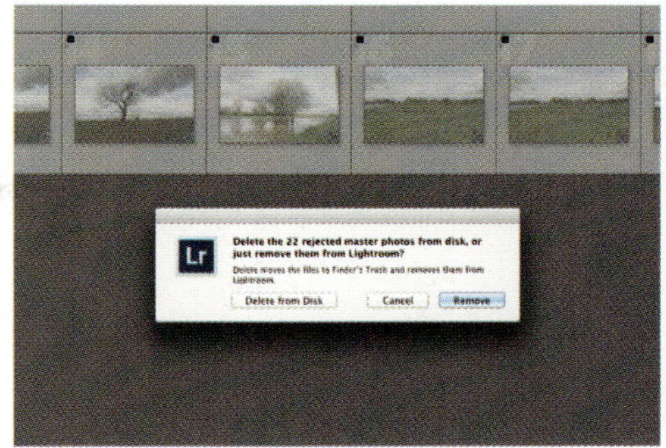

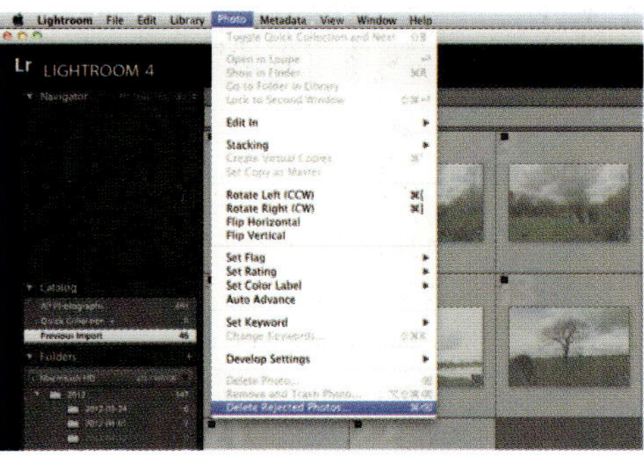

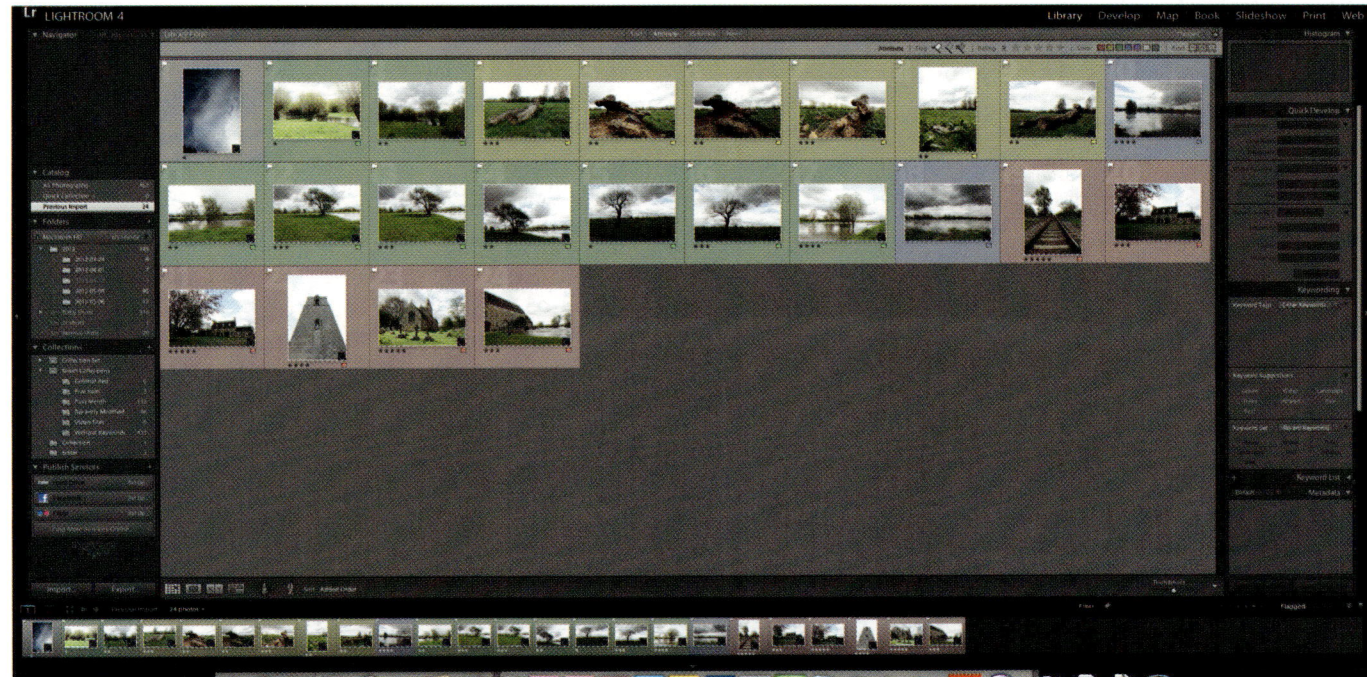

5 Assign a star rating Click the *Flagged* filter, in the Filmstrip, to show your picked images. At this stage, you may have whittled your images down to a suitable number and can move on to the next step; if not, you can choose to either Color Label or Rate your photos to refine your choice. Use the arrow keys to navigate through your selection and use the ***0-5*** number keys to assign star ratings to your images, or the ***6-9*** number keys to assign a Color Rating. You can then go to ***Library>Filter*** by Rating to only display images with an assigned star rating or ***Library>Filter by Color Label*** to display images by colour.

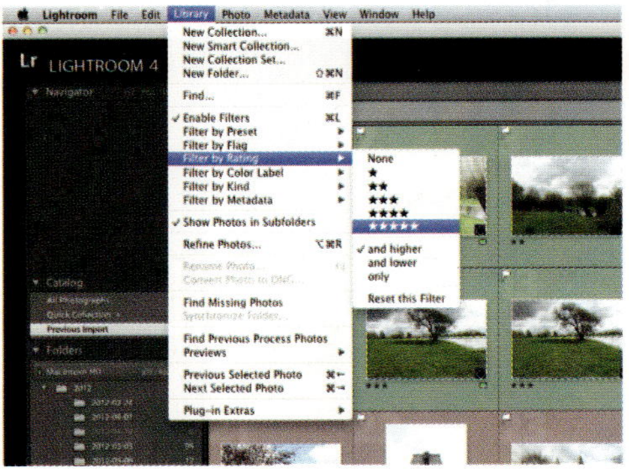

Software compared

Workflow in Photoshop Elements 14

Simplified versions of Lightroom's workflow tools can be found in Photoshop Elements 14 Organizer. Your images can be imported into Organizer using the ***File>Get Photos and Videos*** menu. Elements doesn't offer the same versatility or power that Lightroom does, but tools such as Keyword Tags, Star Ratings and Smart Tags all feature and can be used in much the same way as Lightroom to effectively manage your photo collections.

6 Add Keywords and metadata Adding Keyword Tags to your images can make it easier to find images in your catalogue. Assign a Keyword by selecting one or more images, accessing the ***Keywording*** tab to the right and adding descriptive text such as landscape, portrait, trees, water, wedding, sport etc. Separate multiple keywords with a comma. Your most recently used keywords are saved below the input box. You can also assign Keyword Sets to different genres of photography using the Keyword Set drop-down menu. Next, click on the ***Metadata*** tab and input details such as copyright status, copyright, title and a caption.

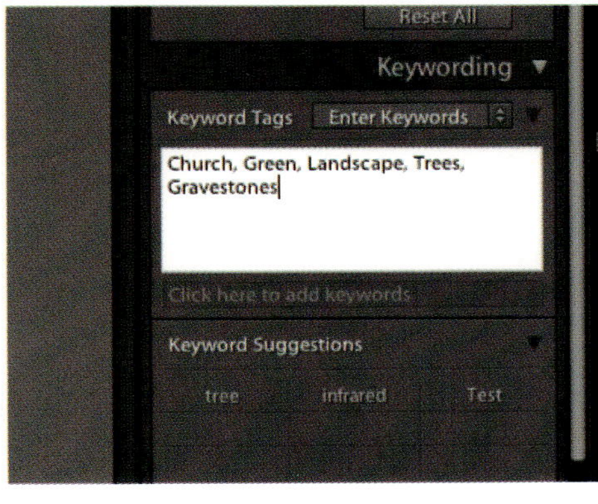

Workflow Part 2

Sorting files can be an overwhelming task, but Lightroom 6 allows you to do it with ease. Here's how...

WHAT SHOULD YOU do with your images once you've imported and selected your collection? Here, we look at indexing your images for easy retrieval, quick developing and the publishing and export options offered within the Library module. All of these features revolve around saving you time and feature in Lightroom 5, 6 and CC – though the latter two also boast face recognition to help organise your portraits. It's best to be methodical at this early stage as the better organised your photo collection, the easier you will find it to locate and sort your images in the future.

1 Collections Lightroom's Collections feature allows you to collate images from different albums and import them into themed folders, such as landscapes, portraits, still-lifes etc. You can create a collection by clicking on the + icon and selecting *Create Collection*. To add images, simply click and drag them into the folder manually, or out of the folder if you want to remove them from the collection. Alternatively, to quickly group images together like those that need more editing, right-click the collection and select *Set as Target Collection*, then right-click an image and select *Add to Target Collection* or press *B* on a selected image. You know when an image is in the target collection as it will have a grey dot in the top right-hand corner.

When you add an image to a collection, the image remains in its original location, so as not to jumble up your library. When viewing a collection in Grid View or in the Filmstrip, you can easily rearrange images into any order by clicking and dragging them. You can view an image's original location by right-clicking on it and selecting *Go to Folder* under the Library tab.

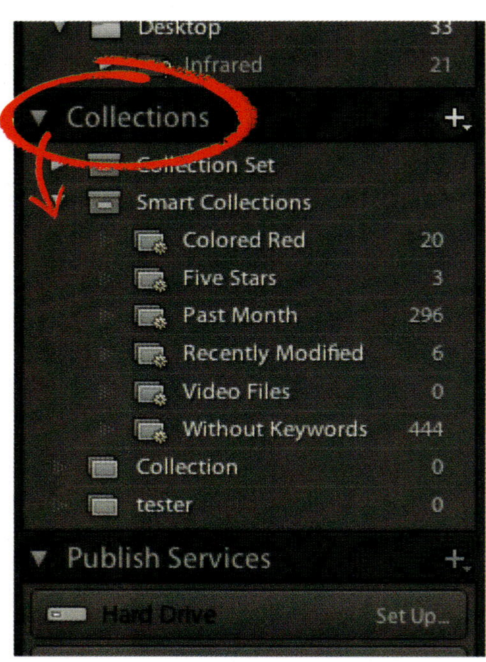

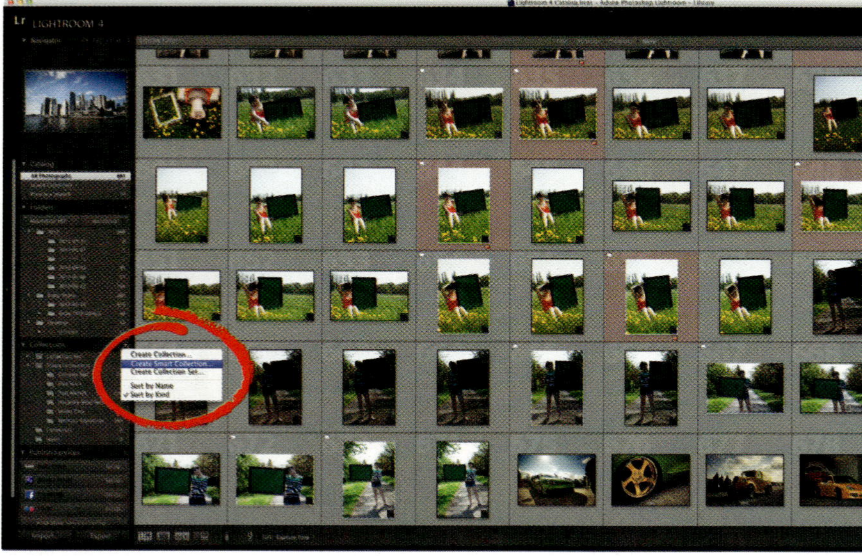

2 Smart Collections You can create a Smart Collection in the same way you would a regular collection, but click *Create Smart Collection* instead. Name your Smart Collection in the dialogue box and use the drop-down menus to set the criteria that the images must meet to be included in that collection (ie Rating is greater than or equal to three stars). You can choose multiple criteria for each collection, so an image is only added if all of the parameters are met. A Smart Collection will automatically pick out images that fit the preset parameters of that collection. Lightroom has some useful standard Smart Collections. Click the arrow to the left of the Smart Collections tab to see them all.

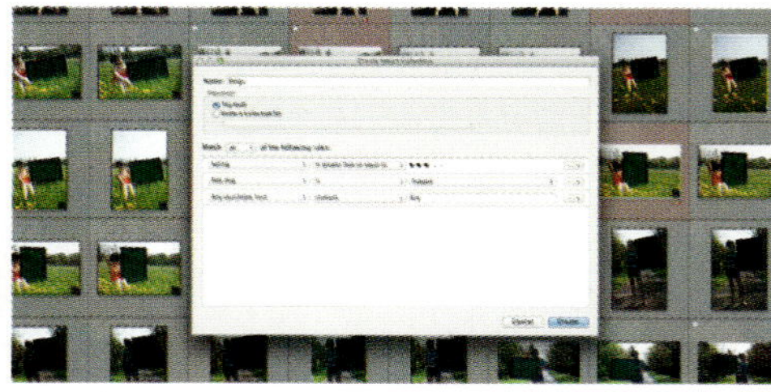

3 Quick Collection If you want to simply group pictures together – perhaps you're not sure what sort of collection you want yet – make sure that no Target Collection is set and simply click on the grey dot that appears in the top-right corner of the image. These images will be assigned to the Quick Collection (the default Target Collection) located under the Catalog tab. From within your Quick Collection, you can Keyword Tag, Rate or Export all of your images conveniently from one place. Your Quick Collection can either be cleared or saved by right-clicking on the Quick Collection tab on the left. Once you save a collection, it moves into the Collections Tab for future access.

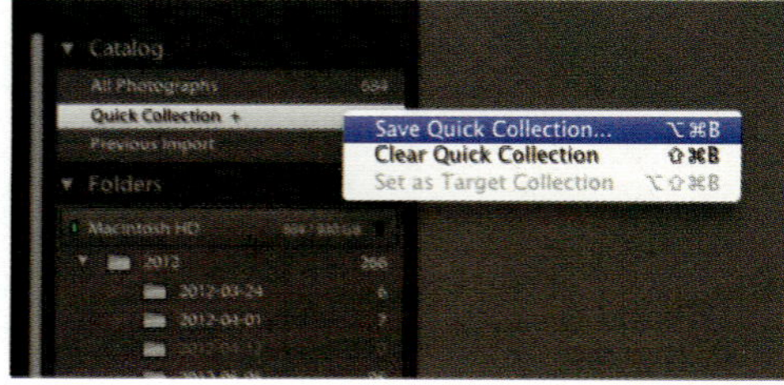

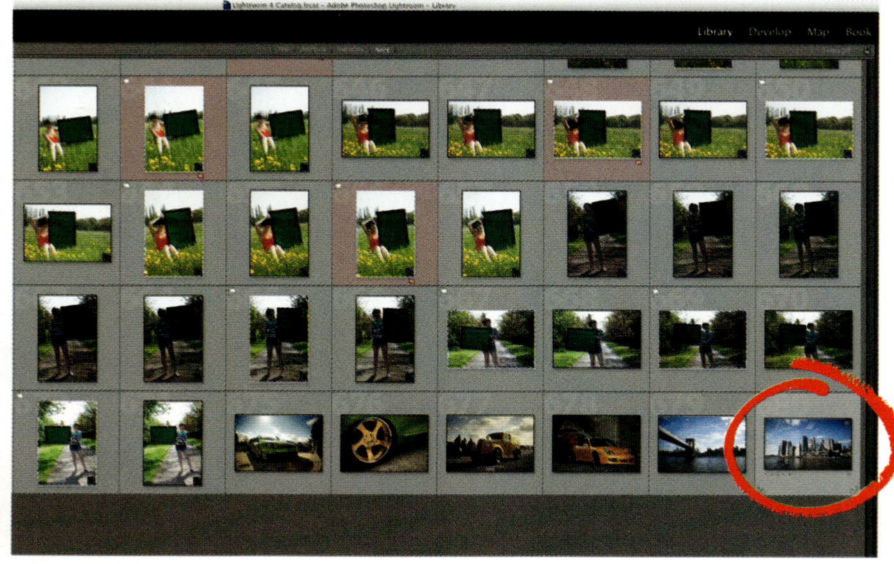

4 Quick Develop The Quick Develop tab, as the name suggests, allows you to quickly edit your images using a scaled-down version of Lightroom's Develop module. By using the Quick Develop tab, you can apply a saved or Lightroom preset to your image or a selection of images, alter the White Balance and apply a tint. The Tone Control tab has an Auto Tone feature that adjusts the Exposure, Clarity and Vibrance of your image based on the histogram – however, results can be hit and miss, so manual adjustment is recommended. For better control and more editing options, we suggest editing images in the Develop module, though it is convenient if you only need minimal editing and a fast export or to publish online.

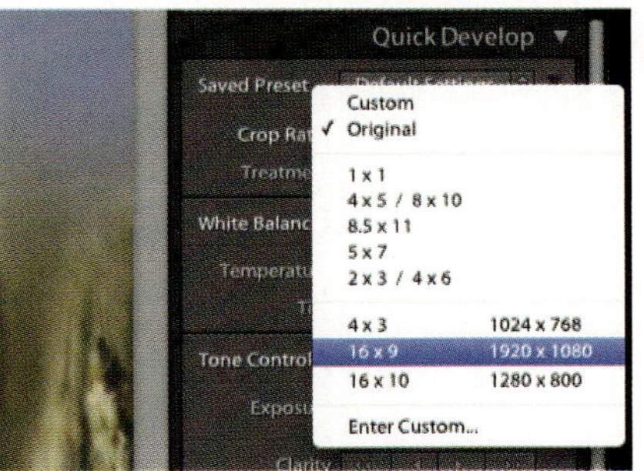

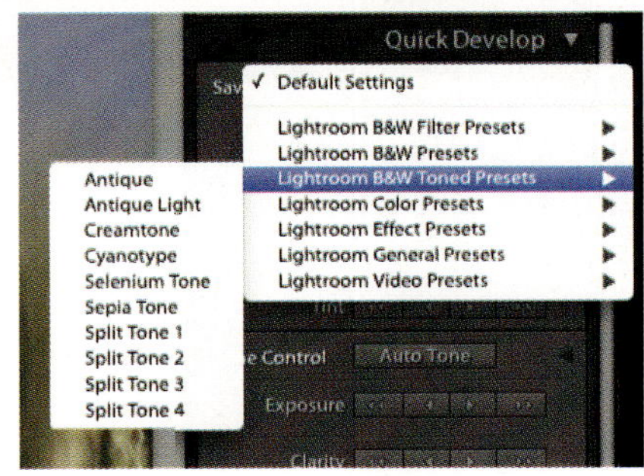

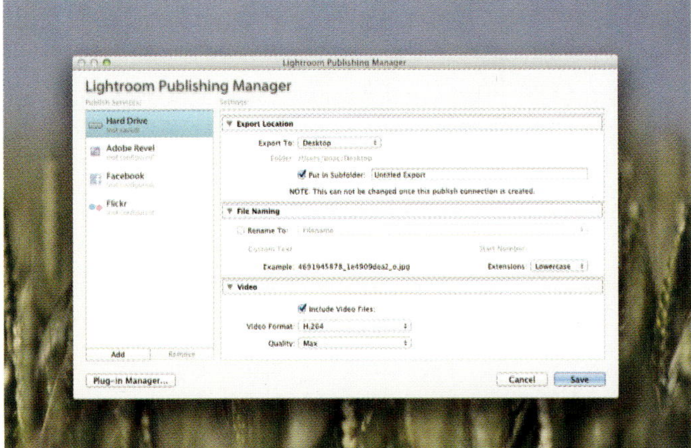

5 Publish Services Publish Services is an extremely useful tool if you want to export a batch of photos or get them online with minimal fuss. The Publish Services tab can be found in the bottom left of the Library module. Lightroom 6 comes with three Publish Services built in: Hard Drive, Facebook and Flickr. Each needs setting up before you can use it – to do this, click on ***Set Up*** next to the corresponding service and fill out the dialogue box as instructed. The Facebook and Flickr services require authorising via your account, but once this has been done, they're ready to use. Additional Publish Services are available to download from Adobe using the Find More Services Online button at the bottom.

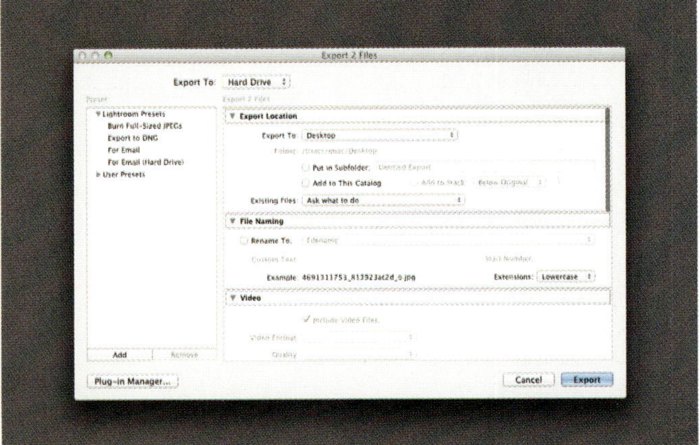

6 Export The Export button can be found to the bottom left of the Library module. Clicking it will export any selected images to your choice of email, Hard Drive, CD/DVD or the Adobe Revel mobile app. Lightroom has some useful presets for exporting images that allow you to tailor the file size and quality, depending on what you plan to do with the images. These export features are quick-fire solutions, but Lightroom 5 and 6 have a range of more detailed options for preparing images for export, such as to a book that is printed by Blurb, a slideshow, print or the web. If you think you want to try these features at a later date, it's worth noting these options are accessible via the main menu bar.

Make your editing more efficient with presets

Presets save you time and effort when processing pictures. Learn how to use Lightroom's and create your own

ALTHOUGH NOT ALWAYS the one-stop solution people hope for, presets are a key part of streamlining your Lightroom workflow. Some argue that the processing stage of creating their images is a carefully constructed process, unique to each image. In reality, if you shoot hundreds or thousands of images in a single shoot, then few people have the time to pore over each image individually. Think of presets like a recipe – they are designed to save you time above all else.

Even if you do enjoy taking time over each image and applying individual unique tweaks, if there is a core selection of adjustments that you frequently make, presets can speed up your workflow drastically and can give you a familiar base from which to start further processing.

A preset can include as few or as many adjustments as you like, from a simple White Balance adjustment right up to multiple Curves adjustments, gradients and noise reduction – all in a single click.

Multiple presets can be applied to a single image, too – but if two applied presets contain the same adjustment then the values from the preset which is applied last will always overwrite the former – so the same multiple presets applied in a different order will create different results. As well as creating your own presets you can also share them, and download presets created by other photographers, which you can tweak and add your own personal touches to.

CREATING A PRESET

1 Make the changes Open an image in the *Develop* module and make the precise changes that you want stored in your preset. Next click on the + icon in the upper-right corner of the *Presets* panel on the left to open the *New Develop Preset* dialogue box.

2 Name your preset Name your preset and select a folder for it to live in; either the existing *User Presets* folder or create a new folder. It's useful to have presets divided into folders based on their application and named appropriately to make them easy to find when you need them.

3 Choose the parameters The tick boxes below allow you to select exactly which settings you want to save into the preset. Once done, click *OK* and your preset will be saved to the Presets menu.

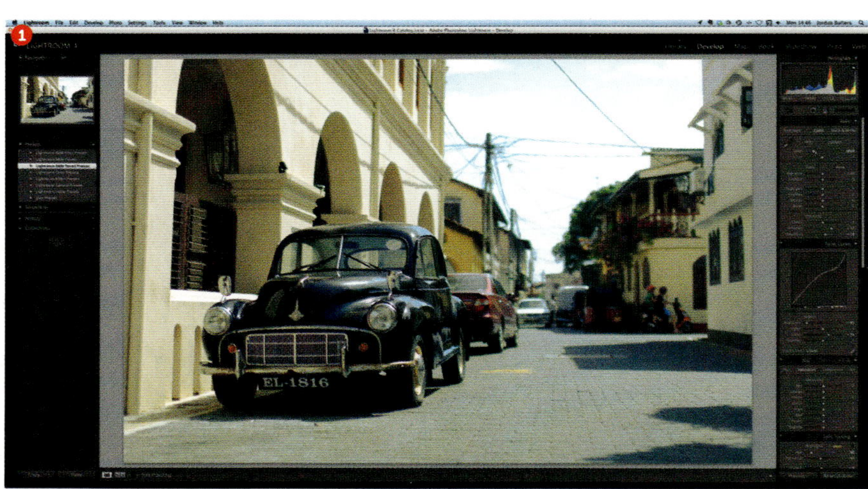

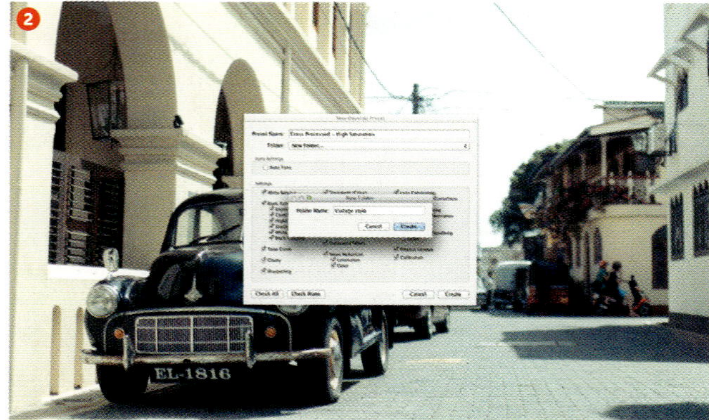

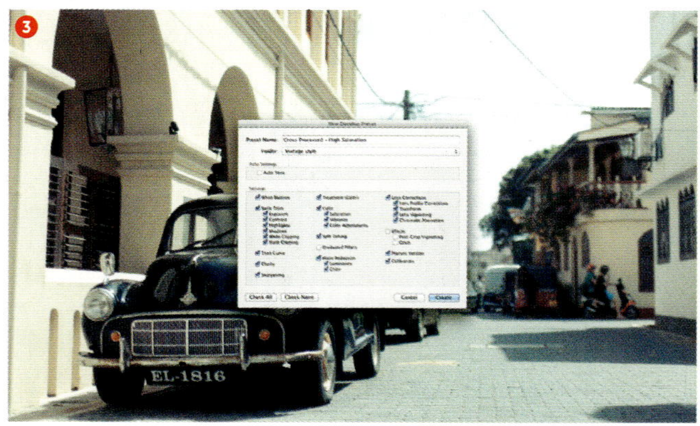

Preset resources

There are literally hundreds of websites out there from which you can download new Lightroom presets; some charge a fee, whereas others are free. Here are some of our favourite resources... Try some out to find out which ones you prefer to work with.

Visual Supply Co

Pricey, but setting the standard for film emulation. VSCO offers three preset packs, 01 contains modern films, 02 contains classic films and 03 contains instant films. Each pack costs $120, but they are really quite good. www.vsco.co

Pretty Presets

Specialising in presets best used for lifestyle photography, Pretty Presets offers a wide range of presets and its website provides plenty of sample images so you can assess what you're buying. Preset packs start at $27. www.lightroompresets.com

Presets Heaven

Presets Heaven adds a new preset each day for you to download. The best thing? They are all completely free! Admittedly, they aren't all great, but there are some gems to be had if you're willing to search. www.presetsheaven.com

Adobe

Adobe offers its pick of its favourite Lightroom presets, as submitted by Lightroom users. Some come with a fee but the majority are free of charge to use. There are hundreds to choose from, too! A great resource. www.adobe.com

USING A PRESET

1 Individual images In the *Develop* module click on the relevant preset in the *Presets* menu and the changes stored within will be applied to your image. To undo, go to *Edit>Undo Preset* or you can click on the *Reset* button in the bottom-right corner.

2 Multiple Images To apply a preset to multiple images, select the images in the *Library* module by holding down *ctrl* (PC) or *cmd* (Mac) and click on each image. Then in the *Quick Develop* menu, use the *Saved Preset* menu to apply the preset to all images.

3 Upon import A useful trick – in the *Import* window use the *Develop Settings* menu on the right-hand side to select the preset that you want to apply upon import. Be aware that this will be applied to all of the images imported at that time.

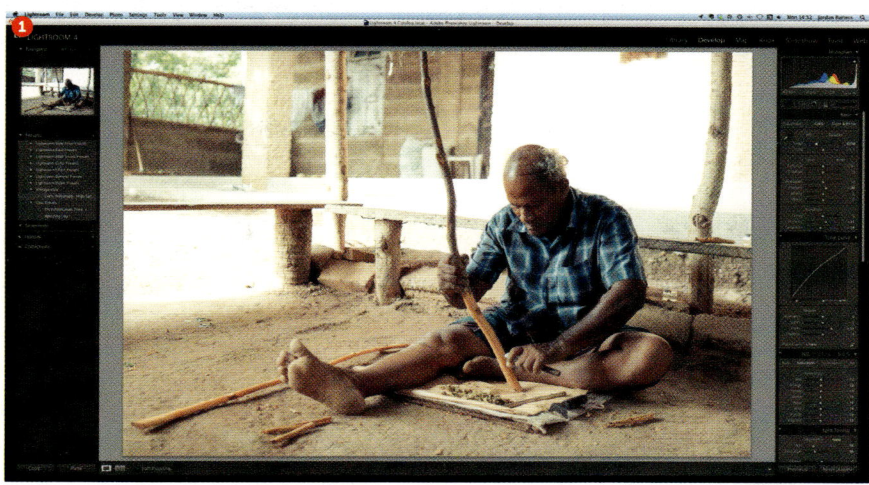

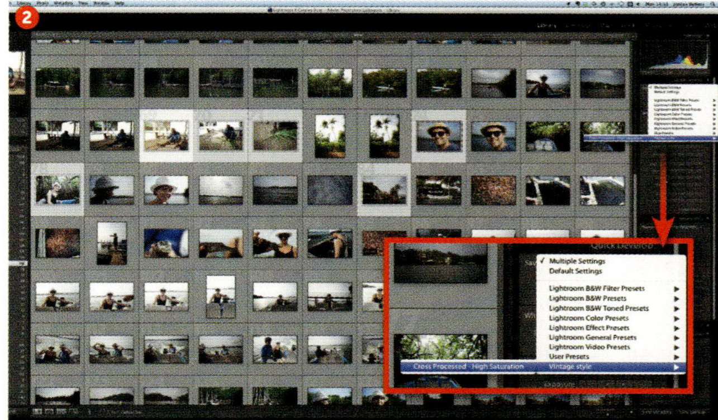

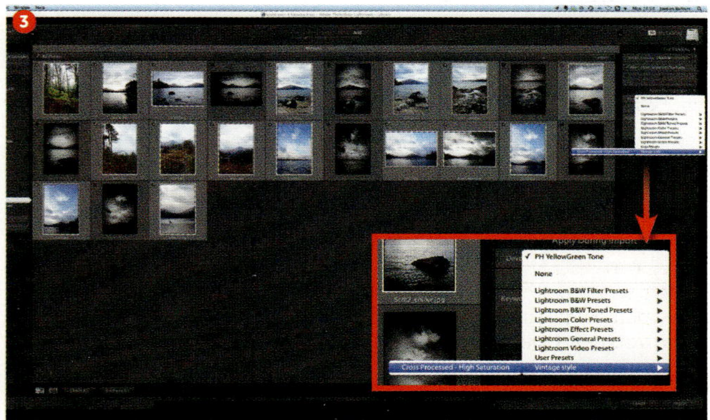

INSTALLING A PRESET

1 Download and unzip With your preset downloaded from the internet, unzip the file into a location that you can easily find again and open Lightroom.

2 Expand the menu In the *Develop* module, open up one of your images and right-click on the *User Presets* folder in the *Presets* menu and select *Import*.

3 Import the preset Locate your file and click the *Import* button – the preset will be imported and applied, ready to use from then on.

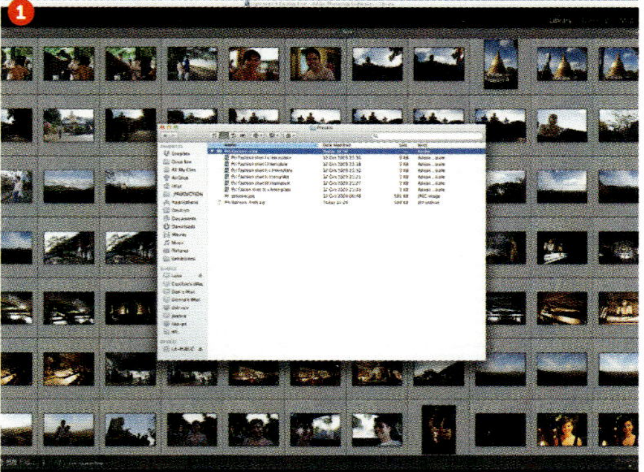

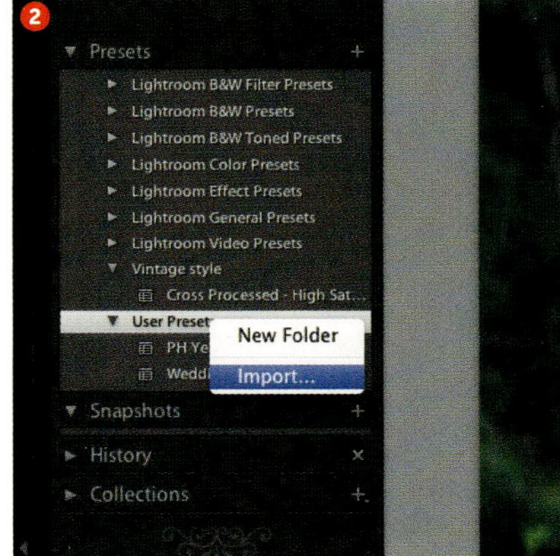

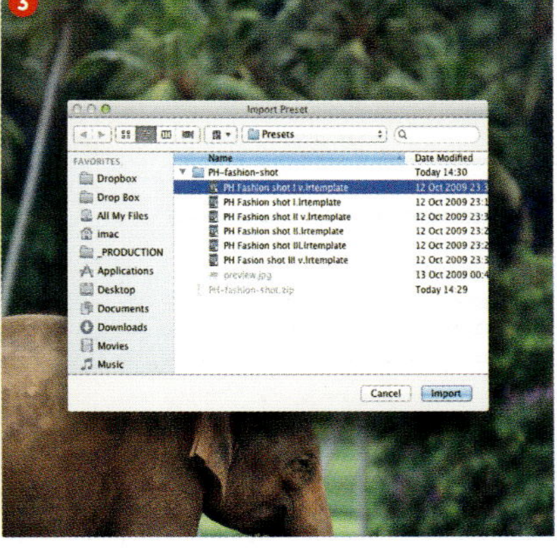

Compatibility

It's worth being aware that although presets created in earlier versions of Lightroom will still work in the latest version, when applied the Develop controls may revert back to that of a previous version, leaving you less advanced editing options. The best way to remedy this is to apply the preset, convert it to the latest process by clicking on the ***exclamation mark*** icon in the bottom-right corner of the image, which may alter the appearance of the image, and then tweak it back to how it was using the newer process. Then simply update the preset by right-clicking on it in the ***Presets*** menu and selecting ***Update with Current Settings***.

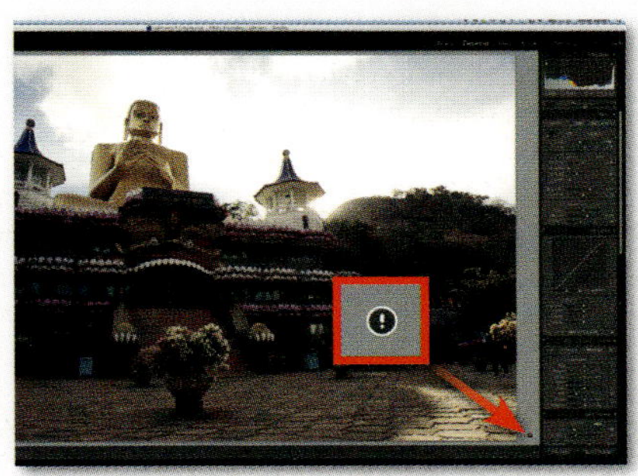

Take control over colour

No one wants dull and washed-out images, but over-saturation can be just as bad. We show you how to take careful control of your colour

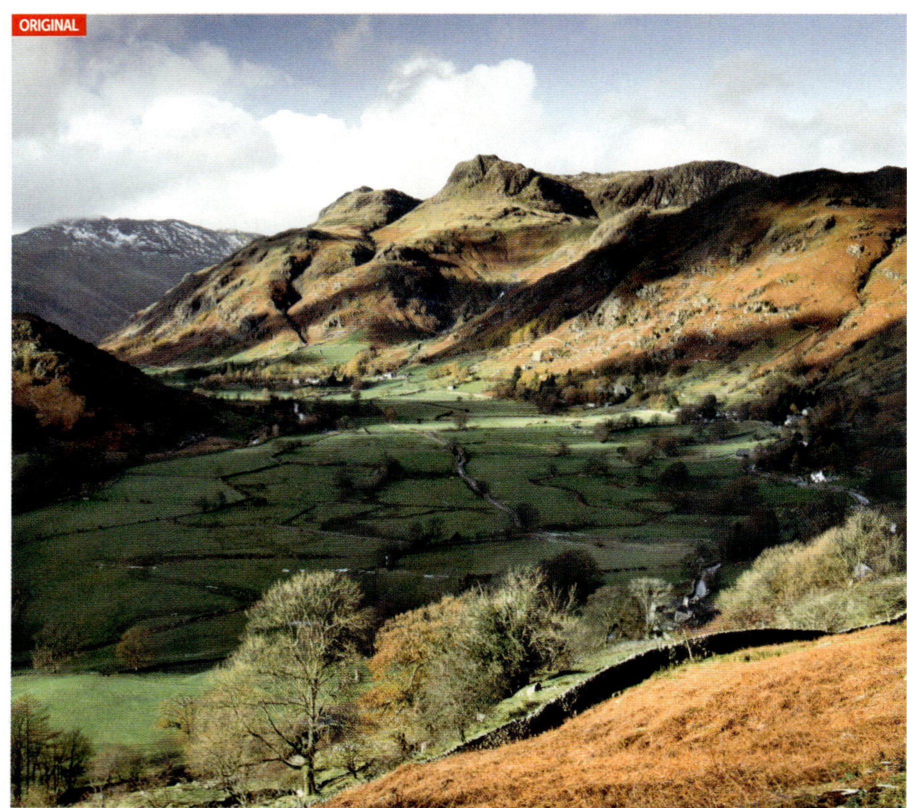

AUTUMN, ESPECIALLY, IS a beautiful time of year for capturing colourful landscapes. Deep blue skies, rustic reds, lush green grass and golden oranges. When shooting to capture colour like this, it's only right to assume that we want to do these fantastic colours justice with realistic reproduction. Failure to replicate the hues we see in real life isn't always down to the photographer – digital cameras are still nowhere near as advanced as the human eye. But there are steps that you can take to ensure good colour reproduction in-camera, such as ensuring that you have the correct White Balance set and shooting under the best lighting conditions. Most of us want to capture maximum detail in our images, which is why we advise you expose your images to the right (meaning you should overexpose your image slightly, but not to the extent where the highlights are clipped). Doing this, though, does sacrifice colour saturation – the brighter the original colour, the worse the image will appear bleached. Thankfully, this can be addressed with Lightroom, as there are a number of controls that allow you to adjust the colours both universally and selectively, based on each individual hue. On the surface, many of the controls, such as Luminance and Saturation, seem to have similar effects but there are subtle differences. For the best results, start to learn what each of the sliders do – starting with the areas covered here...

Know the difference

VIBRANCE AND SATURATION

There's often confusion surrounding Vibrance and Saturation sliders in Lightroom. At first glance they can appear to do much the same thing, but there are clear differences in the results you get from each. The main difference is that the Vibrance slider is designed not to affect colours that are already highly saturated. In most cases, this makes it useful for applying a universal adjustment without over-saturating those colours which are already nice and bright. Furthermore, the Vibrance slider will also not affect hues similar to those found in skin tones. This makes it useful for increasing saturation in portrait shots without turning your subject's skin a strange shade of orange. Take a look at the comparison below to see the difference an adjustment of +75 on each slider makes to the original image.

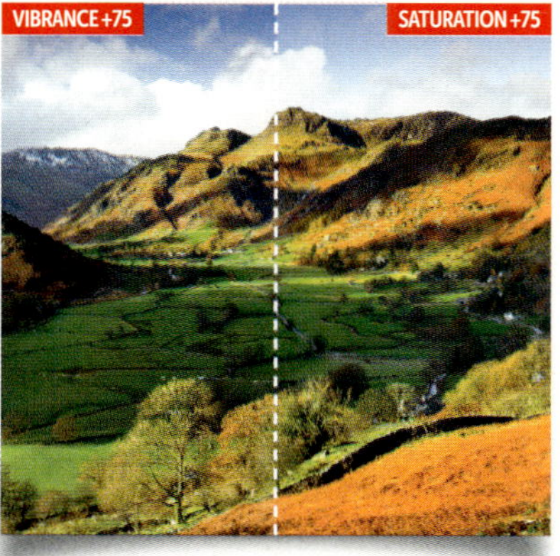

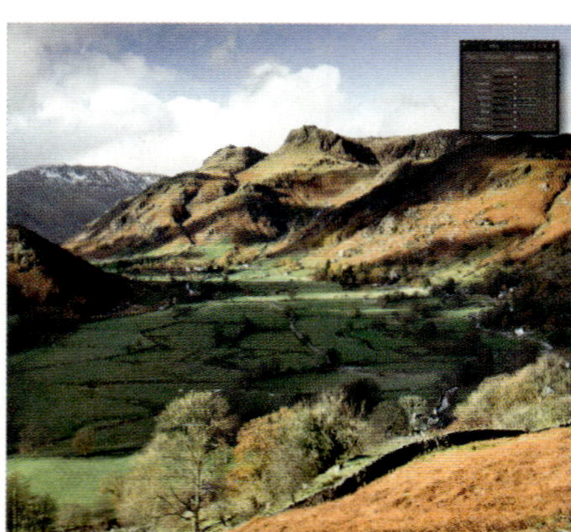

1 Open the image Our image is exposed to the right nicely without any clipped highlights, but the colours have been washed out slightly as a result. Select the *Develop* module and open the *HSL/Color/B&W* tab. Choose the *Luminance* tab to target the image's brightness.

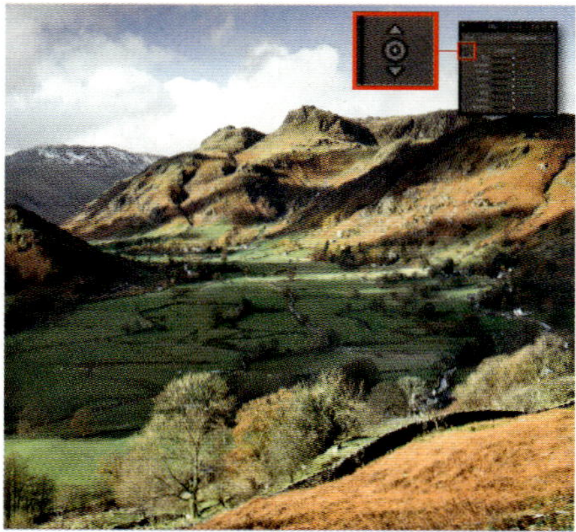

2 Select the Targeted Adjustment Tool One way to make selective adjustments is using the Targeted Adjustment Tool, located to the left of the panel. You can use this tool to make adjustments to a colour range by directly clicking and dragging on the target area.

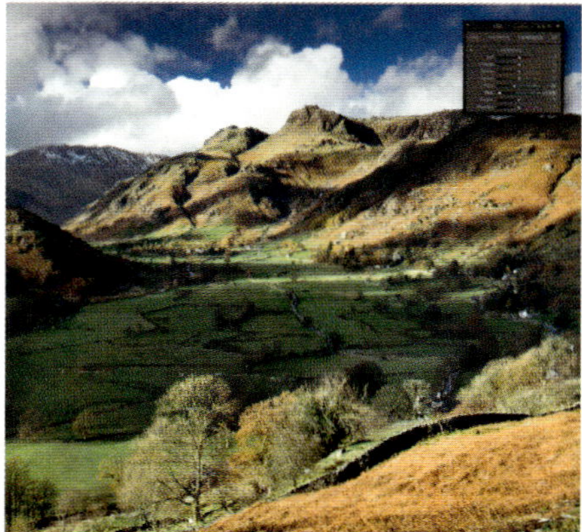

3 Make targeted adjustments Click and hold anywhere on the blue of the sky and drag upwards or downwards to adjust its luminance. Click on the *Saturation* tab, select the *Targeted Adjustment Tool* again and increase the colour intensity of the sky slightly in the same way.

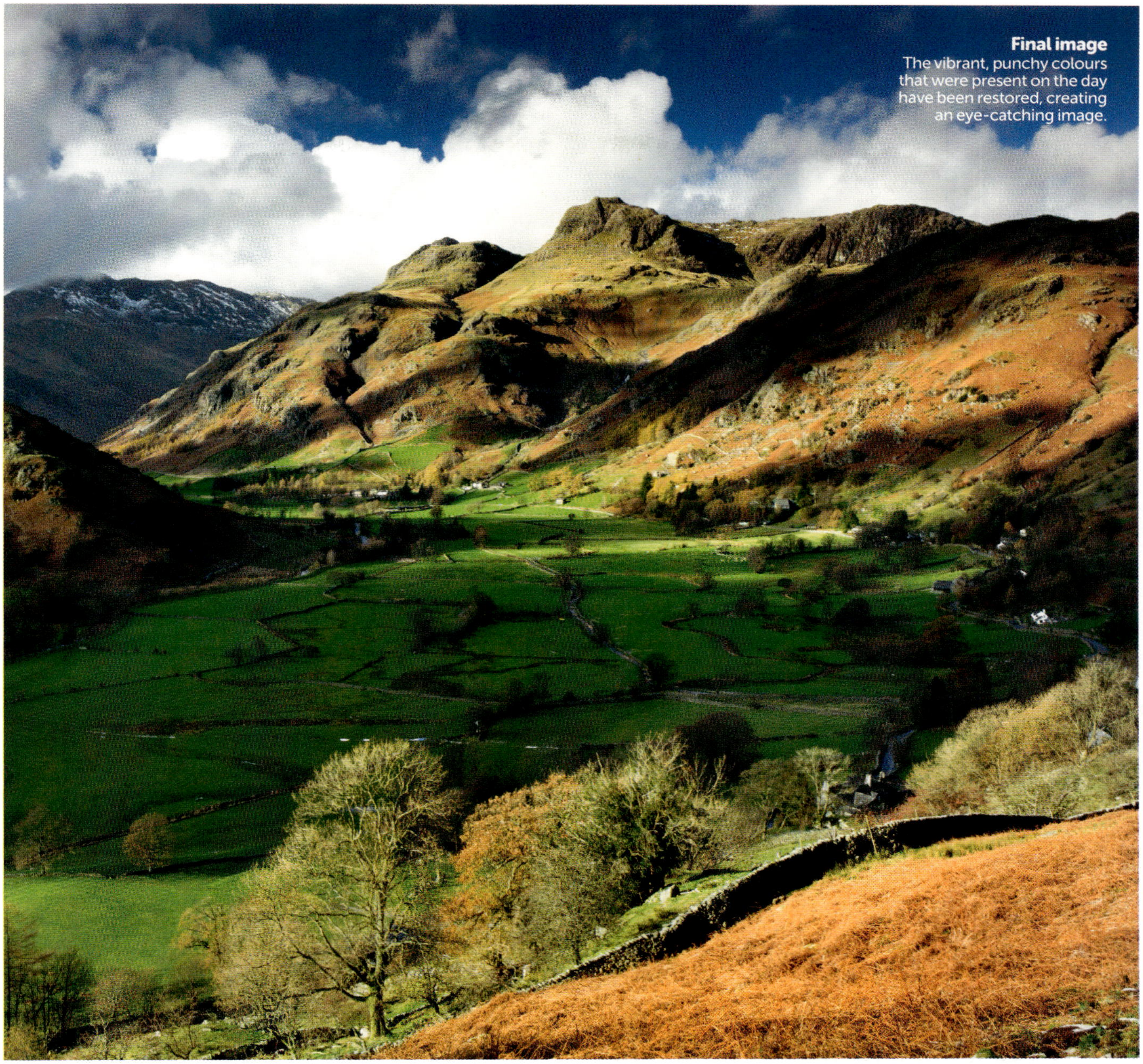

Final image
The vibrant, punchy colours that were present on the day have been restored, creating an eye-catching image.

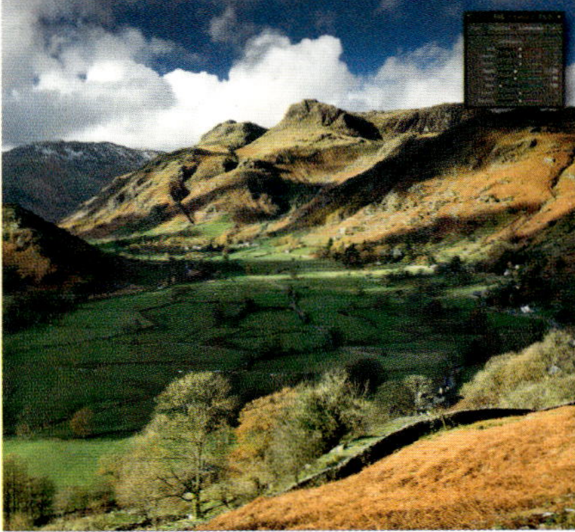

4 Decrease luminance manually As an alternative to the Targeted Adjustment Tool, you can adjust the hues manually using the sliders. Click on the *Luminance* tab again and click and drag on the *Green* slider to increase the brightness of that channel only.

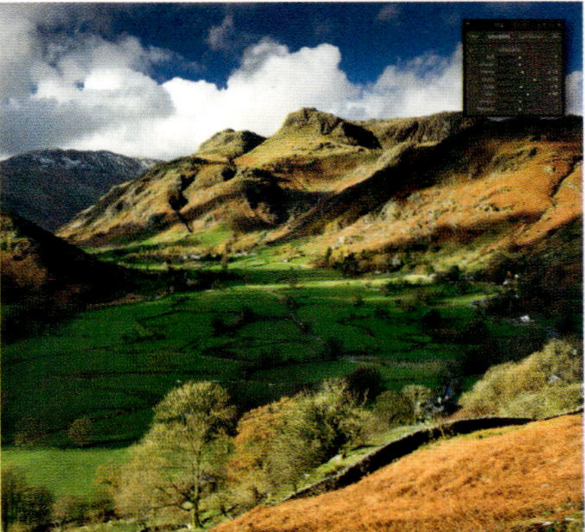

5 Increase saturation manually Click on the *Saturation* tab again and drag the *Green* slider to adjust the channel, being careful not to go too far. The neighbouring channels may need some adjustment, too. This image also benefited from a small increase of the Yellow channel.

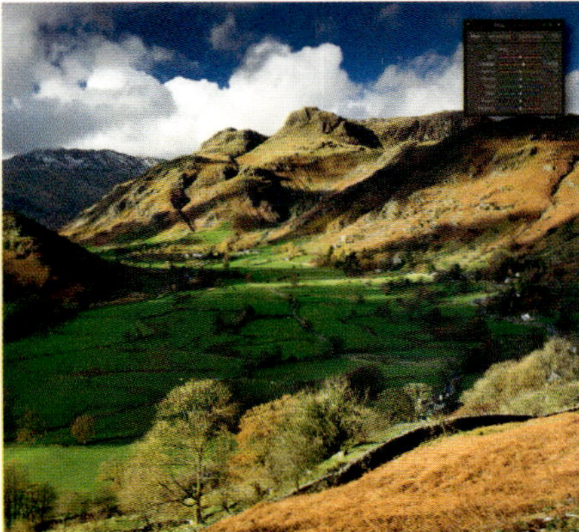

6 Adjust the Hue To change the colour of an area – like these orange hills – select the *Hue* tab. Next move the *Orange* slider until you are happy with the result. You may find only small changes are needed to alter the hue – but be watchful that it doesn't look unnatural.

Colour with Curves

Want complete control over your images without the hassle of multiple tools? Master exposure, contrast and colour using the Tone Curve

THE TONE CURVE is probably one of the more powerful tools within Lightroom. Not only can it be used to adjust the exposure of specific areas of your image individually, but it can increase or decrease contrast, as well as fine-tune the colours and tones present in your shots.

The version of Lightroom that you're using will dictate exactly how far you can go using the Tone Curve. Users of Lightroom 3 are restricted to only being able to adjust the RGB channel as a whole, enabling them to tweak exposure and contrast but not colour. Users of Lightroom 4 onwards have the full capacity to adjust the individual Red, Green and Blue channels, as well as all three together.

Understanding the Tone Curve takes time, but any changes are instantly visible and can be reset without damaging the image in any way. Before starting, make any adjustments to exposure, White Balance and lens corrections. From there, we'll show you the basics of using Tone Curves, but the key is to experiment. With a bit of time and understanding you'll wonder how you ever managed without this tool.

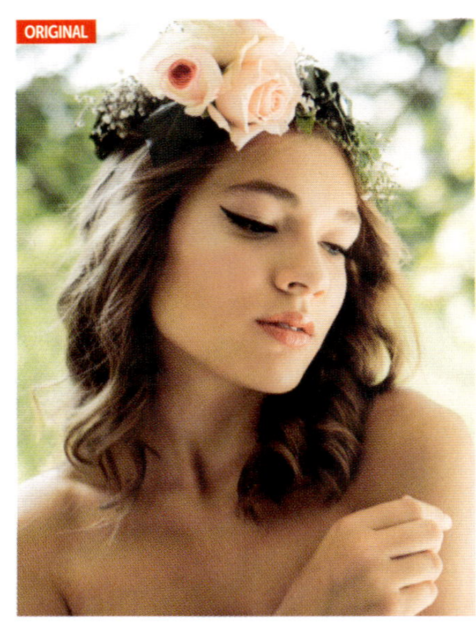

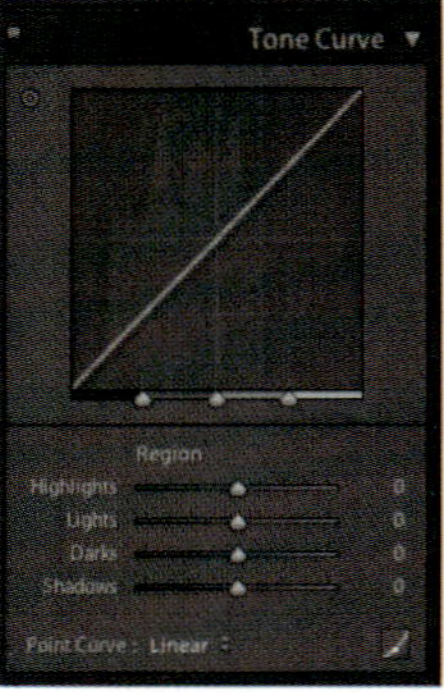

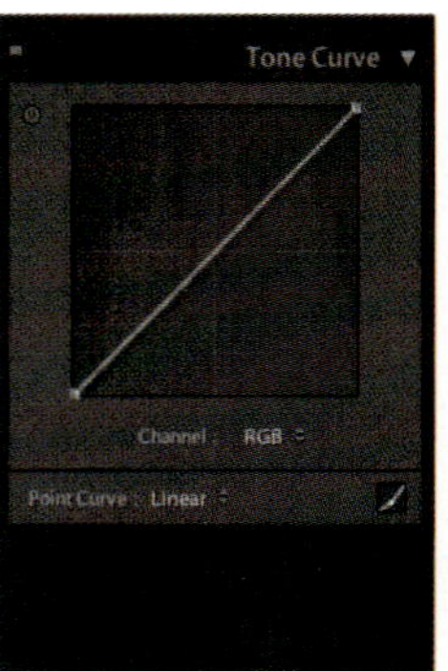

1 ENABLE THE POINT CURVE By default the Tone Curve palette will look as it does above on the left. Click on the *Point Curve* button in the bottom right corner. You'll notice that you now have a choice of channels to edit (above, right). The diagonal line represents the tones within your image, from shadows in the bottom left corner to highlights in the top right.

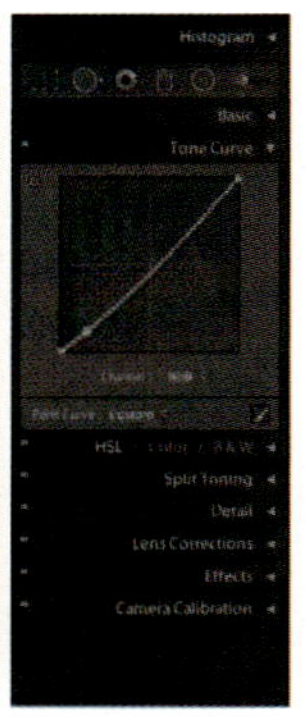

2 ADD A CONTROL POINT With *Channels* set to *RGB*, we'll start by editing the overall exposure and contrast of your image. Click anywhere on the line to add a Control Point. Hold and drag on this Control Point to increase or decrease the exposure of that tone. Here, we've added our Control Point in the shadow area and dragged it down to darken the shadows.

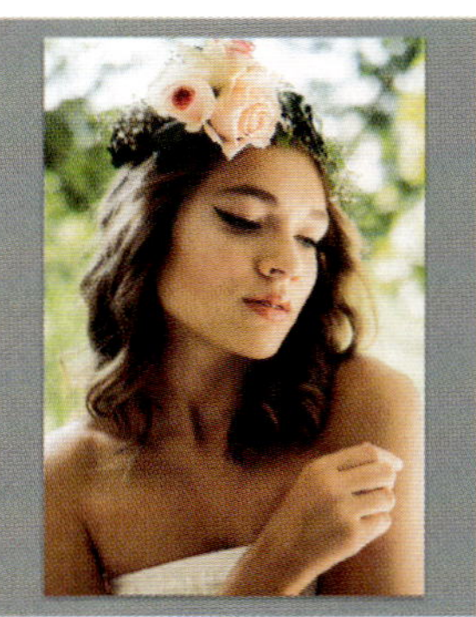

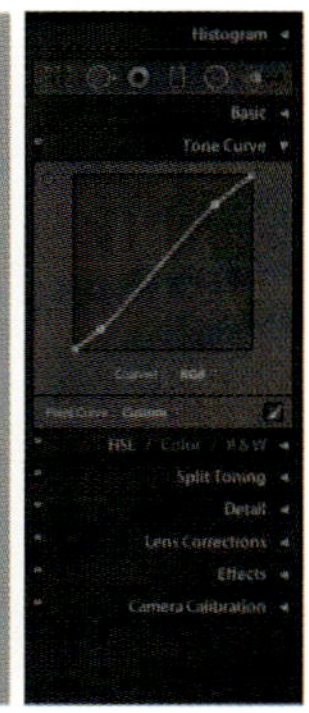

3 ADD CONTRAST As well as up and down, you can drag the Control Point left and right along the line to change the tone that it affects. Click to add a second Control Point to the highlights to adjust that part of your image. Drag this second Control Point to increase the exposure of the highlights. By darkening shadows and brightening highlights, we are increasing contrast.

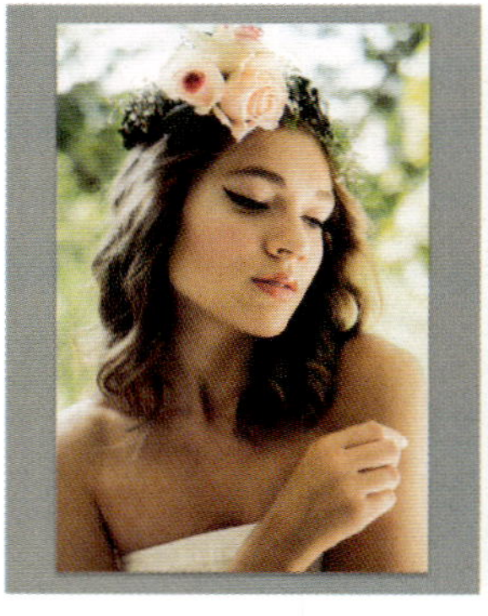

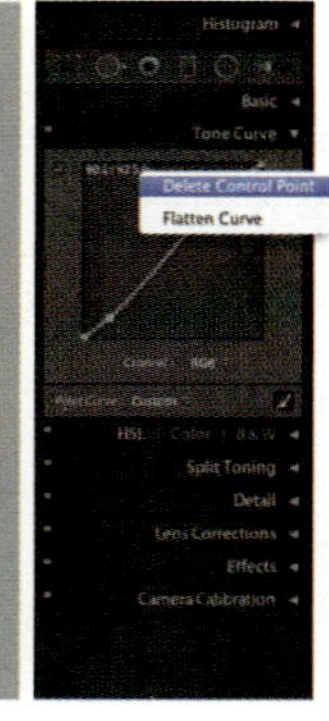

4 REMOVING POINTS This is what's known as an 'S' curve – the sharper and more exaggerated the 'S', the higher the contrast. You can add more points to your curve to further tweak areas, or you can easily delete points by right-clicking on them and selecting *Delete Control Point*. Alternatively, the curve can be reset by right-clicking on the graph and selecting *Flatten Curve*.

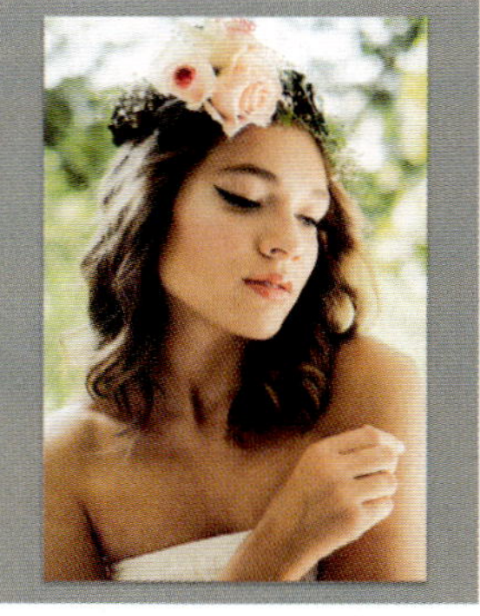

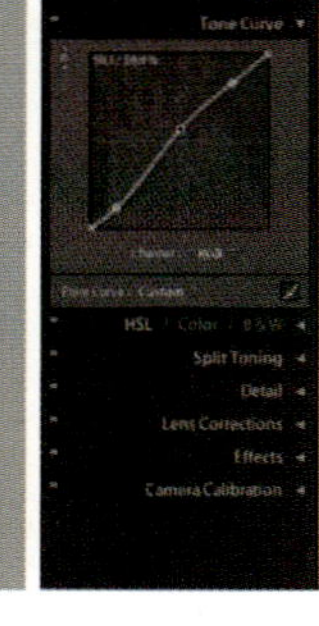

5 ADJUST SELECTIVELY You can also adjust the Tone Curve by clicking and dragging on the area of your image that you want to adjust. First click on the *Targeted Adjustment Tool* icon in the top left of the Tone Curve palette. Then, click on the area of your image that you wish to adjust and drag up or down. The Tone Curve will adjust in situ. Here, we've increased the mid-tones in the skin slightly.

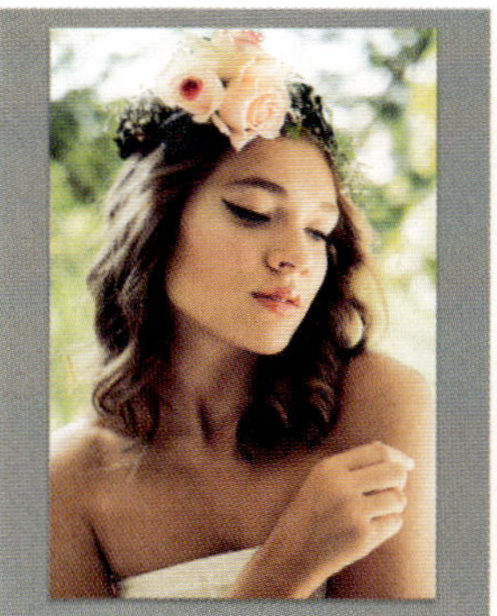

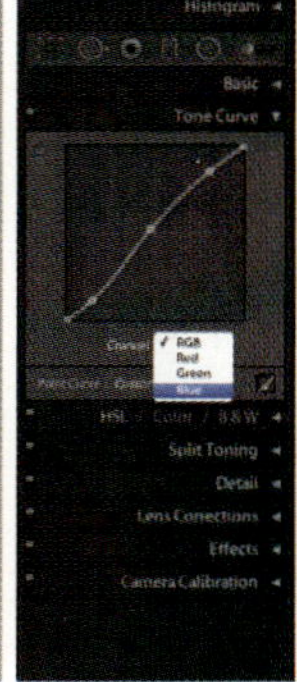

6 EDIT COLOUR CHANNELS Click on *Channels* to adjust the individual colour channels. We want to add some blue to our shadows here, so select the *Blue* channel, add a Control Point to the shadows and drag it up slightly. We also want to add warmth to the skin tones, so we've used the *Targeted Adjustment Tool* to click and drag upwards on a mid-tone area of our subject's skin.

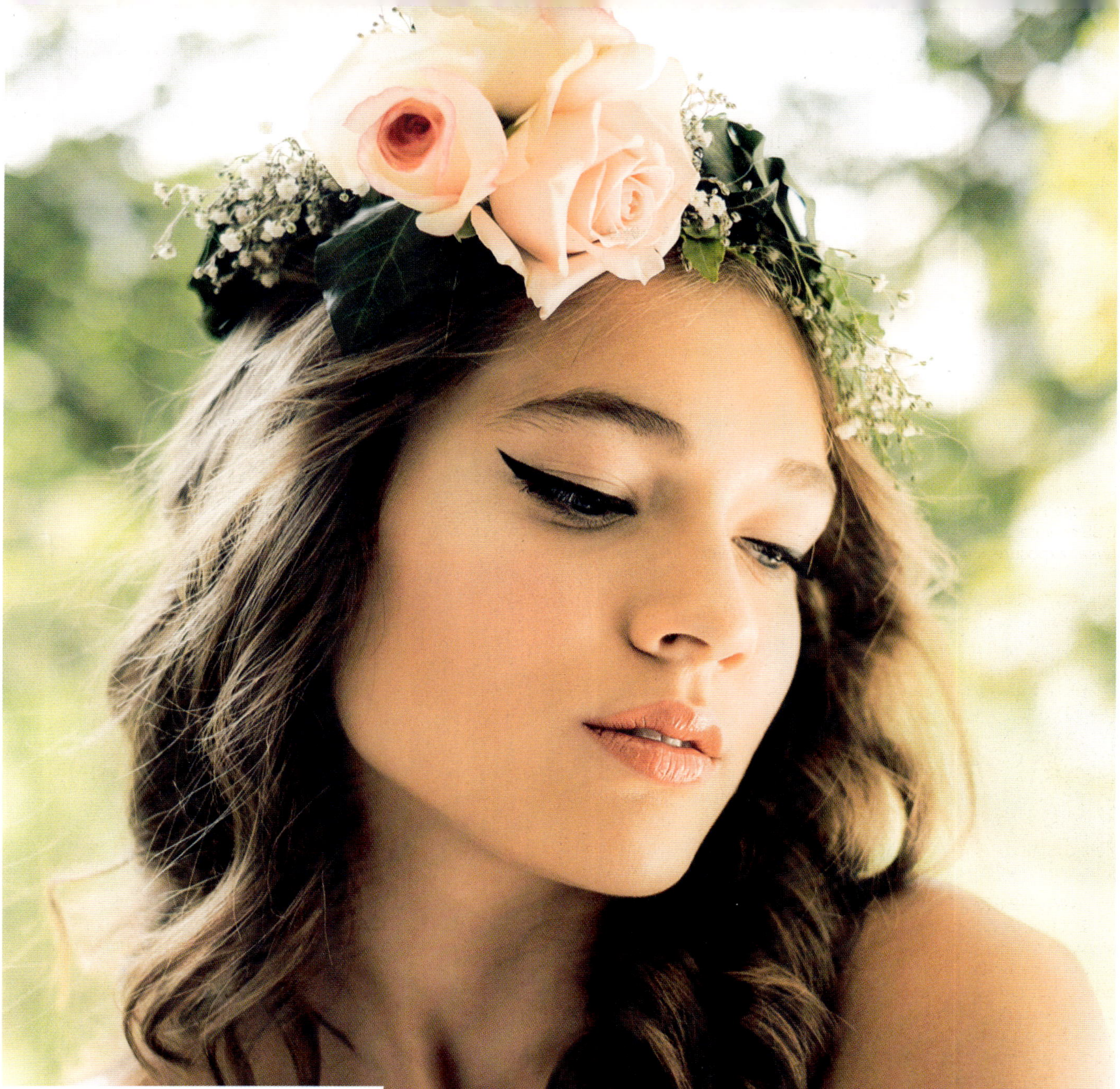

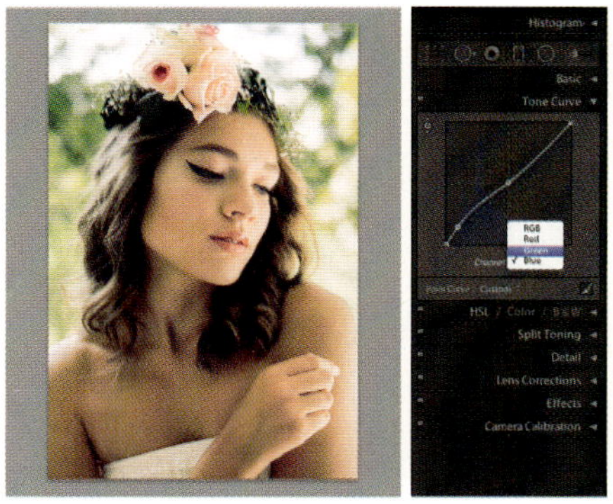

7 FINE-TUNE THE COLOUR Next, we want to boost the greens. Select *Green* from the *Channels* menu and lift the curve between the shadows and midtones. This also lifts the curve in the mid-tone and highlights slightly, tinting our subject's skin. To counteract this, use the *Targeted Adjustment Tool* again to drag down on a skin mid-tone. We've also removed green from the shadows.

The colour wheel explained

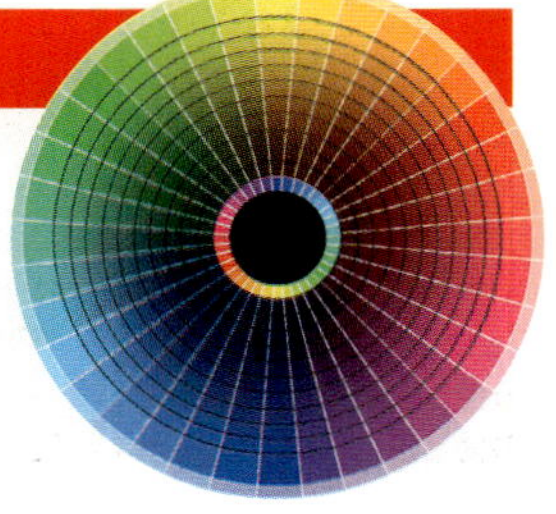

Tone Curves allows you to add or subtract colour across each of the individual RGB channels. Each colour has an opposing colour on the colour wheel. By increasing the curve on the Red channel, for example, you add red to the image. However by decreasing the curve on that same channel, you introduce cyan, as cyan is the opposite of red. Therefore the Green channel can be used to add green or magenta, and the Blue channel adds blue or yellow.

Maximise dynamic range in Lightroom

Expanding dynamic range does not have to mean retina-throbbing HDR effects. Here's how to use Adobe Lightroom for subtle adjustments

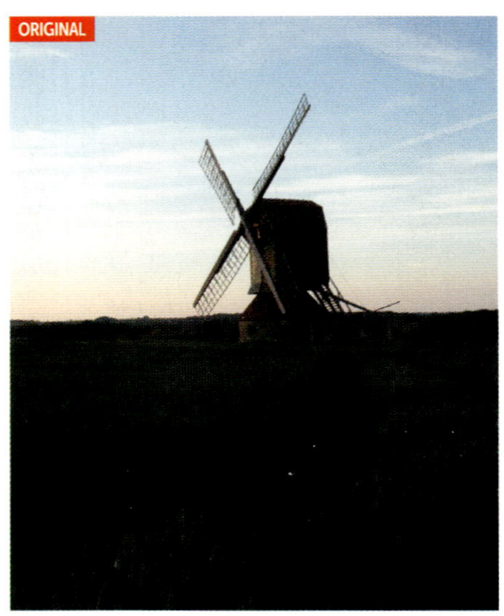

WHEN PRESENTED WITH a scene that exceeds your image sensor's dynamic range, the ideal solution is to use graduated filters to balance the exposure. A set of ND grad filters is invaluable to any outdoor photographer, whether you shoot landscapes, cars, weddings or portraits – at some point or another you'll find yourself reaching for your grads, or wishing you had them with you!

However there are times when using an ND grad isn't practical – scenes where objects stand above the horizon for example, or when you only have time for a quick snapshot and aren't able to fit your filters. Thankfully there are a couple of simple steps that you can take in Adobe Lightroom to expand the dynamic range of your landscape images subtly and naturally.

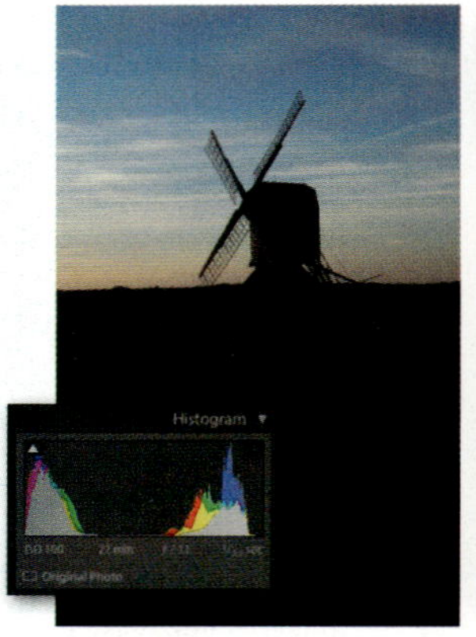
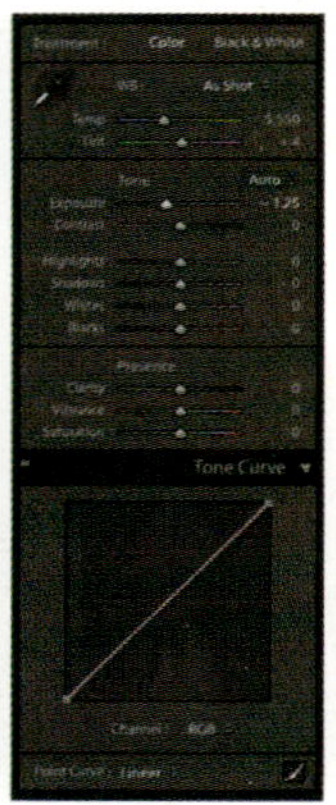

1 CHECK FOR CLIPPING Enter the Develop module and assess the histogram. If the graph is pushed off the end of the scale to the left or the right then there's no data to rescue, so it's not worth wasting your time. Another quick test is to drag the Exposure slider up or down temporarily – this reveals what detail is left in highlights and shadows.

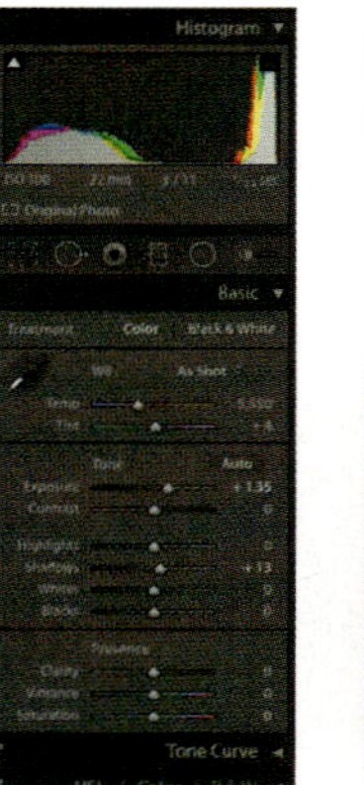
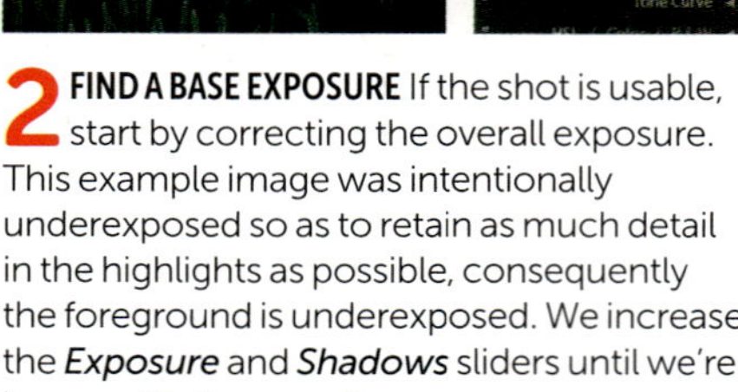

2 FIND A BASE EXPOSURE If the shot is usable, start by correcting the overall exposure. This example image was intentionally underexposed so as to retain as much detail in the highlights as possible, consequently the foreground is underexposed. We increase the ***Exposure*** and ***Shadows*** sliders until we're happy with the overall appearance.

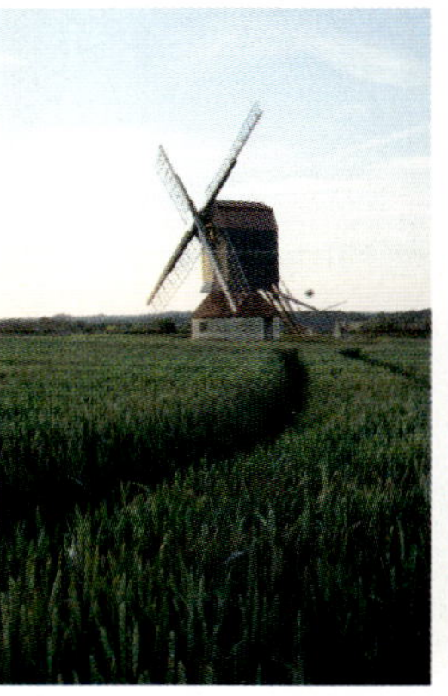
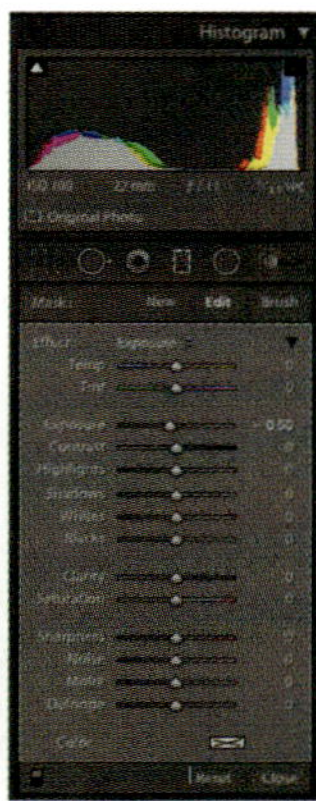

3 RESCUE THE SKY Now it's time to focus on the sky – select the ***Graduated Filter*** by pressing the ***M*** key and reduce the ***Exposure*** slider for the filter to ***-0.50*** at the top of the toolbar on the right. Click where you want the gradient to start, drag downward and release where you'd like it to end – usually around the horizon.

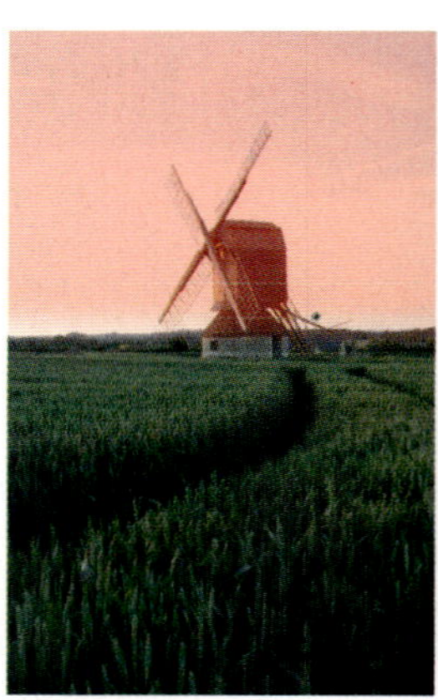
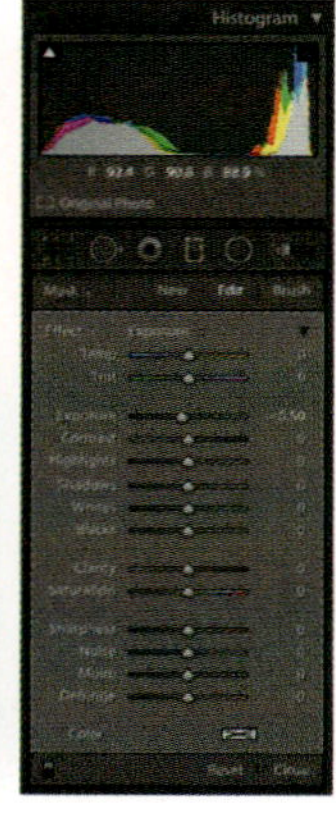

4 ADJUST THE FILTER Above the top line is affected by the adjustment, below the bottom line remains unaffected and the space between is the gradient; the wider the gap between the lines, the softer the gradient. If you're using LR6, you can erase parts of the gradient by going to ***Mask: Brush*** at the top and then selecting ***Erase*** below.

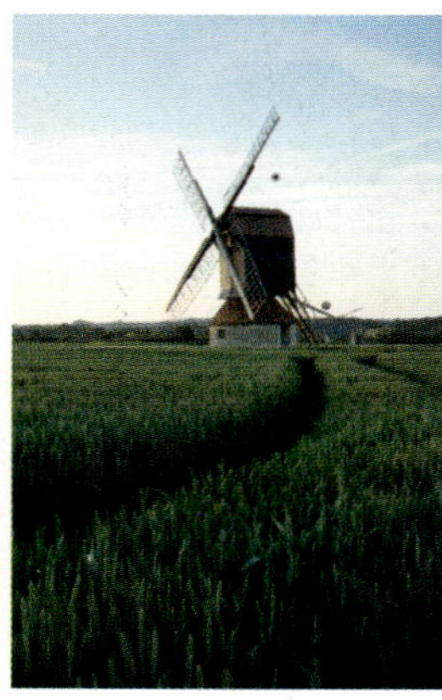

5 ADD A SECOND GRADIENT The idea is to balance the sky and foreground, and not 'over grad' the sky to make it look too dark, which is easily done. Sometimes a second graduated filter can help. If required, click and drag again – the second filter often looks best when applied at a low intensity and when the transition is gradual rather than sudden.

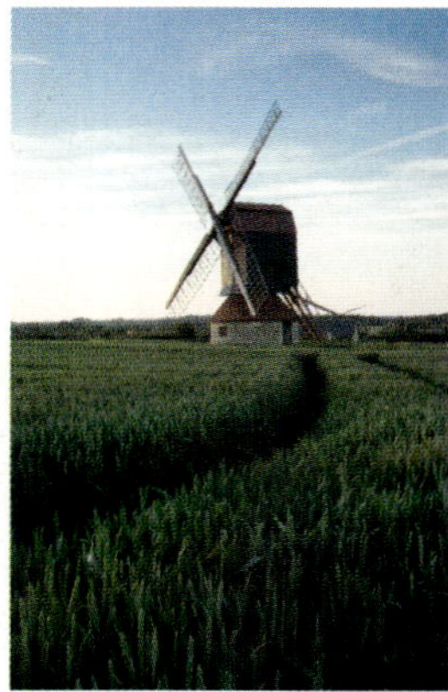
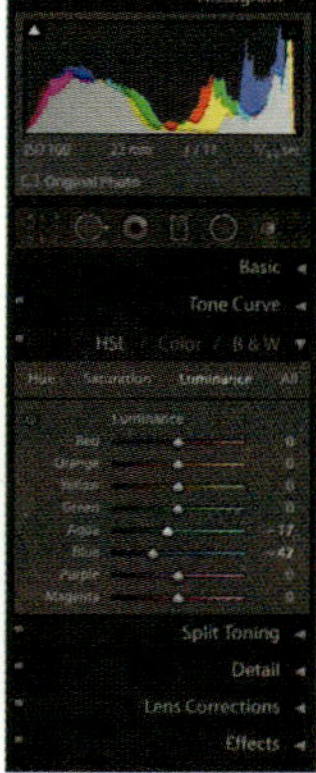

6 ADJUST COLOUR LUMINANCE If graduated filters don't do the job, try adjusting the colour luminance. Under the HSL tab and select ***Luminance***. Darken the ***Blue*** channel to rescue blue skies. Sometimes, slight adjustment to the ***Aqua*** channel is required, too. Just watch for haloing and artefacts where objects stand above the horizon.

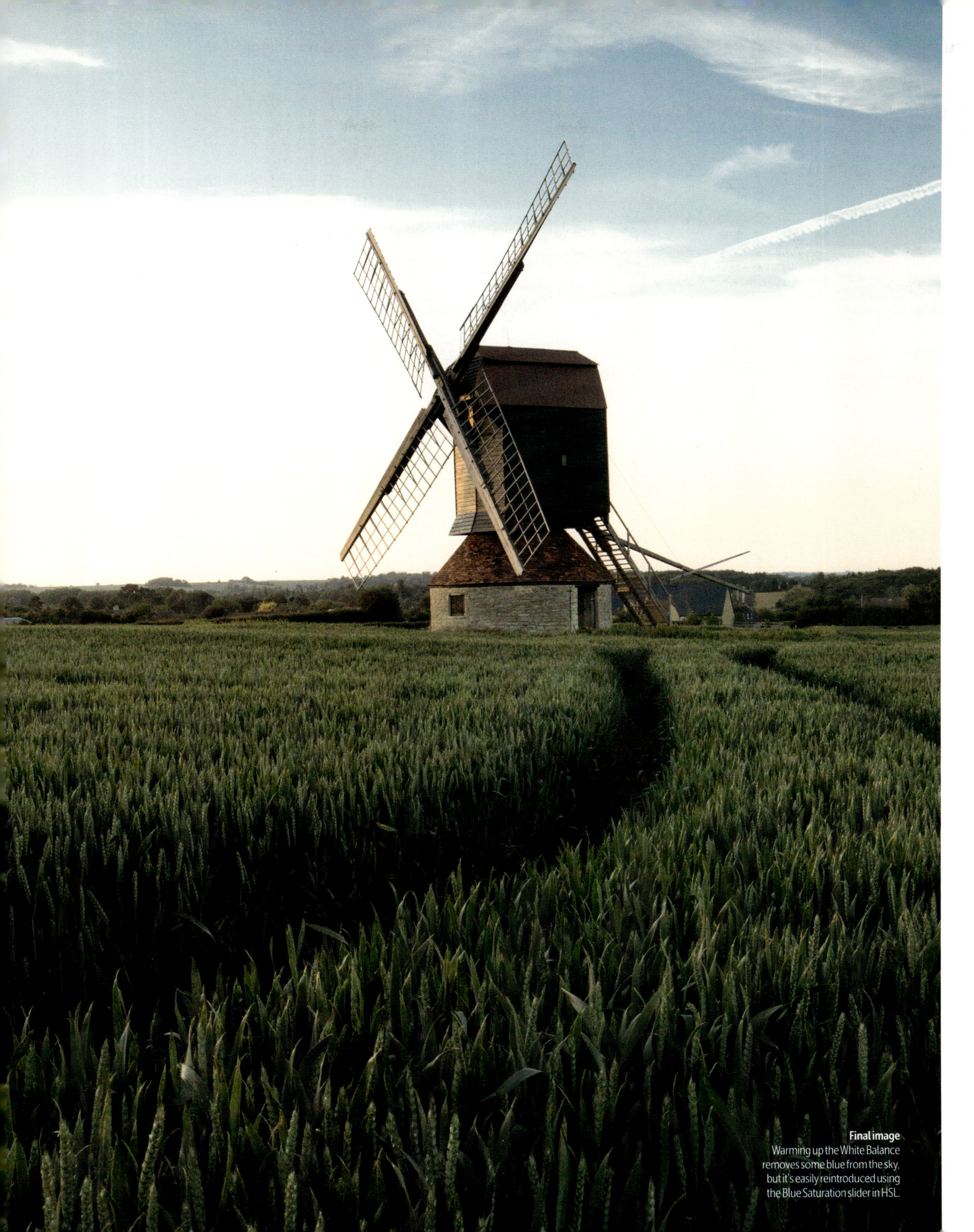

Final image
Warming up the White Balance removes some blue from the sky, but it's easily reintroduced using the Blue Saturation slider in HSL.

Monochrome film effect

Emulate your favourite black & white films by adjusting some essential settings in Adobe Lightroom

WHEN LOOKING AT an image, it's reasonably easy to tell whether that image originated from a digital file or was shot on film. Purists would tell you that film has a certain 'feel' about it, but the reality of it is that there are certain specific characteristics that ring true to film – they mainly comprise of contrast, tonality and grain. Learn how to spot and manipulate these characteristics in your editing process and you can introduce a convincing film aesthetic into your digital files.

The steps below are not a definitive solution and can be easily tweaked to emulate different types of film. It's a good idea to find images shot on the specific film that you want to emulate, and use them side-by-side for reference. For the purposes of this guide we're looking to emulate Kodak T-MAX 3200 – a recognisable black & white film with medium contrast and a coarse grain.

Alternative look

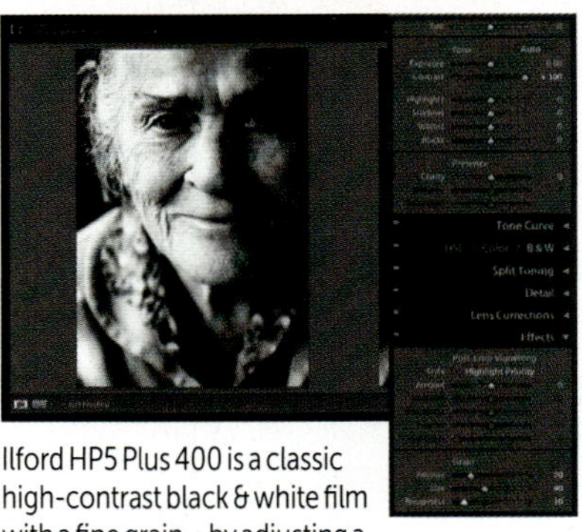

Ilford HP5 Plus 400 is a classic high-contrast black & white film with a fine grain – by adjusting a few of the settings here you can recreate it for yourself. Adjust the ***Contrast*** to ***+100***, reset the ***Tone Curve*** black point adjustment to ***0%*** and alter the grain to ***Amount: 20***, ***Size: 40***, ***Roughness: 0***.

Make your own presets

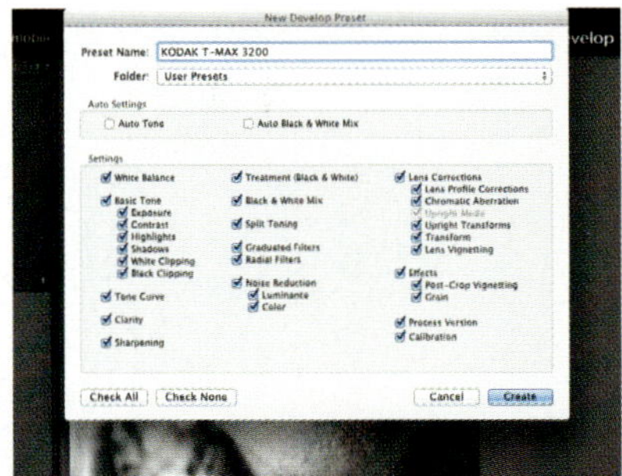

Having made your adjustments, save the settings for future use by clicking on the ***Create New Preset*** button in the ***Presets*** palette. Name the preset for easy reference then, the next time you want to use it, simply click on it from the Presets palette and all of the changes will be instantly applied.

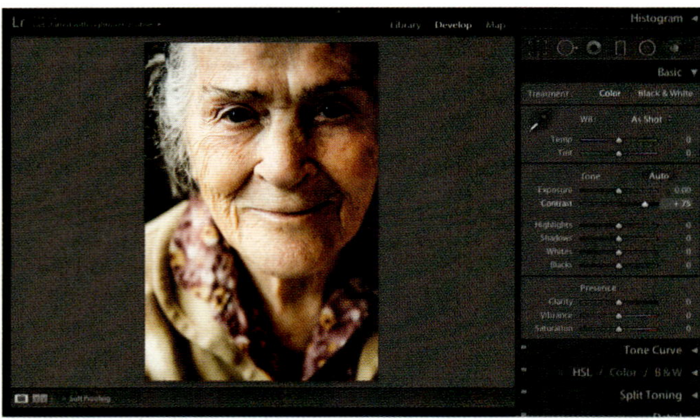

1 ADD CONTRAST: With your image selected in the *Develop* module, use the *Contrast* slider in the *Basic* tab on the right to increase the contrast in your image. The amount of adjustment that you use depends on how much contrast is in your original image, but this can always be tweaked before saving. I've used +75 as a starting point.

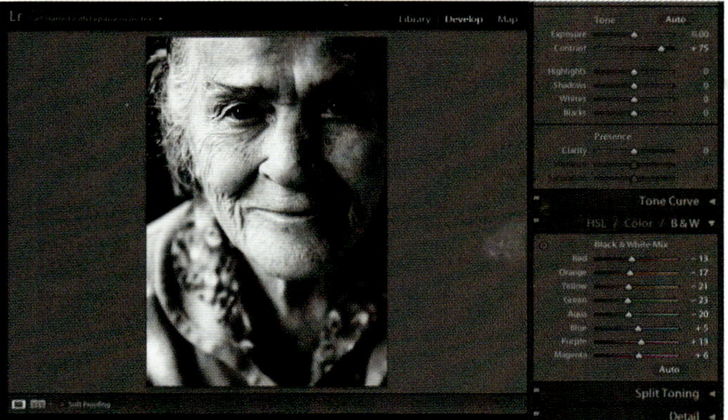

2 CONVERT TO BLACK & WHITE: Converting the image to monochrome is a single step, so go ahead and click on the *Black & White* button in the *Basic* palette. The effect can be tweaked by using the *Black & White Mix* sliders in the *HSL/Color/B&W* palette, just be mindful not to push any of the sliders too far, or you'll lose subtle graduations in tone.

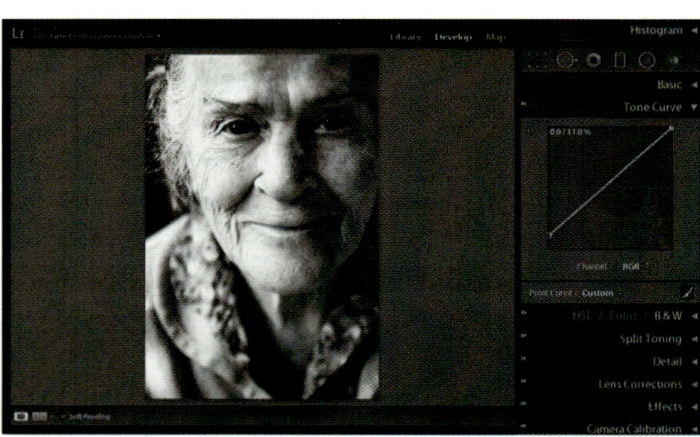

3 REMOVE SHADOW CONTRAST: In the lower-right corner of the *Tone Curve* palette, click on the *Point Curve* button. Then, on the line above, drag the point in the lower-left corner straight upward, as shown. The amount is indicated in the top-left corner; we've gone for 11% to reduce shadow contrast and give the image a matte look.

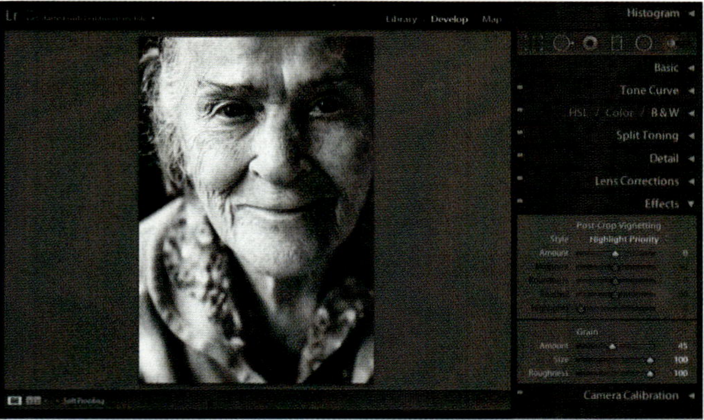

4 ADD GRAIN: Scroll down to the *Effects* palette and increase the amount of grain in the image. The amount used is your personal preference – we're looking to emulate the extreme Kodak T-MAX 3200 film here so have introduced a coarse grain by increasing the *Amount* to *45*, the *Size* to *82* and the *Roughness* all the way to *100*.

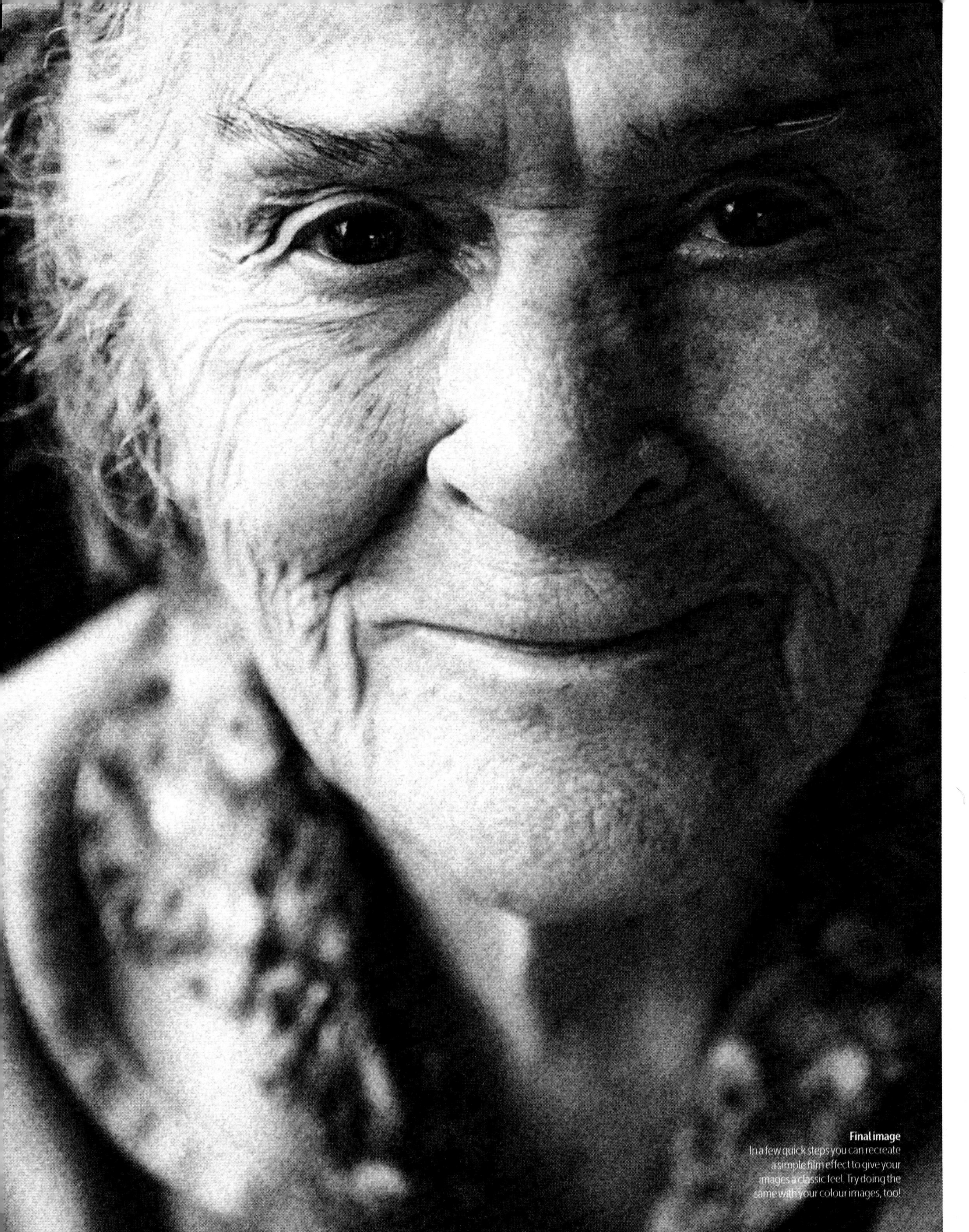

Final image
In a few quick steps you can recreate a simple film effect to give your images a classic feel. Try doing the same with your colour images, too!

How to boost contrast

Recorded a scene that looks a bit bland? Learn how using the histogram in Adobe Lightroom can help to improve its exposure and contrast

THERE'S NO SUCH thing as a 'perfect' exposure, hopefully we've established that by now. In truth, the only correct exposure is the one that the photographer intends to capture – you can over- or underexpose a scene to your heart's content and, no matter what the histogram, or anyone else for that matter, says, if that's the intended result then that's the correct exposure for that image.

The histogram is a key part of both assessing exposure in-camera, and when editing your images, so knowing how to read it is crucial (see the panel opposite for more information). An issue to look out for when both shooting and editing is when the graph comes to an abrupt end at either the left or the right side. This indicates 'clipping', whereby the under - or overexposure is so severe that the data has been lost and correcting that part of the exposure is impossible.

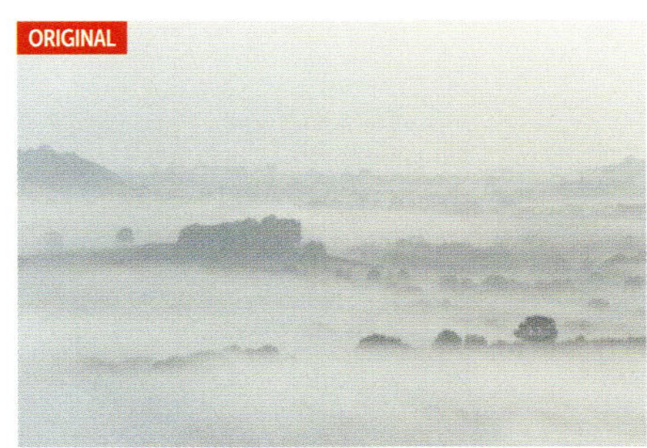

If you're aiming for a wide range of tones in your image, then ideally, you want your histogram graph to reach from the darkest shadows on the left to the brightest highlights on the right. This can be impossible to achieve when photographing low-contrast scenes but, using Lightroom's Exposure and Contrast controls, great results are only a few adjustments away.

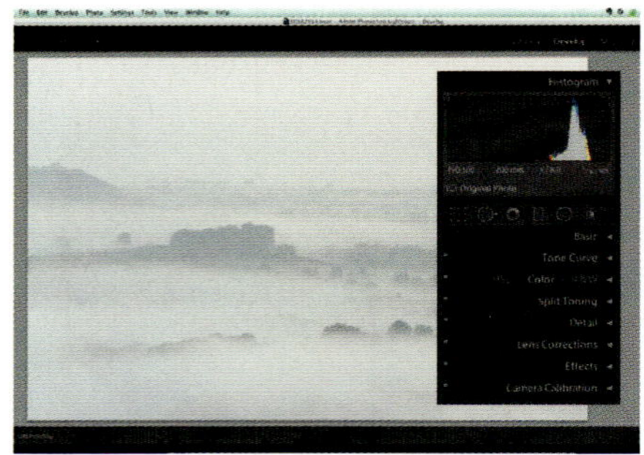

1 TURN ON CLIPPING WARNINGS Before any changes are made, first turn on the highlight and shadow clipping warnings by clicking on the two triangles in the upper left and right corners of the histogram. Any areas of pure black in your image will show blue and any areas of pure white will show red.

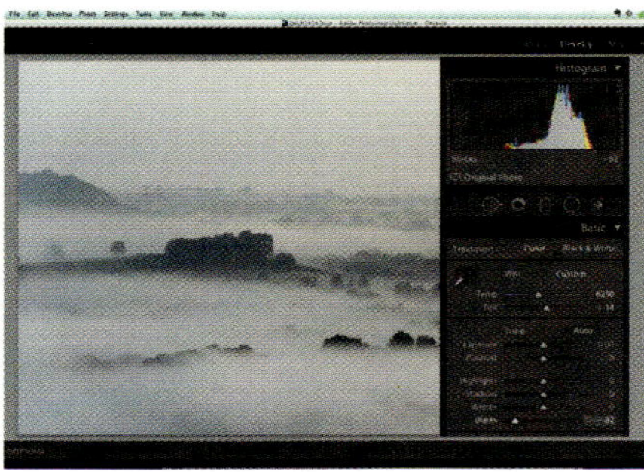

2 SET THE BLACK POINT Reduce the ***Blacks*** slider, keeping an eye on the histogram. This scene contains no true blacks, only shadows, so we stop before the graph reaches the left side. If your image contains a pure black, then reduce the ***Blacks*** slider until just before that area highlights blue.

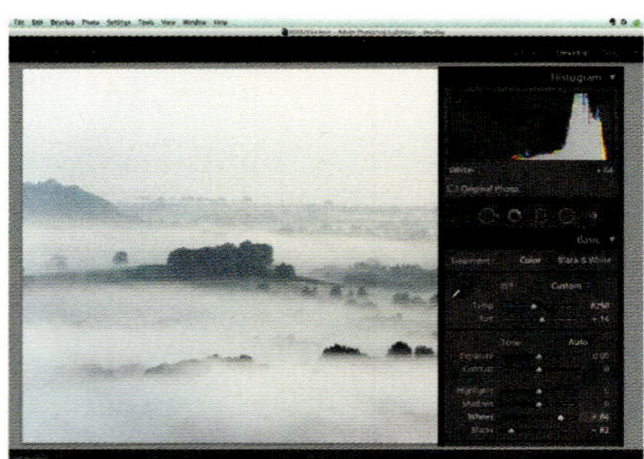

3 SET THE WHITE POINT Now use the ***Whites*** slider to extend the graph to the right. We've stopped before it reaches the far right as this area indicates pure white and the mist should be off-white. Again, if you've an area that should be white then increase this slider until just before that area highlights red.

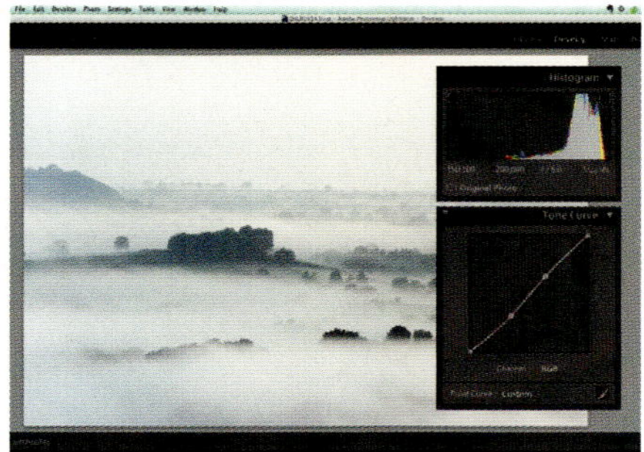

4 INCREASE MID-TONE CONTRAST You'll notice that contrast has been boosted. In the ***Curves*** tab, create a subtle 'S' curve, as shown. This will increase mid-tone contrast. Keep an eye on the histogram – you may need to tweak the Blacks and Whites sliders if the sides of the graph creep out of line.

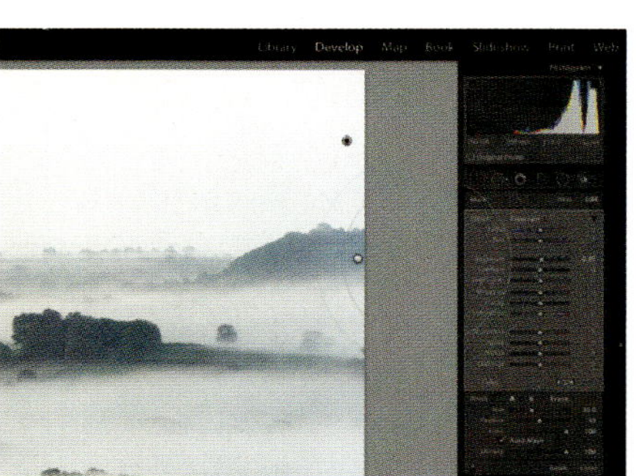

5 MAKE SELECTIVE ADJUSTMENTS There are still areas that need selective adjustment – use the ***Adjustment Brush*** to tackle these. The furthest hills here need more definition, so we use a brush set to ***-0.10 Exposure*** to darken them. Then we use another brush set to ***+0.27 Exposure*** to brighten the sky.

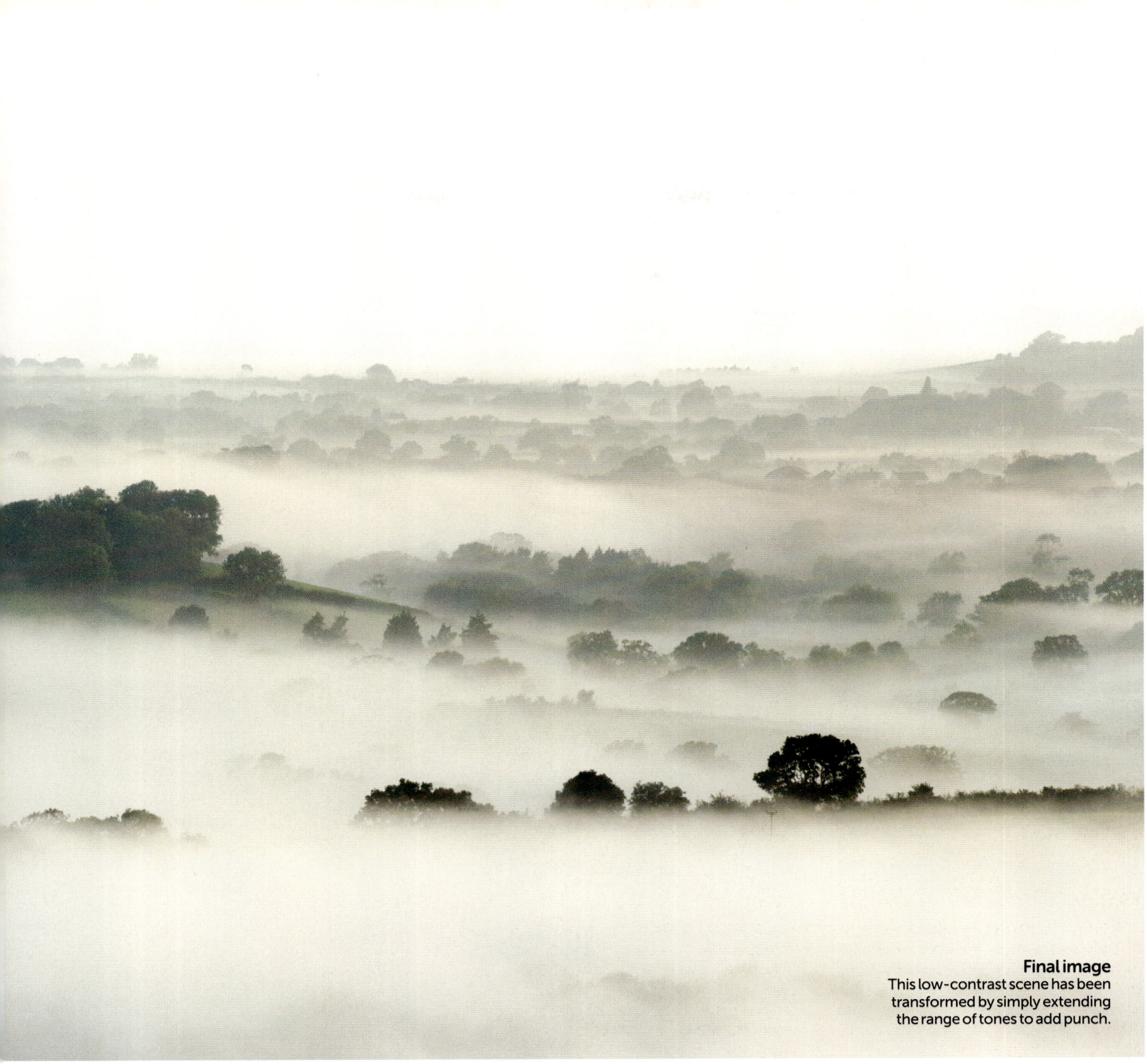

Final image
This low-contrast scene has been transformed by simply extending the range of tones to add punch.

Reading a histogram

Histograms look complicated, but are actually simple to understand. The horizontal axis represents the brightness of your image, and the vertical represents the number of pixels at each brightness level. The left side of the histogram depicts the black and shadows in your image; the right side are the whites and highlights. So, a graph weighted heavily to the left is typical of an image that is quite dark, and one weighted to the right will be bright. This doesn't always indicate under- or overexposure, as the values will depend on the content of the image – for example, a snowy landscape would produce a histogram heavily weighted to the right.

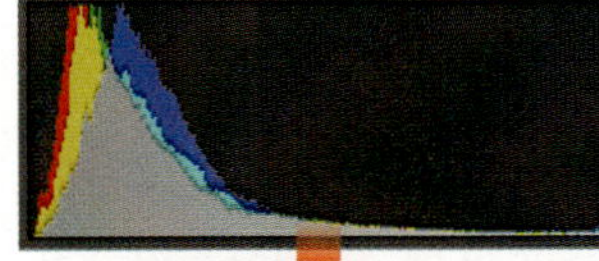

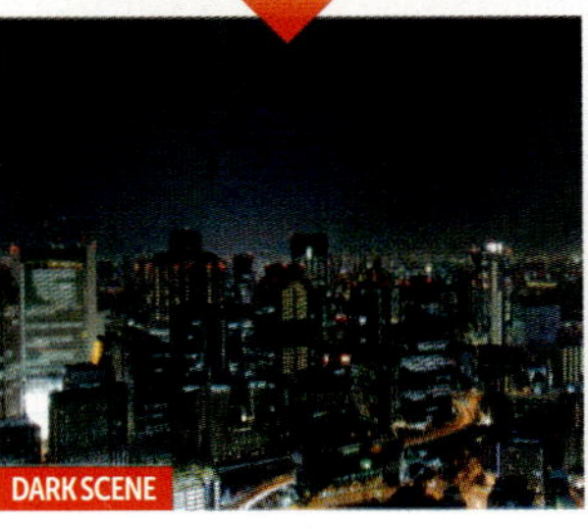

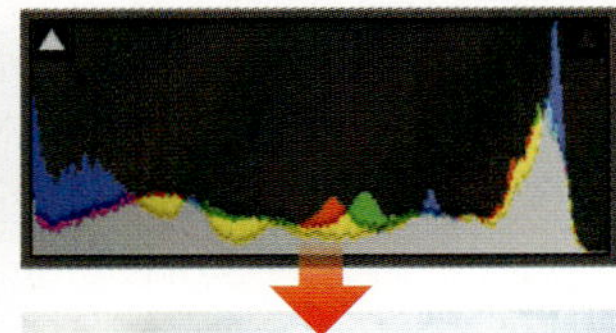

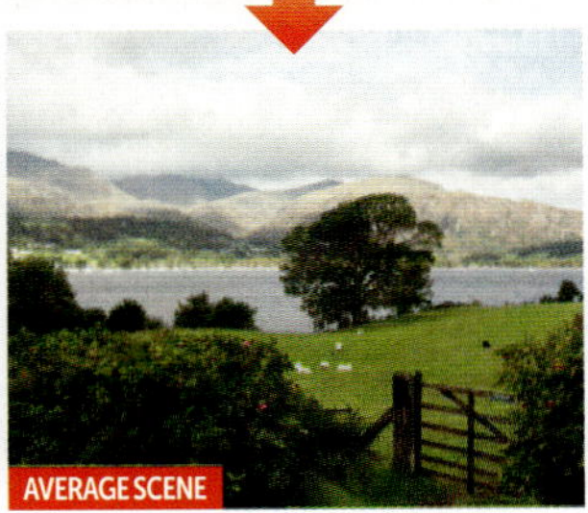

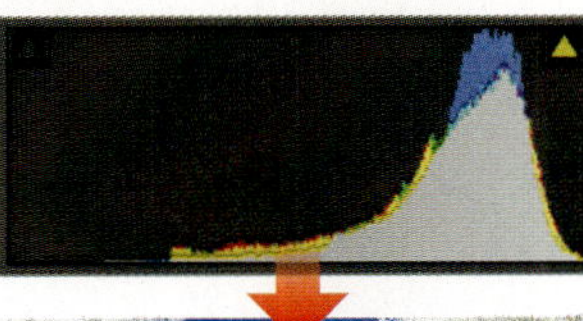

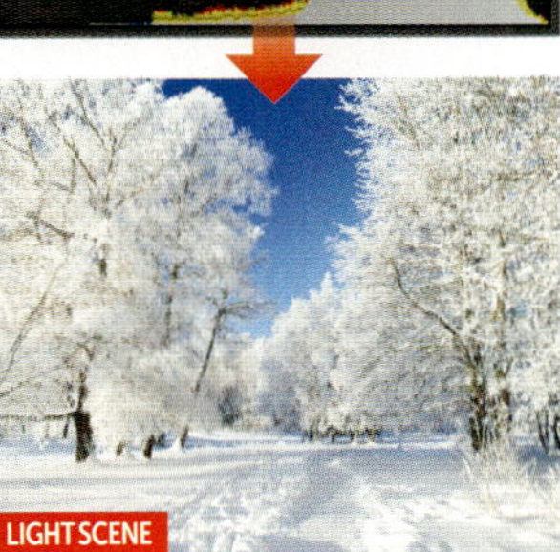

Add flare to your images

Are your backlit outdoor portraits lacking pizzazz? Find out how to quickly and easily add a natural-looking sun flare effect using Lightroom

FOR THE MOST PART, photographers try to do whatever they can to avoid flare. We spend hundreds or even thousands of pounds ensuring that we've got the best optics, with the fanciest, most advanced optical coatings, and we use lens hoods to stop unwanted flare from lowering contrast. But sometimes these ultra-efficient lenses hinder creativity making the fantastic qualities of sun flare that many photographers are now striving to achieve difficult to capture in-camera.

Flare adds atmosphere, conveys warmth and can give your images a summery feel. However, it's not always easy to capture in a controlled manner and too much flare can be destructive to an image, so knowing how to create or add to existing flare is a good technique to get to grips with. To start with, you should always match the direction of existing light in the image. It should always radiate from the sun or sky, too, so strong flares emitting miraculously from the middle of brick walls are a big no. And the colour of the flare should always match the temperature of the light. This effect is best applied to backlit outdoor images – shots taken during golden hour work especially well!

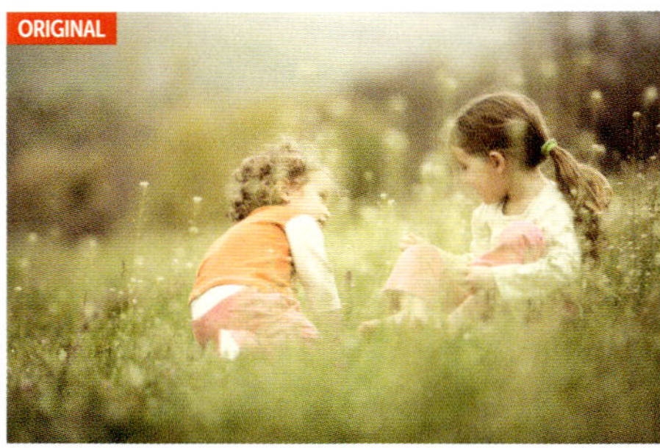
ORIGINAL

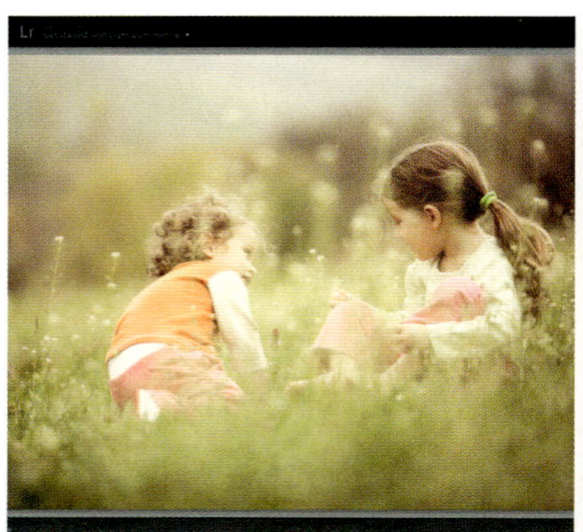

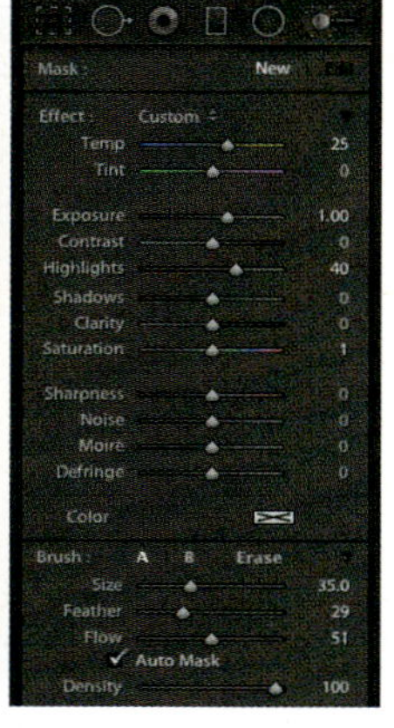

1 SELECT THE ADJUSTMENT BRUSH In the Develop module, select the *Adjustment Brush Tool*. In the Adjustment Brush palette, set the *Temperature* slider to *25*, the *Exposure* slider to *+1.00* and the *Highlights* slider to *40*. This will add brightness and warmth.

Top tip

SAVING YOUR ADJUSTMENT BRUSH
Once you've created your flare brush, you can save the settings for future use by clicking on the ***Effect*** menu in the Adjustment Brush palette and selecting ***Save Current Settings as New Preset...*** We'd recommend saving a couple of different settings at a variety of intensities – one light, one medium and one strong flare, for example.

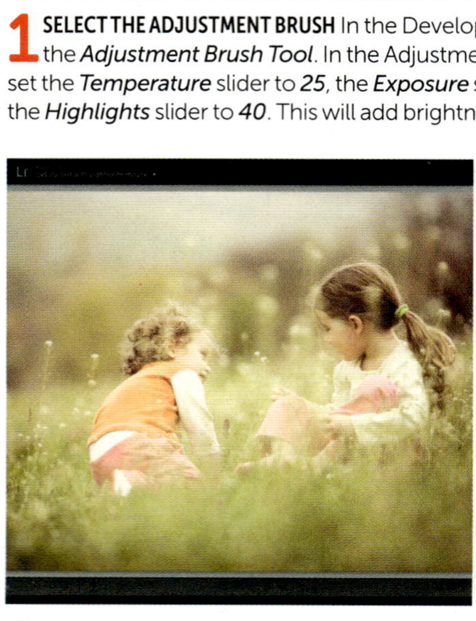

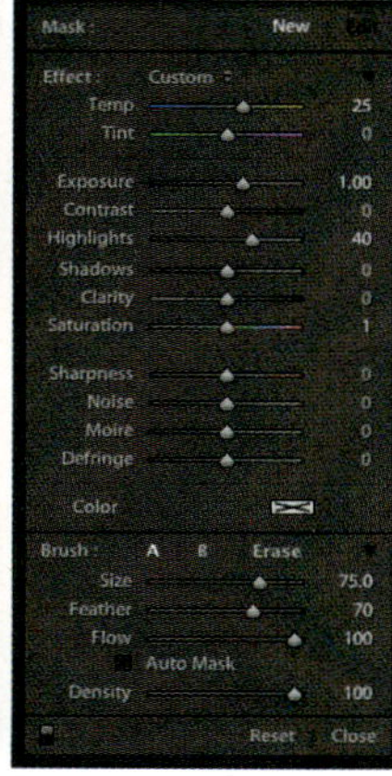

2 SET THE BRUSH SIZE At the bottom of the Adjustment Brush palette, set the brush *Feather* to around *70*, the *Flow* to *100* and the *Density* to *100*, too. Make sure that *Auto Mask* is turned off and set the brush *Size* to *75* – this can also be adjusted with the *[* and *]* keys.

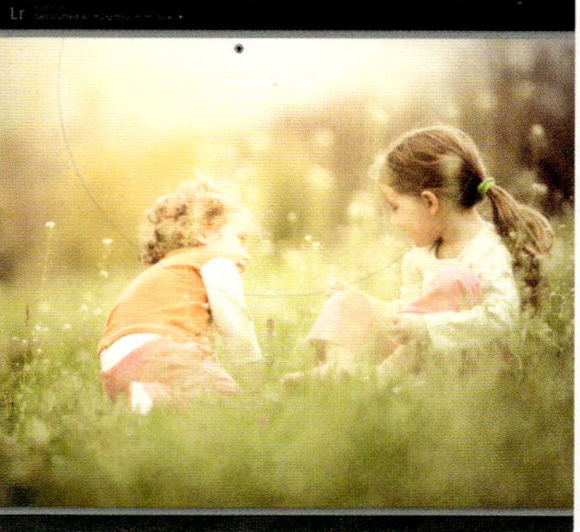

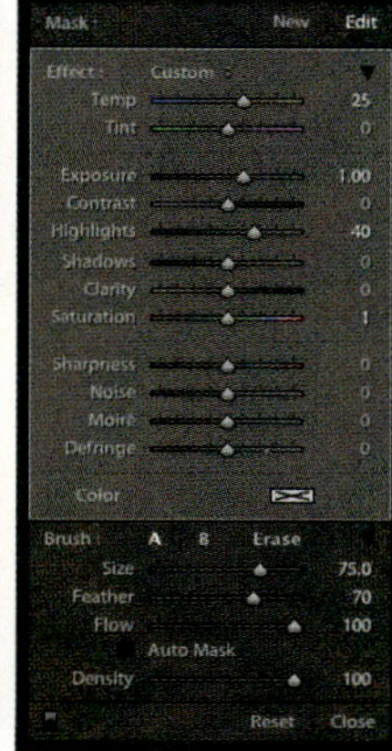

3 ADD THE FIRST BRUSH Creating the flare at the edge of the frame will result in the most realistic results. Identify the direction of light and click once or twice in that area to add the first part of the flare. It won't be perfect yet, so don't worry if it doesn't look right.

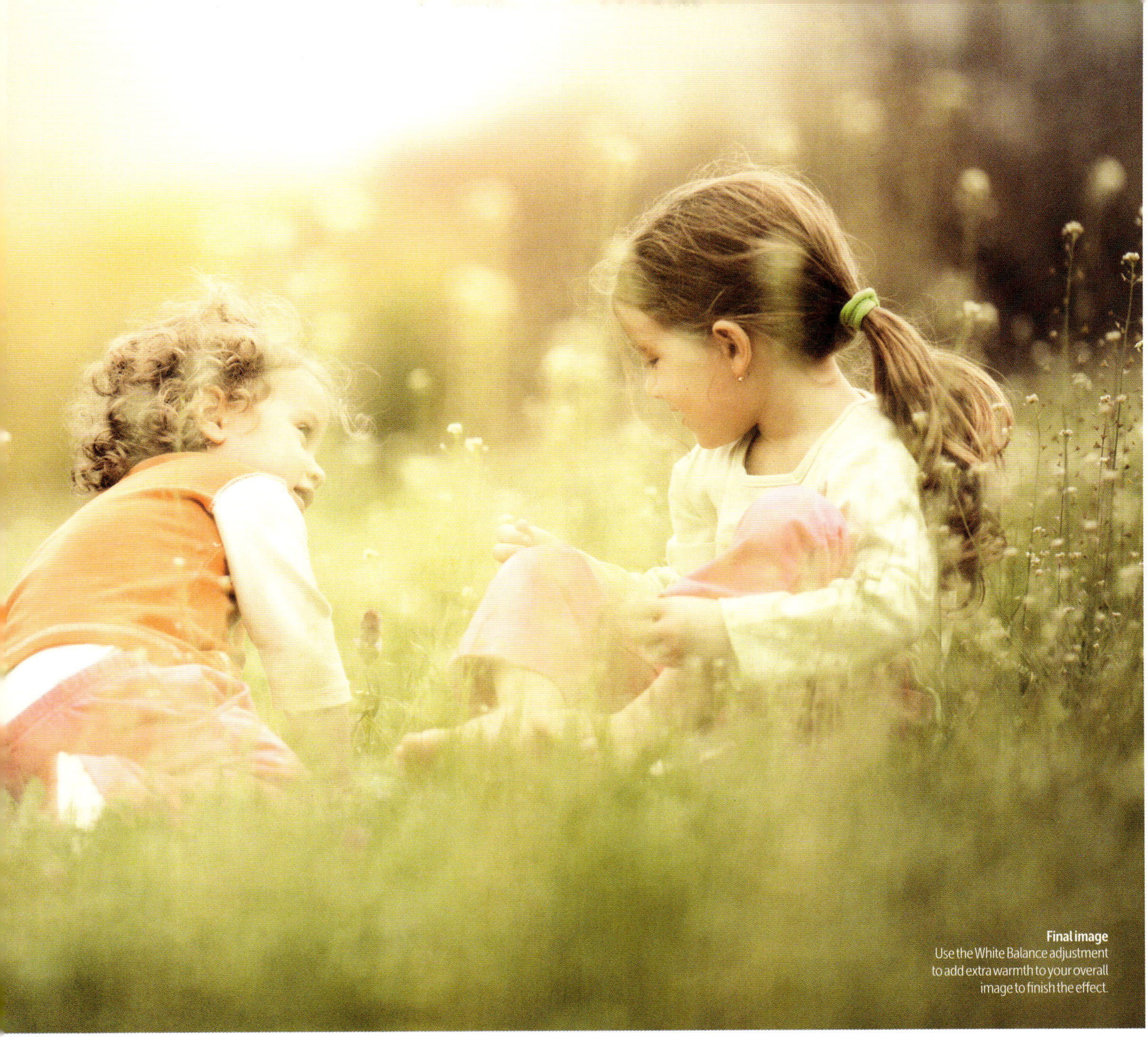

Final image
Use the White Balance adjustment to add extra warmth to your overall image to finish the effect.

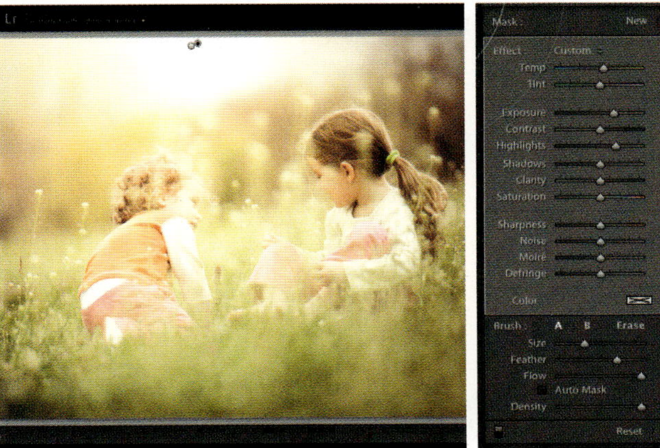

4 ADD ANOTHER LAYER Back in the Adjustment Brush palette, click ***New***. Decrease the brush ***Size*** – the aim is to create the centre of the flare. Set the ***Temperature*** to ***10*** and the ***Exposure*** to ***+1.50***. On your image, click near the centre of your first flare to add a hotspot.

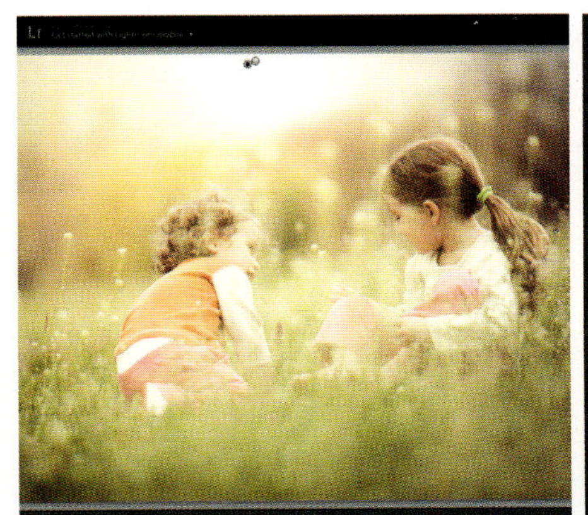

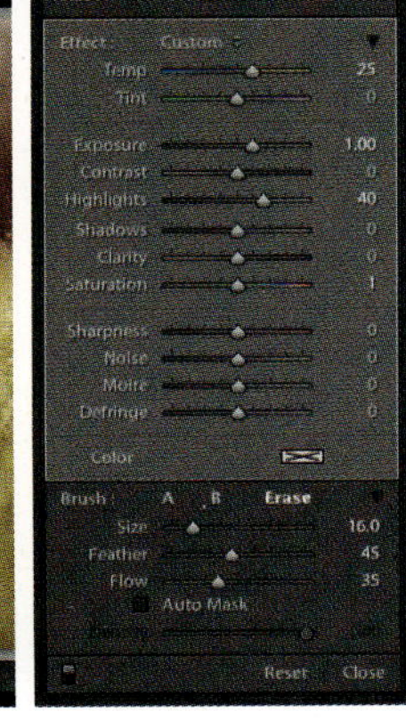

5 ERASE THE EFFECT If the effect is too intrusive, select the flare by clicking on the pin on the image, and select ***Erase*** in the Adjustment Brush palette. Lower the ***Flow*** to ***35%*** and brush back over any areas in which you wish to reduce the effect.

Present pictures with a classic frame

Better known for its workflow capabilities, Lightroom also has some presentation tricks up its sleeve...

ADOBE LIGHTROOM IS a fantastic piece of software for any photographer, and if you shoot any more than a handful of images every time you pick up a camera then you'll know that it's also an invaluable cataloguing and workflow solution. In more recent editions it has also grown in strength as a standalone editing package, allowing you to carry out the majority of basic edits required. However, there are areas that it lacks in, such as not allowing you to use layers or to easily add text and borders to your images. For the first part, we can't really help you, but there is a workaround for the latter issue and it's tucked away in the Print module.

The Print module is usually the place where you end up if you want to print your images directly from Lightroom, but did you know that it also holds templates for triptychs, contact sheets and greeting cards to aid accurate printing? It can also be used to export your images to JPEG, which means that any design or layout that you can come up with for print use can also be applied to an image that you might want to share online or print externally. Here's how you do it...

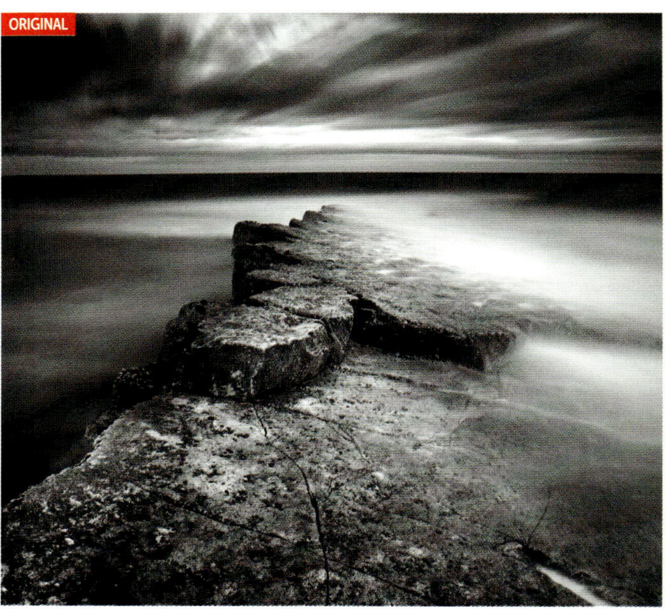

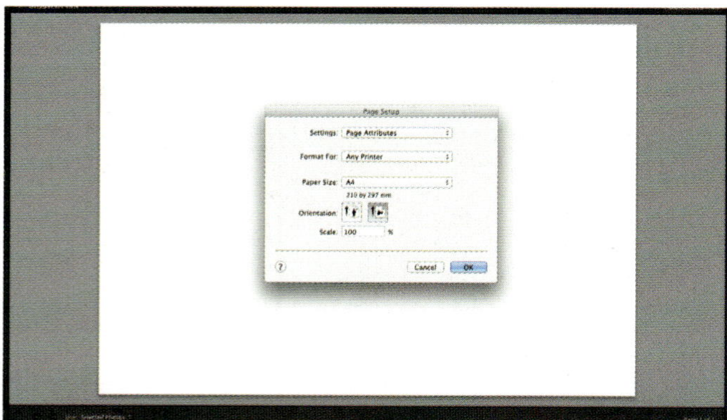

1 SET UP THE DOCUMENT Click *Print* in the top-right corner. Before adding the image you need to set up the page. Click on *Page Setup* in the bottom-left corner and, in the window that opens, select your paper size and orientation. If you're preparing the image for web use, A4 and landscape orientation is best. Click *OK*.

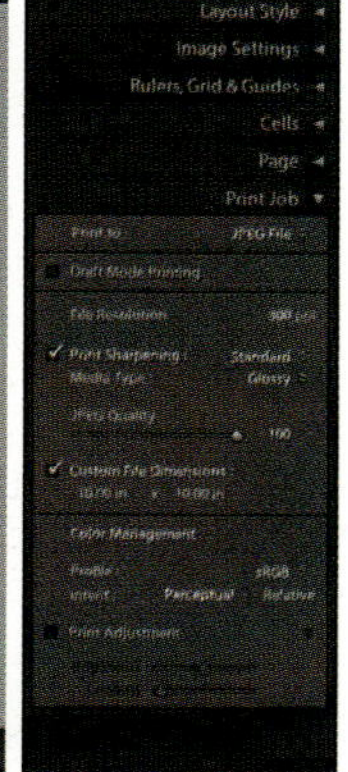

2 SELECT PRINT TO FILE In the *Print Job* palette on the right, set *Print to:* to *JPEG File* and set the *File Resolution* to suit – 300ppi is ideal for print, whereas 72ppi is fine for web use. Set the *Print Sharpening* to *Standard* and *JPEG Quality* to *100*. Use *Custom File Dimensions* settings to change the aspect ratio of your frame.

Save the template

Before you close the Print module, it's a good idea to save this layout in case you want to use it again in the future. In the ***Templates*** palette to the left, click on the small plus (+) sign to save your template. Give it a name that you'll recognise. To find it next time, enter the ***Print*** module and scroll down to ***User Templates***.

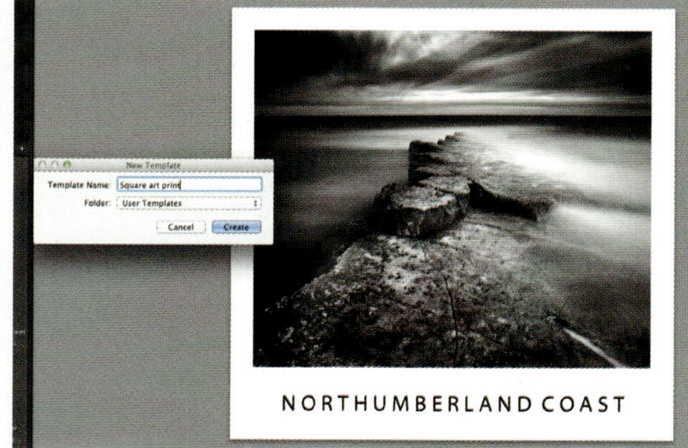

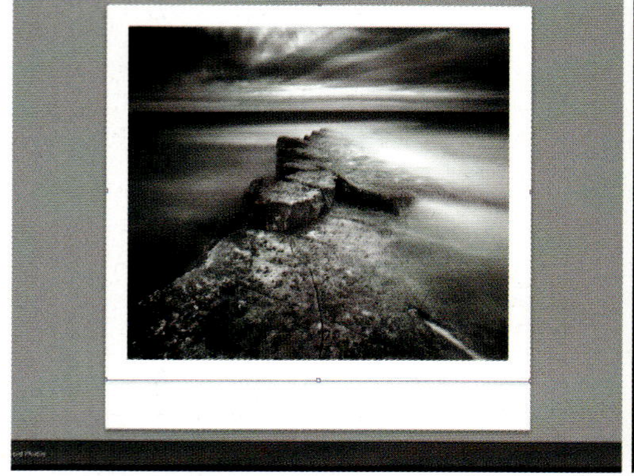

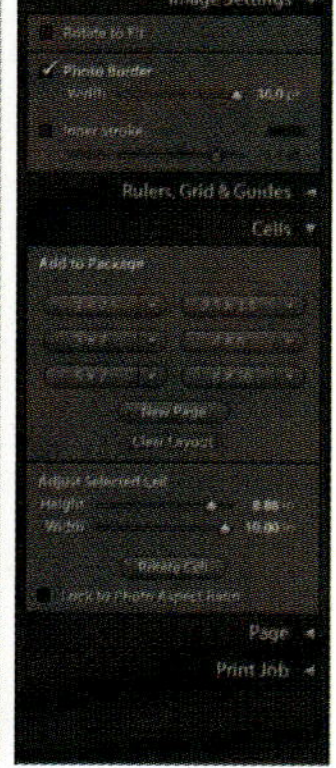

3 INSERT YOUR IMAGE Select *Custom Package* from the *Layout Style* palette, then drag an image onto the page from below and use the anchor points to scale it. In the *Image Settings* palette, increase the *Width* of the Photo Border to suit. Then, in the *Cells* palette, reduce the *Adjust Selected Cell Height* slider to allow room for text.

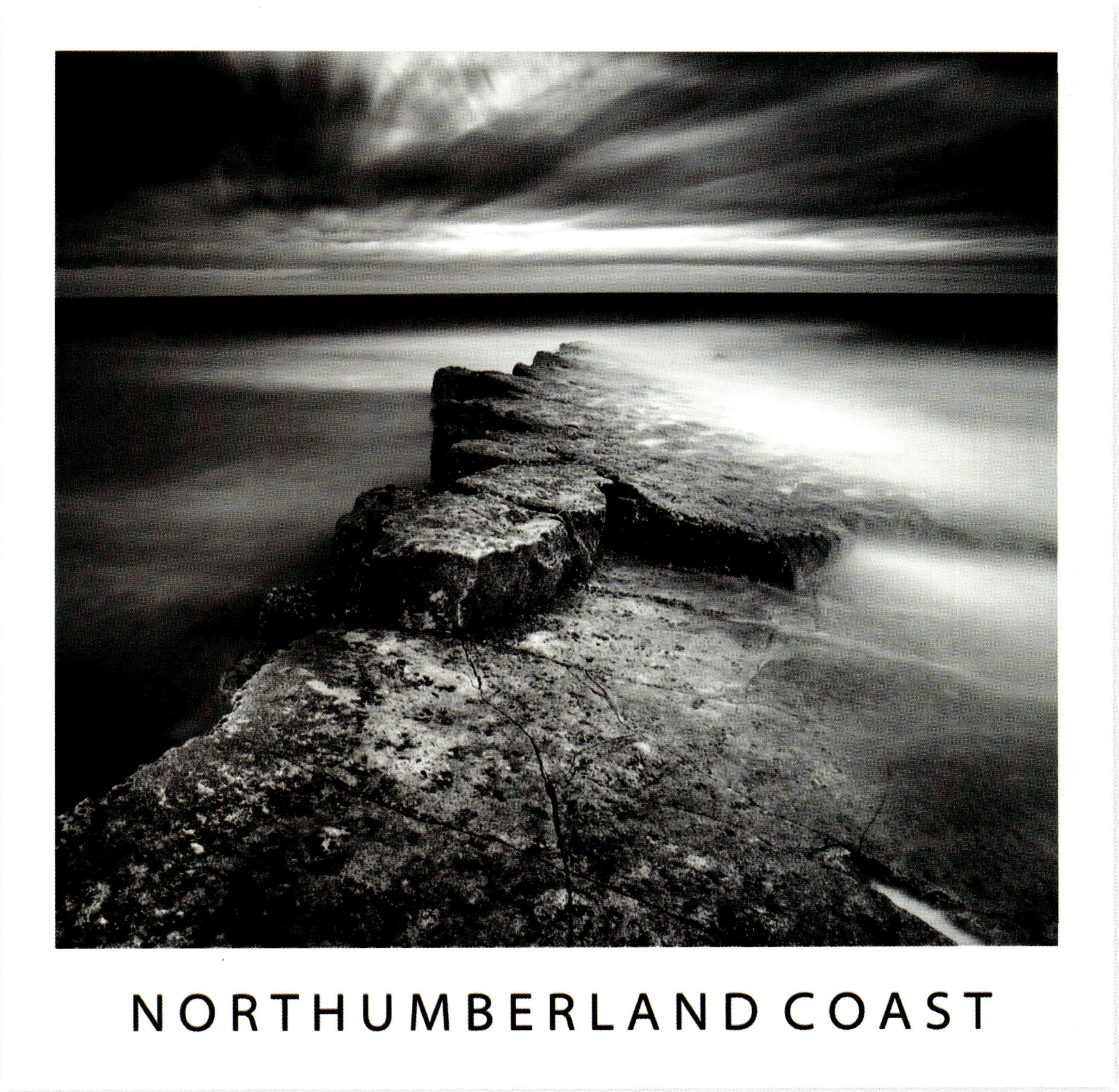

NORTHUMBERLAND COAST

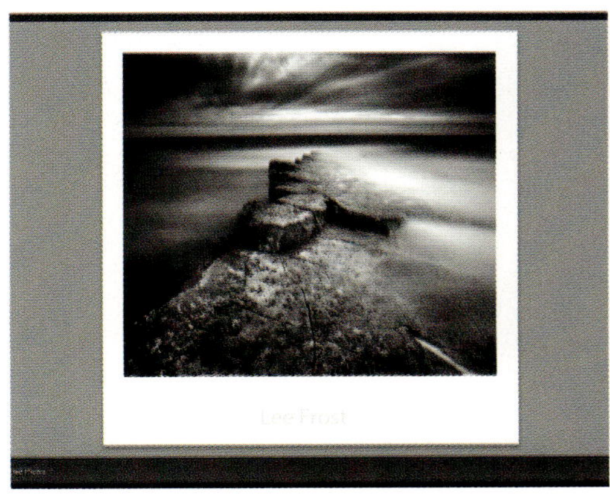

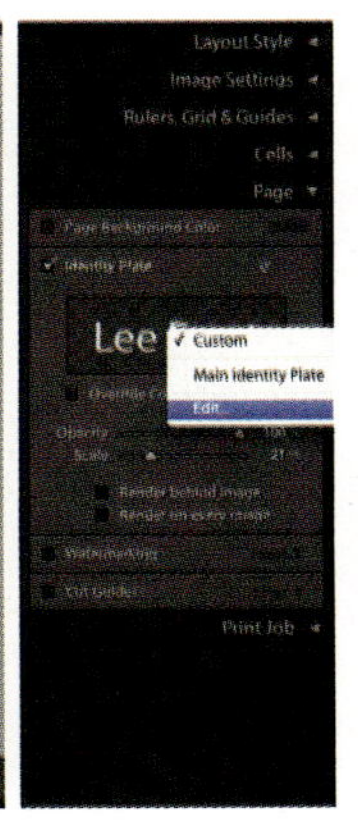

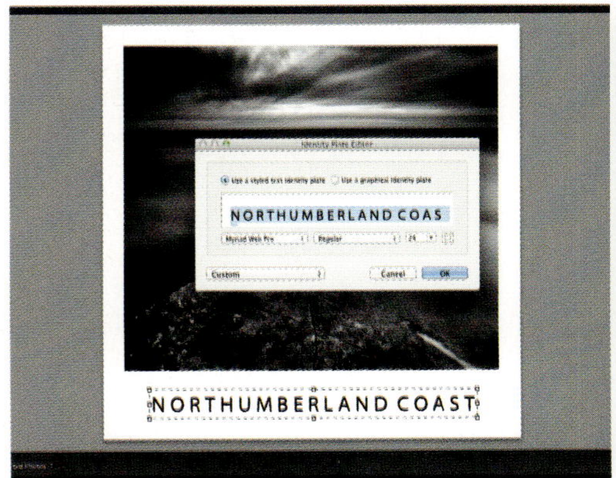

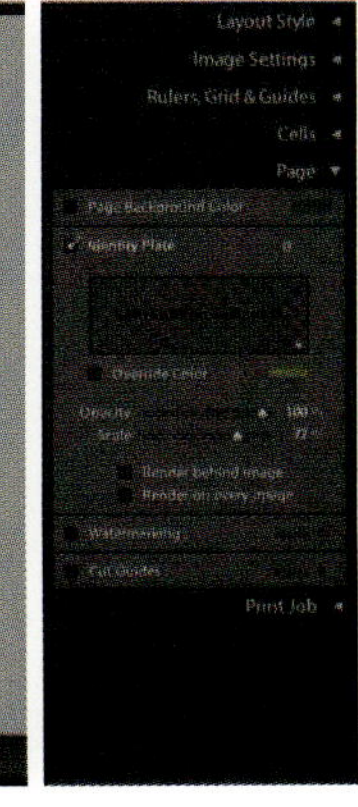

4 POSITION YOUR IMAGE Hold down the ***ctrl*** (PC) or ***cmd*** (Mac) key while dragging on your image to move it around within the cell. Once done, click on the ***Identity Plate*** check box in the ***Page*** palette before clicking on the preview window below and selecting ***Edit*** from the drop-down menu. This will open the ***Identity Plate Editor*** window.

5 INSERT YOUR CAPTION Click ***Use a styled text identity plate*** and, in the text box below, type your caption. Select the font along with the text colour below. Click ***OK***. Back in the ***Page*** palette, use the ***Opacity*** and ***Scale*** sliders to adjust your text. You can also click and drag to reposition it. Once done, click ***Print to File*** to save your image.

Boost black & whites

Do your black & white images lack punch? Learn how to take them from flat to fine-art in five minutes using Adobe Lightroom 6

PROCESSING BLACK & WHITE images is a completely different ball game to working with colour. In fact, take the rule book and fling it out the window with vigour! Forget treading softly and making minute modifications – black & white images, by nature, don't reflect reality so you can afford to take a little more artistic licence when processing them. Adding contrast in abundance, lifting colour luminance, amplified dodging and burning and increasing clarity all sounds like an eye-watering recipe for disaster if you were working in colour, but in monochrome it's a sure way to add impact. Push the boundaries of a colour image too far and telltale signs of overprocessing appear. In this sense, monochrome is much more forgiving. Here are a few easy-to-follow steps to give your black & white shots some extra punch.

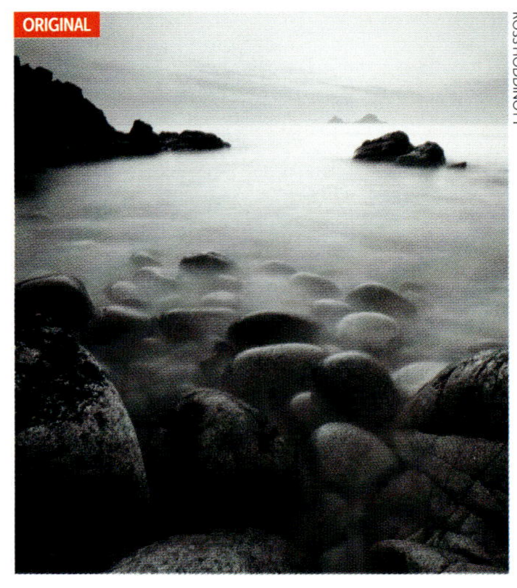

ROSS HODDINOTT

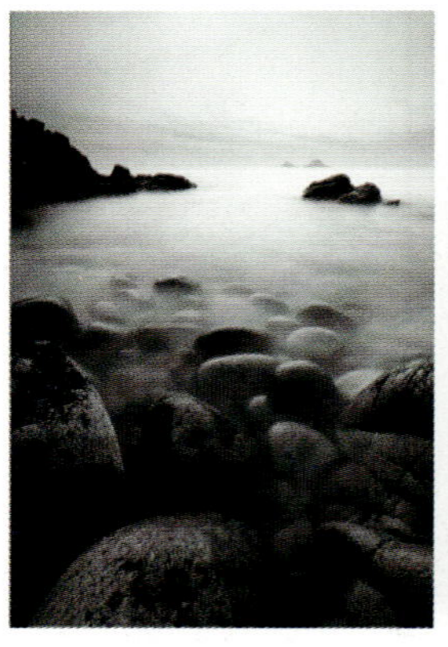

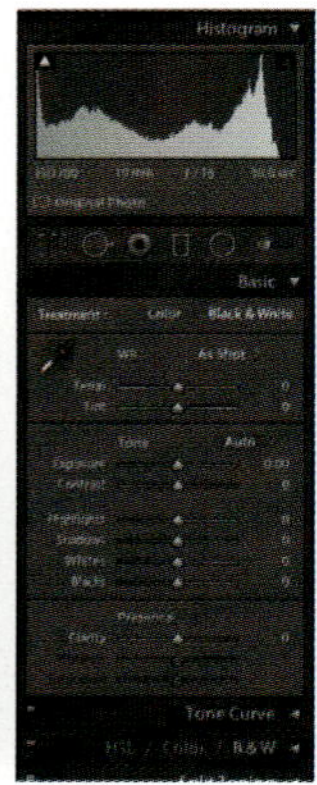

1 CONVERT TO MONOCHROME Load your image into the Develop module and select ***Black & White*** from the ***Treatment*** options at the top of the Basic tab. This performs a rough-and-ready conversion. Once in a blue moon, this will be all that the image requires, but here a bit more adjusting will make it just right. Scroll down to the ***HSL/ Color/B&W*** tab to make further adjustments.

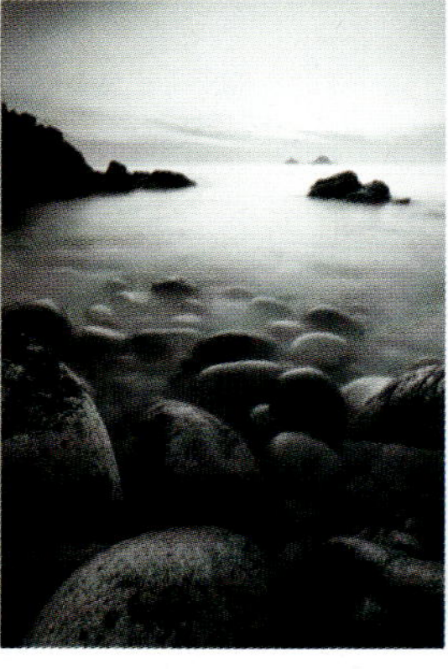

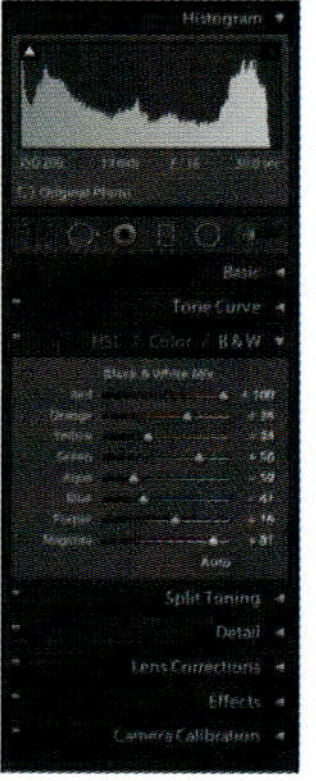

2 ADJUST THE COLOUR MIXER The B&W tab adjusts the luminance of each colour channel. Be mindful that if you adjust two adjacent channels to be vastly different in luminosity to one another then you'll start to see artefacts. Make adjustments, while keeping an eye on the Histogram to make sure that you don't over- or underexpose parts of the image while adjusting.

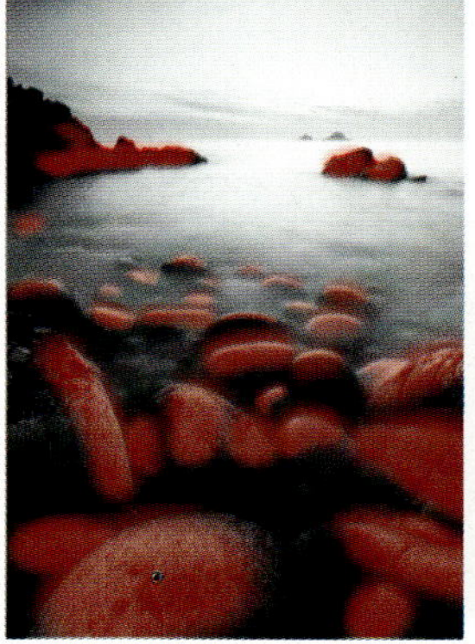

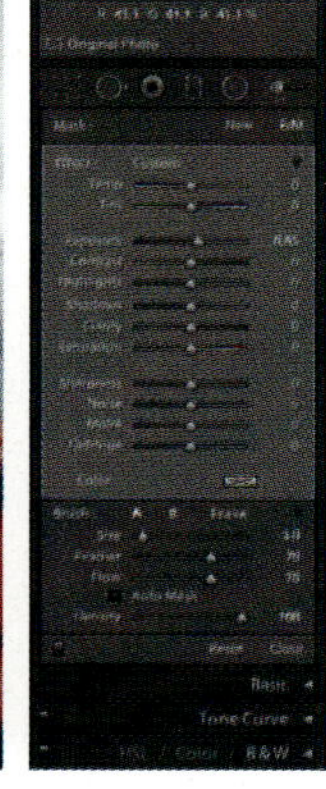

3 USE AN ADJUSTMENT BRUSH Next, select the ***Adjustment Brush Tool*** and, in the ***Brush*** palette, increase ***Exposure*** to around ***0.65***, ***Feather*** to ***70*** and ***Flow*** to ***70***. Choose a brush size with the *[* and *]* keys and dodge (lighten) parts of your image. Aim to enhance existing highlights, such as on the rocks in the foreground, or lift areas of shadow, such as the outcrop in the middle distance.

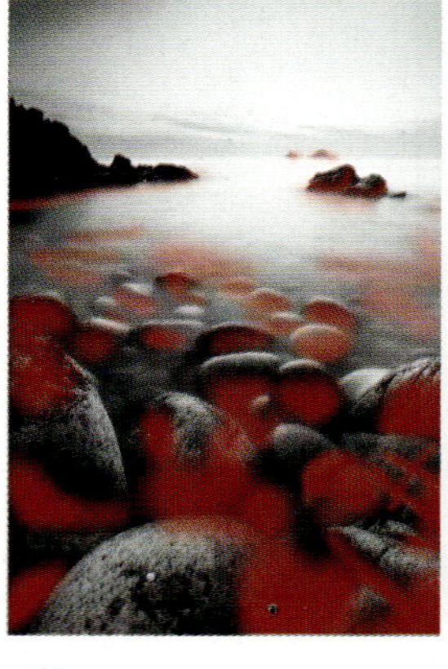

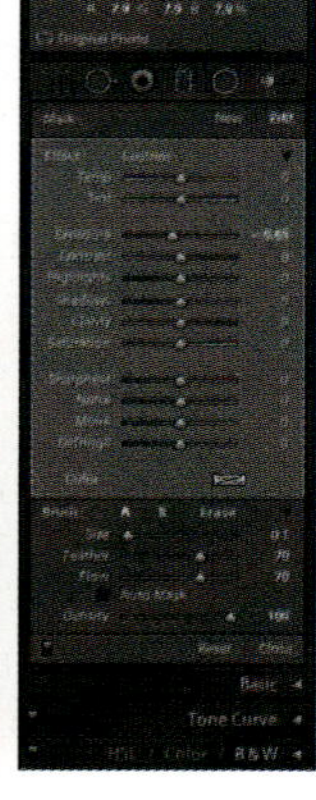

4 BURN TO ADD CONTRAST Click ***New*** at the top of the ***Brush*** palette to create another brush. This time, adjust ***Exposure*** to around ***-0.65***. As before, brush over any areas that need burning (darkening) – this time aim to darken existing shadows and save areas of overexposure. In dodging and burning selectively we are contouring and adding contrast exactly where we need it.

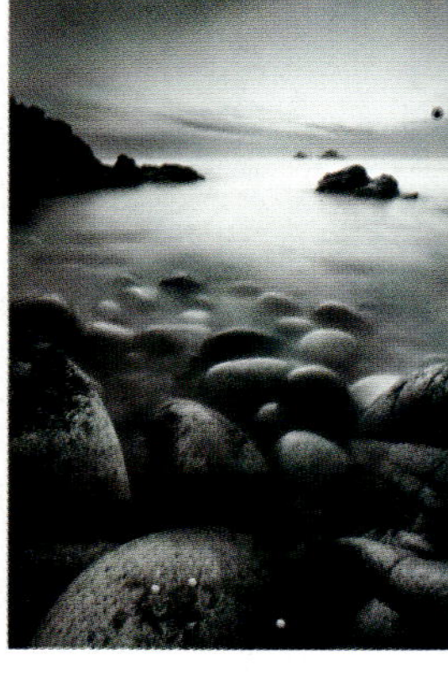

5 SELECTIVE WHITE BALANCE Although we're working in monochrome, adjusting the White Balance still has an effect – this can be done selectively too. Simply create a new brush and use the ***Temp*** slider to adjust the White Balance. Here, a warm brush on the foreground rocks brings out detail and a cool brush on the sky brings back clouds. Every image differs, so you need to experiment.

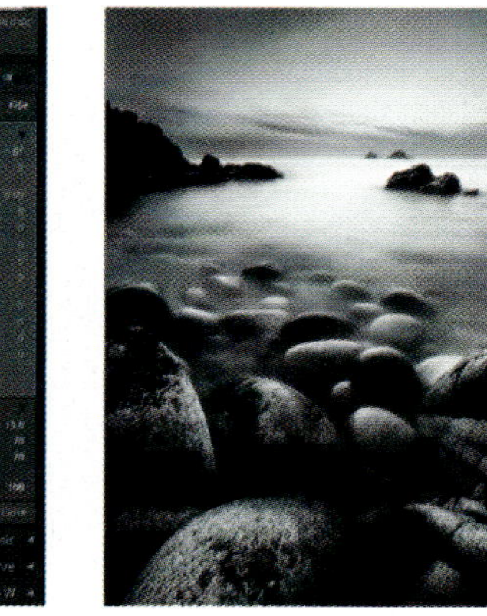

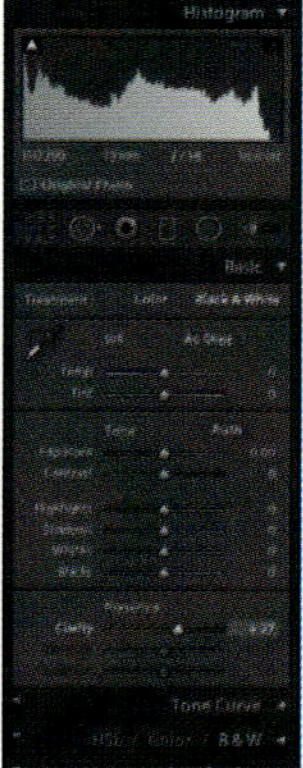

6 ADD DETAIL Back in the ***Basic*** tab, add texture and definition using the ***Clarity*** slider. When working in colour the Clarity slider should be used very sparingly, however monochrome images tend to suit a stronger approach. Gradually increase the ***Clarity*** slider until you're happy with the effect. Again, watch the Histogram as adjusting Clarity can affect your overall exposure.

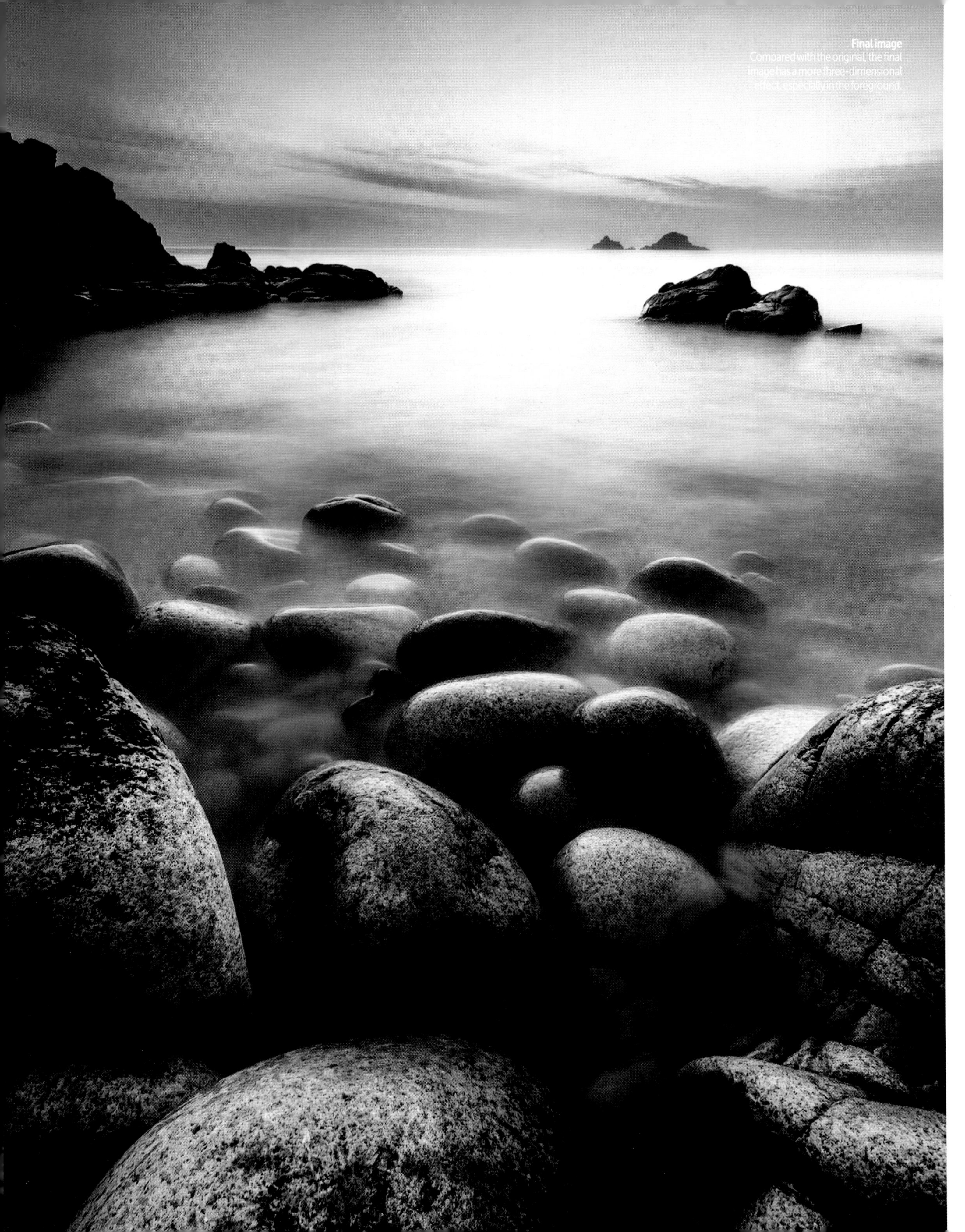

Final image
Compared with the original, the final image has a more three-dimensional effect, especially in the foreground.

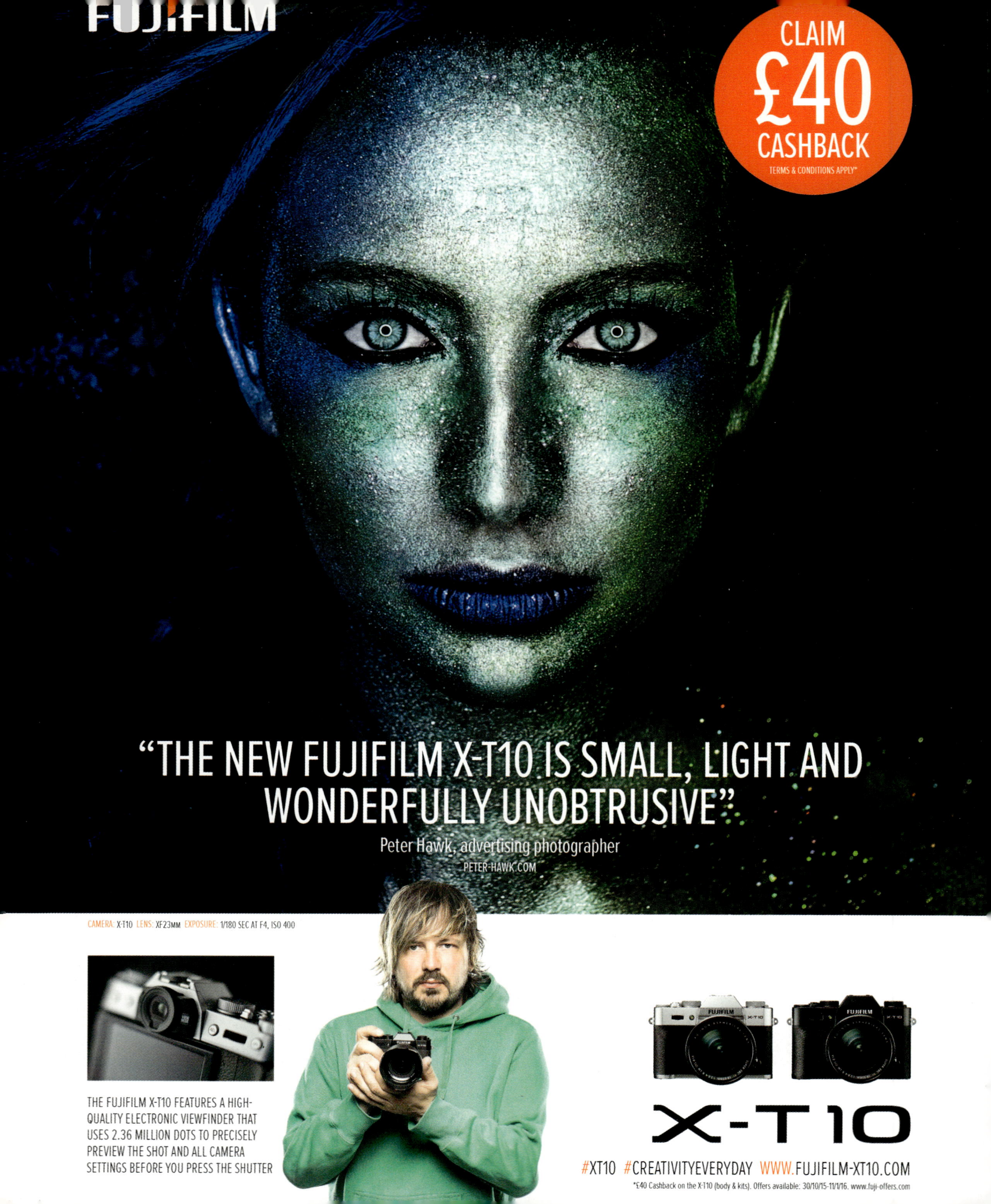

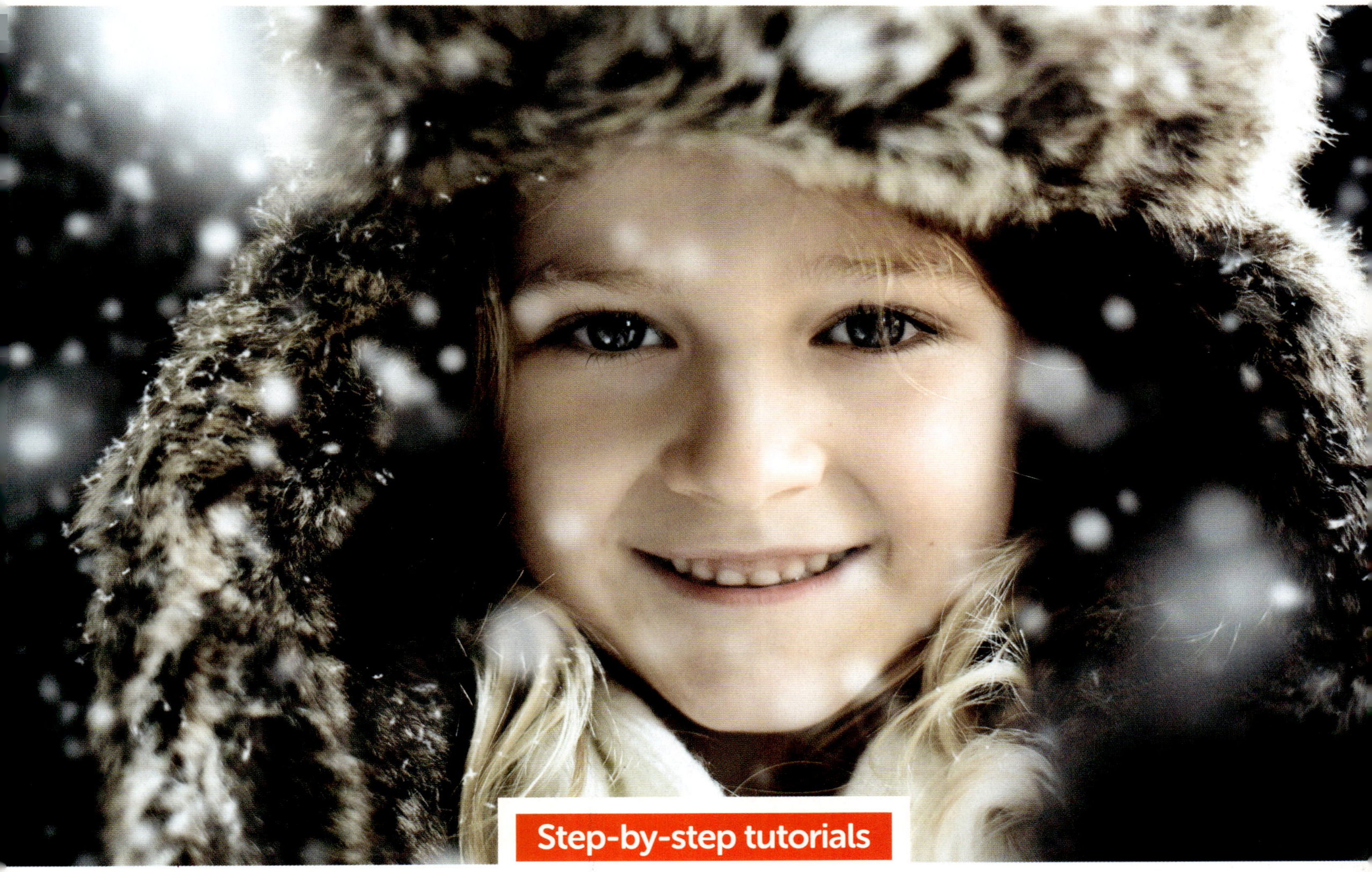

Step-by-step tutorials

PHOTOSHOP

Transform your pictures with minimal effort using our favourite Photoshop skills

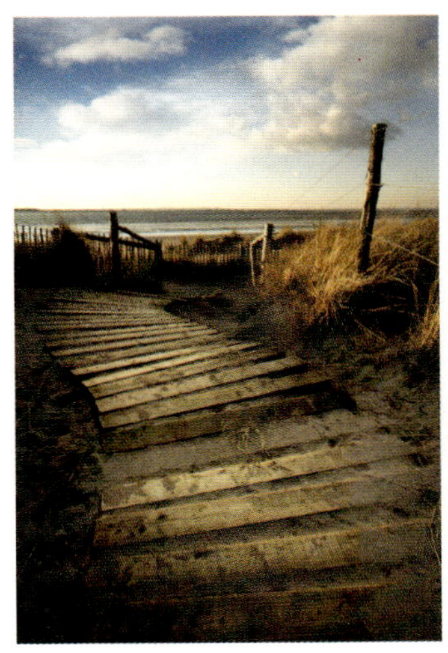
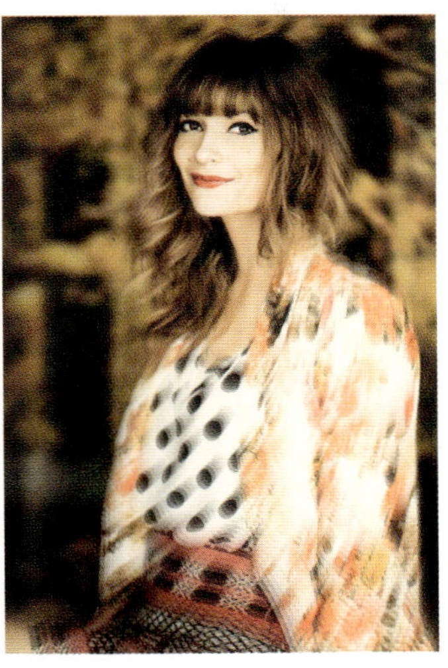
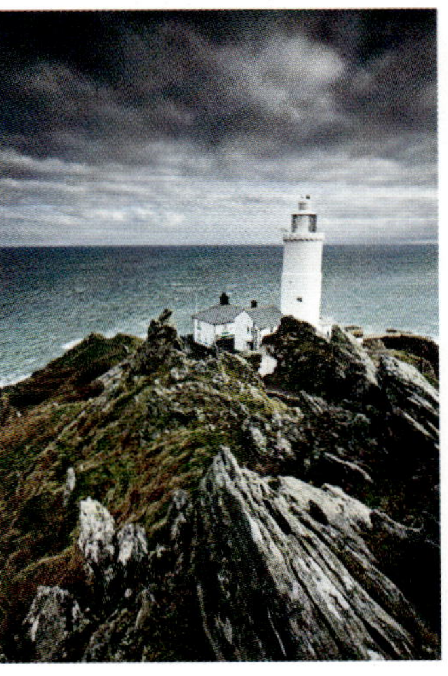
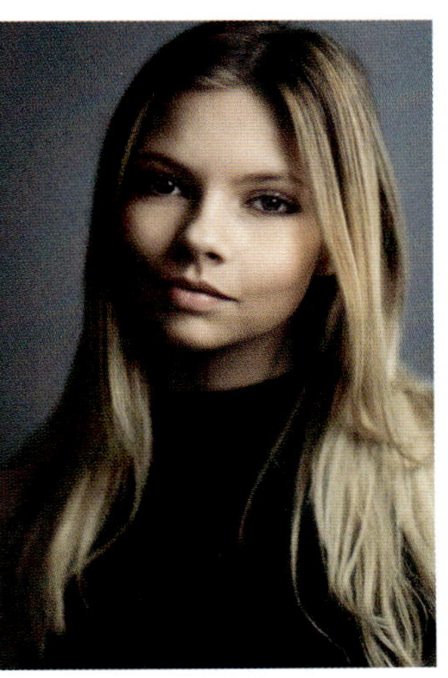

Making manual selections

Smart selection tools are quick and convenient, but when control is paramount, manual selections are usually the best solution

WHILE SMART TOOLS like the Quick Selection Tool, or Elements' Smart Brush, can select areas of colour and strong contrast, what happens when you need to select something that isn't a distinctive colour or is an awkward shape? That's where manual selection tools come into play. They take more time to use as you'll be tracing the area that you wish to select, but it's a good way to make an accurate selection.

For instance, we want to create a dramatic, high-contrast, desaturated final image of this scene. However, as some areas are already high contrast, we only want to boost contrast on specific areas, such as the boardwalk and sky. As the boardwalk has defined edges with sand in between, we're going to need to use both the Lasso and Polygonal Lasso Tools to enable me to make an accurate selection.

Alternative tools

THE PEN TOOL
The Pen Tool is an advanced selection method. Rather than create a selection, the Pen Tool creates a Path. Paths follow vector lines rather than pixel edges, so are ideal for situations when precision is paramount, although the tool takes some time and practice to master.

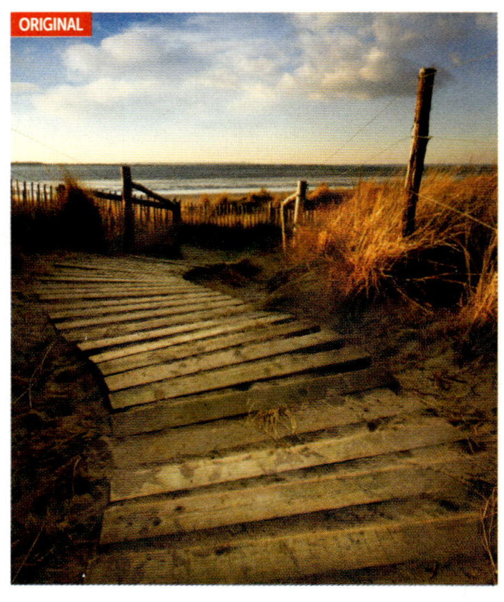
ORIGINAL

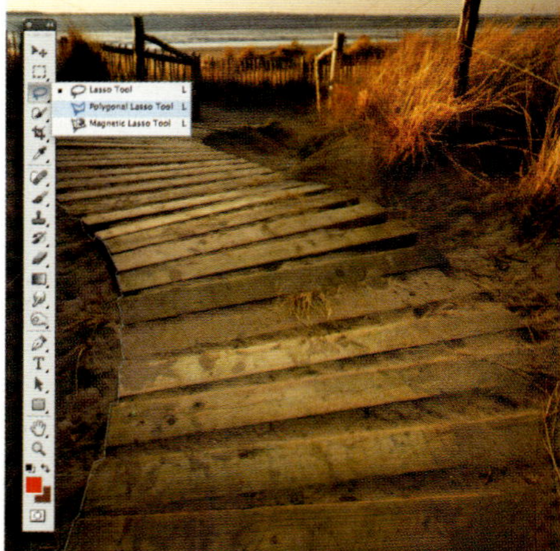

1 Make your first selection Click and hold on the *Lasso Tool* in the toolbar to choose the *Polygonal Lasso Tool*, which is designed to precisely select areas with straight edges. Click once on your image to set the start of your selection before moving the cursor to align with the straight edges of your subject. Periodically click to set the next anchor point.

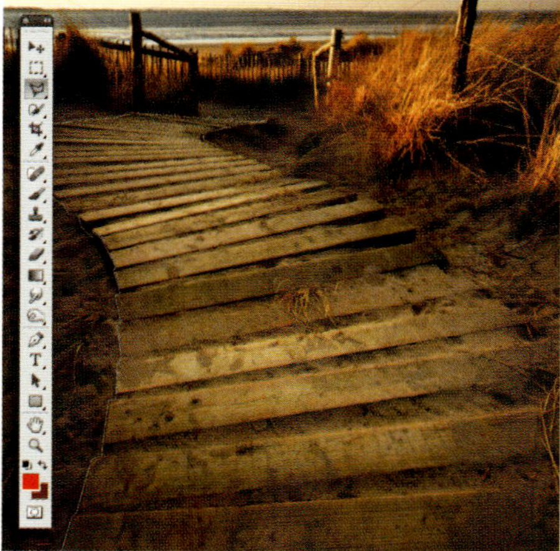

2 Switch between the Lasso Tools If you come to an area that requires you to be more flexible in your selection, hold down ***alt*** to switch to the *Lasso Tool* and trace the cursor around your shape. Release the ***alt*** key to switch back to the *Polygonal Lasso Tool*. Once done, double-click near your selection start point to close your selection.

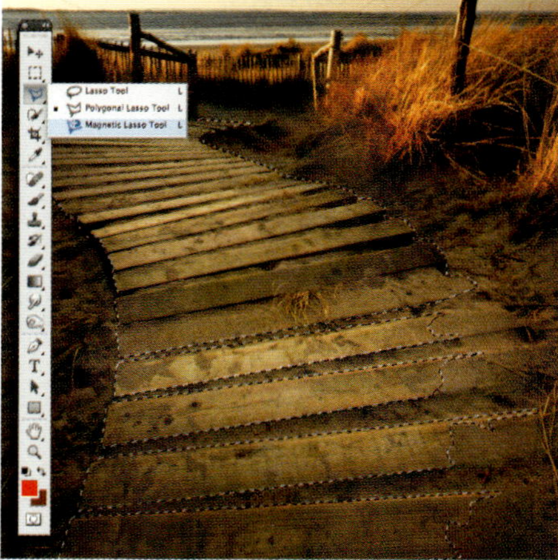

3 Subtract areas To subtract the areas of sand between the boards, hold down the ***alt*** key and select these areas one by one. Upon closing off each selection, that area will be removed from your original selection. Once done, click and hold on the *Polygonal Lasso Tool* in the toolbar to select the *Magnetic Lasso Tool*.

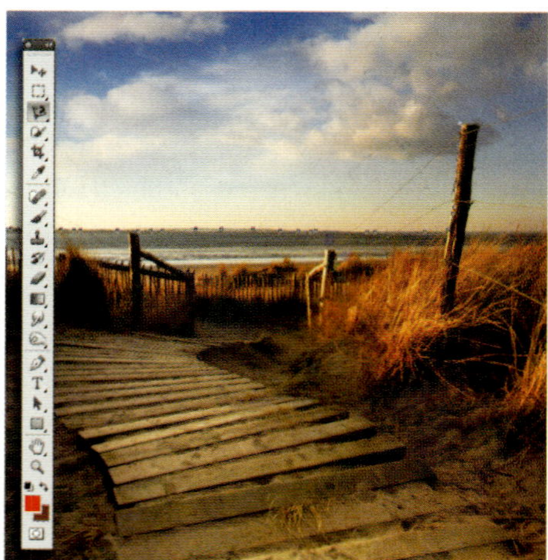

4 Add to your selection Hold down the ***shift*** key to add to the selection and click to set the first anchor point. Trace along the horizon and the tool will anchor to any edges of contrast. If the tool struggles at any point, click once to manually set a new anchor point along that edge. If it places an anchor incorrectly, press the ***backspace*** key.

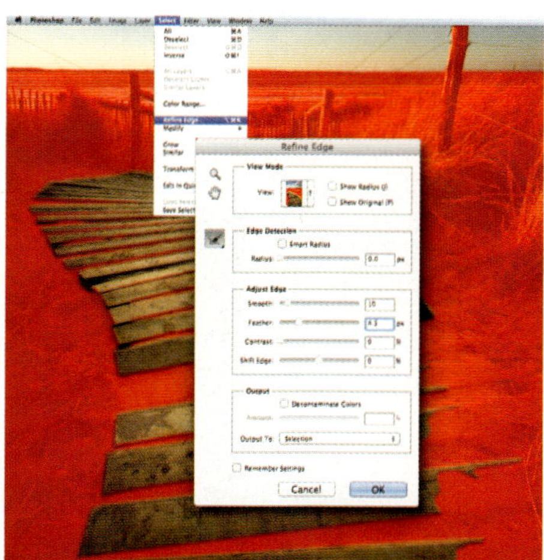

5 Refine the selection With the horizon traced, hold down the ***alt*** key again and click around the edges of the image to close off the selection around the sky. Then go to *Select>Refine Edge* and, in the Refine Edge box, increase the *Feather* to *6.0px* and change *Smooth* to *10*. This will smooth and blur the edges of your selection.

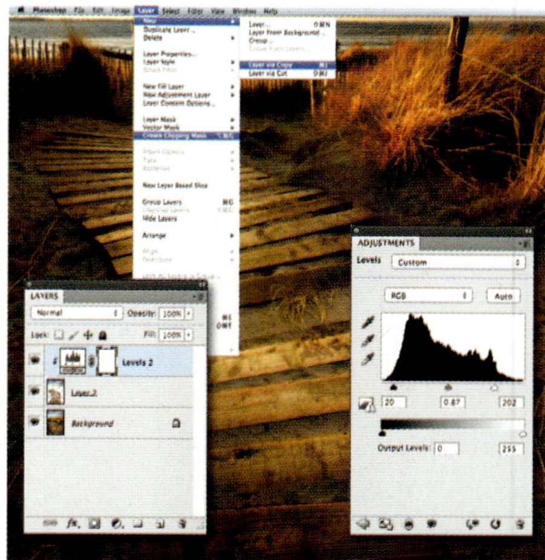

6 Add the adjustments Now you have your selection, create a Pixel Mask by going to *Layer>New>Layer via Copy*. Add a *Levels* adjustment layer and before making any adjustments, go to *Layer>Create Clipping Mask*. Next, in the Adjustments palette, tweak the black, grey and white point sliders to boost contrast in your selection only.

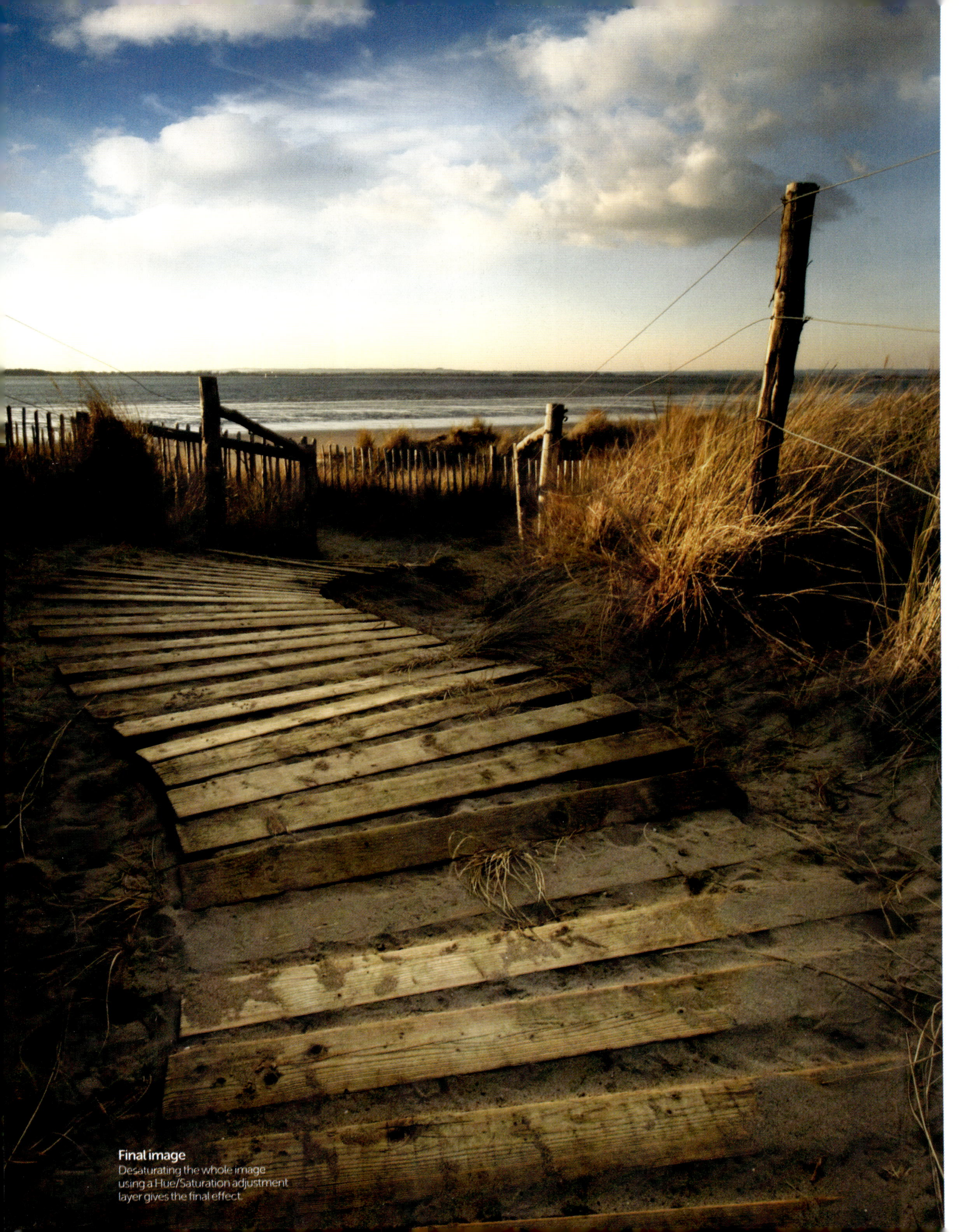

Final image
Desaturating the whole image using a Hue/Saturation adjustment layer gives the final effect

Controlling colour

Make your pictures more vibrant by mastering Adjustment Layers and this neat trick for tweaking each colour channel individually

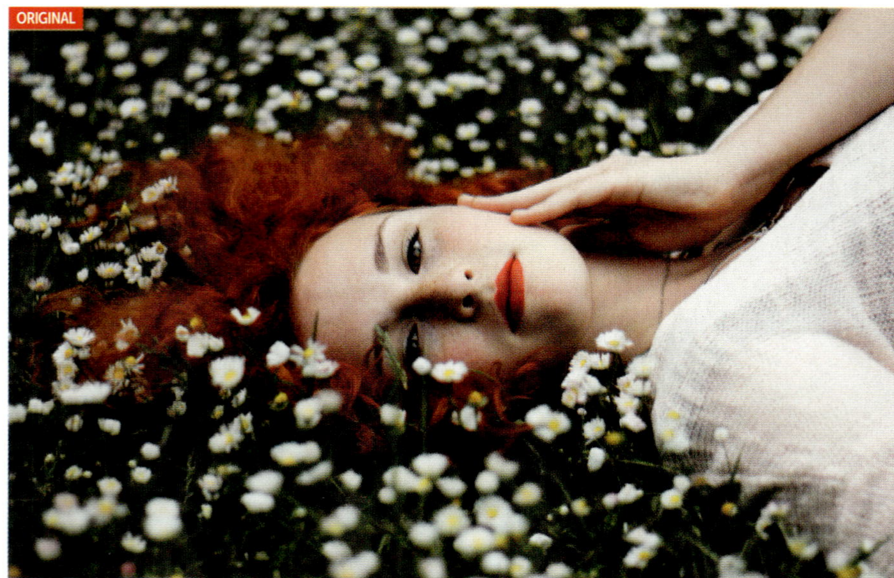

INCREASING IMAGE SATURATION is a delicate process. If your image is lacking vibrance it can end up looking dull and washed out. Perhaps worse, if you're too heavy-handed when it comes to processing your colour images, then image quality is degraded and your shots can end up looking more eye-sore than eye-catching. When working with colour you're constantly walking a fine line between not enough, just right and too much!

A problem that you'll often face when boosting an image's saturation is that some colours look better for being made more vibrant, whereas others suffer from it. Blue skies decorated with white, fluffy clouds often benefit from a boost in saturation, as do green fields and trees, whereas skin tones are more delicate and need a slightly gentler approach. With this in mind it's obviously poor form to just increase the saturation across the whole image and expect to get good results. Selectivity is the name of the game.

Those of you already familiar with Layer Masks will know that you can manually add a Hue/Saturation adjustment layer and then use the Layer Mask to the hide the adjustment from parts of your image. This works great for some images, but can be fiddly when dealing with complex edges or areas where components overlap. We're going to show you a neat little trick that you can use to selectively boost parts of your image, whilst leaving other parts unaffected. Here's how...

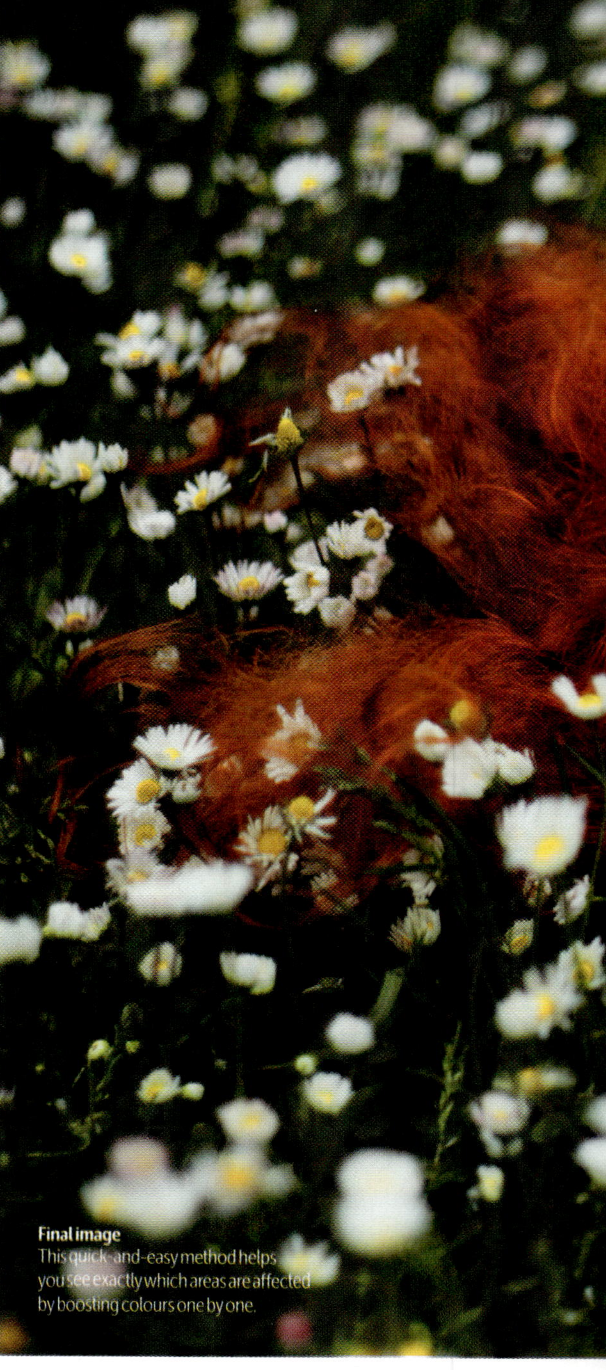

Final image
This quick-and-easy method helps you see exactly which areas are affected by boosting colours one by one.

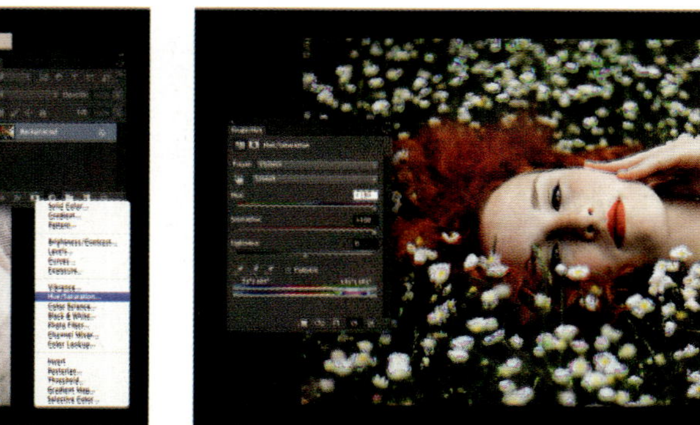

1 ADD AN ADJUSTMENT LAYER In the Layers palette, click on the *Create new fill or adjustment layer* button and select *Hue/Saturation*. Here, we want to boost the grass significantly, and the model's hair and lipstick slightly. Green and red are complementary colours, so the effect should work well.

2 HIGHLIGHT THE COLOURS We're going to work on the grass first. In the Adjustment palette select the *Greens* channel from the drop-down menu. Increase *Saturation* to *+100*. You'll notice that only some of the greens are affected. Increase *Hue* to *+180*. This highlights the areas we are affecting.

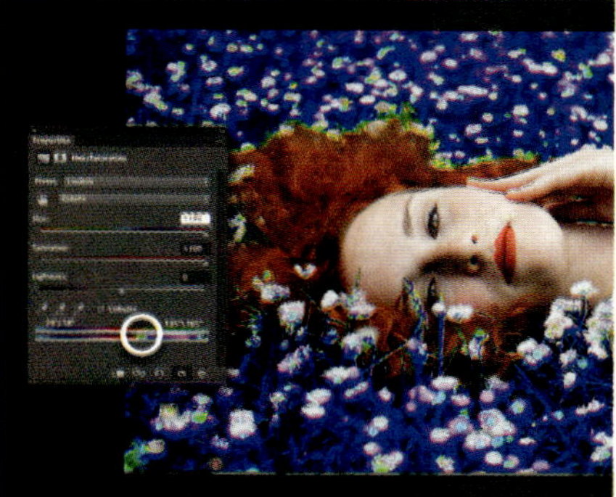

3 TWEAK THE COLOUR RANGE At the bottom there are two colour bars and four markers – two grey and two white. Click in the grey space between the bars, between the first and second markers (circled above) and drag left – this expands the colour range to include yellows, and eventually reds.

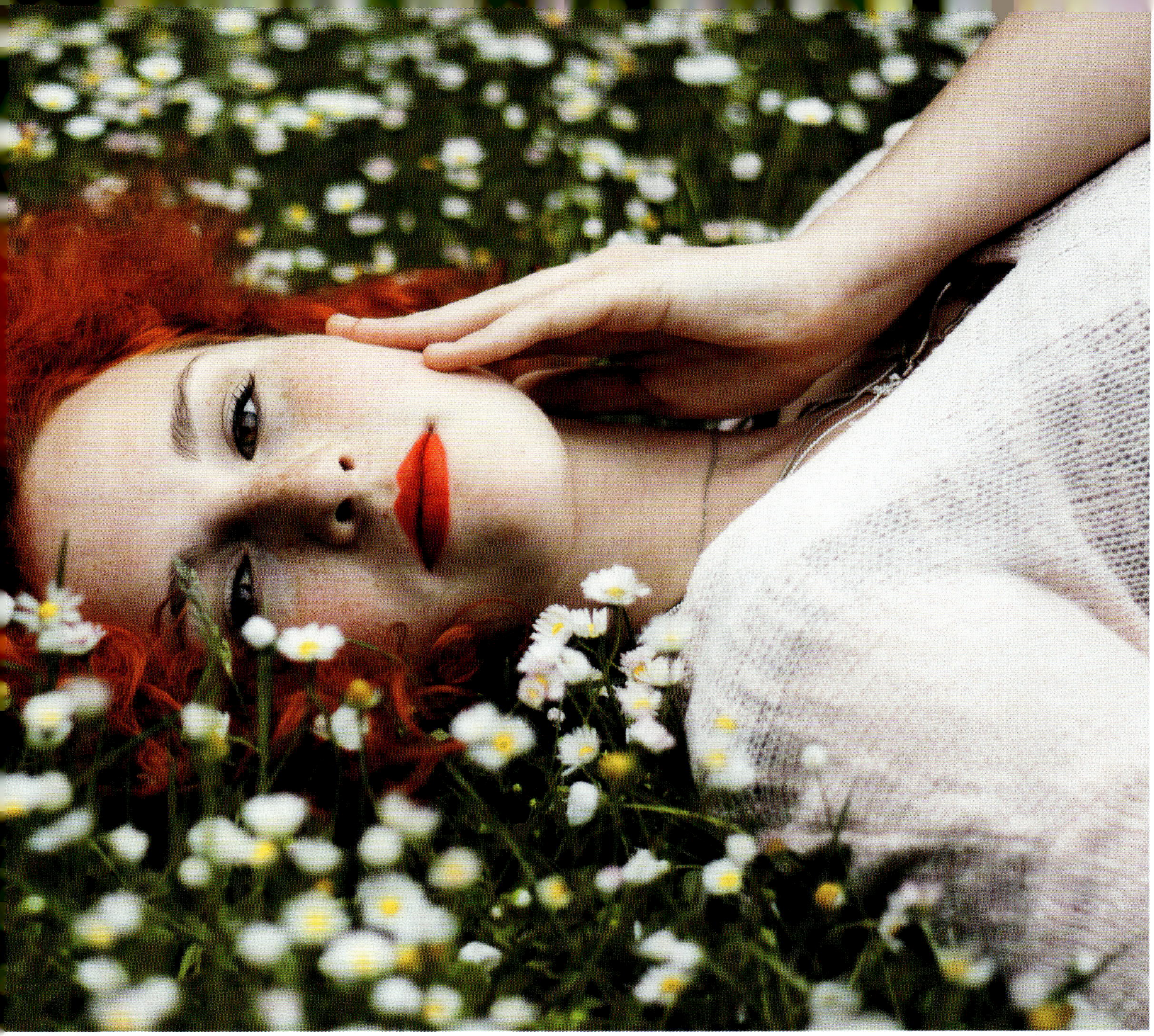

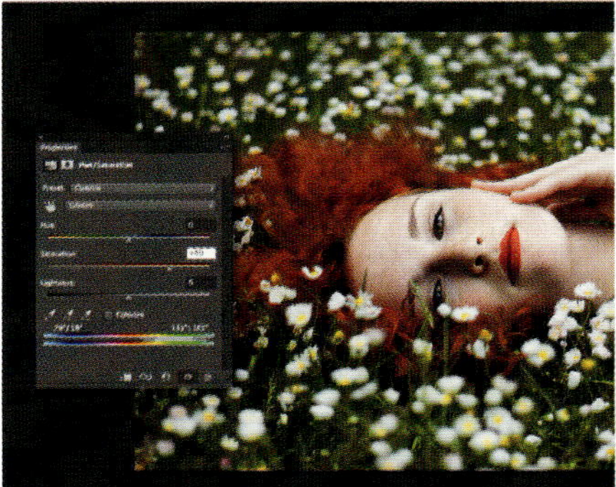

4 DON'T GO TOO FAR Keep going until you include areas that you don't want to affect, in this case the skin and hair, and then slide back the other way to exclude them. Next, reset the *Hue* and *Saturation* sliders to *+0* before gradually increasing *Saturation* until you're happy with the effect.

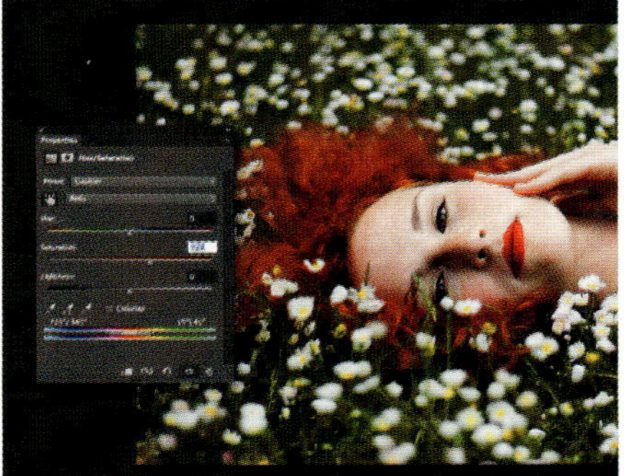

5 TARGET A COLOUR If you're not sure which colour channel to select, an alternative method is to use the *Targeted Adjustment Tool*. Click on the hand icon at the top of the Adjustment palette, then click and hold the colour on your image and drag left or right to adjust the saturation of that colour.

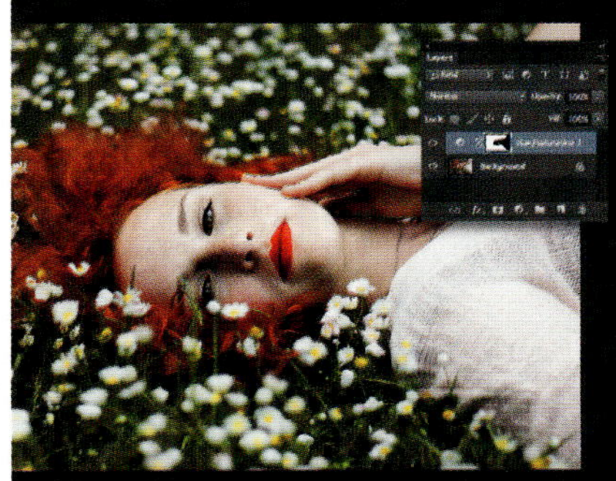

6 MASK THE LAYER This has also affected our subject's skin tone, but this is easily fixed using a Layer Mask. In the Layers palette, click on the *Layer Mask* thumbnail and then select the *Brush Tool*. Choose a soft-edged brush and, with your *Foreground Color* set to *Black*, brush over the area you want to mask.

Add snow to your portraits

You've shot a wonderful wintery portrait, but it's missing one key component: here's how you add a touch of snowy magic...

WHO DOESN'T LOVE a spot of snow? The joy of throwing back the curtains in the morning to be greeted by a winter wonderland is something that resonates with almost everybody, no matter their age.

Shooting during a snow flurry presents fantastic opportunities for dream-like images. Unfortunately, chances for optimum conditions are seemingly few and far between and despite every winter being heralded as the coldest for 100 years, snow rarely materialises. Photographing a winter-themed portrait is simple, but adding a magical element in Photoshop with custom brushes can make it really special.

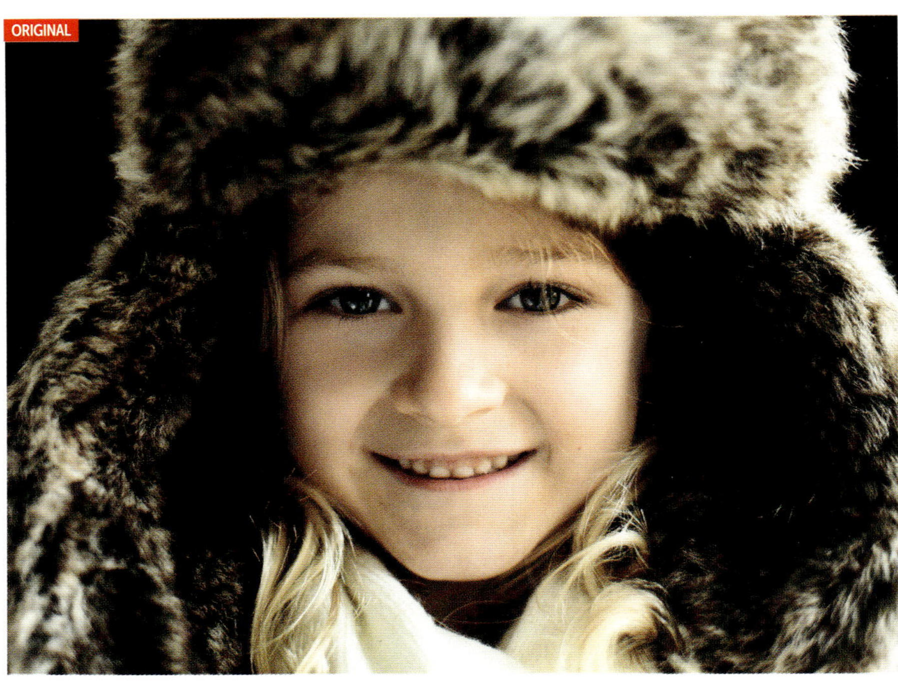

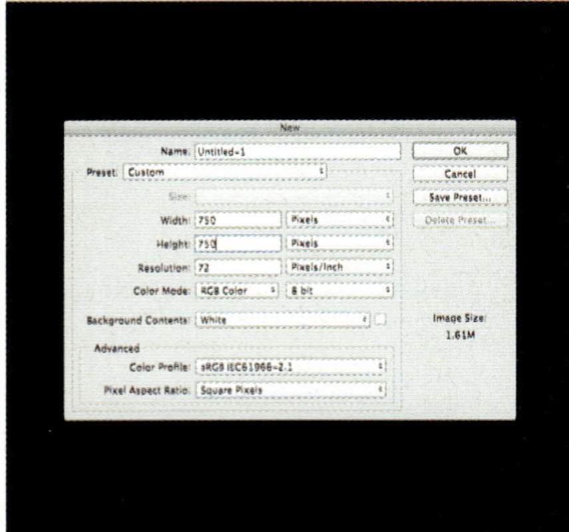

1 OPEN A BLANK DOCUMENT Open a new document by pressing ***cmd + N*** (Mac) or ***ctrl + N*** (PC). Set both the document ***Height*** and ***Width*** to ***750px***, ensure ***Background Contents*** is set to ***White*** and press ***OK***. Select the ***Brush Tool*** and choose a round brush and ***Black*** as your ***Foreground Color***. Set the brush to ***100% Hardness***.

2 CREATE THE CUSTOM BRUSH Adjust your brush ***Size*** and create two dots, one big, one small, in opposite corners, as shown. Then, go to ***Edit>Define Brush Preset*** and give your preset a name. Close this image without saving and open your final image. Go to ***Window>Brush*** to open the Brush palette.

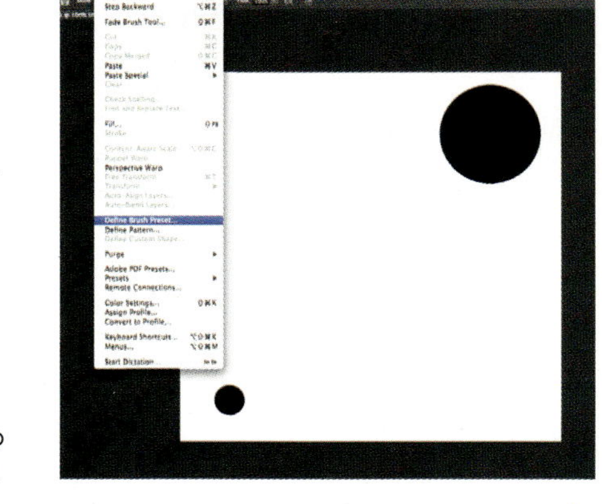

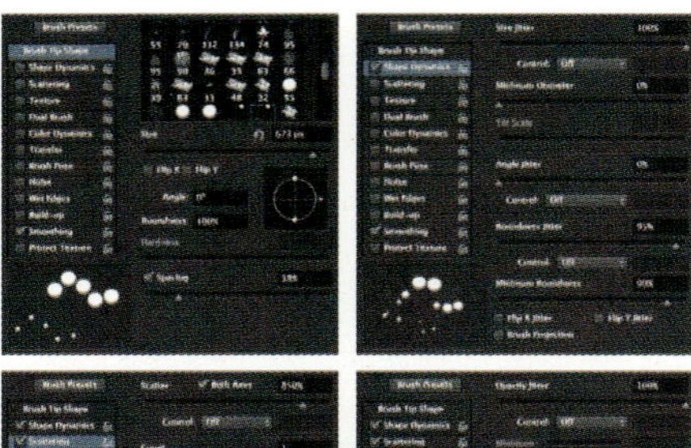

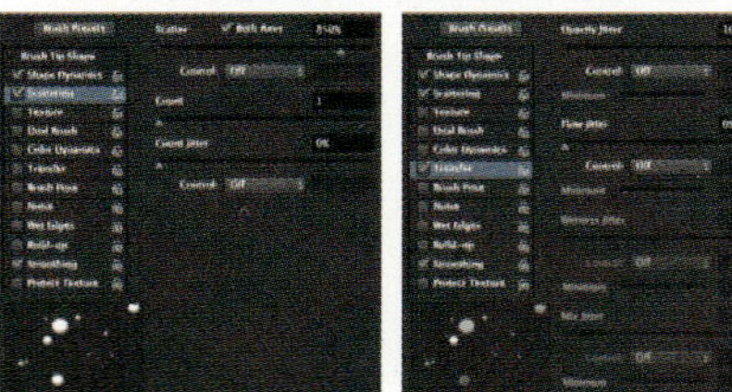

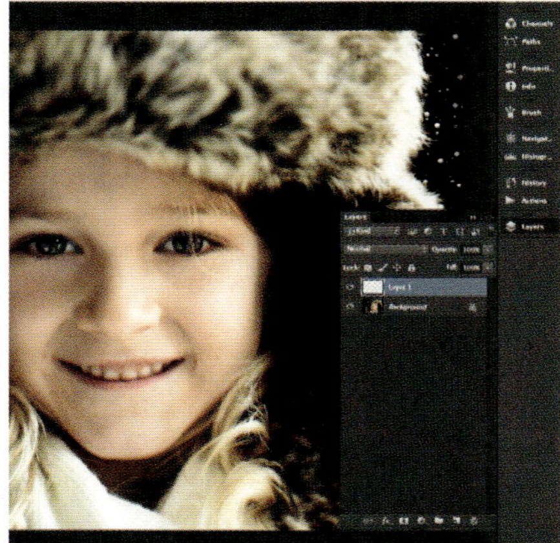

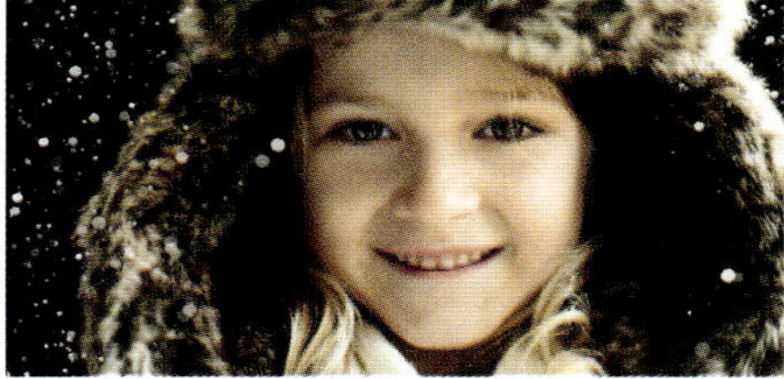

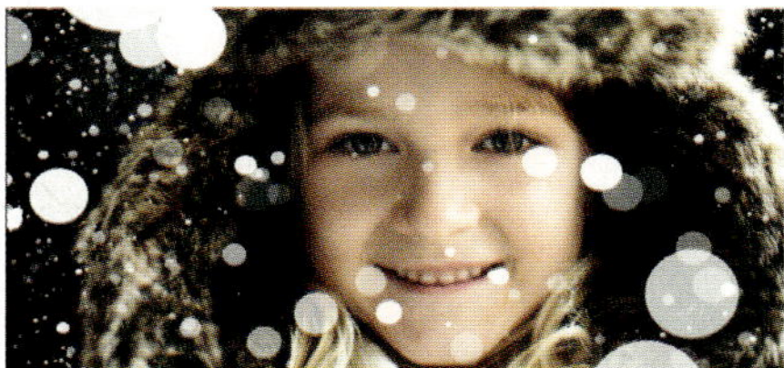

3 SET THE BRUSH FLOW Find your snow brush in the palette and select it. Under the ***Brush Tip Shape*** tab, set the ***Spacing*** slider to ***30-40%***. Click on ***Shape Dynamics*** and set the ***Size Jitter*** to ***100%***, ***Roundness Jitter*** to ***95%*** and ***Minimum Roundness*** to ***90%***. Under ***Scattering***, set ***Scatter*** to around ***850%***, and tick ***Both Axis***. Finally, click ***Transfer*** and set ***Opacity Jitter*** to ***100%***.

4 ADD LAYERS We're going to be adding the snow in layers for added realism. Press ***Shift, cmd + N*** (Mac) or ***Shift, ctrl + N*** (PC) to create a new layer. Set your ***Foreground Color*** to ***White*** and choose a small brush size. Click and paint around the background of your image to add the snow behind your subject. This is the snow that's furthest away, so should be the smallest flakes.

5 REPEAT THE PROCESS Create another new layer, as before, and increase the brush size before painting in the background again, overlapping your subject slightly. Repeat this process two or three more times until you have created several layers of snow, increasing the snow flakes in size for each layer. Paint a few closer flakes in front of your subject too for realism.

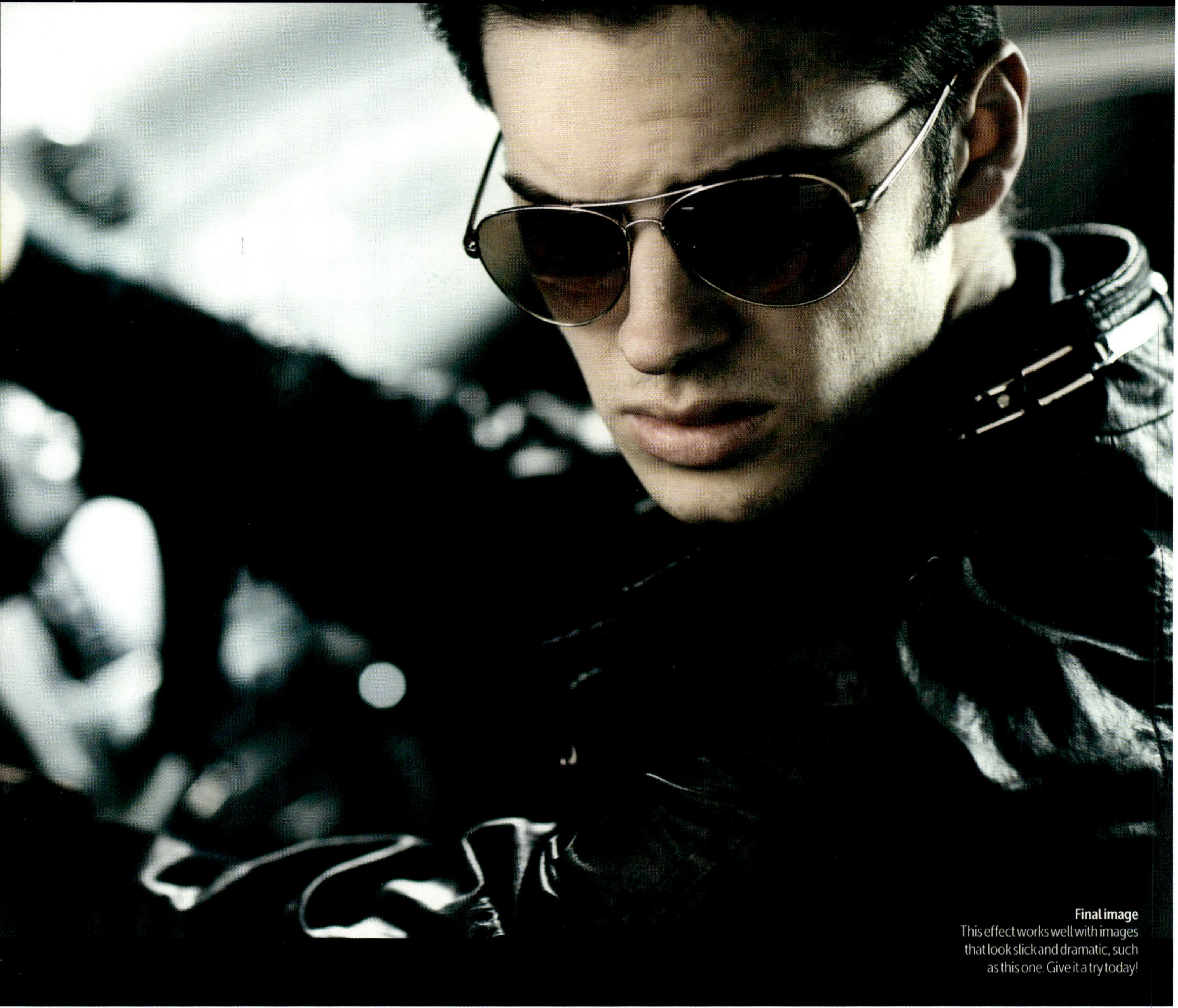

Final image
This effect works well with images that look slick and dramatic, such as this one. Give it a try today!

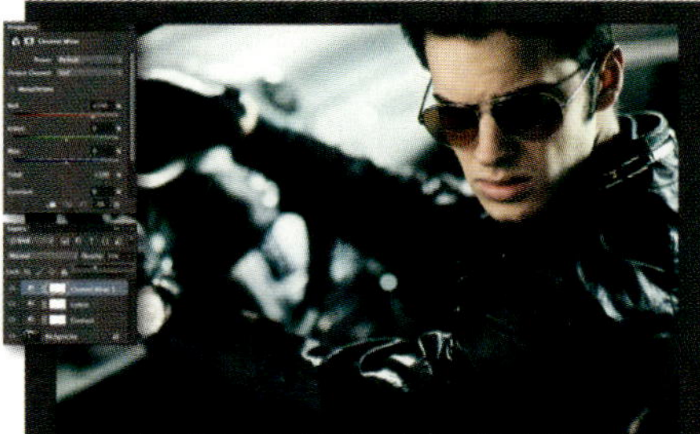

4 ASSESS CHANGES By clicking on the eye icon next to the Colour layer in the Layers palette you can turn that layer's visibility on and off to assess the effect – tweak the Curves graph if required. Once happy, add another Adjustment layer, this time selecting *Channel Mixer*. Set this layer's *Opacity* to around *35%* – this controls the saturation and contrast of our image.

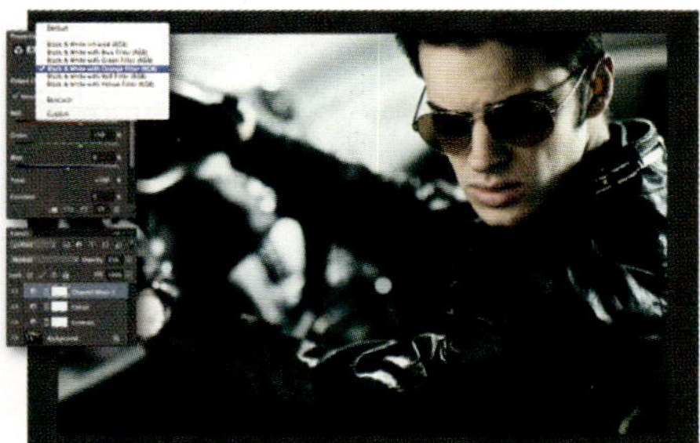

5 DESATURATE COLOURS In the Adjustments palette, use the *Preset* menu to choose a suitable effect for your image. We've found that the Orange, Red and Yellow filter presets tend to work best. These filters will desaturate your image and add contrast – the effect can then be easily adjusted using the sliders below, or by increasing or decreasing the *Opacity* of the layer in the Layers palette.

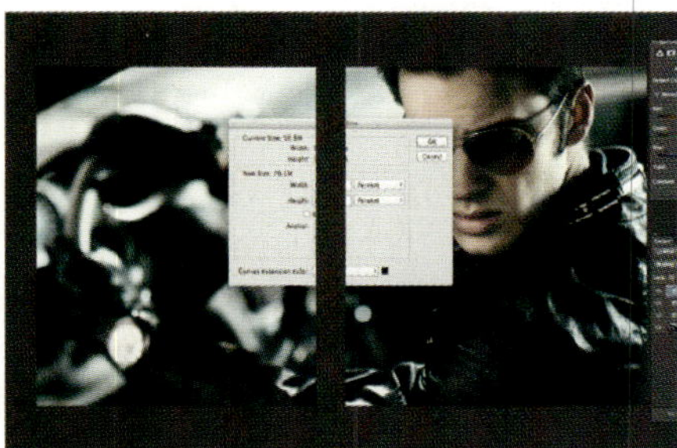

6 CROP AND FRAME A final step to give your image that movie feel is to crop it into a different ratio and add a matte. Use the *Crop Tool* and apply a *16:9* (widescreen) or *2.35:1* (cinema) crop using the top menu bar. Once done, go to *Image>Canvas Size*, change the unit of measurement to *Percent* and set the *Height* to *125*. Change the *Canvas extension colour* to *Black* and click *OK*. The End!

Backdrop colour shift

Fancy a change of scenery? Read on to find out how you can add a subtle tint to a seamless portrait backdrop using Adobe Photoshop...

SEAMLESS PAPER BACKGROUNDS don't come cheap, and are cumbersome too, so keeping a stock of different hues to change them mid-shoot isn't practical. Thankfully, with a little Photoshop trickery you can conduct subtle colour shifts, allowing you to create shoots with more variety, by warming up or cooling down the 'feel of a shoot, or to tweak the aesthetic of your backdrop to suit your subject.

Often adding a hint of colour to a background can completely change the 'feel' of an image. The most pleasing shifts in hue often occur when you warm up or cool down a backdrop by subtly shifting it towards yellow or blue, respectively. That's not to say more adventurous and exaggerated adjustments will not work – experiment with it; the changes are nondestructive and easily adjusted at any time using this technique. It won't work for every colour backdrop, though. A mid-grey seamless offers the most scope for change, as it can be easily lightened, darkened and tinted. A white or black backdrop won't adjust as well, but slight shifts in colour are still entirely possible.

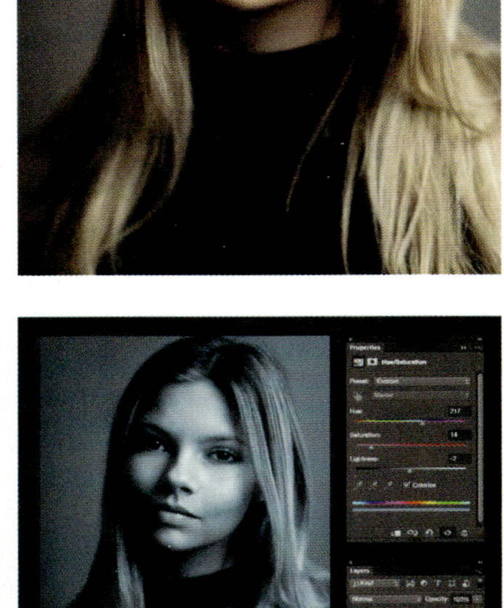

ORIGINAL

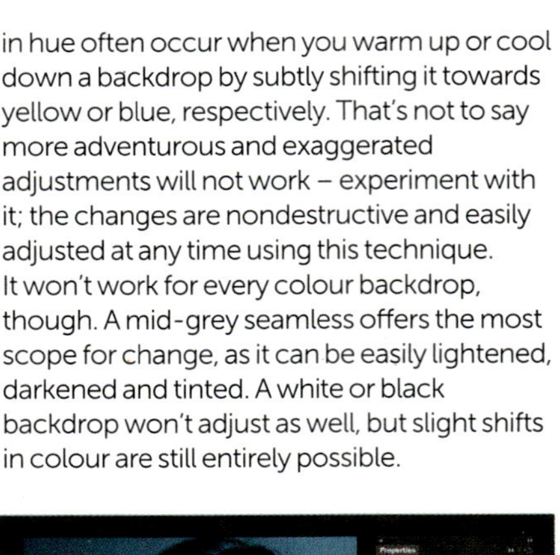

1 TIDY UP FIRST Before you start, carry out any retouching to your image. As we aren't swapping the backdrop, simply tinting it, any existing creases or marks will show through the tint. Then, in the Layers palette, click on the *Add new fill or adjustment layer* button and select *Hue/Saturation*.

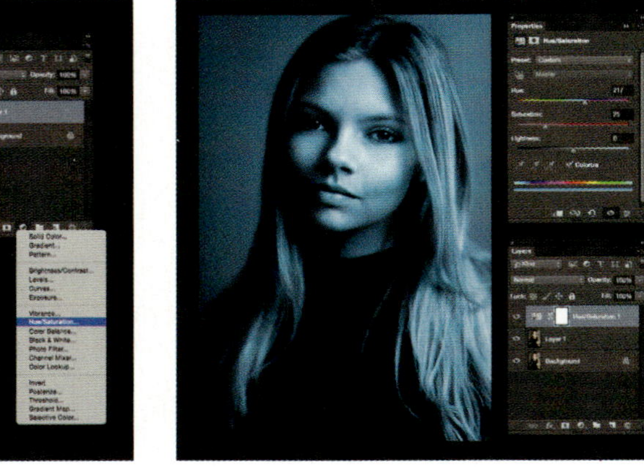

2 ADD THE COLOUR The Hue/Saturation adjustments palette will appear. At the bottom of the palette, click on *Colorize*, which will tint the image. It won't look right straight away and the entire image will be tinted, but we're going to address that momentarily. Start by using the *Hue* slider to choose your tint.

3 FINE TUNE Next, use the *Saturation* and *Lightness* sliders to adjust your ideal background colour. Refrain from pushing the parameters too far or the image will quickly look odd and unnatural. It's tricky to judge at this stage whether you've gone too far, but we'll come back and adjust it again later.

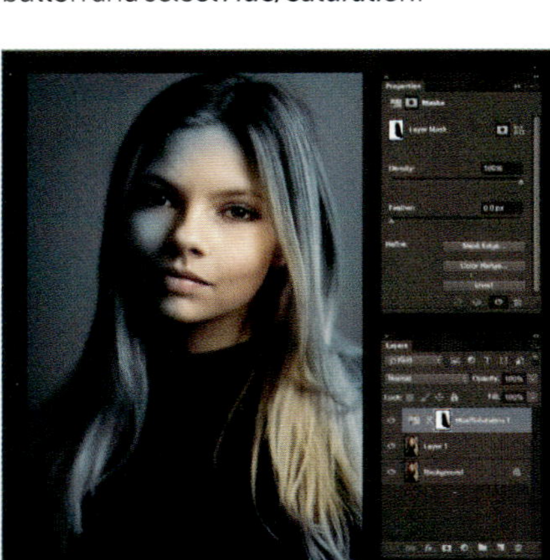

4 MASK YOUR SUBJECT Back in the Layers palette, click on the *Layer Mask* thumbnail on the Hue/Saturation layer to activate the Layer Mask. Select the *Brush Tool* and *Black* as your *Foreground Color*. Using a soft-edged brush at full opacity, carefully brush over your subject to remove the tint.

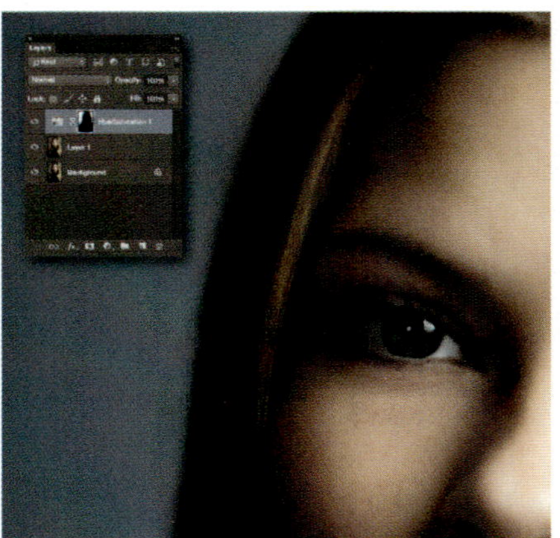

5 TAKE CARE AT THE EDGES Around the edges of your subject it may be useful to use a smaller brush and zoom in. Lowering the brush's Opacity in the top menu bar can help hide the edge of the mask too. If you go too far, simply change the *Foreground Color* to *White* and carefully brush back over.

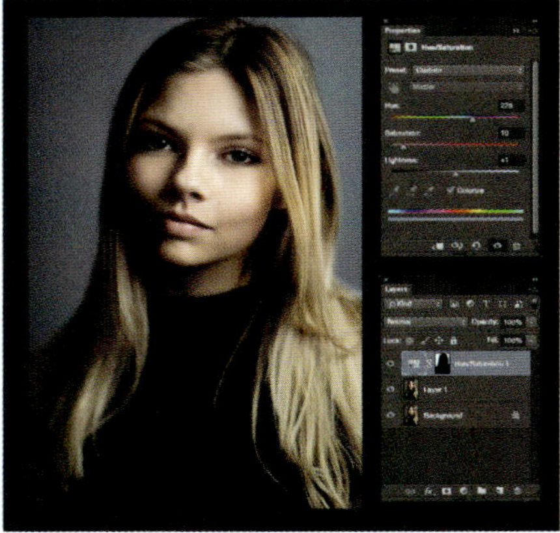

6 FINAL ADJUSTMENTS With your subject masked, head back to the Adjustments palette to make final tweaks to the background colour. Our initial colour choice is too strong, but reducing the Saturation looks more natural. Often you'll only need around *+10 Saturation* to make a difference.

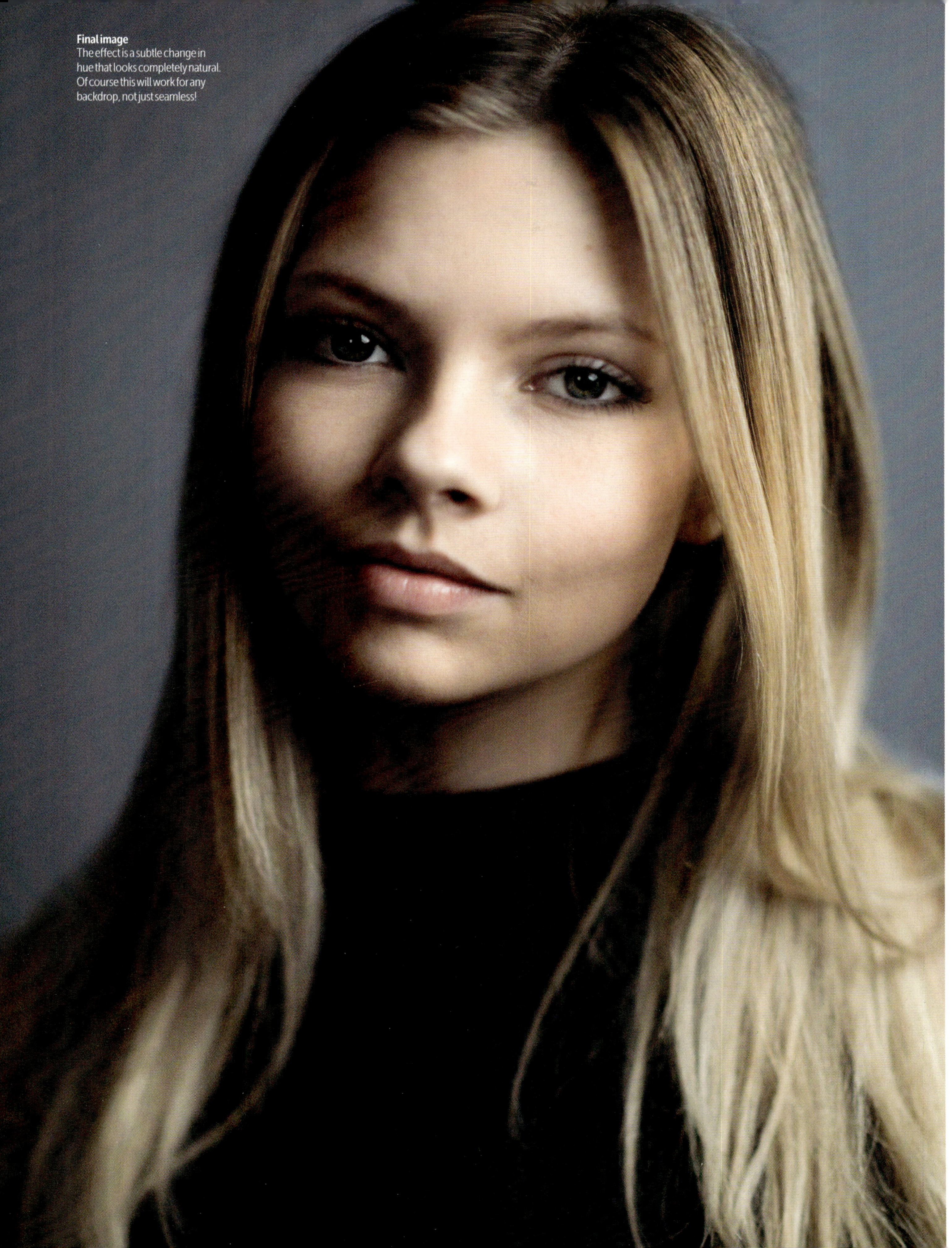

Final image
The effect is a subtle change in hue that looks completely natural. Of course this will work for any backdrop, not just seamless!

Retouching eyes

The eyes are often the point of focus for most portraits. Bring them to life with a few selective adjustments in Adobe Photoshop

THE EYES ARE the windows into the soul, so we think they deserve some extra time and attention when editing your portraits. The eyes are the primary point of focus for anyone viewing a portrait – we are drawn to eyes first and foremost – this is why it's so important to ensure that when you capture your portrait, your focusing is spot-on and the eyes are pin-sharp. Retouching eyes is not just a case of bumping up the exposure – tastes vary from person to person, but the general idea is for your subject's eyes to be bright and crisp, without them appearing to glow in the dark!

Eyes are a lot more receptive to what we'll call 'exaggerated' editing than the rest of the face. Significant increases in saturation, contrast and exposure, applied carefully, can enhance them, whereas similar adjustments would push more delicate features, such as skin, into the realms of bad taste. This makes selective adjustments, such as dodging and burning, and Layer Masks the perfect tools to boost your subject's gaze.

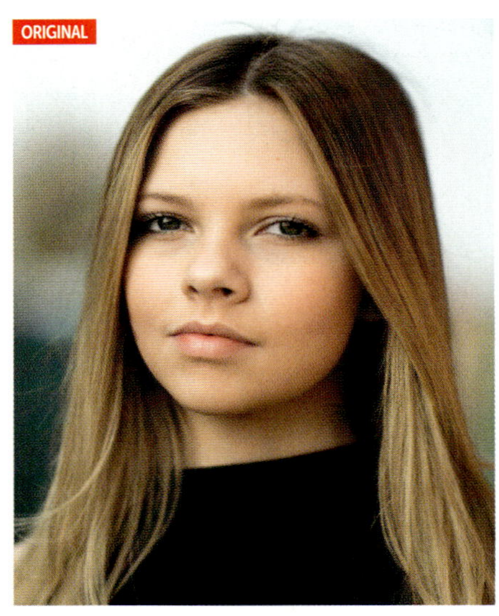
ORIGINAL

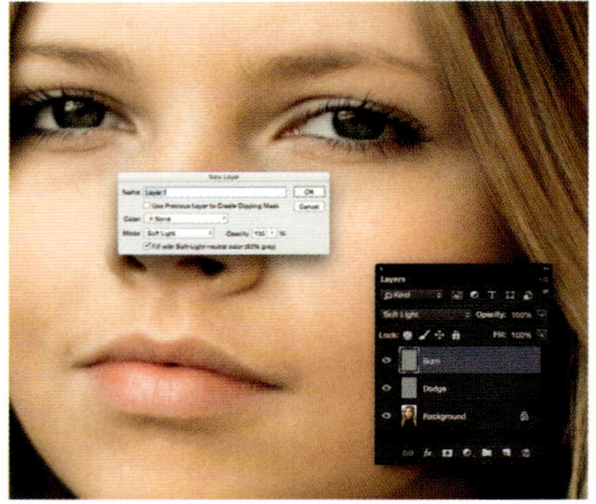

1 CREATE NEW LAYERS Create a new layer by pressing *shift, cmd + N* (Mac) or *shift, ctrl + N* (PC). In the menu that opens, set the *Mode* of your new layer to *Soft Light* and check the box to *Fill with Soft-Light-neutral color (50% gray)* before clicking *OK*. Then press *cmd + J* (Mac) or *ctrl + J* (PC) to duplicate this layer. Rename one of your new layers 'Dodge' and the other 'Burn'.

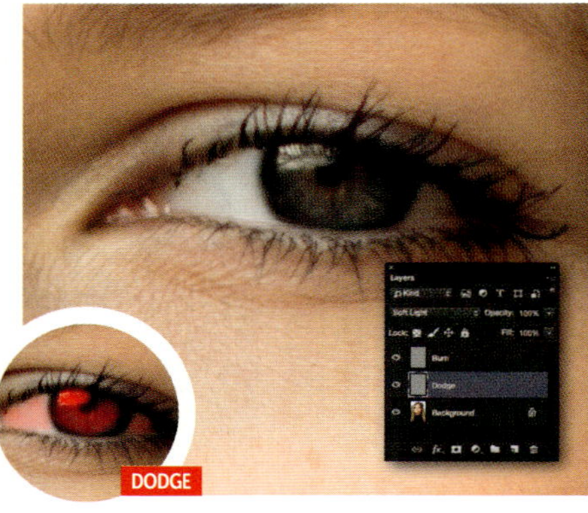
DODGE

2 LIGHTEN THE EYES With your Dodge layer active, select the *Dodge Tool*. In the top bar set *Range* to *Midtones* and *Exposure* to *18%*. *Brush Hardness* should be *0%* and with a brush *Size* that allows you to easily work on the eyes. Zoom in and brush over the whites of the eyes, the iris (the coloured part) and any catchlights in the pupils. We've marked the areas to dodge in red, above.

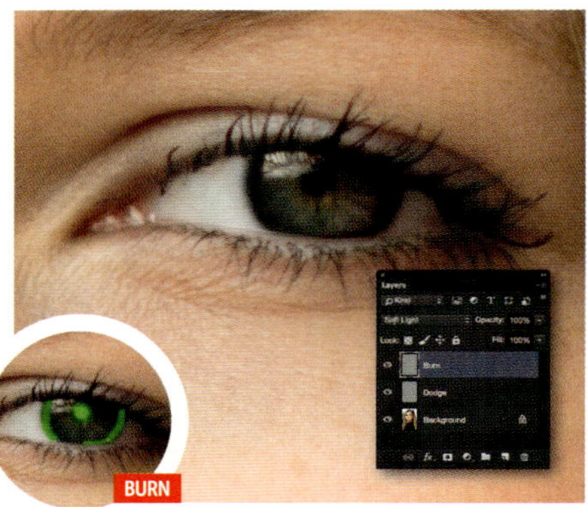
BURN

3 DARKEN THE PUPILS Make the Burn layer active and select the *Burn Tool* – it's in the same group as the Dodge Tool. Set the *Range* to *Midtones* and *Exposure* to *18%*, as before. Use a small brush and darken the pupils. Then, use a smaller brush to burn around the outer edge of the iris – this adds contrast and makes the iris appear three-dimensional. We've marked the areas to burn in green, above.

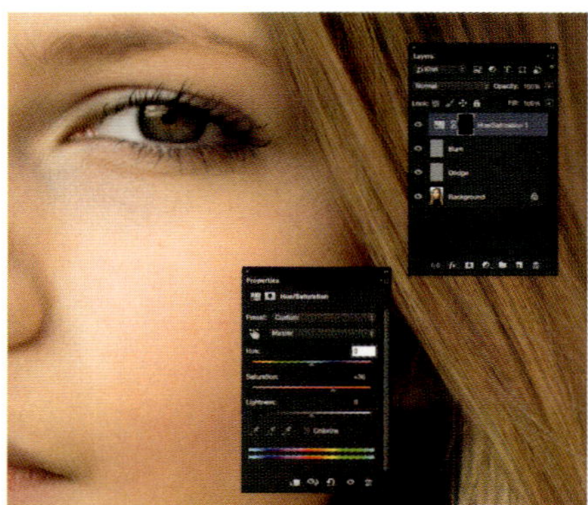

4 BOOST COLOUR Go to *Layer>New Adjustment Layer>Hue/Saturation*. In the Adjustments palette, increase *Saturation*, concentrating on the effect it has on the eyes – ignore the rest of the image for now. Then go to *Image>Adjustments>Invert* to invert the layer mask – this hides the effect. Use the *Brush Tool* with *White* as your *Foreground Color* to brush the colour back into the iris.

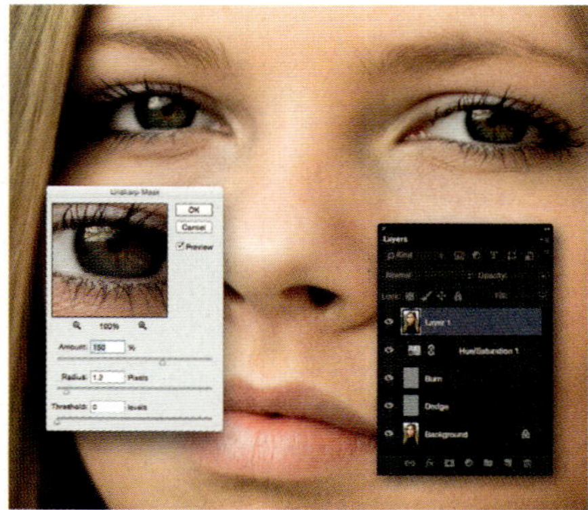

5 SHARPENING In the Layers palette select the top layer, hold down the *alt* key and go to *Layer>Merge Visible*. Then, go to *Filter>Sharpen>Unsharp Mask*. Set the *Amount* to *150%* and *Radius* to *1.2*. Then, go to *Layer>Layer Mask>Hide All* and again, use a soft brush with *White* as your colour to brush around the iris. If you overcook it, reduce this layer's *Opacity* in the Layers palette.

Top Tip: Lightroom users

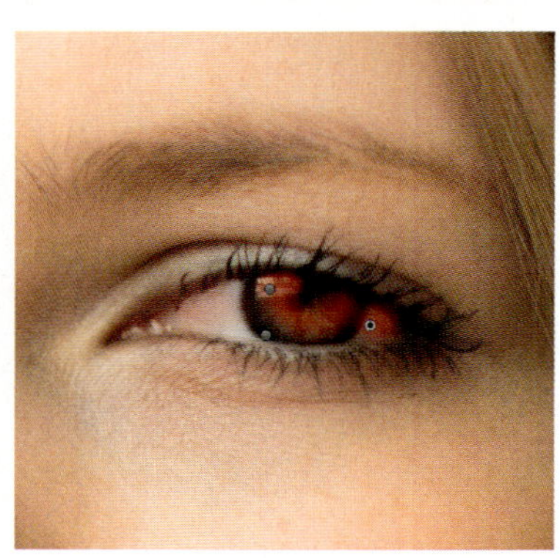

You can make the exact same adjustments in Adobe Lightroom, too – it's even easier in fact. Use the Adjustment Brush coupled with the Exposure, Contrast, Saturation and Clarity sliders to apply the steps above and add extra punch to portraits.

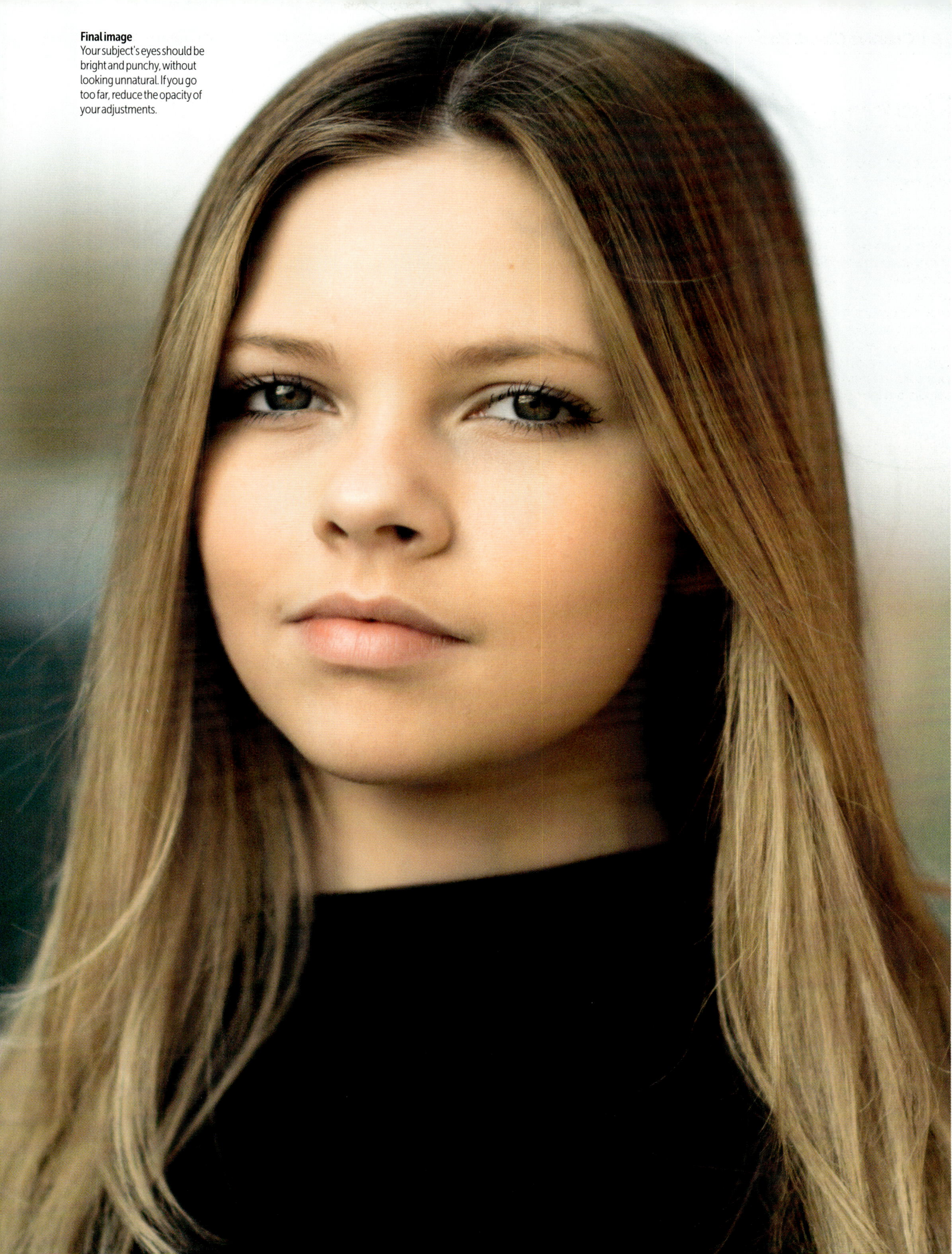

Final image
Your subject's eyes should be bright and punchy, without looking unnatural. If you go too far, reduce the opacity of your adjustments.

ORIGINAL

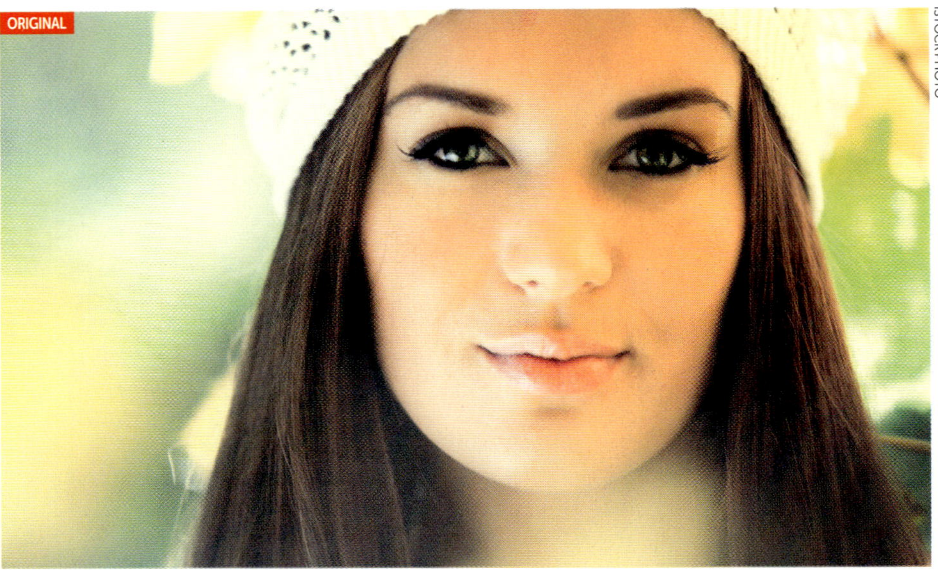

ISTOCK PHOTO

The smart way to sharpen

It's easy to get wrong: the slightest under- or over-sharpening can be detrimental to image quality. Here's how to do it properly...

EVERY IMAGE NEEDS sharpening – even JPEGs that have already been sharpened in-camera – but how do you do it and, more importantly, what's the best way to approach it? There are many, many ways, which is why it's probably the most complex and avoided part of post-production, as it's easier to get wrong than it is right. You have to think of your type of image: what level of sharpening has already been applied in-camera? Do some areas need sharpening more than others? And what's your output going to be? You don't need to sharpen half as much for a low-res web file as you will for a high-resolution print.

With so much to consider, not to mention the many ways to execute the treatment, I'm going to make it very easy for you: use Smart Sharpen, and if your version of Photoshop doesn't have it, use Unsharp Mask (both accessible via Filter>Sharpen). Unsharp Mask has been the preferred method for years, but Smart Sharpen offers more control and better results, due to being able to address specific types of blur and to isolate shadows and highlights. Whichever method of sharpening you opt for, however, we advocate re-editable Smart Filters. Like an Adjustment Layer, converting your image layers to a smart object via Smart Filter will allow you to adjust any sharpening at any stage of editing. Otherwise, when you apply any effect from the Filter menu, it directly affects the image pixels and it's much more complicated to reverse the effects. I've used a portrait for this technique, as it's a good example of when you often need to selectively sharpen to draw the detail out in the features, as opposed to globally which will also alter the smoothness of the skin.

The dialogue box has two options: Basic and Advanced. Start with Basic and use Advanced to reduce any artefacts in the shadows or highlights. While Unsharp Mask targets Gaussian blur, Smart Sharpen targets Lens Blur, too; a more common type of blur in images. By reducing lens blur, you can reduce halos and reveal finer details.

Final image
Just the right amount of sharpening will enhance your shots and give them star quality.

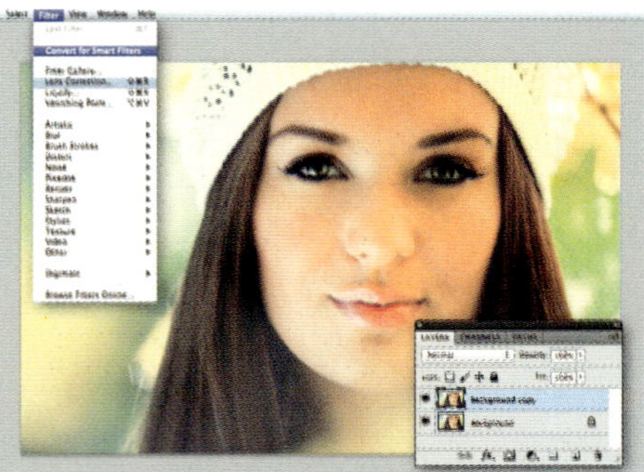

1 Duplicate your image layer Go to *Layer>Duplicate Layer*, click on the new image layer and go to *Filter>Convert to Smart Filters*. Click *OK* if a dialogue box appears. The top layer in your Layers palette should now be a smart object, identifiable by an icon in the bottom right of the layer's image: double-click on the layer to re-edit any filters that you apply at any point in editing.

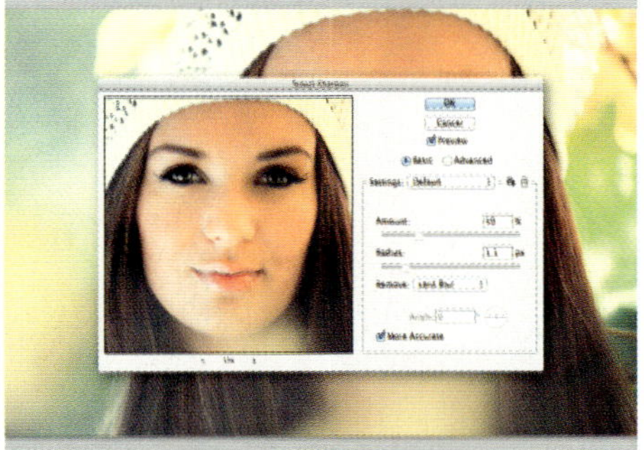

2 Add Smart Sharpen filter With the Smart Filter layer selected, go to *Filter>Sharpen>Smart Sharpen*. Click on the *Remove* drop-down menu to select *Lens Blur* and check *More Accurate* as this will help you target only the areas that need sharpening. Generally, for best results, try to keep the *Radius* within *2px* and adjust the *Amount* slider to between *50-100%*.

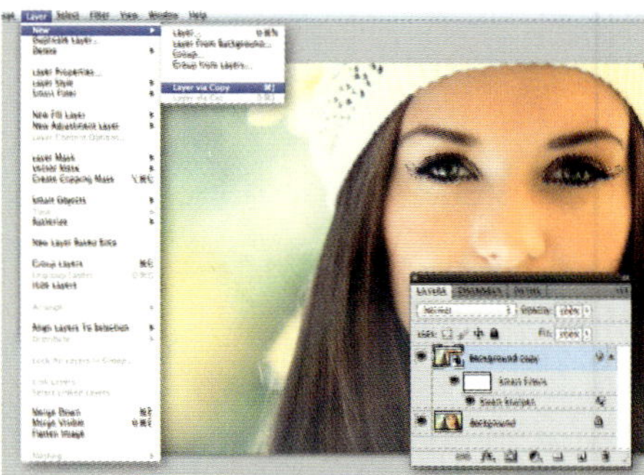

3 Selectively sharpen On some images, you may need to sharpen some areas more than others. A portrait, for instance, usually needs crisp features but soft skin – unless you want every line, pore and wrinkle visible. With the image layer selected, use the *Quick Selection Tool* to draw around the area you want to target – in this case the eyes – then go to *Layer>New>Layer via Copy*.

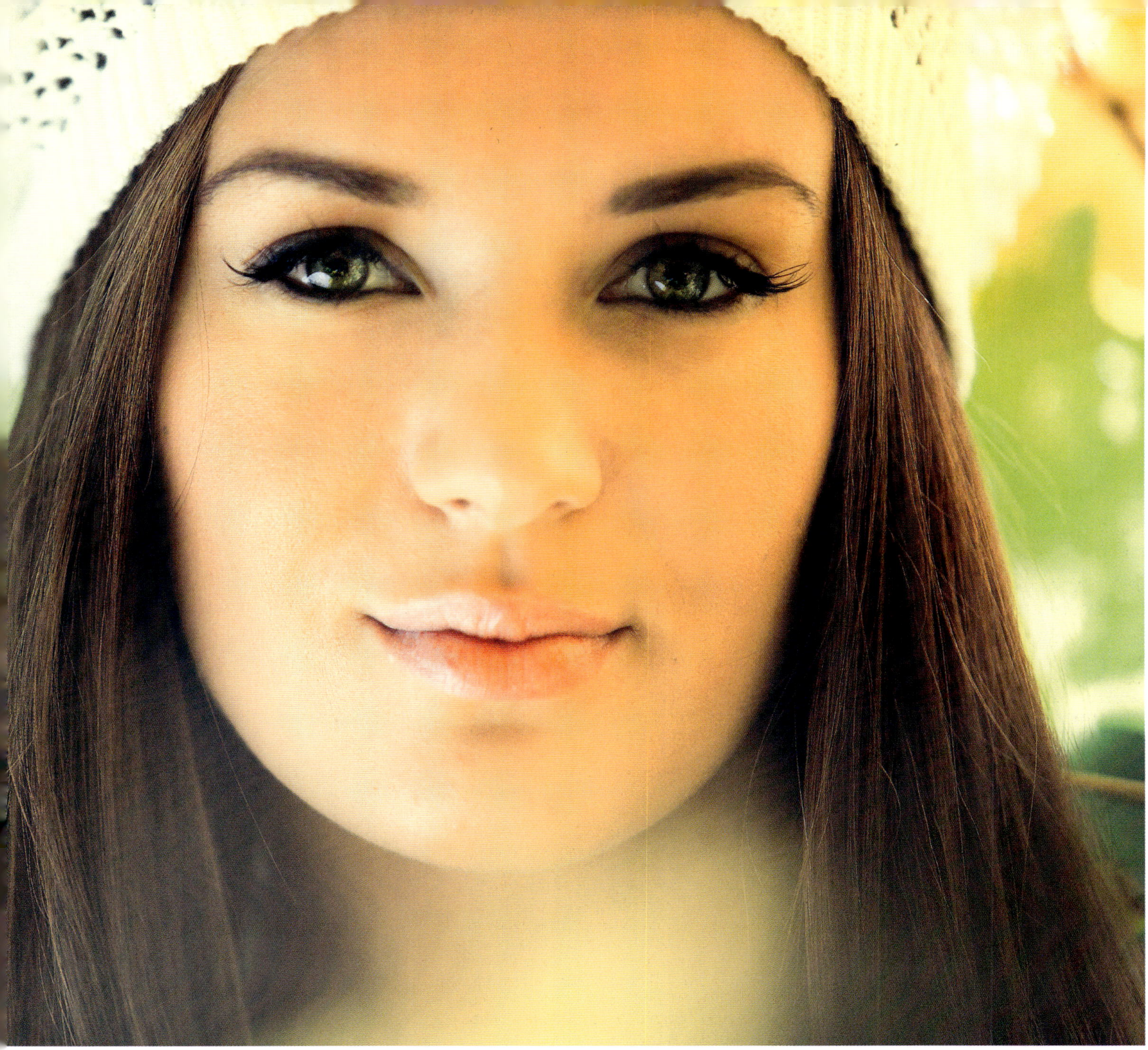

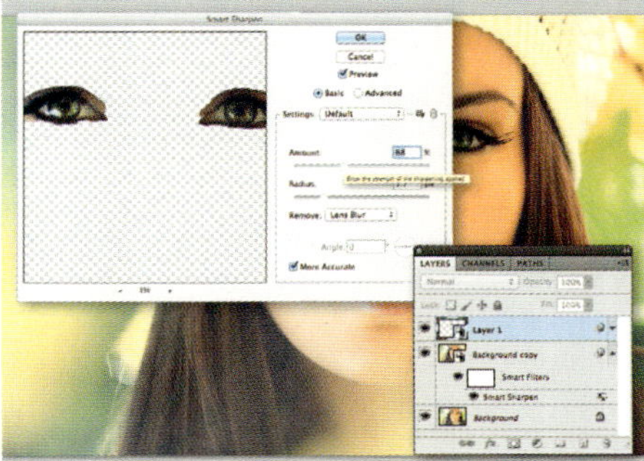

4 Make adjustments Convert the new layer to a Smart Filter as in step one, and again apply the *Smart Sharpen* filter as in step two. We increased the Radius to 2px and the Amount. Once you're happy, click *OK*. Enlarge the preview by clicking on the small *+* to see the effects better and to look for artefacts. To compare the sharpening to the original pixels, click and hold on the preview image.

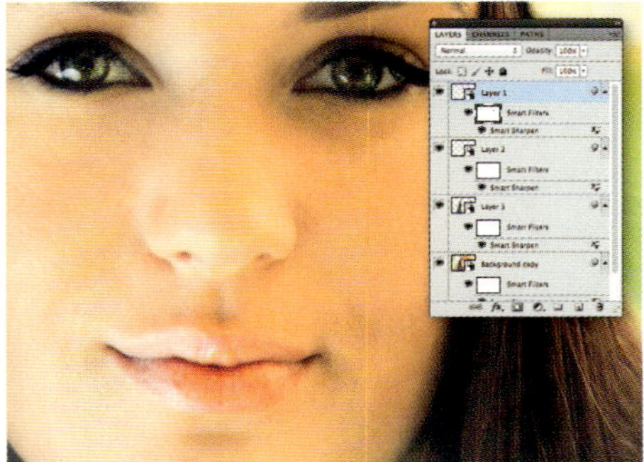

5 Refine the sharpening You can repeat these steps as many times as you want to target different areas of the image that need different amounts of sharpening. If you want to edit any sharpening in the selections, you can do it two ways: either by double-clicking on the Smart Filter or using the attached Layer Mask and Black paint to hide any areas you mistakenly affected.

Common errors

OVER-SHARPENING

It's easy to over-sharpen an image once you notice the details it's revealing, but sometimes you can do more harm than good if you don't recognise the telltale signs of destruction. You need to watch that areas of colour or tonal range don't become pixelated, that artefacts (black and white marks) don't appear or halos form around the areas being sharpened – if this happens, pull back on the adjustment; easy to do if you're working with a Smart Filter.

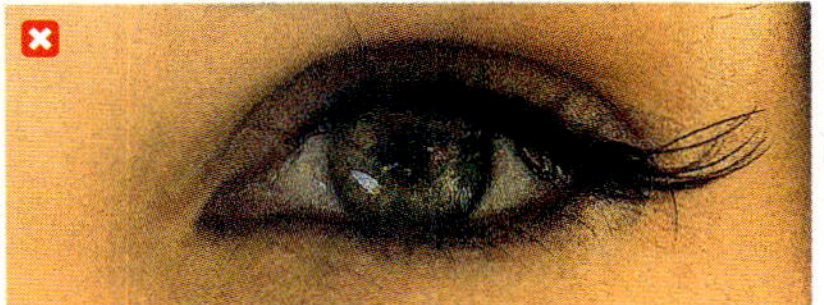

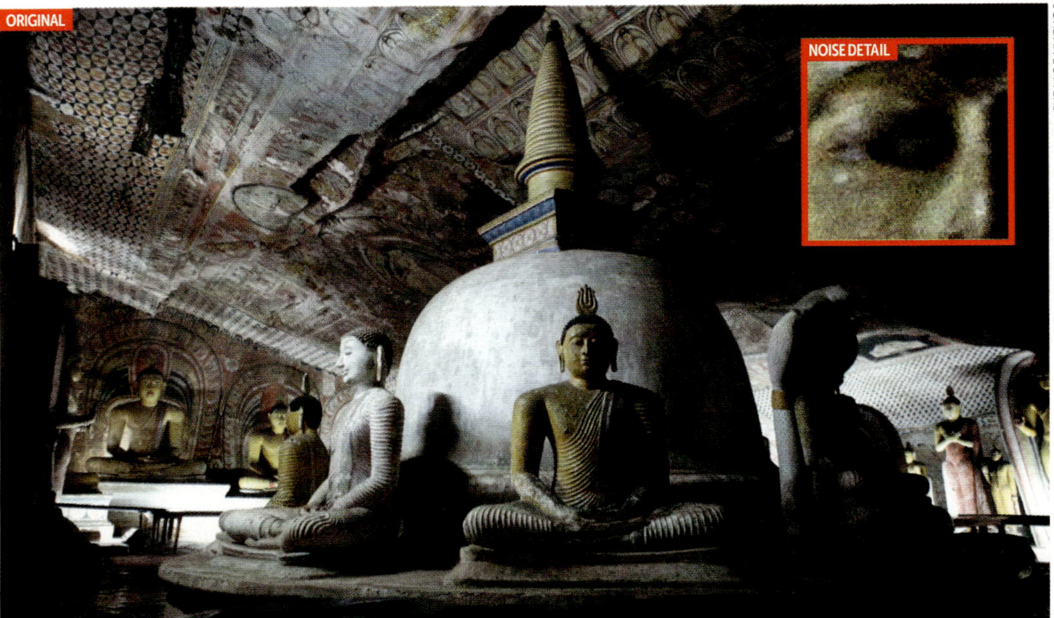

How to reduce noise

Effective noise reduction in Photoshop is fairly simple, but it's easy to go too far. Here's how to get it right

RECENT GENERATIONS OF DSLRs handle noise a lot better than they used to. Shooting at high ISO ratings was previously avoided at all costs unless you wanted to make it look as if you were photographing in a snowstorm. Rarely did you push above ISO 800 unless you absolutely had to. However, thanks to advances in both sensor and processing technology, cranking up the ISO to shoot in low light no longer confines your images to the trash. Of course, using a high ISO isn't the only cause of noise – it can also be affected by long exposures or by over-zealous editing and exposure manipulation.

Photoshop offers excellent controls that allow you to alter the grain in your images. The temptation, though, is to wind the sliders all the way across to eliminate all noise, but it's important to use the controls with restraint. Go too far and you end up reducing image sharpness and losing detail and texture. This is especially noticeable when shooting portraits as excessive noise reduction glazes the skin, making people look like mannequins! When applying noise reduction, compare both the full image and a zoomed-in selection; use the sample area to assess the noise, and the full image to give you an indication of when you've gone too far.

Secrets unlocked

The ***Advanced*** tab within the ***Reduce Noise*** tool is useful if you only have noise on one or two colour channels. First, set the ***Strength*** and ***Reduce Color Noise*** sliders to ***0*** and click on the ***Advanced*** box and the ***Per Channel*** tab. Assess the Red, Green and Blue channels using the grayscale preview to see which channels need noise reduction applying before applying it using the sliders.

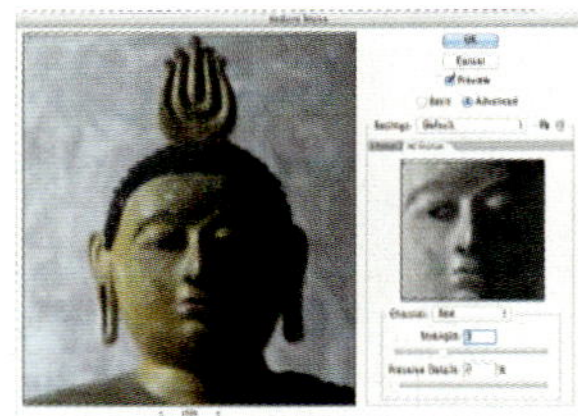

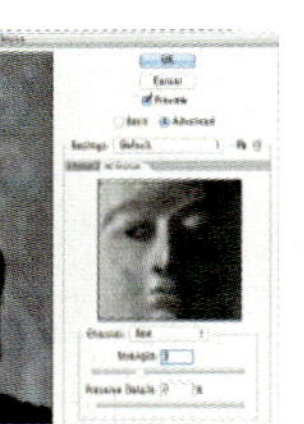

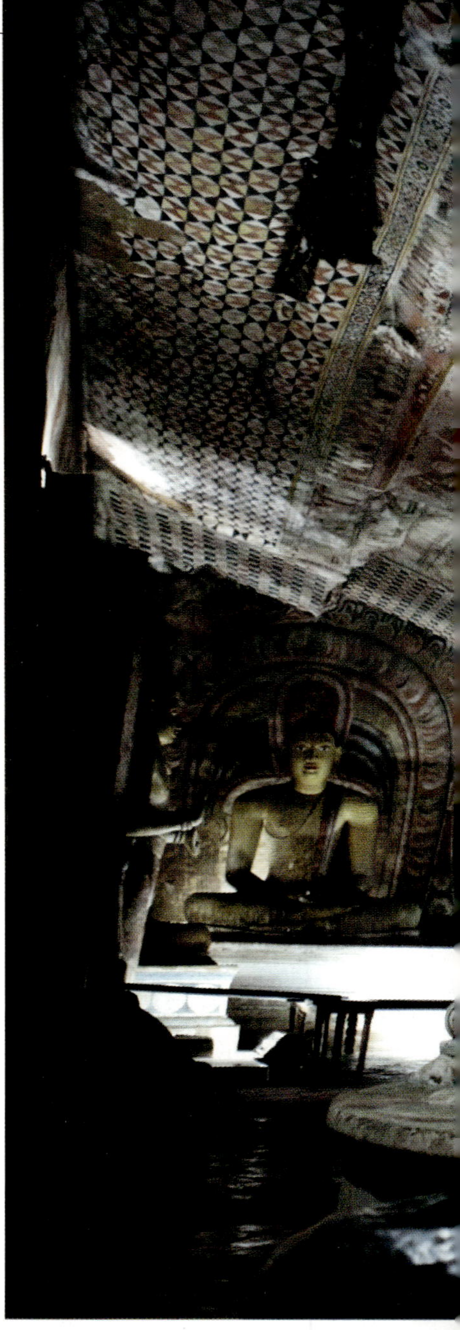

1 Open the image Open your image in Photoshop and go to *Filter>Noise>Reduce Noise*. The Reduce Noise dialogue box will appear, presenting you with a number of parameters to adjust and a 100% zoomed preview window to assess the changes. Click on your main image in the area that you want to preview before making any adjustments.

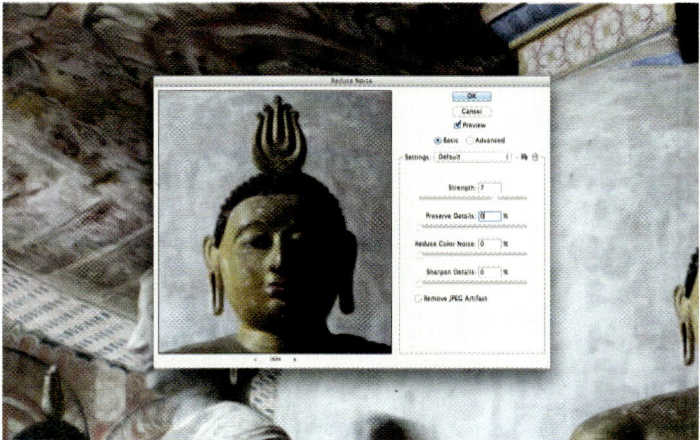

2 Preserve the details By default the Preserve Details slider will be set to 60%. Preserving detail is an important part of noise reduction, but for now move this slider down to ***0%*** as it can also preserve noise too. You should also move the ***Sharpen Details*** slider down to ***0%*** as well, as image sharpening is best done in the final stages of processing.

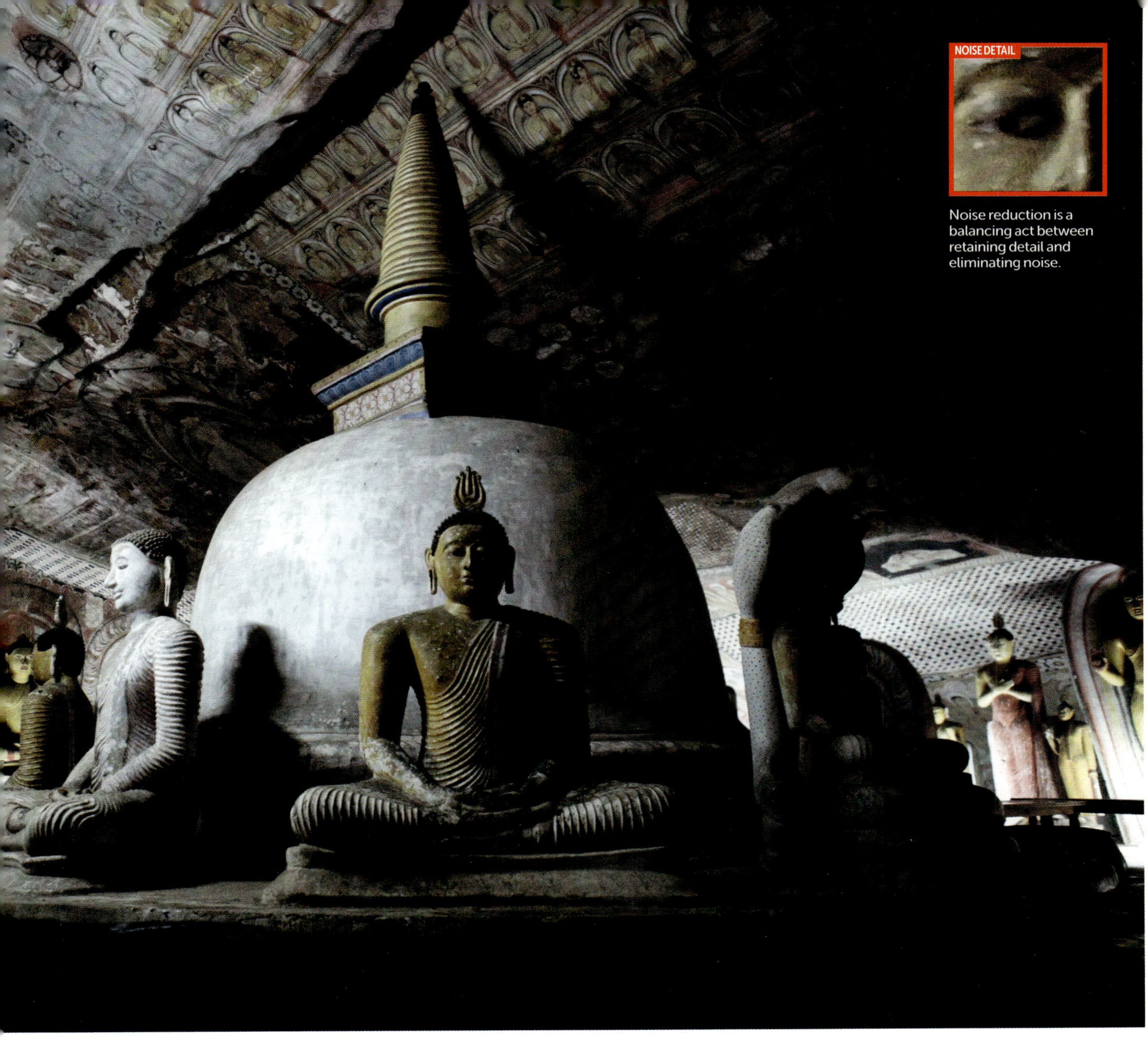

NOISE DETAIL

Noise reduction is a balancing act between retaining detail and eliminating noise.

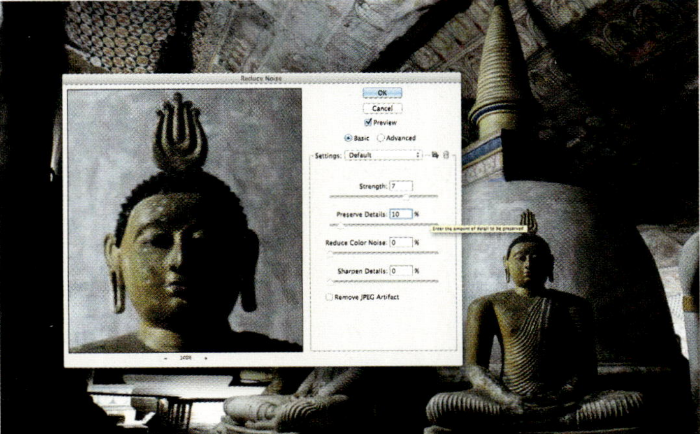

3 Reduce the noise Adjust the ***Strength*** slider to apply noise reduction. Keep a careful eye on the preview window to apply the right amount, being careful not to go too far. Once happy with your selection, start increasing the ***Preserve Details*** slider to bring back lost details, but not going so far that you start to reintroduce the noise.

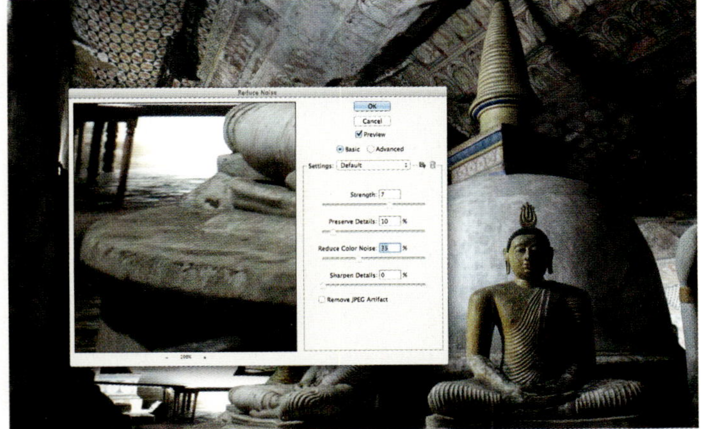

4 Reduce colour noise The ***Reduce Color Noise*** slider can be particularly useful if you have areas of coloured artefacts in your image. As before, use it sparingly as too much colour noise reduction can desaturate your image. Always click on the ***Remove JPEG Artefacts*** checkbox as this can also be used for getting rid of noise caused by JPEG compression.

Breathe life into flat photos

Want to create an HDR effect but don't have Raw files or a set of bracketed exposures? Don't despair! Use Shadows & Highlights...

WE ALL HAVE images that didn't quite render the scene how you remember it. Maybe the sky's not as moody, or the ground is too dark, or maybe the overall appearance of the image lacks contrast or is badly exposed. Well, Shadows & Highlights can resurrect these images. This nifty adjustment is a fantastic photographic tool, which is often overlooked by users since dedicated HDR software like Photomatix and Photoshop actions became available from third-party companies. In the simplest terms, the adjustments allow you to recover detail from over- and underexposed areas by adjusting the Highlights or Shadows controls respectively, or you can improve the overall tonal range using the Midtone Contrast slider. It's really very simple.

The key to success with Shadows & Highlights is subtlety. As with any process that plays with tonal range, HDR included, Shadows & Highlights can produce photographic Frankensteins if used too eagerly. So why not give it a go? The controls may seem daunting at first, but after a little experimentation and with a better understanding of what can be achieved, you may find you'll be using this feature regularly.

Hot key

Alt to reset
When working in Shadows & Highlights, hold down ***alt*** to change the ***Cancel*** button to a ***Reset*** button in case you want to take the filter back to its default settings. You can also uncheck ***Preview*** to toggle between the blurred and original image.

Reset

ORIGINAL

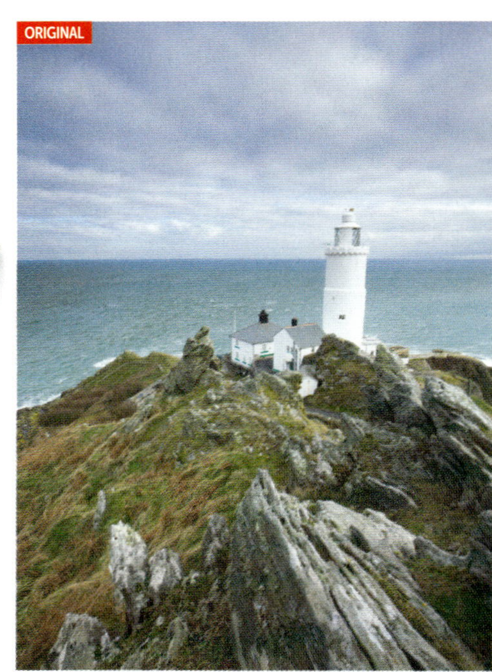

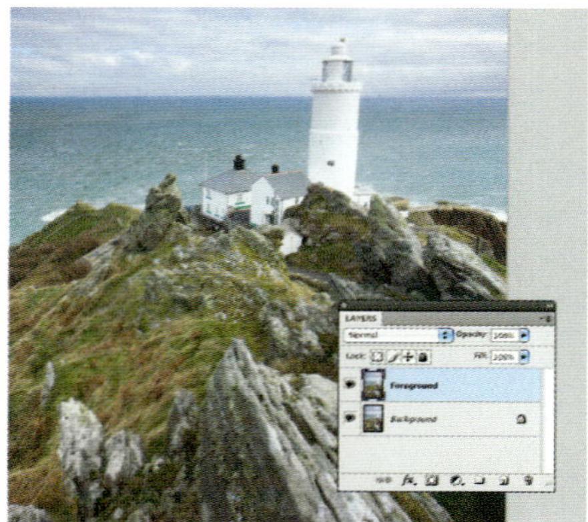

1 Duplicate original Our chosen image is a bit lifeless, yet clearly has potential texture in the sky and detail in the foreground that could be pulled out using Shadows & Highlights. First, create a duplicate layer from the original by going to ***Layer>Duplicate Layer...***, naming the layer accordingly for reference later.

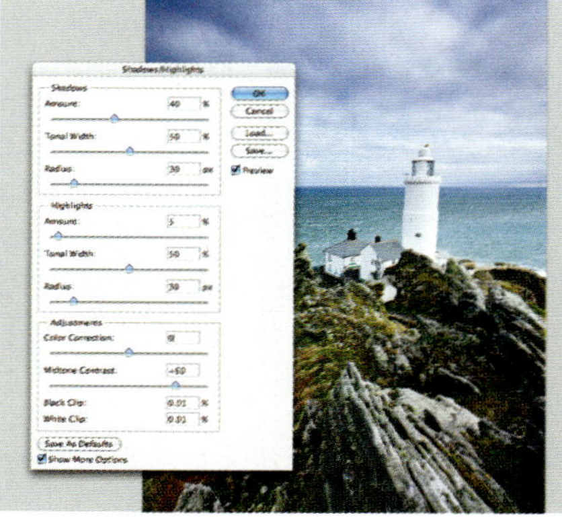

2 Shadows & Highlights On the duplicate layer go to ***Image>Adjustments>Shadows & Highlights...*** As the image is generally flat, concentrate on the ***Shadows*** and ***Midtone Contrast***, with only minor adjustments to the ***Highlight*** field. At this stage you want to be focusing more on getting the foreground right.

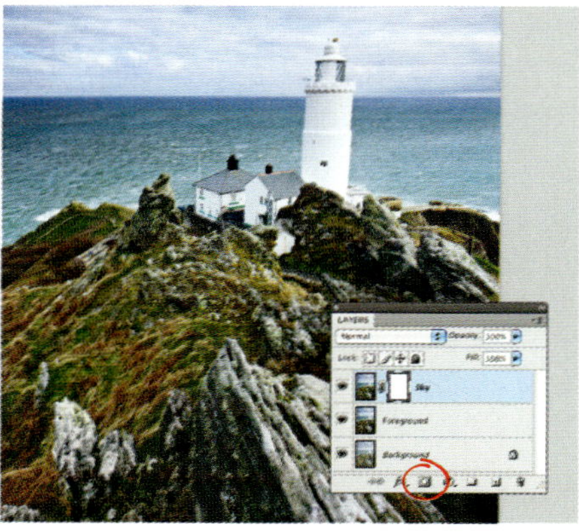

3 Duplicate adjusted layer Now duplicate this edited layer with ***Layer>Duplicate Layer...*** Then add a Layer Mask by going to ***Layer>Layer Mask>Reveal All*** or by clicking on the ***Add Layer Mask*** icon at the bottom of the Layers palette (circled). The purpose of the Layer Mask is so that the next edit only affects the sky area of this layer.

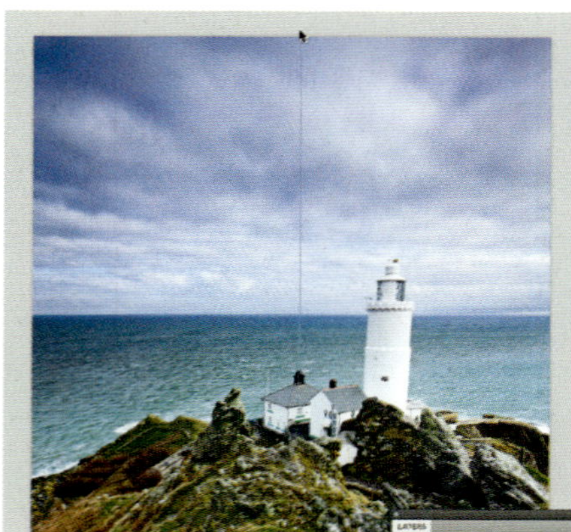

4 Add a gradient Click on the ***Layer Mask*** thumbnail and select the ***Gradient Tool***, ensuring the ***Foreground*** and ***Background Color*** are set to the default ***Black*** and ***White***. With the ***shift*** key held down to ensure a straight line, click near the horizon and drag, letting go at the top of the image. This adds a gradient to the mask.

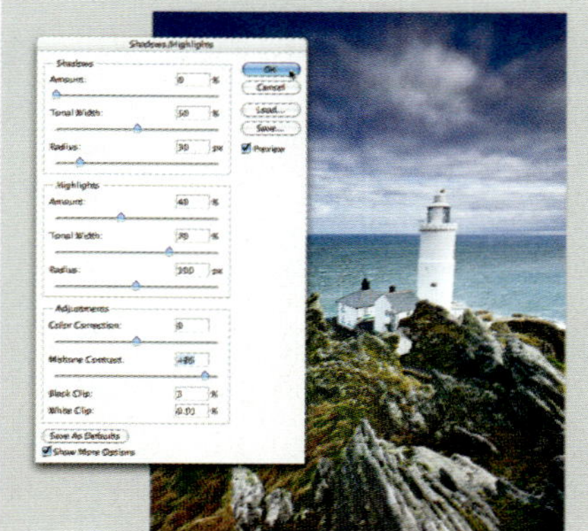

5 Create a stormy sky With the mask in place, any work done will only affect the sky area. Open ***Shadows & Highlights*** as instructed in step two, but this time work mainly on the ***Highlights*** and ***Midtones Contrast*** to pull all the detail back into the sky. You may want to increase the ***Black Clip*** to improve the overall contrast.

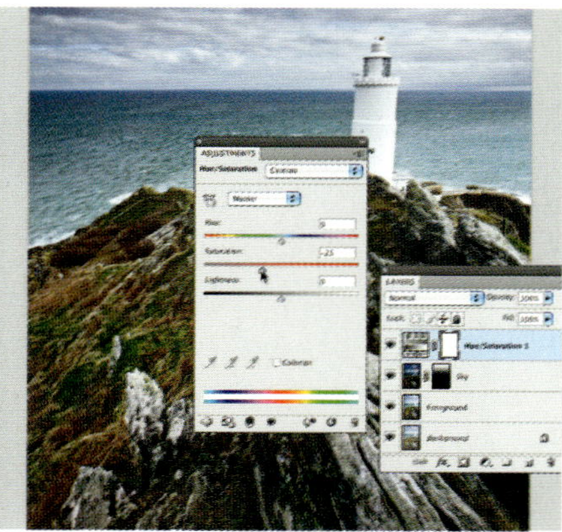

6 Reduce the saturation One final tweak is to remove some of the colour to enhance the storm-like appearance of the image. With the top layer still active, go to ***Layer>New Adjustment Layer>Hue/Saturation...*** and reduce the ***Saturation*** slider by around ***20%***, then click ***OK***. Now save as a ***PSD***, to preserve all the layers.

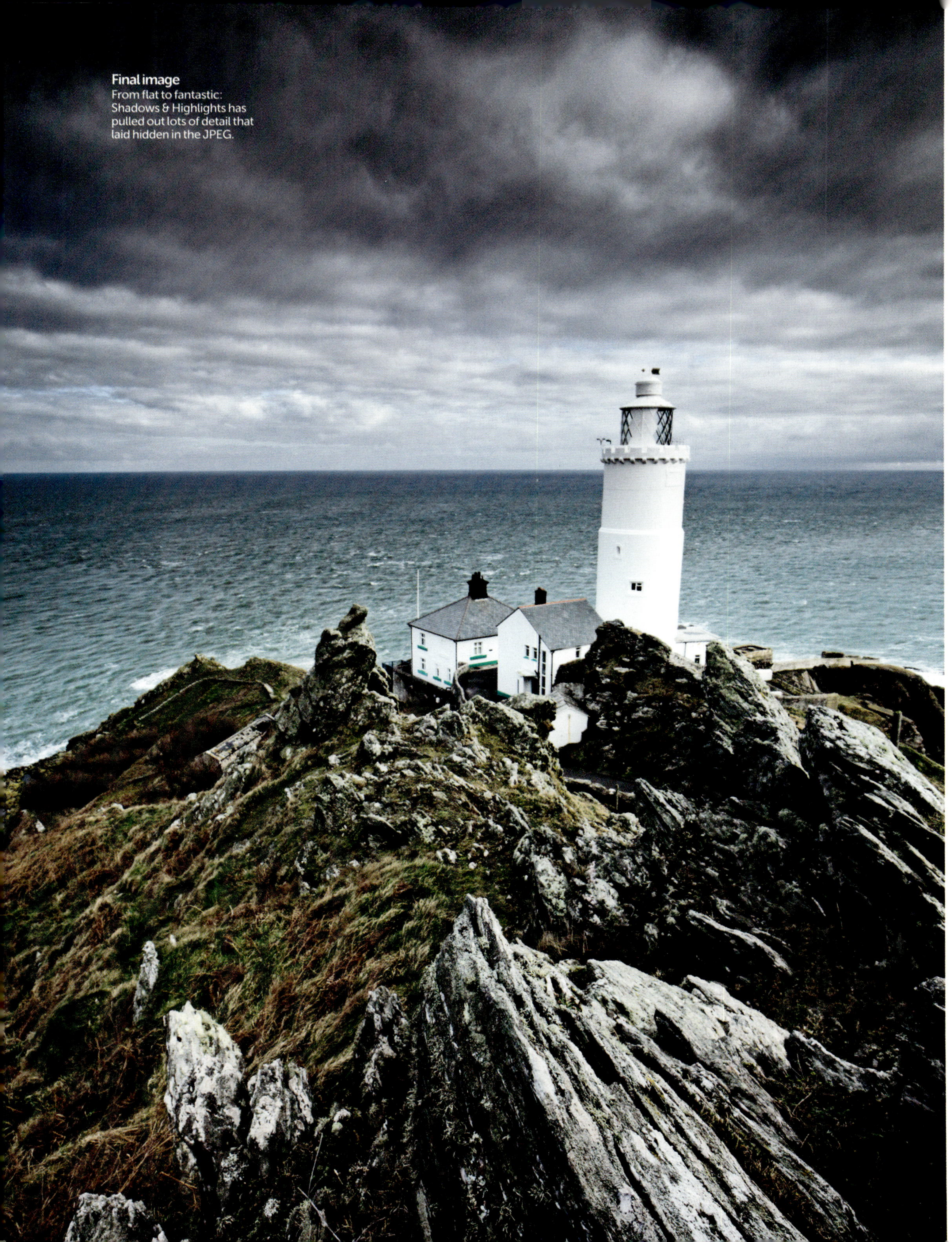

Final image
From flat to fantastic: Shadows & Highlights has pulled out lots of detail that laid hidden in the JPEG.

Advanced retouching skills

Want professional retouching results? This tutorial may take a little time and an eye for detail, but your portrait images will reap the rewards

IT'S EASY TO cake a face in blur or paint over skin for a porcelain finish; the difficulty comes when you want to keep the natural texture but even out and improve the tone. Portrait professionals do it with ease and keep their methods close to their chest, but we have a few secret techniques that we're more than willing to share. Some of you will probably already use quick-fix techniques to smooth skin and reduce imperfections, and it will be all you need for a while, but more seasoned Photoshoppers might be ready to move on to this more thorough and advanced technique. Yes, dedicated software helps you get flawless results, but why spend the money when you already have Photoshop? Layers, Adjustment Layers and Layer Masks are essential here, so make sure you understand how they work as we're skipping the basics. Be prepared for lots of layers, lots of selections and employ your eye for detail, as you'll have to target specific areas – no one-stop-shop global adjustments here! So grab a cuppa, your latest portrait and get ready for a couple of hours' work – the aim is amazing, but undetectable, editing...

How to use...

☑ LAYER MASKS

A Layer Mask allows you to hide detail from the layer it's applied to, revealing the image beneath without erasing it. Select the Layer Mask, then add ***Black*** to the mask to hide image detail and change to ***White*** to restore detail. Use ***X*** to switch between the colours.

1 Cover up dark circles Under-eye shadows can make a subject look unduly tired. The easiest way to brighten a complexion is to minimise these shadows and even out the skin tone. Duplicate your image layer (***Layer>Duplicate Layer***) and select the ***Clone Stamp Tool***, set its ***Opacity*** to around ***20%*** and lightly blend in the new skin. Be careful not to hide all the shadow as you can make the subject look unnatural. If you go too far, use a Layer Mask (***Layer>Layer Mask***) to pull back the effect (see box-out above).

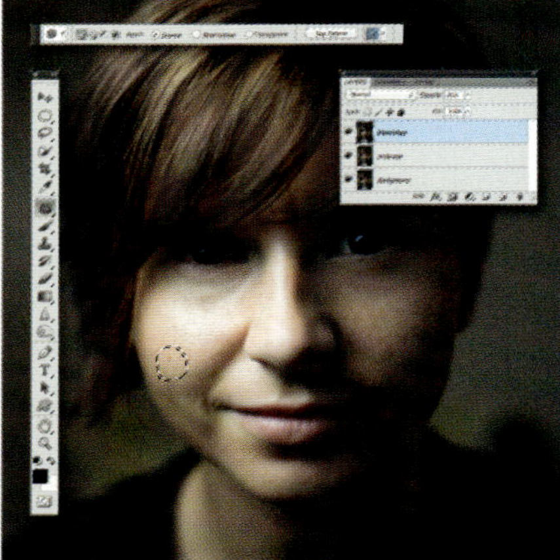

2 Remove blemishes Duplicate your new layer by dragging it down to the ***Add new layer mask*** icon at the bottom of the Layers palette and rename it 'Blemishes'. Select the ***Patch Tool*** from the toolbar and select ***Source*** in the top toolbar. Now draw around a blemish and then click and drag that selection to a clearer area of skin that you want to use to replace it. As you release the mouse or stylus, the selection will blend with the pixels, hiding the blemish. Repeat for all spots, scars and wrinkles that you wish to remove.

3 Smooth the skin Duplicate the 'Blemishes' layer and name it 'Skin Smoothing'. Use the ***Patch Tool*** again, but this time change ***Source*** to ***Destination*** in the top toolbar. Now select an area of skin that's of even tone and smooth texture, then click and drag that selection on top of areas that show visible pores and redness. If the result looks patchy, you should try reducing the layer's ***Opacity*** slider to around ***85%*** and use a Layer Mask (***Layer>Layer Mask***) with a very low opacity brush to smooth the skin's surface.

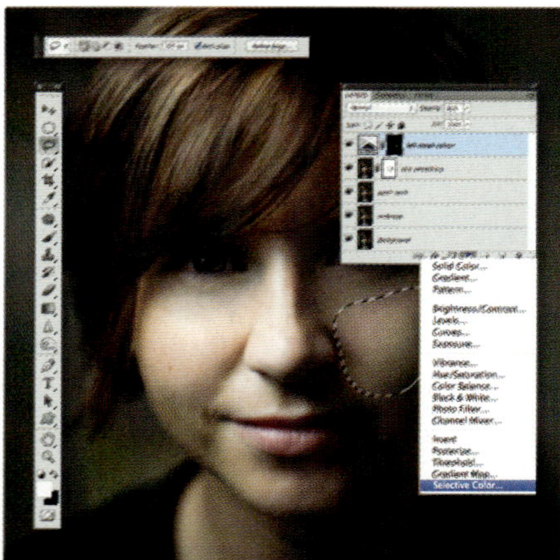

4 Start being selective This stage can take many Adjustment Layers, so try to keep nice and organised by renaming the various layers if necessary. On your last image layer, select the ***Lasso Tool*** and set the ***Feather*** to ***150px*** and loosely select an area of skin of similar tone. Go to ***Layer>New Adjustment Layer>Selective Color*** to create an Adjustment Layer to target that selection. Assess your image and decide what colours are affecting the skin – is it slightly too dark, light, magenta, red or yellow?

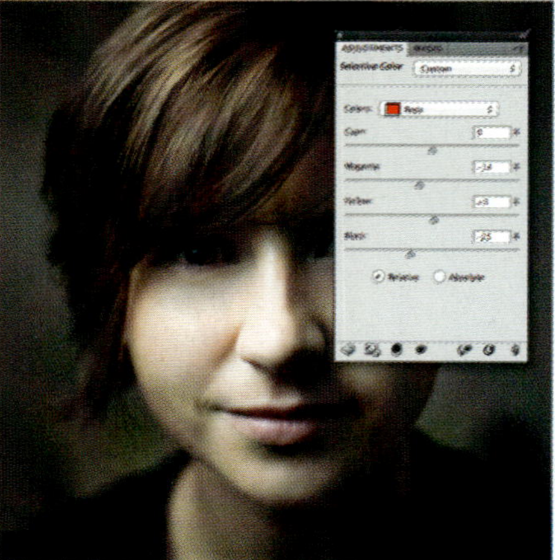

5 Target specific areas In the ***Adjustments*** panel, select the appropriate colour to target from the ***Color*** menu, using the sliders to adjust that colour and even out the skin tone. Repeat the process for different areas of the face, using the ***Lasso Tool*** to create new selections and adding new ***Selective Color*** adjustment layers. As the model's skin had a faint red tinge here, we mainly focused on the Red and White channels to reduce redness using the Black slider. Also try ***Curves*** adjustment layers to adjust local contrast.

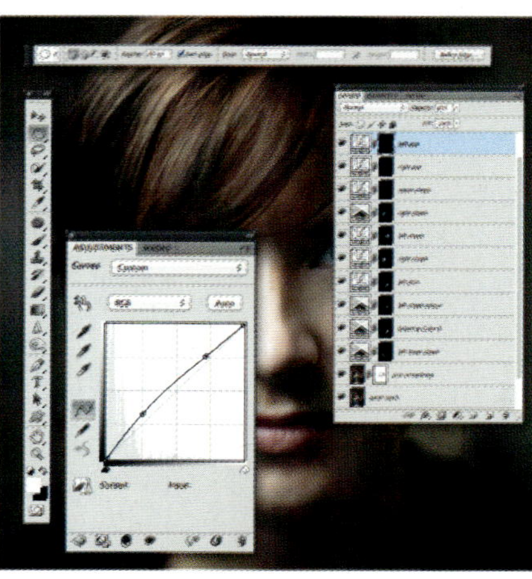

6 Finishing touches Don't rush steps four and five: be prepared to take time over perfecting the colour to ensure that all areas match up. Some colours will suit different areas better than others, so experiment – you can always return the sliders to 0 if needed. Once you're done, use the ***Elliptical Marquee Tool*** with its ***Feather*** set to ***40px*** and select the inner eye. Next add a ***Curves*** adjustment layer and create a soft 'S' shape with the line to increase the contrast of the eye. Repeat for the opposite eye, too.

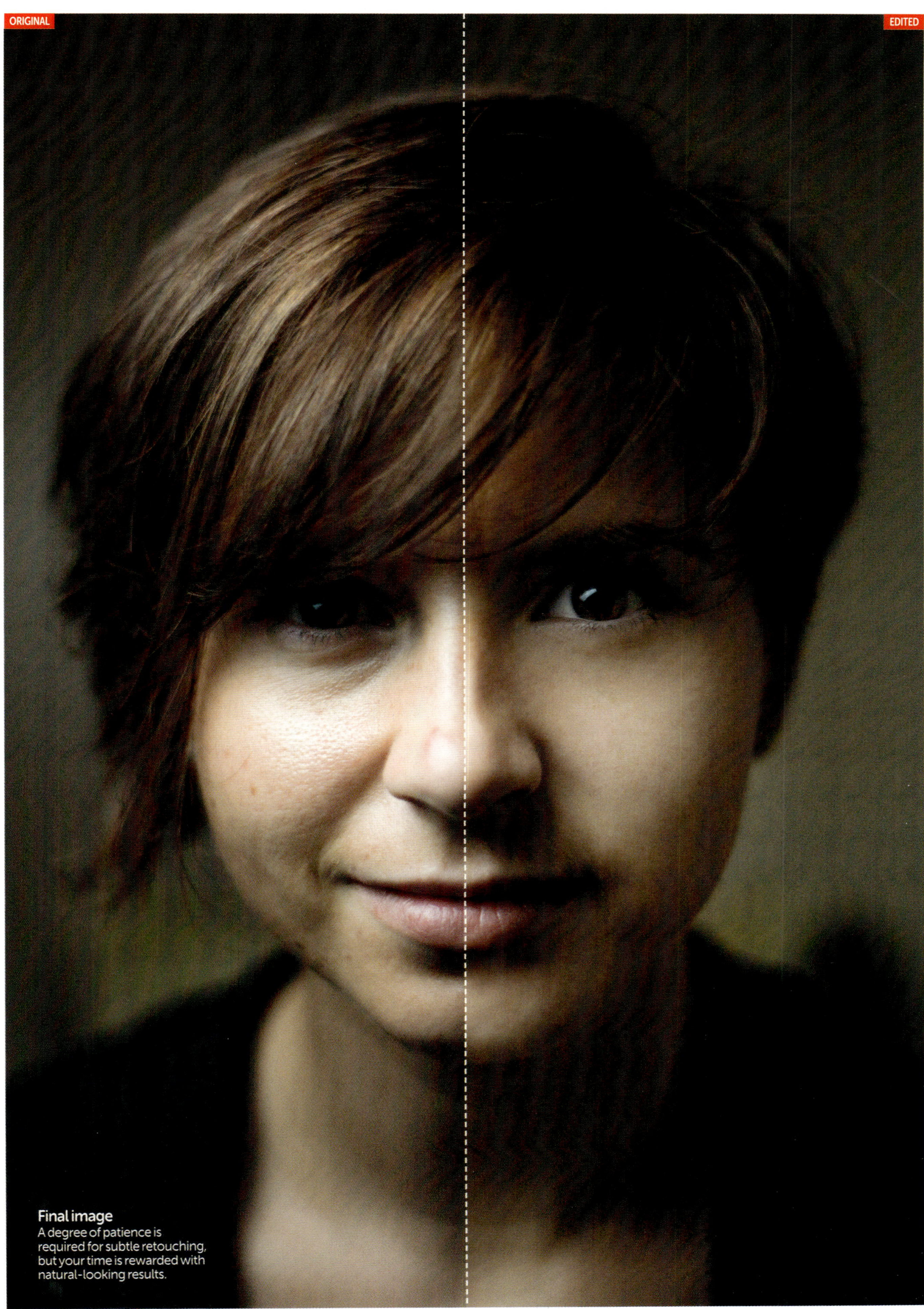

Final image
A degree of patience is required for subtle retouching, but your time is rewarded with natural-looking results.

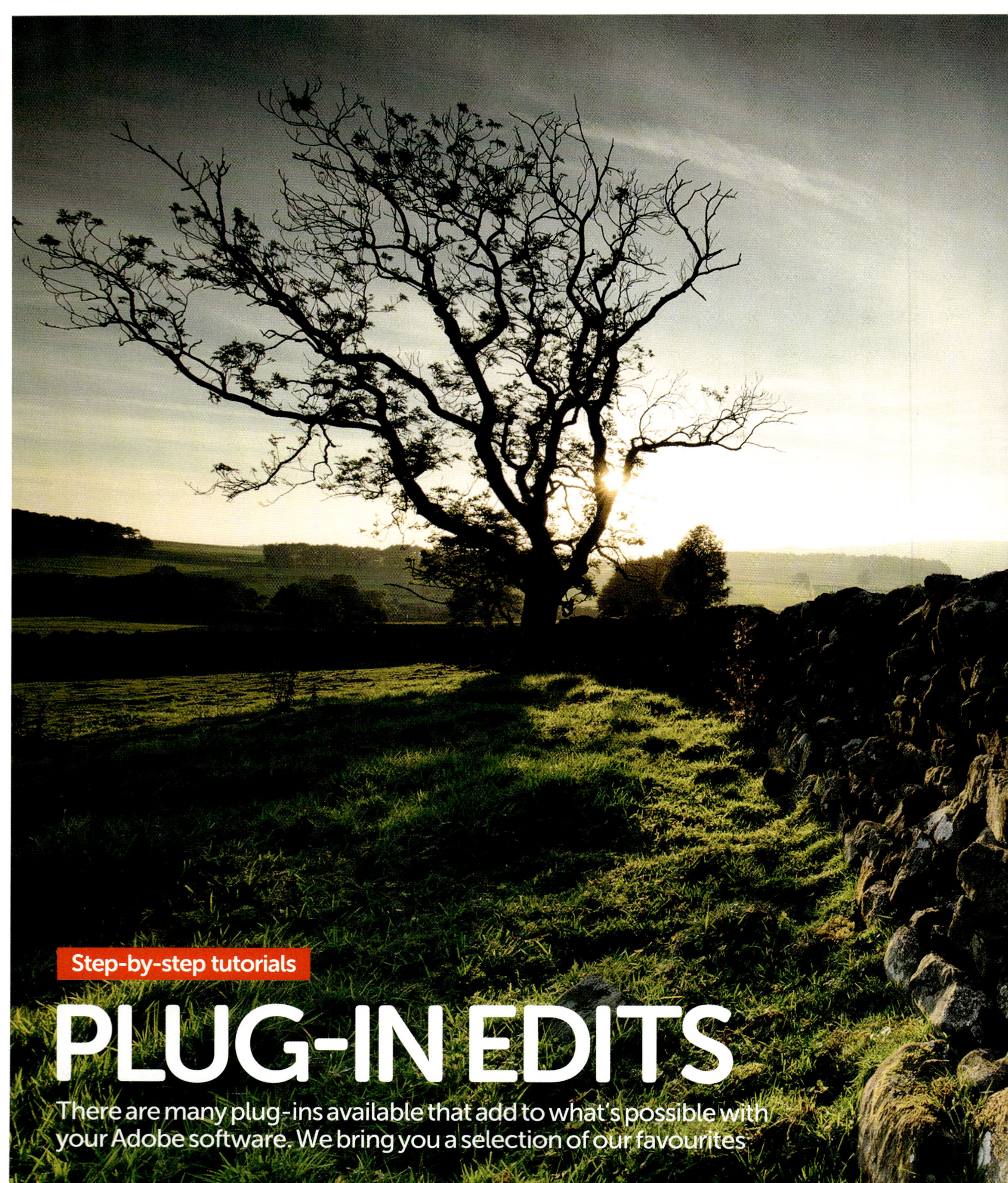

Step-by-step tutorials

PLUG-IN EDITS

There are many plug-ins available that add to what's possible with your Adobe software. We bring you a selection of our favourites

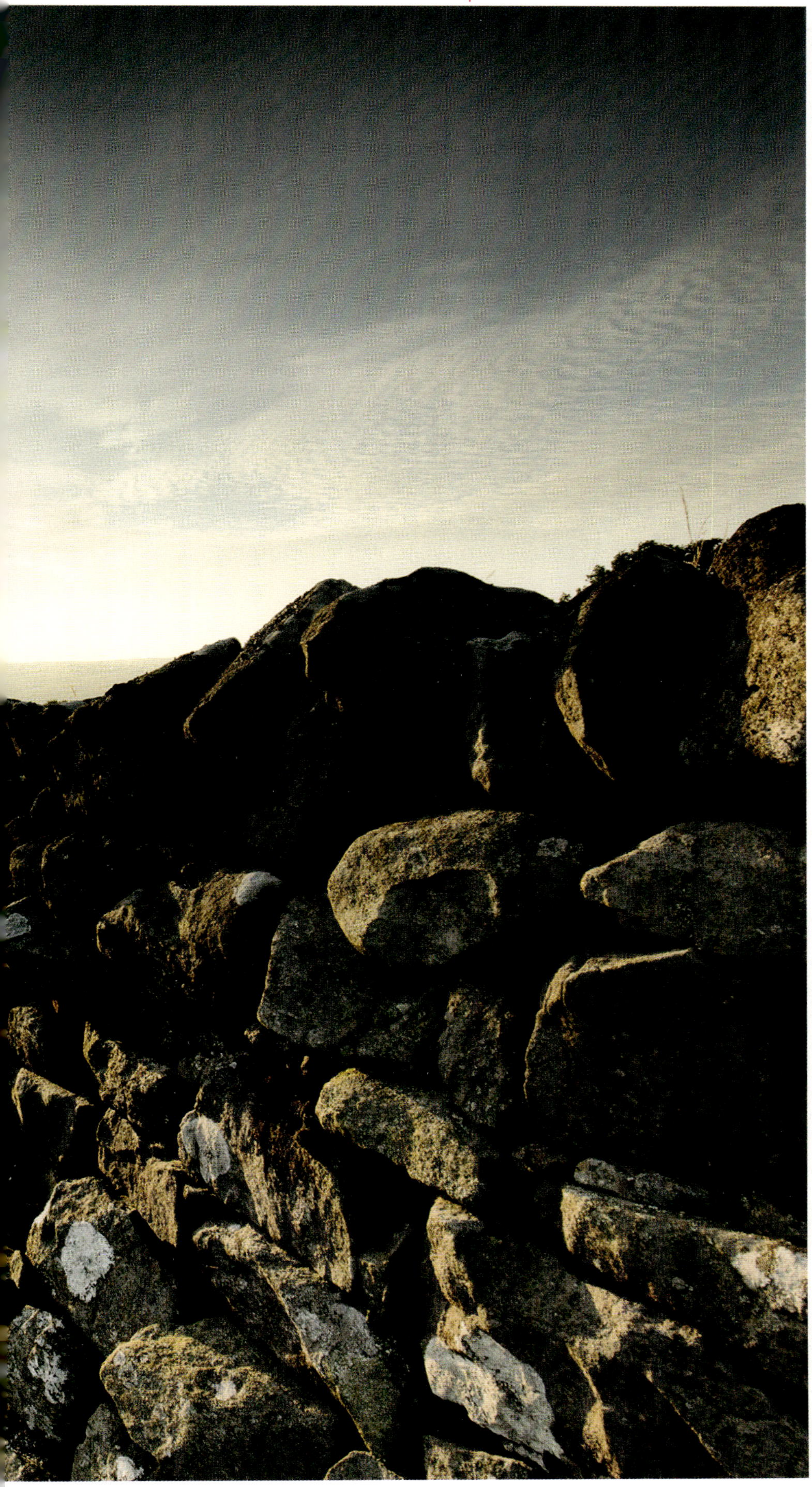

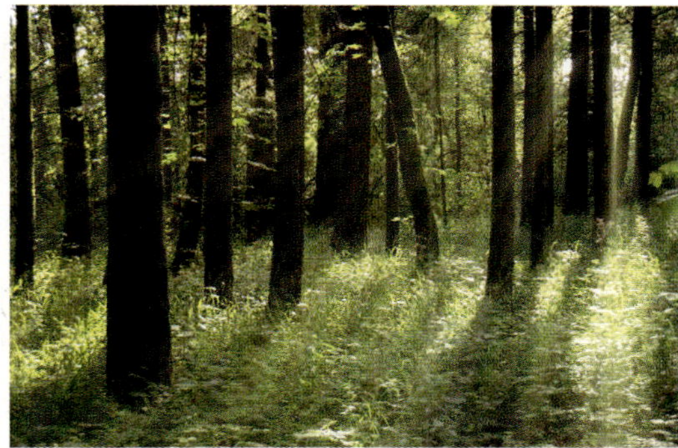

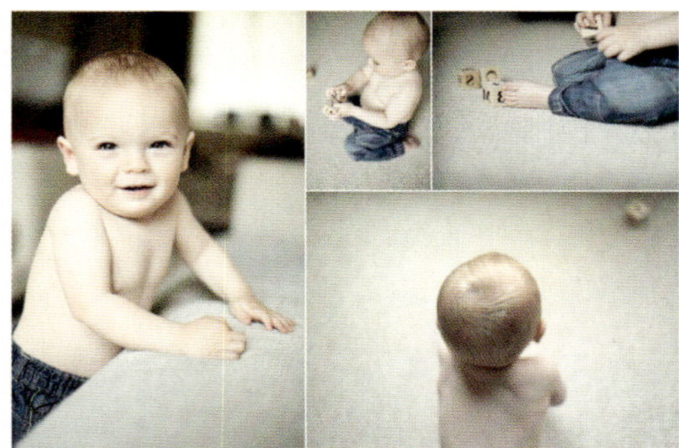

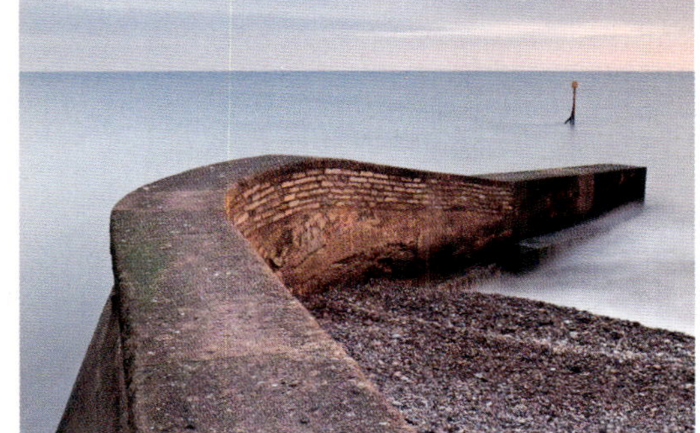

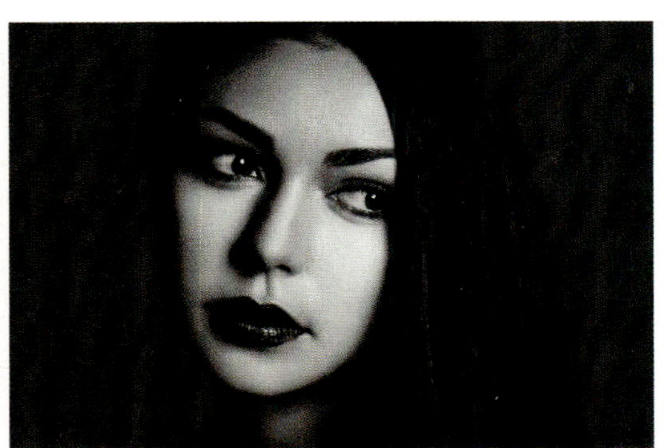

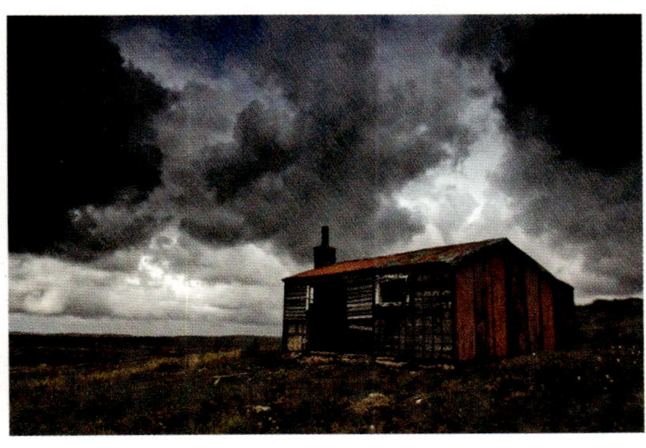

VSCO Film Lightroom plug-in

Made popular for its wide selection of film emulations, we explore the ins and the outs of VSCO film...

EVER SINCE THE advent of digital, photographers have longed to achieve that film look in their images. Presently, emulating film is more en vogue than ever. Cue Visual Supply Co, or VSCO – the experts in film emulation. By shooting, developing and studying a huge selection of films on different cameras, VSCO has created presets that accurately emulate the classic films that we all love and miss so much. Available in five different packs, each costing $119, the VSCO Film Lightroom plug-ins offer users ease and convenience – a one-click solution to style and grade images. This has made VSCO incredibly popular with wedding and lifestyle photographers who want to process hundreds of images quickly and easily.

Due to the large number of variables when it comes to film, there's no one right 'look' for each emulation, so VSCO has provided alternatives. For example, while the standard Kodak Portra 160 preset will offer an accurate representation of that film, a minus (-) symbol indicates a toned-down version and a plus (+) symbol indicates a more extreme look. A double plus (++) symbol indicates that the effects are greatly exaggerated. Some films also have High Contrast (HC) versions – these are typically well-suited to portraits, as they boost contrast while retaining the skin's natural graduations in tone. Finally, VSCO works best with Raw files, as it takes into account the camera that you use, although the presets can also be applied to JPEGs, too.

Go mobile

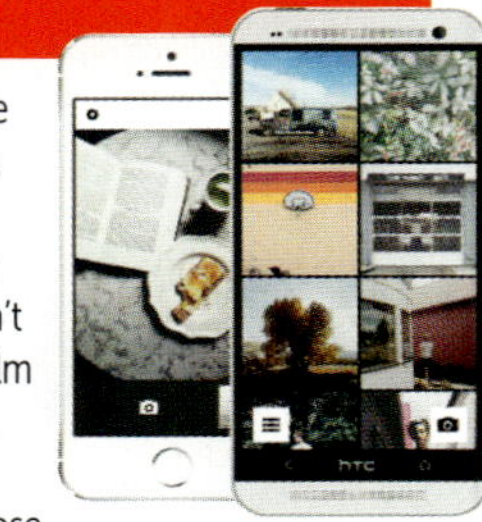

If you want to achieve the same authentic film look on your mobile photos then give the VSCO Cam mobile app a go. It doesn't offer the same specific film emulation as VSCO Film, but there are plenty of film-look presets to choose from and some really useful processing tools. The app is free to download but the extra filter packs cost extra. Download VSCO Cam from the Apple App Store or Google Play for free. www.vsco.co/vscocam

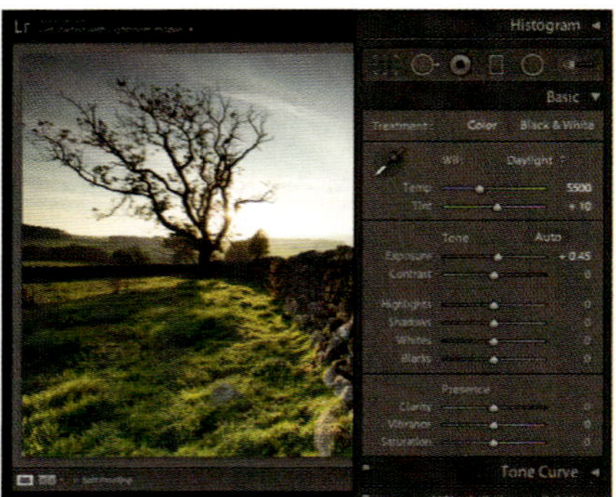

1 MAKE BASIC ADJUSTMENTS

With the VSCO plug-ins installed, first make any adjustments to ***Exposure***, ***White Balance*** and ***Lens Correction*** that are required to your image. Different emulations will have an effect on exposure and can add colour casts too, so further tweaks may be required later on.

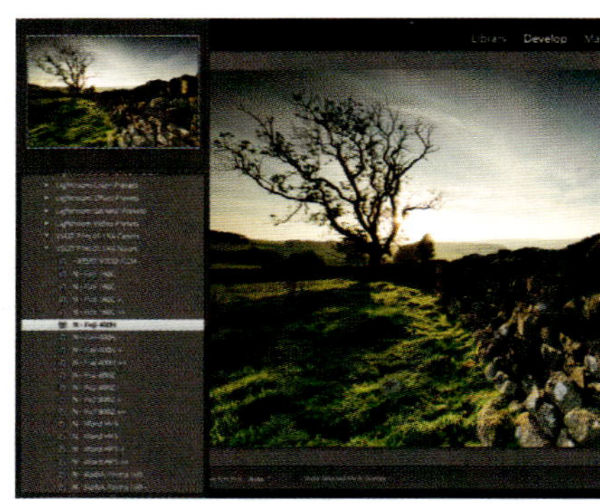

2 CHOOSE A PRESET

From the ***Presets*** list on the left, select the correct folder for your camera make – choose the ***Standard*** folder if it isn't available. Then choose your film – the preview will be updated. Try as many as you like – the settings are reset before the next preset is applied.

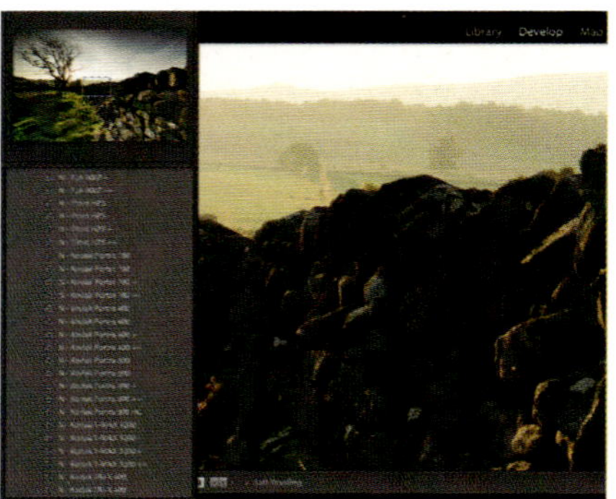

3 FINE-TUNE THE EFFECT

We have settled on the Fuji 400H emulation, but find the grain is a little overpowering. Scroll down to the ***VSCO Toolkit*** and choose the ***Grain-*** preset. Other parameters can be tweaked from within the toolkit or using the standard controls on the right.

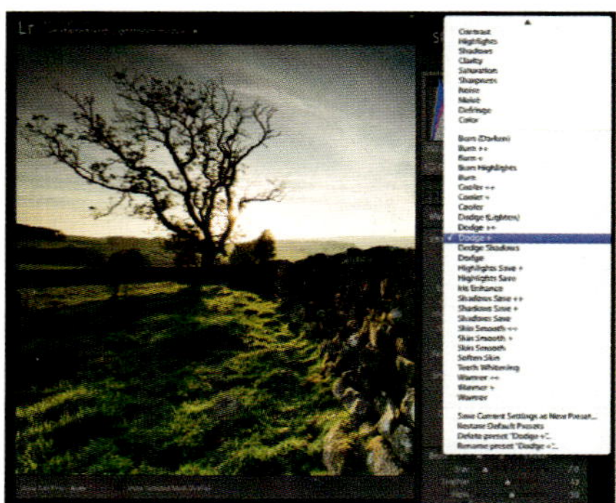

4 MAKE CUSTOM ADJUSTMENTS

VSCO Film also includes custom brush presets for saving time. Click on the ***Adjustment Brush*** to open the palette on the right and select the adjustment from the ***Effect*** menu. The ***Dodge +*** and ***Burn +*** setting are particularly useful for fine-tuning exposure selectively.

TOP FIVE FILMS

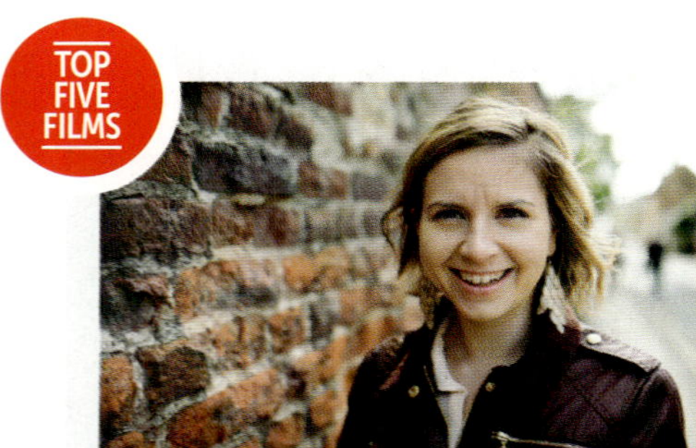

1) Kodak Portra 400 (VSCO Film 01)
A clean and vibrant film that suits well-lit portraits. Delivers fantastic skin tones and saturation.

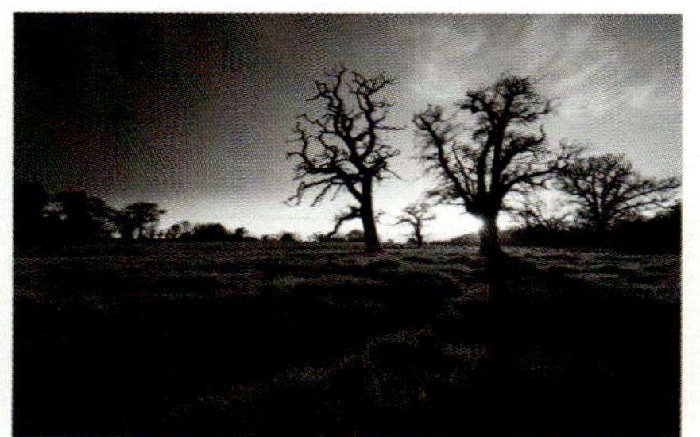

2) Ilford HP5 (VSCO Film 01)
A medium-contrast black & white film with a fine grain and high sharpness. Suited to high-contrast lighting.

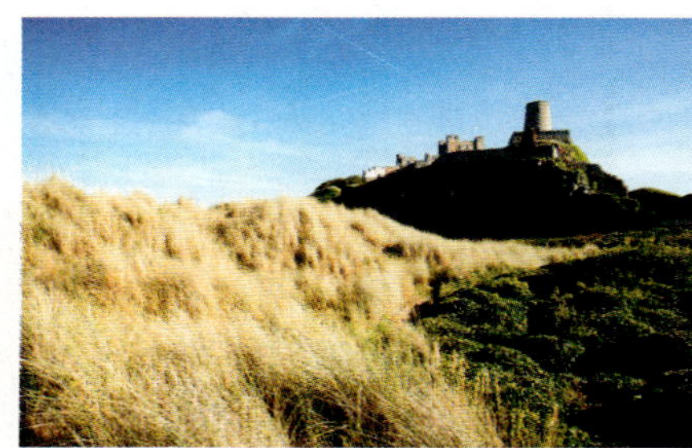

3) Fuji Velvia 50 (VSCO Film 04)
Rich, vibrant, saturated colours and strong contrast. Suited to colourful landscapes.

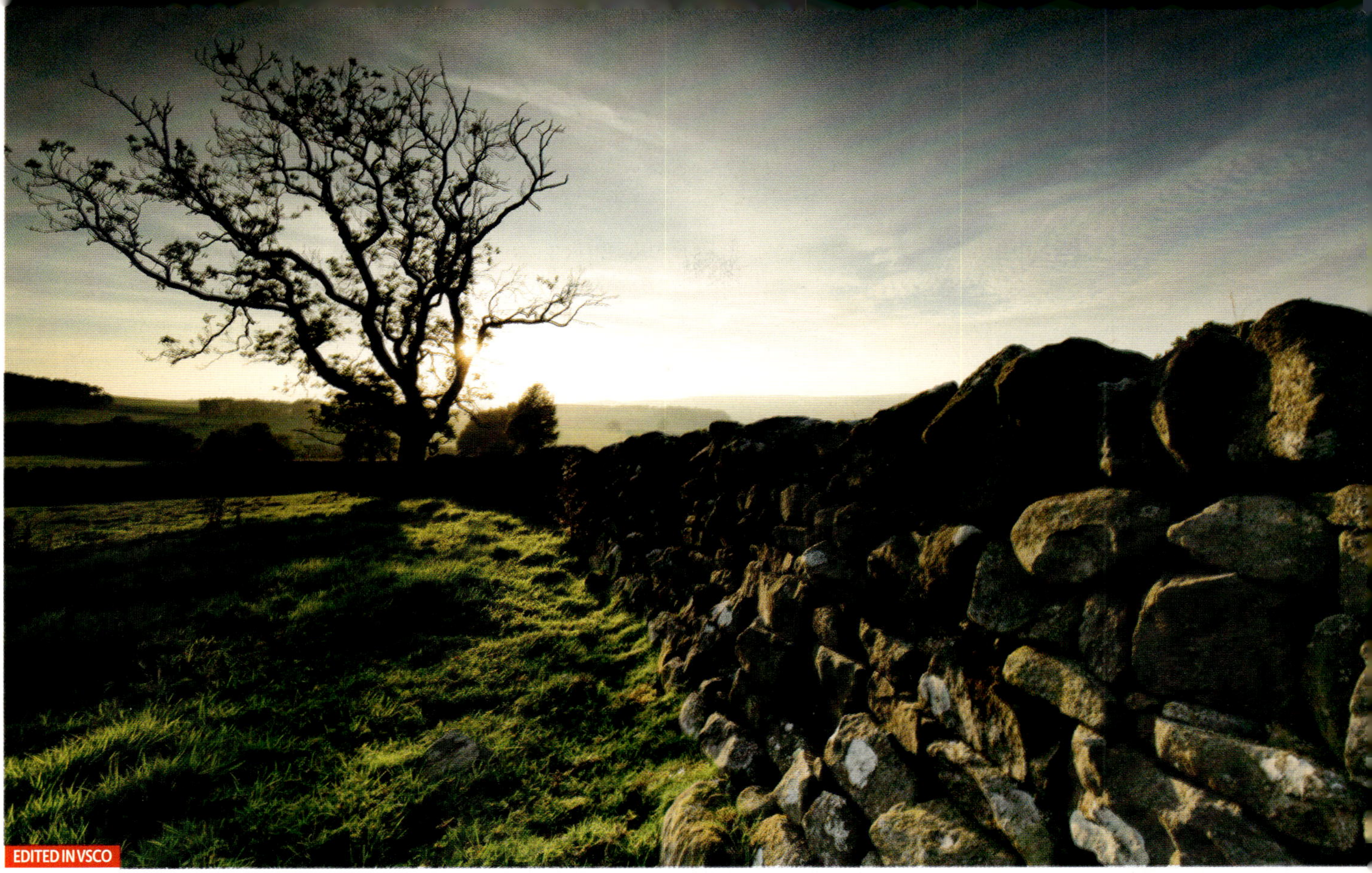

EDITED IN VSCO

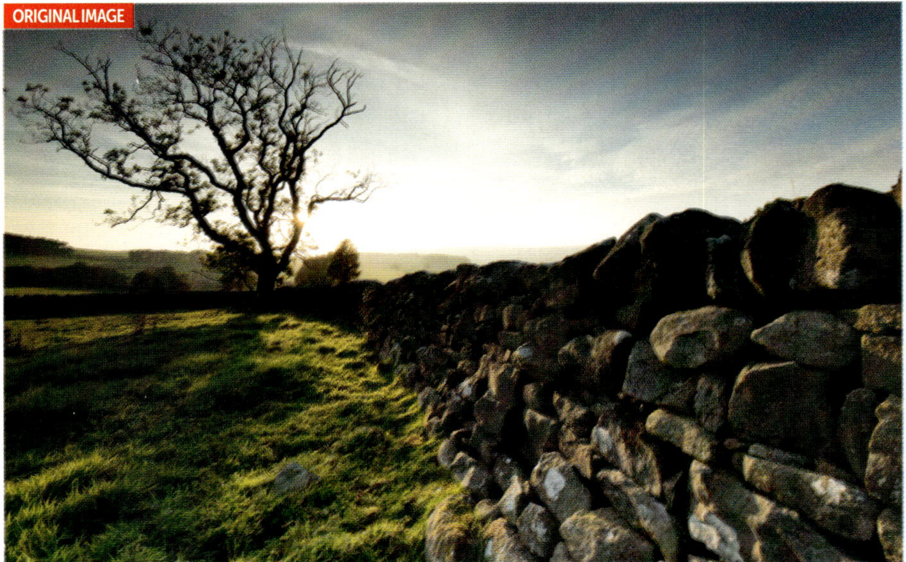

THE VSCO EFFECT: Some films are more extreme than others, but the subtle emulations are often more pleasing. The changes in tone and colour offered by VSCO do a good job of staying true to shooting on film.

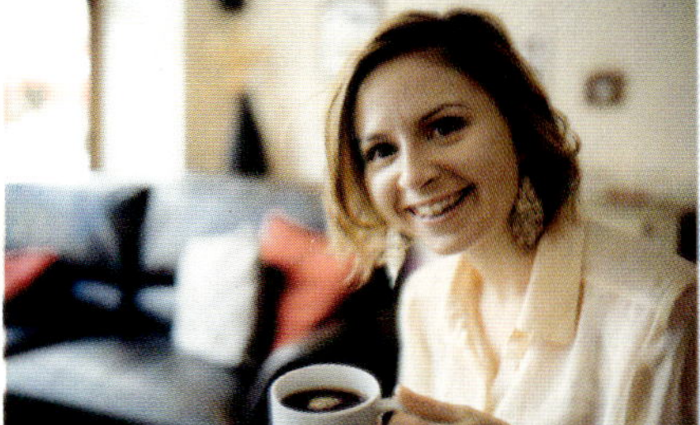

4) Fuji FP-100c (VSCO Film 03)
A medium-contrast, rich film that produces beautiful, glowing highlights. Great for natural-light portraits.

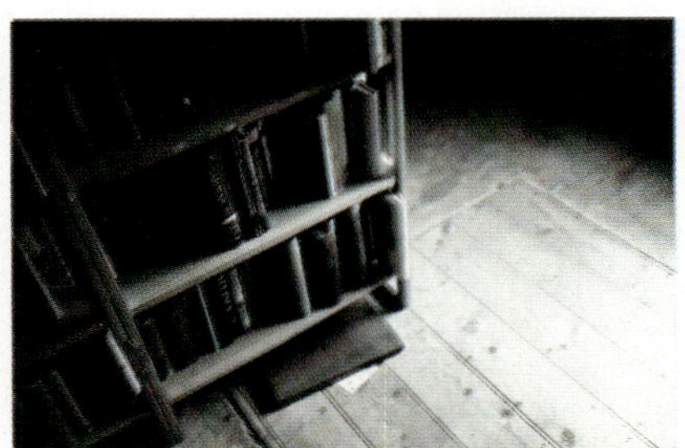

5) Kodak T-MAX 3200 (VSCO Film 01)
High contrast, high detail and high grain. An extreme film that has an instantly recognisable look.

Alternatives

● **Nik Analog Efex Pro –** USD$149
Software required: Photoshop/Elements/Lightroom/Aperture
Part of the Nik Collection so a whole host of other software is thrown in, including the excellent Color Efex Pro and Silver Efex Pro, making this excellent value for money.
www.niksoftware.com

● **Alien Skin Exposure 7 –** USD$149
Software required: Photoshop/Elements/Lightroom/Aperture/Standalone
Offers a large selection of emulated colour and black & white films as well as cinematic looks. Alien Skin's grain is based on real film grain, too.
www.alienskin.com

● **DxO FilmPack –** from £59
Software required: Standalone/Photoshop/Elements/Lightroom/Aperture/DxO Optics Pro
Includes up to 27 black & white films, 39 colour films and 39 designer presets alongside other useful processing tools.
www.dxo.com

● **XeL 2.0 Color –** USD$30
Software required: Lightroom
Lesser known, but XeL offers a huge array of different film emulations. Presets are split into colour, tone and grain, allowing you to apply them selectively. Lightroom only at this point.
www.x-equals.com/blog/

Google Nik Viveza

Viveza's simple yet powerful Control Point feature is perfect for selectively adjusting your exposures quickly and efficiently

THERE ARE COUNTLESS tools available for photographers within Adobe Elements, Lightroom and Photoshop to help them process their digital files, though most assume a certain degree of knowledge in order to get the most out of them. Things can quickly get complicated when you start introducing masks and selections, alongside multiple layers, adjustment brushes and filters. Viveza, part of the Google Nik Collection of plug-ins, aims to remedy this by offering users a simple and straightforward way to make quick and professional adjustments with minimal technical know-how.

Viveza is only available as part of the larger Google Nik Collection (it may sound pricey but, considering that you get seven plug-ins in one, it only works out at just under £13 per plug-in!). To put this into perspective, Viveza used to sell on its own for €100 (and €200 before that), so it's clear to see why the Google Nik Collection is such a bargain! The only caveat is that the Nik Collection isn't a stand-alone product, meaning that you also need Adobe Elements 9 or above, Lightroom 3 or above or Photoshop CS4 or above for it to work.

Alongside a host of easy-to-use universal exposure, contrast and tonal controls, Viveza also offers a fantastic Control Point feature. It's a user-defined area with a feathered edge that allows users to selectively tweak parts of their image, which are then seamlessly blended with the rest of the image, leaving other areas unaffected. Here's how to use them to quickly and easily transform your exposures...

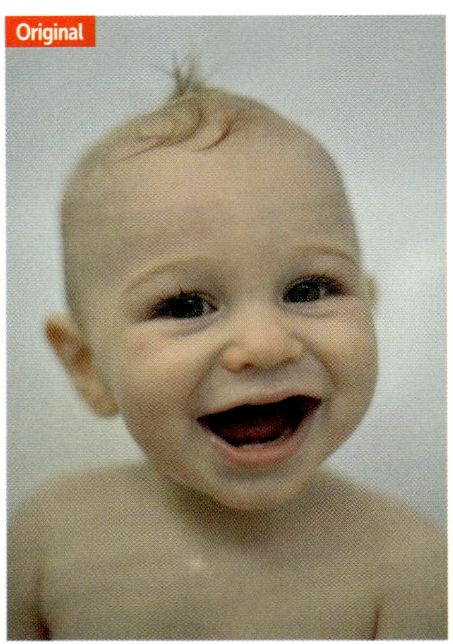

Above: A nice exposure, but the image could really do with a few selective tweaks to really make it pop. This is where the selective adjustments that can be made via Viveza's Control Points system works especially well.

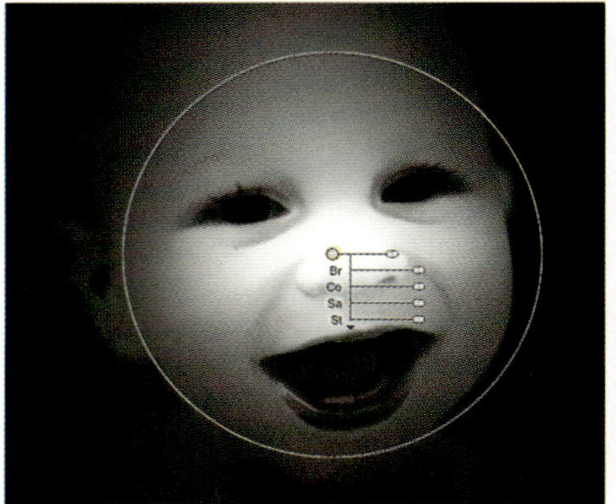

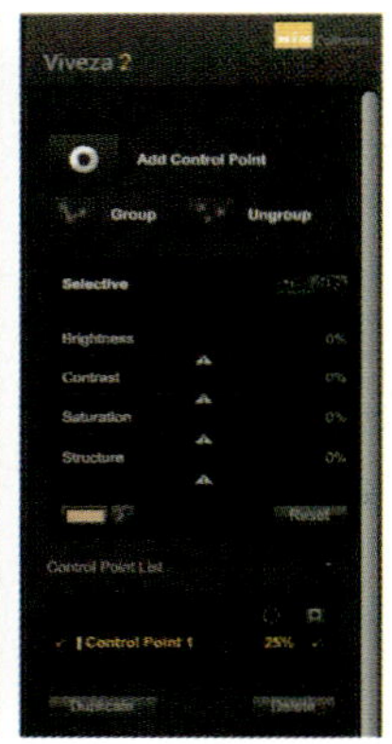

1 ADD A CONTROL POINT Click on the *Add Control Point* button on the right. Drop the Control Point on to the area that you wish to edit and a number of sliders will appear. The top slider controls the size of the adjustment area. Hold down the *cmd* key (Mac) or *Ctrl* key (PC) too while adjusting this to preview the area that will be affected.

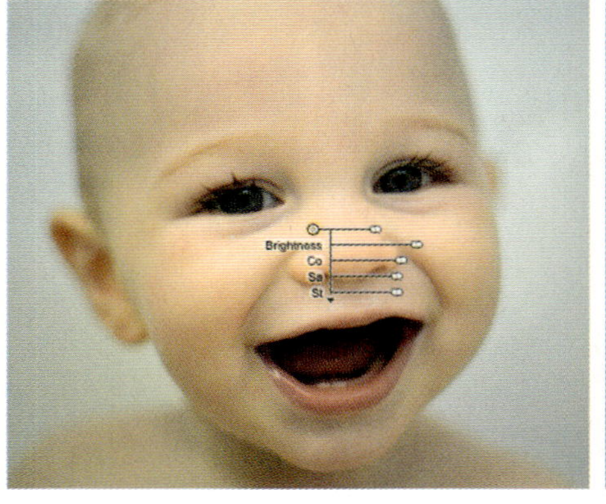

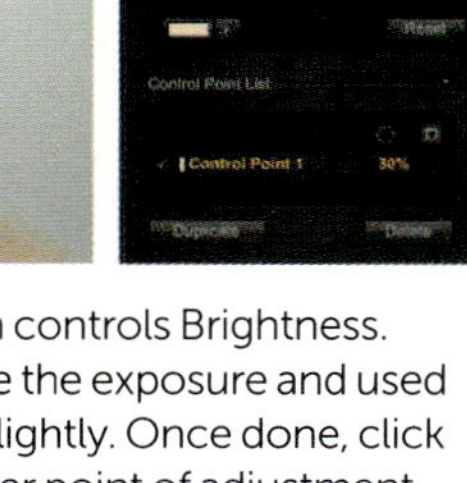

2 MAKE ADJUSTMENTS The next slider down controls Brightness. We've shifted this to the right to increase the exposure and used the Contrast slider below to raise contrast slightly. Once done, click on *Add Control Point* again to create another point of adjustment. I'm going to use this to brighten the eyes, so I click on the first eye.

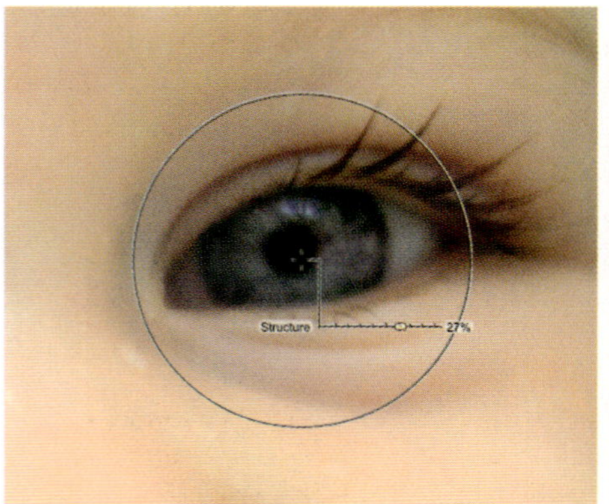

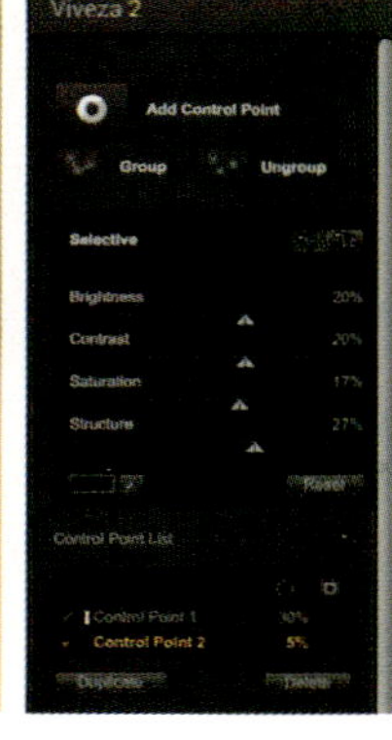

3 ZOOM IN AND ADJUST Use the *Zoom In Tool* at the top to focus on the eye and then adjust the size slider while pressing down *cmd/ Ctrl*, as before, to scale the Control Point. Then use the *Select Tool* to adjust the *Brightness* and *Contrast* again. Also increase the *Structure* and/or *Saturation* slider slightly to better define the eye.

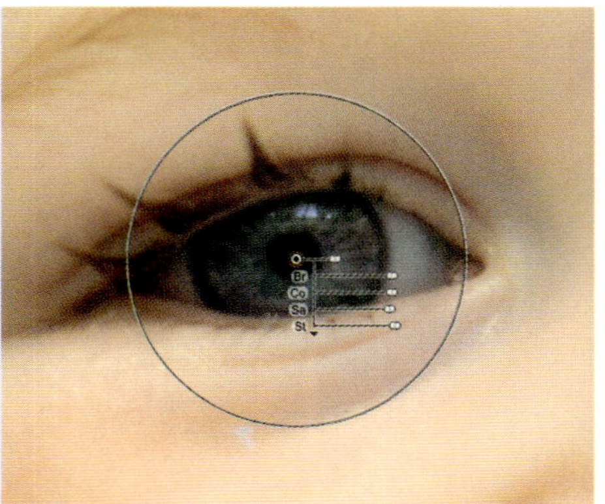

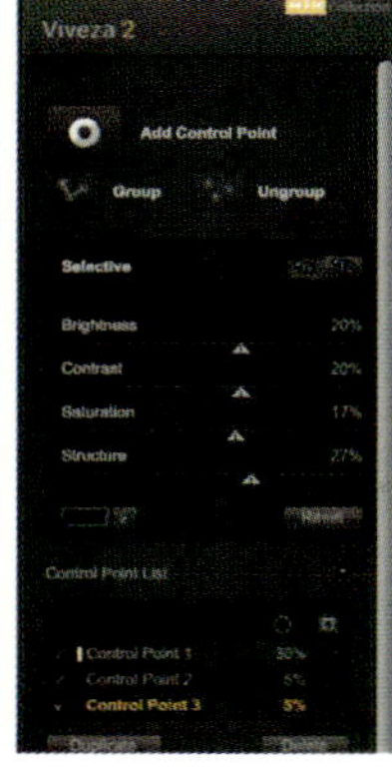

4 DUPLICATE THE CONTROL POINT This Control Point can be quickly duplicated to adjust the second eye. Hold down *alt* and drag off the first eye Control Point to duplicate it. Position it over the second eye and adjust the settings to suit this eye, as before. Control Points can be deleted at any time from the Control Point List on the right.

Final image
We duplicated the original main Control Point and moved it onto the child's body to brighten this area, too.

TOP TIP
Use the Preview tick at the top to check the before and after results. Or, use the Loupe on the right for a closer look

The Google Nik Collection $149

The Google Nik Collection is a host of useful plug-ins to achieve various effects and finishes, all based around ease of use. Here's a quick overview of what they do...

VIVEZA
Adjust exposure, tonality and colour in your images without needing to use Layer Masks, Adjustment Brushes and intricate selections.

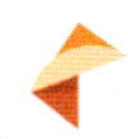

ANALOG EFEX PRO
A selection of film-effect presets, tools and creative effects, this plug-in contains everything you need to give your images an analogue feel.

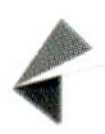

SILVER EFEX PRO
Considered by many to be the best black & white conversion software, it offers plenty of adjustments, including the same Control Point functions as Viveza.

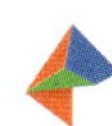

COLOR EFEX PRO
A comprehensive set of colour correction filters and presets for a variety of different looks. A great one-click solution, Color Efex Pro is capable of stunning results in minutes.

HDR EFEX PRO
Achieving desirable HDR effects can be tricky for all but the most experienced. This plug-in makes it really easy, offering presets to suit everything from a subtle look to a complete hyper-real effect.

SHARPENER PRO
It's all in the detail! Offers myriad tools to control structure, contrast and sharpness universally, alongside Control Point features to selectively sharpen your image.

DFINE
Noise reduction, tailored to your camera. Uses unique profiles to carefully reduce noise as well as boasting individual contrast and colour noise controls and selective noise reduction.

Add mood with Rays

Tired of seeking out those elusive God rays only to be let down by the light? We've got just the plug-in for you, and the results it gives are fantastic!

CREPUSCULAR RAYS, God rays, shafts of light... Whichever term you use to refer to them, there's no denying their allure to landscape photographers. You have to have just the right conditions for them to present themselves – a sunny, yet misty morning or evening in a forest or woods with just the right amount of canopy cover will do the trick – not too specific, right?

If you're struggling to make all of these elements align then fear not, the effect can be replicated to a reasonably realistic standard in Photoshop. It's a pretty tricky technique to master if you're doing it manually, but thankfully you don't have to! The clever folks at Digital Film Tools have created a plug-in called Rays to use with Adobe Photoshop, Elements, Lightroom and Apple Aperture, which quickly and easily adds realistic crepuscular rays to your images, with a good degree of adjustability. The software uses existing highlight and shadow areas in your image to determine where the rays should, and shouldn't, be. We're not quite sure how the science behind it works, but here's how you can try it for yourself...

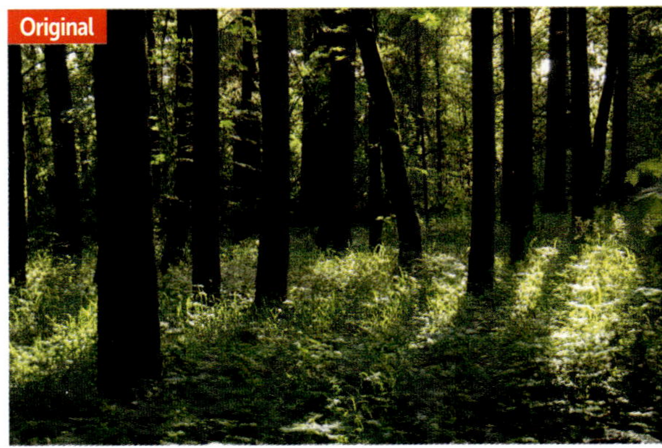
Original

There's an app for that

Alongside the desktop plug-ins there's also a Rays iOS app, suitable for your iPhone and iPad – perfect for adding ray effects to your mobile pictures. Costing just 69p, it offers pretty much the same functionality as the main plug-in and can turn your average snaps into stunning and eye-catching mobile masterpieces! Import or capture your image, add the rays as you would in this tutorial, export and you're done!

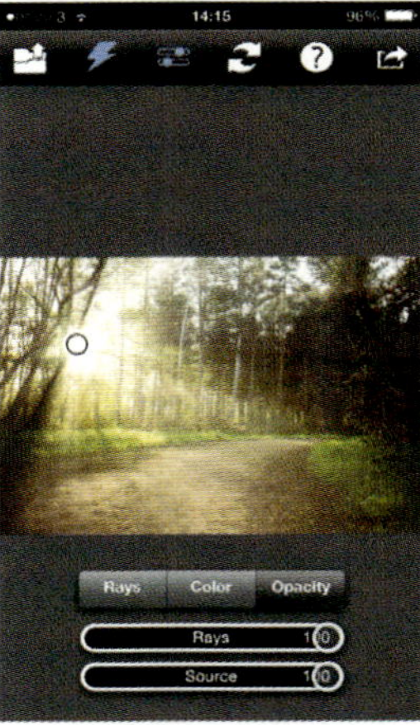

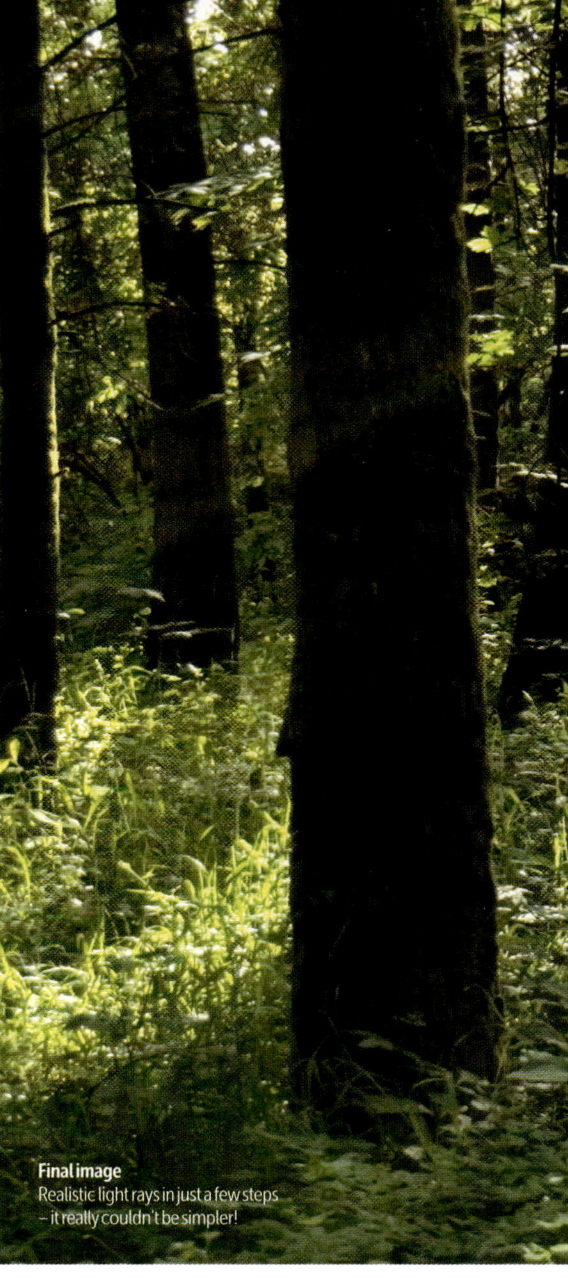
Final image
Realistic light rays in just a few steps – it really couldn't be simpler!

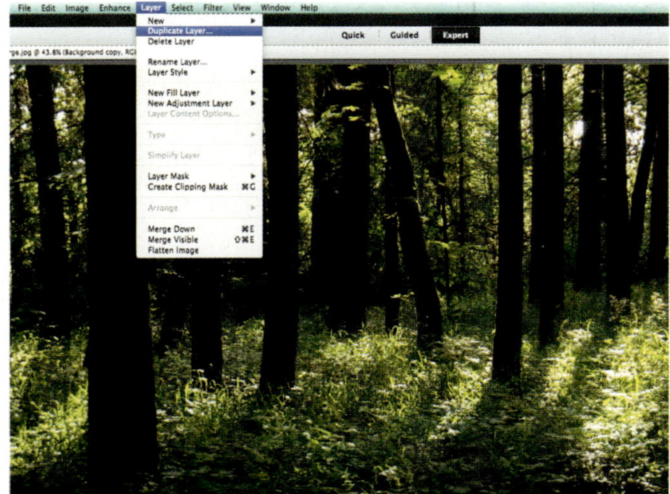

1 PREPARE YOUR IMAGE Open your image in your editing software, as you would normally. We're using Elements for the sake of this tutorial, but the steps taken are similar regardless. Make sure that your image is in RGB Color mode (*Image>Mode>RGB Color*). Then duplicate your background layer by going to *Layer>Duplicate Layer*...

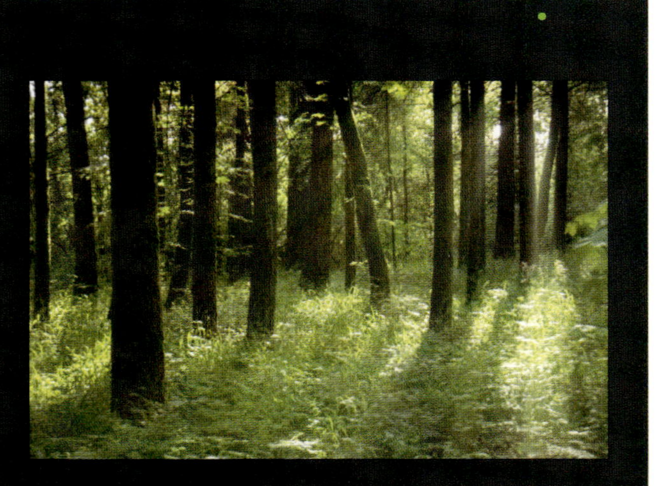

2 POSITION THE LIGHT Go to *Filter>Digital Film Tools>Rays v1.0...* to open Rays. Once open, place your light source by clicking and dragging anywhere on your image. Try to match the position and direction of the light in your image – this may mean placing the light source outside the edge of the image frame.

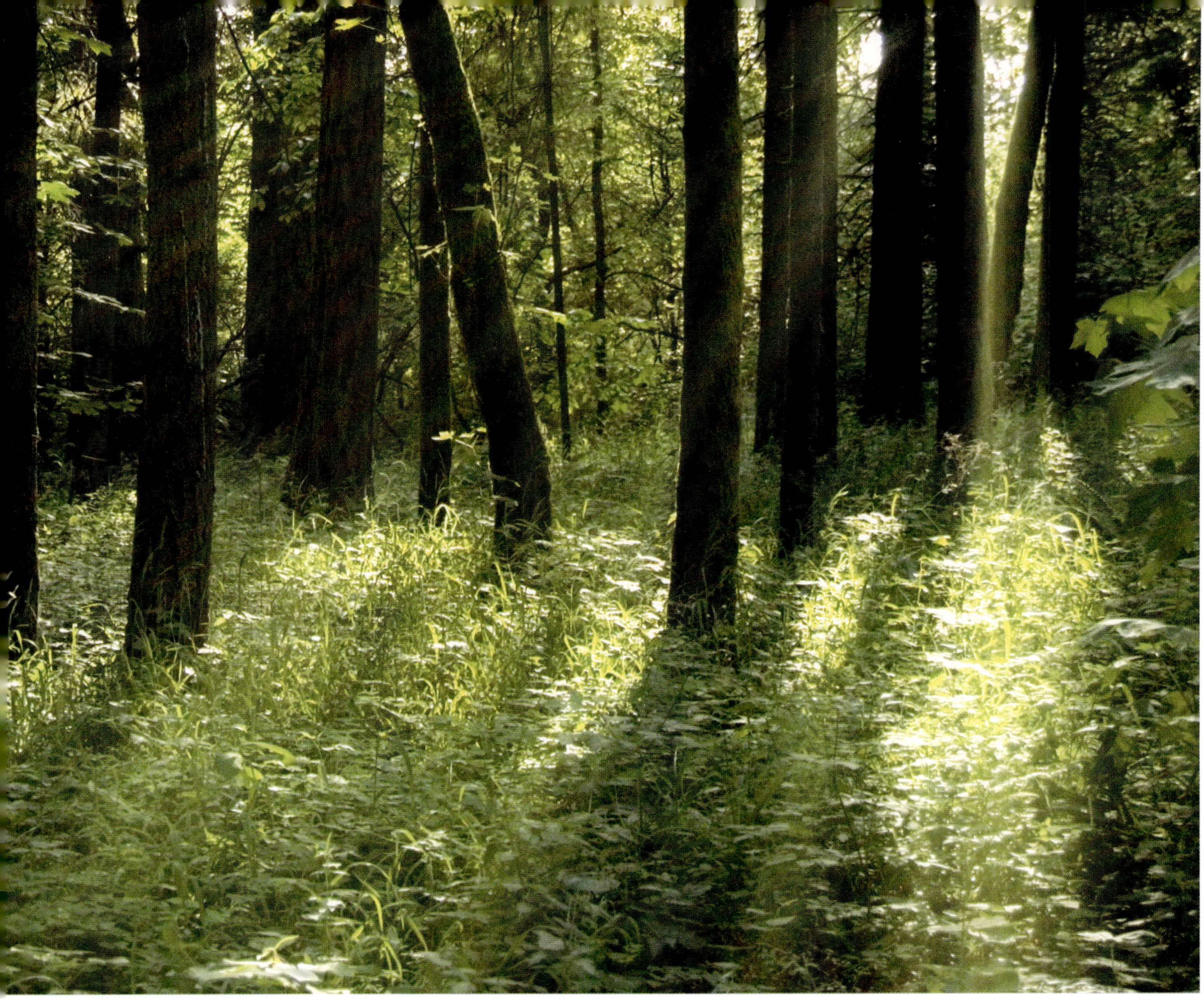

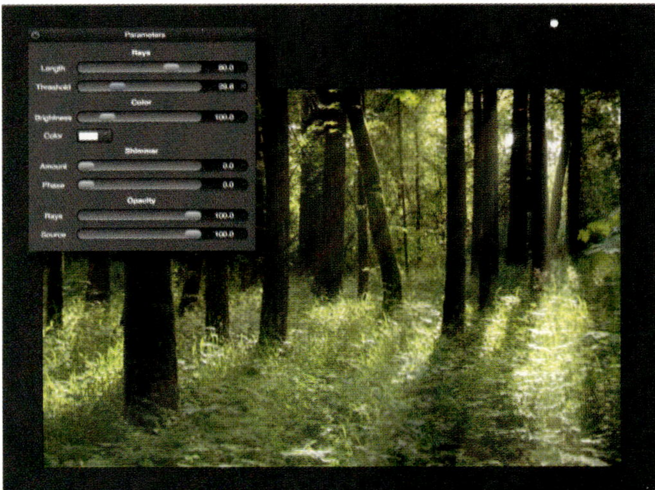

3 ADJUST THE RAYS In the *Parameters* panel, set the *Length* slider to *80* – this adjusts the length of the rays. Next, adjust the *Threshold* to suit your image – between *30-60* usually works well, depending on your image. The higher the Threshold, the fewer rays are generated, but the higher definition the rays become.

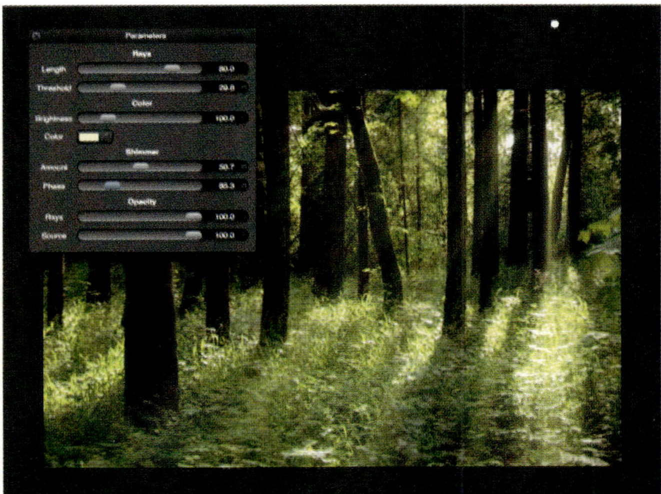

4 CHANGE THE RAYS' COLOUR Use the *Color picker* to match the colour of the rays to the existing light in your image. The *Shimmer Amount* and *Phase* sliders below adjust the randomness of the rays, so tweak these to your liking. Finally, the Opacity sliders at the bottom adjust the opacity of the rays and the source image. Easy!

Tych Panel 2

Want to have manual control over your diptychs, triptychs and collages? Tych Panel 2 is a free Photoshop extension that makes creating them hassle-free, while still giving you control. Here's how to use it...

EVERY SO OFTEN you'll come across a plug-in, piece of software or extension and you'll wonder why the functionality that it offers doesn't come with Photoshop in the first place – Tych Panel 2 is a perfect example of this. Tych Panel 2 is a free extension for Adobe Photoshop CS5, CS6 and CC and was created by Swedish wedding photographer Reimund Trost of Lumens Bröllopsfotografi as a solution for putting together quick and easy diptychs and triptychs to present on his wedding photography blog.

First of all, to download Tych Panel 2, visit: http://lumens.se/tychpanel/. Once downloaded, Tych Panel 2 needs to be installed using Adobe Extension Manager. If you don't already have this, it can be installed for free from www.adobe.com/exchange/em_download/. Once done, simply follow the installation procedure as instructed and the next time you open Photoshop go to *Window>Extensions>Tych Panel* to enable the Tych Panel palette. You're all ready to go...

Know your options

Tych Panel's Options area contains settings that you may find useful. The ***When adding row and columns, maintain...*** option is handy for those uploading to blogs and websites that use a fixed width or height. You can also make the collage panels editable by enabling ***Smart Objects*** in the ***Misc*** tab, allowing you to reorder or swap images without starting over again.

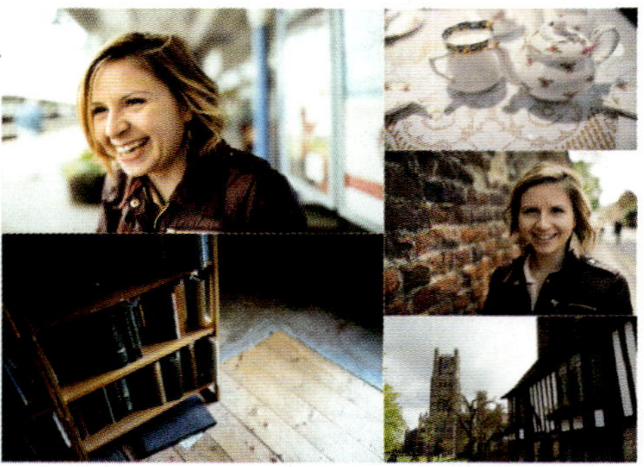

Why not try...

As an alternative to Tych Panel 2, it's worth considering standalone software BlogStomp. It's not free, but it does allow you to create collages, diptychs and triptychs without Photoshop and with minimal fuss. BlogStomp looks at the number of images, along with their orientation, and figures out the best way to arrange them. You can randomise the order of your images, but you can't reorder them manually. BlogStomp costs $49 (£30) for two installations – so you can split the cost with a friend!
www.blogstomponline.com

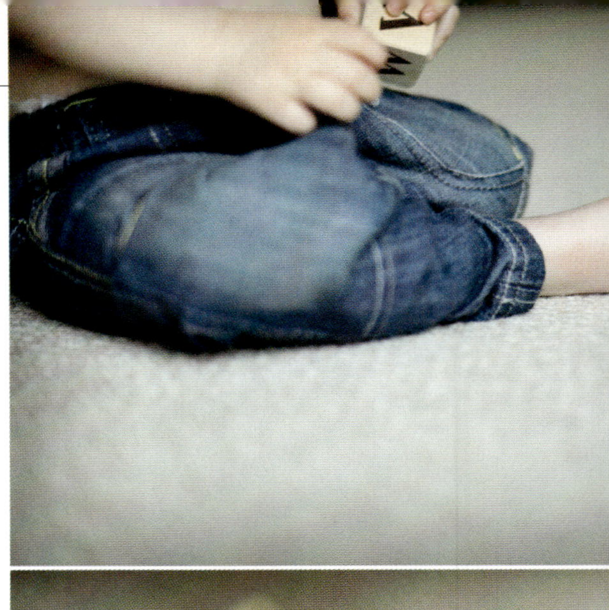

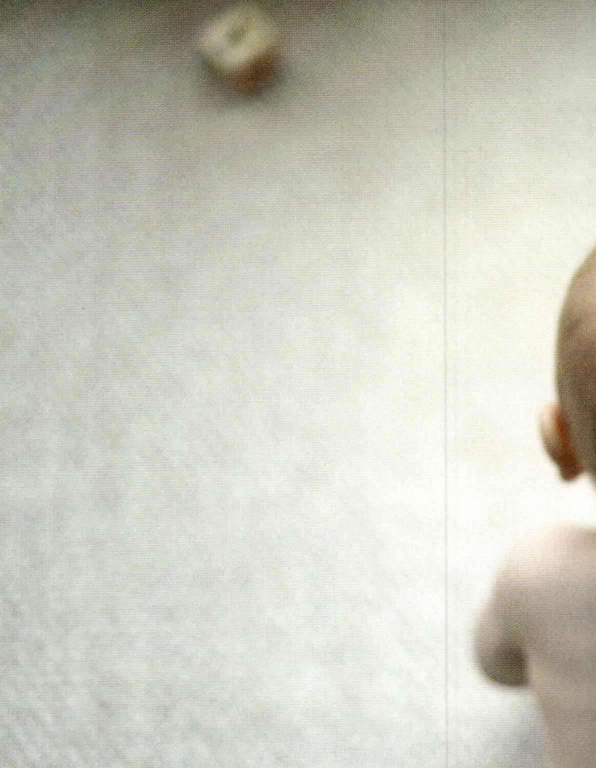

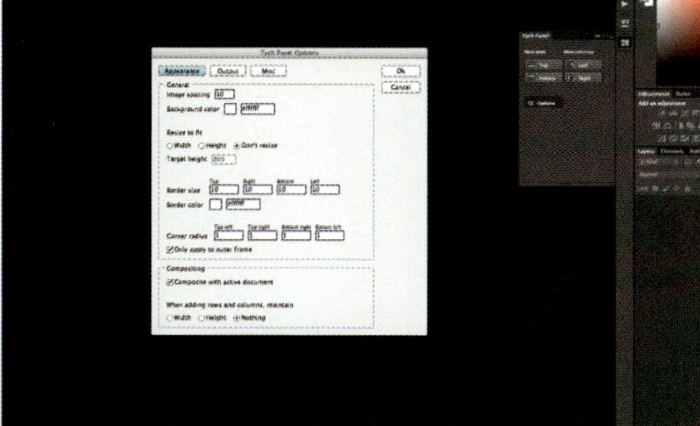

1 SET THE SPACING AND BORDER In Tych Panel 2, click on the *Options* button. Use the *Appearance* tab to set the *Image spacing* and *Border size* in pixels. Selecting the same spacing and border tends to look best. You can also change the spacing and border colour. Use the *Resize to fit* options to set the final size of your collage, too.

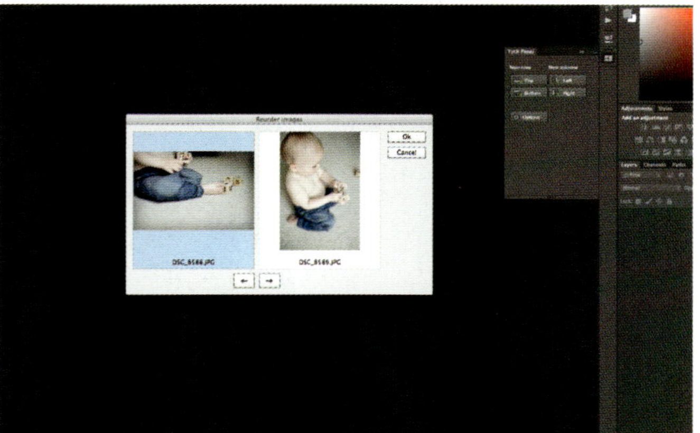

2 SELECT YOUR IMAGES The extension works by adding images in rows and columns – a row or column can comprise single or multiple images. To start off, create a simple diptych: click on either the *Top* or *Bottom* buttons under *New rows* and select your two images. In the *Reorder images* panel, set the image order as desired.

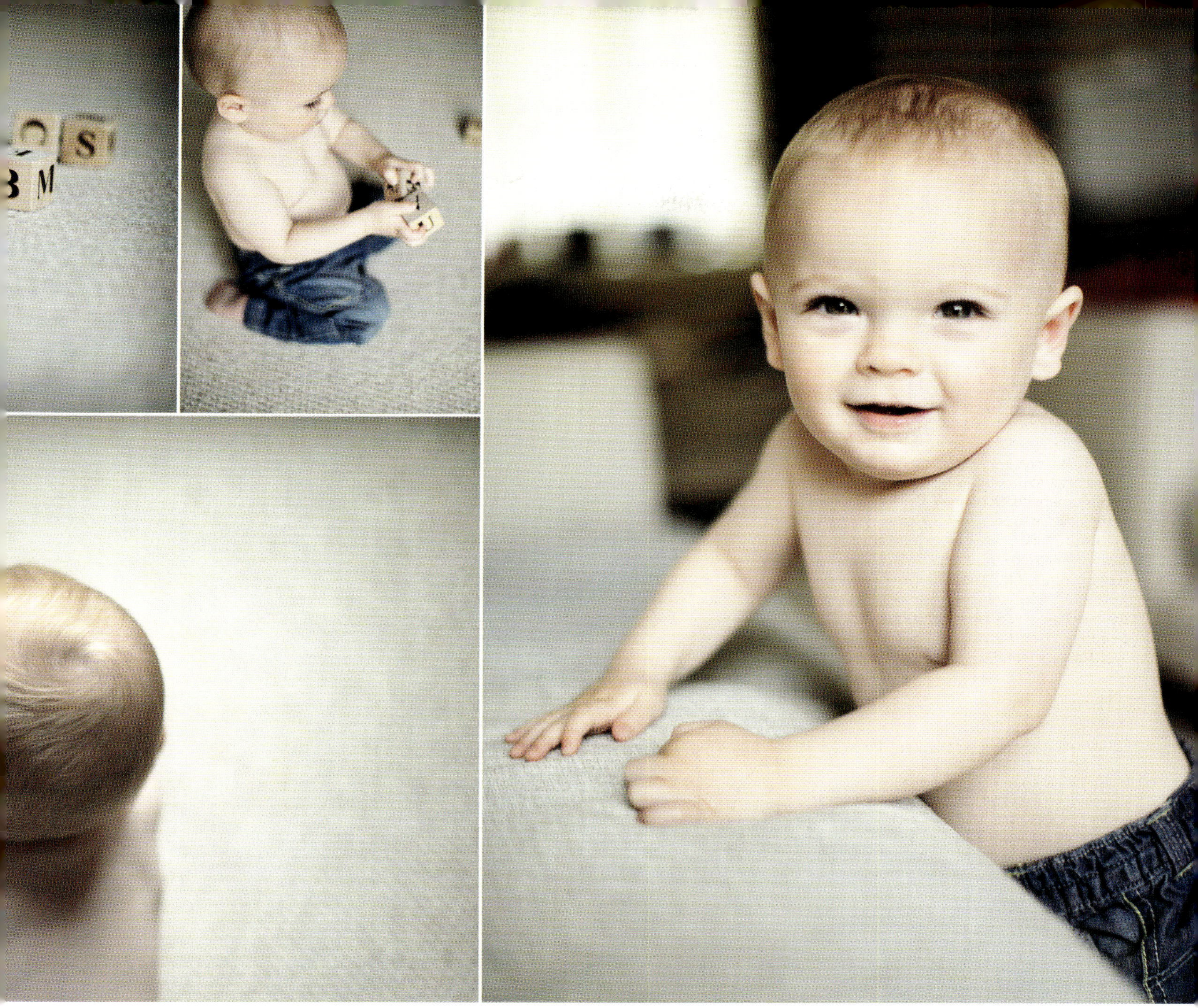

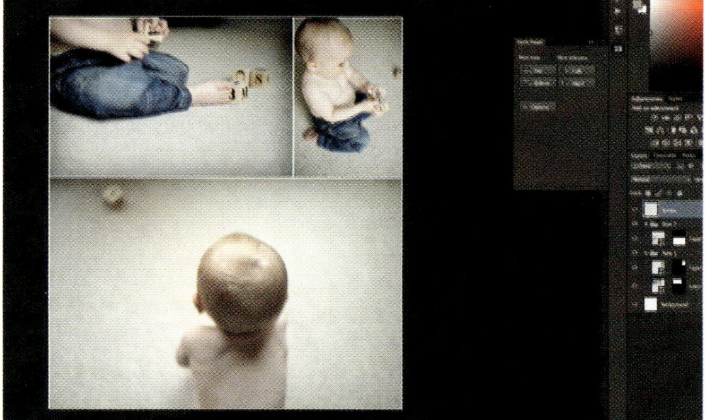

3 ADD A NEW ROW Tych Panel 2 will start to put your collage together using Layers and Layer Masks. Once done, you can add to your diptych should you wish by adding another row or column. We want to add a single, larger image below our diptych. Click on the ***Bottom*** button under ***New rows*** and select the image of choice.

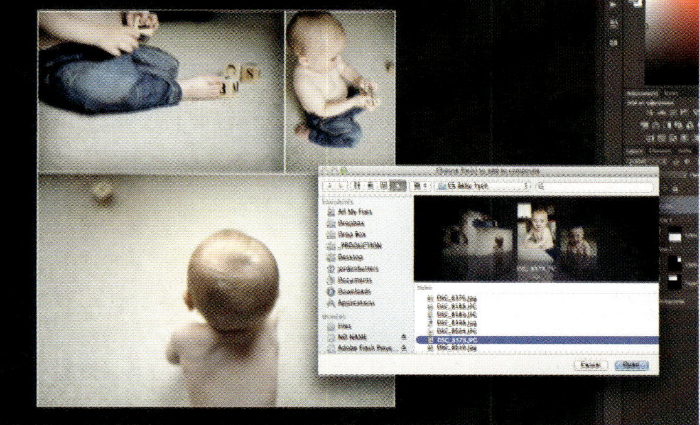

4 ADD A NEW COLUMN The next row or column will be scaled to suit the existing images in the collage. This allows you to add as many additional rows and columns as you wish. We've chosen a portrait-format image to finish off our collage – click on the ***Left*** or ***Right*** button under ***New column*** to add the final image. All done!

Colour themes

Inspired by the hues of an image? Topaz Labs' ReStyle plug-in makes it easy to add colours from one image to another

IN THIS AGE of Instagram filters and off-the-shelf presets, it's never been easier to style the colours in your images. Topaz Labs' ReStyle plug-in is a preset manager with a difference. Boasting more than 1,000 presets, selective adjustments, blending modes and custom presets, it's a powerhouse for colour-toning and offers near-endless options to stylise your images.

While ReStyle's one-click presets are both plentiful and effective, it's the ability to create custom presets that we're going to cover here – specifically, taking the tones from one image and applying them to another. If you've ever seen a colour palette that you like the look of and tried to replicate it, you'll appreciate what a tricky a process it can be. First you've got to identify the colours used in the source image and understand why they work together, then you've got to tone each part of your destination image, adjusting the hues to match those of the first. It's a lengthy process that requires much back and forth and technical know-how. Thankfully, Topaz ReStyle completely takes the headache out of this process.

First of all, head to www.topazlabs.com and download ReStyle – there's a 30-day free trial after which the software costs USD$60. Once installed, you're ready to get started...

ORIGINAL

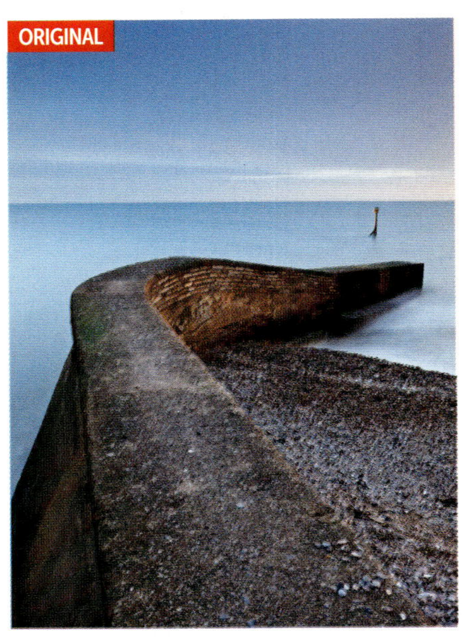

There's an app for that

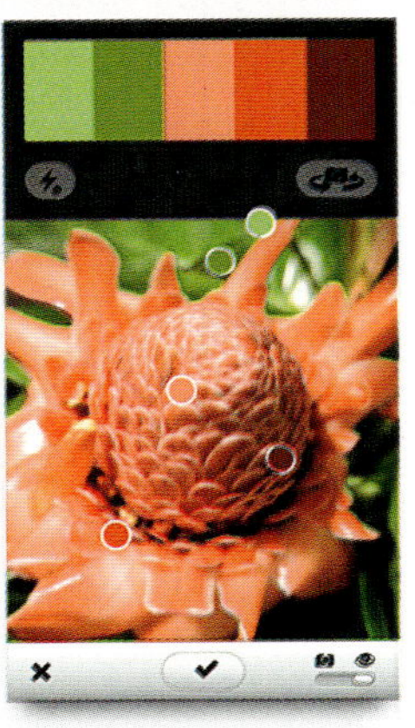

Want to record pleasing or inspirational colour palettes when out and about with your iPhone? Adobe's Kuler mobile app for iOS is available for free, and works in much the same way as Topaz ReStyle. You can use the phone's camera to map colours in front of you and save the theme. Once home, you could even email the theme to yourself and import it into ReStyle to create a preset based on these tones. Visit: Creative.adobe.com/products/kuler

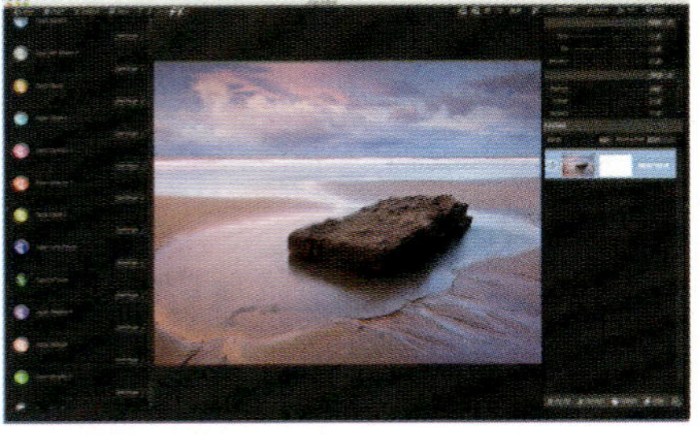

1 OPEN THE PLUG-IN ReStyle can be opened via Photoshop, Elements, Lightroom, Aperture, iPhoto or through Topaz Labs' own photoFXlab, as used here. First, load your source image into the host software before opening it in ReStyle. For Photoshop and Elements users, this is done via the ***Filters*** menu. Lightroom users go to ***Photo>Edit In***.

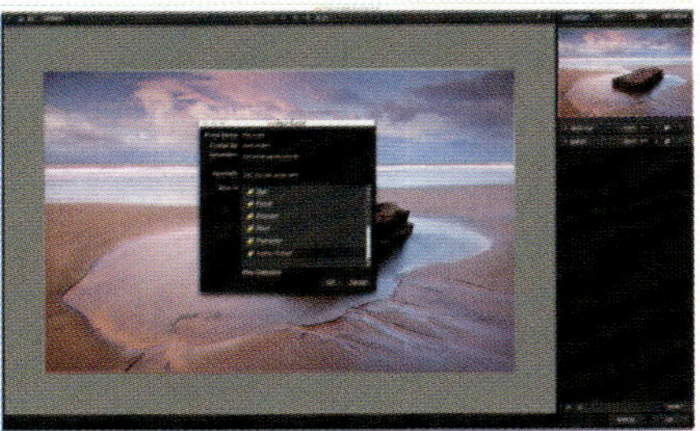

2 CREATE A PRESET With ReStyle loaded, first click on ***Reset*** in the lower right corner, and then click on the + symbol in the opposite corner to map the colours in your image. Give your preset a name, description and keywords to make it easy to find again. You can then save it to an existing collection, or click ***New Collection*** to create your own.

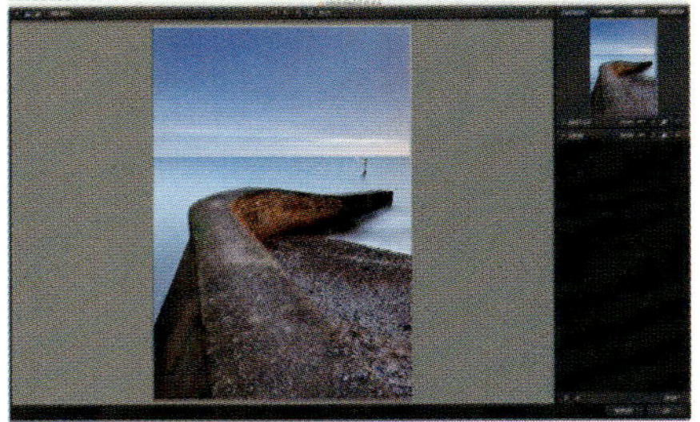

3 OPEN YOUR FINAL IMAGE After ReStyle has finished working, click on the ***Cancel*** button in the lower-right corner to close the plug-in. Back in the host software, close this image without saving and load in the image that you wish to apply the style to. Repeat step one to load this image into ReStyle. Once loaded, click ***Reset*** again.

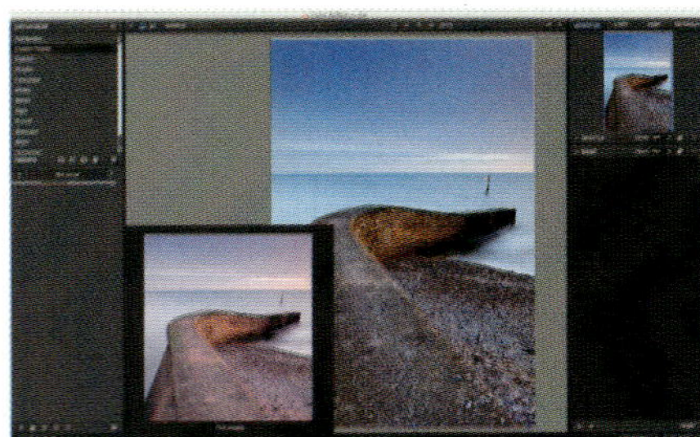

4 APPLY THE PRESET Locate your new preset in the ***Collections and Presets*** panels and click on it to apply. If you're happy at this stage you can save your image by clicking on ***OK*** in the lower-right corner, but we're going to make some other tweaks. To compare your new image with the original at any time, simply click and hold on the image.

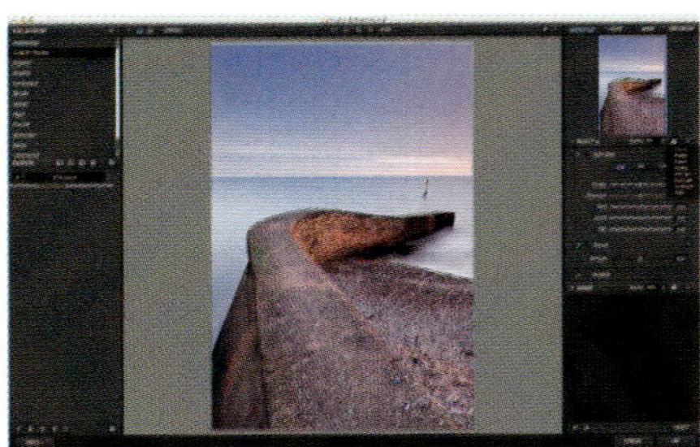

5 TWEAK THE EFFECT At the top of the ReStyle tab you can lower the preset's opacity. To the right of this you can adjust the Blending Mode of the preset. Much like in Photoshop, changing the Blending Mode adjusts how the preset blends with the layer below. You can also customise the Hue, Saturation or Luminosity of each tone.

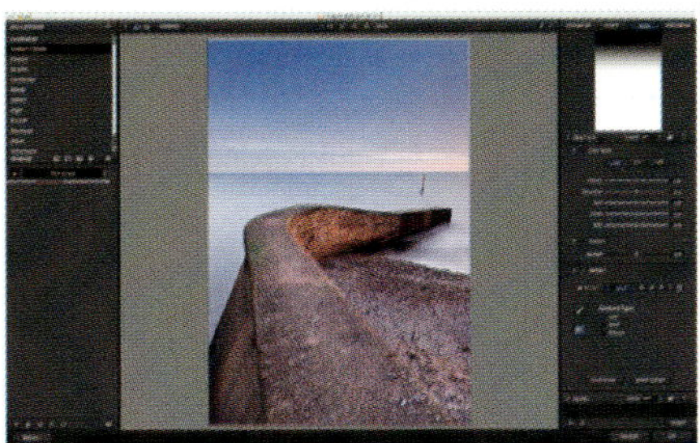

6 ADD A MASK Finally, the Masks feature underneath can also be useful. Click on the ***Tick box*** next to Masks to activate it, select ***Hide*** from the options and use either the ***Brush*** or ***Gradient Tool***, much like in Photoshop, to mask the preset. If you make a mistake, click ***Reveal*** and paint back over that area, or click the ***Reset*** button above.

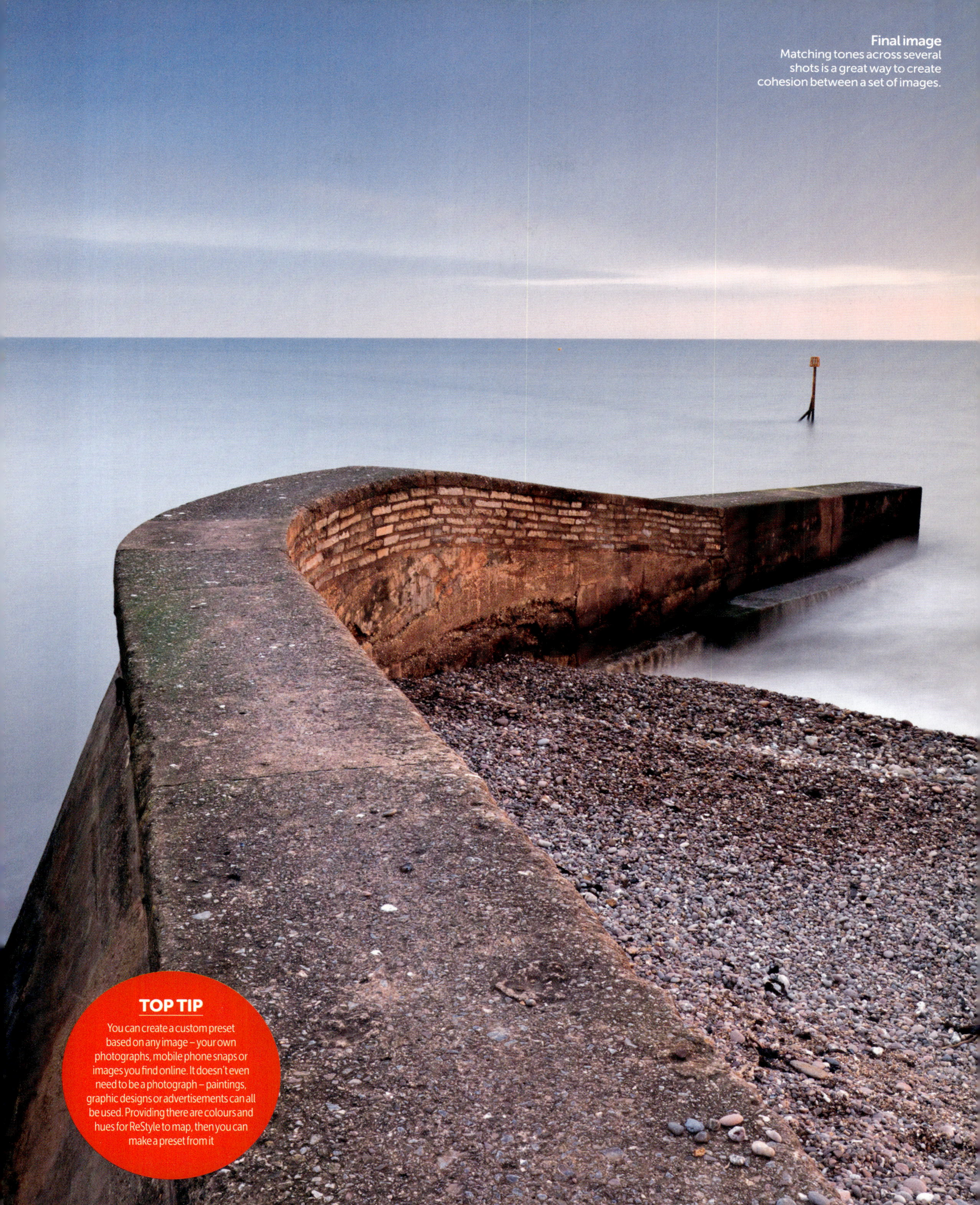

Final image
Matching tones across several shots is a great way to create cohesion between a set of images.

TOP TIP

You can create a custom preset based on any image – your own photographs, mobile phone snaps or images you find online. It doesn't even need to be a photograph – paintings, graphic designs or advertisements can all be used. Providing there are colours and hues for ReStyle to map, then you can make a preset from it

Monochrome with Tonality

Macphun's easy-to-use black & white software, Tonality, makes converting your images to monochrome a doddle. Here's how you use it...

THERE ARE A HUGE number of plug-ins and software packages available that claim to be the ultimate way to convert your images to monochrome. One fairly new product to market is Tonality Pro, from Macphun. This Apple-only black & white conversion software in available in two flavours: Tonality is aimed at amateur and enthusiast photographers and costs £14; while Tonality Pro is aimed at serious enthusiasts and professionals and costs £42. The standalone Tonality package contains the tools that most users will need, while the Pro version adds extra plug-in support for Photoshop, Lightroom, Aperture and Elements along with other more advanced features.

One of Tonality's key features, alongside the vast array of presets available, is layers. Much like Photoshop, effects and adjustments can be added in layers, and then masked so only to apply to select parts of the image, putting a huge amount of selective control in your hands. Alongside the built-in tonal, clarity, exposure and contrast controls are creative effects such as Vignette, Lens Blur and Glow, leaving you with an endless supply of options to tweak and adjust. While we can't run through every feature here, we've provided a quick guide to help you get started and make basic adjustments in Tonality.

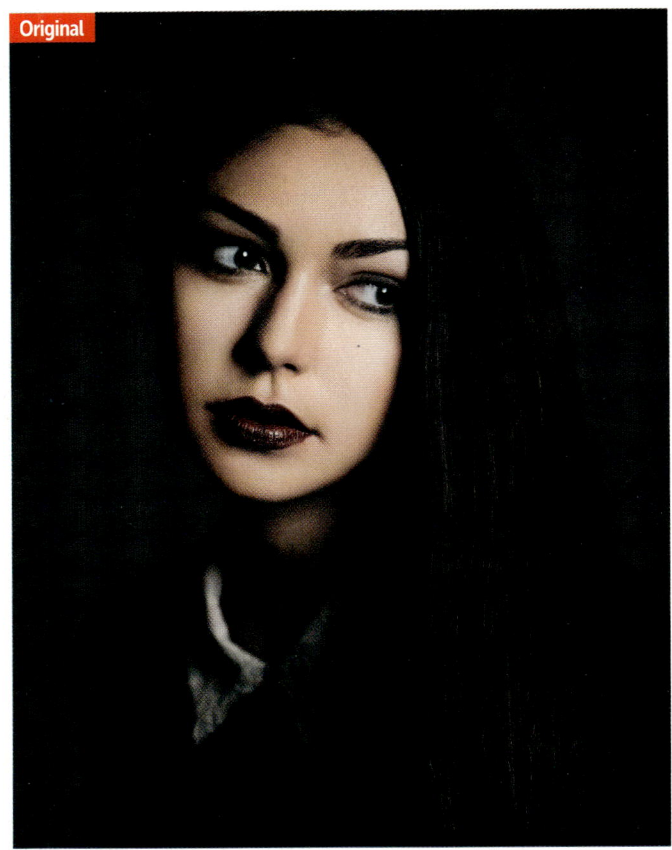

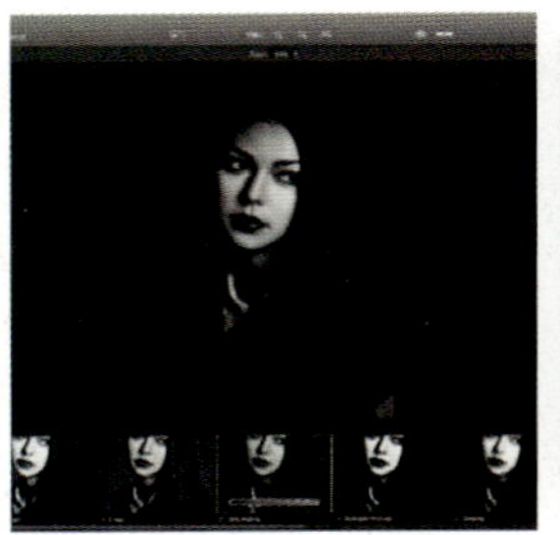
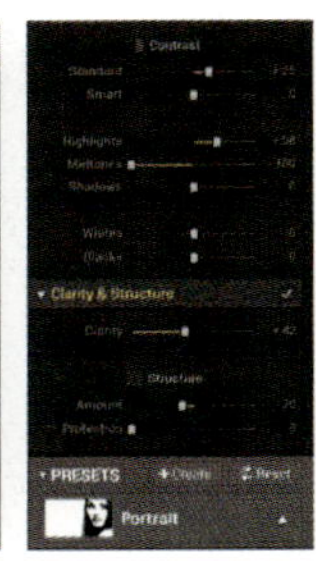

1 TRY A PRESET Load your image into Tonality and start by trying a preset found in the bottom right corner. Selecting the category lists the presets along the bottom – one click and that preset is applied. If none of them suit, click ***Reset*** to the right of Presets and create your own!

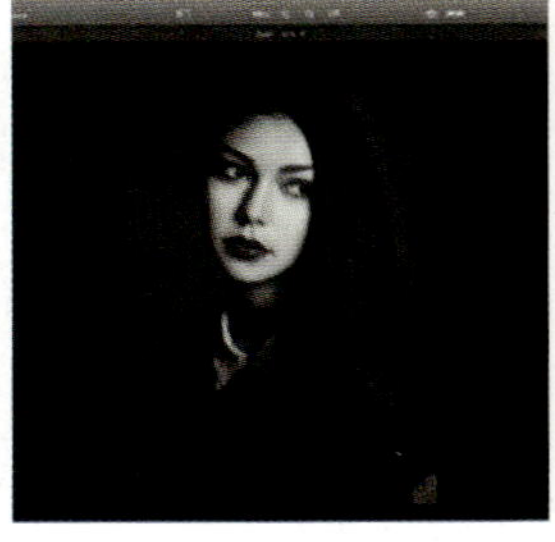

2 ADJUST THE BASICS Start in the *Tone* section on the right by fine-tuning the exposure. Adaptive Exposure allows you to brighten or darken the image whilst preventing clipping. Similarly below, Smart Contrast allows you to add contrast while retaining existing shadows and highlights.

How am I doing?

To compare the changes that you've made to the original, flat black & white image, click at any time on either the ***Quick Preview*** button or the ***Compare*** button for a side-by-side comparison.

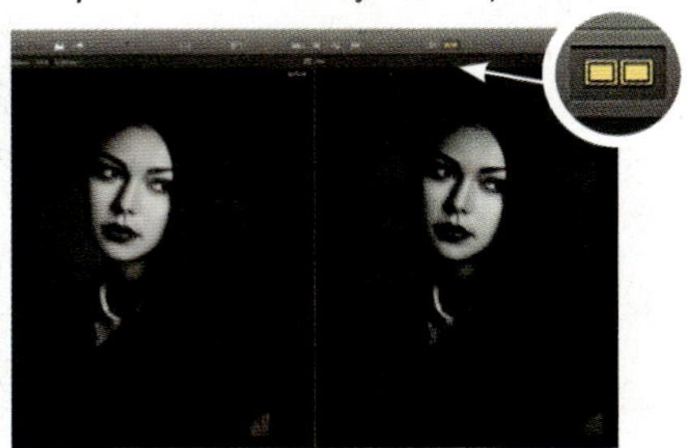

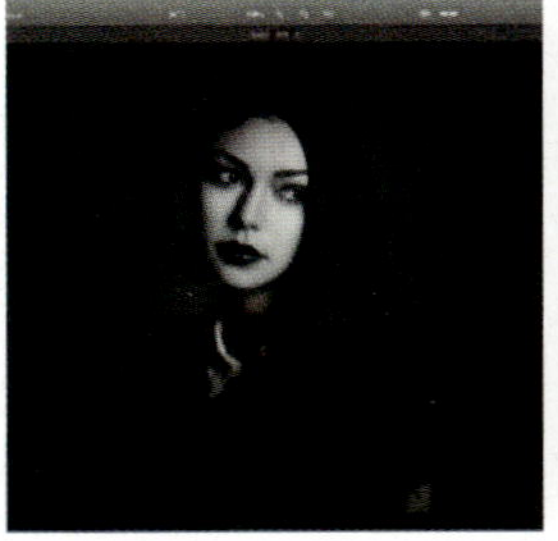
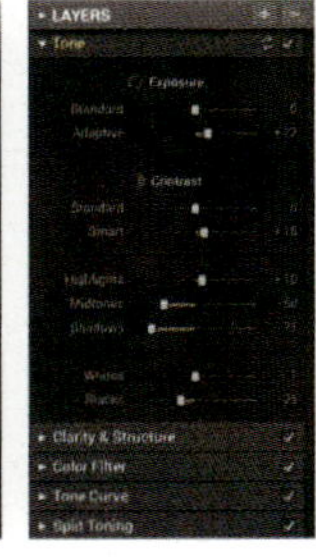

3 TWEAK TONES Use Highlights, Midtones and Shadow sliders to enhance. These aren't smart controls, so keep an eye on the Histogram when fine-tuning them. Adjustments to any one section can be turned off, or reset to default using the controls at the top of each tab.

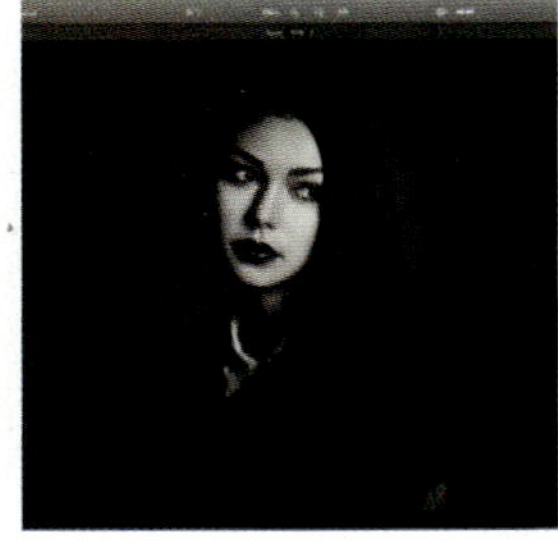

4 ADD DETAIL Clarity & Structure is used to enhance detail, but should be used sparingly. Increasing Clarity adds mid-tone contrast. Structure, on the other hand, finds and enhances edges, ideal for textures and Micro Structure targets fine detail. Protection controls adjust which edges are affected.

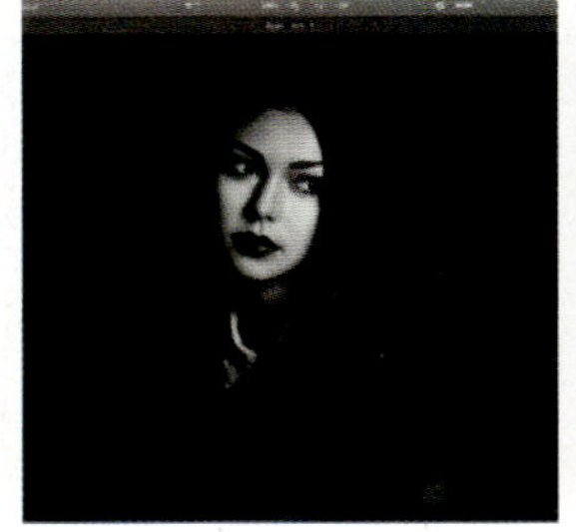
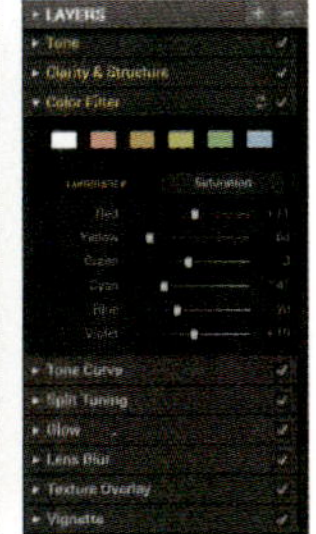

5 COLOUR CHANNELS Color Filters sit below. The Red filter darkens blue skies, the Orange filter smooths skin tones, while the Yellow filter darkens skies slightly. Green and Blue filters are less fruitful, but the latter enhances mist and fog. You can manually adjust the filters using the sliders, too.

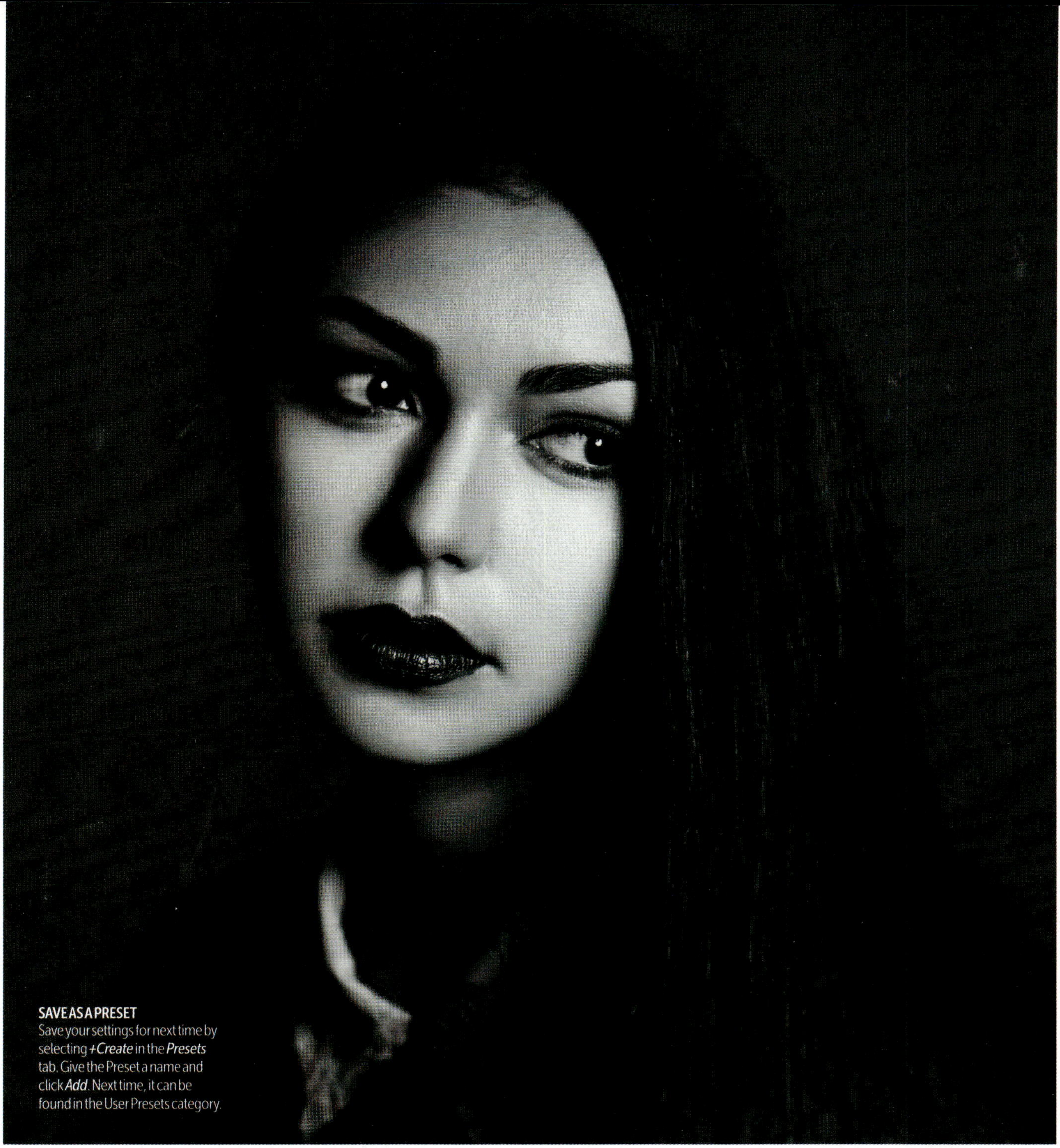

SAVE AS A PRESET
Save your settings for next time by selecting ***+Create*** in the ***Presets*** tab. Give the Preset a name and click ***Add***. Next time, it can be found in the User Presets category.

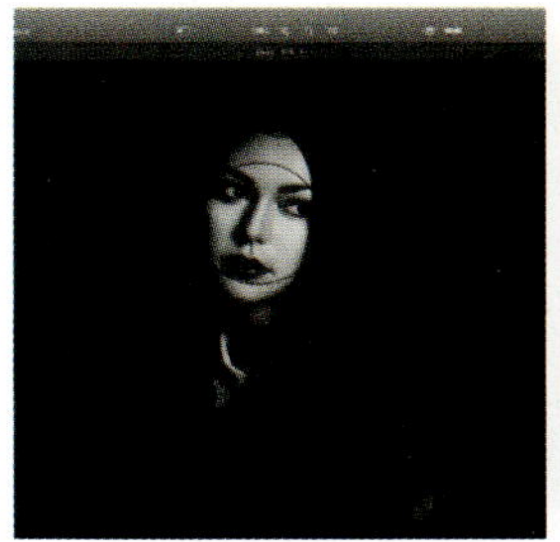
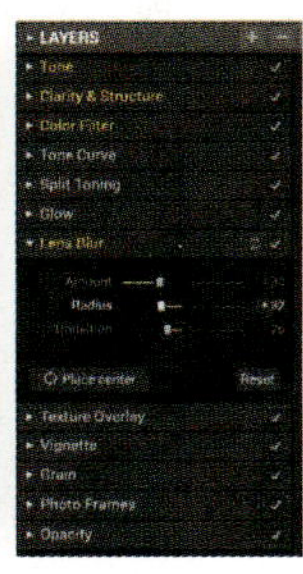

6 ADD SOME BLUR Under ***Lens Blur***, select ***Place Center*** and click on your image to centre the blur. Now modify your blur to suit. Amount adjusts the blur's intensity, Radius changes the size of the clear area and Transition controls the transition between the clear and blurred areas.

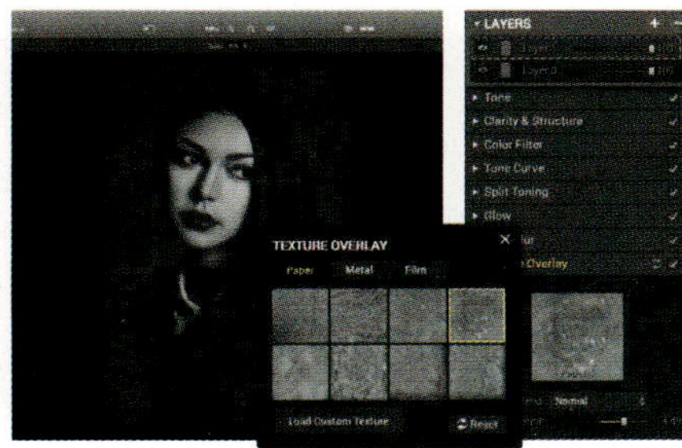

7 USE LAYERS We want to add a texture, but only in select areas. Click on the ***small arrow*** next to ***Layers*** at the top and then select the + symbol to add a new layer. Scroll down to ***Texture***, click ***Select Texture*** to choose your texture from the list and use the ***Amount*** slider to suit your tastes.

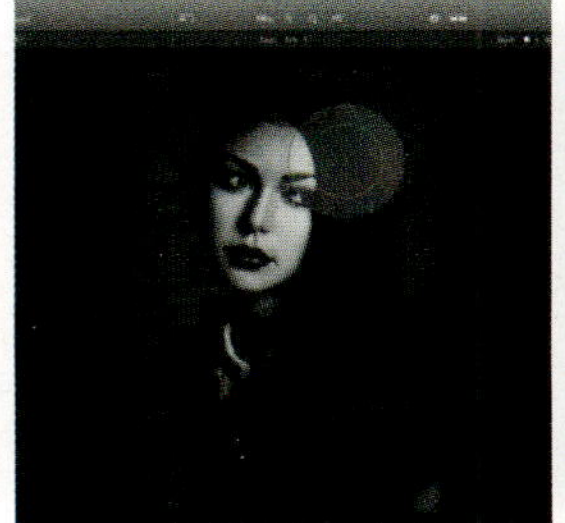
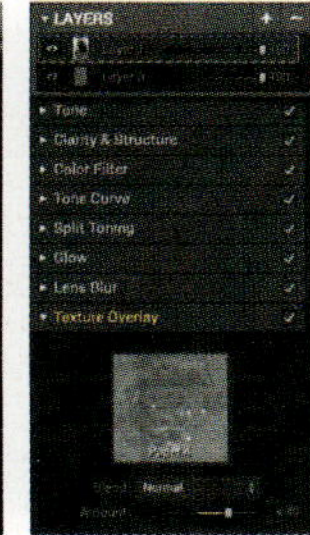

8 ADD A MASK Select ***Brush Mode*** and adjust the brush properties at the top. When you begin brushing, that effect will only show in those areas. Choose the ***Erase Mask Tool*** at the top and brush back over the effect to remove it. You can then set the opacity of the layers in the ***Layers*** tab at the top.

ORIGINAL

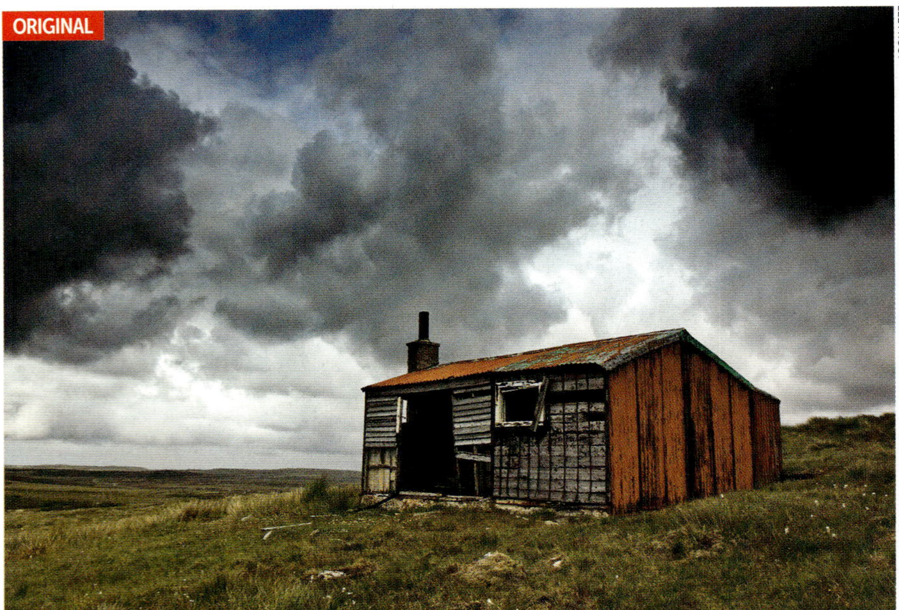

LEE FROST

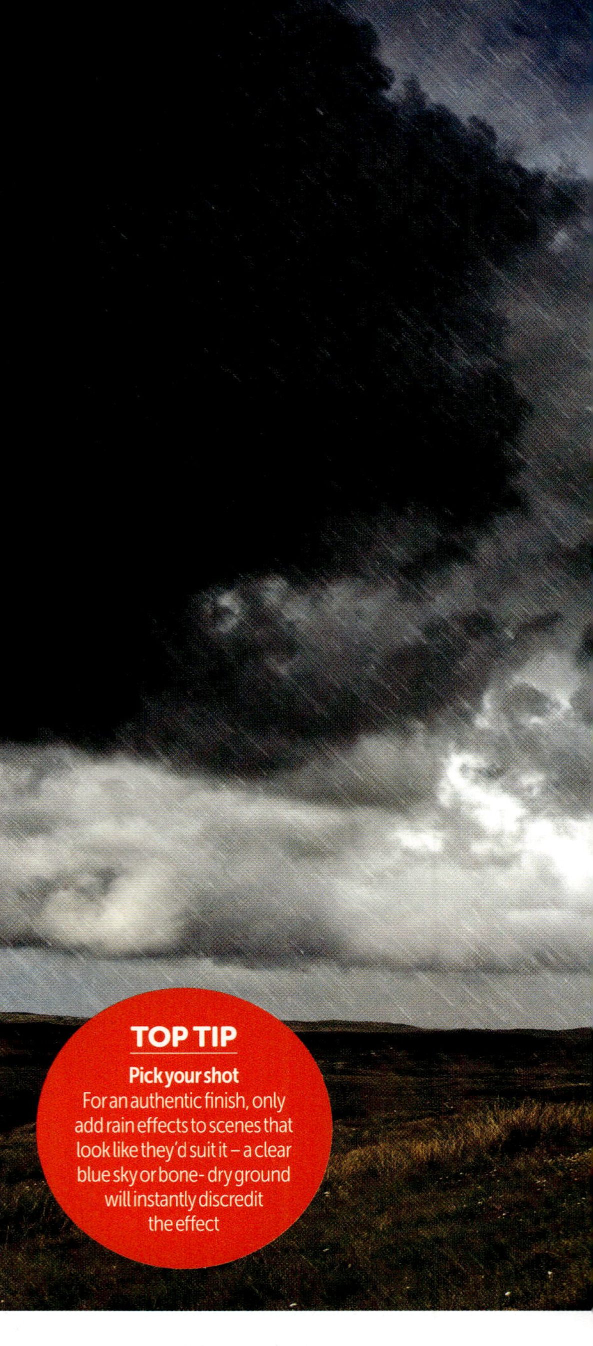

Create realistic rain

Play at being Mother Nature using OnOne software's Perfect Effects 9 plug-in to give your images effortless atmosphere in a matter of minutes

LIVING IN THE UK, it's fair to say we're no strangers to prolonged and unexpected downpours. Landscape, portrait, macro and sports photographers alike will attest that many photographic opportunities have been lost to a surprise interruption of precipitation. However, there are those occasions when rainfall adds to a scene and it's worth sticking it out rather than grabbing your gear and running for cover. Typically, rainfall rarely happens when you want it, so here's a handy way to add a shower to your shots using a nifty plug-in.

This is just one of the many filters, effects, gradients and textures offered by OnOne's Perfect Effects 9 so it's well worth a look. Best of all, at the time of print, Perfect Effects 9 was completely free and available from www.ononesoftware.com/products/effects9free. The app sits as a standalone program, or as an integrated plug-in for Adobe Photoshop CS6 onwards, Elements 11 onwards, Lightroom 4 onwards and Apple Aperture 3.5. The software is also available as part of the larger Perfect Photo Suite 9, which includes six other apps alongside Perfect Effects 9 and costs USD$140. There's also a free 30-day trial should you wish to try out the full suite. What have you got to lose?

TOP TIP

Pick your shot

For an authentic finish, only add rain effects to scenes that look like they'd suit it – a clear blue sky or bone-dry ground will instantly discredit the effect

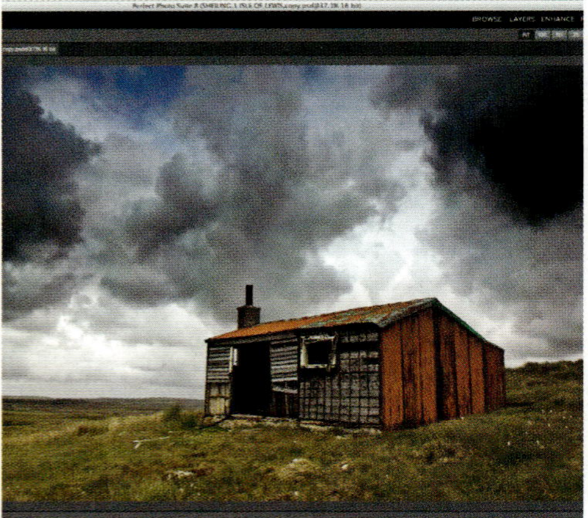

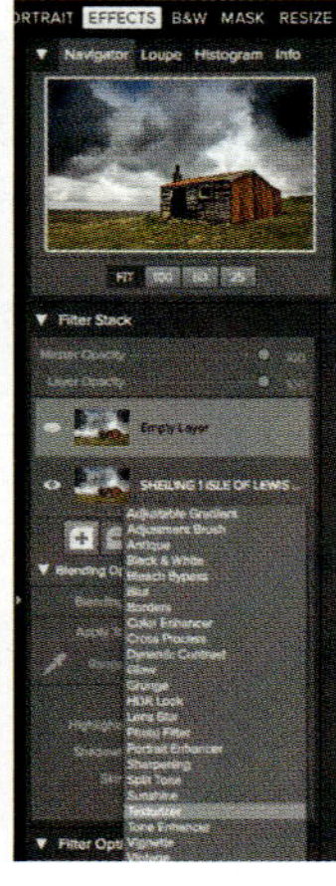

1 OPEN THE FILTER MENU After opening your image in Perfect Effects 9 you'll be greeted with an array of effects that can be selected using the menu on the left. On the right-hand side, under the *Filter Options* tab, click on the *Filter* drop-down menu and select *Texturizer*; this will add a texture to your image, which we're going to adjust next.

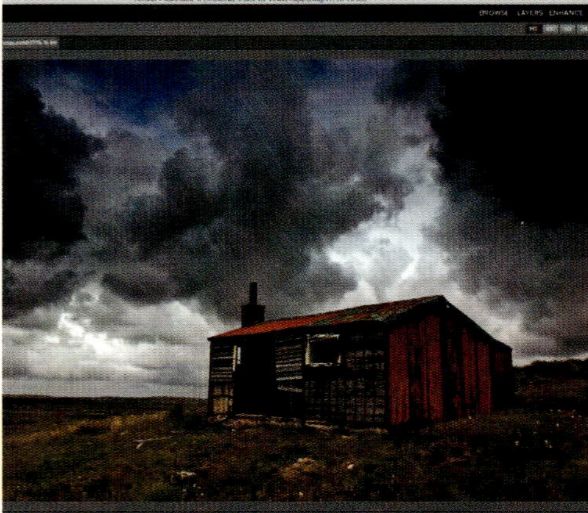

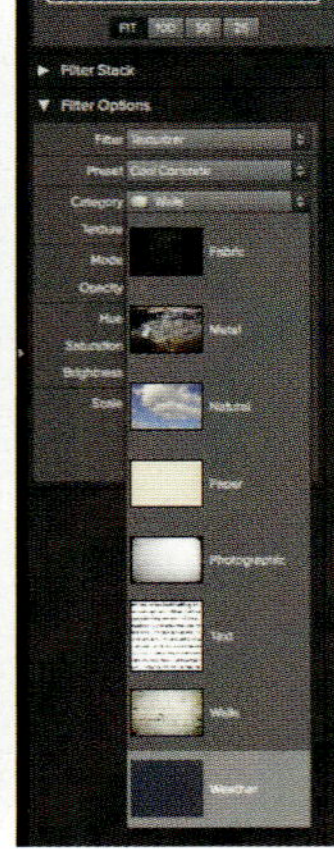

2 ADD A TEXTURE In the *Filter Options* tab, click on the *Category* menu, and select the *Weather* thumbnail at the bottom of the list. This will open a choice of weather effects within the *Texture* drop-down menu. Select one of the three *Drizzle* effects; bear in mind that directional rain tends to look more realistic than perfectly vertical.

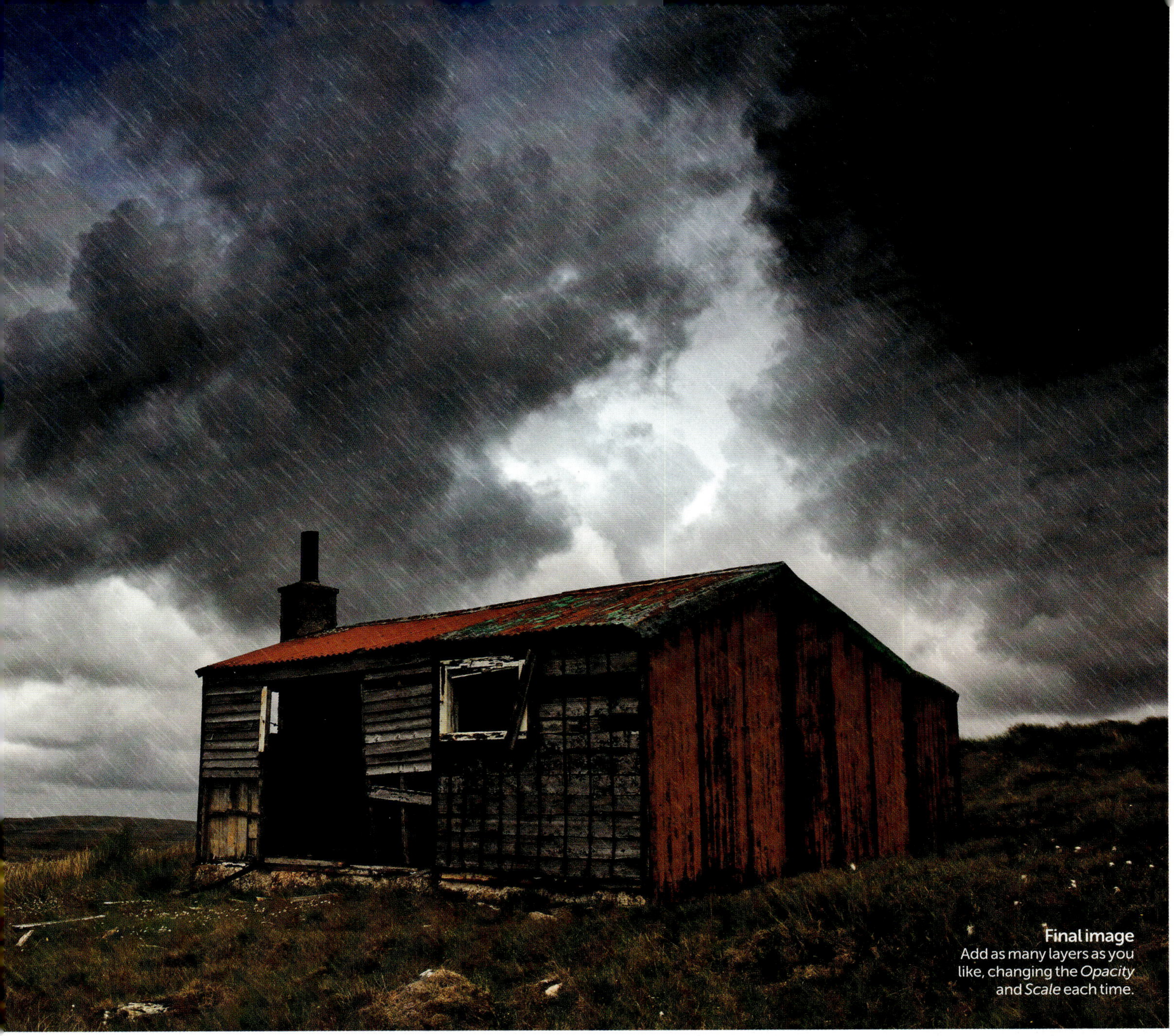

Final image
Add as many layers as you like, changing the *Opacity* and *Scale* each time.

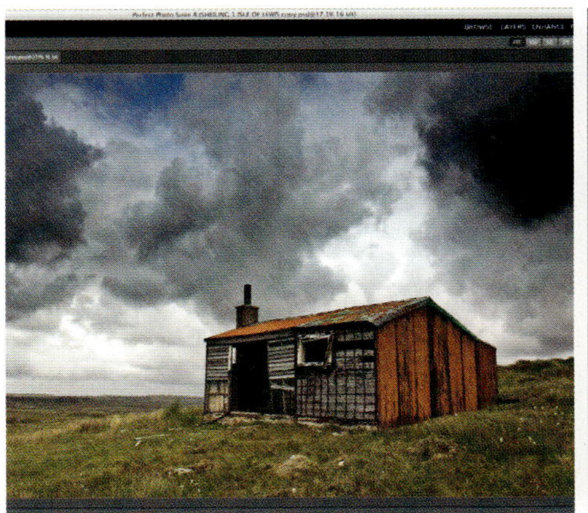

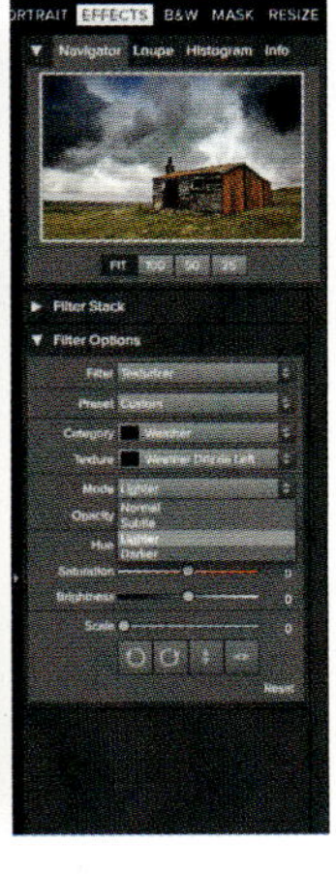

3 ADJUST THE RAIN With your rain effect applied, use the drop-down menu to set the *Mode* to *Lighter*, before lowering the *Opacity* to between *30* and *40*. We're going to apply the rain in layers as this creates a more realistic final effect. This layer forms the furthest layer of rain, so should be less opaque than the next layer.

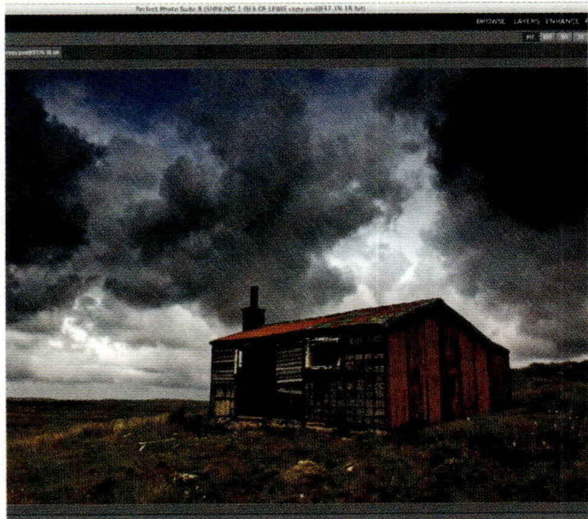

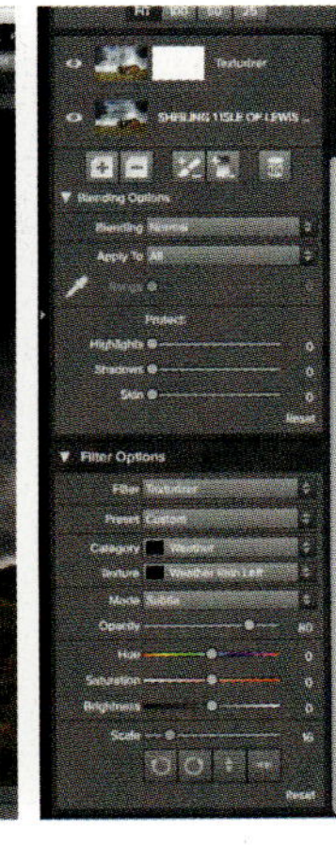

4 ADD A SECOND LAYER Under the *Filter Stack* tab, click on the *Add Empty Layer* button and repeat the previous steps, this time selecting the heavier *Rain* effect, matching the direction of the first layer, of course. Set the *Mode* to *Subtle*, *Opacity* to around *80* and increase the *Scale* to between *15* and *20*. All done!

Fake bokeh with ease

Add lens blur with Topaz Labs Lens Effects' depth mapping facility

THE PROBLEM WITH any software that automatically adds blur is that actual blur is dependent on depth, but images contain no readable depth data therefore the software doesn't know which bits to blur and how much to blur them. Although not fully autonomous, Topaz Labs' Lens Effects is the closest you can get to the real thing, thanks to its clever Depth Map facility. By manually mapping what objects are closest and which are furthest away, Lens Effects allows you to pick focal points and apply blur post-capture. Lens Effects costs $79.99, or you can try it for a free for 30 days at www.topazlabs.com.

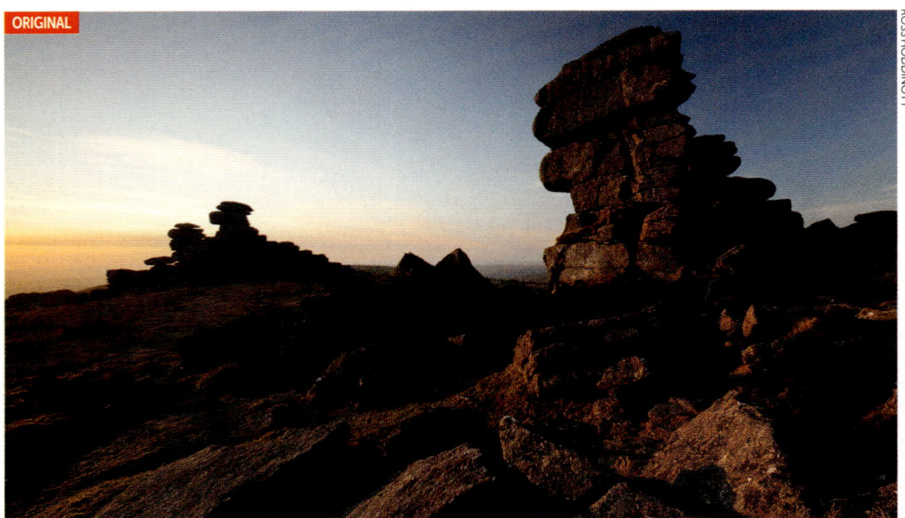
ORIGINAL

ROSS HODDINOTT

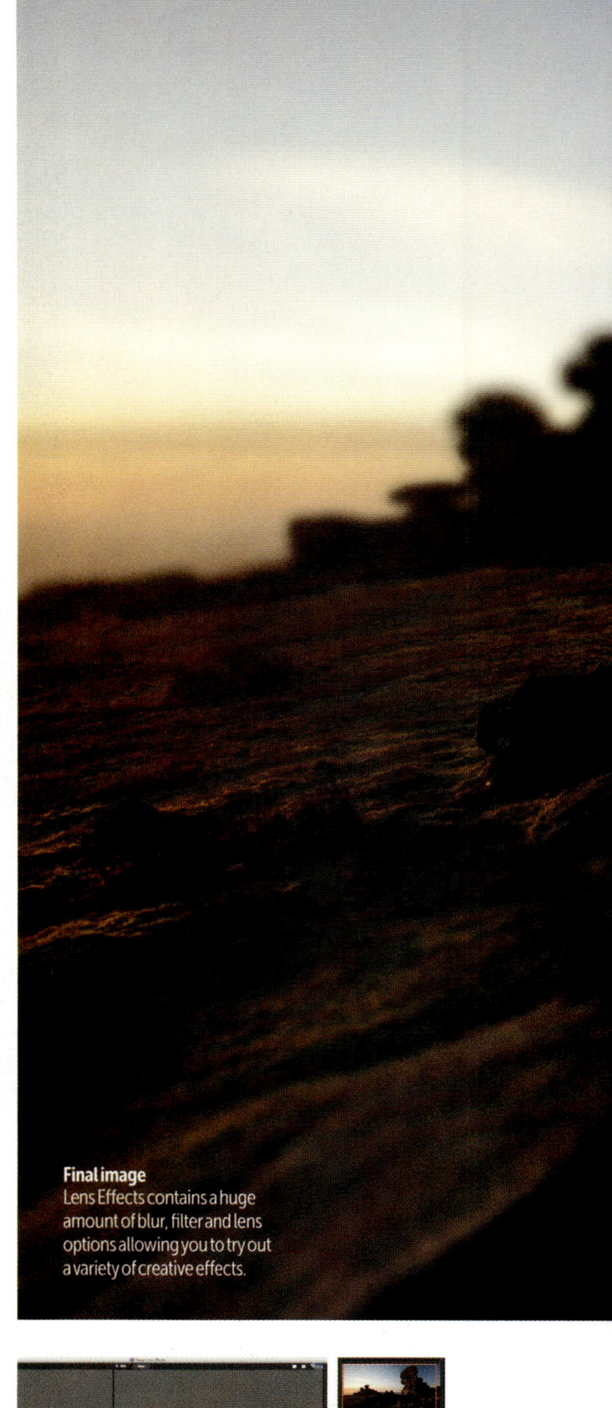
Final image
Lens Effects contains a huge amount of blur, filter and lens options allowing you to try out a variety of creative effects.

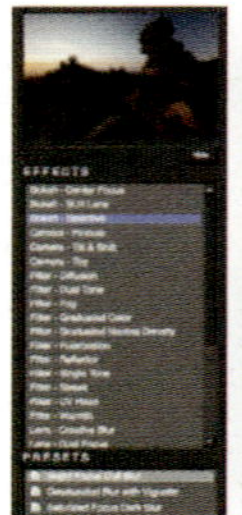
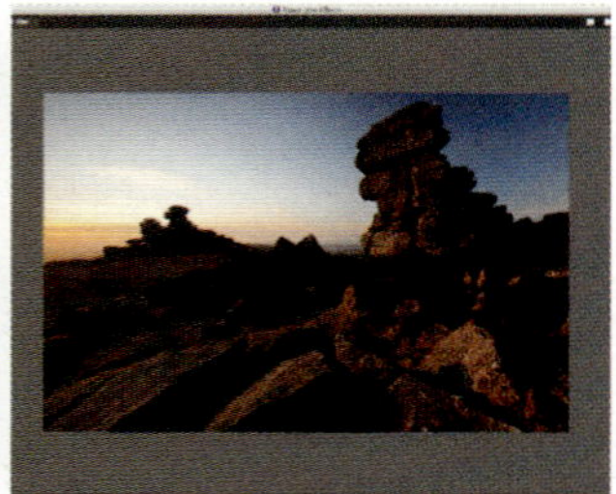

1 LOAD YOUR IMAGE Select *Bokeh – SLR Lens* or *Bokeh – Selective*. The latter allows for greater adjustment and the former contains lens emulations for popular lenses. Your image will be completely blurred, as you first need to assign a depth map to the image. Click on *Edit Depth Map* on the right.

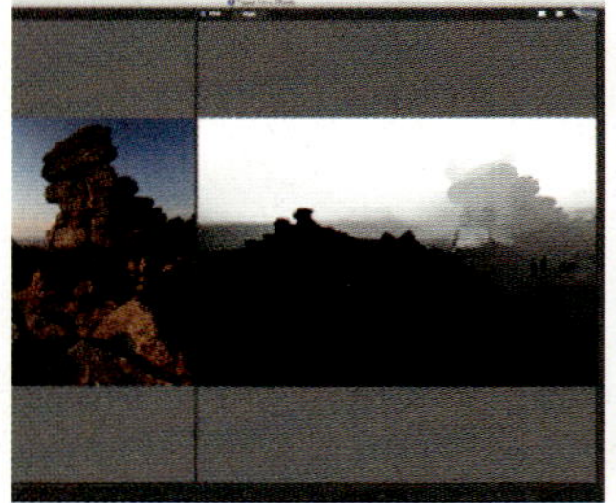
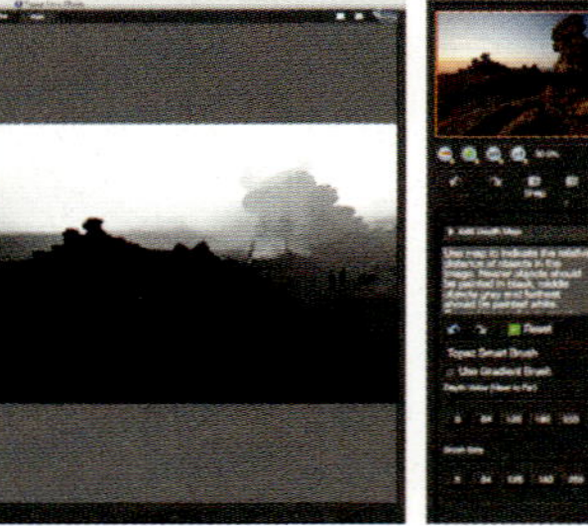

2 SET UP THE GRADIENT You'll see a black and white preview appear – this is the depth map. Black objects are closest and white areas are furthest away. Click *Reset* to clear the depth map and tick the *Use Gradient Brush* option. Use the slider to set your *Gradient Starting Value* to *0*.

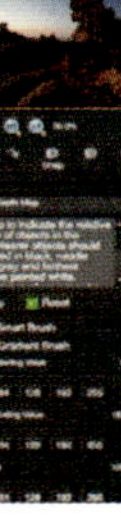

3 ADD THE DEPTH GRADIENT The *Gradient Ending Value* depends on your image. As there's scenery beyond the hill here we chose a value about three quarters along the scale. Click and drag from the closest to the furthest point in your image and repeat until the image is covered with an even gradient.

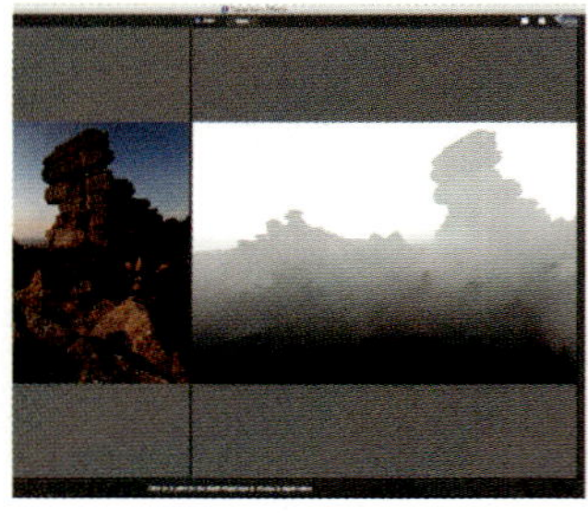

4 FILL OUT THE SKY Untick *Use Gradient Brush* and set the *Depth Value* to *255*. Use a large brush to paint the sky. The smart brush fills in the rest for you. Zoom in and use a small brush near the edges to get a clean selection. Painting the sky white tells the software that it's the furthest thing away.

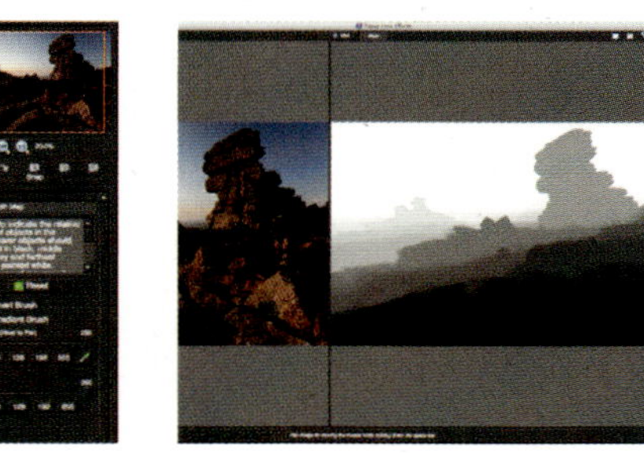
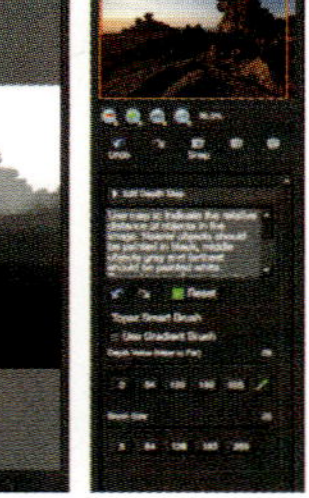

5 REFINE THE DEPTH MAP The depths of the rocks in our image aren't right. Use the *Eyedropper Tool* to select a point in the ground at the same depth as the object in your scene before brushing over it to change its depth. Repeat this, picking different shades for the different objects in your scene.

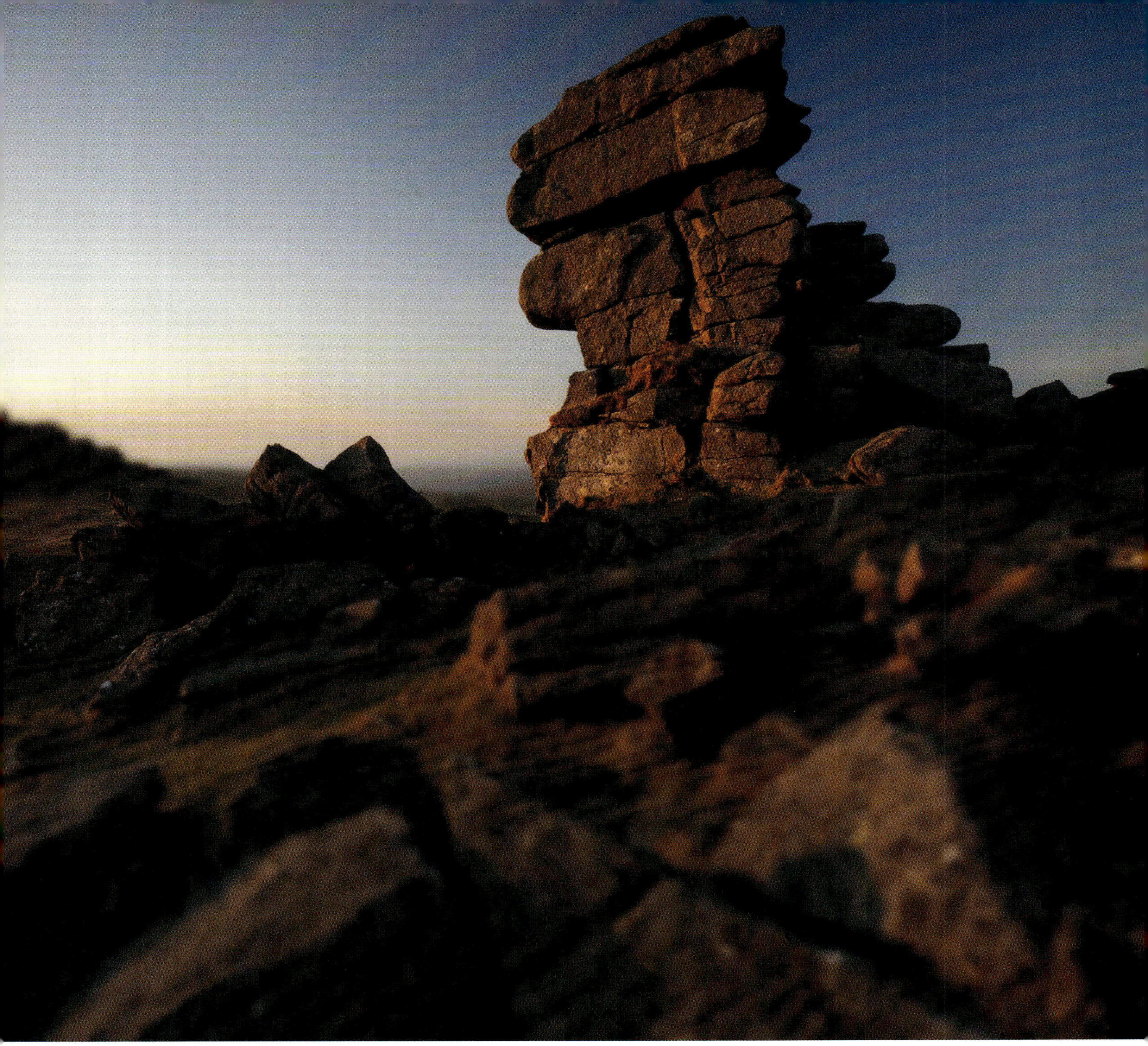

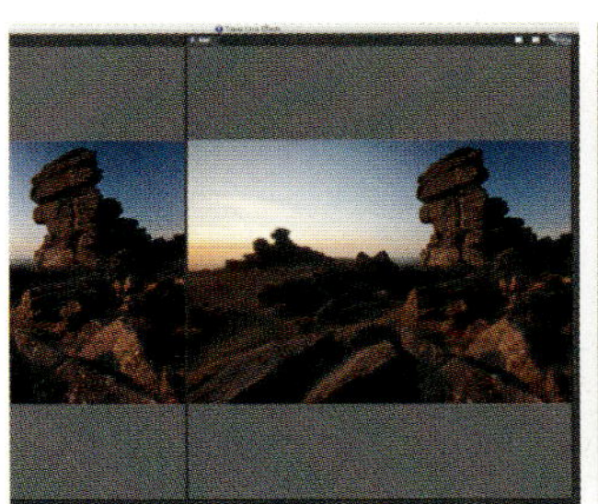
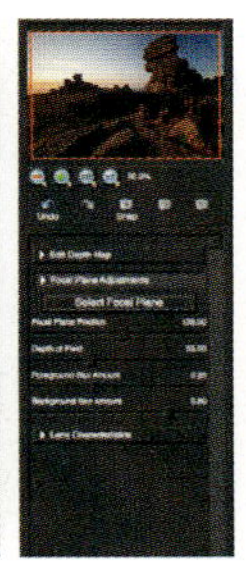

6 ADD THE BLUR Once you're happy, it's time to add the blur. Choose ***Focal Plane Adjustments*** and click the ***Select Focal Plane*** button; this allows you to click on your image to set the focus. From here you can also adjust the Depth of Field and the amount of Foreground and Background blur to suit.

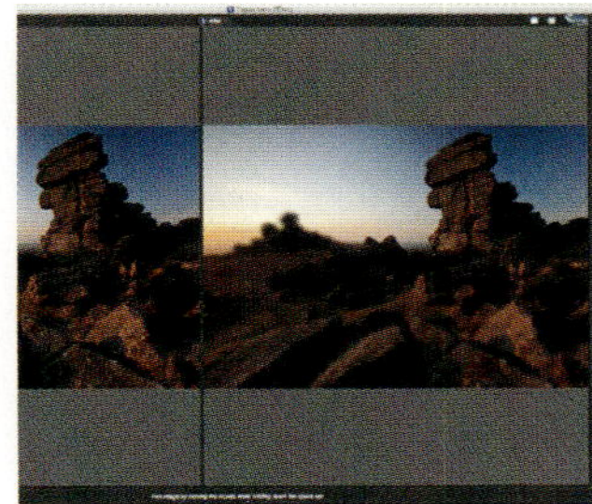
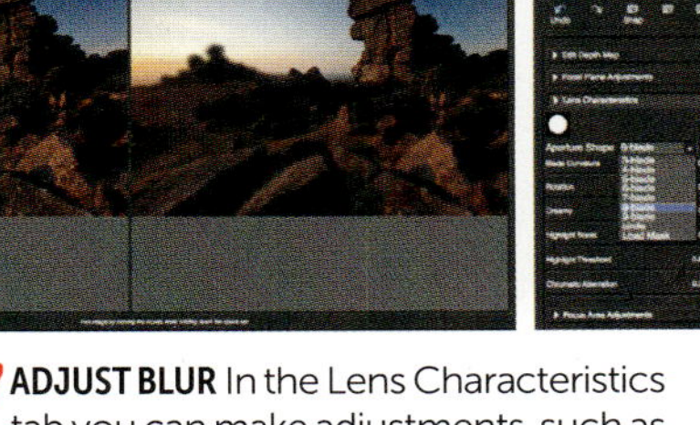

7 ADJUST BLUR In the Lens Characteristics tab you can make adjustments, such as the Aperture Shape, Blade Curvature and how Creamy the bokeh is. You can also control out-of-focus highlights using the Highlight Boost and Threshold sliders. Alternatively, use the Presets menu on the left to emulate a lens.

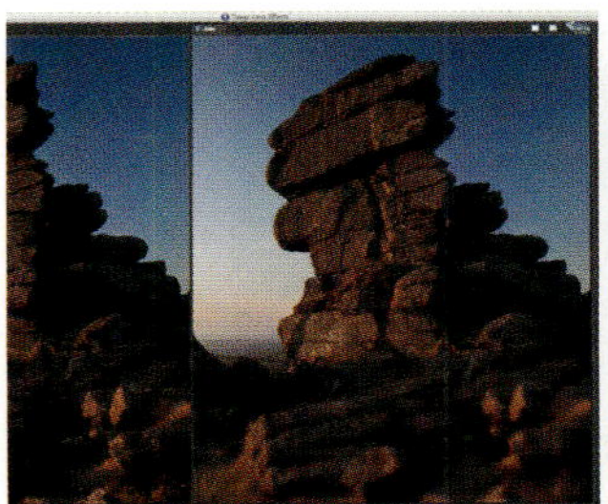
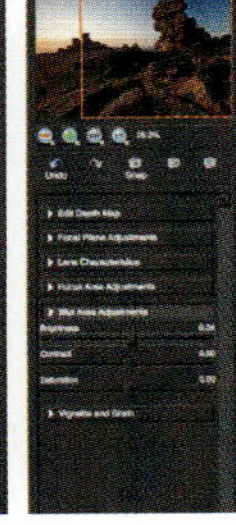

8 ADD SHARPNESS The Focus Area Adjustments tab controls the in-focus part of your image. The Sharpen and Sharpen Radius slider sharpen the focal point. Contrarily, the Blur Area Adjustments tab controls Brightness, Contrast and Saturation of out-of-focus areas.

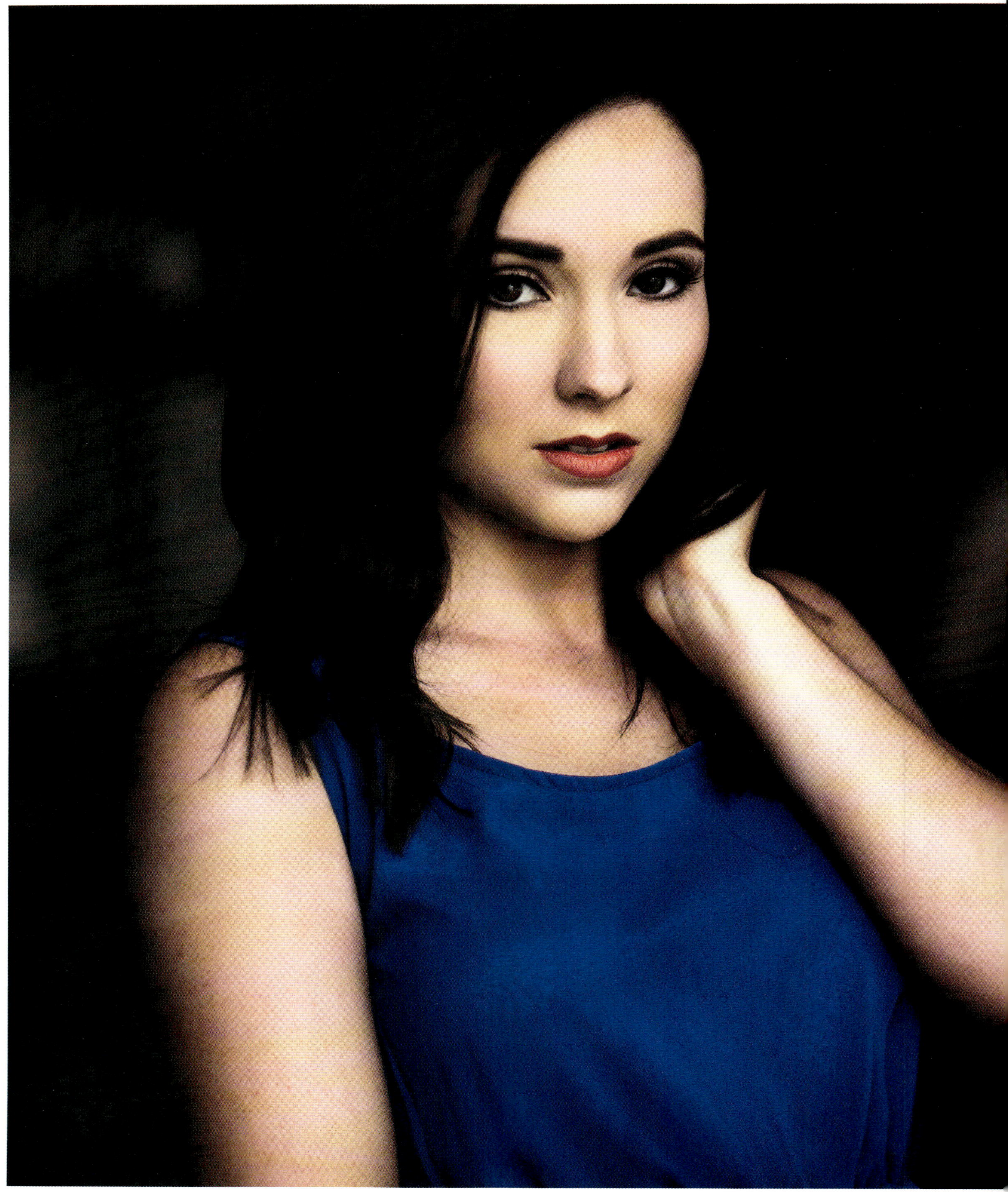

Step-by-step tutorials

SHOOT & EDIT

Try out a trio of fun techniques that will help you to develop your photography and your post-processing skills

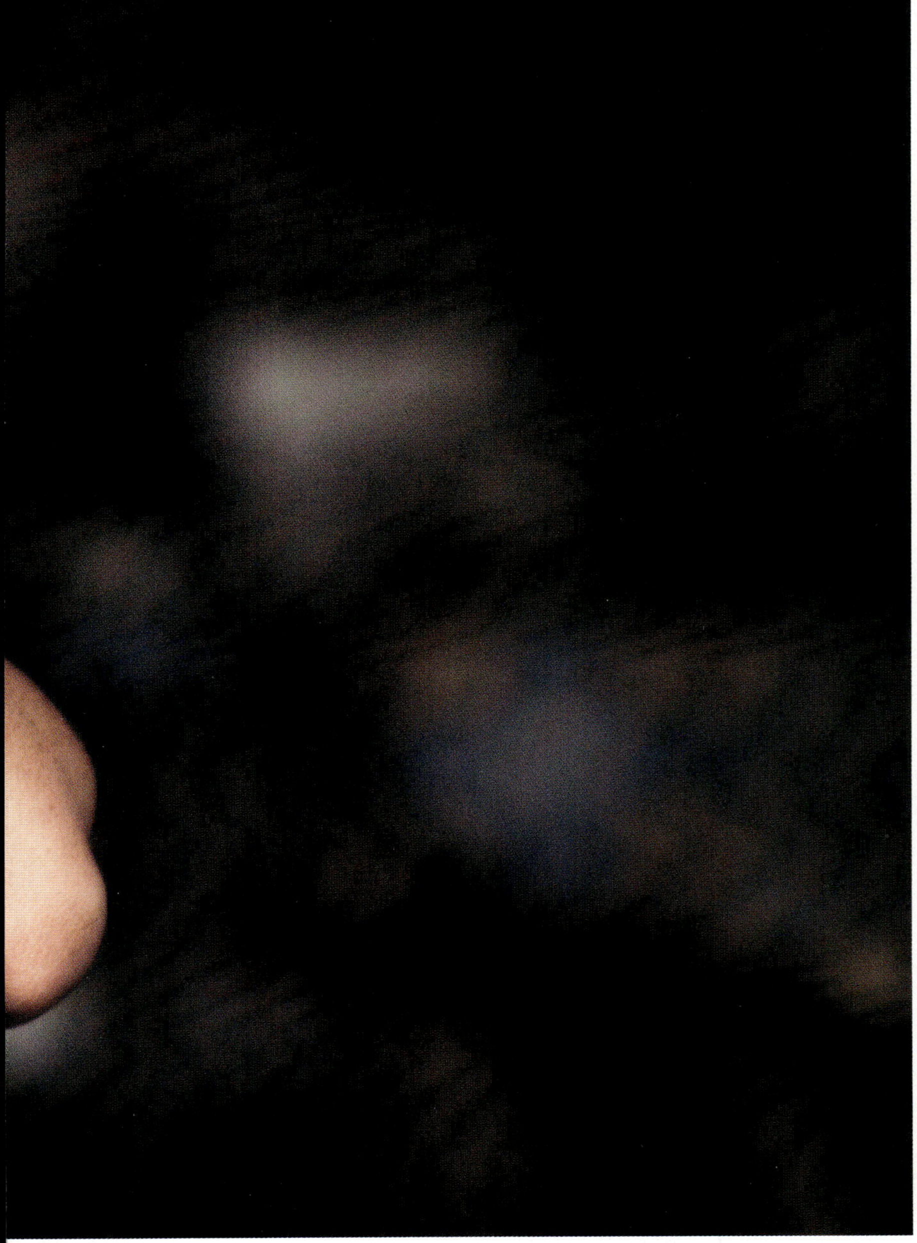

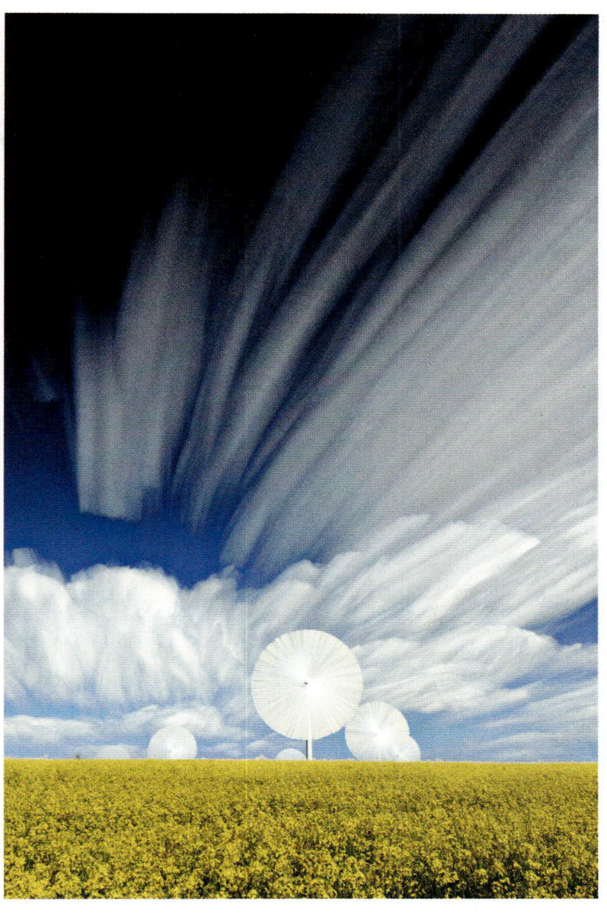

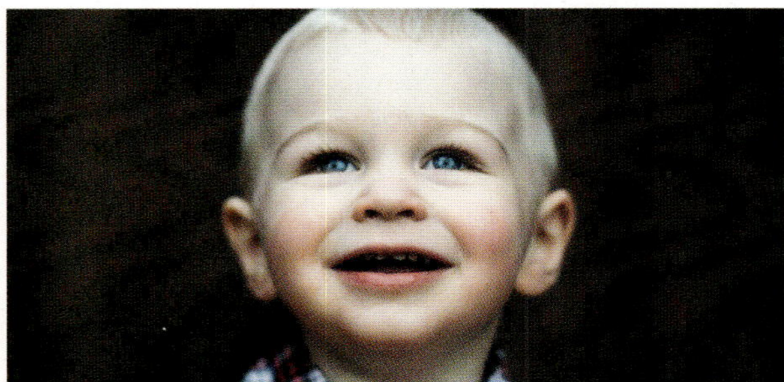

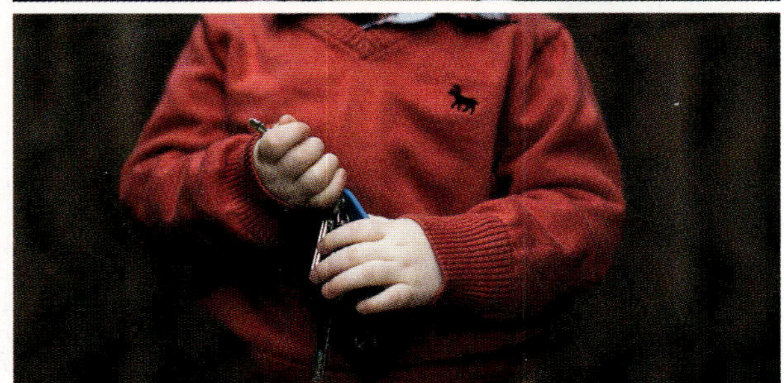

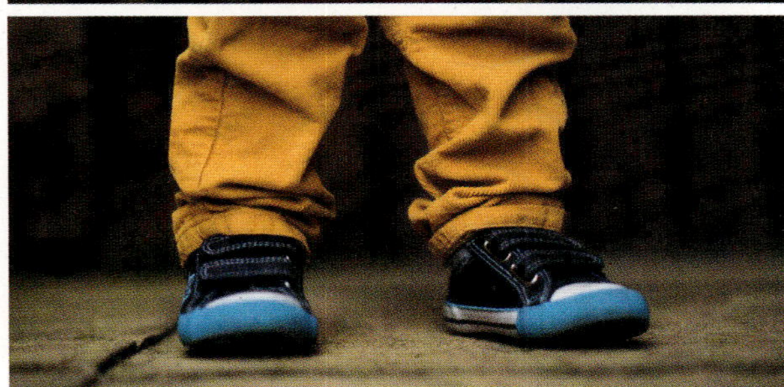

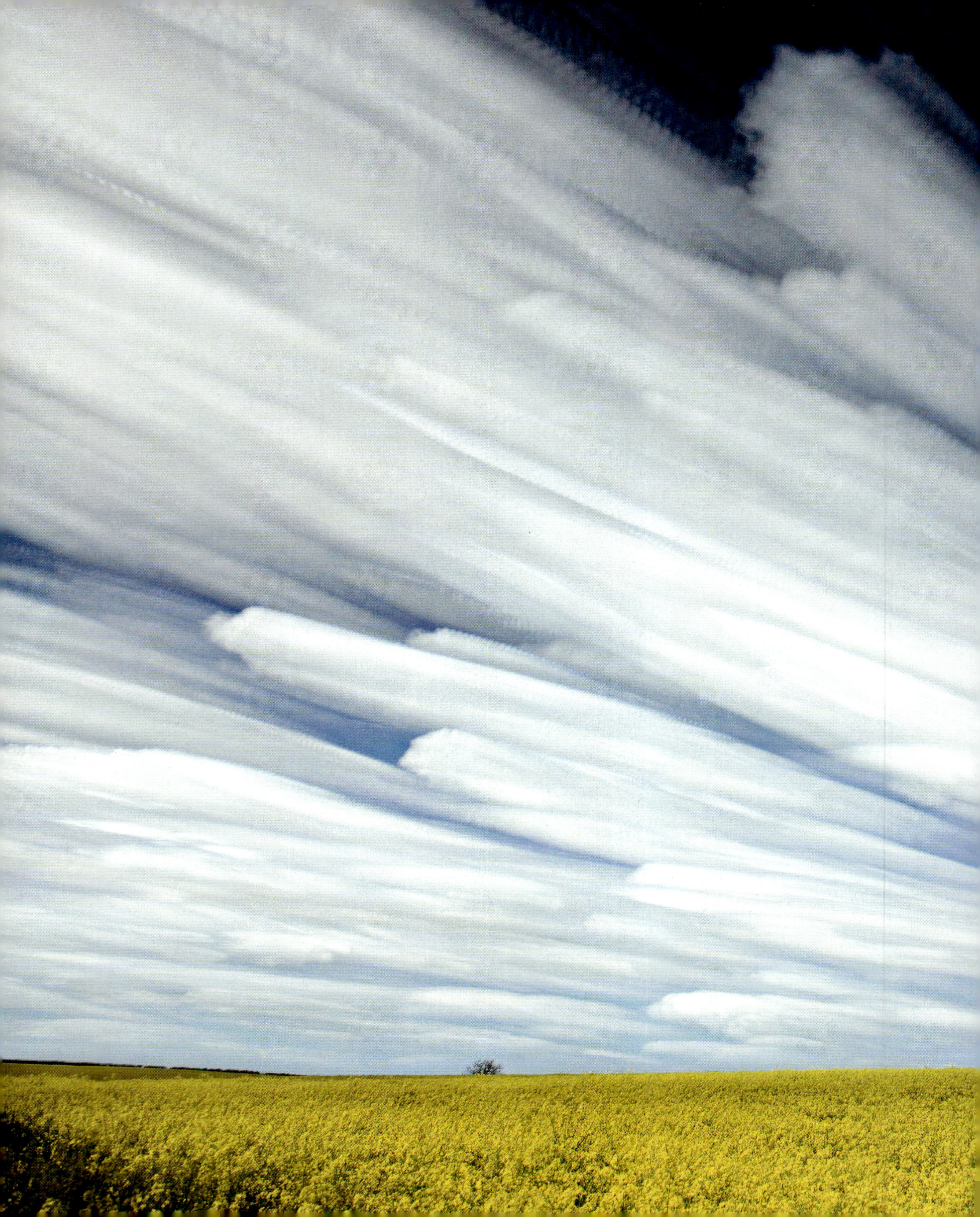

Create a time stack

Make your skies stun by creating a mind-blowing landscape using a time-lapse technique. We show you how to shoot and combine a cloud sequence to create impactful pictures

WE CAME ACROSS THIS technique after seeing the fantastic work of 500px member Matt Molloy (500px.com/mattmolloy). The method for capturing the images are identical to if you were shooting a time-lapse video sequence, however rather than compiling the shots into a video, you overlay the exposures into a single image during processing using Photoshop's 'Lighten' blend mode. By doing this, it has the effect of smearing clouds into unusual and eye-catching patterns. It's actually the exact same processing technique used to compile star-trail images! A windy day will allow you to shoot more movement in a shorter period of time – we shot this tutorial on a relatively still day and, as such, it took around 20 minutes and 600 exposures to compile the final image.

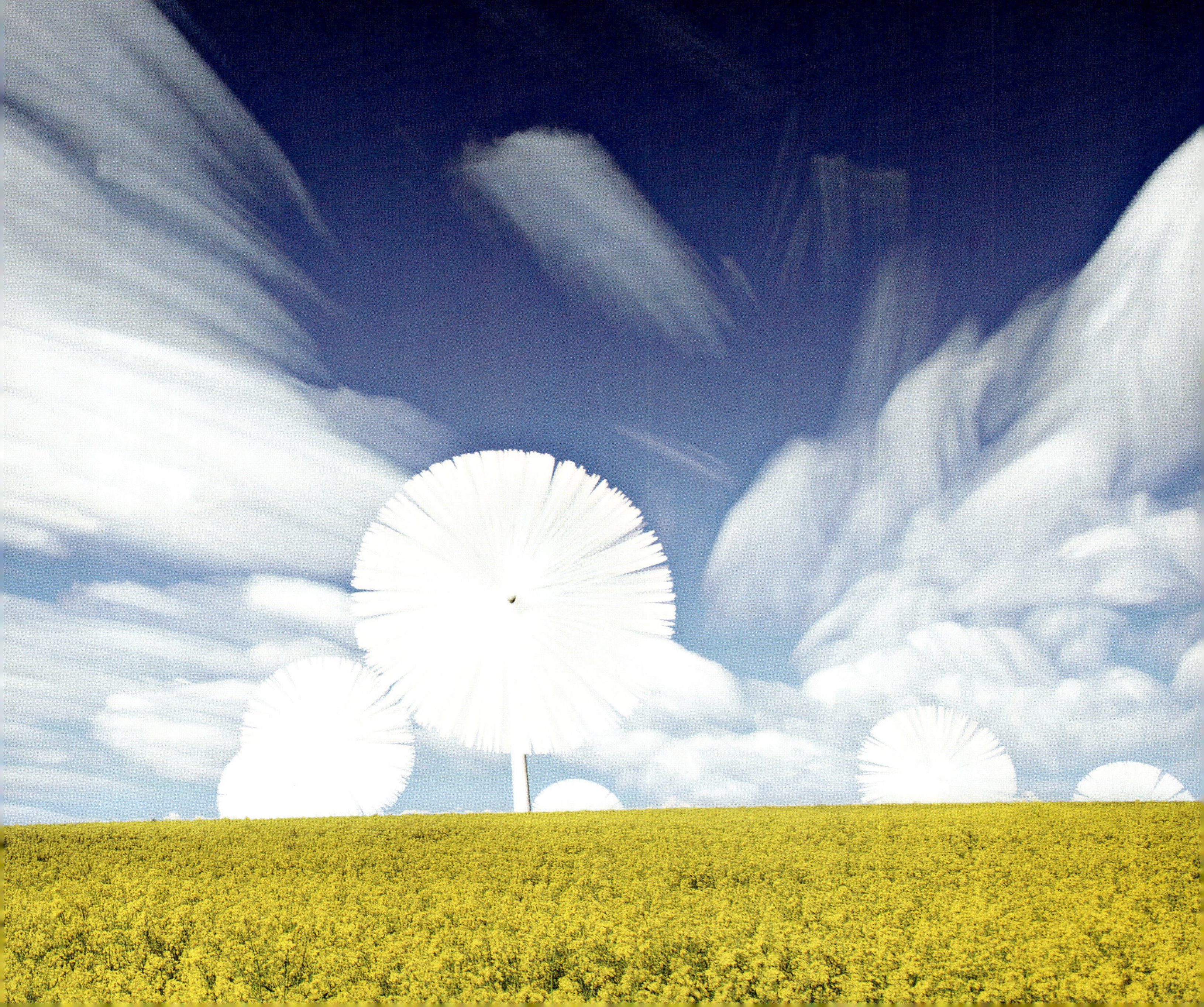

EQUIPMENT: There are a few pieces of kit that you'll need. A wide-angle lens is preferable – ideally a 10-20mm on an APS-C sensor or 16-35mm on full-frame – or else a standard zoom will do. You'll need a good tripod, preferably with a hook to weigh it down if it's windy. An intervalometer is essential and automates the process, triggering your camera every few seconds without you having to press the shutter – these can be had for around £10-15 on eBay or Amazon. Finally, a set of ND grad filters will allow you to balance your exposures.

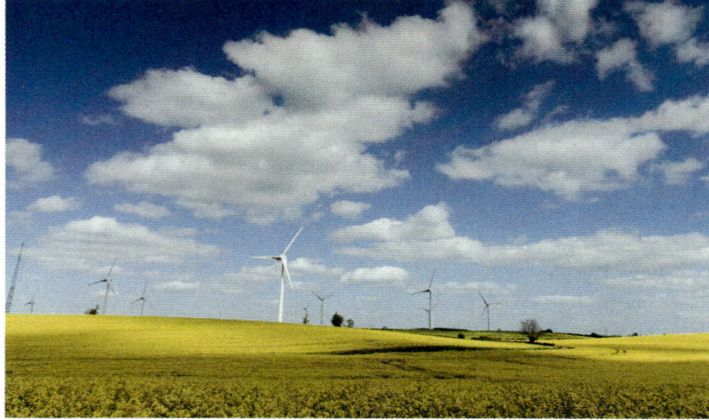

1 CHOOSE A LOCATION Wide vistas work, as do scenes with structures such as pylons, buildings or turbines – these create contrast for the moving clouds. The technique works best when the sun is behind you, or to the side during the day, or in front of you at sunrise or sunset. Check the wind direction too – the effect looks best when clouds are moving towards or away from you, rather than across the frame.

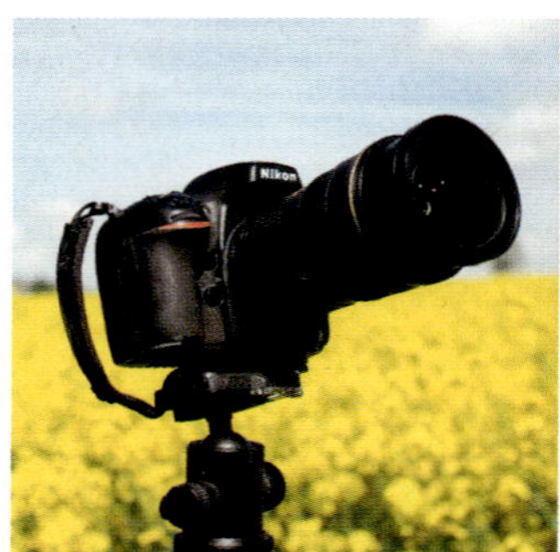

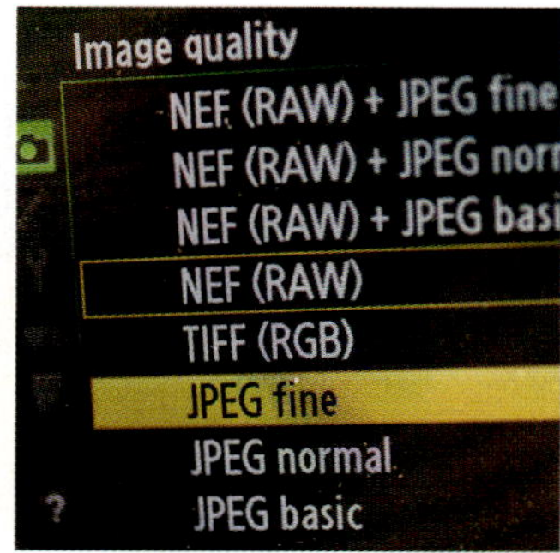

2 FIND THE RIGHT SETTINGS With your camera on a tripod, compose to include plenty of sky. Select aperture-priority mode and a mid-aperture. Set your focus point and then lock your lens to manual focus to stop the focus from changing. In order to fit more shots onto your memory card, and speed up processing, switch your camera to shoot fine JPEG rather than Raw. Take a test shot and check the histogram.

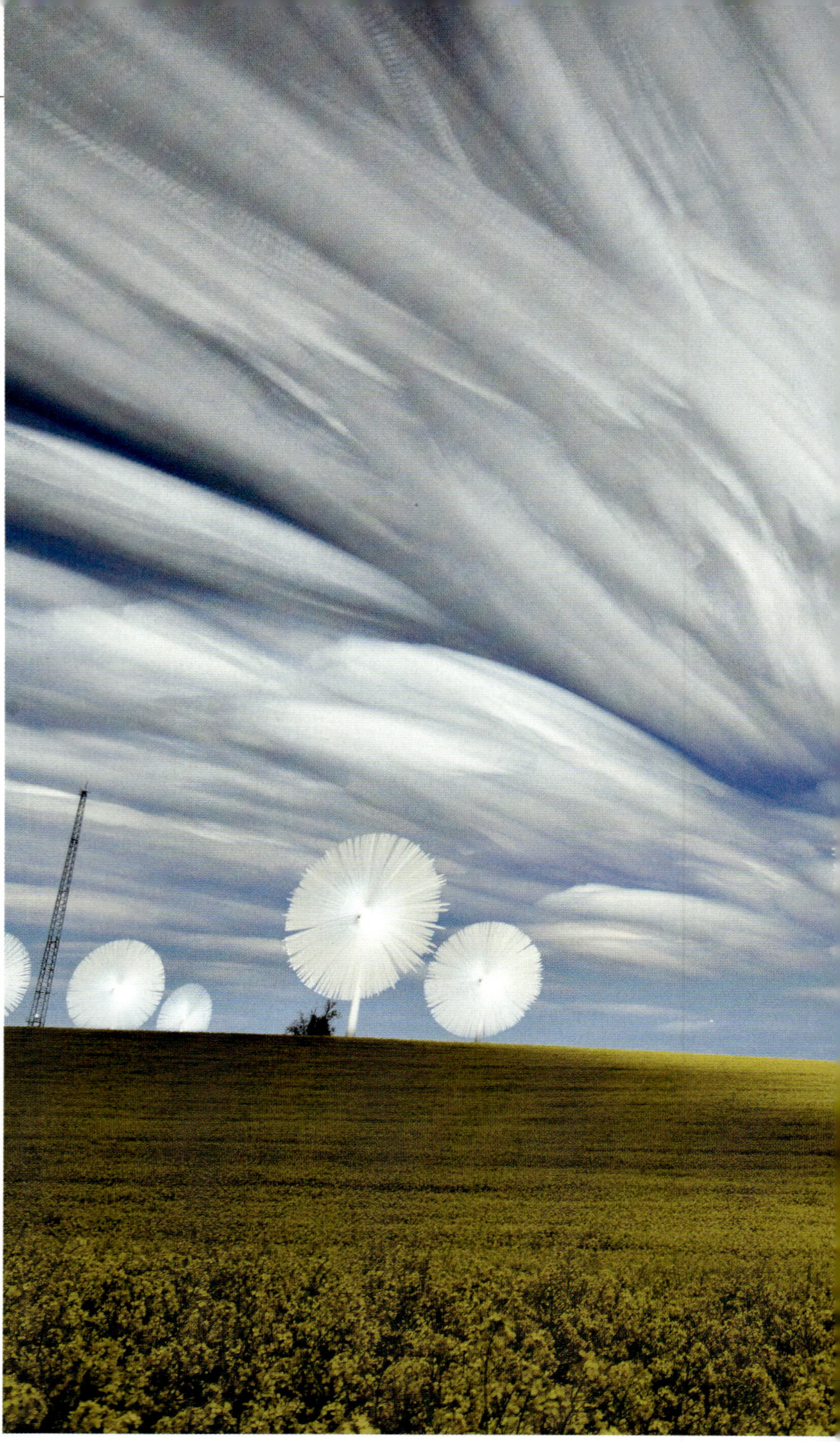

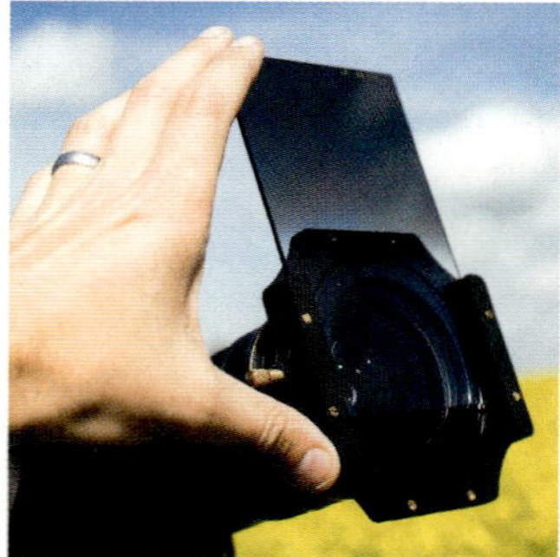

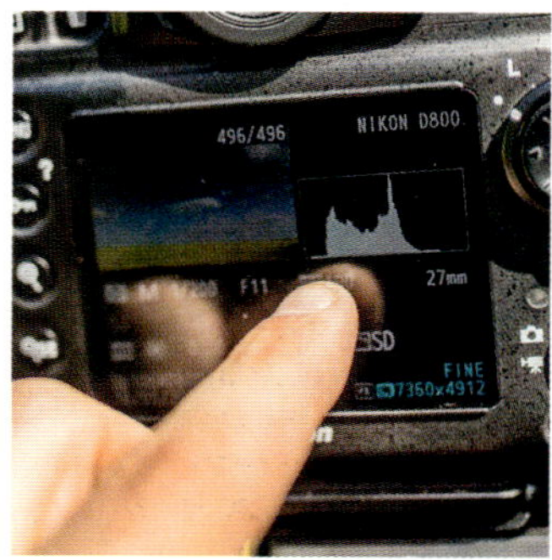

3 FINE-TUNE EXPOSURE You should expose for the brightest part of the scene – usually the highlights in the clouds. This may leave the foreground underexposed, so fit an ND grad filter if necessary to obtain a balanced exposure. I've weighted my histogram to the left to prevent blowing out the clouds. As we'll be dealing with a high number of files we want to get as much right in camera as possible.

4 SWITCH TO MANUAL We want no fluctuation in exposure or White Balance between frames, so we now need to set everything to manual. Select manual exposure mode and, using your test shot as reference, dial the appropriate exposure settings. Set the White Balance to suit the scene – Daylight WB works well for me. If it's a windy day, it's a good idea to hang your camera bag from your tripod to stop it moving about.

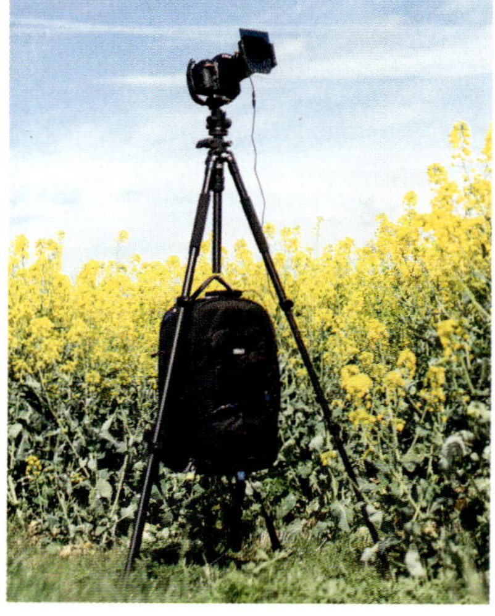

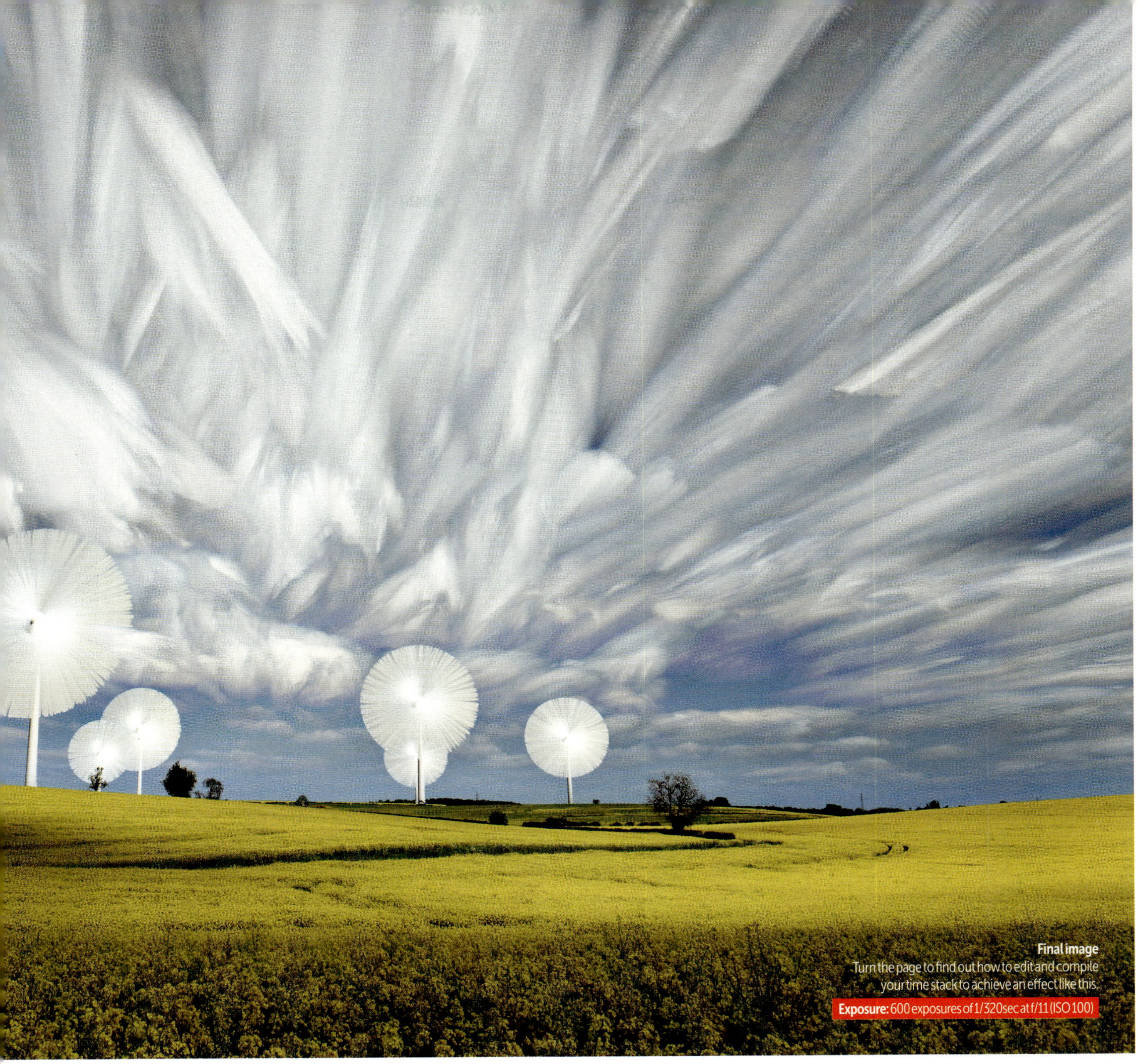

Final image
Turn the page to find out how to edit and compile your time stack to achieve an effect like this.
Exposure: 600 exposures of 1/320sec at f/11 (ISO 100)

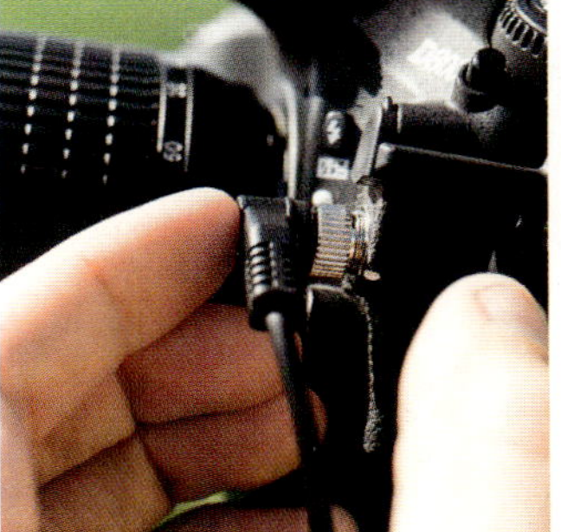

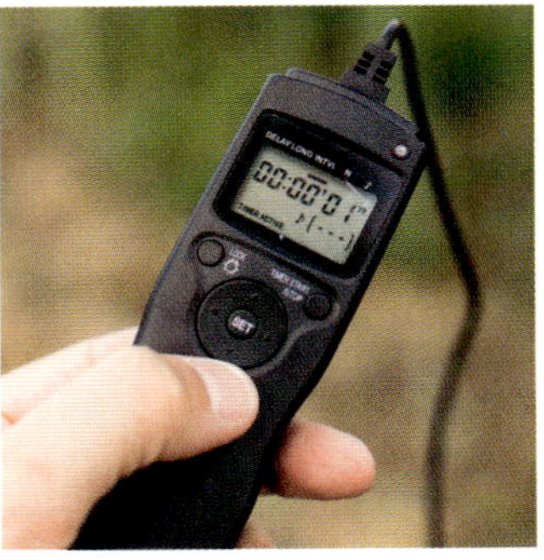

5 SET YOUR INTERVALS Your choice of interval depends on the level of cloud movement and the look you want in your final shot. Fast-moving clouds required a shorter interval between shots than slow ones. A larger interval will create a 'stuttered' effect in the clouds when you compile the time stack, whereas a short interval will create a smoother look. I've opted for a two-second interval between shots.

6 START SHOOTING Press start on your intervalometer and you're away. The number of shots you need depends on the level of cloud movement, but it's best to shoot too many rather than not enough – you don't have to use them all when it comes to compiling it. Watch the sky as you're shooting to gain a measure of how quickly the clouds pass and their direction – it will help you envisage how the final image will look once compiled.

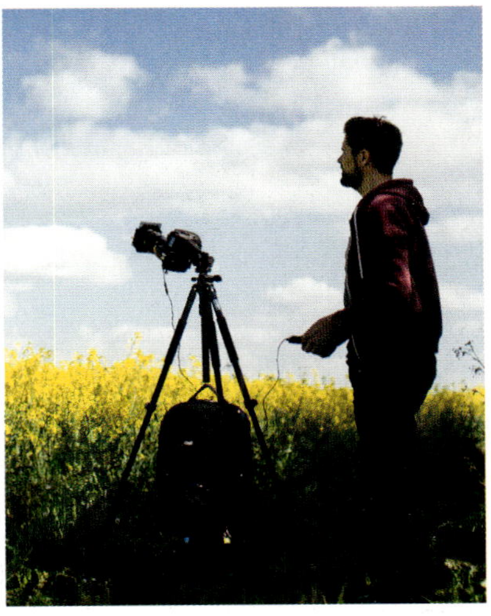

Edit your time stack

With your time lapse taken, it's time to blend the results together into a single, unique time-stack image. Here's how to do it...

THERE ARE TWO ways to compile your time-lapse images into a single file – the quick and easy way, or the hard, lengthy way. The hard way involves cutting and pasting each and every one of your exposures as a new layer onto the previous and setting that layer's Blend Mode to Lighten. The easy way involves simply downloading a clever (and free) piece of software called StarStax (http://bit.do/DSLR_starstax) and letting it do all the hard work for you – we're going to go with the latter.

Once stacked, you can chose to leave it at that, however the resulting image usually ends up looking a bit flat, as the multiple exposures even out the lighting. However, a few select tweaks to contrast and to enhance the sky are all that's needed for a cracking final image.

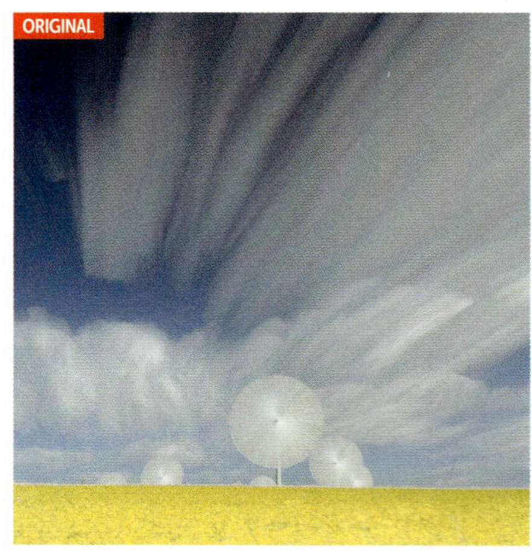
ORIGINAL

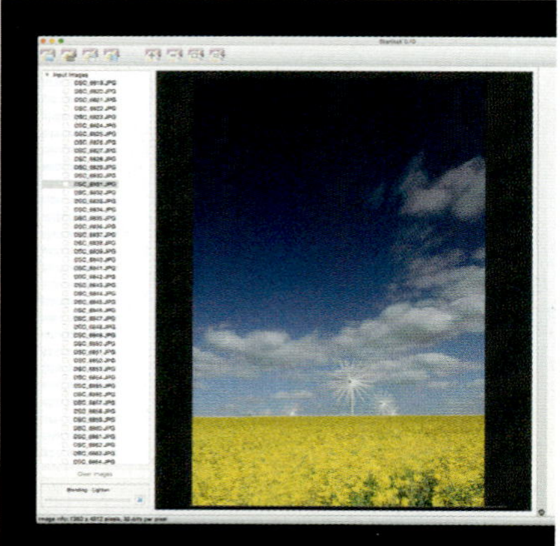

1 STACK THE IMAGES Download your images and open up the StarStax app. Click on the *Open images...* button in the top left and select all of the images that you wish to stack. Make sure the Blending Mode is set to *Lighten* and press the *Start Processing* button. It'll take a while to process – once done make sure you press *Save As...* to save the results.

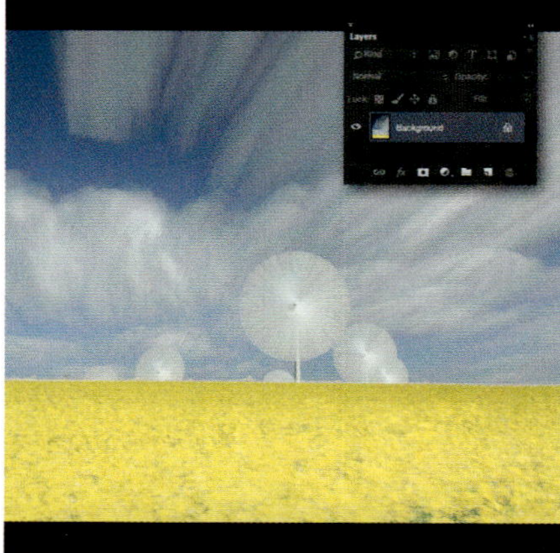

2 FIND A NEW FOREGROUND Open the stacked JPEG in Photoshop. There has been a lot of movement recorded in the foreground of the image, which has turned it into a yellow mess. We replaced the foreground with one from a single exposure to improve it; search through your shots and find a foreground image that you're happy with.

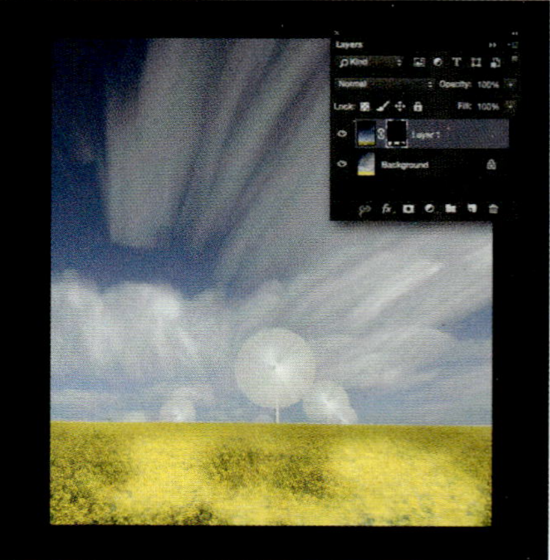

3 CHANGE THE FOREGROUND On your chosen foreground image, go to *Select>All* and then *Edit>Copy*. Back in your stacked image, go to *Edit>Paste*. Then, go to *Layer>Layer Mask> Hide All*. Use the *Brush Tool*, with your colour set to *Black*, and a soft-edged brush, to reveal your foreground on your image, taking care where it meets the sky.

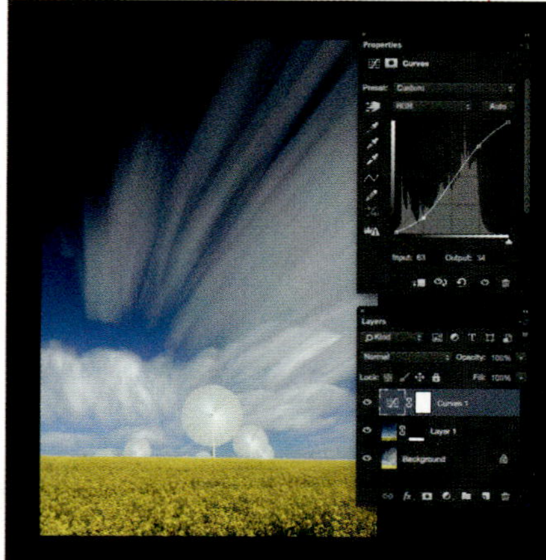

4 ADD CONTRAST Foreground improved, the image is still flat – click on *Add new fill or adjustment layer* in the Layers palette and select *Curves*. In the Adjustments palette, create a subtle S-curve – darkening the shadows and brightening the highlights to add contrast. Be careful not to push the highlights too far and to lose cloud detail.

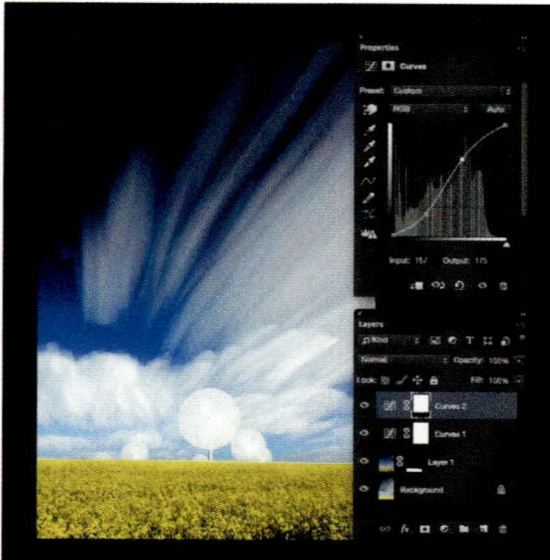

5 ADD MORE CONTRAST Create a second Curves adjustment layer, as before – this time focusing on just the sky. Create a second S-curve in the Adjustments palette to boost contrast in the sky. Once done, select the *Brush Tool* with *Black* set as your *Foreground Color* and brush over the foreground so that the increase in contrast only affects the sky.

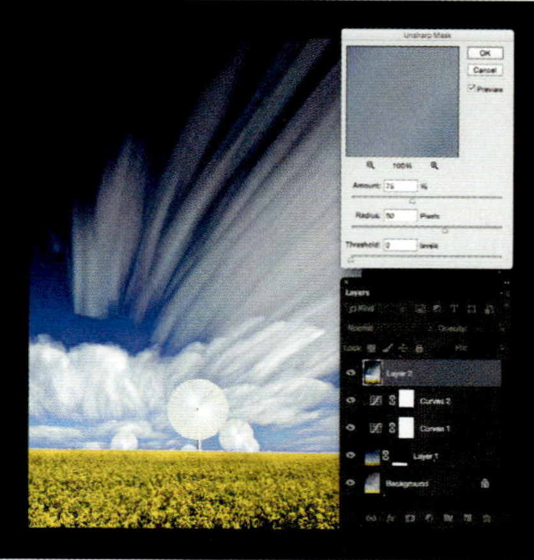

6 BOOST CLARITY An optional step is to boost clarity in the clouds. Hold down the *alt* key and go to *Layer>Merge Visible*. Then, go to *Filter> Sharpen>Unsharp Mask*. Increase the *Amount* to *75%* and *Radius* to *90 pixels* and click *OK*. Next, click on *Add Layer Mask* in the layers palette and use your *Brush Tool*, as before, to mask the effect from all but the sky.

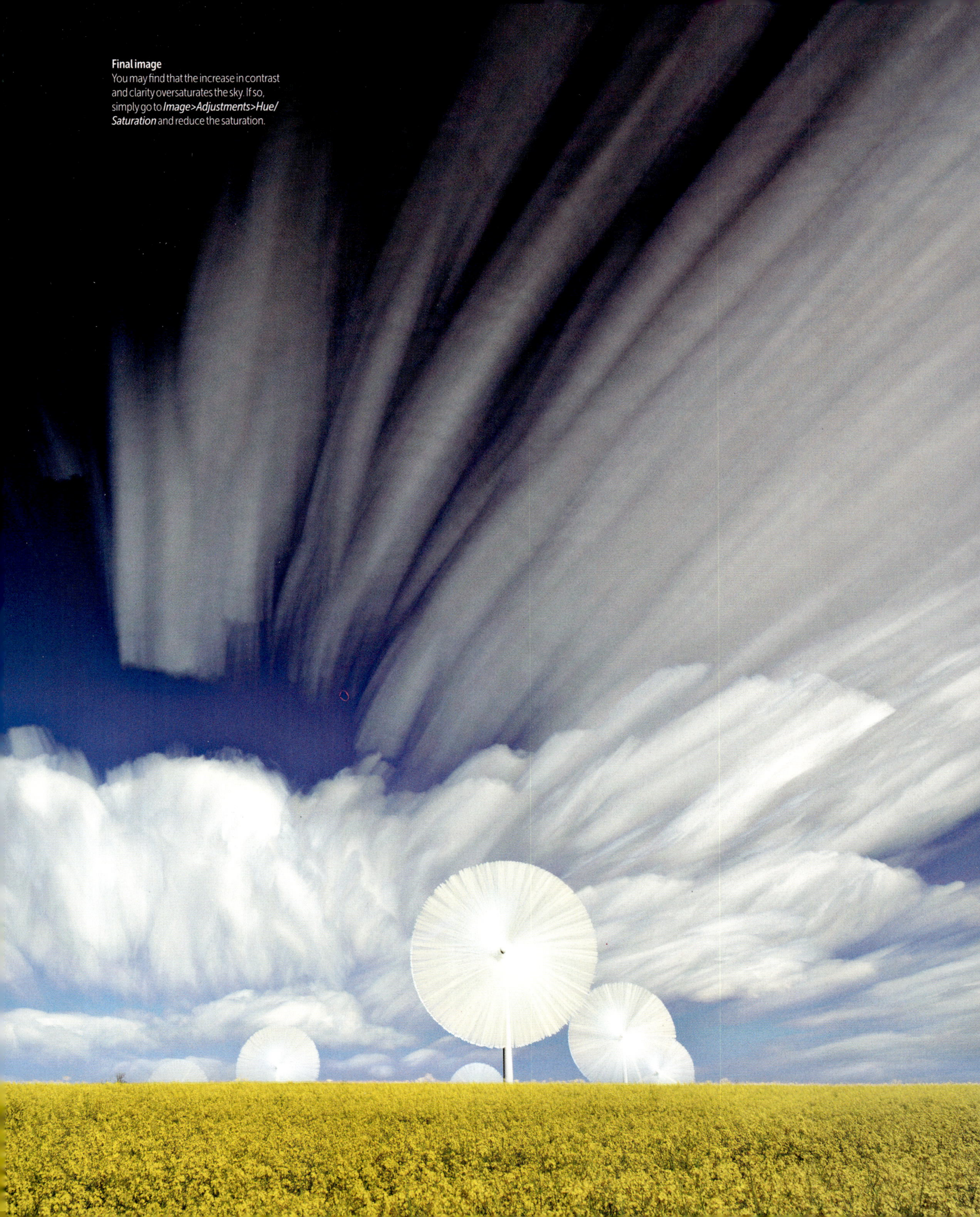

Final image
You may find that the increase in contrast and clarity oversaturates the sky. If so, simply go to ***Image>Adjustments>Hue/ Saturation*** and reduce the saturation.

Daylight portraits

Intentionally underexposing an image would make many photographers question your methods. However, this popular natural-light portrait technique is one many modern photographers are embracing

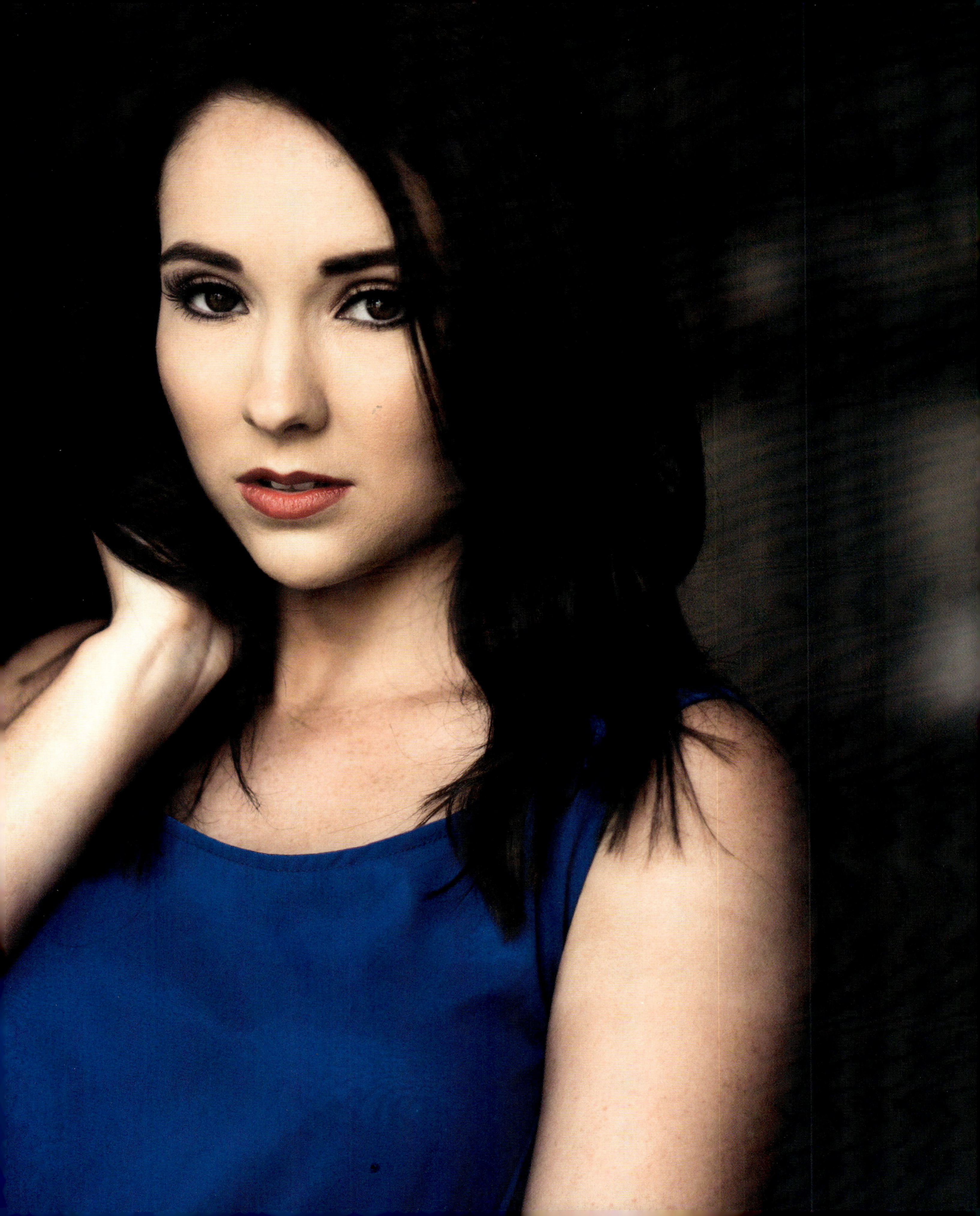

ASK ALMOST ANY top landscape photographer and they'll tell you that exposing to the right, or ETTR, is the best way to get maximum detail out of your Raw files. This is actually true – the light side of the histogram records far more detail than the dark side, so slightly overexposing your files retains more detail. There is, however, a newer school of thought emerging that is becoming increasingly popular with natural-light portrait photographers – intentional underexposure.

Why would you intentionally underexpose a portrait, you may ask? Think about it this way: when using flash you might underexpose the ambient light and then highlight your subject with the strobe to make them stand out against their surroundings. Natural light doesn't often offer the same level of control, although the exposure of your subject can be manipulated by their position to the light and the use of a reflector. There are some situations, however, where you are at the mercy of the light and your surroundings so shooting with post-processing in mind may be your only chance to get the shot that you want. Granted, while you could 'correctly' expose your subject and then darken the background, there's actually less processing involved in underexposing the entire scene and then brightening only your subject. Plus, you now have complete control over the exposure of your subject's skin.

We spotted a local coffee shop when out on a photo walk with our model, Tamrin, and thought that it would make for an interesting backdrop for a portrait shot. The contrast between the dark background and Tamrin's skin and outfit would make her stand out well, so we asked the café owner for permission and set about shooting.

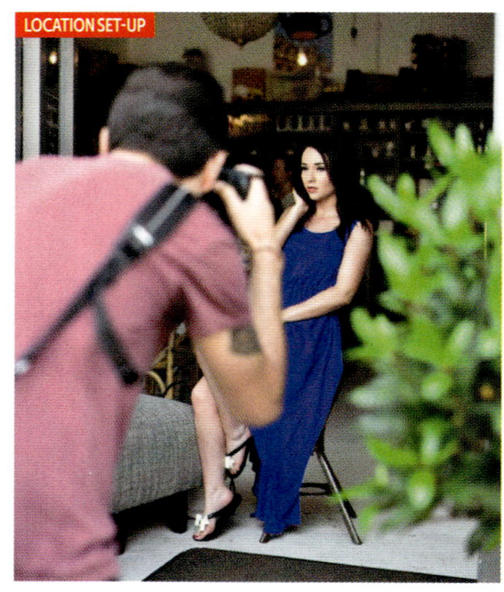
LOCATION SET-UP

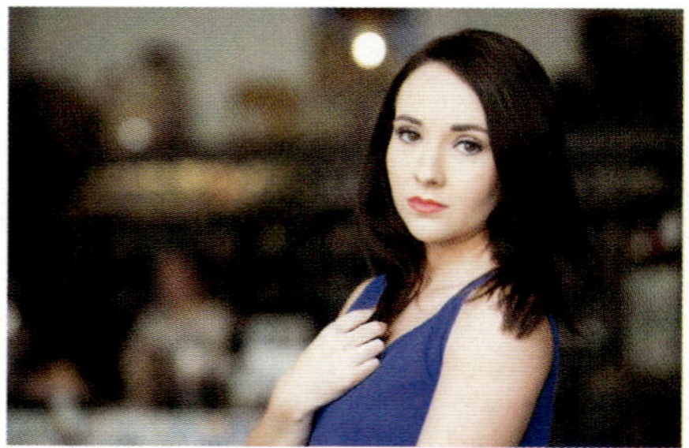

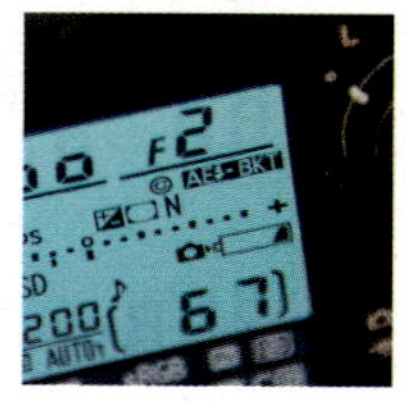

1 FIND THE RIGHT LIGHT Tamrin stands in the doorway of the café, facing the light. A fast prime lens is perfect for this sort of portrait. Select aperture-priority mode and choose a low ISO to maintain image quality. An aperture of f/2 to f/3.5 offers a shallow depth-of-field and a fast shutter speed. Using multi-zone metering, the camera takes into account the dark walls of the coffee shop and compensates for it, overexposing Tamrin.

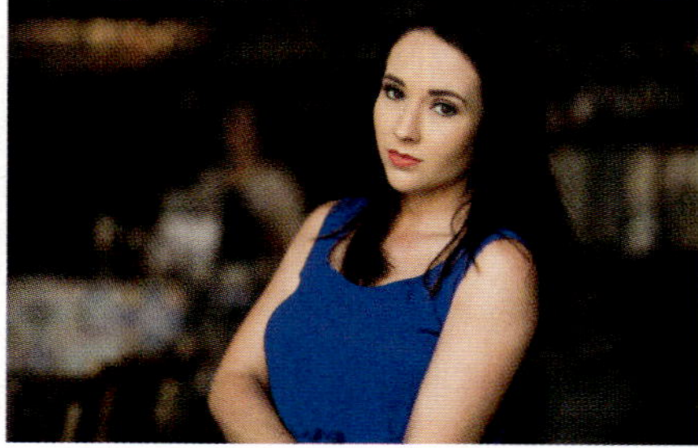

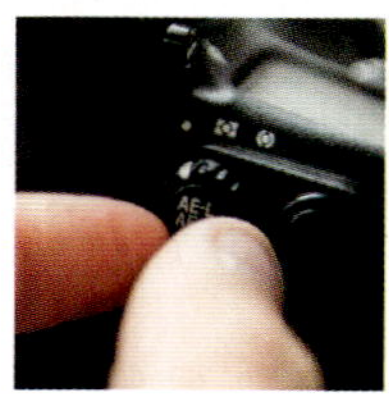

2 USE SPOT METERING Set spot metering and take a reading from the model's face, here it gives a better result but the background is still too bright. Tamrin is in the doorway of the café, and we're stood on the pavement, so we can't move her any further outside to change the ratio of light on her to the background. While we could darken the background in processing, it would be easier to underexpose and then lighten Tamrin's skin in Photoshop.

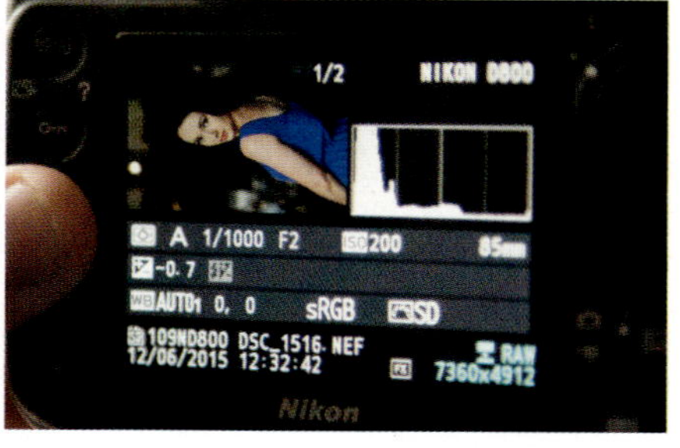

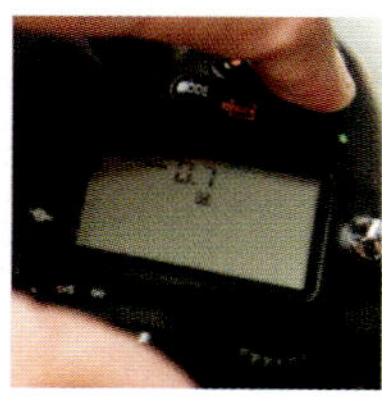

3 USE EXPOSURE COMPENSATION Dialing in exposure compensation of -0.7EV and taking a spot meter reading from Tamrin's face drops the exposure. On the LCD preview the image is dark, but from the histogram we can see that the background exposure is just right and the highlights on Tamrin's skin are in control. We know that we can dodge (lighten) her skin during post-processing and maintain control over the highlights on her skin.

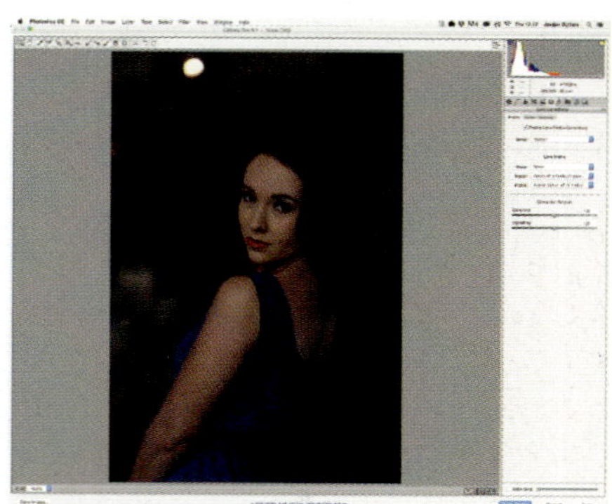

4 RAW ADJUSTMENTS Import the picture into Adobe Camera Raw and make basic adjustments, such as White Balance and Lens Corrections, before opening the image in Photoshop. Next, create a new layer (*Layer>New>Layer*), set the Mode to ***Soft Light*** and tick ***Fill with Soft-Light-neutral colour (50% grey)***. Select the ***Dodge Tool*** from the sidebar and set the ***Range*** to ***Midtones*** and ***Exposure*** to around ***18%*** in the top bar.

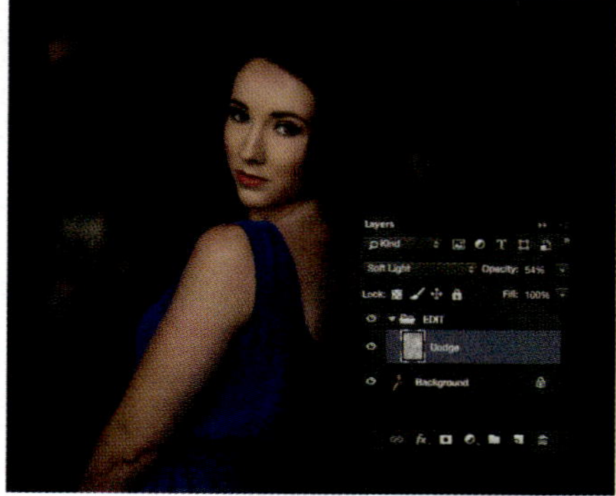

5 LIGHTEN YOUR MODEL Use the ***Dodge Tool*** to gradually increase brightness where needed. We start with a sweep across Tamrin, before zooming in and dodging her eyes and the centre of her face. By building up the brightness where it's needed you can control exactly where the highlights appear on the skin and position them to flatter your subject. We also dodge a few areas of the background to bring out detail where we want it.

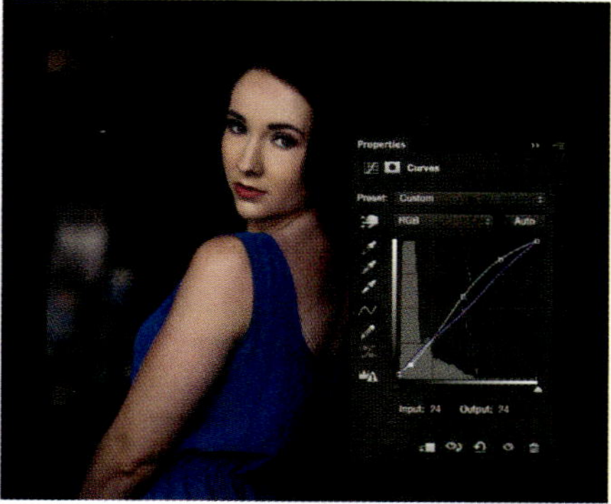

6 ADJUST COLOUR Add a Curves adjustment layer (*Layer>New Adjustment Layer>Curves*) and, in the Adjustments palette, change the ***Channel*** to ***Blue***. Click once in the centre of the curve to add an anchor before dragging the shadows part of the line (near the bottom left corner) up slightly, as shown. This adds a blue tint to the shadows. Then, change the channel to ***RGB*** and create an S-curve, as shown, to increase contrast.

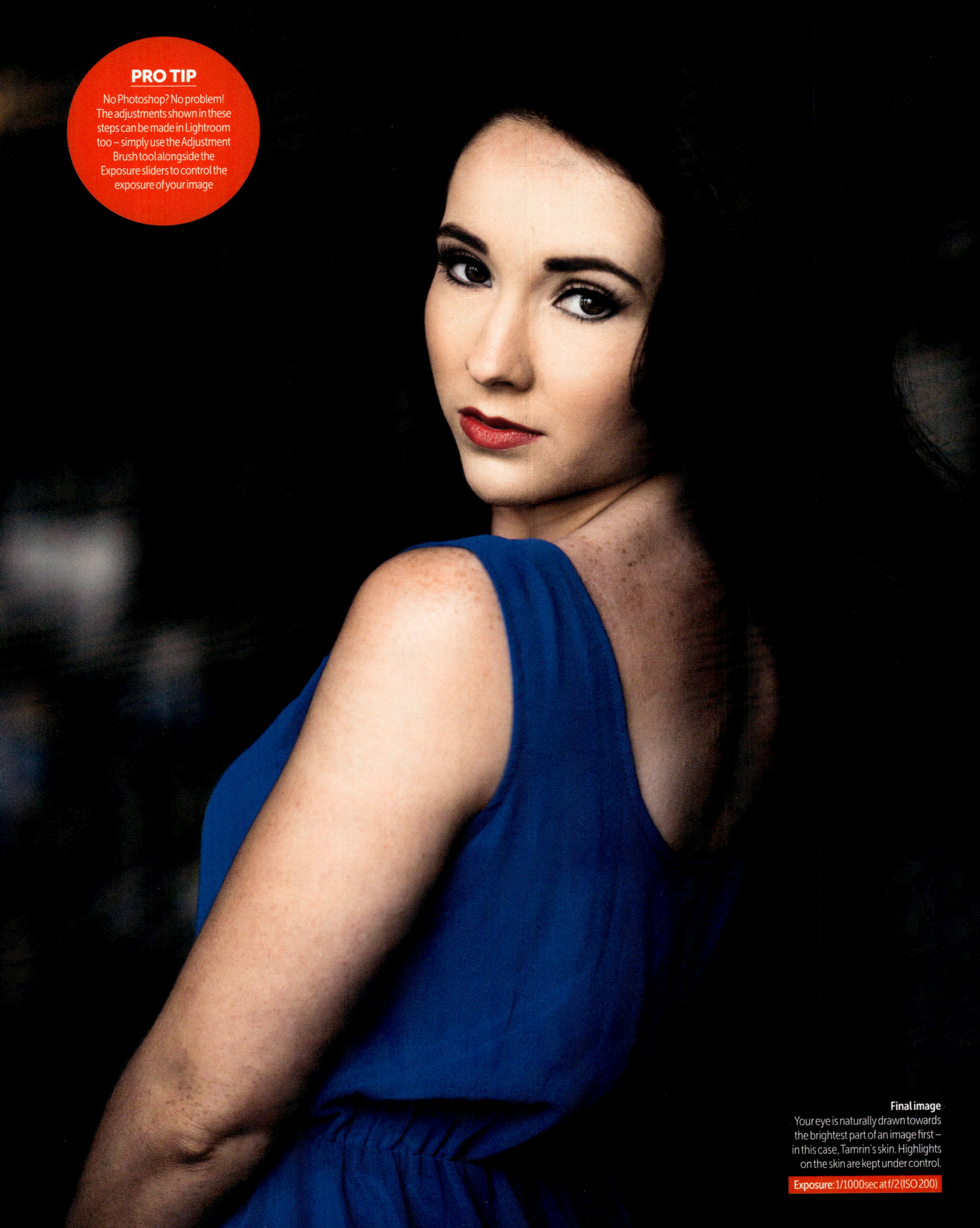

Final image
Your eye is naturally drawn towards the brightest part of an image first – in this case, Tamrin's skin. Highlights on the skin are kept under control.

Exposure: 1/1000sec at f/2 (ISO 200)

Fun triptych portrait

It's time to get creative! The team show you how easy it is to capture your subjects in portions

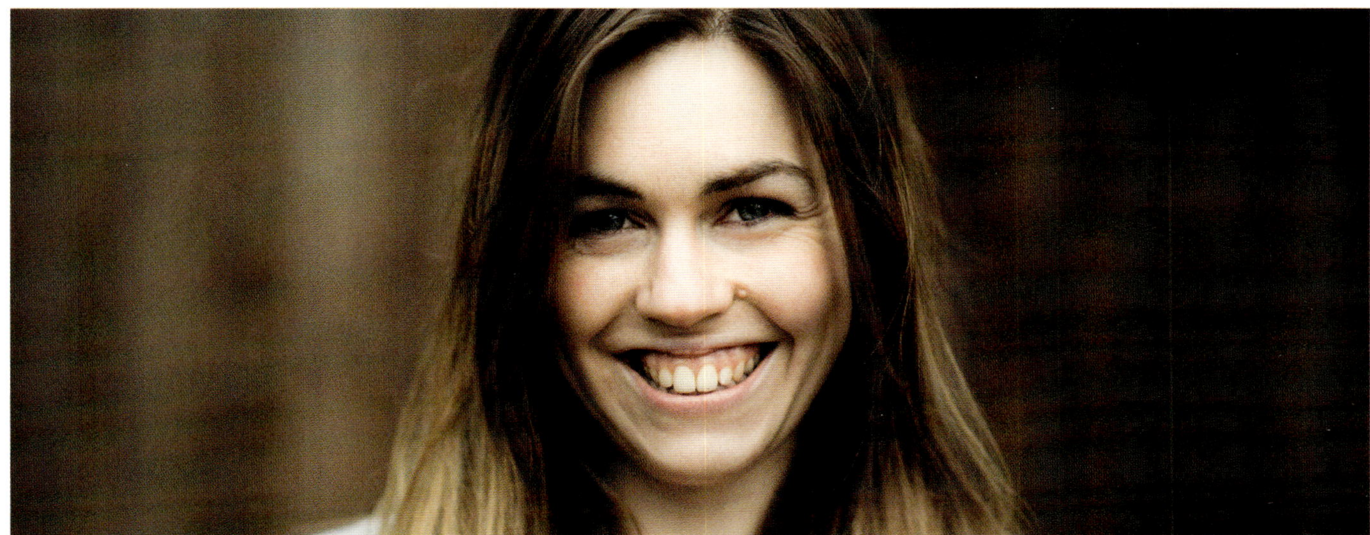

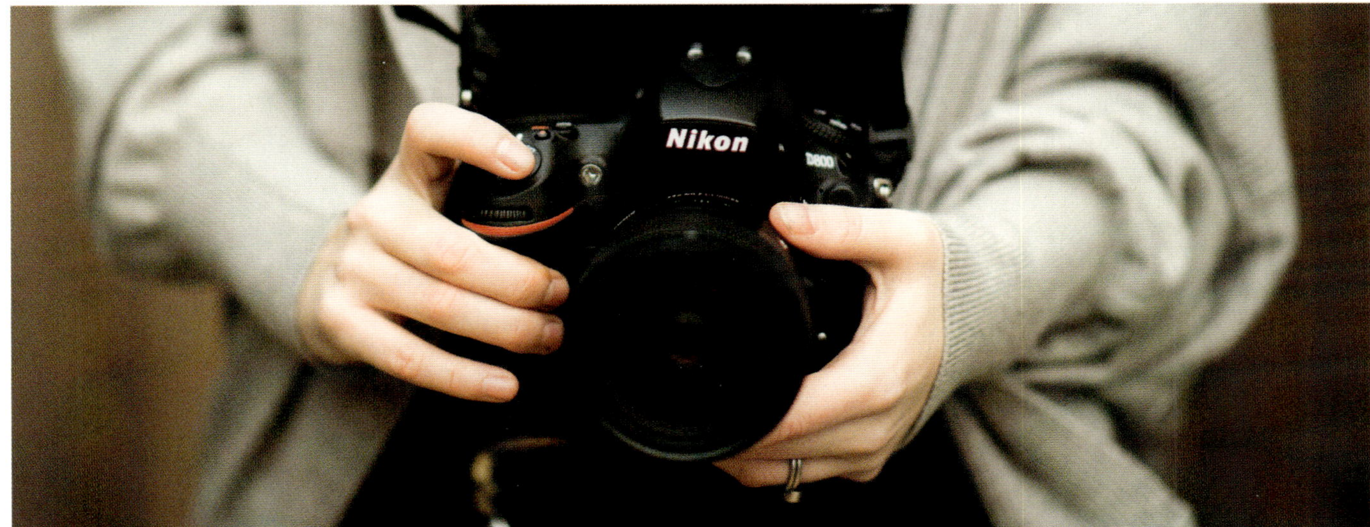

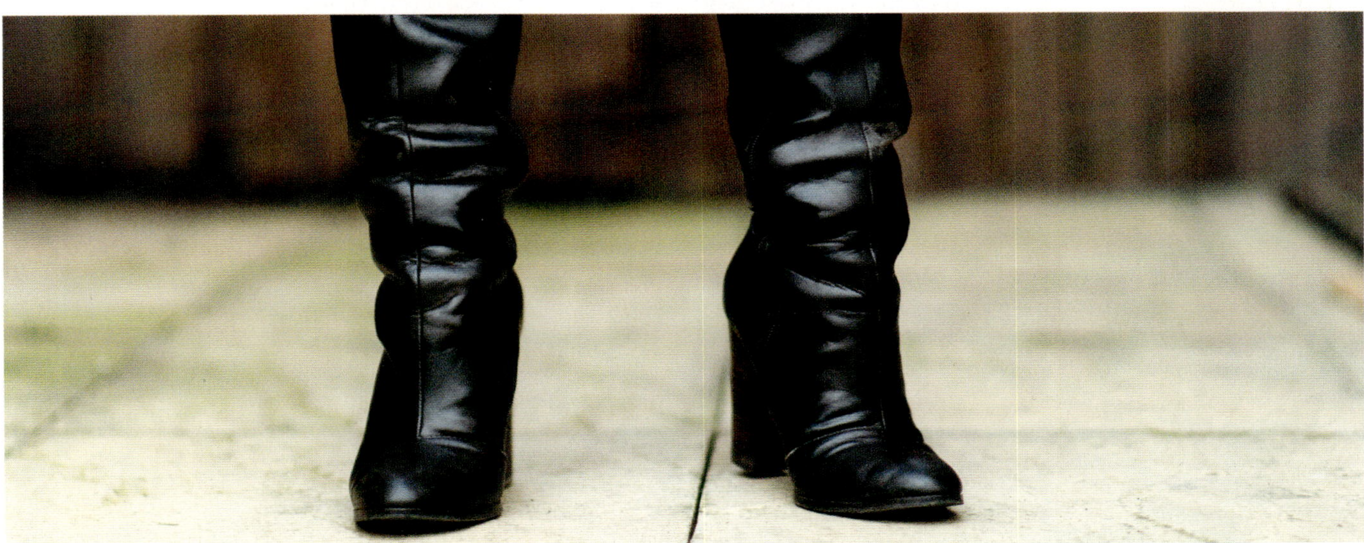

EVER FEEL LIKE you're in bits and pieces? Here's a quirky and creative portrait technique that uses the feeling figuratively! By shooting three individual images of someone's head, torso and feet, before stitching them back together in a triptych, you can create a zany stylised portrait that can't fail to raise a smile.

The popularity of this technique can be credited, in part, to street photographer Adde Adesokan, whose series *Triptychs of Strangers* gained viral success online. Adde used this technique with fantastic and inspiring results and has put together a collection of triptych portraits on Flickr. Check out his take on the idea for yourself, here: http://bit.do/DSLR-adde.

The trick when shooting your own triptych portrait is not to aim for the three images to line up – quite the opposite in fact! Between shooting each segment move in closer, or step further away – you could even switch focal lengths for exaggeration. This creates a disjointed effect that adds to the overall appearance of the final image.

Kit-wise, it's best to keep it simple: natural lighting and your DSLR or mirrorless camera along with a fast prime lens are perfect for the job. We would recommend a 50mm or 85mm f/1.4 or f/1.8 lens, but your kit zoom is fine too. You might want to consider using a reflector if a bit of extra fill is needed, but your best bet is to shoot when the light is diffused by cloud, or in open shade.

Tips for kids

This technique works great for capturing fun images of children and toddlers, too, but be prepared – the child probably won't be as interested in the idea as you are! Capturing the headshot is the trickiest part, particularly if they refuse to stand still! But once that's done the torso shot can be easily achieved by asking the parent to give the child something to hold and distract them. The feet shot can even be done with the parent holding the child in place from the side – shhh, no-one will ever know!

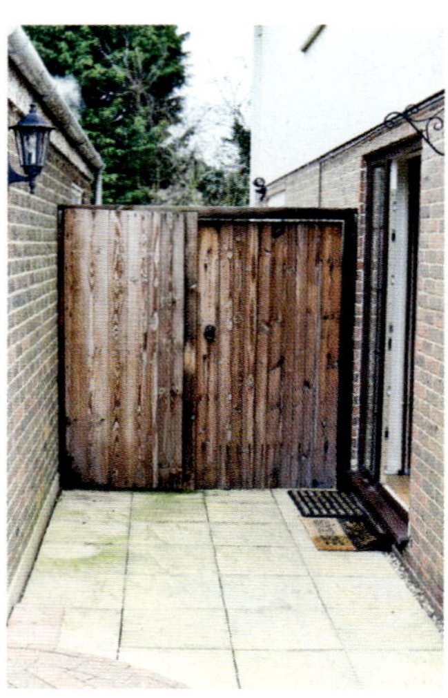

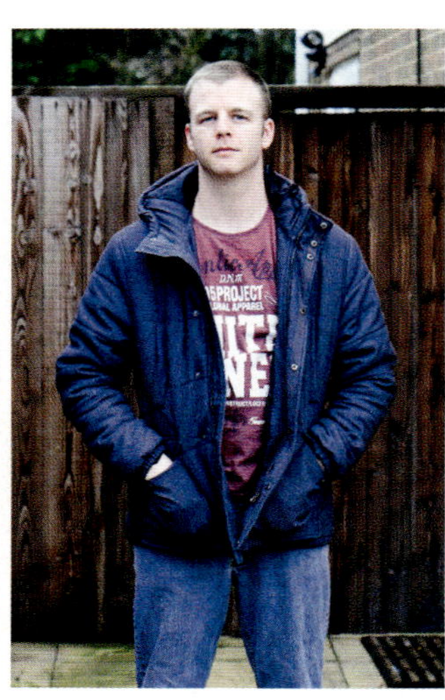

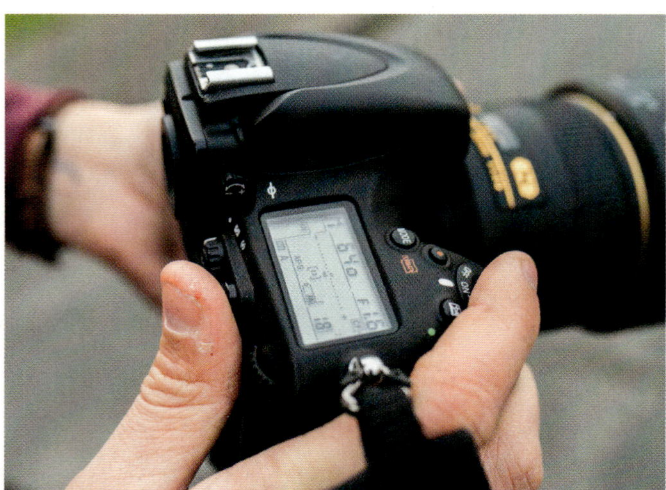

1 FIND A SUITABLE LOCATION As you're shooting a series of images that will sit next to one another in the final result, the lighting and conditions need to remain consistent. Therefore, look for an area of open shade where the light is soft and diffused. Pay attention to the background – it should be clear and free of distractions. Put distance between your subject and the backdrop to help blur it out of focus.

2 ESTABLISH YOUR EXPOSURE Select aperture-priority mode and pick a wide aperture. Choose spot metering and an ISO that gives you a workable shutter speed – ideally faster than 1/100sec. Focus on your subject's eyes and take a test shot. Assess the exposure using the LCD and if you're happy then transfer the settings over into manual mode – this will ensure that the exposure remains consistent for each image.

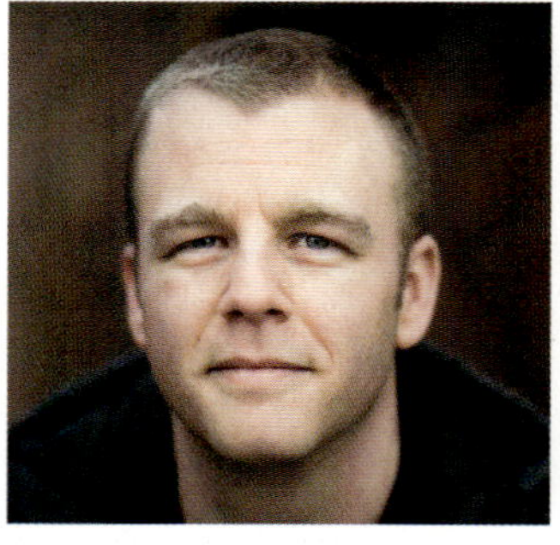

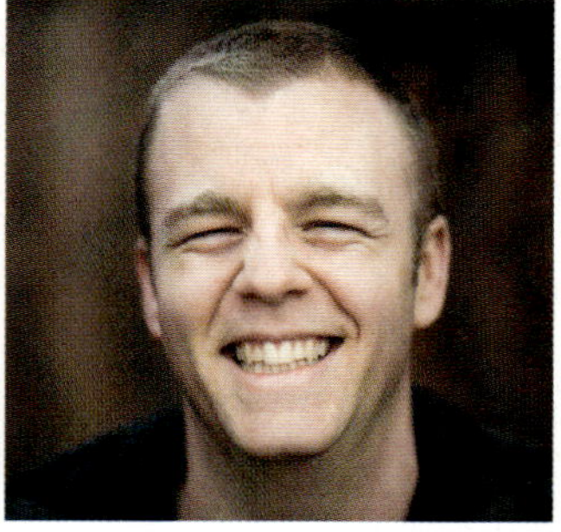

3 SHOOT THE HEADSHOT *(above)* Capture the headshots first as these are arguably the most important and will take the most time. Use a central composition in landscape orientation and look to fill about a third of the frame with your subject's head. Shoot a variety of different looks – from straight faces to smiles to goofy expressions. Also try shooting some closer and further away too – this way you have plenty of choice when it comes to putting together your triptych.

4 CAPTURE THE HANDS & FEET *(right)* Give your subject something to do with their hands – they could play with their phone or twiddle their thumbs, for example. An alternative idea is to let them hold something that represents their job, hobby or personality. When it comes to capturing their feet, don't shoot them straight-on – get down low and ask your subject to angle or lift their feet slightly to give them shape.

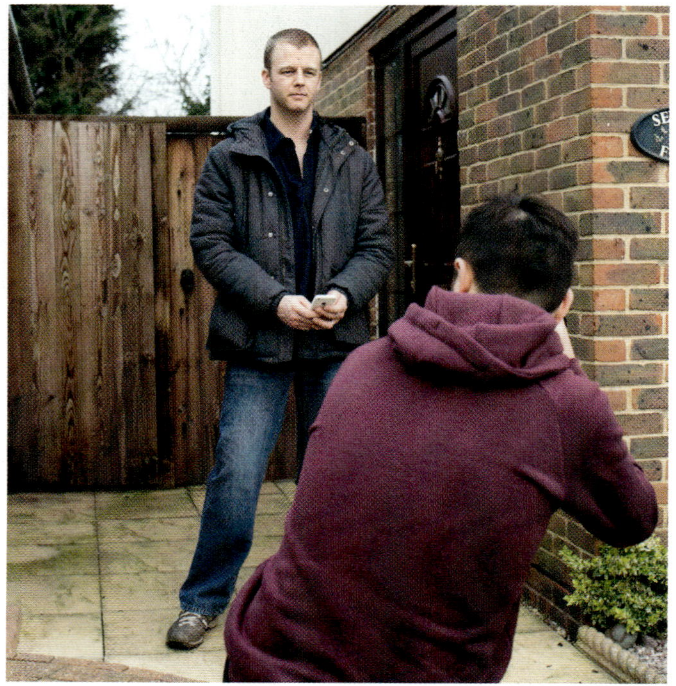

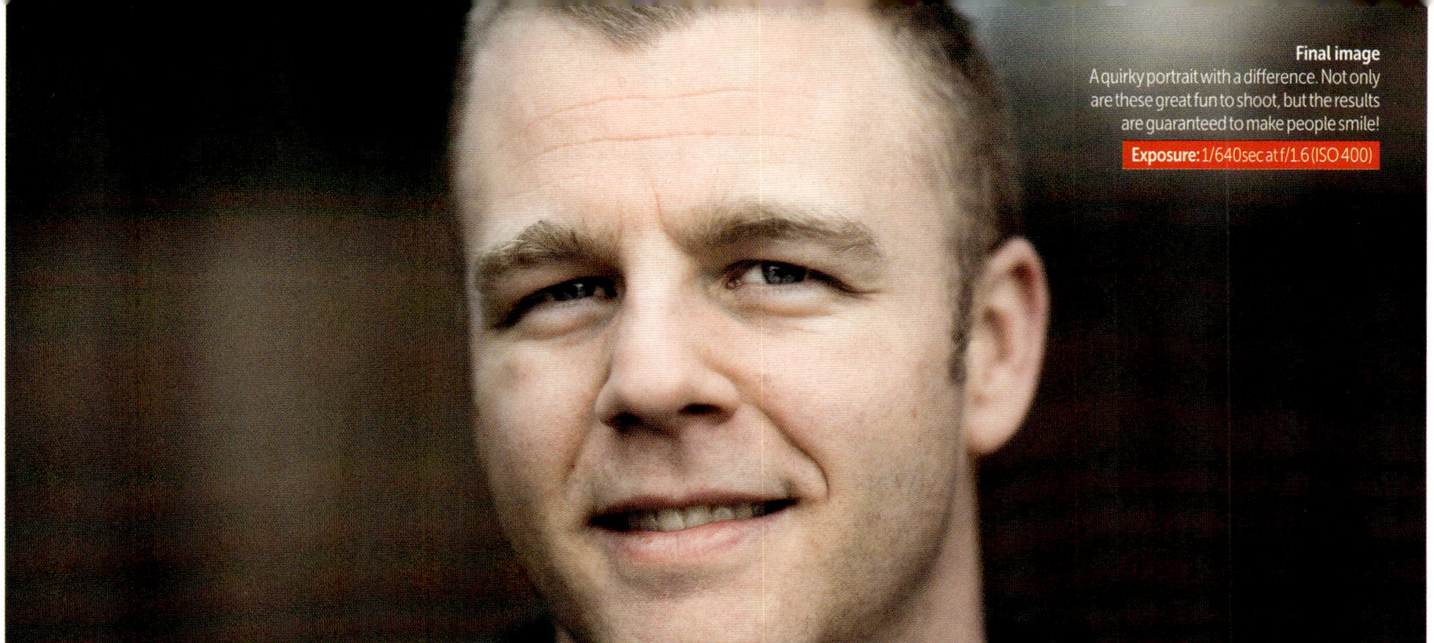

Final image
A quirky portrait with a difference. Not only are these great fun to shoot, but the results are guaranteed to make people smile!
Exposure: 1/640sec at f/1.6 (ISO 400)

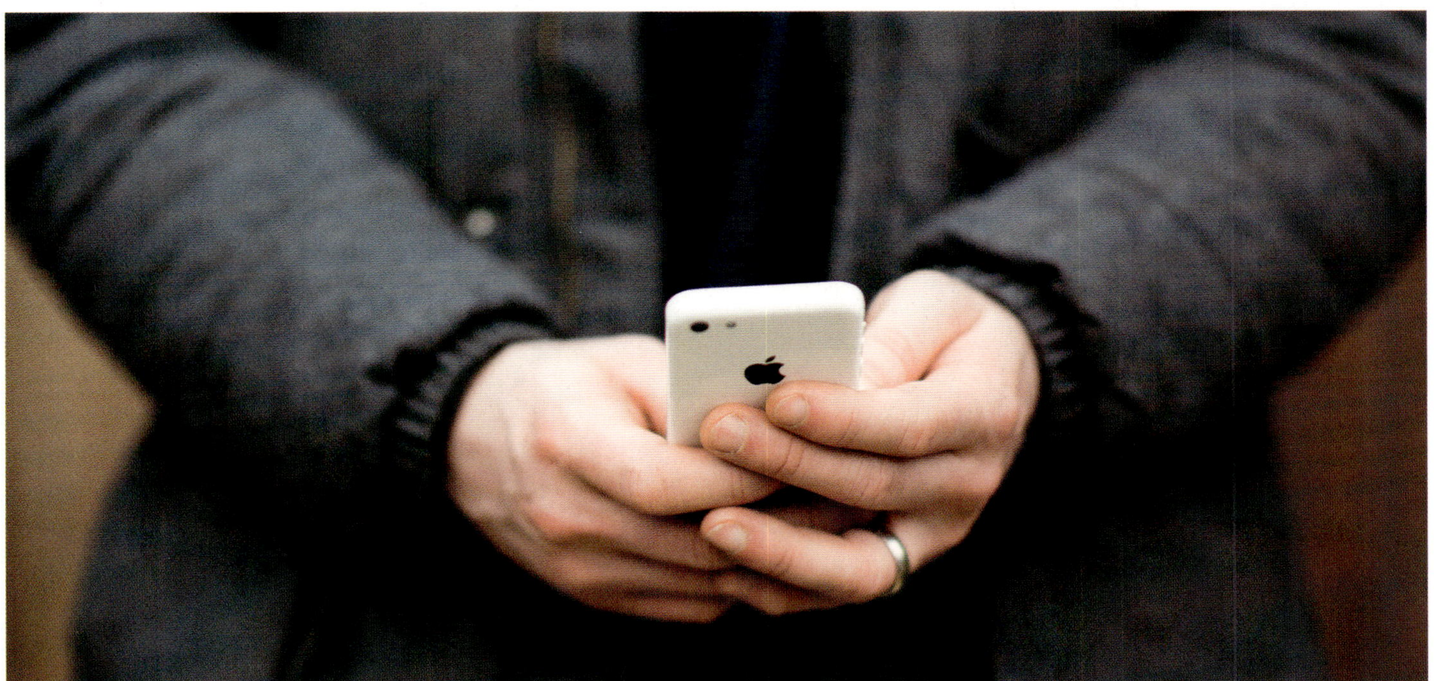

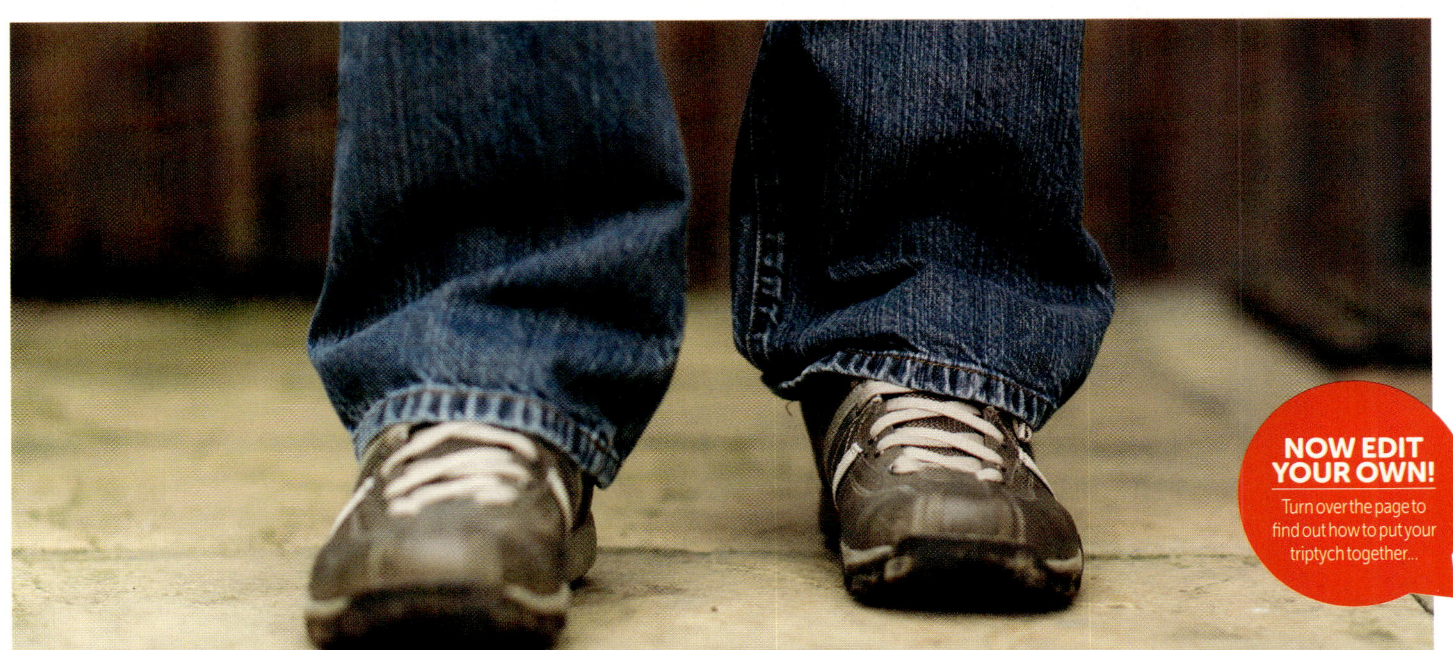

NOW EDIT YOUR OWN!
Turn over the page to find out how to put your triptych together...

Create your triptych

With your images captured, it's time to piece together your triptych portrait in Photoshop

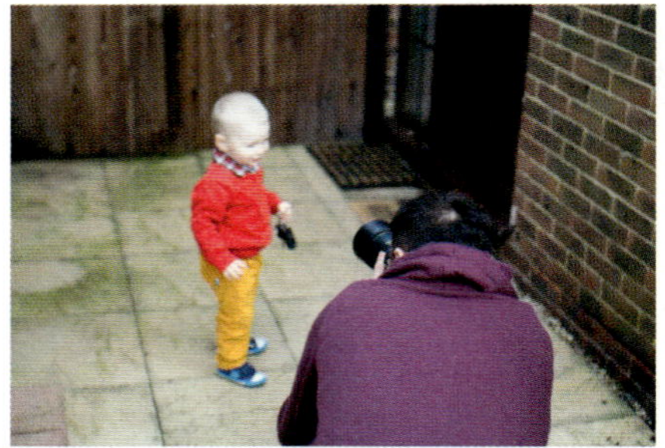

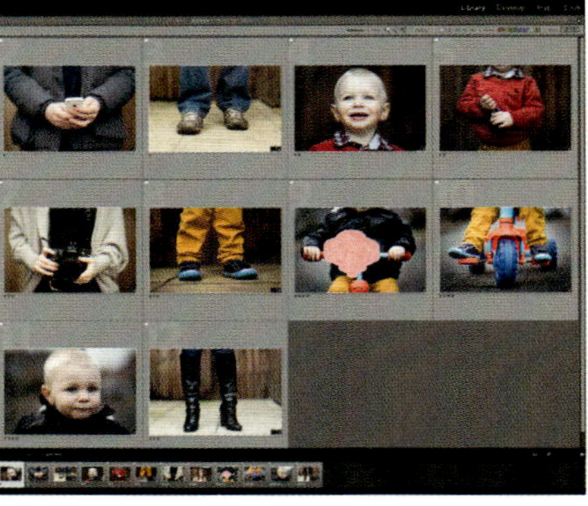

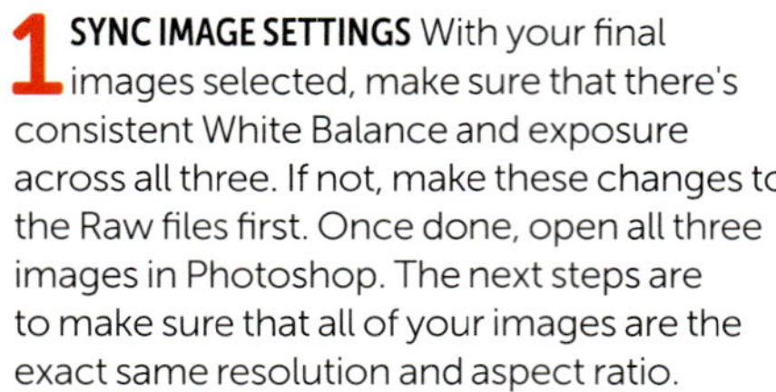

1 SYNC IMAGE SETTINGS With your final images selected, make sure that there's consistent White Balance and exposure across all three. If not, make these changes to the Raw files first. Once done, open all three images in Photoshop. The next steps are to make sure that all of your images are the exact same resolution and aspect ratio.

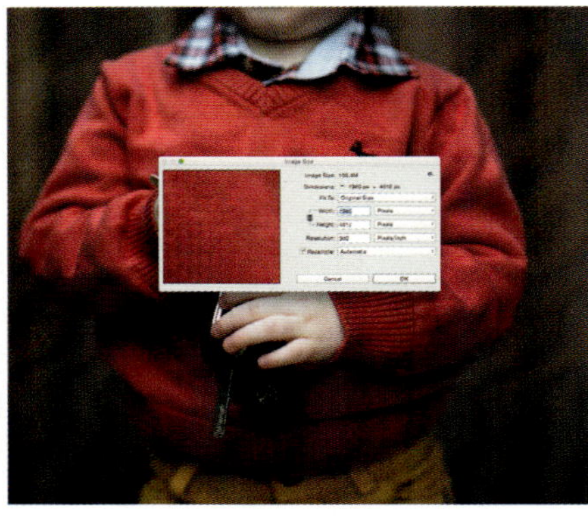

2 MATCH IMAGE SIZES You can skip this step if all of your images are already the same size – we had to crop the Raw files slightly, so all three were different. Check the size of each image by going to ***Image>Image Size***. Make a note of the shortest width from all three and use the same ***Image Size*** menu to make the other two images the same width.

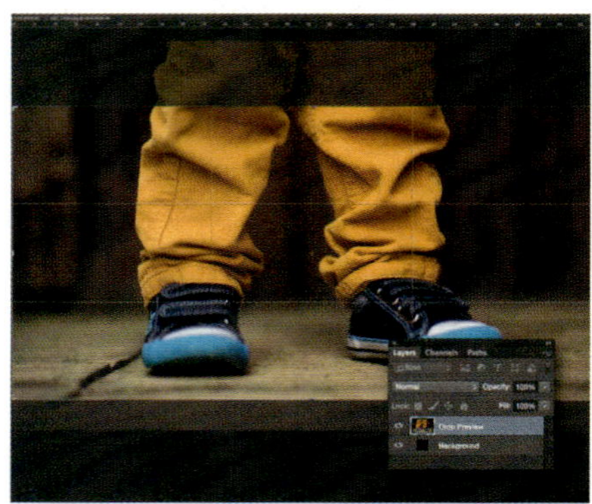

3 MATCH IMAGE RATIOS Next, select the *Crop Tool* and, in the top menu bar, select *Ratio*. In the input boxes to the right, input the image ratio that you want to use – the first box is width, the second is height. We chose *2:1* for our images. Click on your image, line the crop up and press *Enter*. Crop all three images using this same ratio.

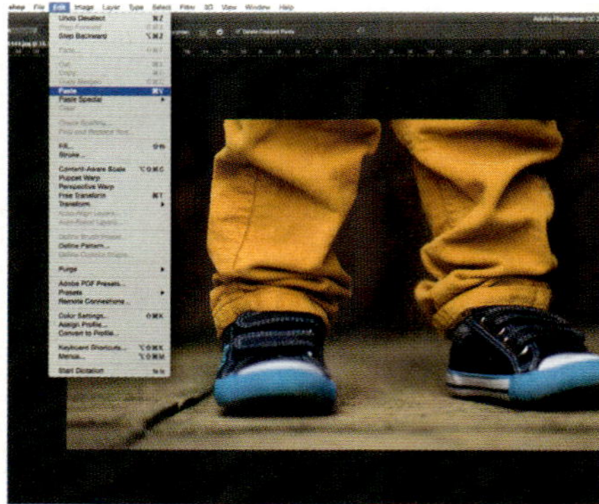

4 COMBINE IMAGES On your torso image, double-click on the *Background* in the Layers palette and click *OK* to unlock the layer. Move over to your feet image – go to *Select>All* and then *Edit>Copy*. Head back to your torso image and go to *Edit>Paste* to paste the feet as a new layer. Repeat for your head image – pasting it onto the torso file.

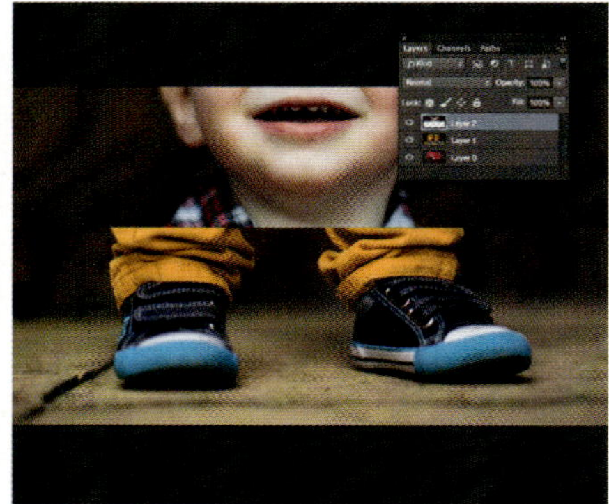

5 MOVE POSITIONS Make sure that Snap is turned on by going to *View>Snap*. Then, activate your head layer in the Layers palette and select the *Move Tool*. Holding down the *Shift* key, drag the layer upwards until it disappears off the top of the frame. The bottom edge of the head layer should snap together with the top edge of the torso layer.

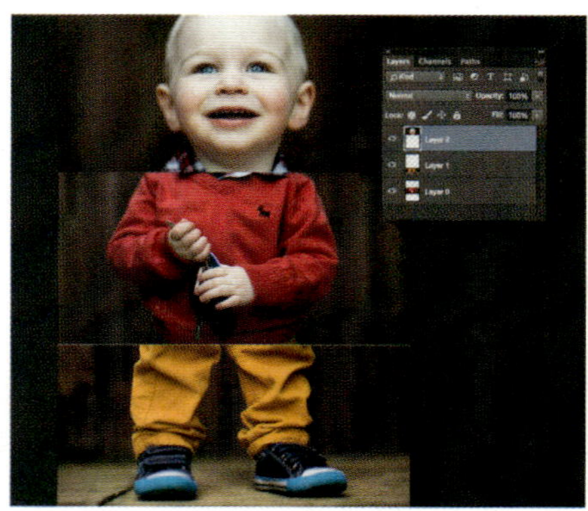

6 REVEAL ALL Repeat this process for the feet layer, holding *Shift* and dragging down until the top edge of the feet layer snaps with the bottom edge of the torso layer. Then, go to *Image>Reveal All* and all three layers will appear, lined up. You might choose to stop here, but we want to add a border between the three images.

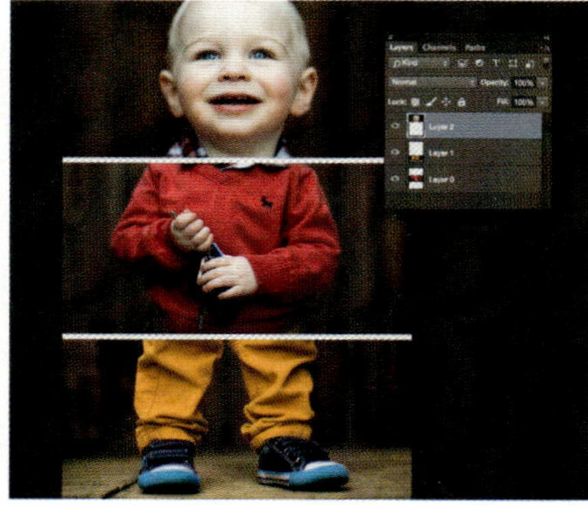

7 ADD SPACING With the *Move Tool* still selected, and your feet layer active, hold down the *Shift* key and tap the *Down arrow* key to create a gap, counting how many times you tapped – each tap is 5-pixels wide. Make your head layer active and repeat this, tapping the *Up arrow* key the same number of times. Go to *Image>Reveal All* again.

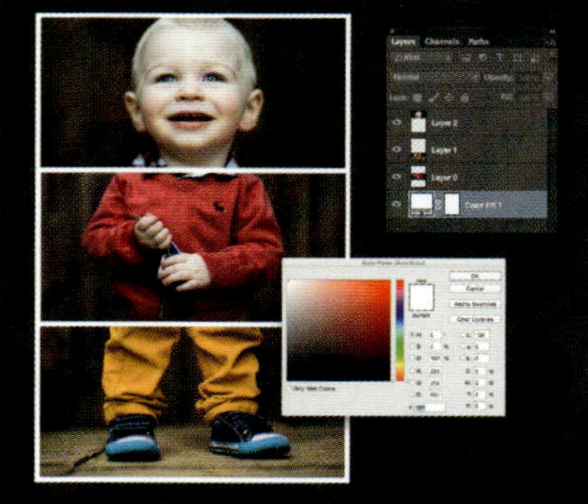

8 ADD A BORDER To add a border, select the *Crop Tool* and then press the *Esc* key. In the top menu bar, press *Clear* and then click on your image. Use the corners to extend the canvas before pressing *Enter*. Then, go to *Layer>New Fill Layer>Solid Color* and press *OK*. Pick your border colour and then, in the Layers palette, drag this layer to the bottom.

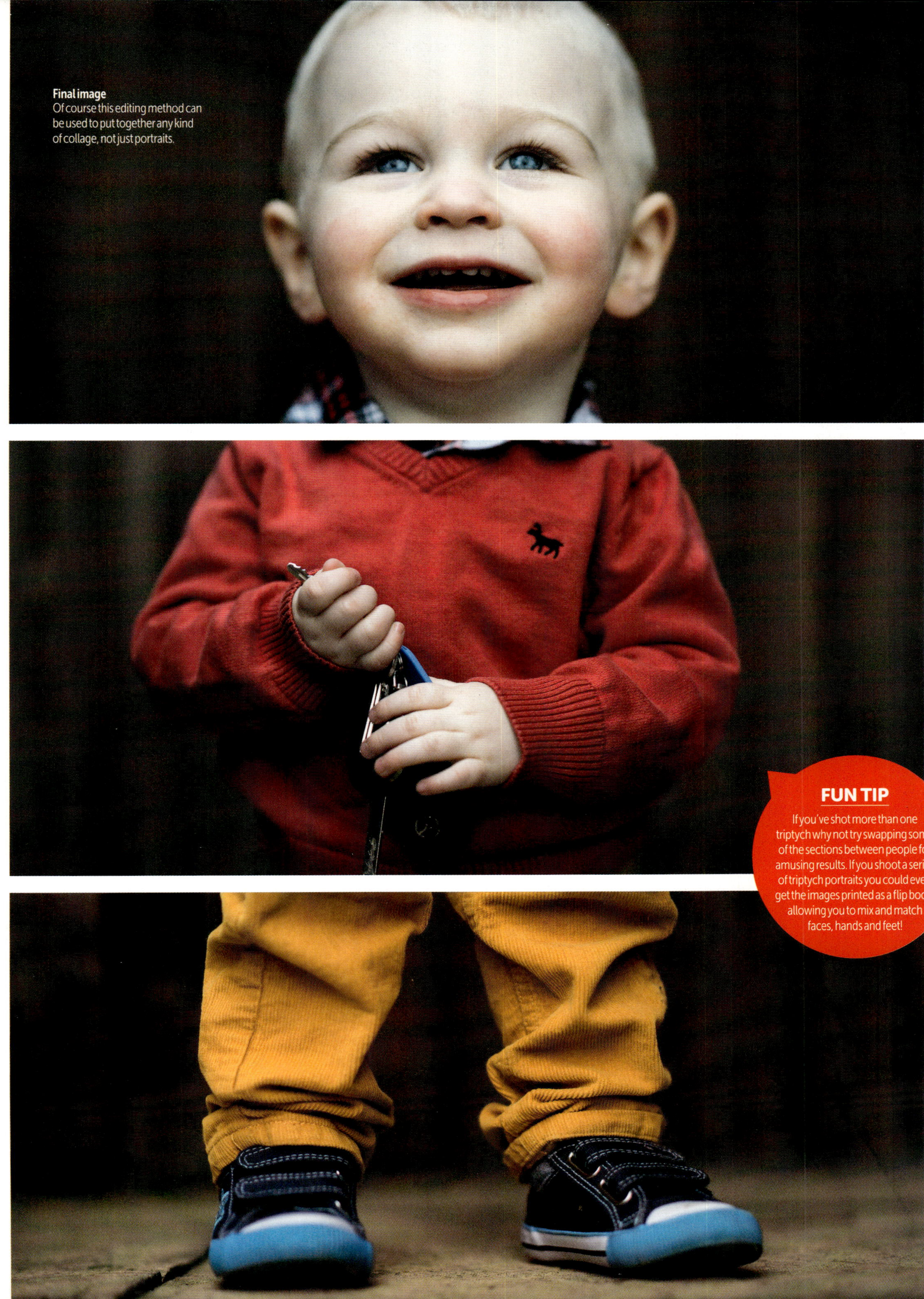

Final image
Of course this editing method can be used to put together any kind of collage, not just portraits.

FUN TIP

If you've shot more than one triptych why not try swapping some of the sections between people for amusing results. If you shoot a series of triptych portraits you could even get the images printed as a flip book, allowing you to mix and match faces, hands and feet!

Subscription Offer

GET 5 ISSUES FOR £5

Digital SLR Photography is the UK's leading magazine for digital SLR photographers of all levels from beginner to enthusiast and professionals. It will inform and entertain you through a unique blend of technique articles, inspirational images, news and authoritative reviews. Covering topics such as landscapes, portraits and close-up photography, this magazine provides a focused and comprehensive read guaranteed to help you get the most out of your photography.

This MagBook has given you a taste of the creative ideas and expert advice on offer every month in *Digital SLR Photography*, so be sure you never miss the chance to improve your photography further by subscribing today. With its step-by-step tutorials and major technique guides, along with inspirational interviews and pictorial showcases, you won't find a more inspiring and informative read anywhere.

Digital SLR Photography's team of experts include several of the UK's leading professional photographers, ensuring you get the very best advice. Our regular contributors include:

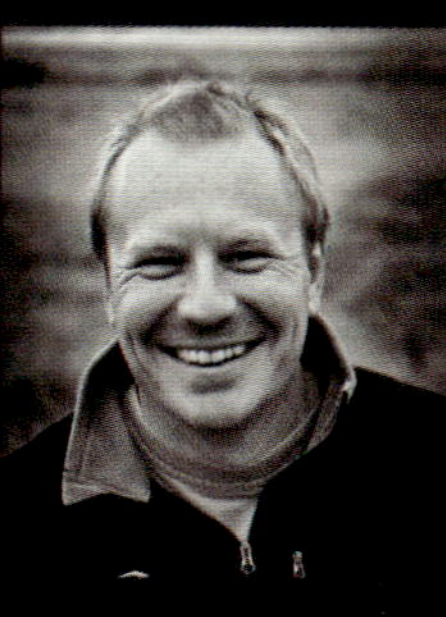

LEE FROST
LANDSCAPE & TRAVEL

A long-standing regular contributor, Lee is a fountain of knowledge when it comes to shooting landscapes and delivering expert tutorials. // **leefrost.co.uk**

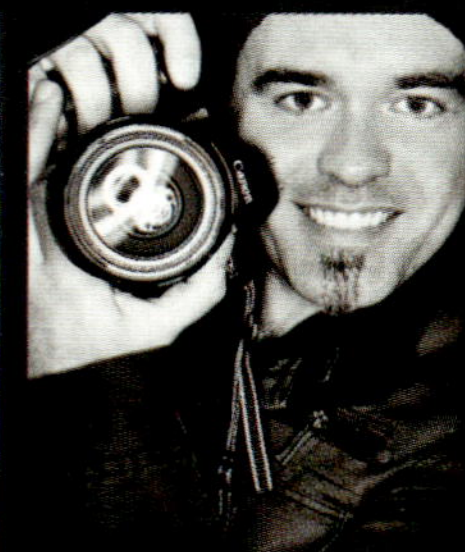

BRETT HARKNESS
PORTRAITS

You either want to be photographed by him or shoot like him. A master of portraits, fashion and weddings, Brett runs regular workshops in the UK. // **brettharknessphotography.com**

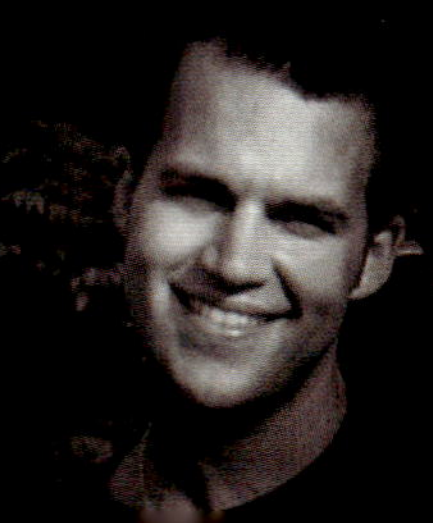

ROSS HODDINOTT
OUTDOOR

He's not only an award-winning nature photographer, a leading expert in landscape and wildlife photography, he's a top tutor, too. // **rosshoddinott.co.uk**

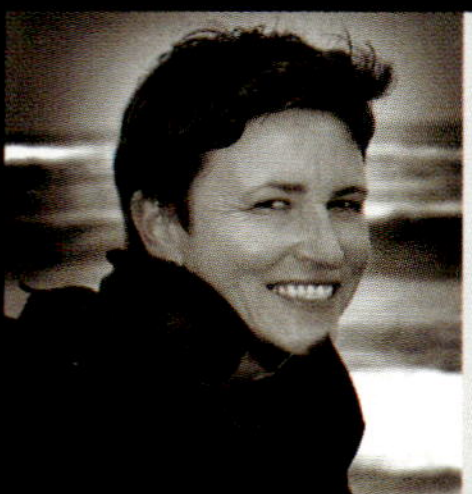

HELEN DIXON
LANDSCAPES

Helen is living the dream, having given up a full-time job to live in Cornwall and become a professional landscape photographer. // **helendixon photography.co.uk**

Choose your package:

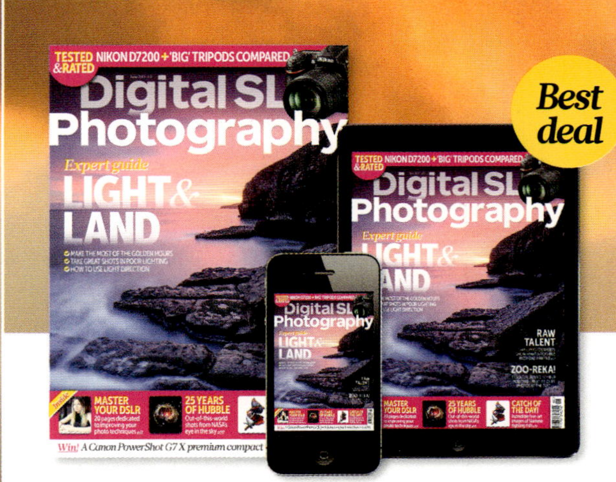

The Full Package

5 issues of ***Digital SLR Photography*** delivered FREE to your door for **just £5**

Over 700 pages of advice and inspiration!

Access to the digital version across all your iOS & Kindle devices*

28% saving on the print edition high street price

77% saving on the digital edition newsstand price

*excludes Kindle eBook readers.

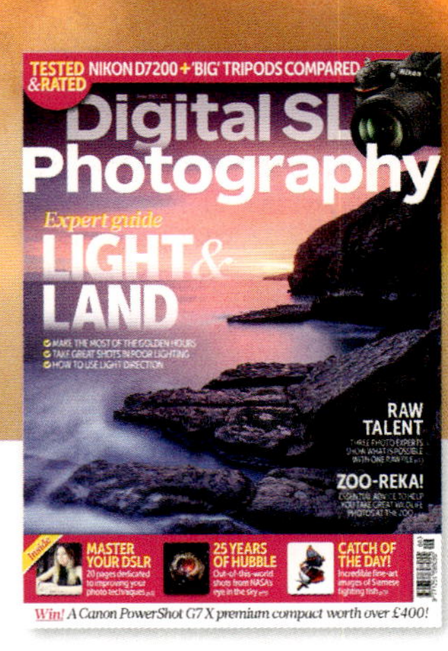

The Print Package

5 issues of ***Digital SLR Photography*** delivered FREE to your door for **just £5**

Over 700 pages of advice and inspiration!

28% saving on the print edition high street price

Photograph: Mark Greenwood

Claim today

Online: **dennismags.co.uk/dslr**

Or call: **0844 249 0482** Calls will cost 7p per minute plus your telephone company's access charge

Offer codes: Quote **G2015BUK** for the Full Package or **G2015PUK** for the Print Package

RAW

You've grasped the basics and become familiar with the features, but now it's time to put the tools into practice and to master the power of Raw for improving the quality and creativity of your photography. Over the next 16 pages, we'll show you how to correct common in-camera errors, capture maximum detail and extend your dynamic range for terrific results

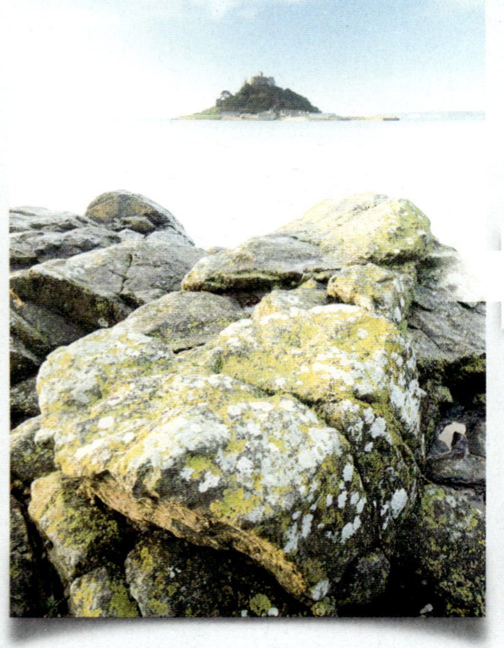

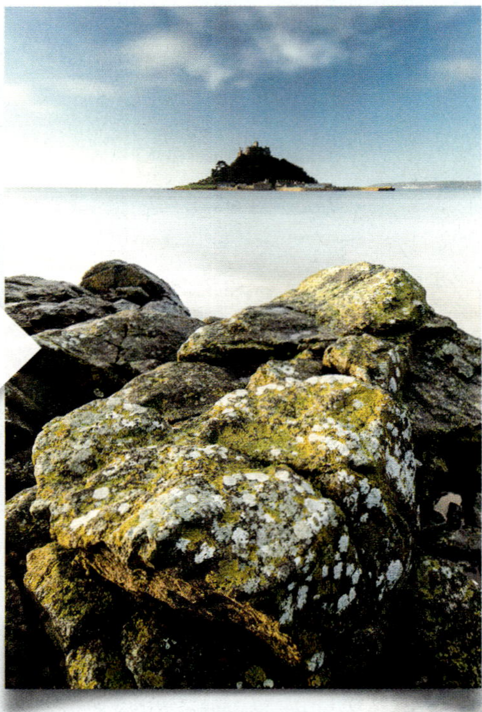

Adobe Camera Raw: the basics

Shooting in Raw has many benefits for the photographer – namely in saving all that lovely data hidden in the shadows and highlights...

What would you do if you were given one million pounds? Buy a new house? Take a luxury holiday or two? Give up the day job to be a professional photographer? Whatever you decide, one thing you probably wouldn't do is to throw away most of that money and try to make the same dreams come true on the small fraction that's left – sounds silly, doesn't it?

So why would you do this with your camera's pixels? You spend a lot of money on the latest technology with the view of getting the best image quality that your budget can buy, and then you, in effect, discard a generous proportion of this data and detail by shooting in JPEG and then wonder why your image quality is not as great as you imagined.

So what should you be using? In short – Raw. These days, digital cameras capture an extraordinary amount of image information and a large part of achieving professional-grade images is knowing how to unlock and capitalise on this detail. Some photographers believe Raw to be tricky and not a format for beginners, while others believe that if you were a good photographer and got the images right in-camera, there's no reason to not shoot JPEG. Both camps are wrong, in our opinion, and the aim of this guide is to show you why and how, with a few adjustments to your workflow, you can dramatically improve your images.

First, Raw is not difficult– it's often more involved than shooting JPEGs because you have to put more thought and time into generating the files to how you want them to look, but it's no different from shooting and processing film, which is what all great photographers did before digital. It's also the most forgiving format, making it ideal for beginners. The format allows you to make human errors without ruining a potentially great image (yes, professional photographers make mistakes too) and allows you to process the image in many different ways – just like you would with a film negative. So for creative photographers, it's really a no-brainer.

If you're still not convinced that Raw is a rookies' format, too, make sure you read how our professional contributors use Raw and why they give it rave reviews.

TOP TIP

Shoot Raw + JPEG

Not only does it allow you to save time and hard drive space by reviewing JPEGs on your monitor before having to convert the Raw files, but you can apply in-camera styles to your JPEGs, like black & white, to preview the results without affecting the Raw data, which you can then adjust later

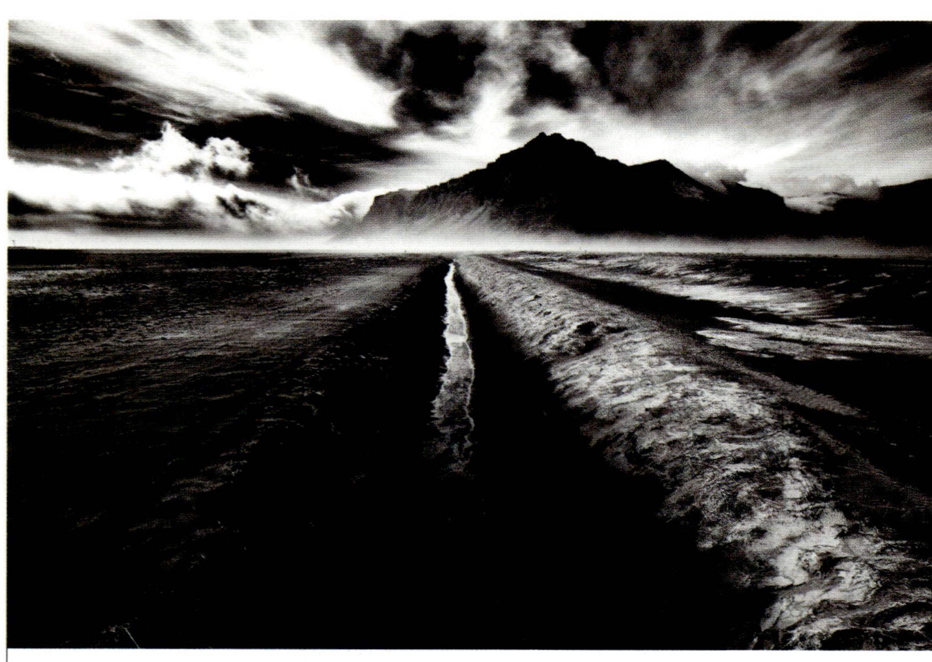

The landscape photographer: **Lee Frost**

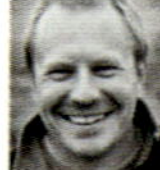

"I want to achieve optimum image quality and the Raw format does exactly that. What's the point in spending thousands of pounds on cameras and lenses, then letting the camera delete data from the images I capture before I've even had the chance to see them on my computer's monitor? A Raw file contains more data than I need, but at least by shooting in Raw I get to decide what stays and what goes. I can also save processed Raw files as 16-bit TIFF files, whereas JPEGs are 8-bit. It's easier to adjust things like colour temperature if you shoot in Raw, too, and I can batch-process Raw files to apply exactly the same settings to each image, which is useful when I shoot a sequence of images to stitch into panoramas. If I forget to specify a WB like Daylight, and instead shoot with AWB, the colour balance of each image may vary – shooting Raw allows for this margin of error." *www.leefrost.co.uk*

Set your camera for Raw

It's so easy: simply select the Image Quality setting via your camera's menu system or top plate and choose Raw or Raw + JPEG, then shoot as you normally would and take comfort in the fact that you're capturing maximum quality. There are a couple of things to be aware of, though, when shooting Raw: first, the image size (see Size matters, page 129); second, a technique called 'exposing to the right'. As the most image information is contained in the highlights, by using your histogram as a guide to slightly overexpose your scene (not so much that you lose detail in the highlights), you can capture a lot more data and detail in a Raw file, which you can then draw out by adjusting the exposure during processing. See page 138 for a more detailed guide for working with histograms.

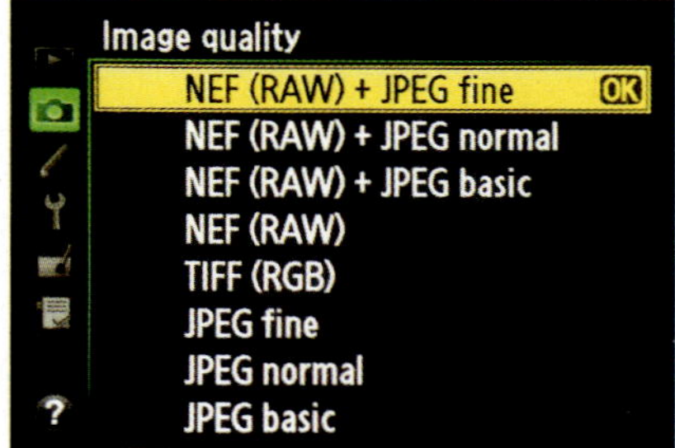

Raw software

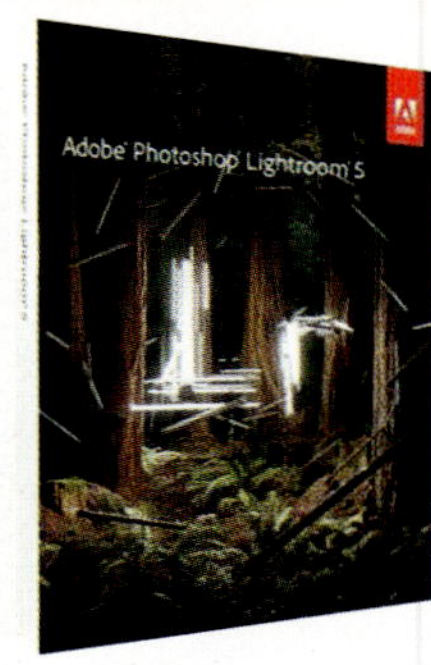

When you buy a camera, the manufacturer provides a CD-ROM with its own Raw processing software. For some, it's sufficient, but many prefer to use third-party processors and for those who already own Adobe software, they have one of the best available. Photoshop's Adobe Camera Raw (ACR) is by far the most popular and powerful editing suites, but versions of this program are also available in other Adobe products, such as Lightroom and Photoshop Elements. In fact, for the most part, the Raw editing capabilities of each are very similar or simplified versions. Capture One is another popular program for some photographers. If you're curious about how each works or how user-friendly you may find them, most can be downloaded as a free 30-day trial.

- **Adobe Lightroom 6** £100 (upgrade £60) Free trial from www.adobe.com/products
- **Photoshop CC** Subscription only £8.57 per month/ £102.30 prepaid for a year Free trial from www.adobe.com/products
- **Adobe Elements 14** £78 (upgrade £63) Free trial from www.adobe.com/products
- **Phase one Capture One** €229 (£146) Free trial from www.phaseone.com/4/
- **Serif Photo Plus X8** £80 Find out more at www.serif.com
- **Manufacturer's software** Free with your camera

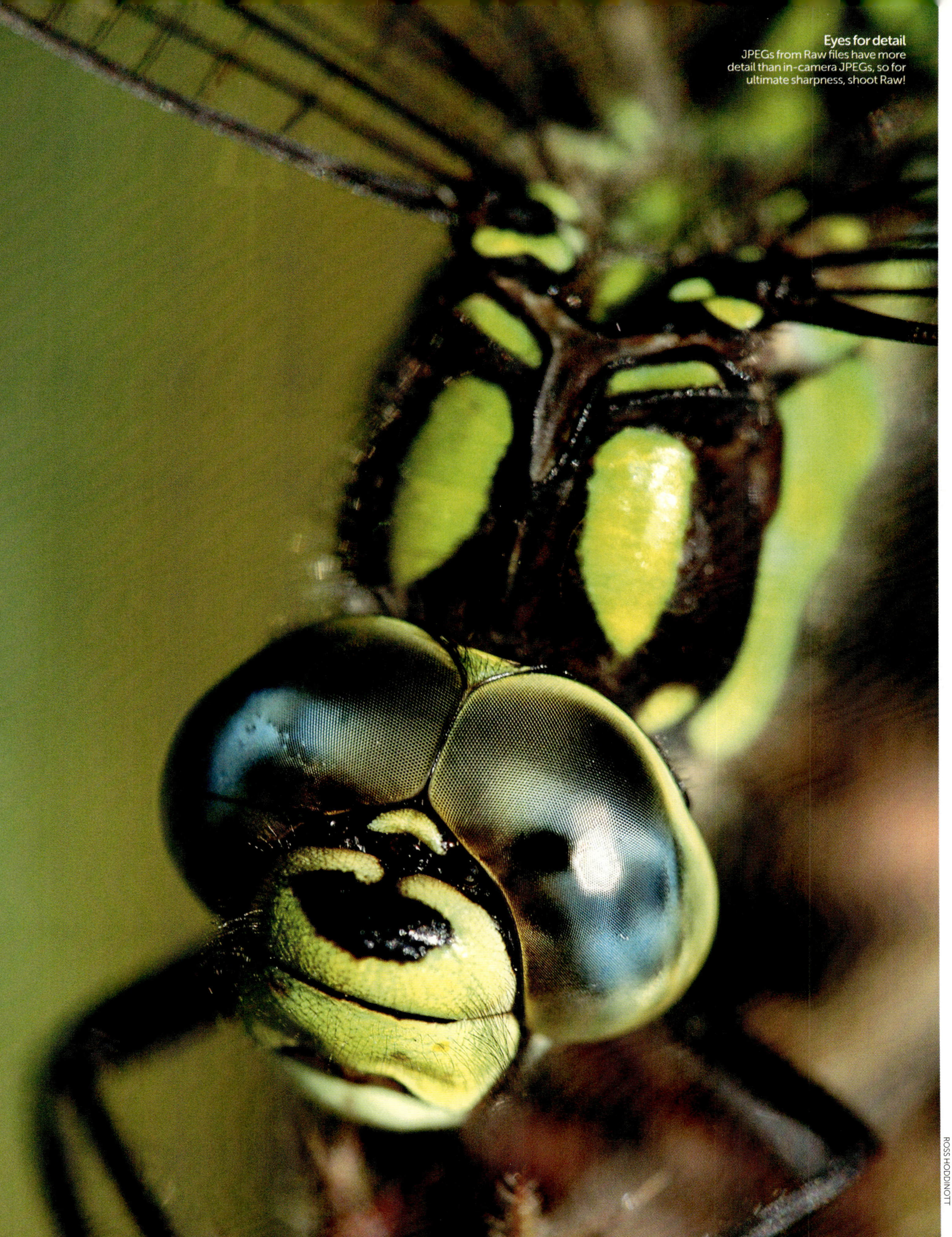

Eyes for detail
JPEGs from Raw files have more detail than in-camera JPEGs, so for ultimate sharpness, shoot Raw!

ROSS HODDINOTT

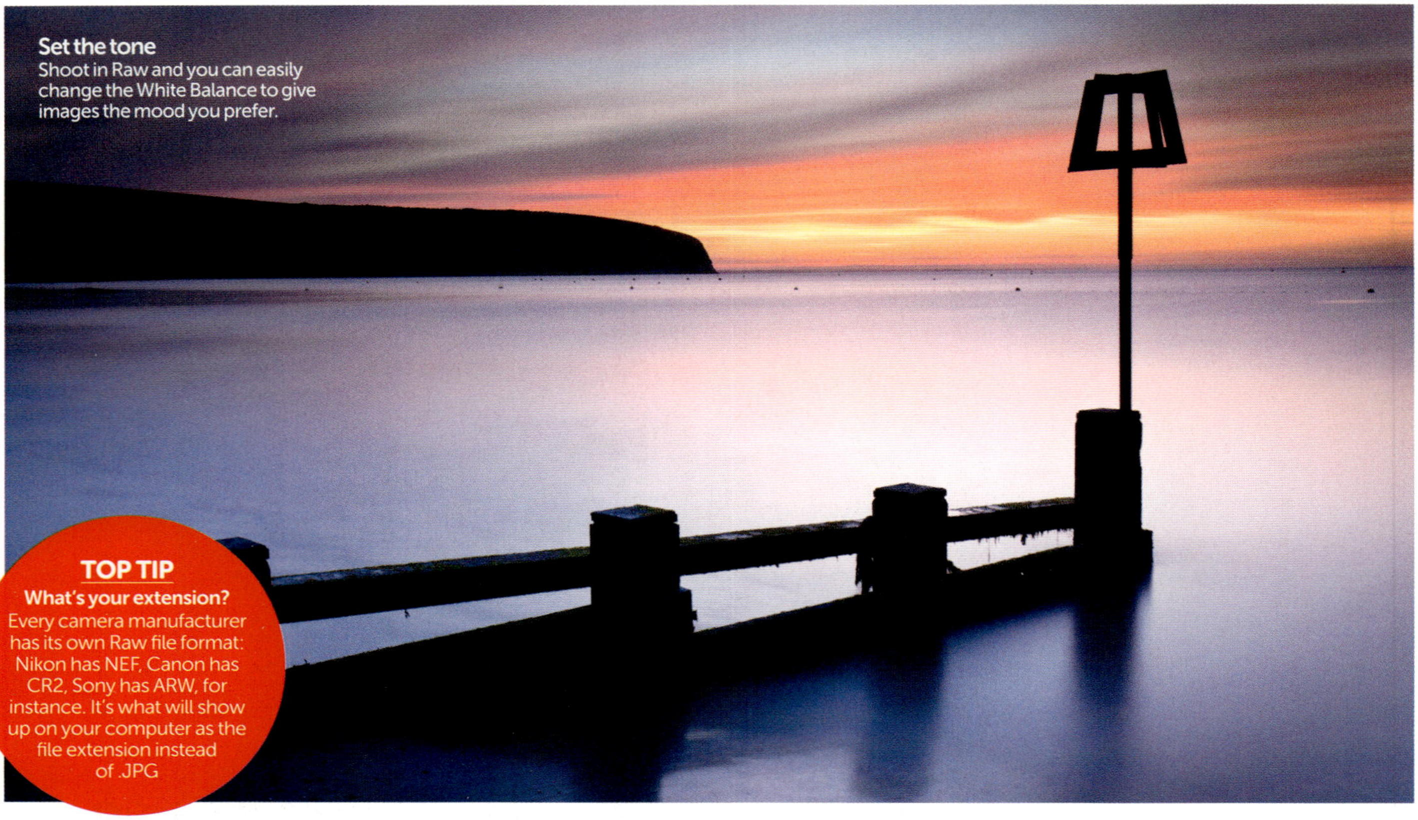

ROSS HODDINOTT

Set the tone
Shoot in Raw and you can easily change the White Balance to give images the mood you prefer.

TOP TIP
What's your extension?
Every camera manufacturer has its own Raw file format: Nikon has NEF, Canon has CR2, Sony has ARW, for instance. It's what will show up on your computer as the file extension instead of .JPG

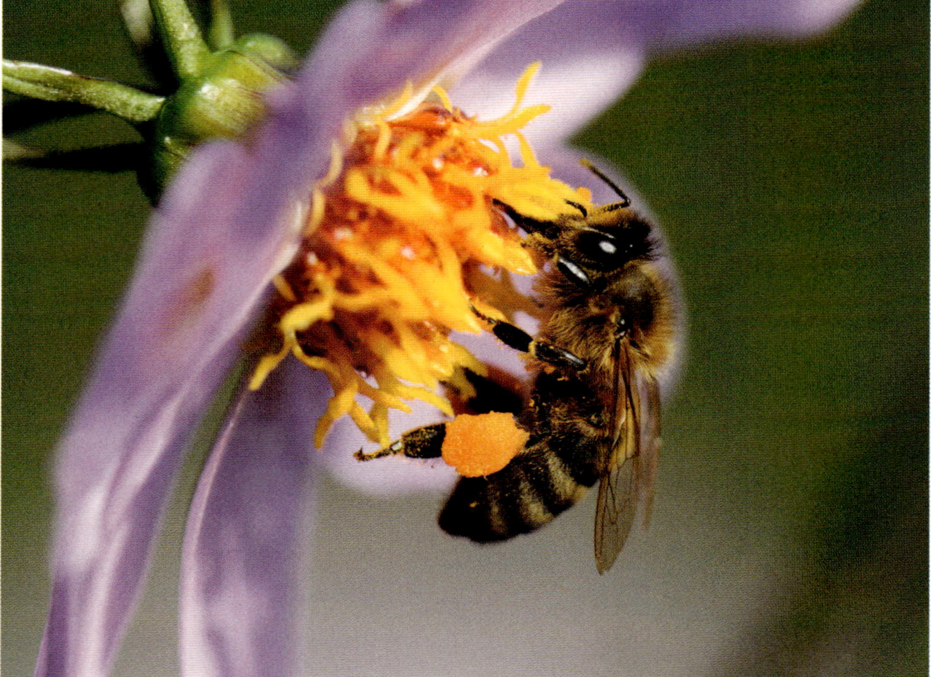

The nature photographer: **Ross Hoddinott**

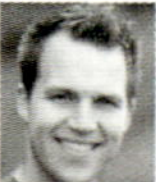

"For nature photographers, the argument for shooting Raw is overwhelming. When shooting wildlife, you have to react quickly to the subject's movement. Often, there isn't time to fine-tune all the shooting parameters, like White Balance, in-camera. However, by shooting in Raw, photographers have the luxury of being able to tweak such things later during editing, without any loss of quality. Due to a Raw file's great flexibility, nature photographers can concentrate on focusing, composition and being creative. Raw files also capture more tonal levels, so image quality is maximised. They also have greater latitude to exposure error, so if you do make a mistake, you are more likely to be able to retrieve the image. Although Raw files are larger and therefore take longer to write to the camera's card, most digital SLRs have such large buffers that shooting JPEGs offers no significant advantage to Raw, even when capturing large bursts of images."
www.rosshoddinott.co.uk

"YOUR RAW IMAGE ISN'T PRINT-READY – IT'S A NEGATIVE WAITING TO BE DEVELOPED. IT'S HOLDING A LOT OF DETAIL FOR YOU TO DRAW OUT"

Understanding the difference between Raw and JPEG might also persuade you. When you take a picture, your camera processes the data captured by the sensor, which, unaltered, is a 12-, 14- or 16-bit uncompressed Raw file (actual depth depends on the camera model that you're using).

A JPEG, on the other hand, has been processed by the camera before the image is saved to your memory card, often after sharpening, colour and contrast adjustments have been applied. The camera also compresses the file down to an 8-bit image as it decides what data is needed for the best photograph and deletes the rest. If you've slightly under- or overexposed your image, chances are that you've lost valuable information that cannot be recovered or corrections made without compromising the image quality. If you had shot in Raw, however, that information would be retained and easily recovered to improve the quality of your exposure and dynamic range. Raw files contain more data than you need to create a successful image and puts you in control of all the creative decision-making. It also means you can use your computer to process your images, which has far more power and controls than a camera.

Do we have you convinced yet? Are you swapping your Quality setting from JPEG to Raw, as you read now? Great. Now what? Unlike a JPEG, your Raw image isn't print-ready – it's a negative waiting to be developed. It's

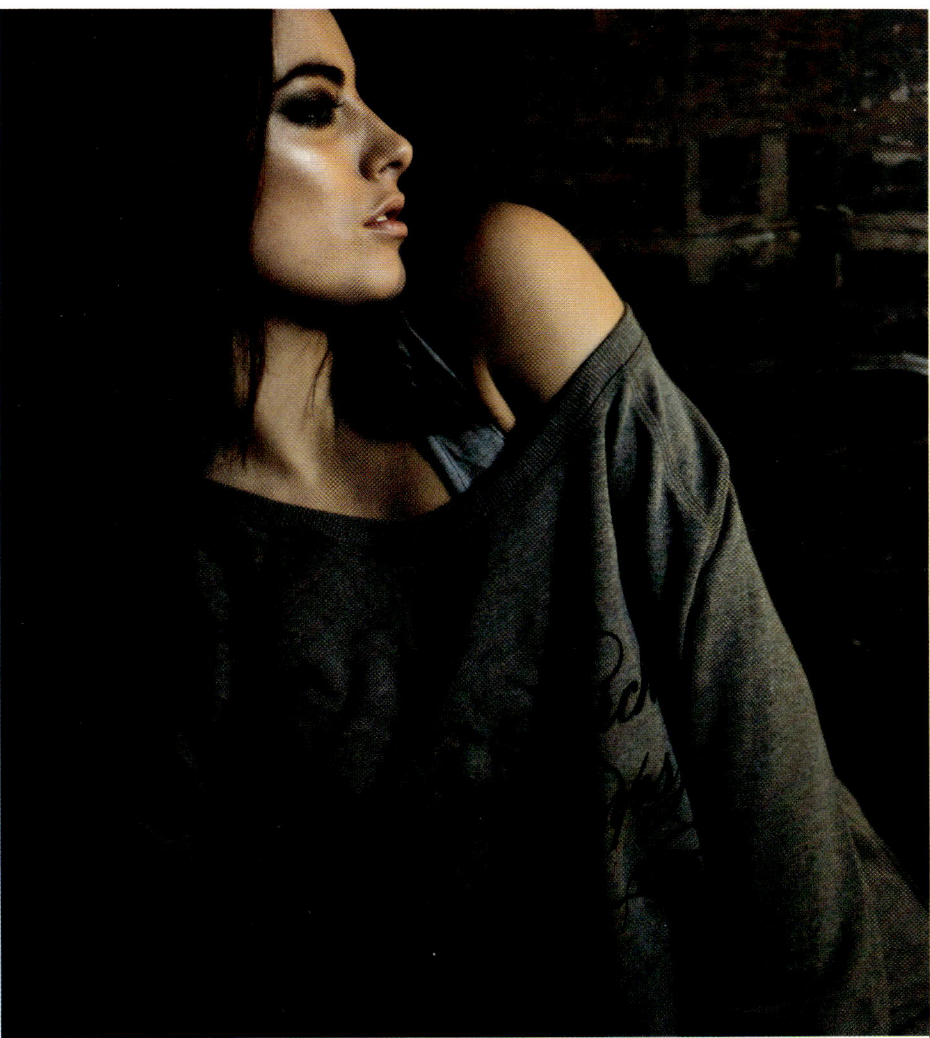

The portrait photographer: **Paul Ward**

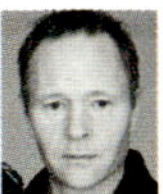

"Up until a year ago, my main priority was being able to get a lot more images on a memory card in case I made mistakes. I thought JPEGs were best. I was wrong: Raw has a lot more benefits. If you get the WB wrong, you can tweak it, whereas doing that in Photoshop on a JPEG isn't very accurate and can be hard to do. If I slightly overexpose a shot, Raw-editing software allows me to pull detail back, which is really handy. Before I moved over to the Nikon D800, whenever I tried to open up shadow areas to reveal detail, I'd get grainy images, but the D800 is amazing for revealing detail in the shadow without introducing noise. It's also useful when creating HDR images. I prefer not to take multiple exposures, as a part of the scene or the model will often move slightly between shots. With Raw I can expand the dynamic range by outputting three different exposures from a single Raw file and merging them together – it's far more controllable and the results are better." *www.paulward.net*

tonally flat, softer than it should be and holding a lot of potential detail in the highlights and shadows for you to draw out.

For many photographers, especially those new to digital editing, the idea of processing and converting Raw files can be daunting and off-putting, but it can be made as simple or as complicated as your skills permit. The beauty of Raw is that, as your skills develop, there's also no reason why you can't return to re-edit the same image again later as long you keep a file in its lossless Raw state, as the image information is never permanently altered. There are several software packages you can use, too, but our preference is Adobe: whether that be Elements, CS, CC or Lightroom. Each has very similar Raw interfaces, borne from Adobe Camera Raw, which we'll show you exactly how to navigate over the page.

Size matters

With increasing megapixels and data collection, one modern challenge photographers are facing is massive Raw files. Depending on your camera's file size, a Raw file can take up to five or six times more space than a JPEG. Not only does this mean high-capacity memory cards, or plenty of spares, but you may eventually need a bigger hard drive and faster processor if your computer is to manage downloading and editing these mammoth images. Add to this that the file size increases as you edit the images until they're compressed, plus the fact that you might want to keep the original Raw file as well as the JPEG, and you'll be needing a lot more storage space than if you stuck with JPEG only. But let's face it, though – the pros of Raw still far outweigh these cons.

Raw FAQs

Q When I open my Raw files in ACR I get areas flashing red and blue. It's really distracting. What does it mean and how can I get rid of it?

A Don't worry, it's only the highlight and shadow warnings! If any of the shadow areas are clipped (pure black with no detail recorded), they will flash blue to let you know and if any of the highlights are blown (white with no detail recorded), the affected areas flash red. It's handy to have these warnings on so that you can identify if the clipped shadows and blown highlights improve as you're making adjustments to the image. If you do want to turn them off, though, just click on the small triangles at the top-right and left corners of the histogram in the Adobe Camera Raw window.

Q I've got Photoshop CS5, Lightroom 6 and Nikon Capture NX, which came with my Nikon D800. They can all process Raw files – which should I use?

A It's entirely up to you, but you're better off sticking with one of the three so you get used to it, rather than chopping and changing between them all. Many Nikon fans use Capture NX, but Lightroom and Photoshop are more streamlined because they allow you to do much more with your images using a single application. Don't forget you have Elements, too, for a simpler and cheaper version of Photoshop if the bigger softwares intimidate you.

Q I've just bought a new DSLR and ACR won't open my Raw files. Do I need to upgrade my version of Photoshop?

A Not necessarily. When manufacturers bring out new camera models, the Raw format used by those cameras usually won't be recognised by the version of ACR you're using in Photoshop as it predated the launch of the camera. When you try to open a Raw file, a message says: 'Could not complete your request because Photoshop doesn't recognise this type of file'.

Adobe issues free updates for ACR that allow you to open Raw files from specified new camera models – you can download them from www.adobe.com. However, whether or not this will solve your problem depends on the version of Photoshop you're using and if the DSLR you bought is a new model or one that has been around for a while. If you're running CS4 or CS5 and your camera is a recent launch, then you'll probably find that the last ACR update issued doesn't include your camera on the list of models covered. If you're running CS6, you'll probably be okay and if you're running CC then you'll definitely have access to any ACR updates for your camera.

If there is no suitable ACR update available for your version of Photoshop, you could either upgrade to Photoshop CC or, alternatively, buy Adobe Lightroom 6 – which will allow you to process Raw files from your new camera and still import into Photoshop after.

Q How should I save my image from Adobe Camera Raw?

A Before you save your image, click on Workflow Options (blue writing at the bottom of ACR) and set the Size, Depth, Space and 300 pixels/inch as the Resolution. If you're not opening your image into Photoshop, click ***Save Image...*** and preferably select ***TIFF*** as your ***Format*** as it retains more information than a JPEG, and set ***Compression*** to ***None***.

Navigating the Adobe Camera Raw interface

New to ACR and confused by all its features? No fear, we will make it clear...

The toolbar

Zoom: Magnify the image to see it in more detail by clicking on the preview image.

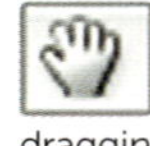

Hand: Navigate around the magnified image by clicking and dragging the Hand Tool.

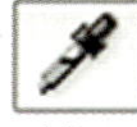

White Balance: By clicking on an image area that's white or grey, ACR can determine the colour of the light the image was taken in.

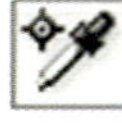

Color Sampler: This allows you to select a colour that you want to adjust by clicking on that area of the image.

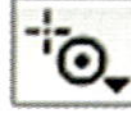

Targeted Adjustment: Instead of using the sliders to make adjustments, drag this tool on the image to make edits.

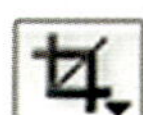

Crop: Perhaps one of the most useful tools, use Crop to change the aspect ratio, to recompose your image or simply remove elements from the edges.

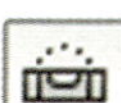

Straighten: Correct a wonky horizon or rotate your image.

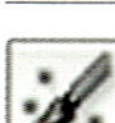

Spot Removal: Use to get rid of sensor spots, dust marks and other unwanted blemishes.

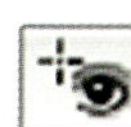

Red-Eye Removal: Click on the subject's pupil to get rid of red-eye in portraits.

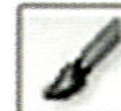

Adjustment Brush: Use this tool to make localised edits to your image by combining it with the tools found in the Basic tab.

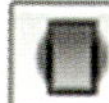

Graduated Filter: Draw a line across your image to apply a graduate effect. You can then adjust Exposure, Brightness, Contrast, Clarity, Saturation, Sharpness and Color of the graduate to suit your picture.

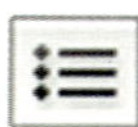

Preferences: Click here to access the Camera Raw Preferences dialogue box.

Rotate counterclockwise & Rotate clockwise: Click on the tools to rotate in either direction by 90°.

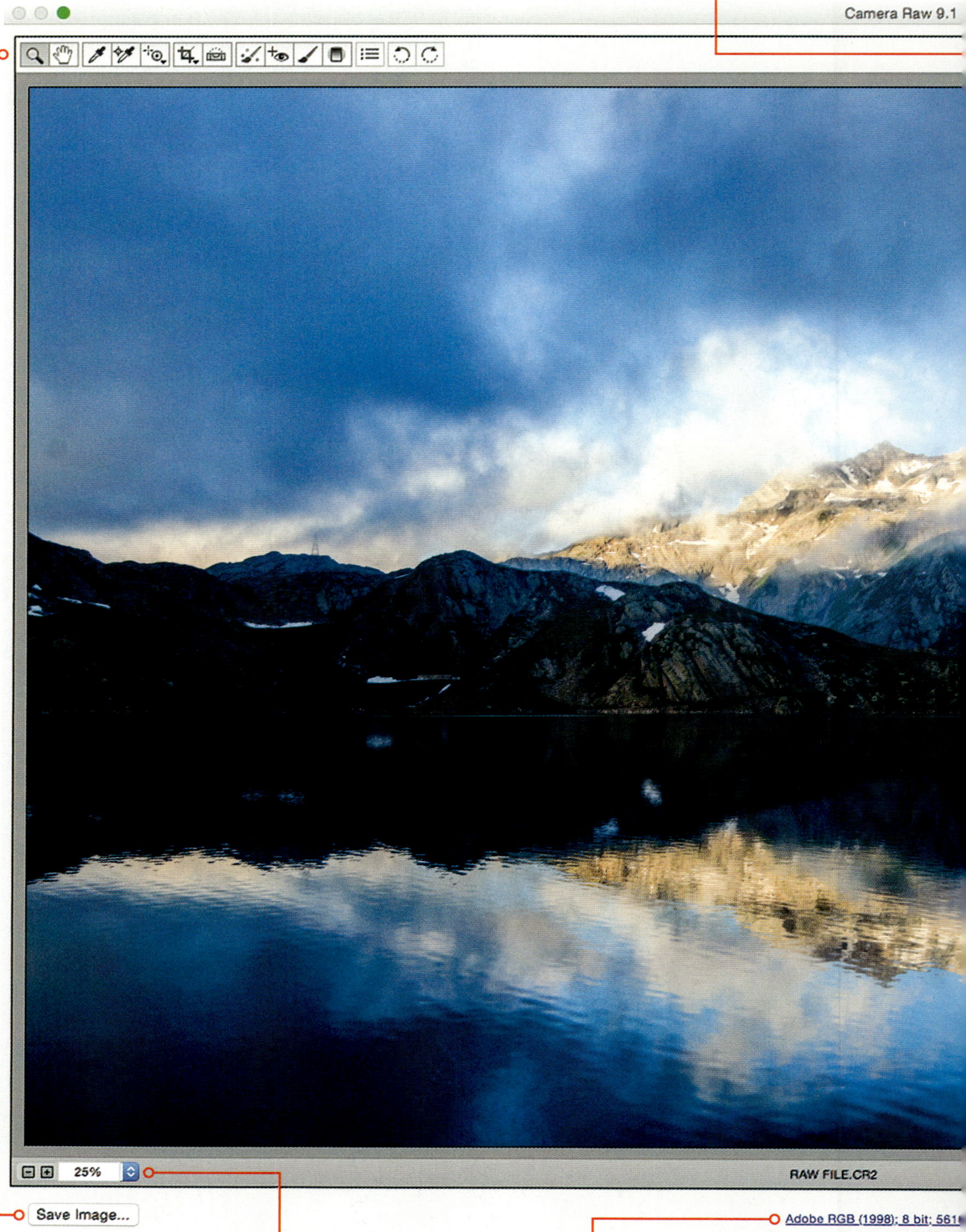

☑ PREVIEW OPTIONS
To see how your adjustments affect your image, make sure this ***Preview*** box is ticked. The button to the right expands or reduces the size of your interface.

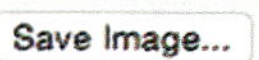

☑ SAVE IMAGE...
Click here to open your Save Options. From here you can select your image Format, File Extension and level of Compression before naming and saving the file.

☑ ZOOM
As an alternative to using the Zoom Tool, you can make more precise enlargements by selecting a percentage from this drop-down menu or using the + or - buttons.

☑ WORKFLOW OPTIONS
By clicking on this blue information line, you can select the best image space, resolution, size and depth to ensure optimum quality.
See page 132 for details.

☑ CLIPPING WARNINGS

Clipping is where detail is lost at the extreme ends of the histogram spectrum – these black and white triangle buttons, when pressed, activate warnings to indicate where clipping has occurred. Areas with lost shadow detail (right triangle) flash blue, while highlights (left triangle) flash red.

☑ HISTOGRAM

Just like on your camera, the ACR histogram shows you the distribution of your exposure information from pure blacks to pure whites. It's a good reference for determining what adjustments you need to make. As you move the sliders, you'll notice the histogram changes its distribution.

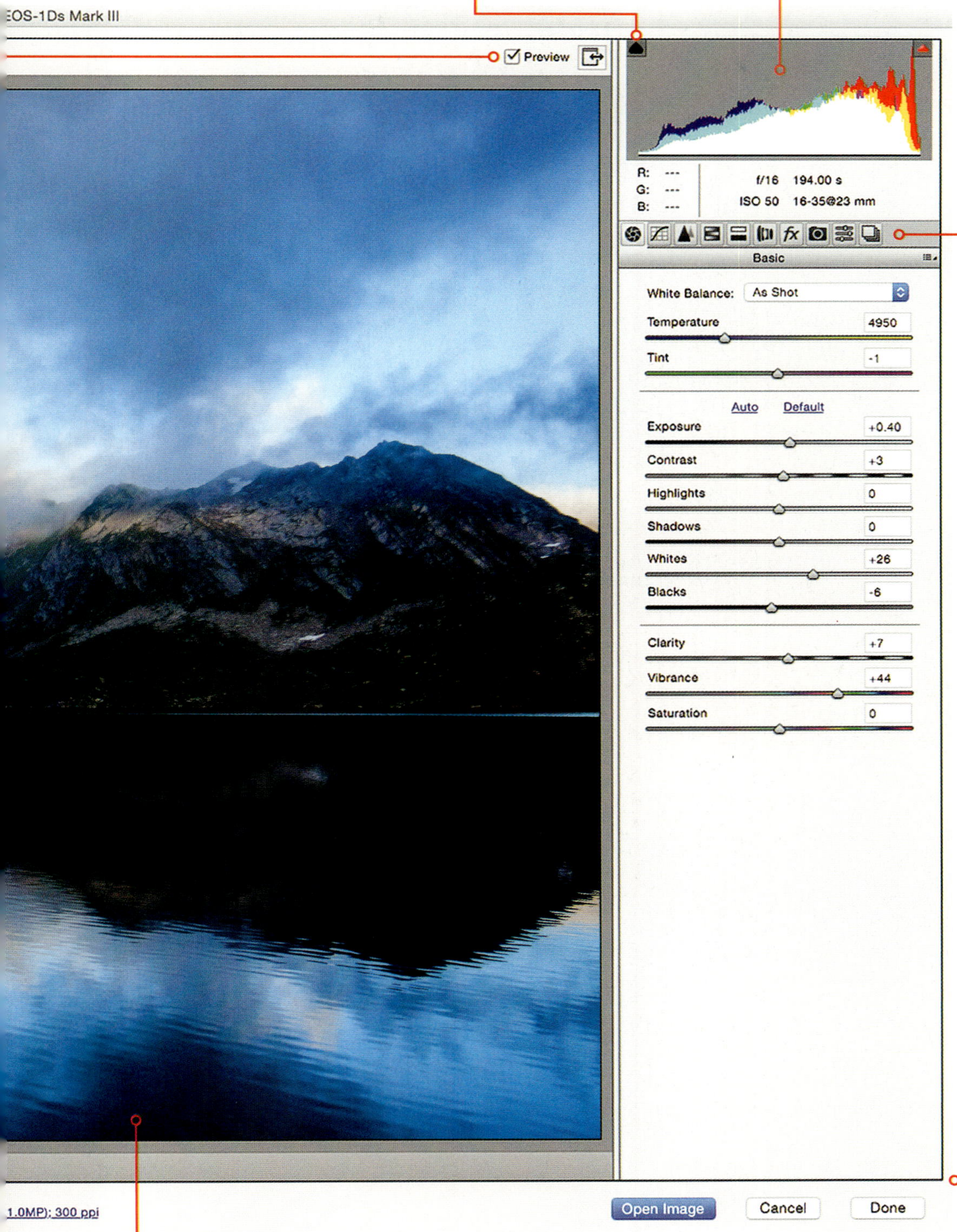

Adjustments

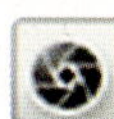

Basic: Arguably the control room of ACR, these tools for the most part are all you need to dramatically transform your Raw images – turn over to find out exactly how.

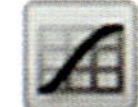

Tone Curve: It functions in a similar way to Photoshop's Curves adjustment, allowing you to manually manipulate the tonal graph to affect your image's contrast.

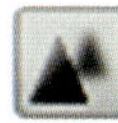

Detail: You can access the Sharpening and Noise Reduction features of ACR via this tab. They're quite straightforward to use, but for more information and tutorials, turn to page 134.

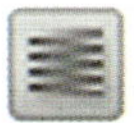

HSL/Grayscale: This tab holds most of the controls you need to alter colour. You have HSL (Hue, Saturation and Luminance adjustments) as well as a Convert to Grayscale box that allows you to use the Grayscale Mix sliders to adjust the various grey tones in your image to improve contrast.

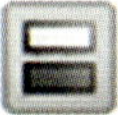

Split Toning: Want to be a bit more creative with colour? The Split Toning tab enables you to adjust the Hue and Saturation of the highlights and shadows separately for duotone results.

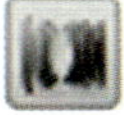

Lens Corrections: A really useful feature and one tab we recommend visiting before you do any editing, especially if you've shot with a wide-angle lens and your image has barrel or pincushion distortion, fringing or vignetting.

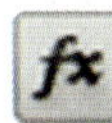

FX: The Effects tab features the more creative adjustments. You can add grain and apply a vignette for artistic results. See page 135 for details.

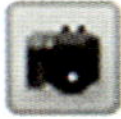

Camera Calibration: Use this tab to apply your in-camera styles, like Vivid and Landscape. You can use the Camera Profile sliders to help calibrate your on-screen image to match your LCD view, if needed.

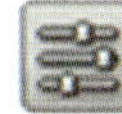

Presets: Create your own presets so you can apply creative or routine tweaks with one click. Simply click ***New Preset*** and then record the adjustments.

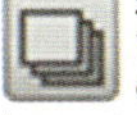

Snapshots: Take 'snapshots' of your editing as you go along to compare the results or to quickly and easily return to an earlier state.

☑ OPEN IMAGE

When you've done all the editing you want to in Adobe Camera Raw, you have the option to open the image in Photoshop for further processing. Instead of clicking Open Image, hold ***alt*** to open the image as a copy – it's useful if you want to apply different techniques to the same Raw file in Photoshop. You can also press ***alt*** to change the Cancel button to Reset, reverting all sliders to default settings.

☑ THE ACR INTERFACE

Adobe softwares have very similar interfaces and capabilities for using Raw, so whether you use Elements or Lightroom, the tools and techniques will generally translate.

Getting started in Adobe Camera Raw

Master these basic Raw adjustments and we promise the quality of your photographs will never be the same again

IF YOU NORMALLY shoot JPEGs, you won't have to know much to notice a dramatic difference to the quality of your edited images once you begin working with Raw.

Just being able to navigate a few basic settings in your chosen software guarantees better results, simply because you not only have a lot more image information stored, and therefore scope for better improvement, but you call the shots based on each image's needs rather than letting the camera apply the same blanket adjustments, like sharpening and colour saturation, to all your pictures.

The best part of editing in Adobe Camera Raw is that it doesn't matter how many errors you make, no amount of editing you do to your Raw file degrades the image quality – unlike a JPEG – so you're free to experiment with consequence until you convert the image to a JPEG or TIFF. And even if you do save your edits to the Raw file, the edits you've made are still completely reversible. Brilliant isn't it!

Most of your key editing tools are housed under the Basic tab and are adjustable using sliders, making them fast and easy to use. If you're only interested in making minimal edits to every Raw file, then this page has all you need to know, and more: Basic is the powerhouse of ACR.

While it has more than enough to get you by, and should keep the learning curve relatively shallow, you and your images would be missing out if you left it there. There is so much more to learn about the way ACR can improve your results and so many techniques that we want to tell you about. But before we get ahead of ourselves, here's a breakdown of what the Basic panel offers and how you can use it to process your best ever pictures.

White Balance

As you'll soon discover, this is one of the most useful tools in your Raw editing arsenal. While the White Balance Tool is great, these controls make correcting any in-camera White Balance errors a doddle once you get the hang of it: simply select a WB preset to match the original scene's lighting conditions or use the sliders for a custom WB.

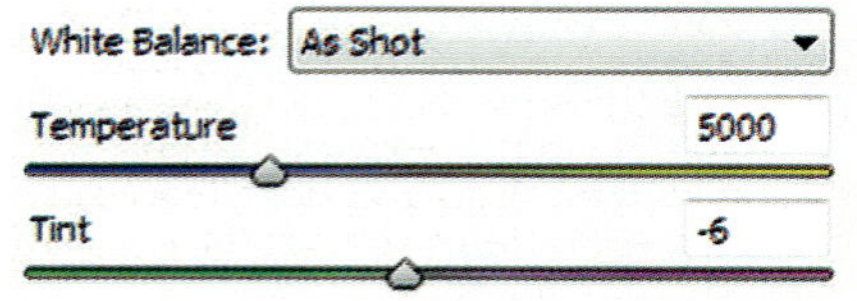

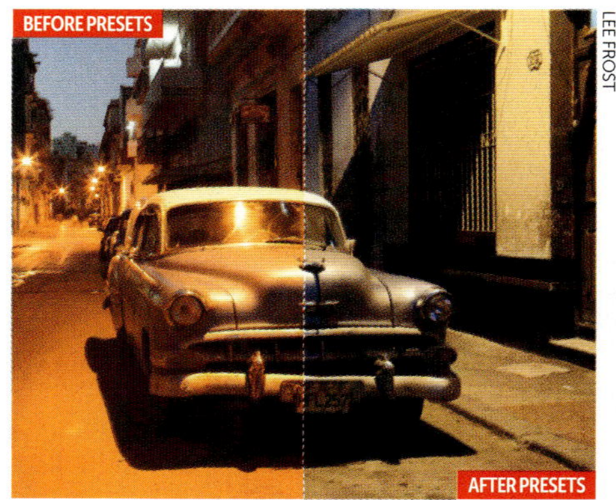

LEE FROST

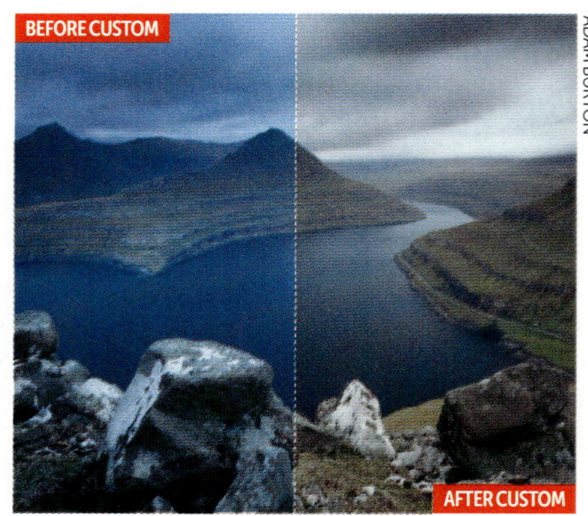

ADAM BURTON

Workflow Options

If you click on the blue text below your preview image in the ACR window, a Workflow Options box opens. Make sure you have ***Space*** set to ***Adobe RGB (1998)*** and ***Depth*** to ***16 Bits/Channel***. Click ***Size*** to see various options: most of which have a – (minus) symbol after them, one that has no symbol and one or two that have a + (plus) symbol at the end. The option with no symbol is the optimum one for your camera and saves your images at maximum resolution. Choose that one. You've paid for those megapixels so you might as well use them. There's no point, generally, in choosing a lower resolution option, and if you choose one that's higher than the resolution of your camera, the files will be interpolated, which you don't usually need – increase the file size later, in Photoshop, if necessary. Also, make sure ***Resolution*** is set to ***300 pixels/inch***.

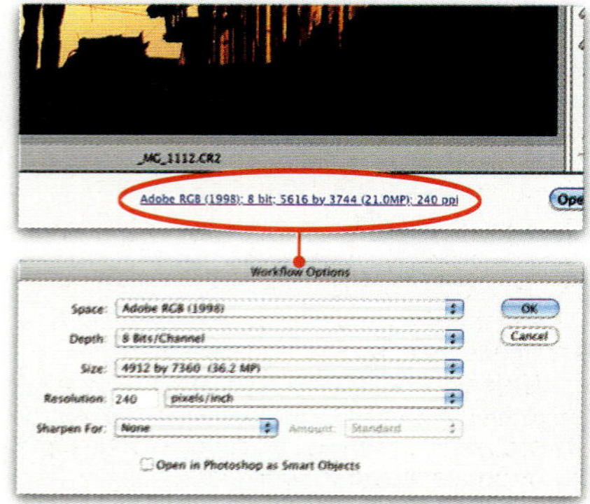

Exposure

Out of all the controls in the Basic panel, ***Exposure*** is the one you're most likely to use every time you make edits. Move the slider to the right to increase or left to decrease the exposure: much the same way as adding exposure compensation to your camera. You can also type in an exposure value, like 2 for two stops, in the box. If your image is dramatically under- or overexposed, combine Exposure with other sliders for the best results and be careful of introducing noise.

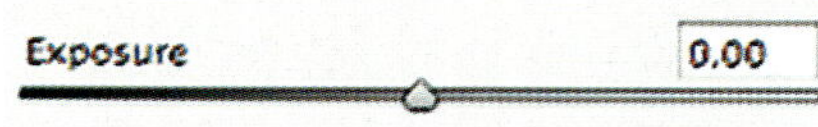

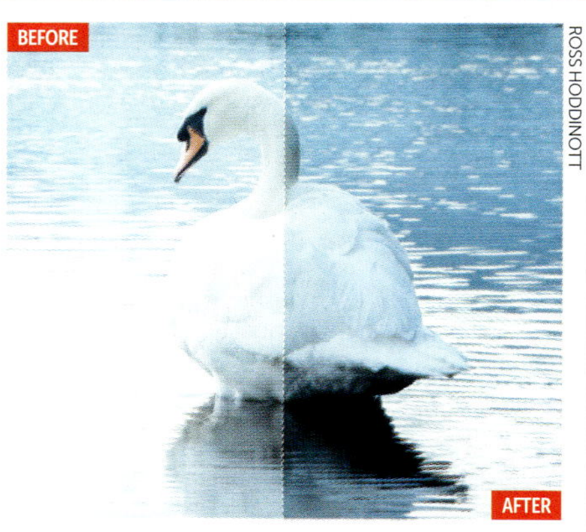

ROSS HODDINOTT

Recovery (Up to CS5)

If you overexposed your image in-camera, then this tool will be your fail-safe option; use it to recover detail that's hidden in the highlights. If you've not clipped your highlights, you can use the slider as generously as you need to, but if you've overexposed to the point where there's no detail to recover, ACR will attempt to reconstruct the detail where two or more colour channels are present. Be watchful of highlights turning grey as a result of trying to retrieve lost detail.

Recovery 0

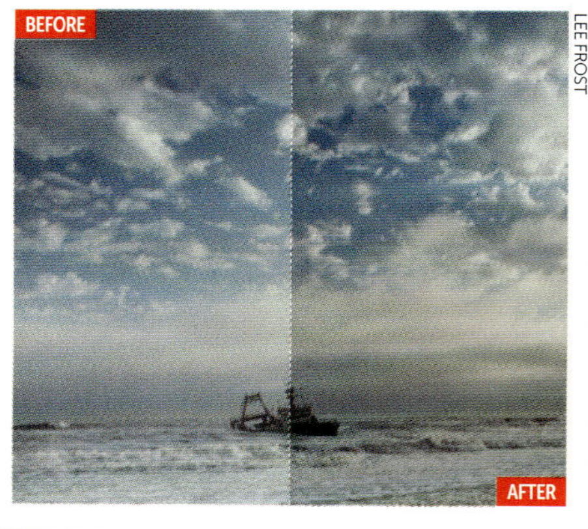

LEE FROST

Fill Light (Up to CS5)

Underexposed your image slightly and want to reveal detail in your shadows? Then this is the tool you'll need to go to once you've tweaked the Exposure. It works in a similar way to if you had used a burst of fill flash when taking the shot, opening up the shadows for a brighter image. Use it in conjunction with the ***Blacks*** slider to improve contrast, but be careful that you don't overdo it or you'll start to introduce noise, halos and the resemblance of an image with ugly hyperreal dynamic range.

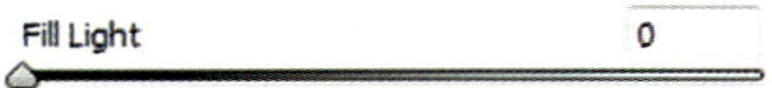

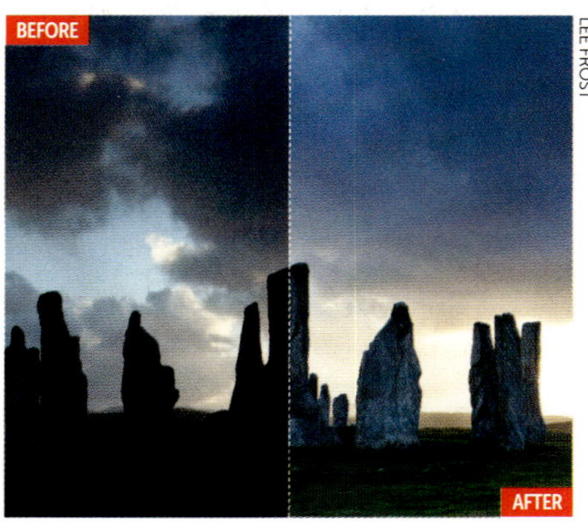

LEE FROST

Contrast

Manipulate the mid-tones, without affecting the pure whites or blacks in your image, to add a little extra punch or to soften tones. Contrast adjustments are best left to the end of your editing process. Be mindful of pushing the slider too far to the left, as this will wash out your image, or too far to the right, as this can cause clipping of shadows and highlights.

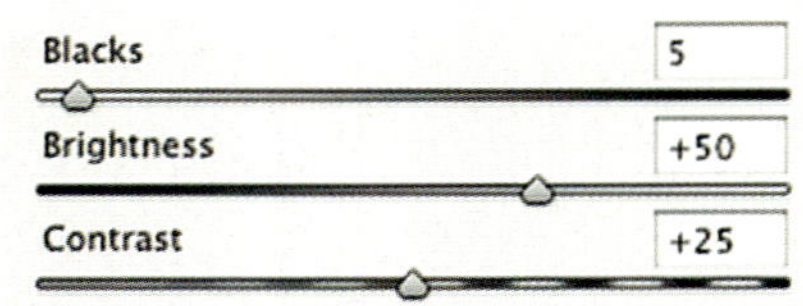

Brightness (Up to CS5)

Quite simply, it does what it says on the tin. Adjust the slider to affect the overall brightness of your image. ACR has more effective tools for doing this, like Exposure, which may be why it's not been featured in the latest version.

Blacks

Target only your darkest areas to add depth to your shadows by increasing the amount of pure blacks in your image. Watch the histogram and the preview images for areas that flash blue to avoid clipping detail.

Clarity

Fantastic for increasing the level of detail in your image, ***Clarity*** is a tool to be loved and loathed. As it targets edge contrast, use it with caution as excess can result in halos and artefacts. CS6 and CC, however, have transformed this tool so halos are now much less of a problem. Zoom in to the image for a better view of your adjustments, which are best made as a final tweak. Combine Clarity with moderate sharpening for the best results: too much of either may hinder image quality.

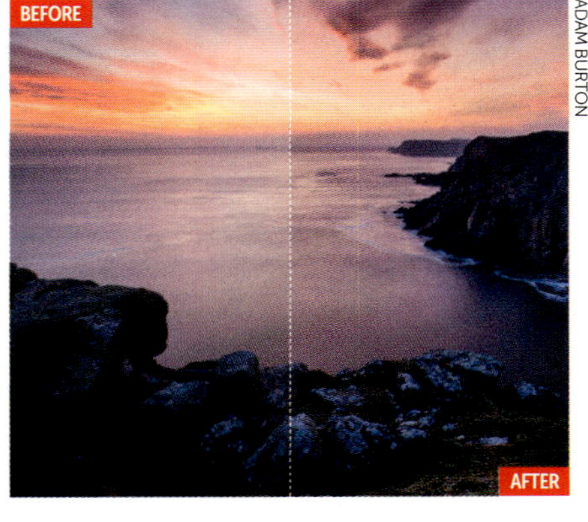

ADAM BURTON

Vibrance & Saturation

Wondering why ACR has both these sliders? It's simple: ***Vibrance*** targets areas that are not already saturated, while ***Saturation*** enhances all colours equally.

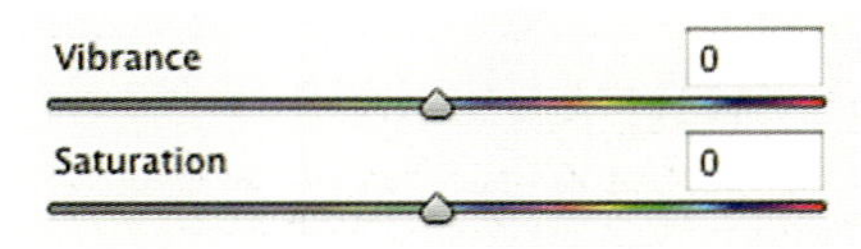

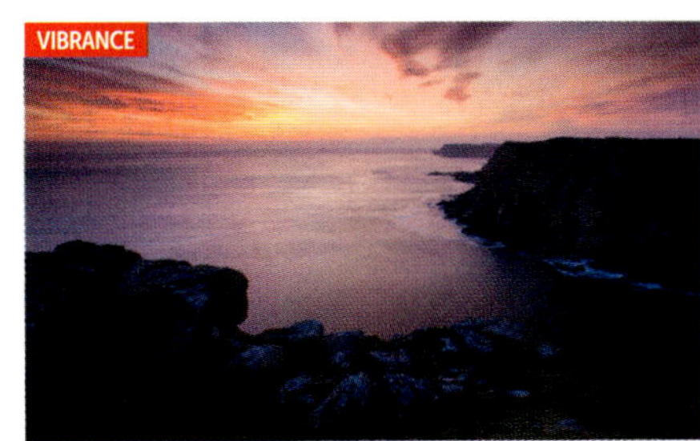

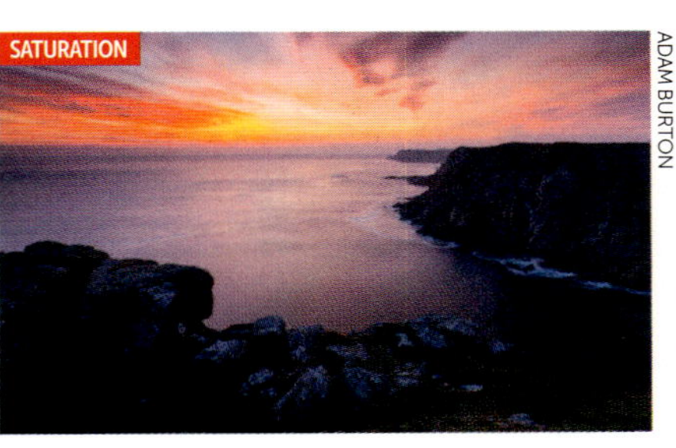

ADAM BURTON

Adjustment Brushes

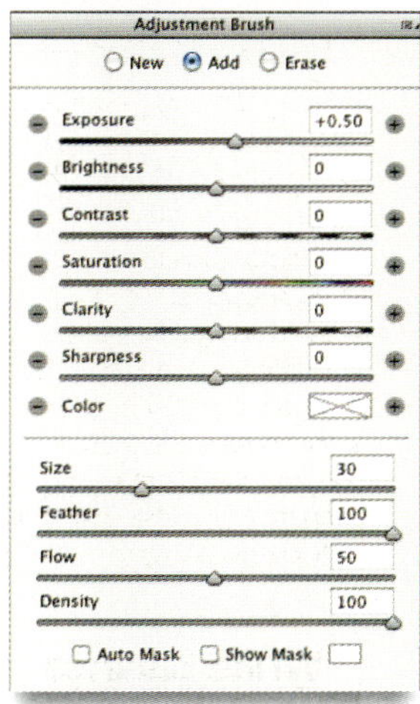

While the Basic tab holds the key to your fundamental editing tools, every adjustment you make to your image using the sliders affects your Raw file globally. But what if, after you've made all of your adjustments, there are areas of the image that are in need of further work? Do you open it in Photoshop to destruct the pixels using the Dodge/Burn Tools or arduously use Adjustment Layers with Layer Masks for selective editing? Well, while the latter option is still a preference over the former, you don't even have to leave ACR to make these localised changes – that's what the Adjustment Brush is for.

Once you select the ***Adjustment Brush*** from the toolbar, the Basic panel converts to the Adjustment Brush panel, featuring some of the same sliders: Exposure, Brightness, Contrast, Saturation, Clarity, Sharpness and Color. In CS6 and CC, you also have the benefit of Noise Reduction, Moire Reduction, Defringe, Clarity, Saturation, Shadows, Highlight, Tint and Temp.

In CS5, CS6 and CC, there's also a sub-category that affects the brush's properties such as Size, Feather, Flow and Density. You can use the brush to target specific areas of your image and then the required adjustment slider to edit that section without interfering with the rest of your image.

The ***Auto Mask*** feature is really useful for helping you to isolate areas of your image. For every new area you want to target or adjustment you want to make, click ***New*** at the top of the panel. If you want to delete an adjustment at any point, hover over the adjusted area to reveal the pin (a green node) – if it's not visible, just click ***Show Pins*** at the bottom of the panel. Click on the ***pin*** and then ***Backspace*** to delete. Alternatively, you can always press ***Erase*** and brush over the area again to remove the adjustment.

New to CS6 & CC

- **Highlights:** This new tool is incredibly powerful: drag it to the left to recover highlight detail – like Recovery in CS5 – or the right to brighten highlights with minimal clipping. Use in combination with the ***Whites*** slider for extra punch.
- **Shadows:** Use this slider by moving it to the right or left to brighten or darken shadows and mid-tones, respectively, and to recover detail in the shadows.
- **Whites:** Drag this new slider to the left to reduce any clipping to the highlights – similarly to Recovery in earlier CS versions – or the right to introduce specular highlights.

Advance your skills with these top tools

Want to know how to use the other highly effective features in ACR? Here are a few...

TOP TIP
Further reading
For monthly in-depth tutorials on how to apply these tools and Raw processing techniques in Lightroom and ACR, read *Digital SLR Photography* magazine

HAVING COVERED THE basics, you should at least be able to now dabble with processing your Raw files and start to notice the difference to your images. Some photographers, after making basic ACR exposure and contrast adjustments, prefer to open their image in the main Photoshop suite to apply any distortion correction and sharpening, rather than continuing to edit in ACR. It's really a matter of choice.

If you do choose to make some, or all, of your extra adjustments in Photoshop, we strongly advise not compressing your Raw file first, but to open your Raw image as a copy or object to ensure the best results – otherwise you'll lose data and quality.

Depending on your preferred ACR workflow, some of the tools featured in this section, such as Camera and Lens Correction, defringing and vignette removal, might become your first port of call before making any edits in the Basic panel. Whatever your preference is, it's worth knowing what they do and how they work.

Lens Corrections

Different lenses exhibit various defects depending on factors like f/stop and focal length, one of which is distortion. But this is simple to correct in ACR. Select the ***Lens Corrections*** tab and click ***Profile***, then ***Enable Lens Profile Corrections*** for automatic adjustments based on the lens you've used. You can also use the ***Distortion*** slider if it's not sufficient. See Vignetting and Fixing Fringing for more information on further common corrections.

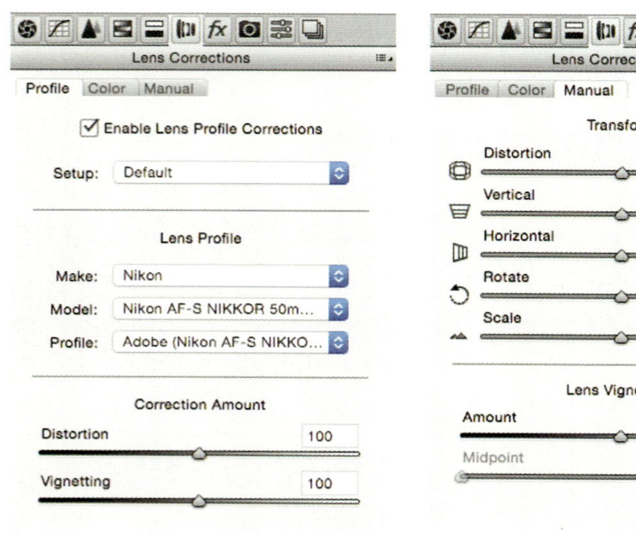

BEFORE

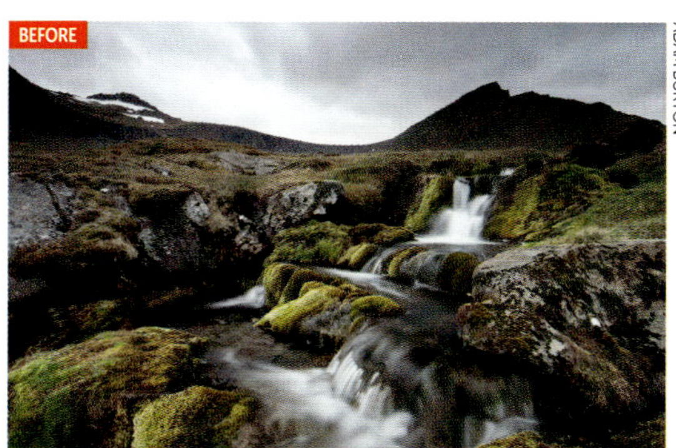

ADAM BURTON

AFTER

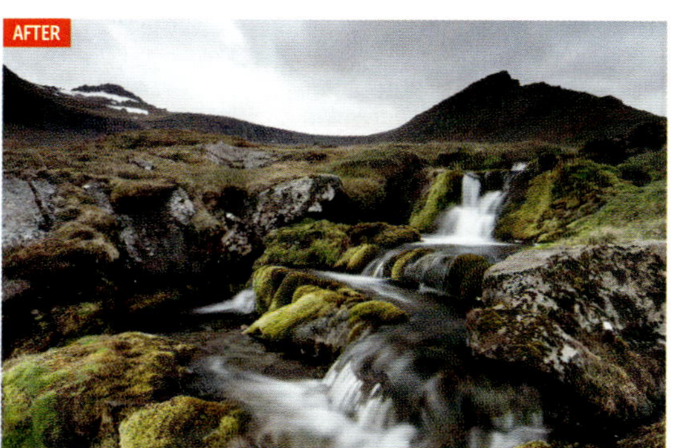

Sharpening

A lot of photographers to leave sharpening to Photoshop, or at least after all other editing has been done, as it arguably offers more control and allows you to alter the level of sharpening depending on the output (ie web or print). ACR's sharpening, however, located in Detail, is based on the same algorithm as Photoshop's Unsharp Mask, so is very effective. Sharpening in ACR also has the benefit of being nondestructive and reversible, whereas in Photoshop this is a lot more difficult to achieve. However you decide to sharpen, know that it's an essential step as, unlike a JPEG, no in-camera sharpening has been applied to a Raw file.

BEFORE

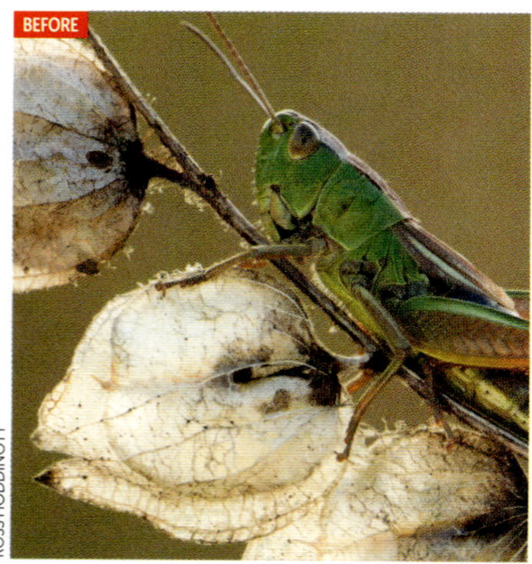

ROSS HODDINOTT

AFTER

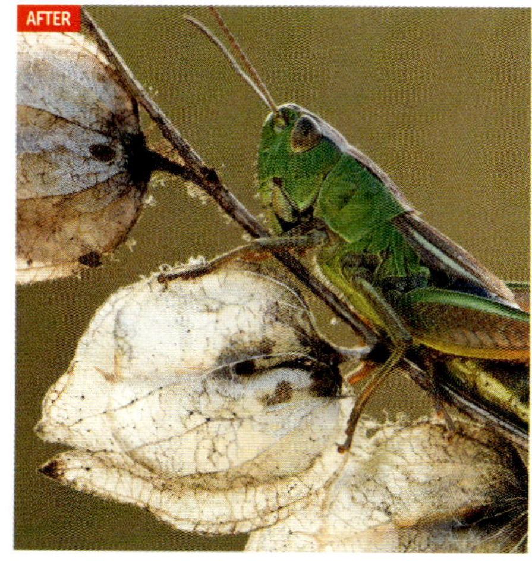

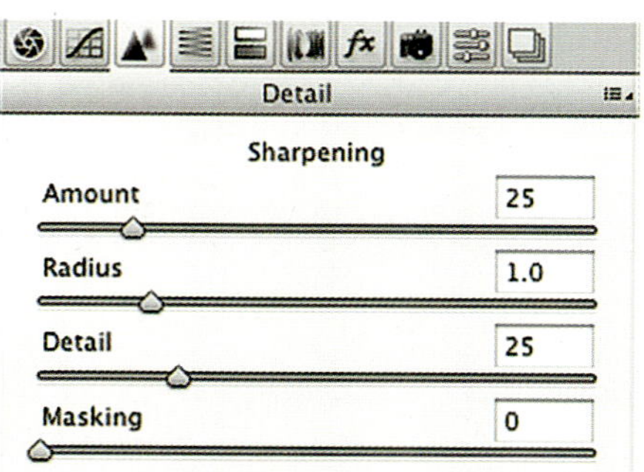

Amount: This affects edge definition. The higher the Amount, the more edges are sharpened. Be careful of adding artefacts by going too far as it can be detrimental to your image.

Radius: Adjust the size of the details that sharpening is applied to. Use a high ***Radius*** for large details and a low ***Radius*** for fine details.

Detail: Use to sharpen high-frequency data. Set it low to remove blur around edges and high for making texture much more pronounced.

Masking: Leave this slider set to ***0*** so the other sliders affect the whole image or ***100*** to restrict tweaks to the strongest edges. Press ***alt/opt*** to see the areas masked.

Tone Curve

The next tab along from Basic is Tone Curve, and it works in a similar way to Curves in Photoshop. As Raw files are notoriously flat, this section can become really useful and an alternative to some of the Basic sliders once you've got the hang of it. You have two options: Parametric and Point. Under the *Point* sub-tab you can select a preset that affects the brightness and contrast, or you can adjust the line intersecting the histogram manually, like you would in Curves. If Levels was more your style, stick with the default *Parametric* sub-tab as it allows you to use the sliders, which can be more manageable, to target *Highlights*, *Lights*, *Darks* and *Shadows*. Move the sliders to the left to lighten, or right to darken those specific tonal bands. You'll notice as you change the sliders that the graph line changes shape – the higher you set the contrast, the steeper the curve will create an 'S' shape. In Lightroom 6 and Photoshop CS6/CC, you can also select specific colour channels to edit – great if you only want to affect the contrast of Red, Green or Blue, or apply a creative cross-processing technique to your images.

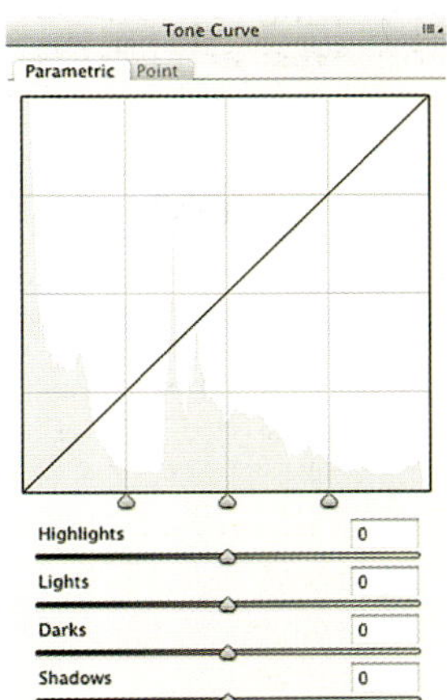

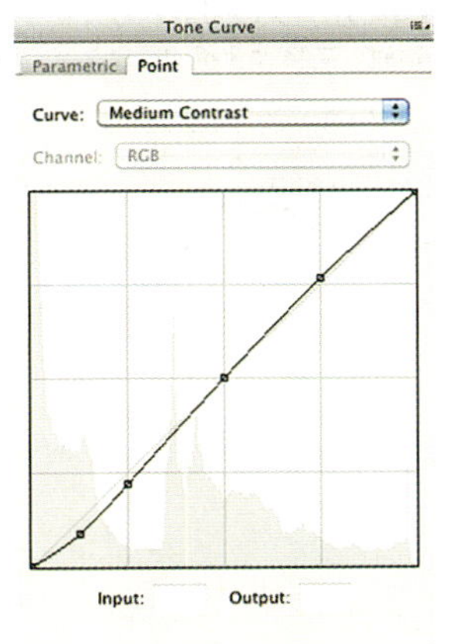

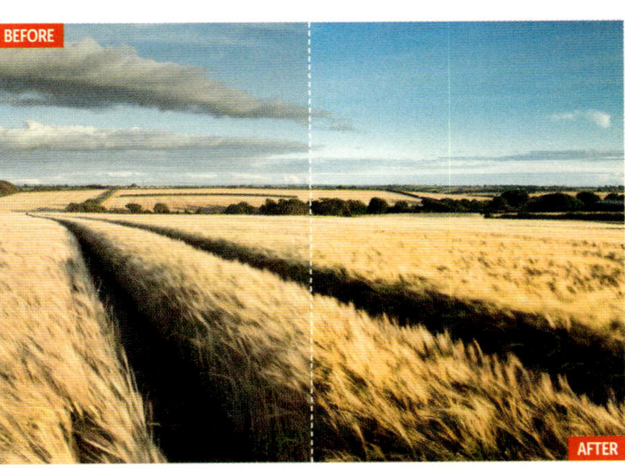

Fixing fringing

ACR makes fixing colour fringing incredibly easy: click on *Lens Corrections* then the *Manual* tab (CS5) and select *Defringe: All Edges* or the *Color* tab (CS6/CC). Here you can correct purple and green fringing independently. Zoom in to your image to at least *100%* to judge the results.

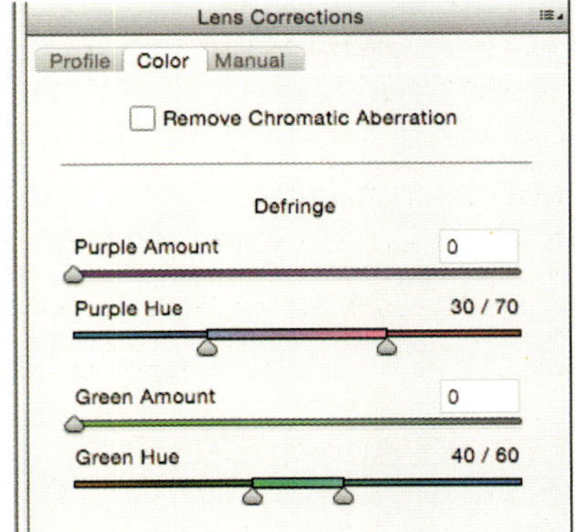

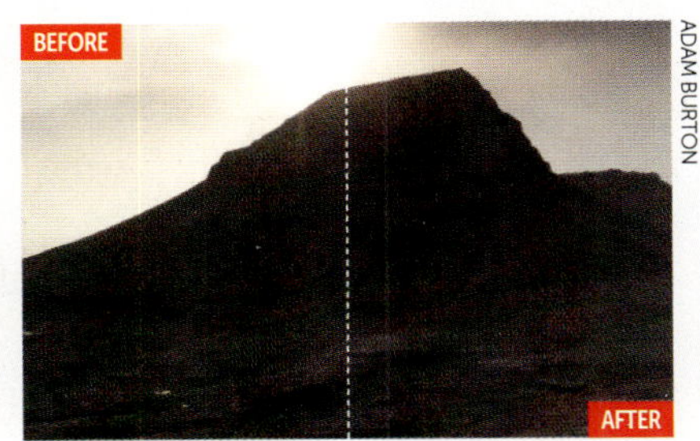

ADAM BURTON

Vignetting

Lens corrections: Often if you've used a wide-angle lens, your image may suffer from slight vignetting (darkening of the corners). To correct this, click on the *Lens Correction* tab and use the *Amount* slider under *Lens Vignetting* to lighten or darken the edges to reduce the amount of cropping you may need to do. The *Midpoint* slider is useful if your vignette encroaches beyond the corners.

Lens Vignetting
Amount 0
Midpoint

Artistic effect: Vignetting, when controlled, can be an artistic finishing touch. In this case, use *Post Crop Vignetting* under the *Effects* tab. Choose a *Style*: *Highlight Priority* to protect your highlights; *Color Priority* to preserve hues; *Paint Overlay* to blend the original colours with the vignette. You can then adjust the following settings: the *Amount* to lighten or darken the corners; *Midpoint* to affect the spread of the vignette; *Roundness* to decide its shape; *Feather* to adjust the softness; and *Highlights* to control contrast.

Post Crop Vignetting
Style: Highlight Priority
Amount 0
Midpoint
Roundness
Feather
Highlights

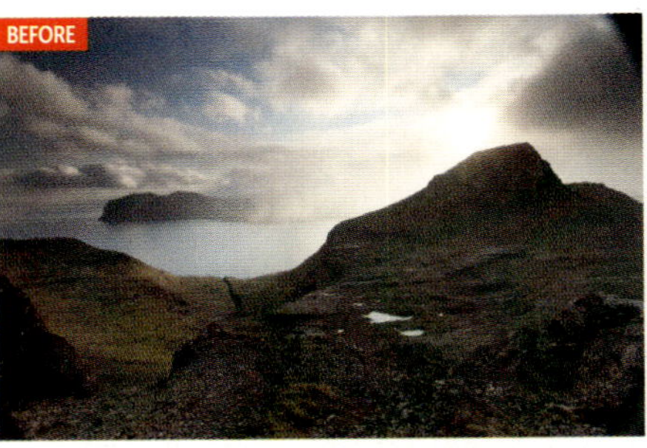

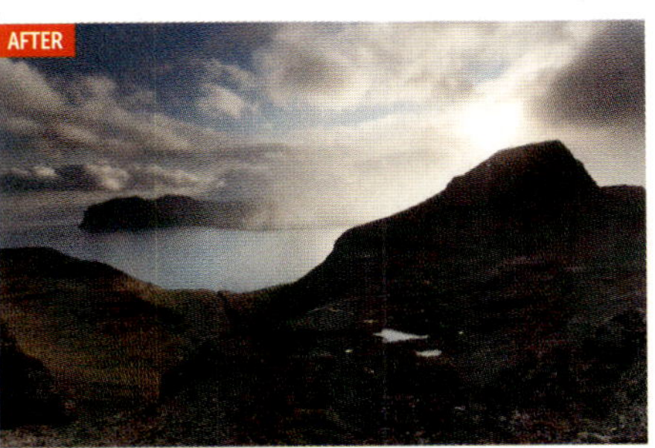

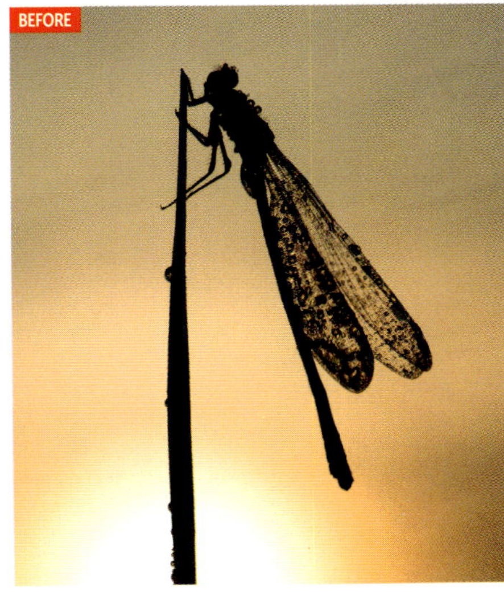

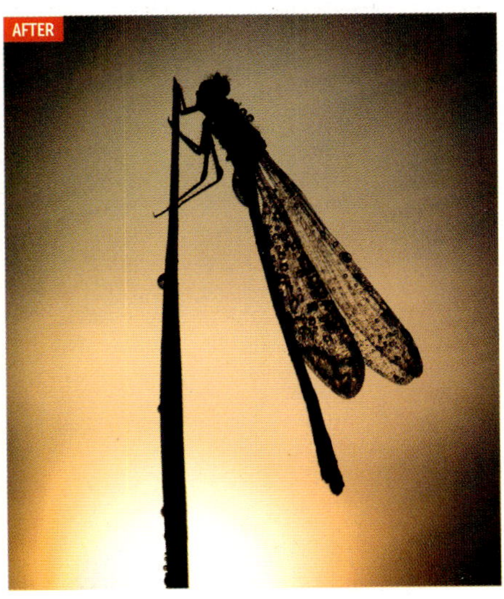

How to manage colour with Camera Calibration

Perfect Photoshop's colour rendering and take control of your Raw editing process with a more efficient workflow

IT'S ONE AREA Of Adobe Camera Raw that often gets ignored, but it holds a few tricks and treats you might be interested to know about – especially if you like your in-camera presets or your shadows often have a colour cast. The eighth tab along the editing suite in ACR, Camera Calibration, offers a few practical and creative profiles for adjusting and improving the colour rendering of your pictures. Each profile is calibrated to get the best from your camera or to correct its unwanted colour behaviour, so it can be a really useful tool if you know how to use it. Your default profile is Adobe Camera Standard, which is excellent and very rarely – if ever – will you need to change from it. But if you want to experiment with your colour rendering, this article should show you how. Plus, if you routinely apply the same settings and treatments to images in Adobe Camera Raw, you might be interested in the section on creating and applying Presets in order to save you valuable editing time.

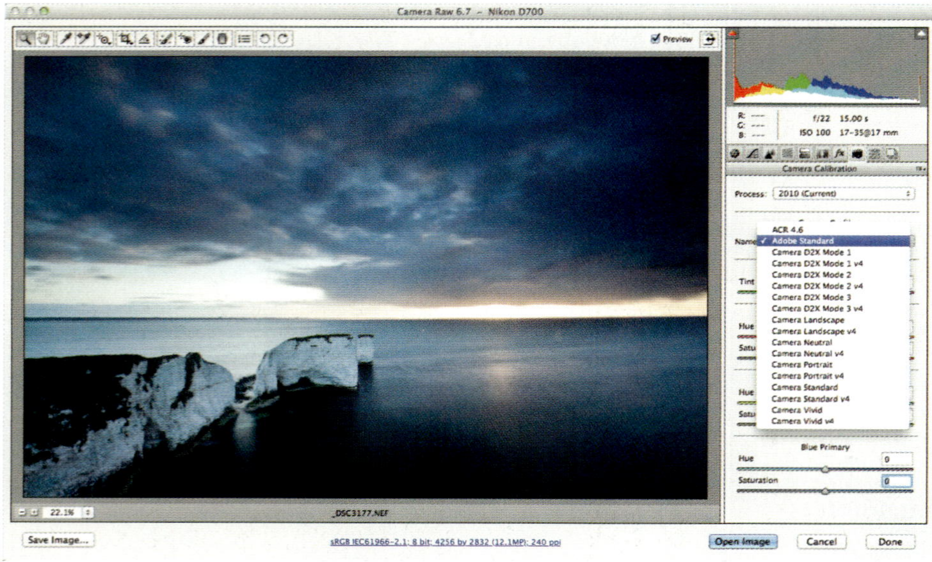

Applying profiles

If you previously shot in JPEG and liked the look of some of your camera's built-in colour profiles, you may be missing them now you've converted to Raw processing. These profiles (otherwise known as Picture Styles or Picture Controls on your camera) can be accessed via the Camera Profile section and affect your Raw file's saturation, colour and contrast to varying degrees. Depending on your camera, there may be many to choose from: some familiar, others not; some effective for making your images richer and colours punchier, while others simply ruin them. It can be fun to experiment with the different profiles and there's no harm in clicking on them because any adjustments made in ACR are nondestructive – but you'll probably find the best results come from your camera's more familiar Picture Styles.

For the example image opposite, shot on a Nikon D800, there are the following options: Landscape, Neutral, Portrait, Standard and Vivid, plus an alternate version for each. You could apply these settings in-camera if shooting in JPEG of course, but when shooting Raw, all colour, contrast and sharpening adjustments are discarded, requiring you to specify the look using the controls in ACR.

The beauty of being able to apply profiles after capture, rather than in-camera, is that you can use them as a base to be refined by other settings. It also means that you can process the same image multiple times to different effect. If you create a style you like, you can always save it as a Preset, to be applied to future images with a click of a button (see panel for details).

Saving a Preset

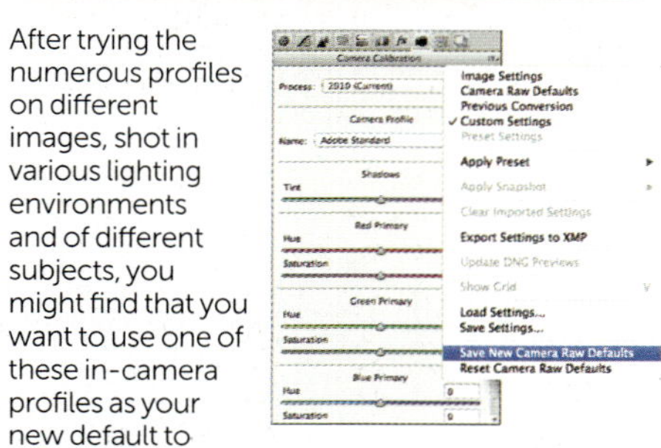

After trying the numerous profiles on different images, shot in various lighting environments and of different subjects, you might find that you want to use one of these in-camera profiles as your new default to apply to all images imported into ACR. If that's the case, select that profile from the *Camera Profile* drop-down menu in ACR and then click on the drop-down menu in the top right of the *Camera Calibration* panel. Scroll down and click on *Save New Camera Raw Preset*.

Saving a Preset

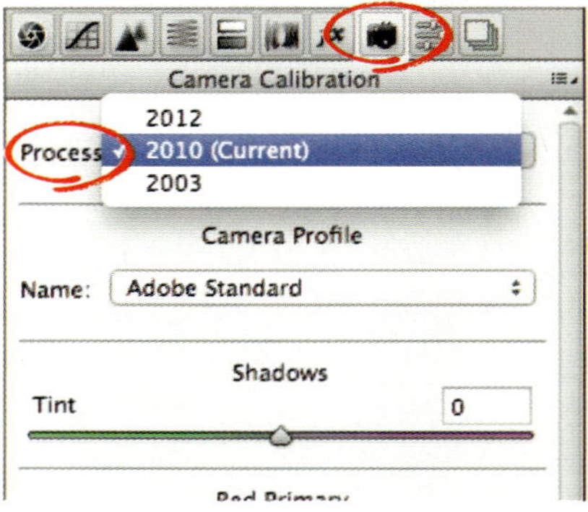

PROCESS These profiles are compatible with older versions of Adobe Camera Raw. Choose a different ACR profile if you want new images to maintain a consistent look to match with older photos.

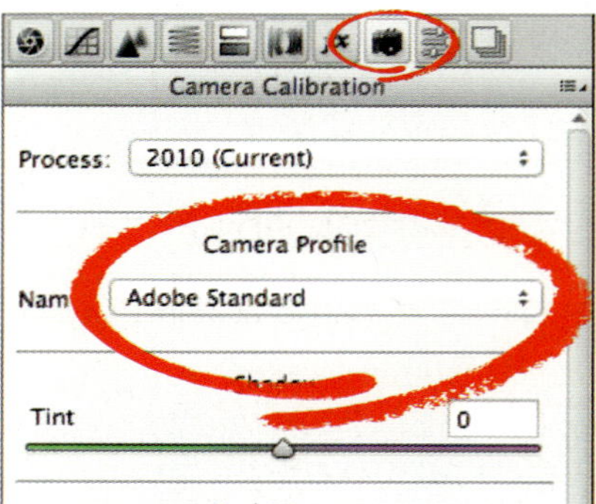

CAMERA PROFILE Sets the profile you want to use for your image.

ADOBE STANDARD This profile improves the colour rendering of your camera – especially warm tones such as reds, yellows and oranges. There's an Adobe Standard profile available for every camera.

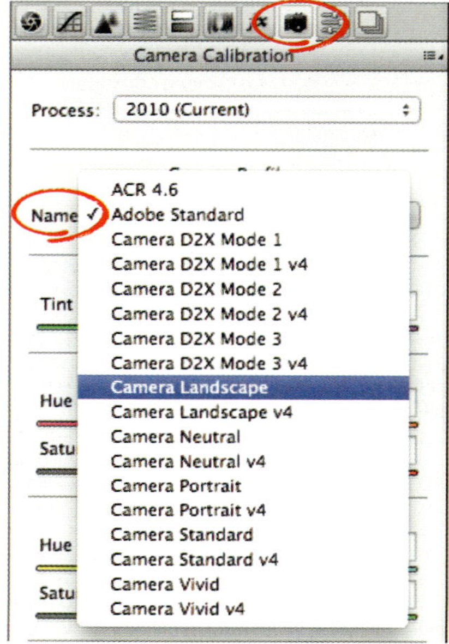

OTHER PROFILES These profiles attempt to match the camera manufacturer's in-camera Presets as closely as possible.

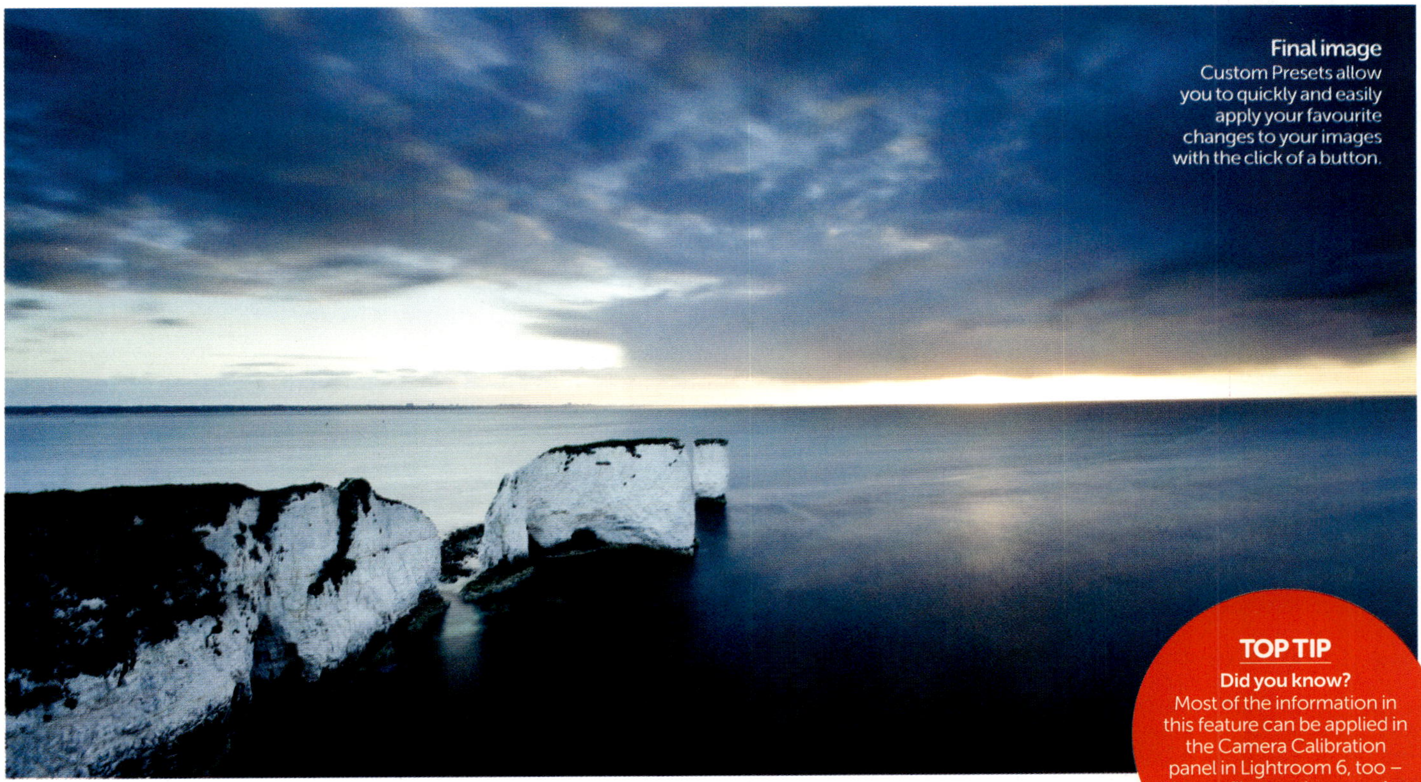

Final image
Custom Presets allow you to quickly and easily apply your favourite changes to your images with the click of a button.

TOP TIP
Did you know?
Most of the information in this feature can be applied in the Camera Calibration panel in Lightroom 6, too – the profiles are the same for both Adobe softwares

Adding and applying Presets

Whether you're creating a new colour style, calibration profile or want to be more efficient by saving your basic or creative editing process to apply to future images, the Presets panel in ACR is just what you need. Here's how to make the most of it...

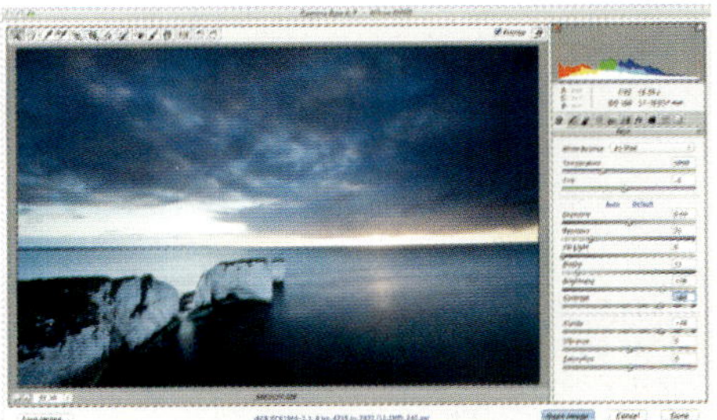

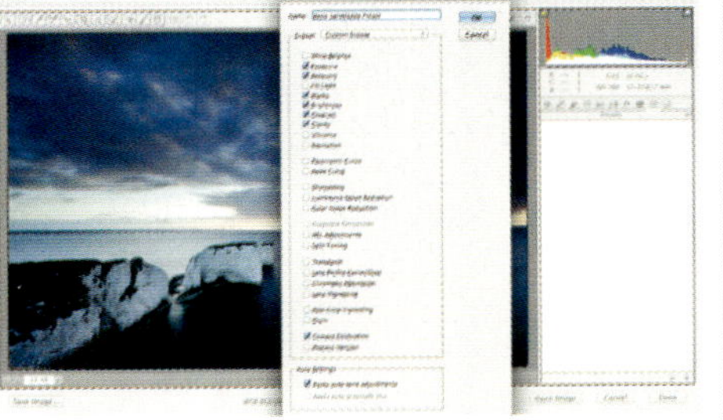

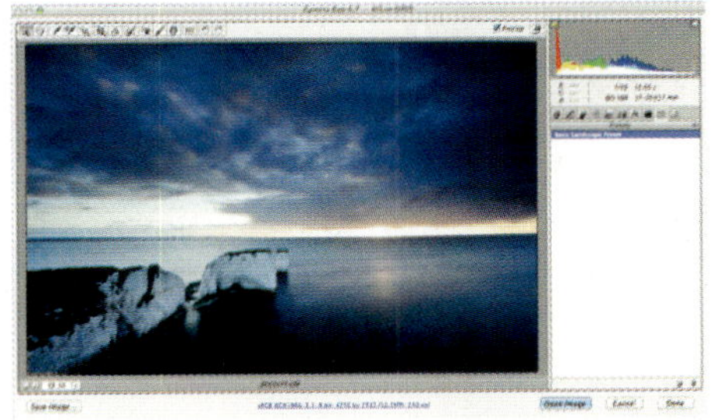

1 Make adjustments In your usual fashion, make all the adjustments that you want to apply to your future Raw files. It could be as basic as correcting exposure by a couple of stops, a combination of sharpening and improved clarity, a complete colour overhaul or a black & white conversion treatment – whatever you want.

2 Create the Preset Click on the *Preset* panel in ACR – this will be a blank panel until you add a preset. Down in the bottom right-hand corner of this panel is a *New Preset* icon, click on it to open the control panel. You can now select all the adjustments that you've just done and would like to save within this preset. Give it a name and click *OK*.

3 Apply the Preset You should now see that your new Preset is visible in the panel, ready to use. To check it works, open a new Raw file and then apply your Preset by clicking on it in the *Preset* panel. You can create as many Presets as you want and delete any Preset by clicking on the *trash can* icon in the bottom of the panel.

Fine-tune colour

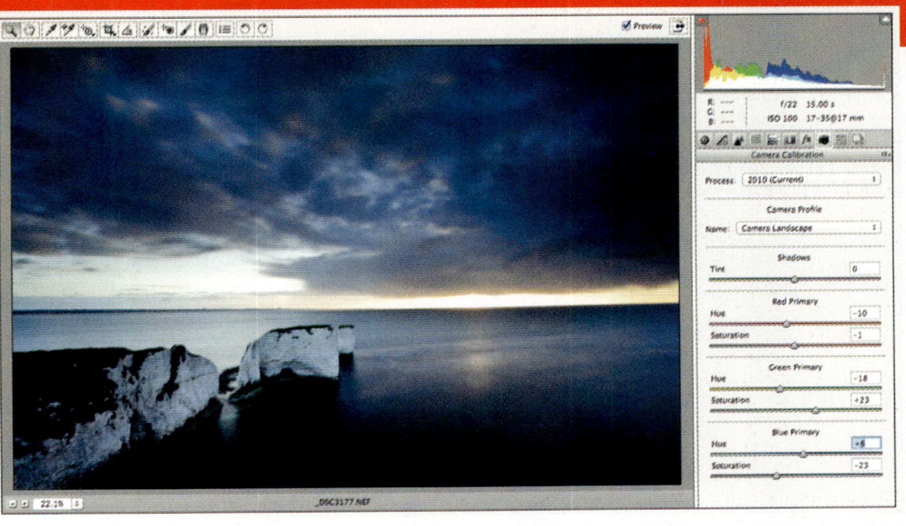

You can adjust how Photoshop interprets the colours captured by your camera by using the controls in the Camera Calibration panel and saving it as a Preset (see panel on opposite page). Some images from certain models of camera can have a slight magenta or green tint to the shadows, which can be corrected here using the *Shadows* slider to adjust the colour and make it more neutral.

Keep the *Camera Profile* set to *Adobe Standard* for the best colour rendering for your particular camera. If that doesn't do the trick, you'll need to refer to the *Red, Green* and *Blue Primary* sliders to change the hue and saturation of that individual channel. If your picture has a green cast, pull the *Hue* slider away from *Green* until the image looks neutral. Adjust the *Saturation* slider afterwards, too, if required. If the tint is consistent across your images, you can save these settings as a Preset so you can apply it to all subsequent Raw files, saving you valuable time in editing.

How to 'expose to the right'

Maximise the detail in your Raw data with this professional technique

IF YOU'RE NOT familiar with the term 'exposing to the right' (ETTR), despite sounding like something you could get arrested for doing, it is actually a Raw-only technique designed to help you maximise image quality. The principle is to push your image's exposure as far towards overexposure as possible, without clipping highlight areas. You do this by increasing the exposure length until the majority of pixels are grouped to the right of the histogram's mid-point – with the brightest pixels nuzzled to the far right. While ETTR images look awful initially – too bright and lacking in contrast, and require more time, thought and effort to process – the final result is an image boasting more tonal information and smoother tonal transitions.

Most digital sensors have a usable dynamic range of around six stops and can – at the very least – capture a 12-bit image, capable of recording 4,096 tonal levels. The more tonal levels available, the smoother the transition between the tones in an image will be. However, these tonal levels are not spread evenly throughout the brightness range of the sensor. So, while you might assume that each stop in the six-stop range is capable of recording an equal number of tones, in fact, each stop records half the light of the previous one. Half of the tonal levels are devoted to the brightest stop (2,048), half of the remainder (1,024 levels) are devoted to the next stop, and so on. As a result, the last and darkest of the six stops boasts just 64 levels. Therefore, if you do not utilise the right of the histogram you are wasting a large percentage of the data your camera is capable of recording.

Underexposed images contain less detail and data than a 'correctly' exposed image, and while you can attempt to lighten them during processing, the tonal transitions will not be as smooth and the risk of posterisation (abrupt changes in tone and shading) is greatly enhanced. In contrast, if you intentionally do the opposite – exposing to the right so that more data is recorded in the sensor's brighter stops – you will capture far more tonal information and image quality will be maximised. This is easy to illustrate by taking two images: one shot at a 'correct' exposure and the other exposed to the right (see below). The difference in file size can be several MB as the ETTR image has more data recorded. Even though many sensors are now 14-bit, giving photographers more tonal levels to play with, the principle is exactly the same – the sensor's brightest stop contains the most quality.

To get the most out of an ETTR file, a good processing technique is essential, but it's not difficult. You just need to adjust the Raw file's Exposure, Brightness and Contrast until the image represents the original scene. Another benefit of ETTR is less noise. Noise is most obvious in shadow areas – by biasing exposure towards the highlights, it is kept to a minimum.

So, while it remains important not to actually overexpose images to the degree where the highlights are blown, the benefits of exposing to the right are impossible to refute for Raw shooters. Here's a quick guide how to do it...

Secrets unlocked

☑ HIGHLIGHT WARNING To help ensure you don't actually clip the highlights when practising exposing to the right, switch on your camera's highlights warning. This is designed to warn you if any pixels are overexposed. Affected areas will flash. If this happens, adjust exposure accordingly by selecting a faster shutter speed, then reshoot so that no clipping occurs.

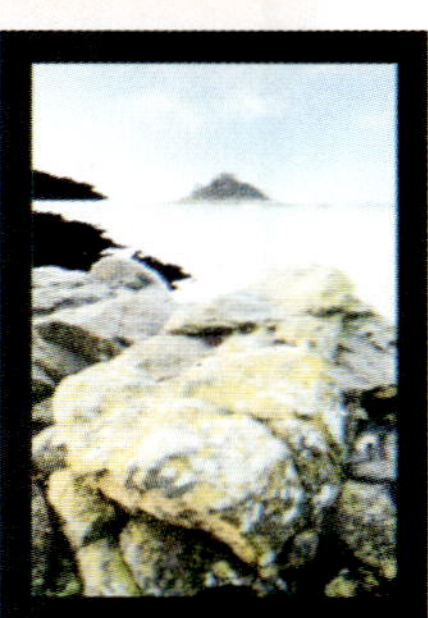

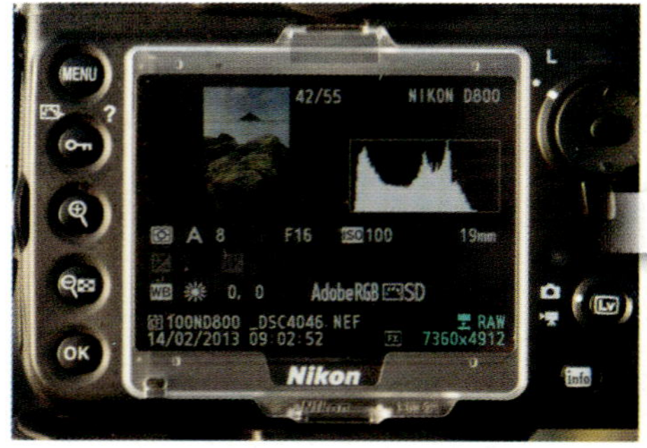

☑ 'CORRECTLY' EXPOSED This image and its histogram look fine: taken in aperture-priority, the camera has achieved a technically 'correct' exposure. However, the gap to the right of the graph indicates that the brightest stop of the sensor isn't being fully utilised, meaning valuable data is being wasted. The original Raw file is 43MB in size.

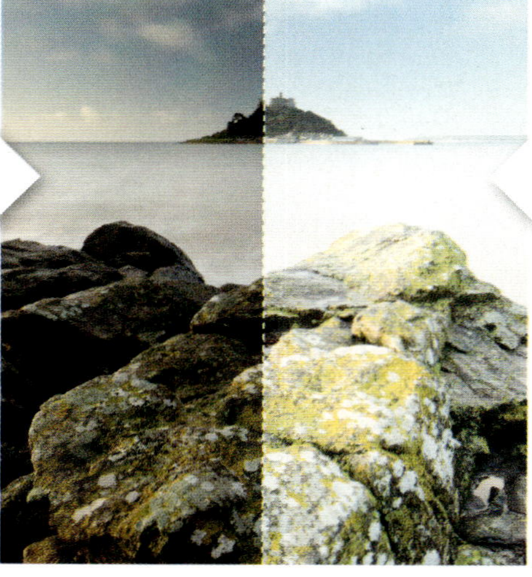

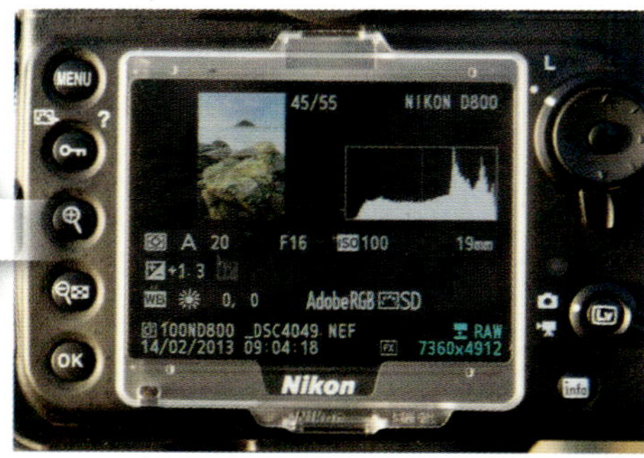

☑ OVEREXPOSED Exposed-to-the-right images might look too bright and washed out, but valuable data has been recorded, maximising image quality. In this case, the ETTR image is 43.3MB in size – more than 0.3MB larger than the 'correctly' exposed image. The extra data helps to prevent posterisation and noise is also kept to a minimum.

1 Achieve the result In order to push the exposure to the right to capture more tonal levels, you need to apply in-camera positive exposure compensation. How much depends on the scene and its level of contrast, so review the histogram. Start by applying 1/3-stop increments until the pixels reach the right-hand edge of the histogram. In this instance, we applied +1.3EV to achieve this.

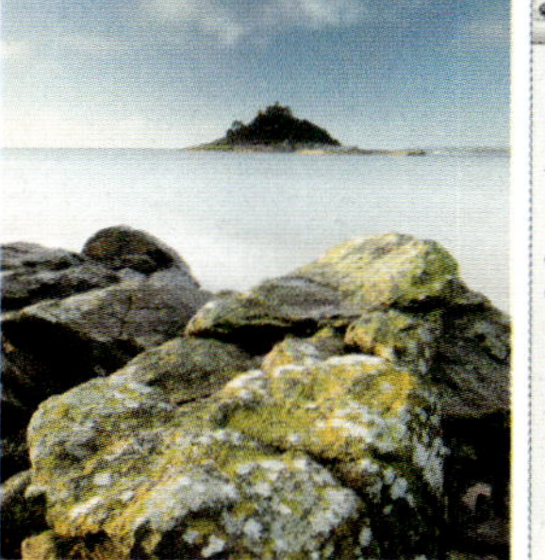

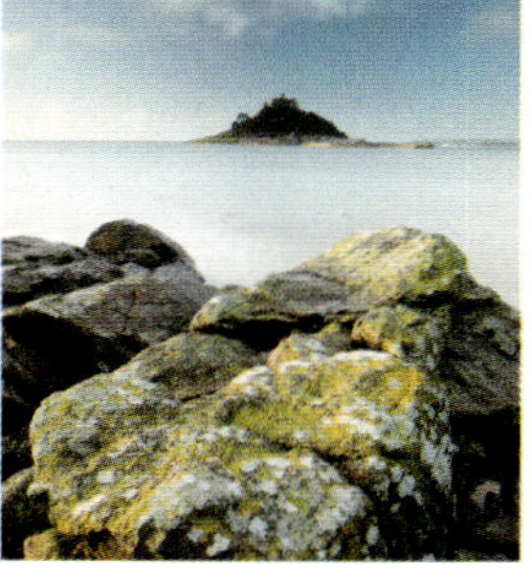

2 Recover detail Every ETTR image needs some processing. In ACR, use the *Exposure* slider under *Basic* or *Tone Curve* to ensure the tones in the image are spread evenly across the range of the histogram. Doing this should help restore the image's natural contrast. You may also find you need to use the *Blacks* and the *Recovery* (or *Highlights* slider, depending on your ACR version) to retrieve detail.

3 Boost the colour ETTR images rarely need many further adjustments. However, a small degree of *Vibrance* and tweak to the *Contrast* slider might help give your final result a little more punch. Although ETTR files do require the photographer to spend more time working on a computer, the high image quality of the final result makes it an essential and worthwhile technique.

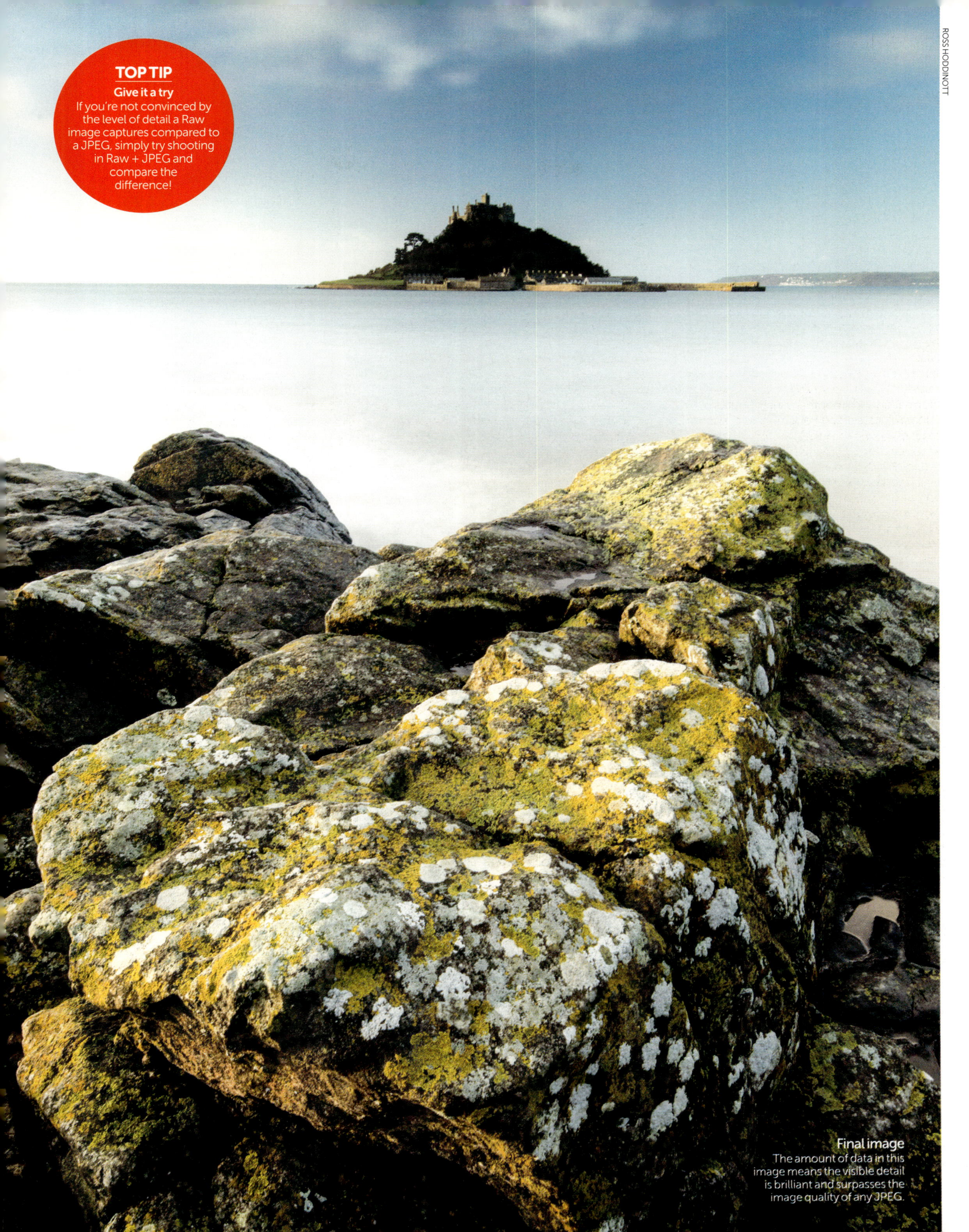

Final image
The amount of data in this image means the visible detail is brilliant and surpasses the image quality of any JPEG.

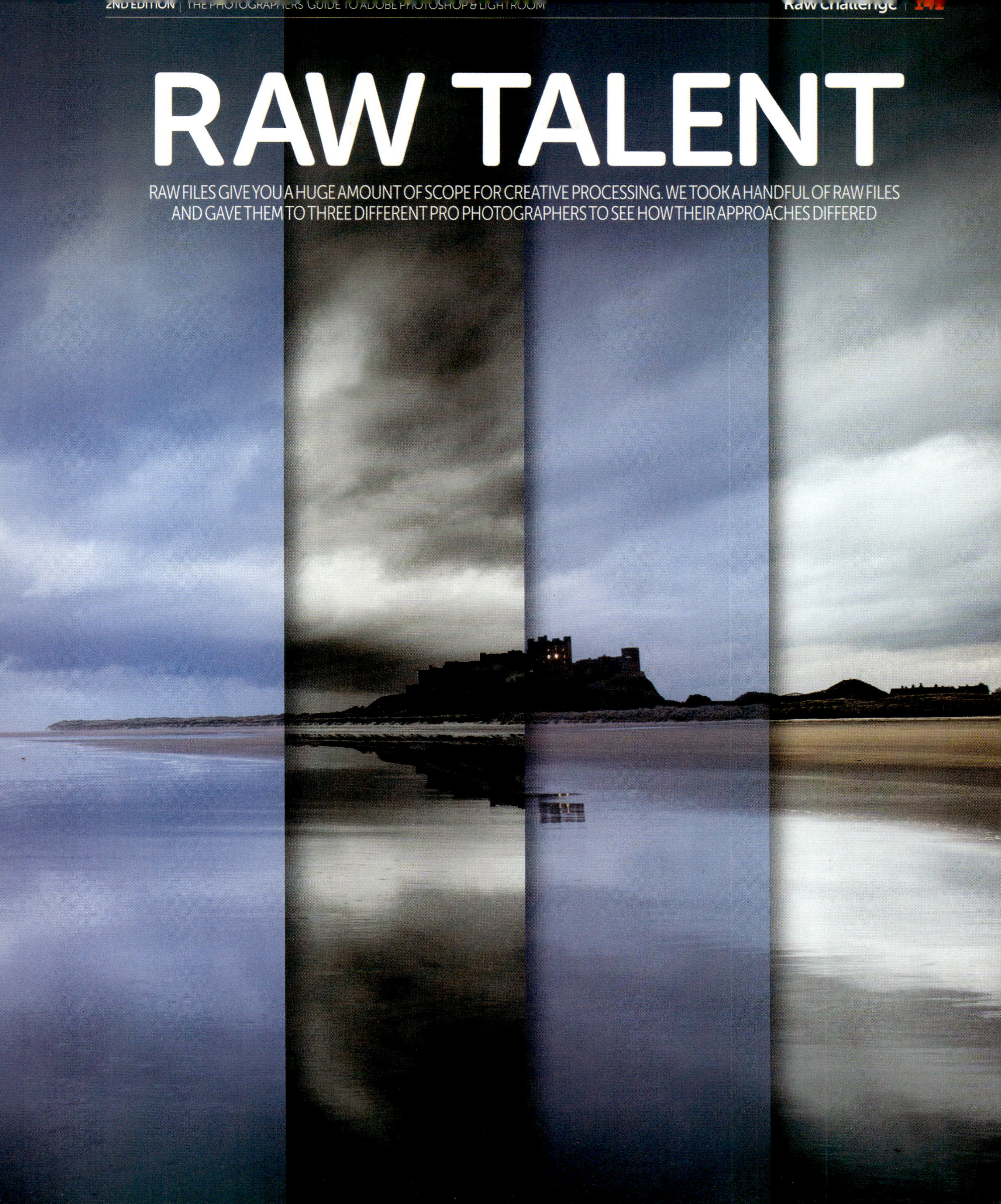

RAW TALENT

RAW FILES GIVE YOU A HUGE AMOUNT OF SCOPE FOR CREATIVE PROCESSING. WE TOOK A HANDFUL OF RAW FILES AND GAVE THEM TO THREE DIFFERENT PRO PHOTOGRAPHERS TO SEE HOW THEIR APPROACHES DIFFERED

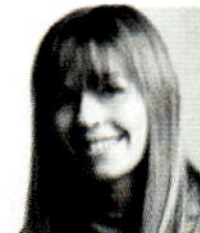

Raw challenge 1: Caroline Schmidt

Strong colourful clothes can often distract from a subject's face but a black & white conversion can easily avoid this

SUCH A VIBRANT portrait might call for some colour treatment, but strip the colour away and there is also a wide tonal range with strong separation between the subject and background. It's a good candidate for a black & white conversion. You might think me crazy to strip such as strong image of its rainbow colour, but sometimes a busy, graphic image can look better black & white.

When importing images into Lightroom for shortlisting, I'll often use its B&W Presets to preview what an image might look like converted to monochrome at varying contrast levels – it gives a good indication of what I can do to them in Photoshop.

While you can just as easily use Lightroom to develop your black & whites, I prefer Photoshop ACR when I know I may need to do more detailed work on the image later on. There are a thousand and one ways to convert an image using Adobe software, and you can do all your Raw editing in Lightroom – especially if you've presets and actions to make workflow faster – but this is my preferred method.

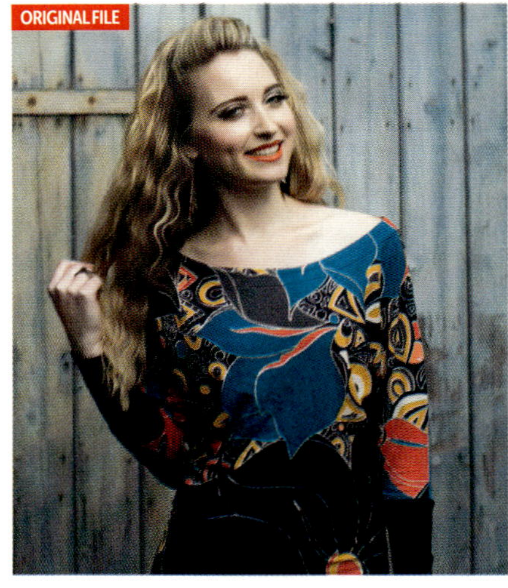

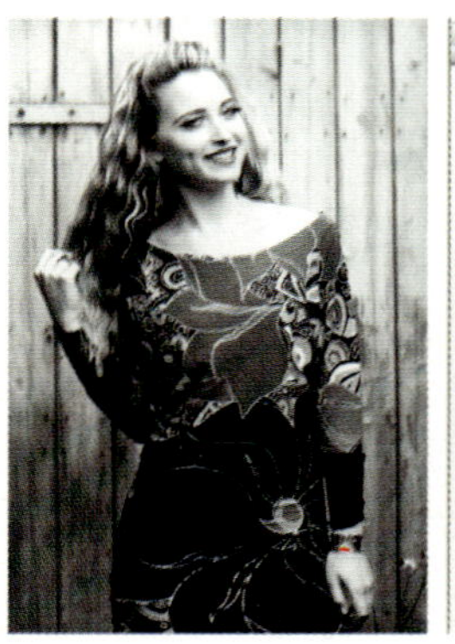

1 CREATE A BASE EXPOSURE Opening the portrait in ACR, my first stop is to click *Auto* under the *Basic* tab to see how it compares to the original exposure. The in-camera exposure is quite atmospheric, so a blanket automatic adjustment brightens the mid-tones and evens out the histogram, but weakens the style of lighting used when the shot was taken. I increase the *Contrast* slider and then brighten the *Whites* and darken the shadows with the *Black* slider.

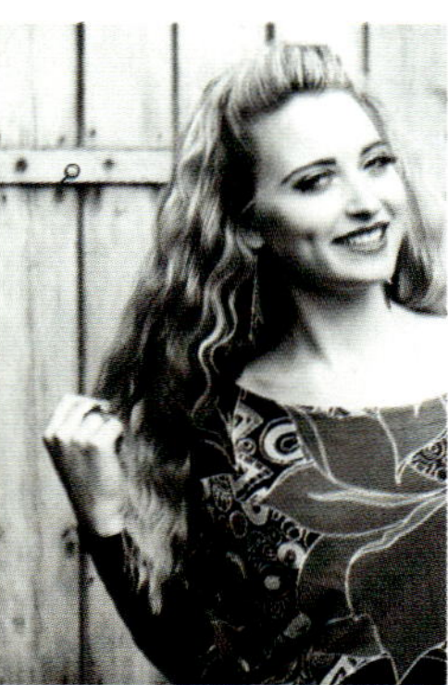

2 EDIT THE BACKGROUND One reason this image looked like a good candidate for black & white was the texture of the wood. Editing the contrast to brighten or darken mid-tones is best done in Raw as it's nondestructive and less fiddly than using layer masks in Photoshop. I click on the *HSL/ Grayscale* tab and *Convert to Grayscale* to preview the image in black & white. I then use the *Adjustment Brush*, adjusting the brush size and settings to reveal detail in the wood.

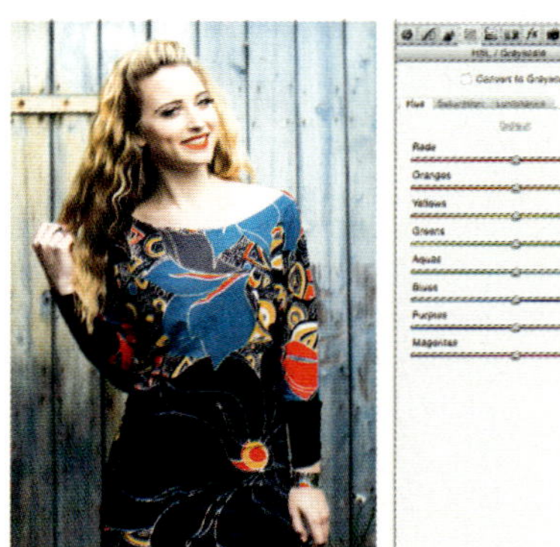

3 SHARPEN AND OPEN Before opening in Photoshop, I click the *Sharpen* tab and zoom into the model's eye at 100%. It's slightly soft, so I increase the *Radius* to *1.4* and the *Amount* to *66*, looking for symptoms of oversharpening. I untick *Convert to Grayscale* before I click *Open* to make further edits in Photoshop. If I convert in ACR, I'll export in Gray Gamma, not Adobe RGB, which contains the colour information I need for the best conversion.

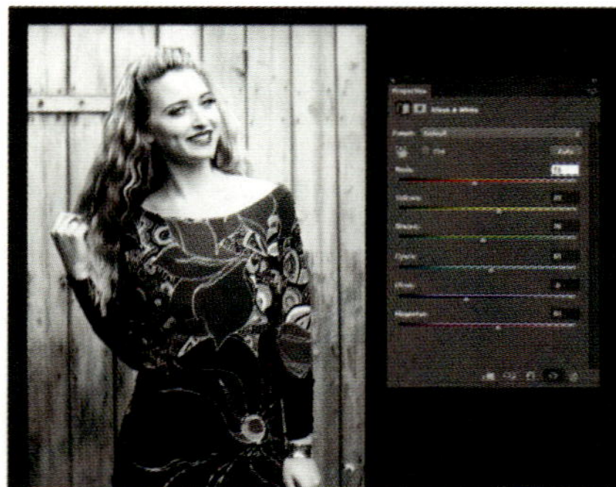

4 TURN BLACK & WHITE One of the best ways to convert to monochrome and to manipulate colours is using a Black & White adjustment layer, which allows you to tweak the tone based on specific colour channels. I quite like the look of the image as a black & white, so I only make a few tweaks to reduce the *Red* channel to dim her red lips and dress, increase *Yellow* to brighten her blonde hair and skin and decrease *Blue* to darken the blue paint on the wooden door.

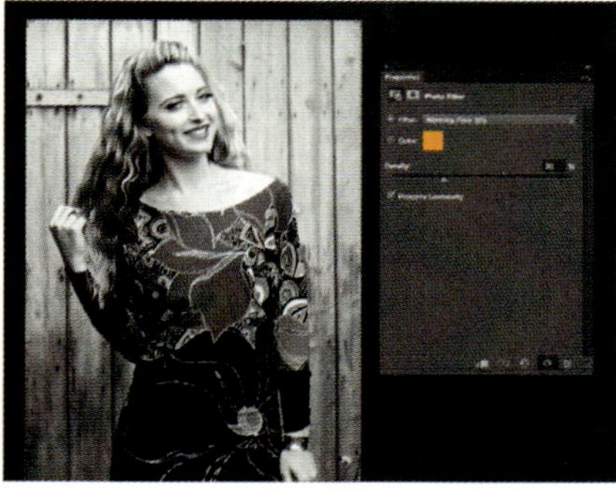

5 ADD WARMTH A high-contrast black & white can look stark, which suits certain subjects, but for portraits I prefer a warmer tone. While you can duo or monotone an image, subtle effects tend to look more natural. For this image, I apply a *Photo Filter* adjustment layer (*Layer>New Adjustment layer*) and select *Warming Filter* from the drop-down menu. I leave the *Density* at *30%* but control the effect by varying the layer's *Opacity*: 5-10% does the trick.

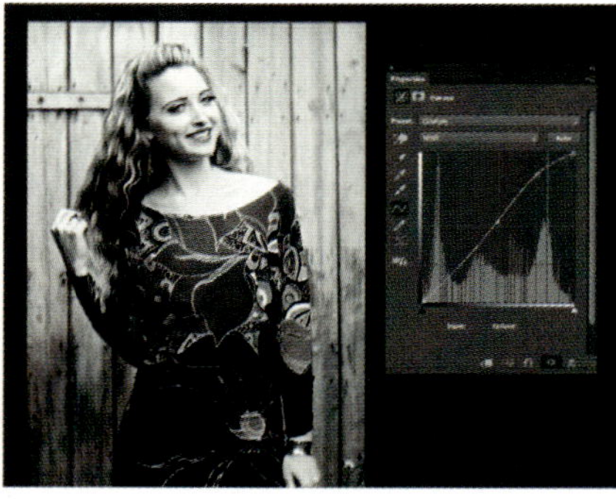

6 FINAL TOUCHES To add a subtle but bright haze to the top of the image, I add a *Gradient Fill* adjustment layer selecting *Foreground to Background* and *White* as the colour, tweaking the *Radius* for the best angle. I repeat using *Black* as the colour, angled at the bottom of the frame, for a vignette. I adjust both layers' *Opacity* to get the effect that looks best, and finish the shot off with a slight increase in highlights using a *Curves* adjustment layer.

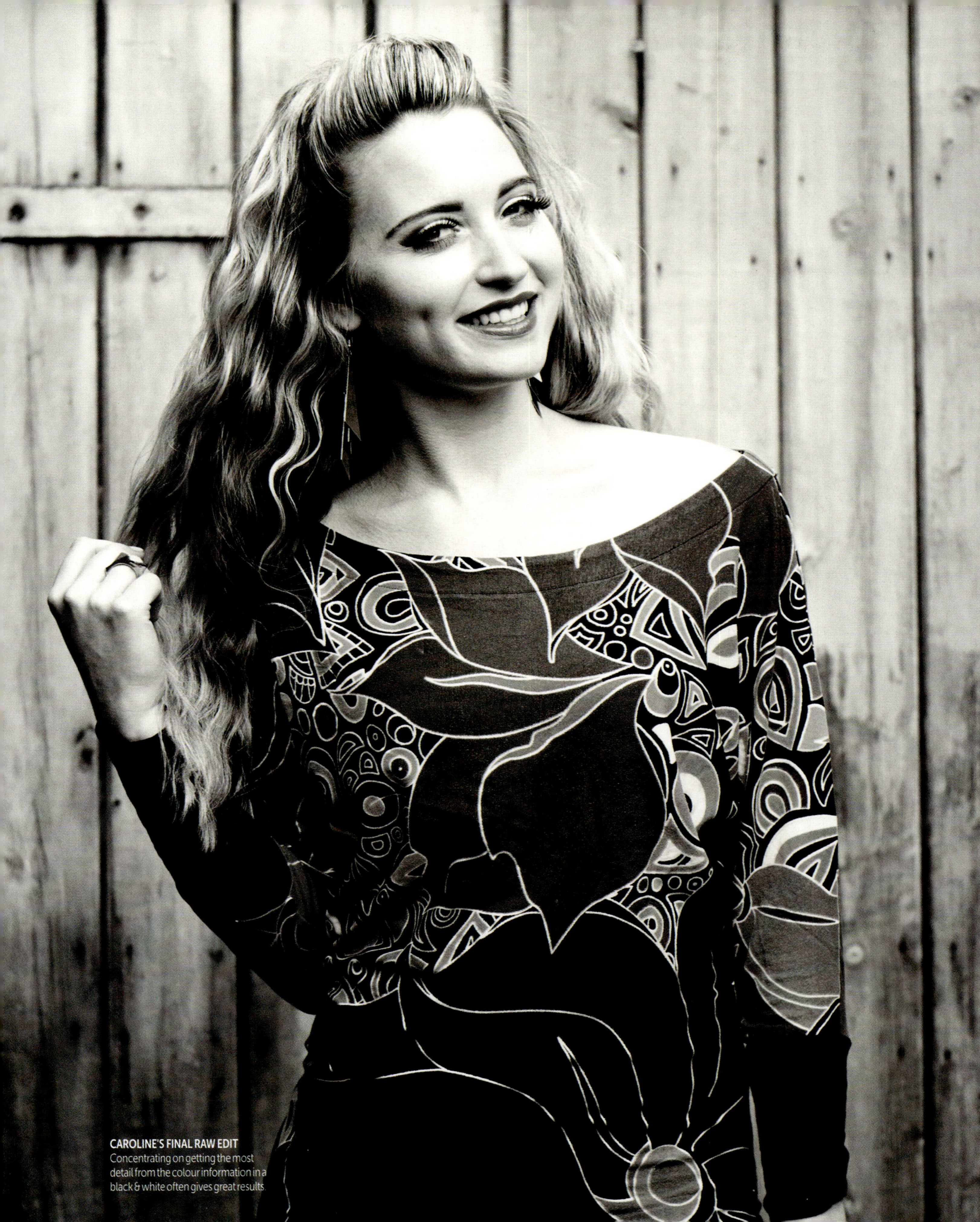

CAROLINE'S FINAL RAW EDIT
Concentrating on getting the most detail from the colour information in a black & white often gives great results.

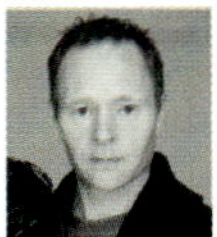

Raw challenge 2: Paul Ward

Professional commercial photographer Paul Ward talks you through his process for editing colourful portraits

EVEN THOUGH I always aim to capture a shot as close to perfect as I can in-camera, knowing that I can tweak the highlights or push up the shadows is a comforting fail-safe, especially when I'm shooting for clients, but the biggest benefit for me is the White Balance adjustment. White Balance is easy to misjudge in mixed lighting and shooting Raw means you can rely on the flexibility it offers when editing. It is possible to adjust the colours on a JPEG file but it doesn't look that accurate and can degrade the image slightly if used too heavily.

When I first opened this Raw file, I was instantly struck by how blue the tones were, and not surprising as it was shot at a White Balance of 4700K. Because of the model's blonde hair and the rustic looking door, I thought that it might look even better with a brighter and warmer finish. As it's outdoors I knew that my custom lens flares might work well too and add to the 'summery' effect. I always spend a fair amount of time covering blemishes, removing hairs and brightening skin, although this model's skin is beautifully even already.

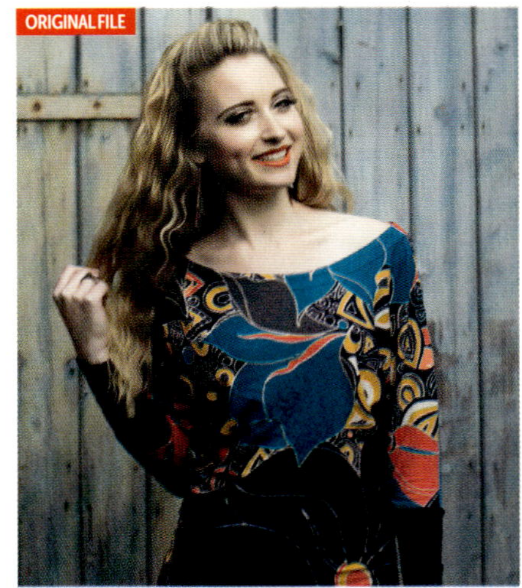

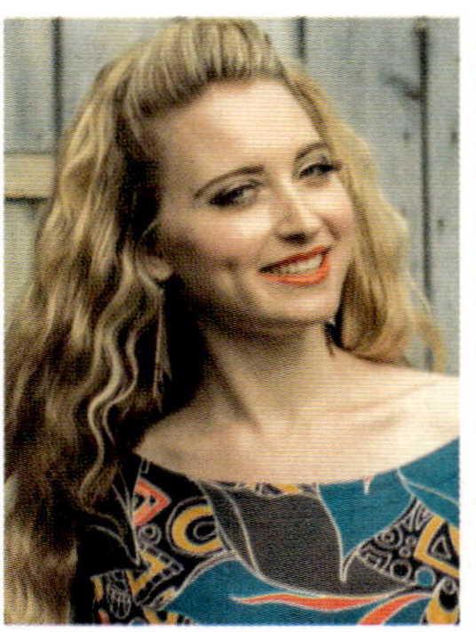

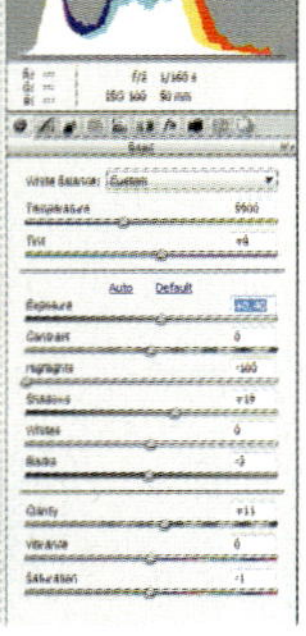

1 CHANGE THE WHITE BALANCE To add warmth to the image, I set a custom White Balance by moving the ***Temperature*** slider to a higher value, giving the image a golden look. I then drag the ***Highlights*** slider to ***-100*** to recover all overexposed areas in the image, and push ***Shadows*** and ***Clarity*** up slightly to boost the contrast and sharpness. Before opening the Raw file in Photoshop, I also adjust the noise reduction sliders to get rid of the little grain in the image.

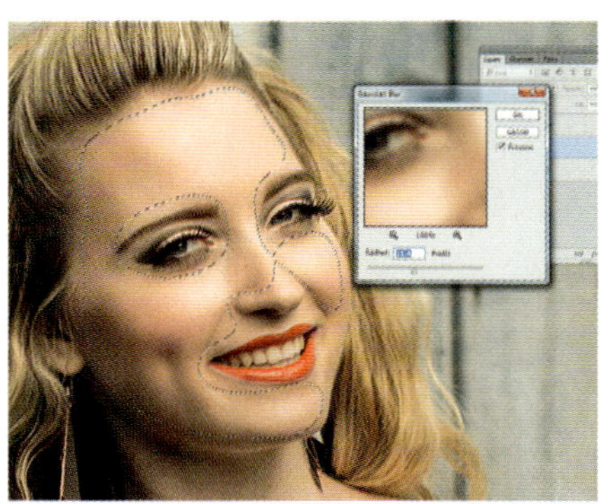

2 USE FREQUENCY SEPARATION In Photoshop, I start to work on retouching the skin using a technique that's called Frequency Separation. It's quite an advanced retouching process but highly effective. It uses multiple layers, blending modes and blurring/ sharpening techniques to smooth skin and remove blemishes, while retaining texture and detail. (Read issue 81, August 2013, of *Digital SLR Photography* to find out how to master this pro retouching technique.)

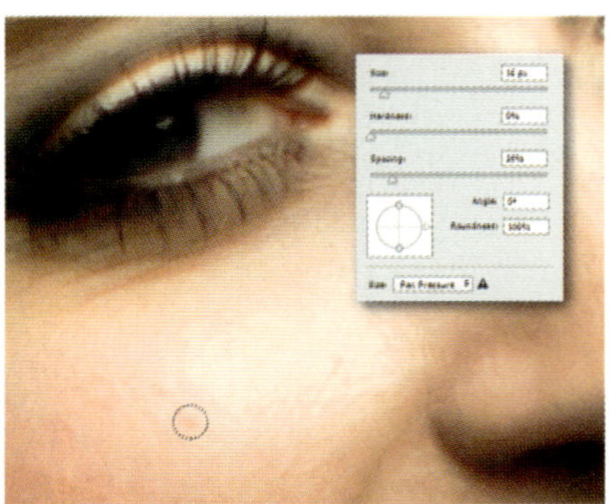

3 RETOUCH THE SKIN After the skin's been polished, I switch between using the ***Healing Brush Tool*** and the ***Clone Stamp Tool*** – using a fairly small, soft-edged brush for both – to tidy up the skin, to cover any blemishes and remove stray hairs. I tend to find zooming into areas of the skin as much as 300% makes it easier to refine the tiny details, like pores and to remove small hairs along the hairline, which on a wider view can create a cleaner finish.

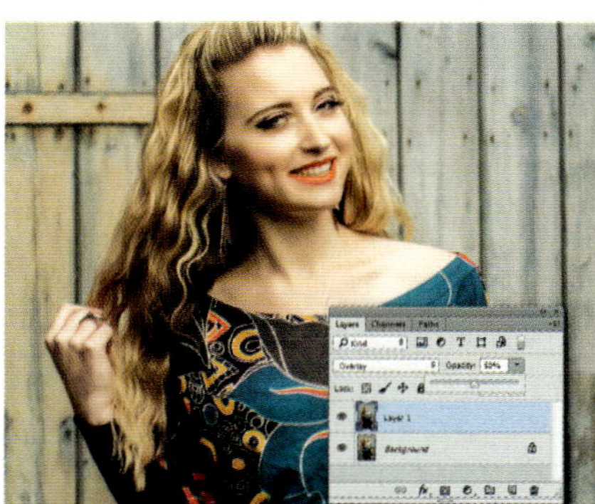

4 INCREASE SATURATION I duplicate the Background layer by dragging the layer down to the ***New Layer*** icon at the bottom of the Layers palette. At the top of the Layers palette, I change the new image layer's ***Blend Mode*** to ***Overlay*** using the drop-down menu to boost the contrast and increase the saturation. At 100% opacity the Overlay layer is overpowering, so I make the image slightly opaque by reducing the layer's ***Opacity*** slider to ***50%***.

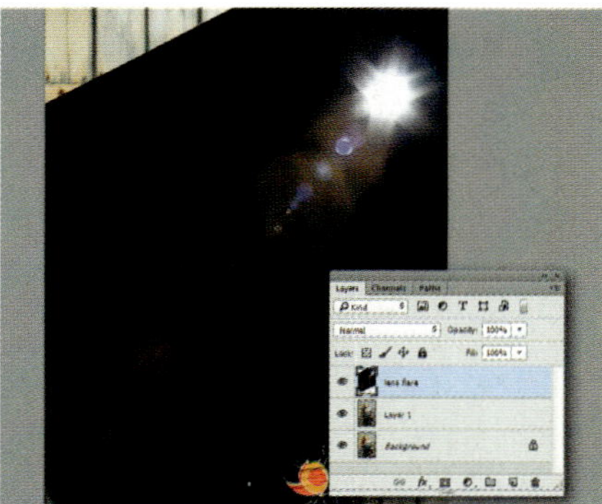

5 ADD LENS FLARE I shot lens flare using a large black piece of cardboard with a 1cm hole. I put a flash behind the hole and took shots of the card using an M42 fit lens. I added it to a black canvas in Photoshop so that I can have quick access to a wide range of lens flare styles. When I want to add lens flare to an image to enhance its 'summery' feel, I copy and paste the image on to a new layer and rotate it using the ***Transform*** functions to the desired angle.

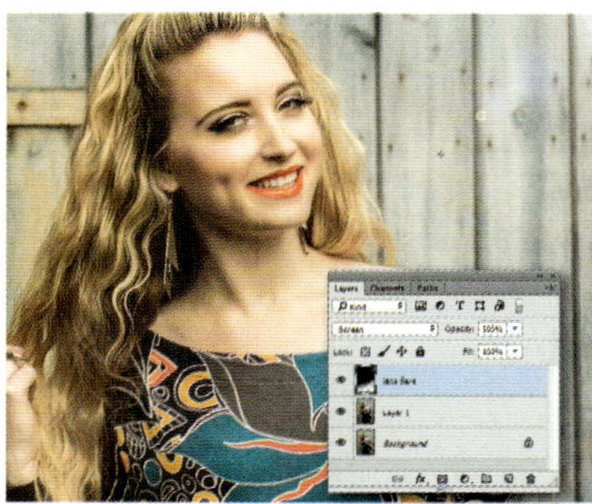

6 BLEND IN THE LENS FLARE With the lens flare layer in position, I change the layer's ***Blend Mode*** from ***Normal*** to ***Screen***, which removes the black leaving only the lens flare visible. I use the ***Eraser Tool*** with a large, soft brush to work over the image removing any hard edges that may still be visible where I've rotated the lens flare layer. Next, I flatten the layers (***Layers>Flatten Image***) and save the file as a TIFF (to retain the layers) and a JPEG. Hey presto!

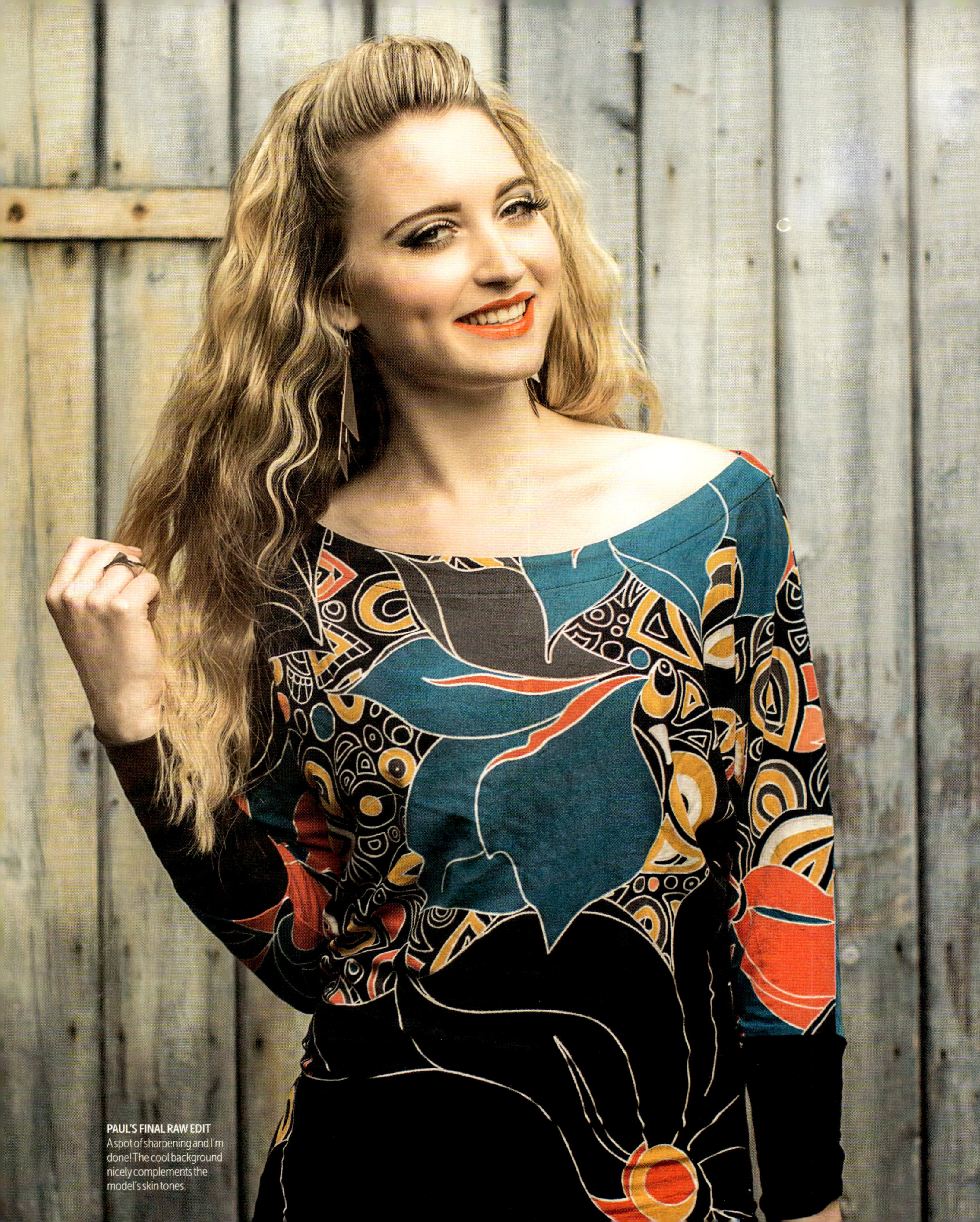

PAUL'S FINAL RAW EDIT
A spot of sharpening and I'm done! The cool background nicely complements the model's skin tones.

Raw challenge 3: Jordan Butters

For retouching portraits and working selectively, Jordan prefers the editing power of Photoshop CC

I'D CONSIDER PORTRAITS to be some of the trickiest types of photographs to retouch and edit. Why? I think it may be because we're so used to seeing people's faces in photographs that any instance in which someone's skin is a bit too smooth, or their eyes brightened just a smidgen too much, seems to stand out like a sore thumb. For this reason alone when retouching portraits, I'll often finish my edit before powering down the computer, but then revisit the picture the following day – a fresh set of eyes can often give you a new perspective on whether you've got it just right, or over-egged it.

This is a really nice portrait with great lighting, but there's a lot going on. The model's dress is quite busy and the background, although photogenic, is competing for attention. The model's skin looks quite good straight out of camera, so I'll most likely be focusing my time in Photoshop CC on making the colours in the image work well together, and adjusting exposure selectively to allow the model to really stand out against her surroundings.

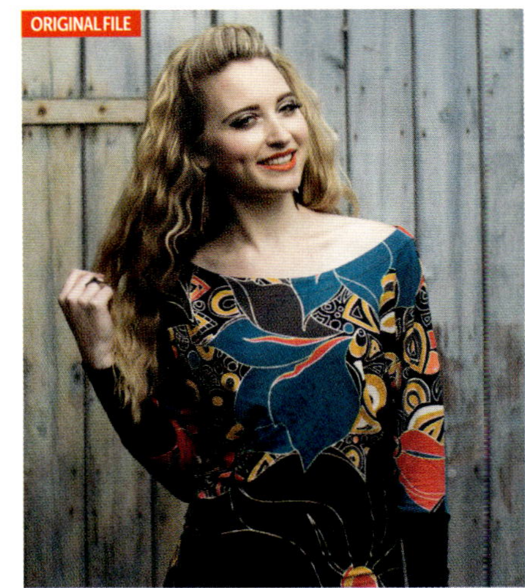

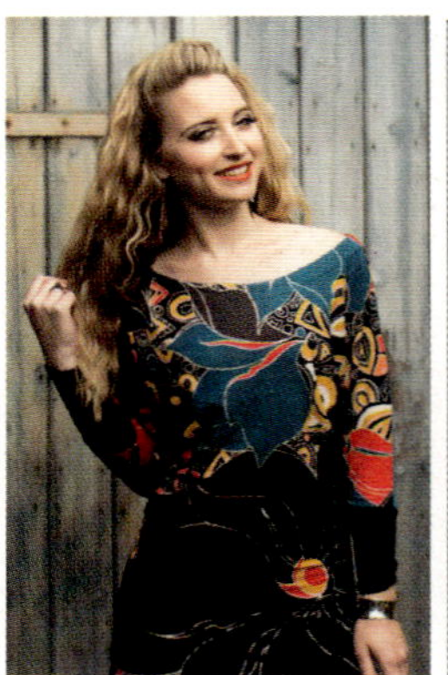

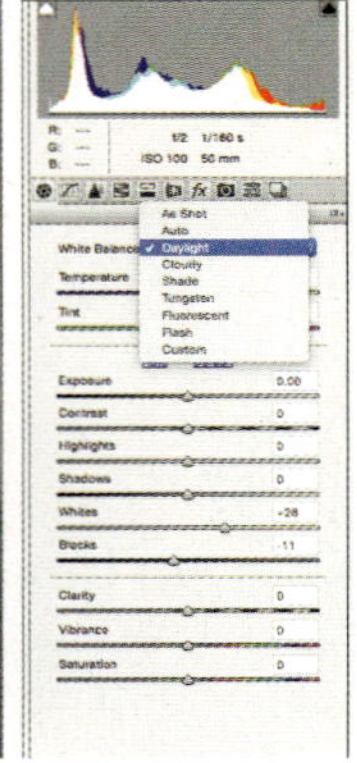

1 RAW ADJUSTMENTS I'll be doing most of my adjustments within Photoshop CC, but there are some that are best done in Adobe Camera Raw first. I'm guessing the image was shot using natural light or flash with a similar colour temperature. I set the *White Balance* to *Daylight* before applying profile *Lens Corrections*, which removes any vignette and distortion.

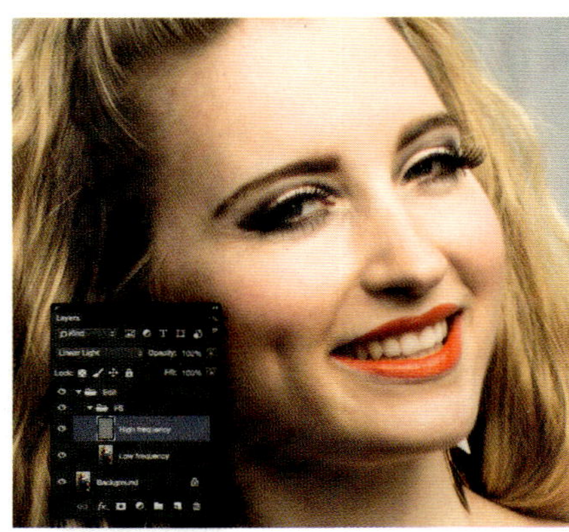

2 FREQUENCY SEPARATION The model here has good skin, but I always start portrait retouching with a spot of frequency separation. I have an action set up for this in Photoshop so it's a one-click step. I use the *Clone Stamp Tool* on the low frequency layer to smooth out the skin tones and then the *Patch Tool* on the high frequency layer to remove blemishes and lines.

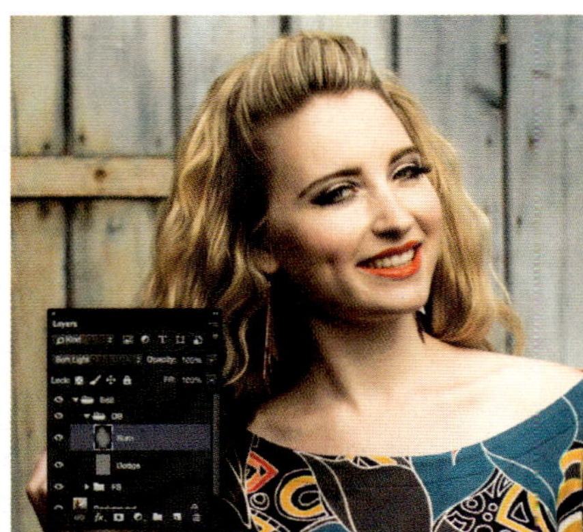

3 DODGE AND BURN Next, I add two new layers, both set to *Soft Light* and filled with *50% grey*. On one layer I use the *Dodge Tool* to brighten the eyes and remove some shadows. On the other layer I use the *Burn Tool* to add a vignette to the background Upon initial review I've overdone the dodging, but drawing down the *Opacity* on this layer easily solves this problem.

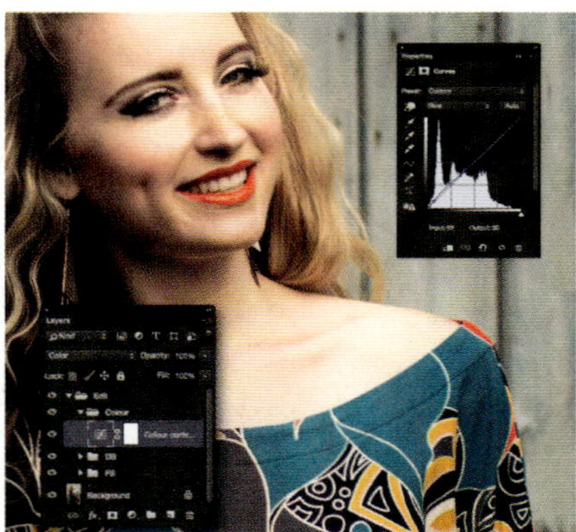

4 ADJUST COLOUR Next, I concentrate on colour. I create a new *Curves* adjustment layer and set its *Blend Mode* to *Color*. In the *Blue* channel I add blue to the shadows before adding an anchor point to the mid-tones to prevent the highlights from taking on a yellow tint. I switch to the *Red* channel, anchor the mid-tones again and remove red from the shadows, which adds a teal tint.

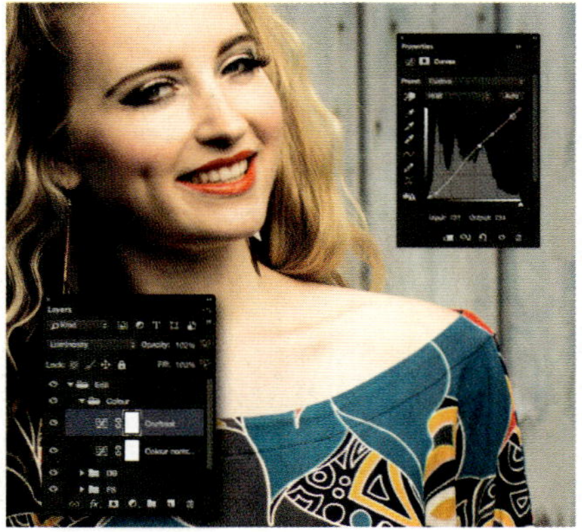

5 ADD CONTRAST Adding another *Curves* adjustment layer with the *Blend Mode* set to *Luminosity* allows me to adjust the contrast without affecting colour. I create an S-curve, adding contrast, however this makes the skin too bright. Using the *Targeted Adjustment Tool* I am able to concentrate on the skin tones and reduce the brightness, without sacrificing contrast.

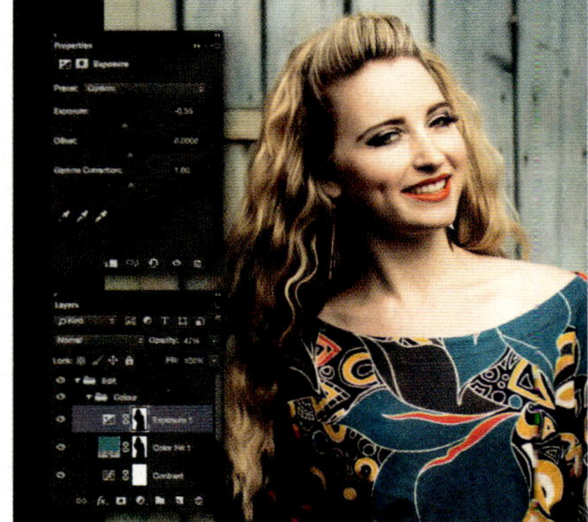

6 TWEAK BACKGROUND The background is distracting for me. I add a *Solid Color* adjustment layer, choosing a teal tone, before changing the *Blend Mode* to *Soft Light*. I then mask this effect, so that it only affects the background. The backdrop is slightly too bright however, so I add an *Exposure* adjustment layer and reduce the brightness using the same mask.

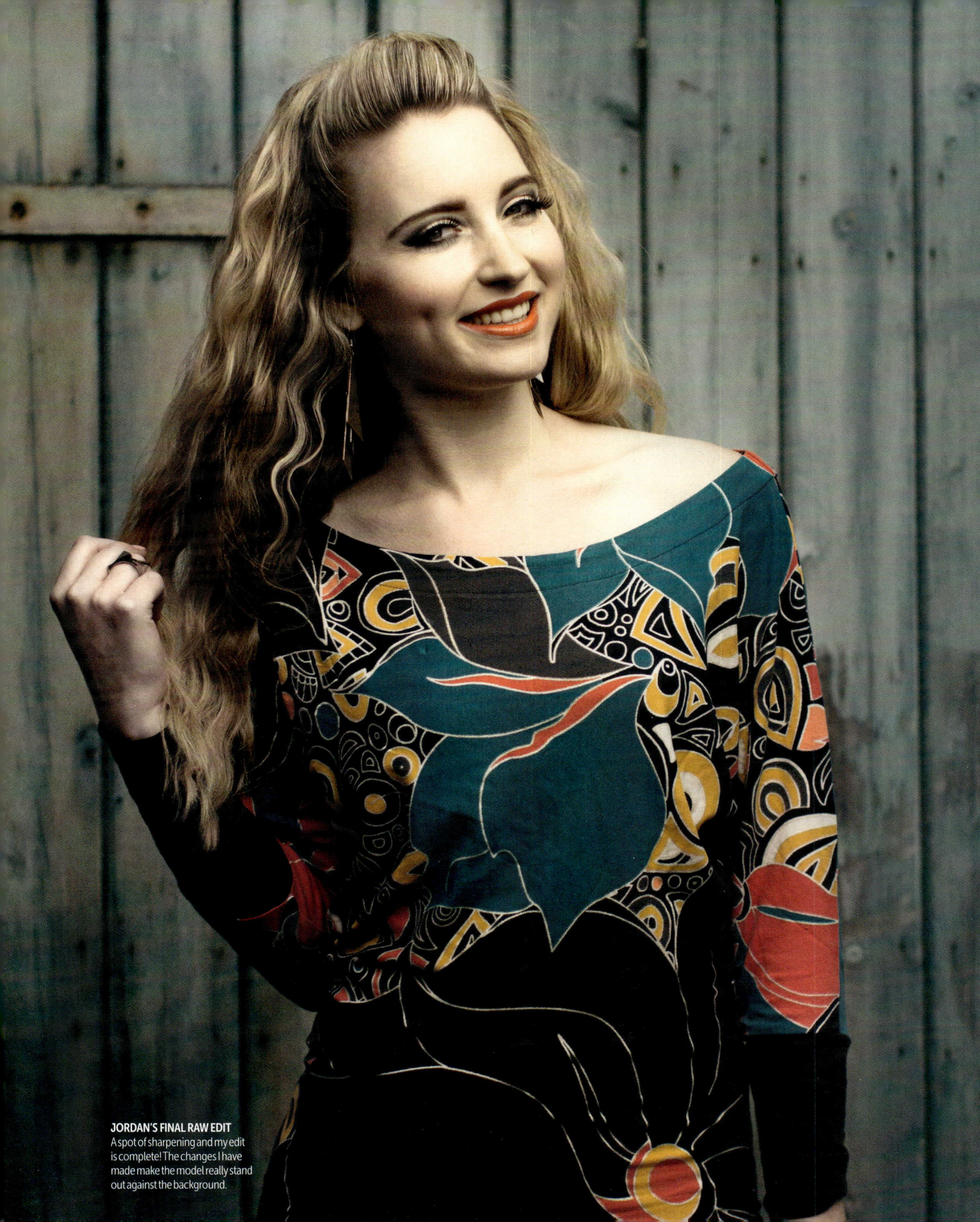

JORDAN'S FINAL RAW EDIT
A spot of sharpening and my edit is complete! The changes I have made make the model really stand out against the background.

ORIGINAL FILE

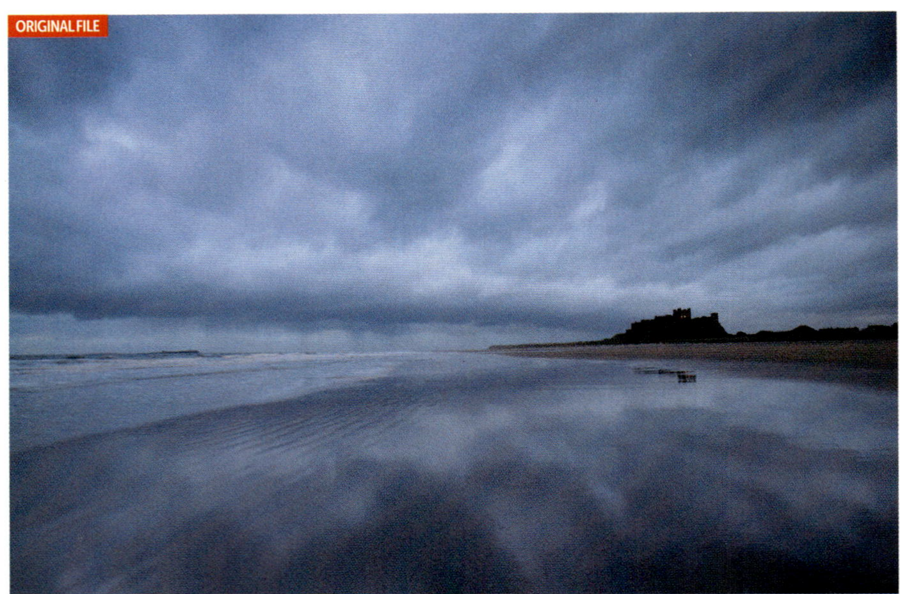

ADAM BURTON

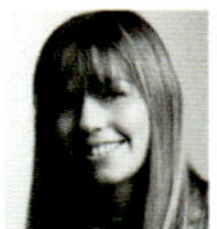

Raw challenge 1: Caroline Schmidt

Experimental editing usually results in discovering your emerging style and, for me, that's a flare for the dramatic

A BROODING LANDSCAPE with striking reflections and tonal detail is crying out for huge contrast adjustments. With a JPEG file, you have to be especially careful in how you go about edits so not to introduce quality-degrading noise and artefacts. This is why Raw is such a valuable file format: it provides much wider margins to expand exposure information. Thankfully Adam's exposure is spot-on, so I can concentrate on polishing the colour and contrast. Had the file been under or overexposed, I might not have been able to be so demanding on the data without a detriment to quality.

While Adobe Camera Raw (ACR) and Lightroom are fine places to make all Raw edits, I prefer to use ACR for base adjustments then continue to edit the Raw files in Photoshop to utilise the flexibility of Layers, Layer Masks and Blending Modes.

This challenge will be an interesting experiment in technique and vision. While Jordan and I have often worked on the same photo shoots, it's amazing how different our images can look – especially after we've finished editing the pictures – as our styles are polar. Adding Adam to the mix should yield interesting ideas and results.

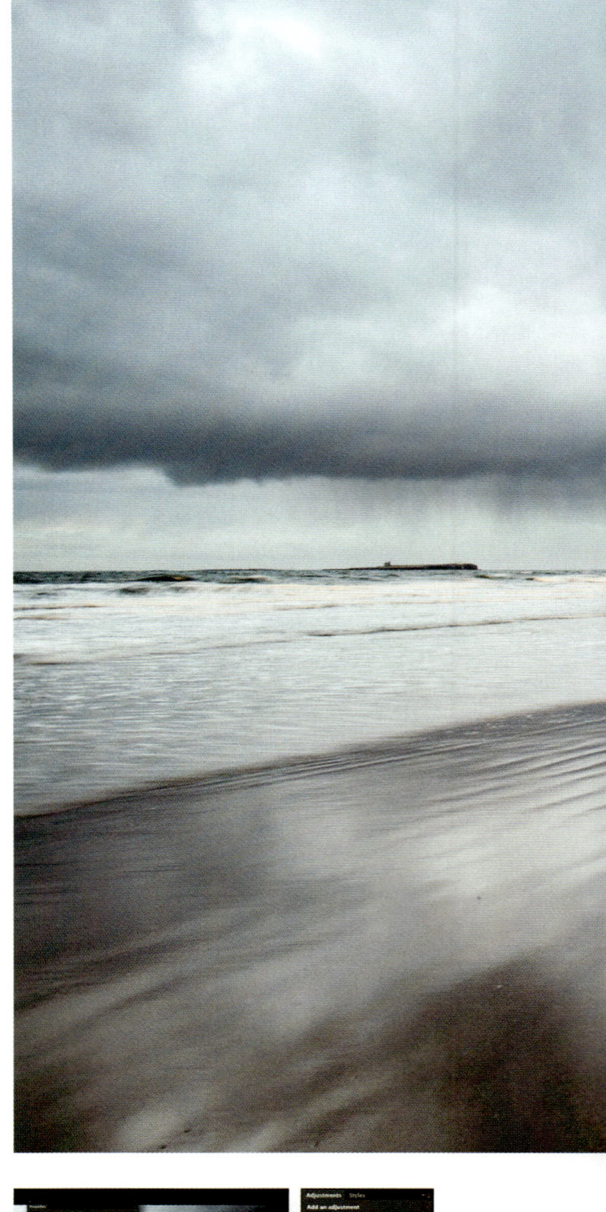

"RAW IS SUCH A VALUABLE FILE FORMAT AS IT PROVIDES MUCH WIDER MARGINS TO EXPAND EXPOSURE INFORMATION"

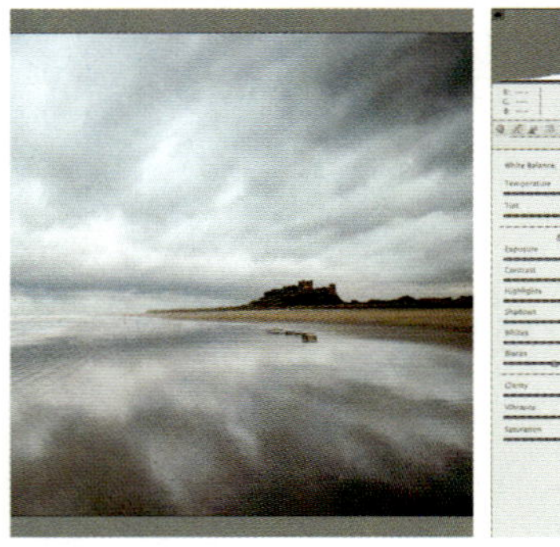

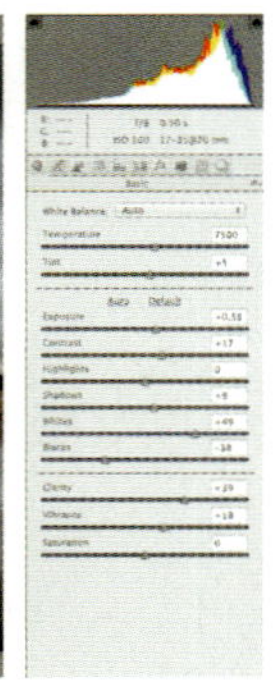

1 OPEN IN ACR In its Raw form this image looks strong, but a click of *Auto* neutralises the White Balance, deepens Blacks and brightens Whites. The *Clarity* slider should be used carefully to avoid halos but where there's a lot of mid-tone, this feature increases contrast as well as sharpness. I use the *Straighten Tool* to correct the slight skew on the horizon.

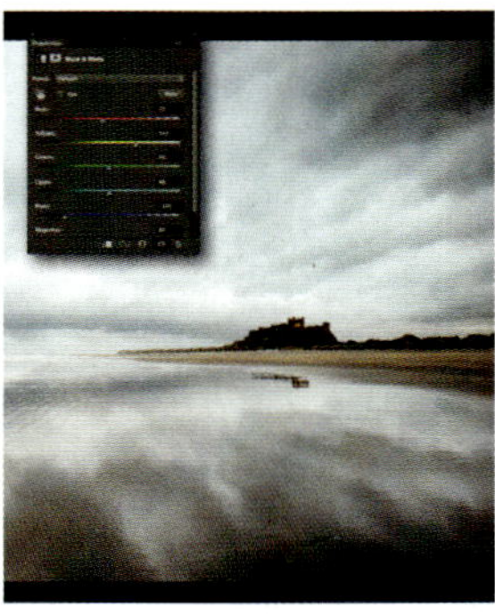

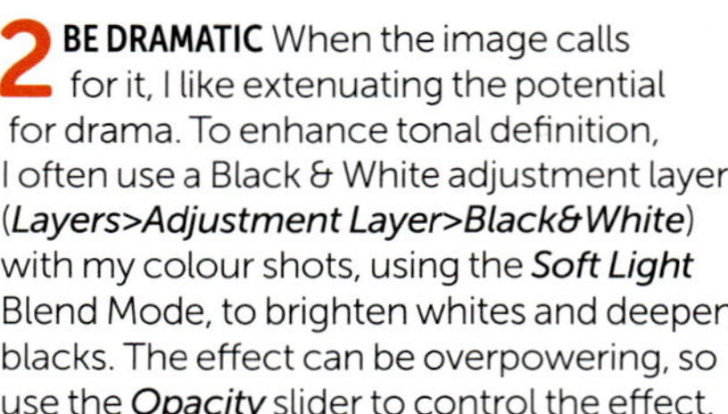

2 BE DRAMATIC When the image calls for it, I like extenuating the potential for drama. To enhance tonal definition, I often use a Black & White adjustment layer (*Layers>Adjustment Layer>Black&White*) with my colour shots, using the *Soft Light* Blend Mode, to brighten whites and deepen blacks. The effect can be overpowering, so use the *Opacity* slider to control the effect.

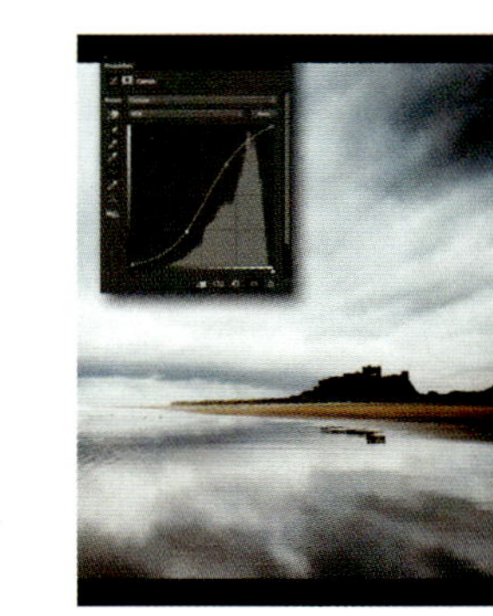

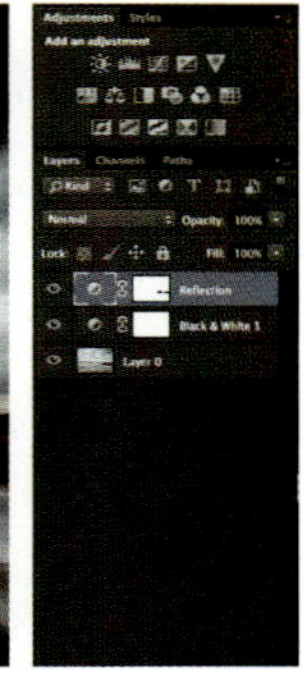

3 TACKLE IN SECTIONS Global adjustments are often good enough but, occasionally when there's strong interest in different areas of the image, I like to work in sections so not to lose highlight or shadow detail. Tackling the reflection first, I add a *Curves* adjustment layer and boost the contrast with a loose S-curve, then use the attached *Layer Mask* to hide or reveal the effect (see step 4).

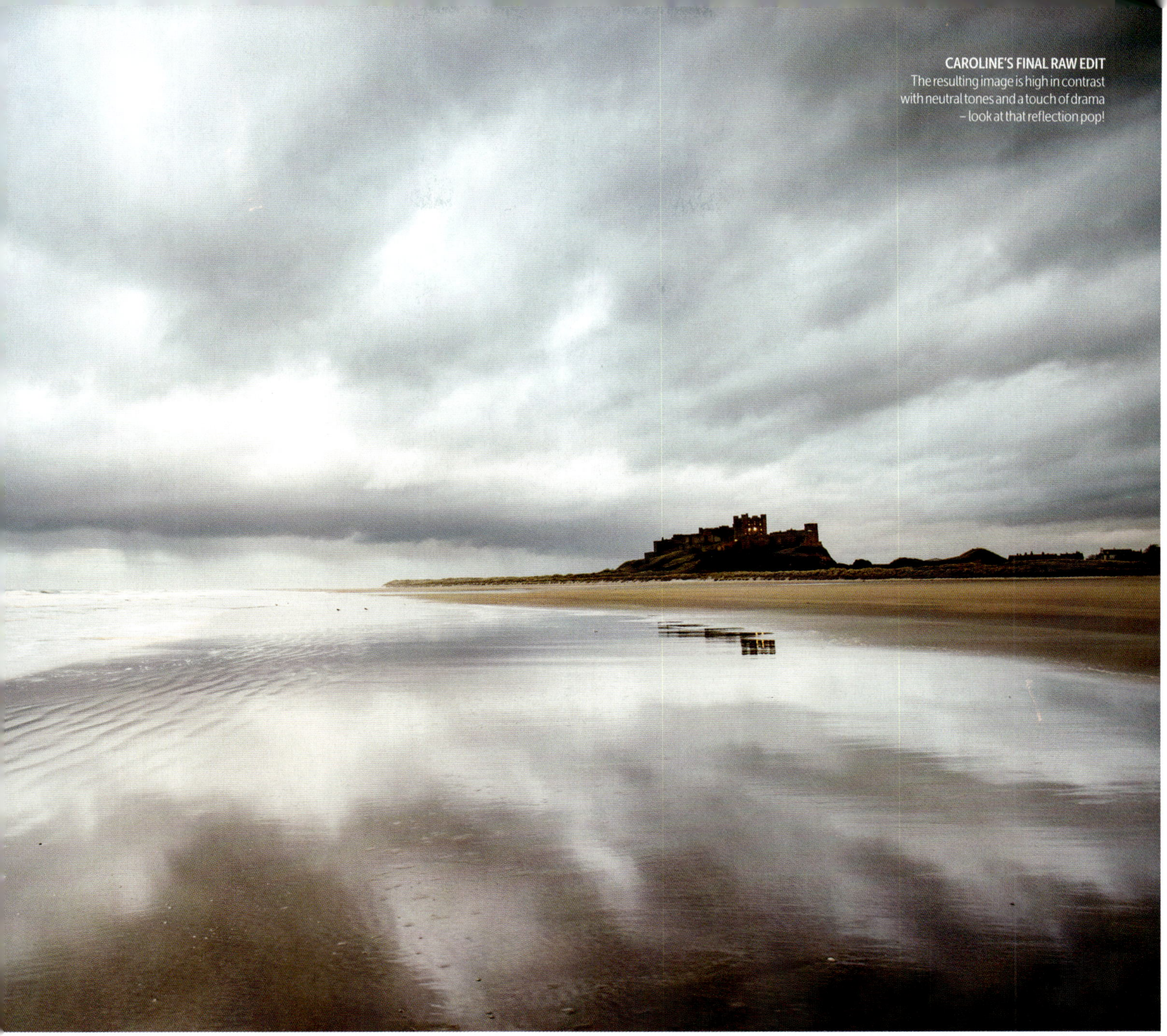

CAROLINE'S FINAL RAW EDIT
The resulting image is high in contrast with neutral tones and a touch of drama – look at that reflection pop!

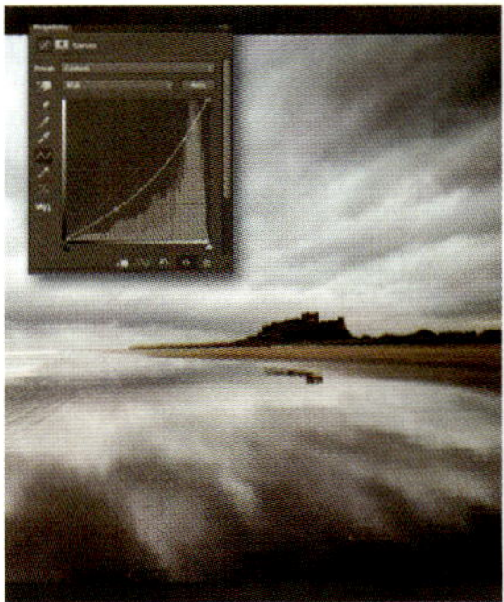
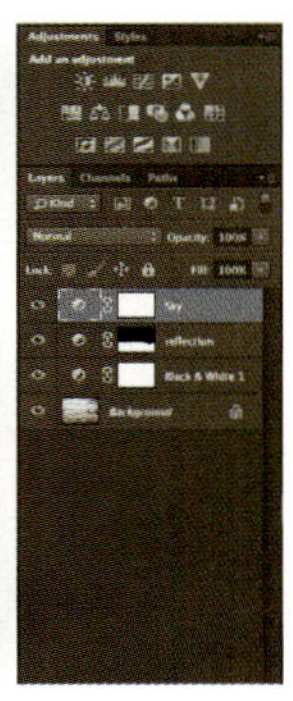

4 ADJUST THE SKY Repeating the previous step, I correct the sky with another *Curves* adjustment layer and use the *Layer Mask* to hide the effect everywhere else but the sky. As it's easier to reveal the effect than mask it, I *Invert* the Layer Mask then use the *Brush Tool* with the *Background color* set to *White* to reveal the sky, varying the brush's *Opacity* to diminish the effect in areas.

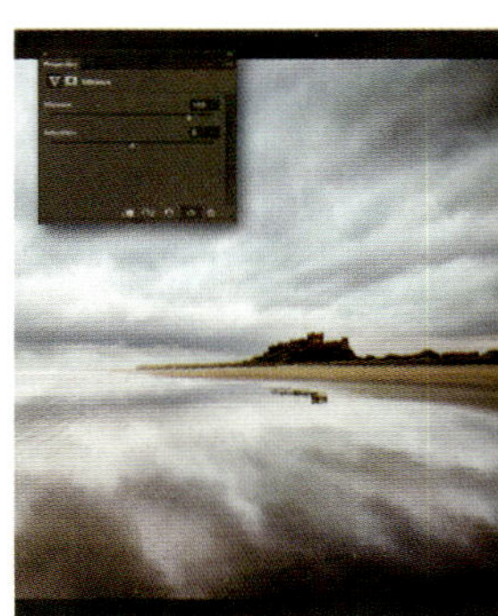
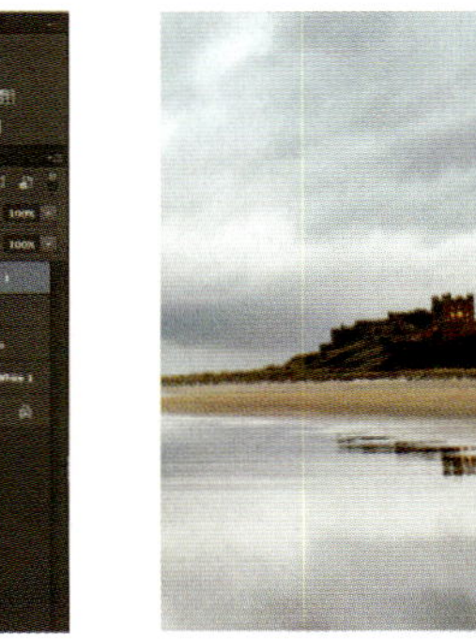

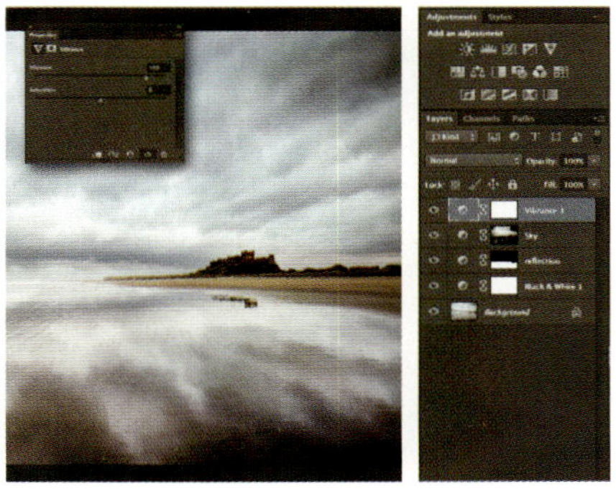

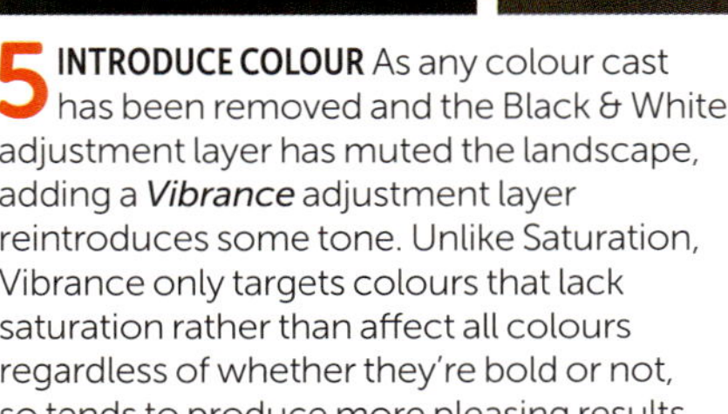

5 INTRODUCE COLOUR As any colour cast has been removed and the Black & White adjustment layer has muted the landscape, adding a *Vibrance* adjustment layer reintroduces some tone. Unlike Saturation, Vibrance only targets colours that lack saturation rather than affect all colours regardless of whether they're bold or not, so tends to produce more pleasing results.

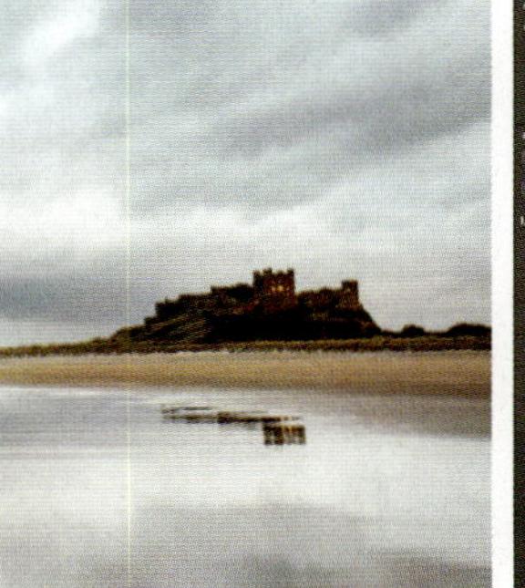
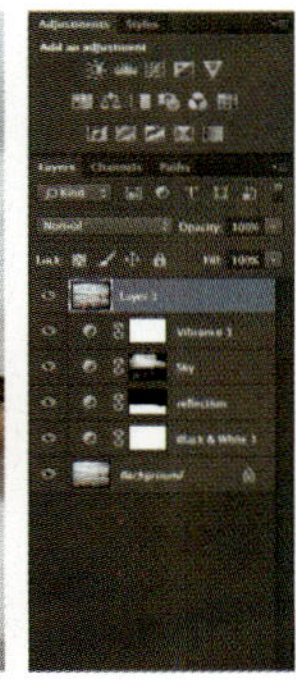

6 CLEAN UP THE SHOT As a final step, I zoom in to the image and use the *Clone Stamp* and *Healing Brush Tools* to remove sensor dust and marks. A small crop of the image tightens up the composition and a little sharpening using Unsharp Mask (*Filter>Sharpen>Unsharp Mask*) crispens the details. I'm happy with the results – I wonder how it compares to the other two...

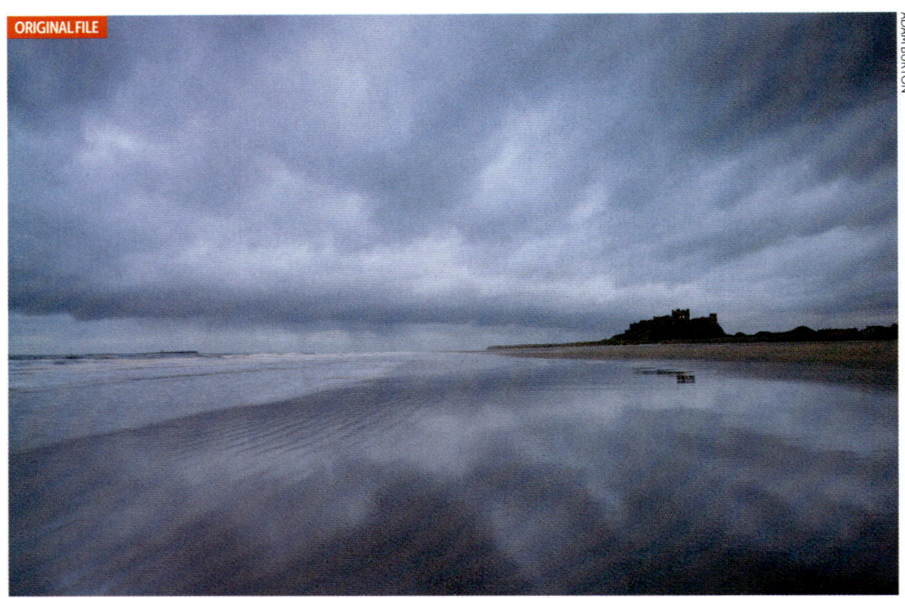
ORIGINAL FILE

ADAM BURTON

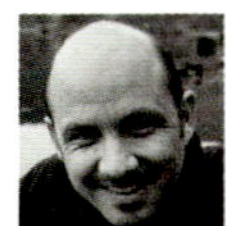

Raw challenge 2: Adam Burton

Landscape photographer Adam Burton's subtle processing style aims to improve but stay true to the original scene

WHENEVER I PROCESS a picture, my priority is to retain the authenticity of the original scene. It is important to me that I keep my picture true to the conditions that I witnessed, or as far as I can remember and for that reason I try to do minimal processing.

When I say minimal, think subtle. All of my pictures are captured in Raw and, as such, there are certain small adjustments that I apply to every image to bring the file to life. For me, it is a case of polishing the picture through a series of subtle changes, rather than creating a very different image through heavy-handed processing.

This image of Bamburgh Beach in Northumberland was captured at the end of a glorious day, when dark menacing clouds rolled in to swallow up a lovely sunset. With strong reflections in the water and just a hint of sunlight reflecting on the castle windows, the remainder of the scene was dark and foreboding; this particularly appealed to me and was the reason I fired the shutter.

I was very happy with the wide composition, bringing a sense of space to the picture. But after downloading the image, the Raw file felt a little flat compared to my memory of the scene and this was my main consideration while post-processing.

"AFTER DOWNLOADING THE IMAGE, THE RAW FILE FELT A LITTLE FLAT COMPARED TO MY MEMORY OF THE SCENE"

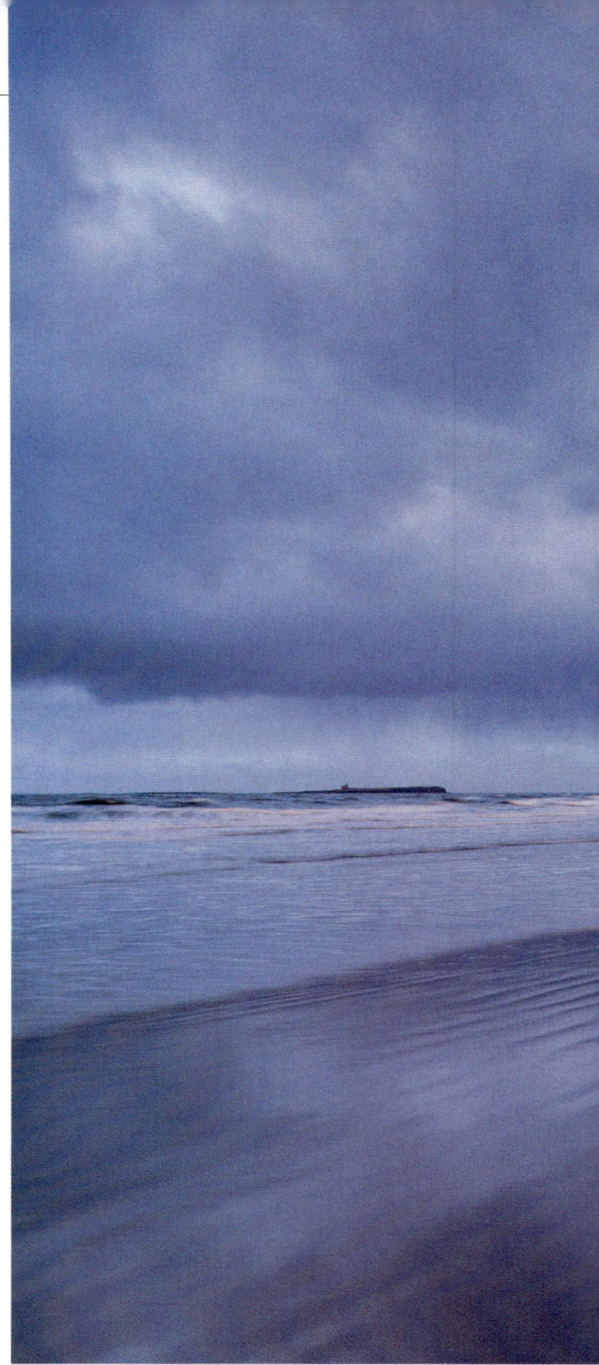

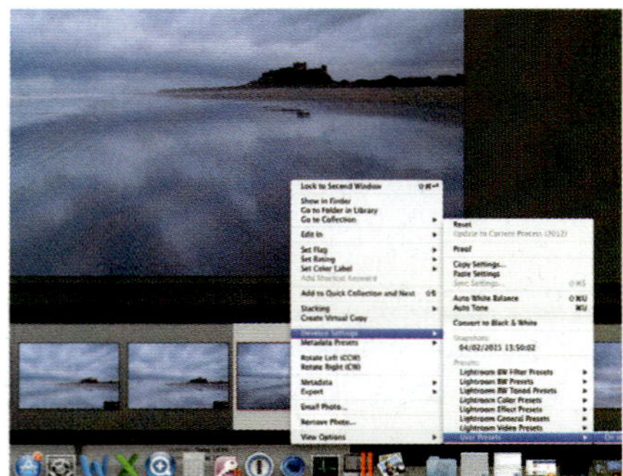

1 STANDARD ADJUSTMENTS After importing the file into Lightroom, I apply a series of generic adjustments. I always apply capture sharpening upon import using the *Sharpen – Scenic* preset. Next, I select the *Lens Corrections* tick boxes *Enable Profile Corrections* and *Remove Chromatic Aberration*. As these changes are universal, I have them saved as a User Preset.

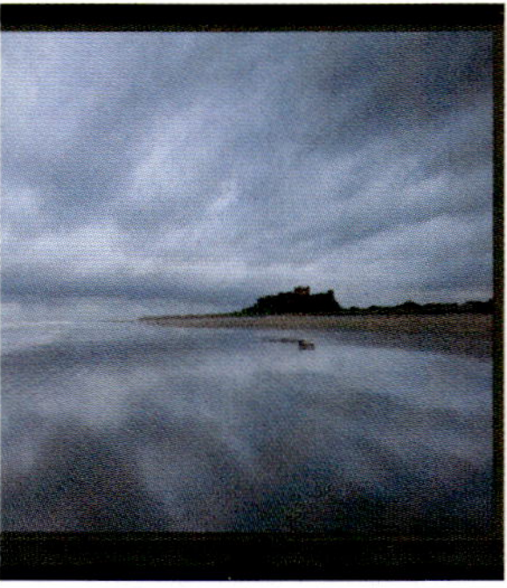

2 WHITE BALANCE My camera is always set to Daylight White Balance and for many situations this does not need to be changed in Raw processing. However in low light, such as when this image was captured, Daylight White Balance can give the picture a noticeable blue cast. To compensate for this I manually adjust the *White Balance Temperature* from *5150* to *5353*.

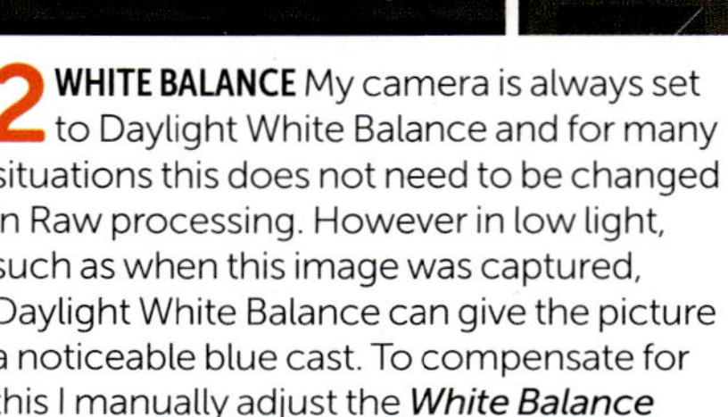

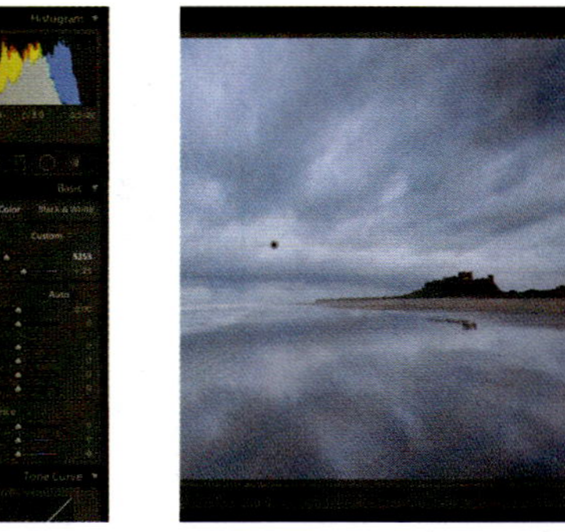

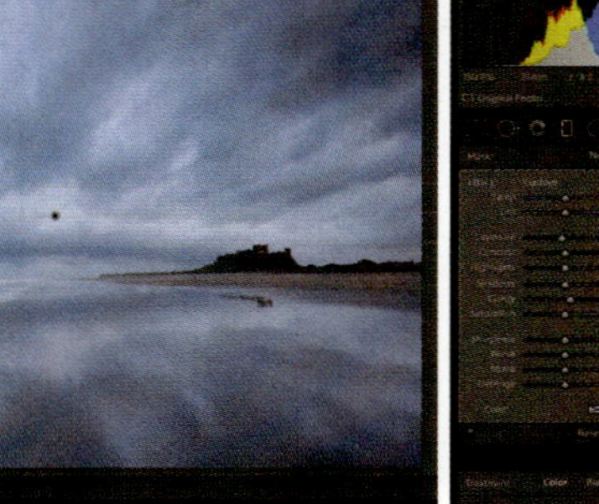

3 APPLY A GRADUATED FILTER Although I always use ND grad filters on my camera, I chose to add a digital ND grad filter to intensify the drama in the sky and also to balance the sky with the darker reflections. I reduce the *Exposure* by *-0.30* and increased the *Clarity* by *+16*. The grad is pulled down to just above the castle as I don't want to further darken the building.

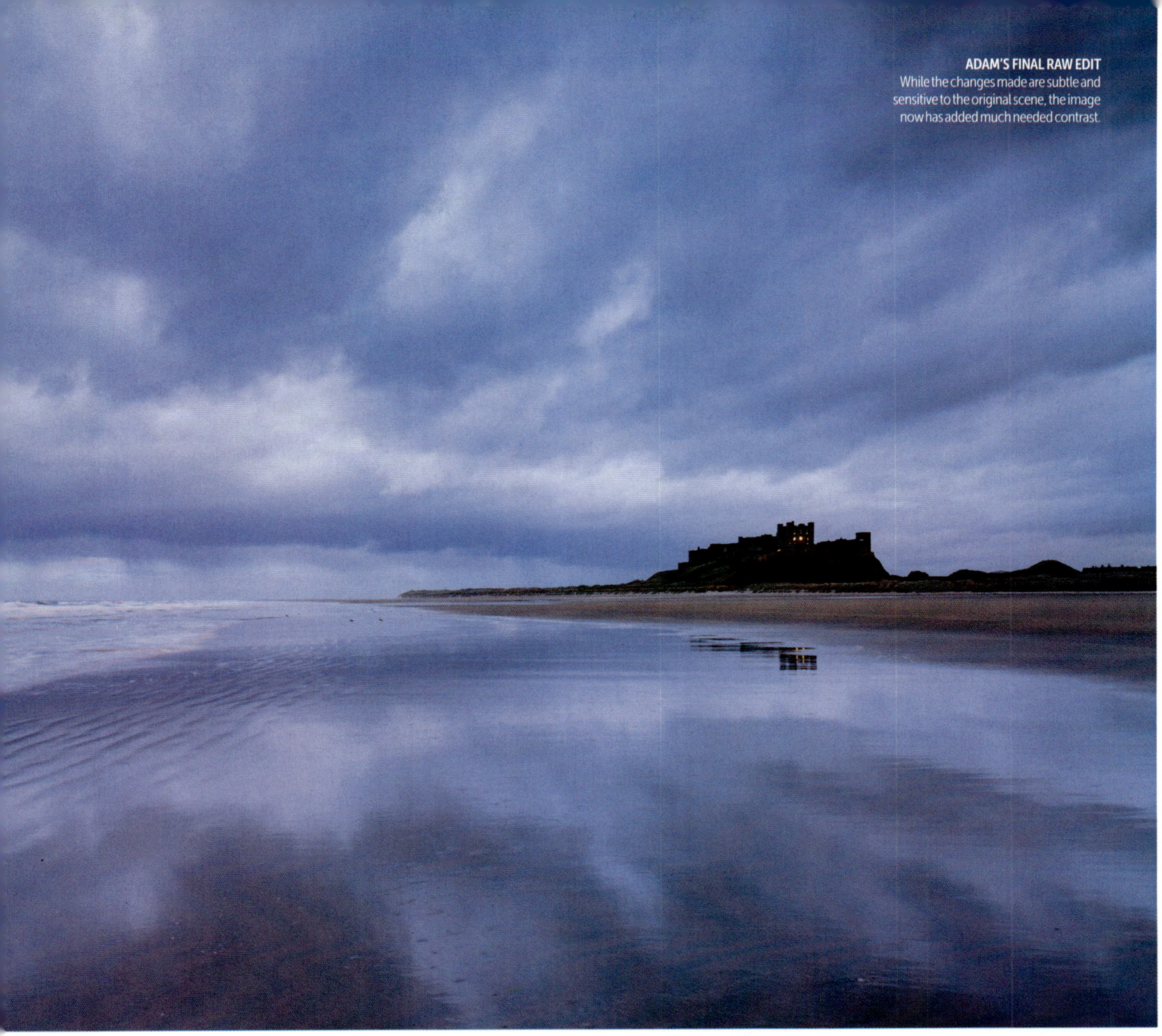

ADAM'S FINAL RAW EDIT
While the changes made are subtle and sensitive to the original scene, the image now has added much needed contrast.

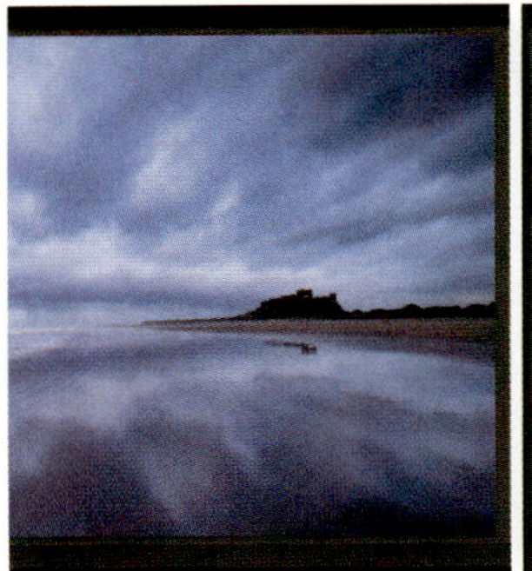
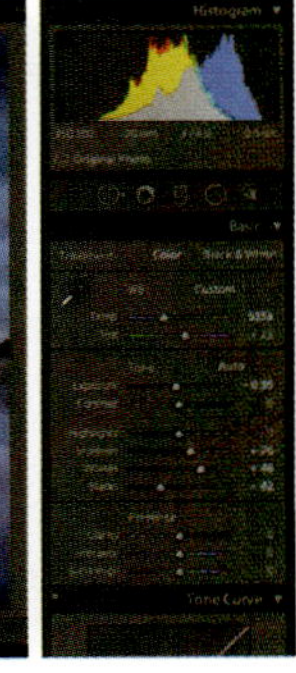

4 EXPOSURE ADJUSTMENTS I darken the *Exposure* slightly to *-0.30*, but want the castle to be lighter, so increase the *Shadows* by *+26*. I usually stretch the White and Black points across the histogram until just before each clipping triangle lights up. Here, a substantial increase of *+48* for the *Whites* and *-42* to the *Blacks* is used and instantly makes the picture more punchy.

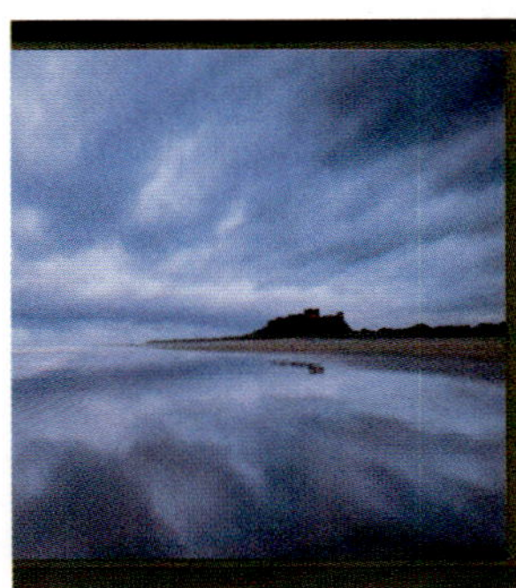
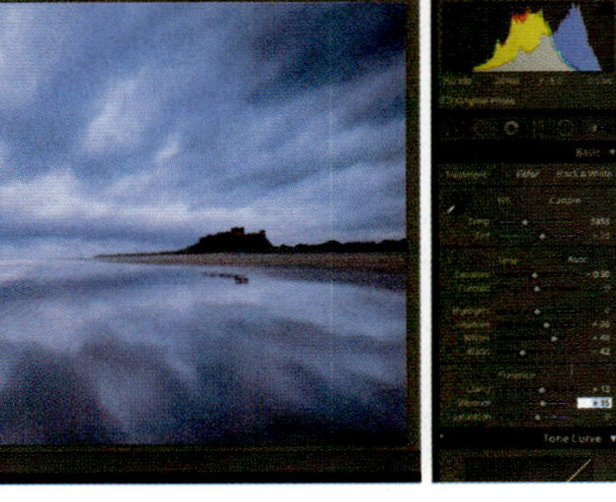
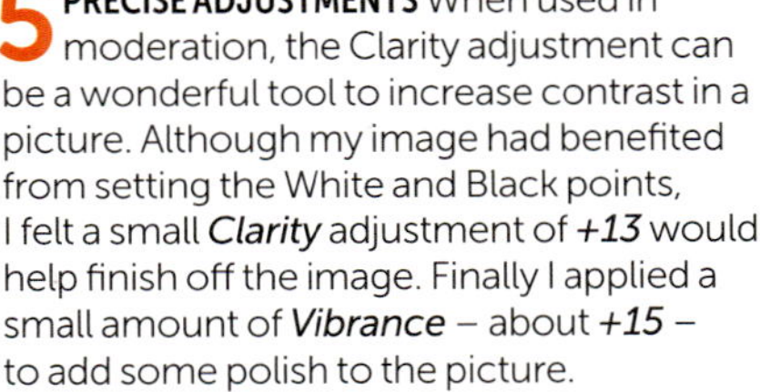

5 PRECISE ADJUSTMENTS When used in moderation, the Clarity adjustment can be a wonderful tool to increase contrast in a picture. Although my image had benefited from setting the White and Black points, I felt a small *Clarity* adjustment of *+13* would help finish off the image. Finally I applied a small amount of *Vibrance* – about *+15* – to add some polish to the picture.

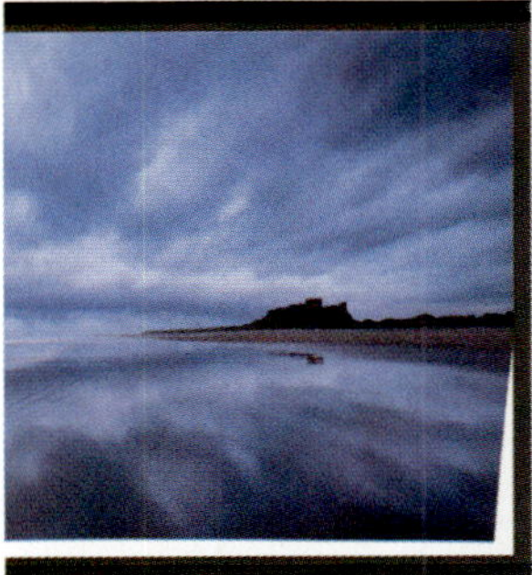
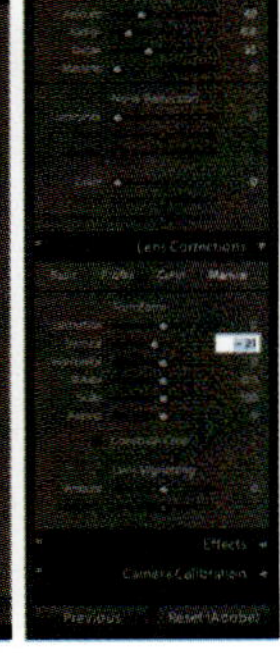

6 LENS CORRECTIONS I'm ready to export the image to Photoshop for fixing the dust spots and the wonky horizon. However, something is bugging me about the castle. As it's positioned close to the edge of the frame, lens distortion is causing it to lean. In *Lens Corrections*, I set *Vertical* to *-21* to correct for this, and clicked *Constrain Crop* to crop the edges. Much better!

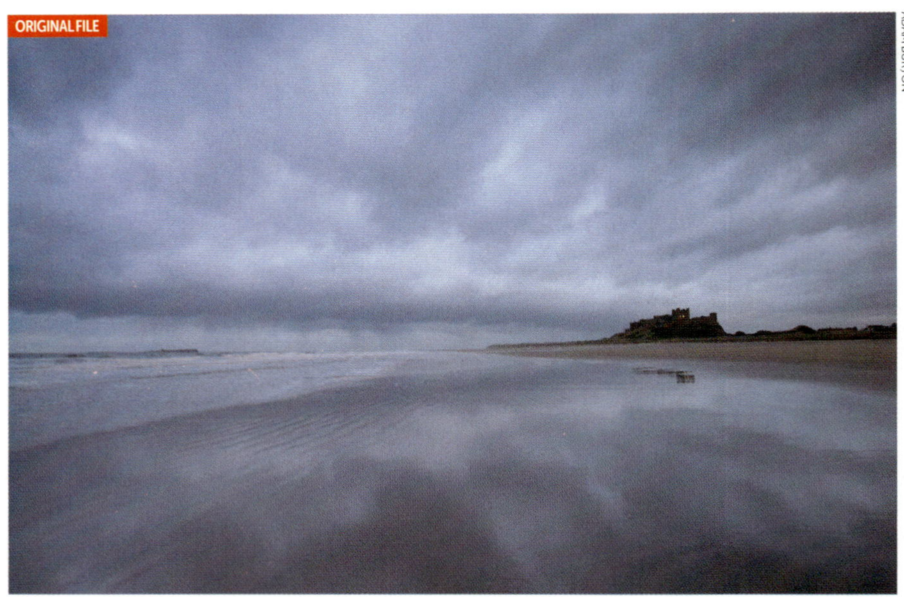
ORIGINAL FILE

ADAM BURTON

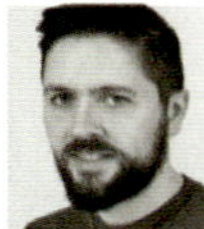

Raw challenge 3: Jordan Butters

We give one of our Photoshop experts free reign to see what he can come up with – purists look away now!

BEING GRANTED THE privilege of working on someone else's Raw file is a pretty rare occurrence, but an interesting experiment. Photographers are understandably precious about protecting their images – we take a lot of time, care and attention towards making sure our exposures are the best that they can be. With that in mind, I want to do justice to Adam's Raw file, while at the same time explore a more creative approach outside of straightforward editing.

Raw Tip

Find your own approach: any one effect can have several different methods of delivery, with similar results. Experiment and find one that works for you

I know Adam is an advocate of getting it right in camera, and his editing style reflects this, so I want to push the boat out (coastal pun fully intended) to create something a little bit different. This is the opposite of Adam's purist approach, so it'll be interesting to see how our final images differ!

One blessing is that Adam's Raw file is perfectly exposed for the scene, so no drastic recovery to the highlights is required in Adobe Camera Raw, meaning I can get straight to work in Photoshop.

> "THIS IS THE OPPOSITE OF ADAM'S PURIST APPROACH, SO IT'LL BE INTERESTING TO SEE HOW OUR FINAL IMAGES DIFFER!"

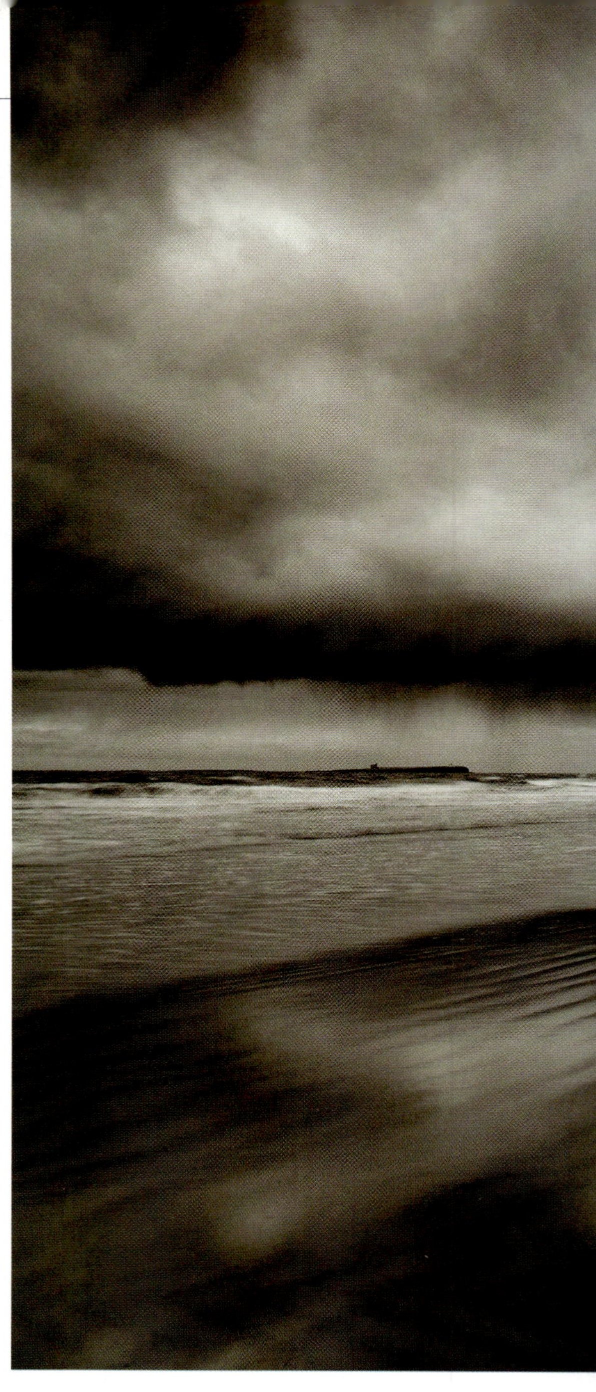

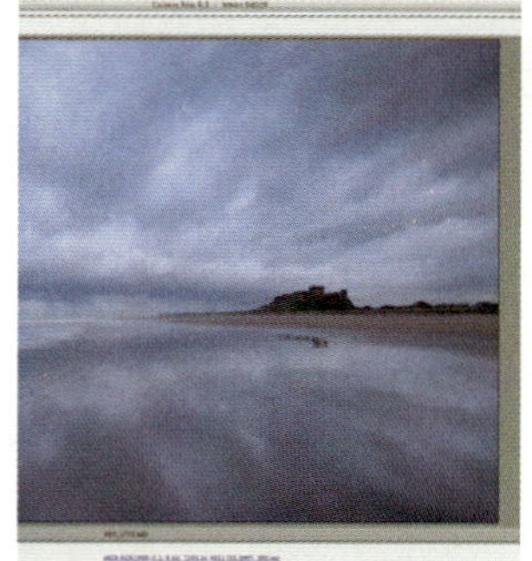

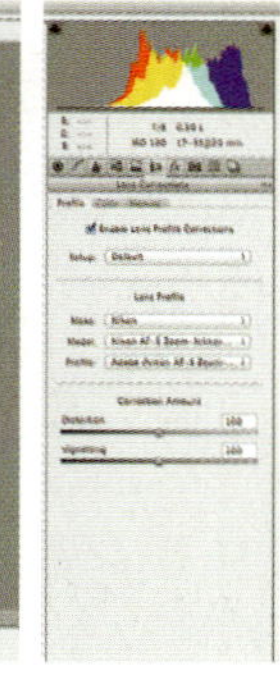

1 BASIC ADJUSTMENTS Thanks to the relatively flat light, there's plenty of scope in the histogram to boost contrast. Opening the file in ACR I try various White Balance settings, however feel that a high-contrast black & white approach will suit the brooding sky best. I use *Lens Corrections* to fix distortion and straighten the horizon using the *Straighten Tool*.

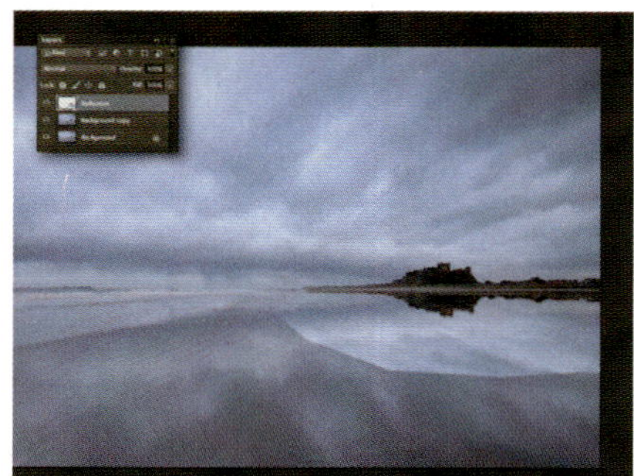

2 FAKE THE REFLECTION The purists may hate this, but I decide to make more of the castle's reflection. In Photoshop, I use the *Lasso Tool* to select the castle and some sky before copying and pasting it as a new layer. I then use the *Transform* command to flip the selection upside-down and add a *Layer Mask* with a soft brush at a low opacity to blend the genuine and faux reflections.

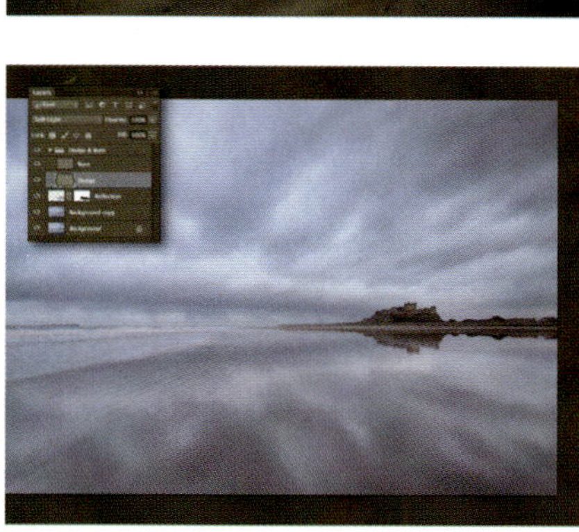

3 DODGE & BURN When it comes to fine-tuning areas of an image, my favoured approach is to dodge and burn. To do this without altering pixels, I create a new layer with its *Blend Mode* set to *Soft Light* and fill it with *50% Grey*. I then use the *Dodge Tool* set to *midtones* at *18%* to brighten where needed. This is repeated for areas that I want to darken using the *Burn Tool*.

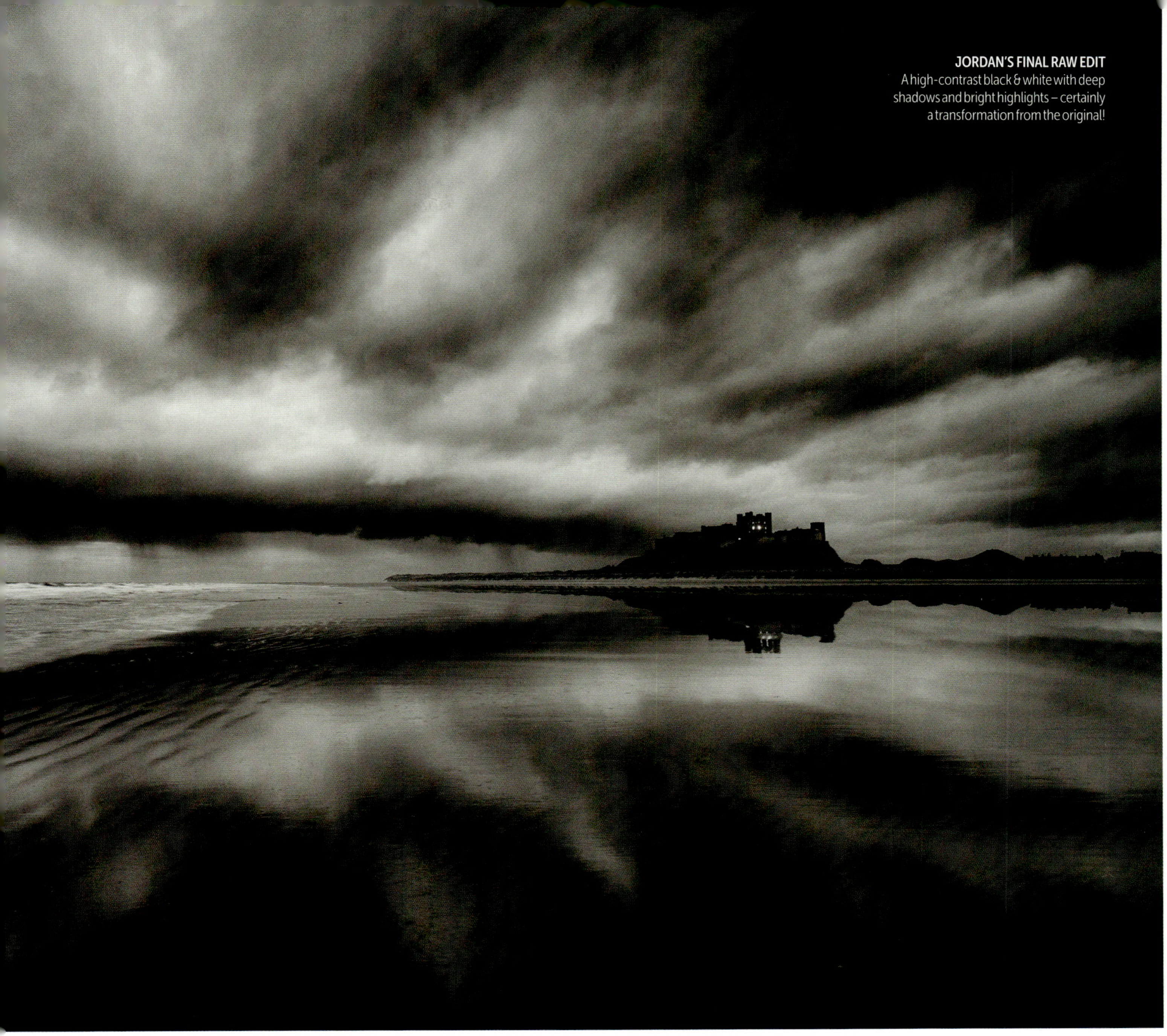

JORDAN'S FINAL RAW EDIT
A high-contrast black & white with deep shadows and bright highlights – certainly a transformation from the original!

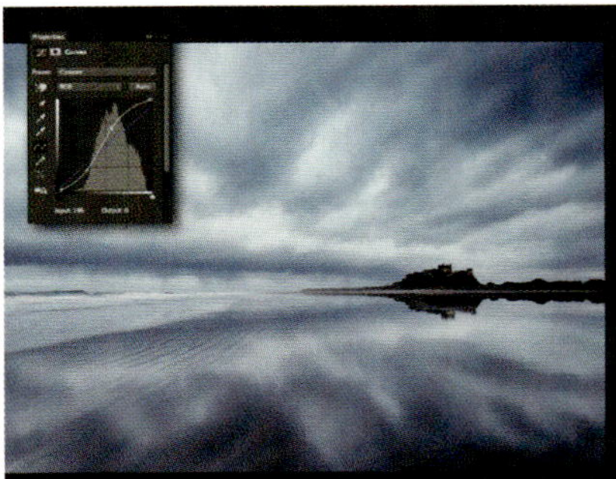

4 INCREASE CONTRAST There are several ways to boost contrast but I like using a ***Curves*** adjustment layer (***Layers> Adjustment Layers>Curves***) as it allows for fine adjustments. I add an exaggerated S-curve to the ***RGB*** channel, before selecting the ***Blue*** channel and removing blue from the highlights – this adds yellow, as it sits opposite blue on the colour wheel.

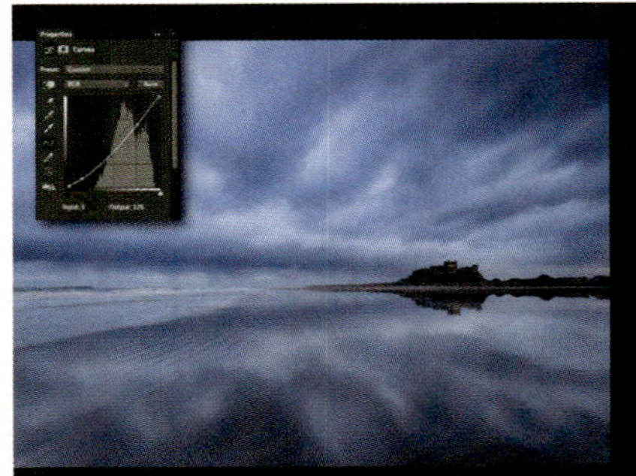

5 ADD A GRAD FILTER We're getting there now. I want to over-grad the sky to make the most of those clouds, so I add another ***Curves*** layer. I reduce the exposure from the lower to upper mid-tones, making sure that the shadows and highlights are kept intact so as not to reduce contrast. I then use a gradient layer mask so that only the sky is affected, much like using an ND grad filter.

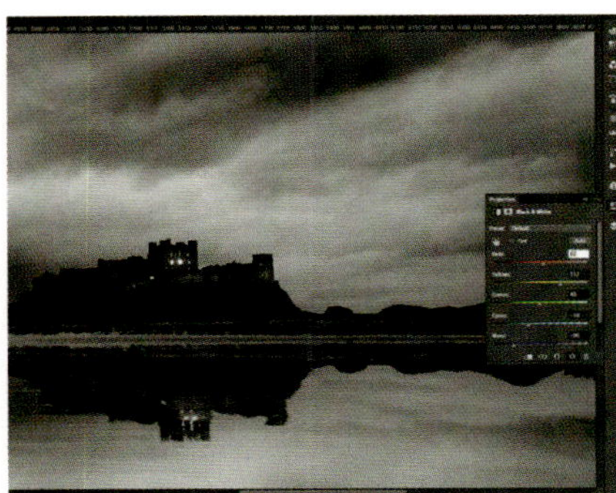

6 CONVERT TO BLACK & WHITE With the tonal changes made, I convert the image to mono using a Black & White adjustment layer (***Layers> Adjustment Layers>Black & White***). In the Adjustments palette, I decrease the ***Blue*** channel and increase the ***Yellow*** channel – this makes the castle pop. Finally, I go back and tweak Curves to increase contrast a touch more. All done!

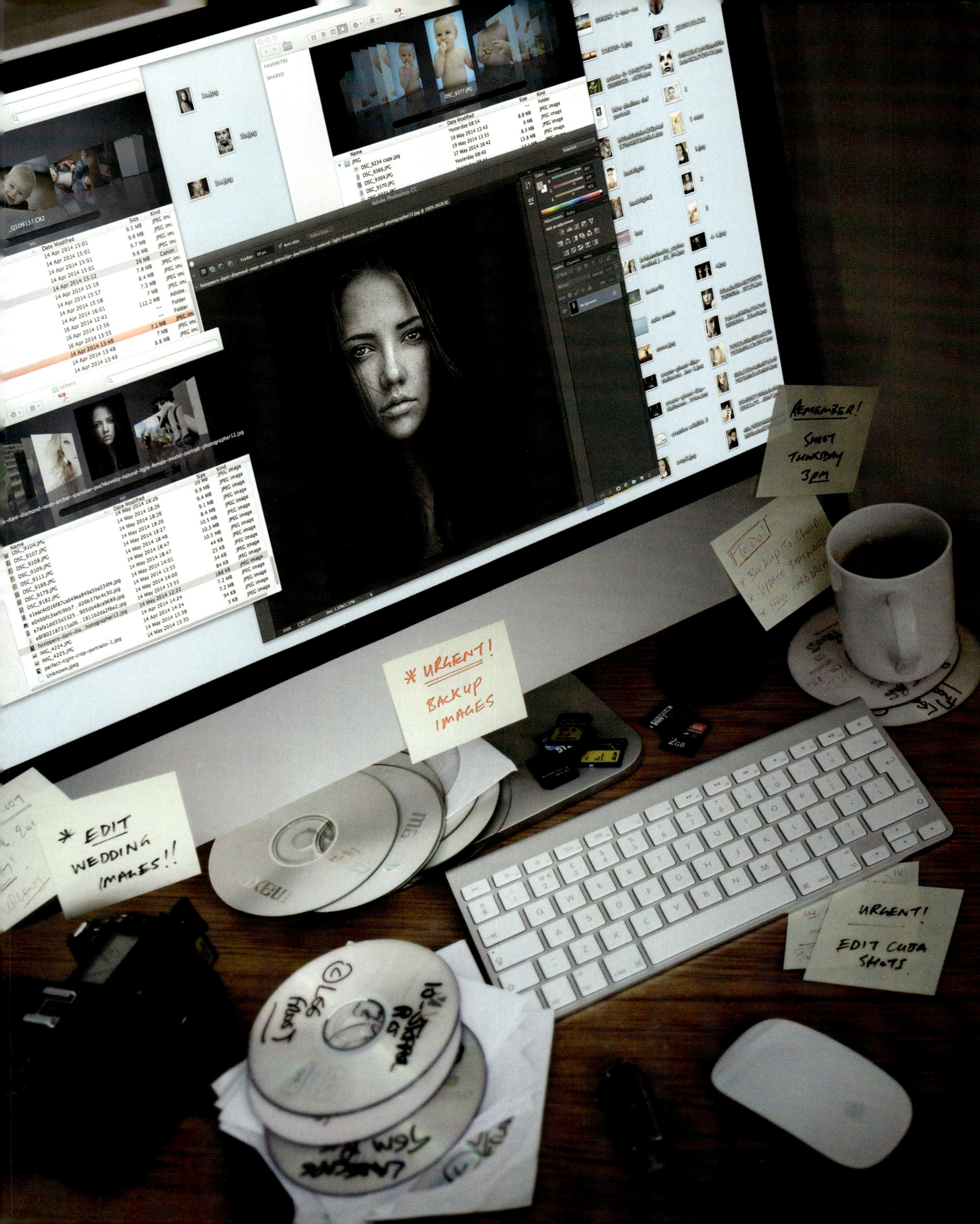
REMEMBER!
SHOOT THURSDAY 3PM
* URGENT!
BACKUP IMAGES
* EDIT WEDDING IMAGES!!
URGENT!
EDIT CUBA SHOTS

Spring-clean your photo workflow

Tired of a messy machine, of losing images or finding duplicates? It's time to clean up your act. Follow these essential steps to help you organise and archive your images for an efficient workflow

THINK OF AN IMAGE you shot a few years ago. Got it? Now I dare you to try to find it on one of your backup discs in less than three minutes. If you can, stop reading now. Seriously, turn to page 158 or go pick up your camera: there's nothing we can do for you here. For the other 99.9% of you, tear this feature out and stick it to your monitor as a reminder.

Most of us would like to think we could put our hands on an image, not overwrite any files and have everything safely secured in backup hard drives – but we don't. In fact, for most of us we operate a system of organised chaos and that means we know the image is in one place – that 2TB external hard drive – somewhere, and if you had a week you might be able to find it.

Who can blame us though: we're photographers, we'd rather shoot than sort. But with high-capacity memory cards storing more images than ever and masses of external hard drive space costing pennies, it is no wonder we end up in such a mess.

I'll take a long-shot and say most of us are guilty, at some point, of dragging and dropping images from memory cards on to our hard drive for a quick edit, or to format a memory card, with every intention of returning later to organise properly – but never do. Before we know it we're looking at folder upon folder of obscurely digit-named images, different content on different hard drives and preparing ourselves to spend hours in a vain attempt to sort out this 'organised chaos'. Sound vaguely familiar?

Professionals can't afford to misplace images, to risk overwriting files or to waste valuable minutes searching for a client's pictures: they need a rigid workflow system to stick to religiously and it should be no different for the rest of us.

1) START WHEN YOU SHOOT

A structured workflow should start in the camera, not the computer. Making sure your images are time-stamped with the right date is the first step towards organising your photos – it makes it much easier once you come to search for files chronologically. You can also add geotagging, which allows you to add location information and customise your camera's file names. The latter is useful if you want to identify images from different cameras as you can change the start of the file name to MKII or D800, for instance. Alternatively, you could bookmark the shoot, but just remember to change the file name before your next session.

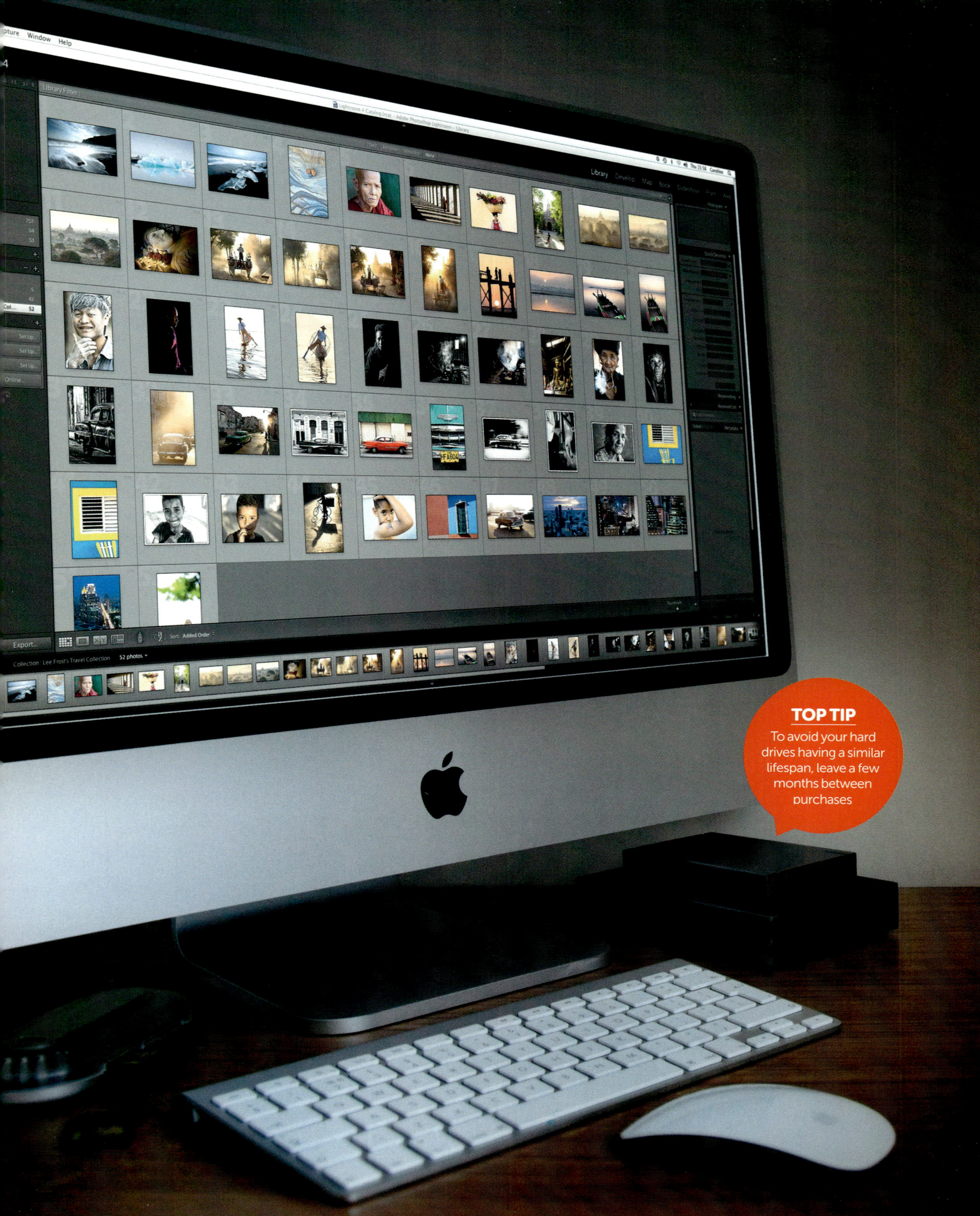

TOP TIP

To avoid your hard drives having a similar lifespan, leave a few months between purchases

2) MANAGEMENT SOFTWARE

A software program that helps you to manage, sort, search and archive your images is essential for a smooth workflow. The best programs let you catalogue and browse all your images as well as edit from Raw, without affecting the original pictures. Adobe Lightroom would be the preferred choice, while Adobe Photoshop Elements and Apple's Aperture 3 also offer similar features at a lower price.

The essential tools you need to look for are the ability to batch-name groups of images, edit metadata and add keywords as soon as you import the files from your camera. It should also have a search-and-sort facility like a rating or tagging system, the ability to backup to create an archive and export files to other editing software or social media.

If you didn't create a custom naming scheme in the camera, you'll want to select a name that reflects the image content so once the software imports the files they already have the appropriate file names and sequential numbers. Embedding metadata, keywords and copyright info not only makes it easier to search for images but can protect them and improve your SEO rating once you load them up online. You can set your system up to add your copyright information (if you've not already got it set up in-camera) on import and manually add the keywords to each photo. With Lightroom, you can also catalogue images into Collections, allowing you to collate images from different albums into themed folders, or images you rated similarly, to improve searchability. You should also set up your system so that backup copies are generated and stored on an external drive as images are imported and also export edited images to your hard drive.

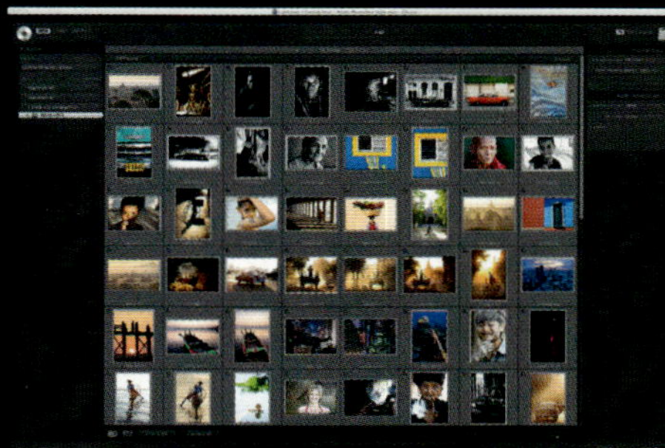

Managing manually

If you decide to not use management software, like Lightroom, you should make sure that you have a sound filing system and prudent backup procedure. You could set up a level of folders starting with year and month, and then within each month set up subfolders named by date, subject or shoot like '20/05/2014 Bella at the Beach'. Within these folders I suggest creating four separate folders: Originals, Working, Edited and Web. As soon as you take your files from your memory card, download them into the Originals folder, which from here on out never get touched; this is your archive. You can then sort through the images to edit, convert from Raw and save to the Working folder where you'll store your PSD files. Once you've got your final image, you then save it as a JPEG or TIFF for print to your Edited folder. Your Web folder is there for those images you watermark and resize for blogging, social media and your website. Just remember to keep it simple and always put your photos in the right folders when downloading from your camera.

3) STORE & SAVE

Once you've got your images organised, you'll want to back them up. The easiest way is to have an external hard drive, but one is not enough to ensure the safety of your files – especially if you delete the images from your computer to optimise performance. Like computer hard drives, external hard drives have a lifespan, so relying on just one is a mistake. Aside from hard drive failure, you risk power outages, viruses and worms, not to mention fires, floods or theft. A burglar is not going to take your computer but leave your hard drive and nor is a flood going to differentiate between the two, so at the very least you should have two drives in two separate parts of the house. Better still in two separate houses. You can pick up 1TB external hard drive for as little as £40 and there's a constant flow of reviews online, if you're unsure. Check out our sister site, Expert Reviews (www.expertreviews.co.uk) for in-depth tests. A few of our favourites include Western Digital's My Passport Ultra, the LaCie Minimus, Buffalo DriveStation 2T, Seagate Backup Plus and Samsung 1TB M3 Portable Hard Drive.

While you can manually drag and drop to your backup disc, life can be made easier with software that automatically updates a connected external hard drive. Programs like Time Machine (Apple Mac) update regularly, while others let you schedule your backups for when you sleep. But how do you make sure your secondary cloned backup has all the same files? You sync them. Programs like FreeFileSync, Robocopy and Toucan Portable can help Windows users, while SuperDuper and Carbon Copy Clone work for Macs. You could also sync the devices to your Cloud storage, your piece of the pie in the sky, which can be linked to multiple devices at various locations. An even safer option is to manually update your clone drive by copying files from your master – this is a preferred option as you're in control of your backups' integrity but takes time and may mean you have weekly or monthly gaps in your backup, unless you do it daily.

While two backups are good, three is even better. Some photographers use a third hard drive or store their important files and image collections to CD or DVD, which is a valid option but can become expensive and result in insurmountable disks and drives over time. The Cloud – online storage – is arguably a better solution. Most providers do offer free space, but for the sizeable amount of images photographers want to keep safe you'll likely be looking at a monthly fee for unlimited storage space, in the range of £3-£10 per month, depending on the features you want from your service plan. Providers like Just Cloud, SOS online backup and MyPCBackup allow you to set automatic archiving that you can also sync to multiple devices, even if they're off site. Some backups clone and archive your whole hard drive, while others let you be more selective. Some let you share files while others offer the invaluable option of restoring lost or corrupted files from their archives. With Cloud storage, however, you do risk the third-party system becoming compromised or the company closing, which is why we advise you to operate a system of multiple independent devices. There you have it: a foolproof way to protect your important images. So don't delay, set up your backup today!

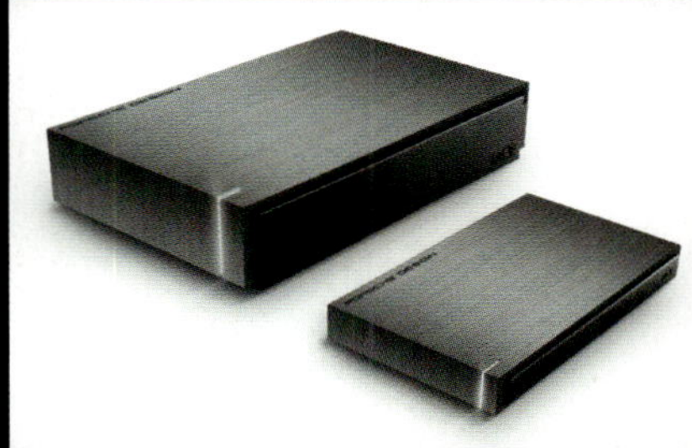

RAID or NAS?

RAID (redundant array of independent disks) is a fancy external hard drive with expandable storage as it can contain multiple drives in one enclosure. There are several levels of RAID, but most of us only need to be concerned with RAID-1 as it works by automatically copying backed-up data to each drive, creating two or more mirrored hard drives. NAS – network attached storage – can also contain multiple drives in one enclosure but enables you access via different computers or mobile devices.

Spring clean checklist!

- ✔ Invest in decent image management software such as Lightroom
- ✔ Establish and stick to a filing system
- ✔ Invest in multiple backup solutions
- ✔ Add custom names and metadata to images on import
- ✔ Sync your system to make backups automatically or back up manually daily

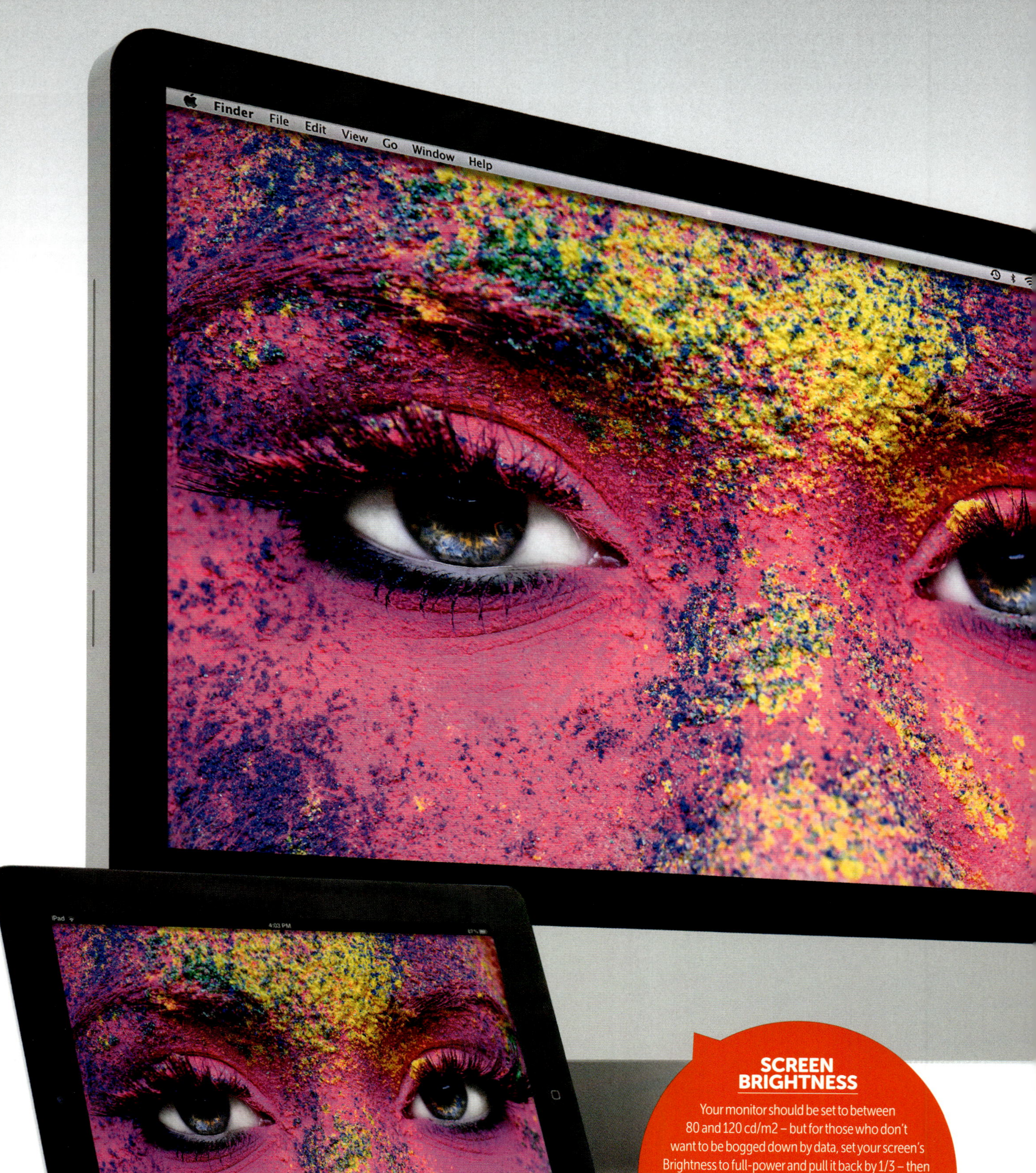

SCREEN BRIGHTNESS

Your monitor should be set to between 80 and 120 cd/m2 – but for those who don't want to be bogged down by data, set your screen's Brightness to full-power and pull it back by 1/3 – then you'll be in a similar ballpark. Most people like the punch of their screen on full brightness, but you really want to be working at 2/3 brightness for accurate rendering. There's also the added bonus that you're being greener by saving energy and you're also extending the life of your monitor

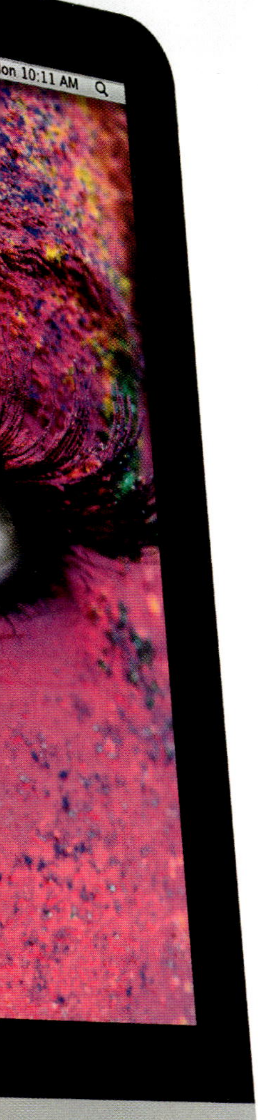

True colours

Do you know your sRGB from your CMYK, or a Spyder from a Munki? And why do your prints look different on your iPad and your iPhone? Caroline Schmidt clears up the confusion about controlling your colour management in this uncomplicated guide to calibration

FORGET PRINTS FOR the moment, let's cater to those photographers whose images live on-screen and never make it into a frame. While it's sad but true, most of us now enjoy our images on monitors, be it computers, digital photo frames, smartphones or tablets. But what if I was to tell you that no two screens are ever the same, and that the amazing images that you're spending considerable time to develop – and using to show off your talents – are not being seen how you intended. Would you be surprised?

We put faith in expensive technology and expect each product to follow an industry standard, so that when we filter images through these pieces of tech, like a camera to monitor or iMac to iPad, they should look the same – or at least very similar. The truth is the parameters between products can be vastly different, and you have to take control over your colours in the same way you would calibrate a new lens for precise focusing. This isn't just for the professional pedantic who can tell a slight colour shift or Pantone blue PMS322 from Pantone PMS323, it's for every photographer who wants their whites to be pure white and their colours and detail to be true to life.

Most people don't realise that they have a problem until something changes in their system, they notice their images on someone else's monitor or make their debut in a magazine. Some people are lucky and buy a camera, monitor and printer that work well together without any management, and it's only when they buy a new printer or view their images on a calibrated device that their colours look shocking.

Ultimately, you want what you capture in camera to be the same as you see on screen, and what you see on screen to look the same in print – and to know the easiest route to get there. So how do photographers make their colours consistent? They curse an awful lot, read loads of books and get terribly confused – then get a piece of solid advice. The advice is that if you want to view your images consistently across all devices, calibrate your screen so it syncs with any other calibrated screen, be it a high-street printer, a lab or mobile device.

Calibration: What's the point?

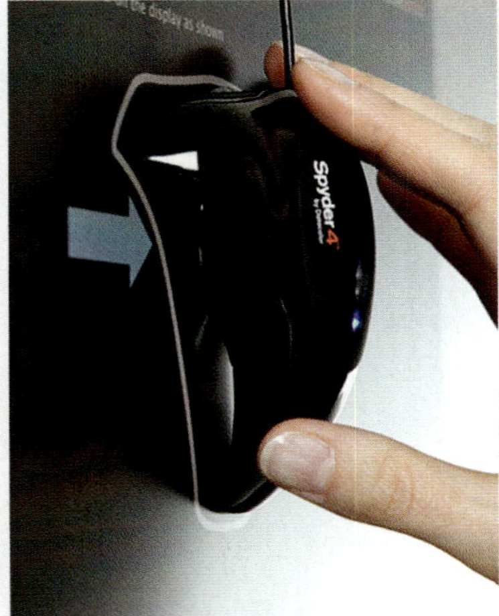

- Every monitor renders images differently, unless they're calibrated. That goes for iPads, iPhones, Android devices, TVs, laptops, desktop monitors and LCD and LED displays, not to mention different makes and brands available. By calibrating your monitor you can at least feel assured that whoever is viewing your images is also viewing them on a calibrated monitor – and if they're serious about photography, the chances are they will be.
- Displays change over time; recalibration ensures that you return your monitor back to its initial reference state for brightness and colour to get consistent results.
- Why spend precious time creating images in-camera, perfecting them on the computer to then print them to a printer that doesn't match your on-screen colours? Now that's pointless.
- Wide-gamut displays have a tendency to look oversaturated without calibration.
- Your punchy black & white might look grey and muddy on the majority of calibrated monitors if you've not taken the time to control your monitor's brightness, white and black points for perfect highlights and shadows. Similarly, colours won't look true to life and any colour corrections and toning will be futile.

Colorimeters

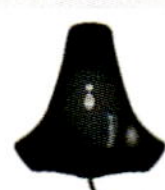

DataColor Spyder5Pro £125
This mid-range product, available from Datacolor, adapts to ambient light changes and features a full-spectrum, seven-colour sensor. It can be used to calibrate your computer, TV, iPad, iPhone and Android devices using the free SpyderGallery App.

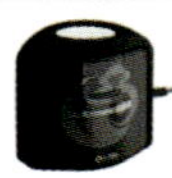

ColorMunki Display £110
Offering advanced controls with a fast and intuitive interface, X-Rite's ColorMunki Display offers photographers the tools and guidance they need, plus the scope for greater control, should it be required. There's also a free ColorTRUE mobile app to calibrate iOS and Android devices.

ColorMunki Smile £67
A simple, no-frills calibration device for laptops or desktop monitors. Designed to take the stress out of calibration for amateur photographers, Smile does everything for you aside from plug itself in.

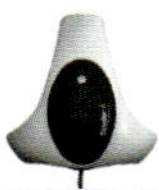

DataColor Spyder5Express £89
A does-what-it-says-on-the-tin product that offers a quick calibration solution if all you want is true-to-life colours, a device to calibrate all your displays and minimal hassle. The Spyder5Express particularly suits photographers who only display their images digitally.

Calibration kits

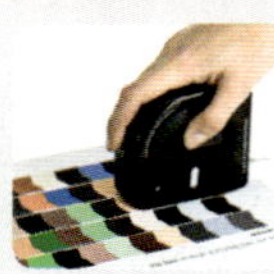

ColorMunki Photo £320
An all-in-one colour control solution by X-Rite Photo, which calibrates your camera, monitor and printer. It offers a truly simple approach in a convenient and portable package that provides accurate monitor-to-print matching. It also comes with a Macbeth Mini Colour Checker Chart for ACR profiling for digital cameras, and a free ColorTRUE app for calibrating Apple iOS and Android devices.

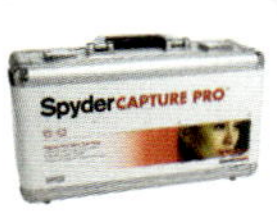

Spyder Capture Pro £360
Get Datacolor's complete camera and monitor calibration bundle: SpyderLenscal for precise focusing, SpyderCube for control, contrast and white balance, SpyderCheckr for colour balance and SpyderElite to calibrate your monitor.

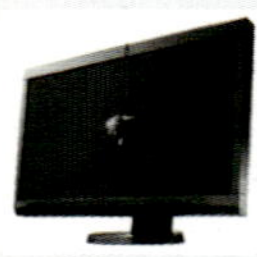

EIZO ColorEdge CS230 23-inch monitor £450
Aimed at entry-level users for photo editing, the CS230 adjusts calibration using its built-in SelfCorrection sensor, which makes it easy to maintain an initial colour calibration by automatically re-adjusting the monitor when scheduled to do so. You still need to purchase a colorimeter for the initial calibration.

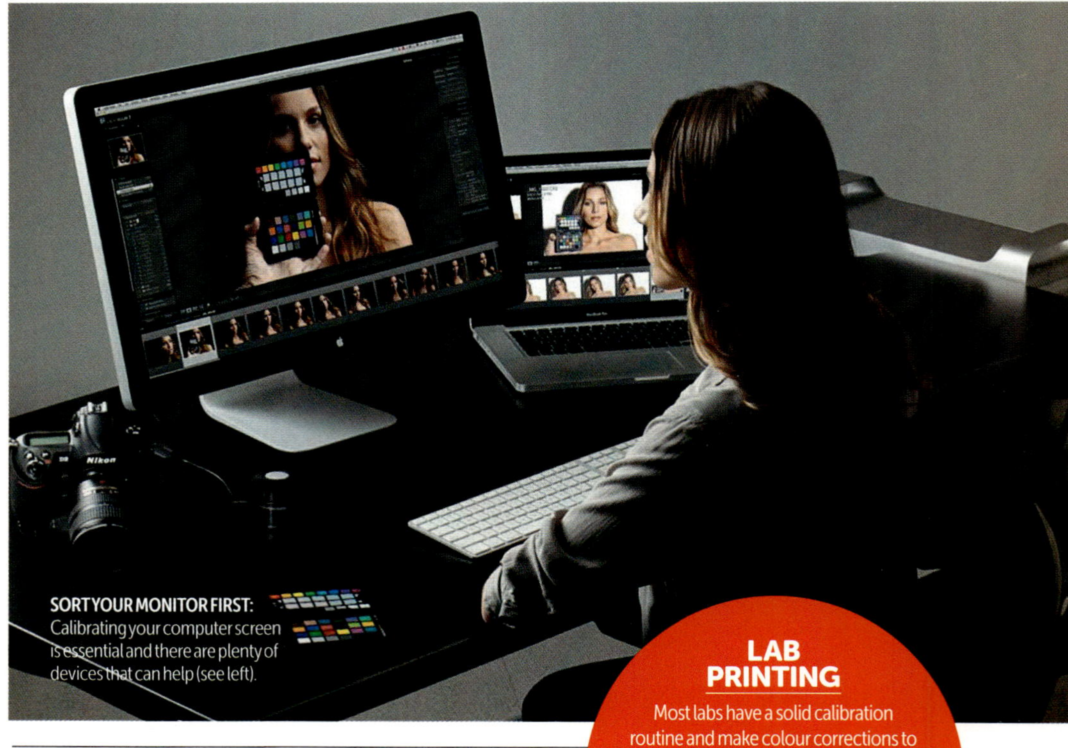

SORT YOUR MONITOR FIRST: Calibrating your computer screen is essential and there are plenty of devices that can help (see left).

LAB PRINTING

Most labs have a solid calibration routine and make colour corrections to prints to ensure the best standard, so by having your screen calibrated too you're minimising the margin for error. Labs work in sRGB, so if you create your images in any bigger colour space you'll find that your colour transitions are stripped away

THREE STEPS TO MAXIMISING DETAIL AND COLOUR IMPACT

In an ideal world, colour management should begin in-camera and end with the printer, but for correct colours it's the monitor calibration that should take priority, followed by the camera and the printer...

1

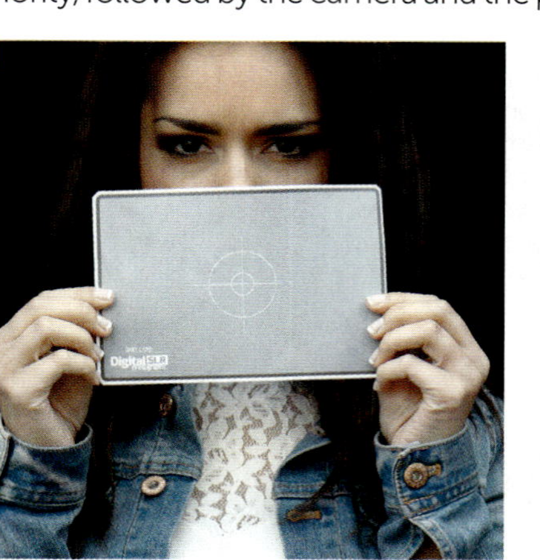

2

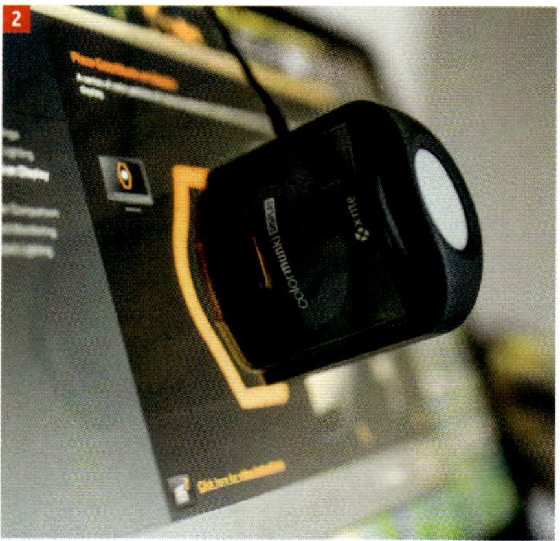

1 Correct in-camera: Use a simple grey card to set your White Balance. This neutralises shifts in colour temperature and makes colours true and more vibrant.

2 Use a colorimeter: The most essential part is a calibration unit for your monitor so that you can maximise the colours on it. Any new computer will be set up for general use and be horribly bright, with a limited range of colour. A calibrated monitor will open out all of the half and three-quarter tones, so that you can see more detail in the shadow transitions.

3 Adjust your printer: There's the least margin for error with prints but people still expect printers to be able to recreate exactly what's on their screen. The problem is that the screen has the biggest margin for error, which is why calibrating it is so important.

3

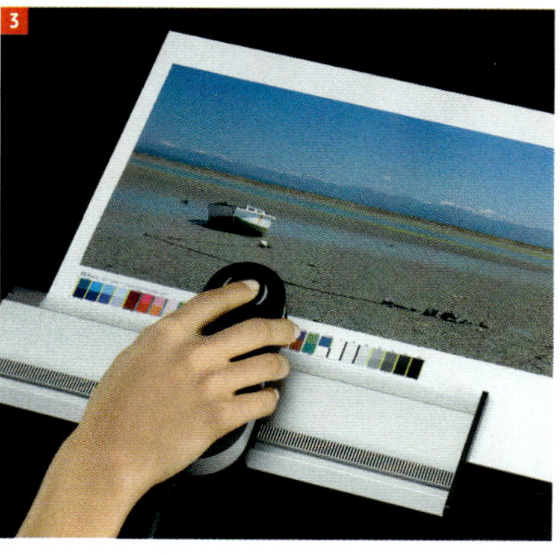

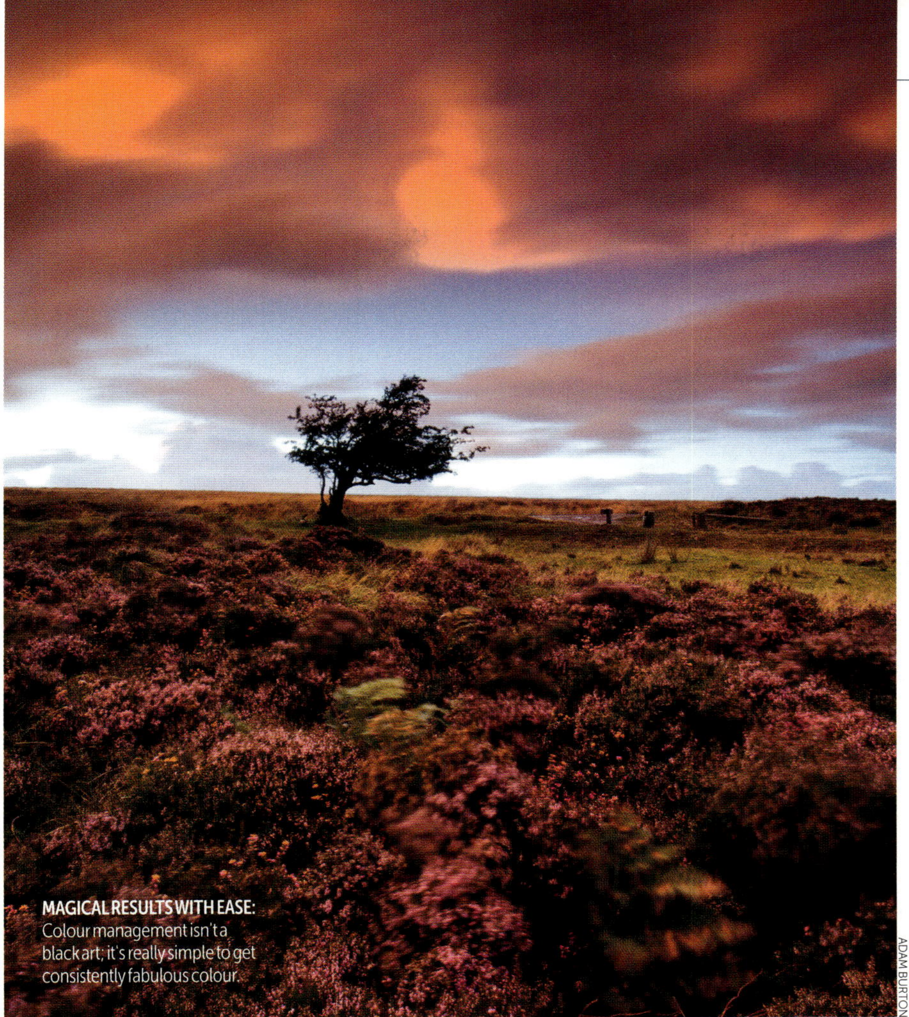

MAGICAL RESULTS WITH EASE: Colour management isn't a black art; it's really simple to get consistently fabulous colour.

HOW TO CALIBRATE YOUR MONITOR

It's so easy to get professional-grade colour these days that a monkey could do it, or at least a ColorMunki. All you need to do is buy one of our recommended colorimeters (see far left), install the software, attach the colorimeter via its USB and follow the on-screen Wizard instructions. Simple. Some products offer more advanced options if you want to develop or customise your calibration, but the essential features are fully automated. You may need to recalibrate your monitors every few weeks to compensate for changes that occur over time, but quite often you'll find that your colorimeter will remind you of this.

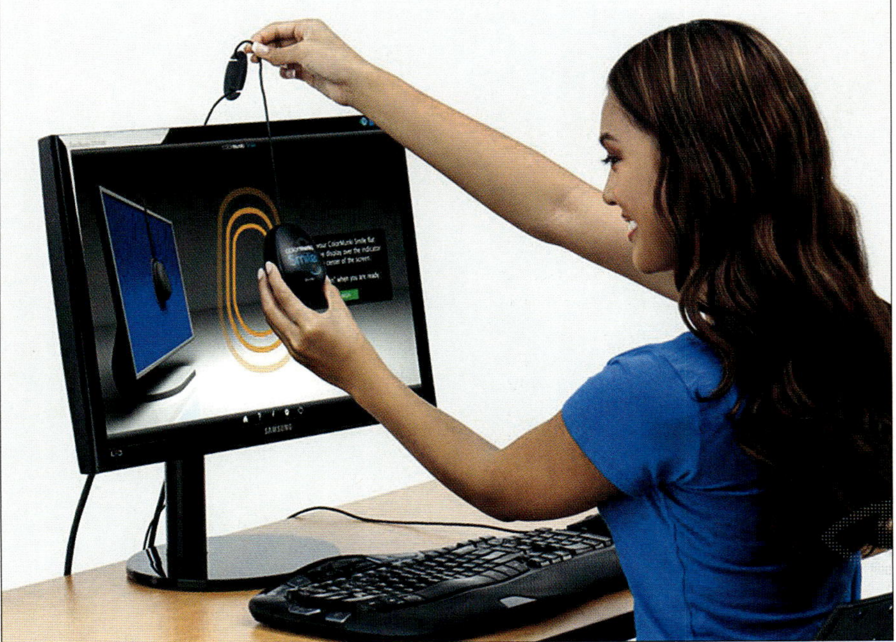

Jargon: Know your terms

- **Colour gamut:** The range of colours you can see and that your screen reproduces. You cannot do anything to adjust this, as it's a mixture of capabilities from your monitor and graphics card. As a rule of thumb, the more expensive the monitor the wider its gamut will be.
- **Candala per square metre (cd/m2):** This is the measure of light emitted per unit area – it's used to specify the brightness of a display device. Most desktop monitors have luminances of 200 to 300 cd/m2. The sRGB spec for monitors targets 80 cd/m2 and, typically, calibrated monitors should have a brightness of 120 cd/m2.
- **Colour space:** The main three colour spaces that photographers work in are: sRGB, Adobe RGB and Profoto RGB. Each one has a different colour gamut, which makes it easier to reproduce colour and retain shadow, as well as highlight detail and saturation on different devices set to the same colour space. Most devices tend to work within sRGB and you may find that they strip out the extra data from larger colour spaces, such as Adobe RGB or Profoto RGB, because they are not able to identify the colours.
- **Profiling:** Means a very similar thing to calibrating in that you're working to a set standard. Profiling is the creation and calculation of that standard for accurate colours, while calibration is the process of correcting colours.

Colour spaces explained

Which colour space should I use?
ProfotoRGB, Adobe RGB and sRGB are the main ones. ProfotoRGB, preferred by Lightroom, is a huge colour space, but there isn't a device on the market that can replicate it so it's not practical for editing in. Adobe RGB has a wider gamut than sRGB so if you're printing your work commercially, use this. sRGB is good because most cameras can capture it, most monitors work within its colour gamut and it will give you consistent results. Anything viewed on the web should be sRGB.

What's the point of soft-proofing?
It's a method of previewing before committing to the print, by applying a 'canned' profile provided by a printer to your image to emulate the effects on your image on screen. The type of paper you use will also affect the colours and soft-proofing is a way of previewing this.

How does ambient light affect my monitor?
The brightness of the room, the position of the screen and even the colour of the walls can have an affect on how colour and contrast is perceived on screen. Most colorimeters have Ambient Light detectors to help neutralise the effects, but if yours doesn't, avoid multiple light sources hitting your screen and calibrate your monitor in the dark.

What if my monitor's gamut isn't wide enough?
It won't display the colour, but the closest it can. For instance, green in spring is made up of yellow and different shades of green – if your monitor cannot pick up the subtlety it will just display the same green rather than reproduce the details.